IRON DESTINIES,
LOST OPPORTUNITIES

*Books by Charles R. Morris*

Iron Destinies, Lost Opportunities: *The Arms Race Between the U.S.A. and the U.S.S.R., 1945–1987*

A Time of Passion: *America, 1960–1980*

The Cost of Good Intentions: *New York City and the Liberal Experiment*

# IRON DESTINIES, LOST OPPORTUNITIES

*The Arms Race Between the U.S.A.*
*and the U.S.S.R., 1945–1987*

CHARLES R. MORRIS

*A Cornelia & Michael Bessie Book*

HARPER & ROW, PUBLISHERS, New York
*Cambridge, Philadelphia, San Francisco, Washington*
*London, Mexico City, São Paulo, Singapore, Sydney*

We would like to thank Princeton University Press for permission to quote from Herman
Kahn, *On Thermonuclear War*. Copyright © 1960 by Princeton University Press.

FIRST EDITION

Designer: Sidney Feinberg

Copy editor: Ann Adelman

Indexer: Maro Riofrancos

Library of Congress Cataloging-in-Publication Data

Morris, Charles R.
  Iron destinies, lost opportunities.

  "A Cornelia & Michael Bessie book."
  Bibliography: p.
  Includes index.
  1. Arms control—History. 2. Nuclear arms
control—United States—History. 3. Nuclear arms
control—Soviet Union—History. I. Title.
JX1974.M587  1988      327.1'74'09      87-45650
ISBN 0-06-039082-4

88  89  90  91  92  RRD  10  9  8  7  6  5  4  3  2  1

*To my mother*

# Contents

*Acknowledgments*    ix
*Introduction*    xi

### PART I. THE ORIGINS

1. The Uncertain Alliance    3
2. The Beginning of the Cold War    23
3. "An Action Short of War"    42
4. From Berlin to the Yalu    57

### PART II. SUPERIORITY AND DOUBT

5. In Stalin's Wake    81
6. Eisenhower    94
7. The Technological Imperative    120
8. The Failure of Dwight Eisenhower    147

### PART III. AMERICA AT THE CREST

9. The Summons of the Trumpet    163
10. Winning the Arms Race    179
11. Vietnam Prelude: The Road from Bandung    199
12. Hubris    212

### PART IV. THE SHIFTING BALANCE

13. Decisions in the Kremlin    235
14. "Mad Momentum"—ABMs, MIRVs, and SS-9s    246

15. The Technology of Long-Range Destruction    269
16. SALT and the Shifting Military Balance    286

### PART V. THE JAGGED COURSE

17. The Bear Stretches    315
18. Arms Control Revisited    334
19. Images of War    348
20. Rearming America    373

### PART VI. FORTY YEARS AFTER

21. New Opportunities?    405
22. The Military Balance, 1987    418
23. Lessons and Reflections    435

   *Notes*    445
   *Works Cited*    505
   *Index*    529

# Acknowledgments

An author invariably imposes on friends. Three deserve special mention. Andrew Kerr, my business partner, took an active interest in the project from the beginning and tolerated an excessive level of absence—both physical and mental—with good spirit during its prolonged gestation. Jan Lodal was unfailingly and spontaneously generous with his time, his immense knowledge of weapons issues, and his contacts in the defense community. Ed Hamilton undertook a massive, written, line-by-line critique of an earlier draft that was both challenging and enormously helpful. A number of other friends—Evan Davis, Dave Downes, Greg Farrell, Diana Murray, Herb Rosenzweig, Ivan Selin, Claude Singer, Jon Weiner—read and commented on all or part of various drafts. Doug Love led me through some mathematics of weapons effects that overmatched my rusty calculus. Cynthia Smith, of the University of Hawaii, double-checked thousands of notes and weapons details conscientiously and indefatigably and made innumerable astute suggestions. I'm grateful to them all. I consider it a privilege to work with my editor, Mike Bessie, and my agent, Tim Seldes. Finally, but not at all least, my wife, Beverly, and my children, Michael, Kathleen, and Matthew, managed to endure yet another book with affection and good humor.

# Introduction

A ballistic missile is one of the dazzling technological achievements of the modern age. The Minuteman missile, the mainstay of the American force, 60 feet long, sleekly lethal, graceful as a Brancusi sculpture, can erupt from a deep underground silo on barely a minute's warning; it can carry three warheads, each with more than fifteen times the explosive power of the atomic bombs that devastated Hiroshima and Nagasaki, and place them each within several hundred feet of a target in the Soviet Union 8,000 miles away. The newer MX missile carries ten warheads and is even more accurate. There are 1,000 Minutemen and MXs buried in silos in a broad swath through the center of the American continent. The Soviet Union has even more land-based missiles than the United States and bigger ones. Their modern SS-18 and SS-19 missiles carry more than 5,000 warheads, all of them accurate enough, in theory at least, to destroy America's Minutemen and MX missiles in the ground.

On the average day, some thirty-five huge American and Soviet missile-launching submarines lurk deep beneath the world's oceans, playing a deadly game of cat-and-mouse with the other side's trailing attack submarines, using powerful computers to search out each other's presence in the smear of random sound from fish and tidal flux. The United States carries almost twice as many warheads on its submarine missiles as the Soviet Union does, with as many as fourteen packed onto a single missile. A single American submarine could launch two nuclear warheads at *every one* of the top one hundred Soviet cities. Most amazingly, the newest generation of American submarine-borne missiles, despite being launched from drifting underwater platforms, will achieve the same few hundred feet of accuracy as the most modern land-based missiles.

Both sides are deploying new cruise missiles, inexpensive, small, and deadly, that can be launched from any platform, a moving ship, a bomber aloft, a truck or a train. The cruise skims across the earth's surface, zigzagging through mountain ranges and man-made obstacles, too low for aircraft defenses, too small for most radars (remember Mathias Rust, the German teenager who flew his little plane to the Kremlin?), tracing a route from maps stored in its memory, and homing on its target with almost perfect accuracy. The nuclear infrastructures of both sides are filled out with satellites, communications, and radar networks—the American network stretches throughout the world—to detect impending attacks and direct their own forces. The early warning and battle management components, like the huge "phased-array" radars, electronic eyes that can sweep across the sky in millionths of a second, tracking hundreds of objects at a time, are technological marvels as imposing in their own way as the missile forces themselves.

The lethal majesty of the strategic nuclear arsenals obscures the immense investments both the United States and the Soviet Union have made in their conventional forces. Spending on President Reagan's "Star Wars" program and all other American nuclear programs accounts for less than 10 percent of total American defense outlays. The Soviet Union maintains 5 million men under arms, the United States more than 2 million, and the NATO allies another 3 million. America's forces are spread worldwide, its force projection abilities symbolized by fifteen giant carrier fleets, huge floating military bases that bring American atomic bombers and nuclear and conventionally armed missiles within range of any target anywhere in the world. The Soviet Union's conventional power is centered in its fleet of more than 50,000 tanks and the great weight of mechanized artillery, troop carriers, tactical bombers, and short-range missiles poised for *blitzkrieg* war in Central Europe.

Leapfrogging technological genius drives the conventional arms competition as much as the strategic one. Antitank missiles with special warheads to blast through tank armor cast doubt on Soviet tank power; a Soviet technical breakthrough in armor construction threatens the obsolescence of most NATO antitank weapons. Homing missiles endanger tactical aircraft; electronic jamming devices confuse the antiaircraft missiles. The newest generations of American precision-guided weapons—not yet in operation—threaten the mass destruction of entire Soviet tank brigades. Soviet guided missiles, launched at long range by ocean-prowling bombers, could wreak similar havoc against the mighty American carrier fleet.

American military spending each year amounts to about three years' worth of national economic growth. The Soviet burden is much greater, since it matches or exceeds American spending on an economic base only half the size. Military spending is not a total waste. The Defense Department, for example, virtually created the American microchip industry and sustained it during its infancy. But the economic success of countries like Japan, which diverts little of its scientific and engineering talent into weapons design, can hardly be fortuitous. The immense level of American defense spending also bears much of the responsibility for the large budget deficits that have strained world finances throughout the 1980s. In the Soviet Union, the decades of emphasis on the military have created shameful investment imbalances, an economy that is slipping from second to third rank in the world, and a consumer standard of living that is still mired in the 1950s.

Against a forty-year history of competitive arming stands the single, massive fact that the world has thus far avoided a nuclear war. It must be left to metaphysicians to debate whether that happy forbearance has been because of, or in spite of, the existence of the vast stores of weapons. Even so, no one could have conceived, three or four decades ago, that the opposing armories would grow to such size. Not even the most enthusiastic advocate of nuclear deterrence would argue that *10 billion tons* of TNT equivalent explosive power is the essential minimum for deterrence.

The obvious question, then, is: how did we get here? The purpose of this book is to help trace out the answer to that question, and perhaps draw some lessons that might be helpful in the decades ahead.

A note on usage: I have strenuously avoided the use of all but a handful of the most common military acronyms; my objective was to avoid the necessity for a glossary of terms. In choosing among the various English transliterations of Russian, Chinese, and Arabic names, I have tried merely for consistency.

# PART I.

------------------------------------------------------------

# THE ORIGINS

CHAPTER 1

---

# The Uncertain Alliance

## The Big Three

Franklin Roosevelt dropped out of sight after his inauguration to a fourth presidential term on January 20, 1945, making no public appearances and issuing no public statements for almost two weeks. Astonishingly, to a modern age accustomed to obsessive press attention to every detail of a President's daily schedule, there was virtually no speculation on his whereabouts until rumors began to emanate from Cairo early in February that Roosevelt had travelled to the Crimea for a "Big Three" meeting of the Allied wartime leaders—Roosevelt himself, Winston Churchill, the prime minister of Great Britain, and Joseph Stalin, the General Secretary of the Communist Party and president of the Council of People's Commissars of the Soviet Union. Charles de Gaulle issued a testy statement that if such a conference was indeed under way, none of its conclusions could be binding upon France. The meeting had been in progress for almost a week before it was officially announced in England that Churchill would miss the opening of the British Trade Unions Congress because he was conferring on a ship "somewhere in the Black Sea" with Roosevelt and Stalin.

Roosevelt had left the United States by ship shortly after the inauguration to meet with Churchill on the island of Malta in the Mediterranean. From Malta, a party of some 700 British and American officials flew in two dozen military planes to Yalta, a summer resort on the Black Sea. At the airfield, the entourage was greeted with a sumptuous banquet of smoked sturgeon and salmon, caviar, white and black bread, cheese, butter, and the finest vodka, champagne, and brandies that could be ransacked from Russia's starving land. The parties drove separately on newly finished roads to the collection of Czarist summer palaces where the meetings would be held—the Black Sea ship story

3

was a wartime security ruse. Armed sentinels stationed every hundred yards along the six-hour drive fired salutes, and woman guards waved bright kerchiefs and scarves. Churchill's car was intercepted by Vyacheslav Molotov, the dour Soviet Foreign Minister—Stalin's train had not yet arrived—and the prime minister, grumbling how Roosevelt had managed to slip by, was spirited off to yet another enormous meal.

Roosevelt set up shop in the Livadia Palace, a favorite home of the Czar Nicholas, built shortly before the Russian Revolution for 2 million gold rubles. The top delegations luxuriated in enormous bedrooms—the doughty Admiral Ernest King had the Czarina's boudoir—but colonels and majors were crowded as many as sixteen to a room. The plumbing was execrable. Roosevelt had the only private bath, and the entire British delegation had only two. On the third day, Navy personnel were discreetly called in to exterminate the bedbugs.

Roosevelt was almost universally acknowledged as the world's supreme politician. Virtually single-handedly, he had steered his country to its late perception of the global dangers of fascism and nazism, orchestrated its entry into the war, and maneuvered all the threads of the Western command into his own fingers. His dazzlingly diffuse intellectual style—following his thought process was "very much like chasing a vagrant sunbeam around an empty room," said his Secretary of War—gave the impression of superficiality. But Roosevelt's management of the war effort belies such judgments. In broad strategic terms, his judgment was superb and he had the confidence to insist upon it. Roosevelt understood that the United States could successfully fight on two fronts at the same time; he grasped the primacy of the war in the North Atlantic, the necessity to defeat Germany first, the importance of North Africa, the proper time for a European invasion, and the nature of a Pacific naval strategy. After the war, Churchill, who did not pay compliments lightly, remarked that Roosevelt was "the most skillful strategist of them all." Better than Marshall, his interlocutor asked. "Yes, better than Marshall," Churchill replied.

For Roosevelt, "the possibility that something might turn up he could not deal with seemed never to cross his mind." "I think," he wrote to Churchill in 1942, "I can personally handle Stalin better than either the Foreign Office or my State Department. Stalin hates the guts of all your top people. He thinks he likes me better." After he met the dictator at Teheran in 1943, he described him as "the very heart and soul of Russia, and I believe we are going to get along very well with him and the Russian people—very well indeed." He told Henry Wallace that "the United States and Russia are young powers. . . . England is a tired old power." After Yalta, he told the American people that "agreement was reached on every point. And more important . . . I may say, we achieved a unity of thought and a way of getting along together."

To a certain extent, of course, Roosevelt's optimistic appraisals of Stalin were politicking. He wanted to entice both Russia and the American people to join in his vision of a postwar world order. In private conversations with de Gaulle, he betrayed greater cynicism. Certainly Charles "Chip" Bohlen, probably the leading Soviet expert at the State Department, and Averell Harriman, the Ambassador to Moscow, both of whom were close advisers, harbored few illusions about the Soviet system. Before the war, too, Roosevelt had made some fierce anti-Soviet remarks, and just before his death it appears that he was sharply revising his hopes of cooperation with the Russians. Indeed, who is to say that, given better health and more time, he might not have had greater success. Stalin, Harriman remarked, seems to have feared Roosevelt most of all. Churchill would pick your pocket for a kopeck, Stalin once told Milovan Djilas, "but Roosevelt goes only for the larger denominations."

Roosevelt's sunny optimism is often contrasted with Churchill's gloomy realism about the Russians. But Churchill too was frequently given to the delusion that he could somehow "manage" Stalin. Churchill had insisted on travelling to Moscow by himself some three months before Yalta to discuss a postwar settlement with the Russian leader. Roosevelt, infuriated, had demanded that Harriman accompany him. But Churchill managed to shake the dogged Harriman off and, alone with Stalin, made his celebrated "percentages" proposal—that they would exercise their influence over the Balkans as follows: Greece, 10 percent Soviet, 90 percent British; Rumania, 90 percent Soviet, 10 percent British; Bulgaria, 75 percent Soviet, 25 percent British; Hungary and Yugoslavia, 50:50. Churchill listed the divisions on a piece of paper; Stalin simply made a check with his big blue pencil. Then Churchill, perhaps embarrassed at his own cynicism, proposed that they burn the paper. "No, you keep it," said Stalin.

Churchill's own great influence on the historiography of the war has undoubtedly contributed to the exaggeration of his prescience about Soviet intentions in Europe. Eisenhower and Marshall's refusal to mount an attack from Italy through the Ljubljana Gap to Vienna to forestall Soviet control of Austria and all the Balkans is often presented as the classic contrast of American naivete with British geopolitical realism. Churchill's insistence, however, was not nearly so vigorous as sometimes portrayed, and the narrow confines of the Gap, still well defended by the Germans, held the seeds of a military disaster. Similarly, the latterday assertion that Eisenhower could have reached Berlin before the Soviets is at best arguable; and Marshal Zhukov permitted the Americans and British access to their agreed zones in any case, and matched Eisenhower's pullback from his end-of-war position in Germany with a Soviet pullback from its own end-of-war position in Austria to pre-arranged lines.

Churchill's view of the Russians wavered through 1944. At times he was sunk in gloom. ". . . although I have tried in every way to put myself in sympathy with these Communist leaders," he said, "I cannot feel the slightest trust or confidence in them. Force and facts are their only realities." And in the spring, he told Anthony Eden, his Foreign Secretary, "broadly speaking, the issue is: are we going to acquiesce in the communisation of the Balkans and perhaps of Italy?" But during the same period, he told reporters that Stalin's position on Poland was "reasonable." Then in the fall, Churchill was outraged at Stalin's cold refusal to supply, or even to allow the Allies to supply, the Polish underground fighters during the Warsaw Rising; for eight dreadful weeks the Polish partisans were slaughtered by the Nazis while the Russian armies were encamped on the Vistula, a relatively short distance away.* Yet Churchill made his trip to Moscow within weeks of the Rising, and told Stalin, "there are no matters which cannot be adjusted between us when we meet together in a frank and intimate discussion." Even after Yalta, when Churchill was generally depressed by the Polish settlement, he rallied his spirits to report: "Marshall Stalin and the Soviet leaders wish to live in honourable friendship and equality with the Western democracies. I feel that their word is their bond. I know of no government which stands to its obligations, even in its own despite, more solidly than the Russian Soviet government."

But of the two Western leaders, only Churchill had an imagination of the epic and purple proportions required to grasp even an inkling of the monstrous reality behind the squat, pock-faced, often charming, Joseph Stalin—a paranoid, bloody-handed tyrant, a psychopath who

*The issue is not quite as black-and-white as it appeared in 1944. Rokossovsky, the Soviet commander, was clearly overextended by the time he reached the Vistula, and the Rising was premature. But Stalin's refusal, at the height of the massacre, to allow Allied supply planes to land or take off from Soviet soil was vengeful. He certainly understood that the decimation of the Polish underground would make his own pacification of Poland that much easier.

had created a pathological state in his own image. Hitler surpassed him only in the surgical, so very German, efficiency of his cruelties. Stalin's death list was the greater, built up over years of exercising an Oriental despotism on a scale vaster and more far-reaching than any man had ever before conceived. Djilas, who knew him well, confers on him "the glory of being the greatest criminal in history. . . . For in him was joined the criminal senselessness of Caligula, the refinement of a Borgia, and the brutality of a Tsar Ivan the Terrible." Stalin has the unique distinction among tyrants that rather than killing merely "enemies who had actually opposed" him, he wreaked his vengeance as well on "friends and colleagues, who had done nothing and constituted no danger to him."

Stalin came to his policy of terror only by degrees. After consolidating his power in the late 1920s, he began enforcing agricultural collectivization in Kazhakstan. Ever more heavy-handed methods were used as the peasants resisted, with the result that livestock were slaughtered, crops were disrupted, and famine ensued. It soon became apparent that as the famine spread, peasant resistance to collectivization collapsed; so famine was then applied as deliberate policy in the Ukraine. Robert Conquest estimates that at least 11 million people, perhaps as many as 14 million, died in Stalin's rural terror, with a minimum of 7 million directly starving to death and another 4 million dying in labor camps as a result of mass deportations in the name of "dekulakization"—kulaks were middle-class peasants, and by definition enemies of the state.

Resistance to Stalin's rural depredations surfaced in the Communist Party's Seventeenth Congress in 1934, and he unleashed a violent repression upon his own party, first engineering the assassination of Sergei Kirov, a rising young party moderate. The years between Kirov's murder and the war were a delirium of midnight arrests, sudden disappearances, secret executions, and show trials in which heroes of the Soviet Union debased themselves with fantastic "confessions" of vast spy rings and underground armies dedicated to the downfall of Mother Russia and the Great Leader himself. Of the eleven other original members of the Bolshevik ruling elite who survived to 1937, all died by Stalin's hand. Of 1,966 delegates to the 1934 Congress, 1,108 were executed or imprisoned. Of 115 members of the 1934 Party Central Committee, 98 (by some counts, 110) were shot. When Stalin turned against the military in 1937, he executed 3 of 5 Marshals, including the revered Tukachevsky, 14 of 16 army commanders, all 8 admirals, 60 of 67 corps commanders, and 357 of 596 divisional and brigade commanders.

The Terror reached down into the lowest levels of society, and the nation was coerced into becoming a vast network of informers. For turning in his own father, twelve-year-old Pavel Morozov was proclaimed a hero of the Young Communist League, and a statue of him was erected in his village square. A careful estimate is that by the end of 1938, there were 17 million people in prison or labor camps, and that a million people were executed in that year alone. Demographers discovered after the war that the population of the Soviet Union was 20 million lower than they had anticipated after accounting for the deaths attributable to the war.

Stalin seems to have taken a rough pleasure in his nation's debasement. He apparently personally dictated some of the more absurd confessions, and occasionally watched the show trials from behind a curtain, as the prosecutor, Andrei Vyshinsky—the same Vyshinsky who dealt with the West as Deputy Foreign Minister after the war—put his victims through their paces, as often as not with Western correspondents in attendance, most of whom detected little untoward in the proceedings. Most bizarre was the Terror's insistence that its victims "confess." The medieval Inquisition similarly redeemed both the sinner and its own purposes, and Stalin's confessions were as readily extorted by torture, although of a brutal and ham-handed variety compared to the exquisite cruelties of episcopal Spain.*

The despotic nature of Stalin's rule was known in broad outline to Western specialists, although it was diplomatically forgotten when the heroic struggles of the Soviet Union proved to be the major turning point in the war against the Nazis. Giving due credit to English steadfastness after Dunkirk, and to the great contribution of American materiel, the Alliance could never have prevailed without the immense sacrifices of the Russian people. Anglo-American deaths in both theaters in World War II did not exceed 1 million. Russia's are estimated at 20 million. But even in 1945, gratitude and the glow of the approaching victory could not quite obscure the underlying strains in what was

*In Arthur Koestler's fictional account of a show trial in *Darkness at Noon,* often taken as an account of Bukharin's trial, the defendant confesses because of his loyalty to Bolshevism. Solzhenitsyn makes the point specifically: "Bukharin devoted [himself] . . . to the dialectical elaboration of the judicial lie: for Bukharin it was too stupid and futile to die if he was altogether innocent (thus he *needed* to find his own guilt!)" It is a good tale but not true. After a year's imprisonment, Bukharin admitted his guilt, but in terms that were obviously defiant and that made a nonsense of the charges, much to Vyshinsky's exasperation. His fifty-four co-defendants, however, all made abject confessions; but apparently all of them, unlike Bukharin, were physically tortured. The show trials, though mad, were not without method. Bukharin's trial, for instance, succeeded in discrediting *all* former Bolshevik leaders except Stalin, and "grudgingly," Lenin.

never more than an alliance of last resort. The public doctrine of Bolshevism, after all, muted though it may have been during the war, challenged the very legitimacy of Western governments and proclaimed that the historic mission of the Soviet Union was to hasten their doom. More important, Stalin's cynical pact with Hitler in 1939, and his jackal grab for eastern Poland and the Baltic states, had figured mightily in starting a shooting war in the first place. Had Hitler not turned upon him, Stalin might have been sharing the spoils of a different table.

Tensions were evident well before 1945. Stalin was embittered by Roosevelt's failure to deliver on a much-too-casual promise to open a second European front in 1942. Nor was he placated by the North African invasion, since he considered it directed more at preserving the British Empire than at easing pressure on Russia. His irritation grew when the unexpected resistance of the Vichy French in Africa meant that a European invasion had to be postponed again in 1943—although most military writers agree that an invasion attempt at that time would have been suicidal. And the Russians were insulted by the American need for gratitude for the lend-lease aid. During the Siege of Stalingrad, one minor official exploded: "We've lost millions of people, and the Americans want us to crawl on our knees because they send us Spam!"

The exasperation was reciprocated by the American foreign service professionals, who were particularly offended by the Russian peasant style of bargaining. The Soviets seemed to regard the vast flow of lend-lease goods as their due, and rarely even acknowledged the aid. General John Deane, whom Roosevelt had handpicked to head the military mission to Moscow and mend relations, wrote how at innumerable Russian banquets: "These toasts go down past the tongues in the cheeks. After the banquets we send the Soviets another thousand airplanes and they approve a visa that has been hanging fire for months. We then scratch our heads to see what other gifts we can send, and they scratch theirs to see what else they can ask for."

Even at the height of the war effort, Stalin's obsession with secrecy obtruded on normal relations. He refused to allow Allied pilots to overfly Russia, no matter what the reason, and was always reluctant to exchange military information. He would not permit the Americans to establish air bases in Siberia to use against Japan, even after he had agreed to enter the Pacific War, and it was somehow always difficult to arrange the release of American fliers whose planes had been downed over Russia. For their part, the Americans and the British took pains to keep their progress on the atomic bomb a secret from the Soviet Union.

The lack of trust is evident in the gnawing fear of both the Soviets and the Western Allies that the other would make a separate peace with Hitler. Anglo-American fears eased when the Soviets began their triumphal march westward after the victory at Stalingrad. But even in the spring of 1945, just before Roosevelt's death, Stalin became nearly hysterical when the Americans insisted on excluding Russia from preliminary talks on the surrender of German forces in Italy—the Germans, it was feared, would not surrender to Russians. Stalin bluntly accused Roosevelt of unilaterally easing peace terms and allowing the Germans to transfer troops to the Eastern front. Roosevelt protested his "bitter resentment" at "these vile accusations" and elicited a grudging statement that was perhaps the closest Stalin ever came to making an apology.

If Western-Russian relations were strained, those between the United States and Great Britain were not nearly so close as the existence of the latterday "special relationship" might imply. A number of influential Americans, including Harry Hopkins, believed that "British imperialism loomed as much a potential threat to peace as Soviet-Russian Communism," and Hopkins told Churchill's doctor on the way to Teheran that "you will find us lining up with the Russians." Roosevelt thought that the British Empire was an anachronism, and was determined not to put American power at the service of a postwar colonial restoration, an attitude that provoked "much friction, and some heated exchanges" with Churchill. The Permanent Secretary of the British Foreign Office, Sir Alexander Cadogan, remarked wryly how Churchill's manners were tested by "explanations from the President about other powers' higher morality." At the time of the Yalta Conference, the *New York Times* published a think-piece on "America and Britain: Rivals or Partners," and C. L. Sulzberger cautioned that while the United States had "no base of conflict" with the Soviet Union, it could be drawn into postwar controversies by imperial Britain.

The British were fully as ambivalent as the Americans. Edward Stettinius, Roosevelt's Secretary of State, wrote of "the emotional difficulty which . . . any Englishman has in adjusting himself to a secondary role." Or as de Gaulle commented, with evident satisfaction, "The British did not conceal their gloom . . . at finding themselves dispossessed of the leading role." In 1946, for instance, despite a previous agreement between Roosevelt and Churchill, the two countries quickly agreed to chart independent courses in the development of nuclear power. Stalin was well apprised of Anglo-American frictions. Soviet officials were approaching Americans with the message that "Americans and Russians should stick together and solve the problem without British interference," at about the same time as British diplomats were being asked "why we worked so closely with the Americans . . . [since] we had much more to gain by working with the Russians."

## Yalta

The conference at Yalta, one of the those "woolly and bibulous" exercises in summit diplomacy, in Cadogan's waspish phrase, marked in many ways a high point of Allied cooperation; but at the same time it threw into sharp relief all the root divisions that were ultimately to lead to the Cold War. The conference was as much Roosevelt's idea as anyone's. With the end of the war in sight, he was anxious to begin settling the postwar order, and started pressing for a summit conference as soon as his election was assured in 1944. Several months were devoted to finding a site agreeable to Stalin, who refused to travel beyond territories controlled by the Red Army, and who insisted, in any case, that he could not leave Russia while he was directing the massive Soviet war effort.

Neither Churchill nor Roosevelt was at his best at Yalta. Roosevelt was dying—the obvious deterioration of his health was a shock to a number of observers—and Churchill was despondent over the palpable slippage of British influence and his own growing political difficulties at home, "spending hours of his own and other people's time simply drivelling," according to the weary Cadogan. Stalin, by contrast, was at the height of his powers, buoyed by his great military victories in the East, a virtual deity at home, and armed with a set of precise and absolutely concrete objectives. Cadogan wrote home, "I think Uncle Joe much the most impressive. The President flapped about and the PM boomed, but Joe just sat there taking it all in and being rather amused. When he did chip in, he never used a superfluous word, and spoke very much to the point."

The military review at the start of the conference enhanced the Soviet psychological edge. The British and the Americans were facing less than half the number of German divisions as the Russians, but their advance had been disrupted by the great German counterattack in the Ardennes. At the request of the Western Allies, Stalin had accelerated his winter offensive schedule to relieve pressure on Eisenhower's troops; and after a "whirlwind offensive," over a million Russian troops were massing on the Oder and Neisse rivers, within striking distance of Berlin. Roosevelt and Churchill were appropriately admiring.

Stalin's own attitude toward summit diplomacy may also have wavered between cynicism and hope. At one point, when Churchill proposed in a toast that the three great powers could preserve world peace for a hundred years, Stalin responded with genuine emotion. And in a rough way, in a bargain between equals, he would keep his word—after his fashion, that is, or as he told Hopkins, "the Soviet Union always honors its word, except in cases of extreme necessity." He refused to help the Greek Communists in their fight against the British, for instance, at least partly because he had told Churchill that Greece was within the British sphere of influence. The enormous gap in comprehension between the West and the Soviet Union, however, was a fundamental problem. As Harriman remarked, "words have different connotations for the Soviets." Stalin never understood why the Americans and the British kept resorting to high-flown declarations of principle. Declarations, he said to Anthony Eden, are "algebra"; he preferred the "practical arithmetic" of politics. In a revealing exchange at Yalta one evening, Churchill, after a number of brandies, declaimed on the rights of small nations: "The eagle should permit the small birds to sing, and care not wherefor they sang." Stalin merely growled that small birds better watch their step when the eagle was around, and then proceeded to berate Roosevelt for allowing Argentina to support the Nazis. If Argentina had been in *his* sphere of influence, he stated darkly, he would have taught it the hazards of an independent political line.

Stalin's bargaining position was made all the stronger by the failure of Roosevelt and Churchill to concert theirs. As often as not, Roosevelt, with his natural politician's instinct for compromise, slid into the position of mediator between Churchill and Stalin. Churchill and Stalin had diametrically opposed positions on the future of Germany, for instance. In the long tradition of British balance-of-power politics, Churchill wanted a strong France and a rehabilitated Germany to serve as counterweights to the looming Soviet power in Central Europe, and was thoroughly exasperated by the Americans' apparent inability to understand what he was talking about. He believed that the punitive policy toward Germany in 1919 had paved the way for Nazism and feared "chaining England to Germany's corpse." It was the one issue that caused Stalin to lose his temper. He wanted to see Germany emasculated, and was counting on German raw materials and capital equipment to rebuild his own ravaged country, the more so since the United States had recently shown a disposition to attach political conditions to postwar loans.

Roosevelt airily dismissed Churchill's balance-of-power worries—the new supranational peace-keeping mechanisms would make them irrelevant, he hoped—and he skittered between all sides on most of the other issues. At first, he stunned the British by siding with Stalin against granting great power status to France in the postwar administration of Germany, then he switched sides and persuaded Stalin to go along by volunteering that American troops would leave Europe within two years after the war. On reparations, Roosevelt endorsed a plan, in the fall of 1944, that would have "pastoralized" Germany, breaking it up into small duchies and stripping it of its industry; but he later admitted the plan was a "boner." He seemed to switch again at the start of the conference when he told Stalin privately that he felt "bloodthirsty" on Germany, but in the plenary sessions, began to slide toward Churchill's position, particularly as it became clear that the United States would end up footing the bill, just as it had for the reparations exacted after World War I. Stalin finally challenged Roosevelt's vacillations directly, and Harry Hopkins slipped his boss a note that it was Uncle Joe's turn to win one. Roosevelt then pushed through an agreement that the Soviet figure of $20 billion in reparations would be the "basis for discussion" at a postconference reparations commission to meet in Moscow. This was something less than a final commitment, but the American minutes of the meeting leave a clear impression that Stalin had won a significant concession from the President.

Churchill and Roosevelt also had quite different interests in Asia. For Roosevelt, an overriding objective of the conference was to secure Soviet participation in the war against Japan; in a private meeting with Stalin, he freely gave away Chinese and Japanese territory to that end, and expressed the hope that he and Stalin could create a postwar Asian dispensation without involving the British. The secrecy of his backstage dealings—neither Truman nor Byrnes was certain of the details of the Asian territorial concessions a year later—helped create the "black legend" of Yalta. For his part, Stalin bargained shamelessly—how could he persuade the Soviet government to join the Pacific war, he pleaded, unless he brought home major territorial concessions? He wanted the Kurile and lower Sakhalin islands from Japan, leases at Port Arthur and Dairien, Outer Mongolia separated from China, and control of the Chinese eastern and Manchurian railroads. In grasping for Chinese territory, of course, he displayed little sensitivity for his ally, Mao Ze-dong, one of a long series of perfidies that eventually culminated in the Sino-Soviet split.

The central issue of the conference, however, was Poland, and here Roosevelt and Churchill were relatively united. The Polish question is often presented as a confrontation between the principle of self-deter-mination and *realpolitik* concepts of spheres of influence. But no one at Yalta disputed that Poland was within the Soviet sphere of influence, a fact that Churchill's "percentage" proposal of the previous fall merely confirmed. Roosevelt, his public rhetoric notwithstanding, had tacitly accepted at the Teheran Conference in 1943 that Stalin's writ would run in Poland, and at Yalta both he and Churchill anxiously reassured Stalin that he should have only "friendly" nations on his borders. There was, in any case, little choice in the matter, since Poland was already occupied by the Red Army. The issue at Yalta was never whether Poland would be a Soviet satellite, but how the Soviet Union would exercise its power—for it was beginning to dawn on Western diplomats just what Stalin might mean by "friendly."

The basic problem in ensuring a "friendly" Poland was that self-respecting Poles hated the Russians. Russia and Poland had been ene-mies for centuries. Only five years had passed since Stalin had agreed with Hitler to take a huge chunk of eastern Poland in exchange for giving the Nazi dictator a free hand in the West. Less than twenty years before that, Lenin had suppressed his anti-imperialist scruples long enough to conquer most of eastern Poland until he overextended him-self trying to take Warsaw itself. Marshal Pilsudski, probably the most revered Polish leader between the wars, regarded Russia as an "Asiatic monster, covered with European veneer."

The Soviet "liberation" of Poland fully supported Pilsudski's judg-ment. In the same month as the Yalta Conference, a British report said that the Soviet Army was "plundering the people in an alarming man-ner . . . stripping the people of provisions, taking watches and valuables, and raping women." And another report the next month described the population in Soviet areas as "far worse than before . . . the Red Army completely devastated the countryside, looting absolutely everything movable." Stalin himself may have ordered the massacre of thousands of Poles. There was no trace of some 9,000 Polish officers who had been held in Soviet prisons at the outbreak of the war; when pressed on their whereabouts, Stalin only muttered that they had been assisted to "es-cape to Manchuria." Finally, there was the circumstantial evidence of the mass grave at Katyn Forest, now accepted as convincing by most historians, that in 1940 the Soviets had executed more than 4,000 Polish officers in cold blood, each with a single shot in the back of the head. Later, when asked about the Polish officers, Lavrenti Beria, head of Stalin's secret police, said that there had been "a grave mistake" and that they were not available. Poles did not need long memories to mistrust Stalin.

The Polish leaders, most of whom were established in an émigré outpost in London, regarded any move toward a European settlement with deep suspicion. These were the same stiff-necked patriots who, unlike the Czechs, had gone to war with Germany rather than acquiesce in territorial concessions, and they had no intention of giving up eastern Poland to Stalin. Churchill sympathized with their position, but had little patience with their stubbornness, and took it upon himself to explain the facts of life. Nobody was going to war to restore Polish boundaries, he told the London Poles, adding brutally: "If you want to conquer Russia, we shall leave you to do it." Churchill's remonstrations might have had more effect if it had not been for Roosevelt's dissimulations. At Teheran, he had told Stalin that he understood Russia's need for buffer states against Germany, but confided that he could not say so publicly because of the importance of the Polish vote at home. With his eye on the 1944 elections, he persisted in encouraging the London Poles in the belief that he would support their territorial claims, when he had no intention of doing so, and almost certainly stiffened the Polish opposition to any postwar compromises with the Soviets. When asked at one point how he planned to extricate himself from the growing Polish muddle, he said he would appeal to Stalin to do the right thing "on grounds of high morality."

As far as Stalin was concerned, there was no longer a Polish problem. He had assured himself of the country's official loyalty by establishing a "friendly" government composed primarily of little-known but suitably subservient Polish Communists—the so-called Lublin government, from the name of the city where it was organized. All of the apparatus of the Soviet police state was being put into place by the time the Western governments began raising the Polish question at Yalta. Beria's NKVD, officering the Communist partisans, had embarked on a virtual civil war against the Polish Home Army, the largest Nazi resistance movement in Europe, and were apparently under orders to search out and kill the more active and aggressive Polish resistance leaders.

Churchill and Roosevelt opened the discussions on Poland by addressing Stalin's territorial demands—Stalin wanted all the territory he had gained by his pact with Hitler, pushing the Russo-Polish border west to the "Curzon Line" drafted by the British and French at the close of World War I. Since Stalin was one of the world's greatest leaders, Churchill and Roosevelt asked, might he not be "magnanimous" and not take quite so much? Stalin professed to be shocked. How could he be "less Russian than Curzon and Clemenceau?" He could "not even return to Moscow" if he made such a concession, he expostulated. The matter was closed. Churchill and Roosevelt then shifted focus to the undemocratic nature of the Polish regime and pressed Stalin hard over the next several days. Could a new government be formed incorporating the London Poles? A flat "No" from Stalin. Would Poland hold free elections? Of course, Stalin assured them—the Soviet Union was a democratic country. Could Westerners observe the elections? Again a flat "No." Stalin needled Churchill throughout. Who, he asked, had elected de Gaulle, whom Churchill supported so strongly as the leader of free France? Did Churchill's eloquence on behalf of self-determination apply to India as well? He was sorry Churchill could not get information from Poland. Oddly, he himself was having trouble getting information from Greece. Not that he *needed* information from Greece, he hastened to add, for he had agreed that Greece was within Churchill's sphere of influence.

Finally, Stalin resorted to country-bazaar bargaining. Roosevelt proposed at one meeting that the Poles themselves be invited to Yalta to discuss matters. The next day, Stalin announced that his delegation had been trying to contact the Lublin Poles to invite them to the conference. Alas, they didn't have their phone numbers. Molotov, however, had drafted a new position on Poland. But it was still being typed, so perhaps they might discuss the United Nations. Whereupon Molotov, to Roosevelt's surprise and delight, read a paper that dropped the most extreme Soviet demands on voting procedures in the new organization—Stalin had previously demanded that each of the sixteen Soviet republics have its own vote. It was a topic dear to Roosevelt's heart, and one on which the Soviets had been intransigent. Roosevelt and Churchill expressed their gratification at Stalin's change of heart. Molotov immediately announced that his paper on Poland was ready, and although Churchill continued to fight a rearguard action, it was clearly the West's turn to compromise.

As Stalin pressed his proposal, Roosevelt asked how soon there might be free elections in Poland—for then the character of the interim regime would not be so important. "Perhaps a month, perhaps two," Stalin answered. Churchill hastened to assure Stalin that he would not be held to such a pledge until the fighting ended. Roosevelt proclaimed himself satisfied with the timetable, and a deal was struck essentially following the outline of Molotov's paper. The Lublin Poles were recognized as a legitimate interim government, although it was to be "reorganized on a broader democratic basis" to include additional but unspecified party representatives. "Free and unfettered elections" were to be held "as soon as possible." Stalin got his Curzon Line boundary with only minor digressions; and it was agreed that Poland would get "substantial accessions of territory" from Germany in compensation, although it remained for Stalin's troops to secure the boundary on the western Neisse River that he wanted. Stalin readily agreed to some "algebra"—a "Declaration on Liberated Europe" that satisfied Roosevelt's Wilsonian impulses—and the conference ended in an atmosphere of amicability.

Churchill was depressed over the Polish settlement, but even he acknowledged that it was "probably the best that could be gotten." The British Foreign Ministry staff were more optimistic because of the "spirit of frank cooperation" that characterized the discussions. The Americans were elated. Roosevelt's Secretary of State, Edward Stettinius, said that, "clearly . . . the Soviet Union made greater concessions to the United States and Great Britain than were made to the Soviets." Harry Hopkins proclaimed "the dawn of a new day. . . . We had won the first great victory of the peace—and by 'we' I mean *all* of us, the whole civilized human race."

### First Frosts

Relations quickly ran downhill after Yalta. It soon became evident that Stalin had no intention of permitting the "free and unfettered" elections he had promised in Poland. The barbaric behavior of the Red Army confirmed Churchill's worst fears. In the first weeks after Soviet troops liberated Vienna, the medical clinics counted 87,000 rape victims. Germany was much worse. Civilians were crucified, babies had their heads broken, rape was almost a matter of right. Stalin reported with pride that "no single German" remained in the area to be given to Poland. "I fear that terrible things have happened during the Russian advance through Germany to the Elbe," Churchill brooded in May.

Even more ominously for the Yalta agreements, only days after the conference ended, Vyshinsky strode into the office of King Michael of Rumania, who was trying to form a cabinet, and demanded that the government be dominated by Communists. He slammed the door so hard when he left that the plaster cracked. The Red Army presence in Bucharest left little room for argument. At the same time, it was becoming clear to the Soviets that, despite the apparent reparations accord at Yalta, the United States would never agree to the level of compensation Stalin wanted, and would probably not make up the difference with loans on terms the Soviets could accept. Roosevelt's death made the Soviets even less inclined to expect continued good relations with America.

During his first week as President in April 1945, Harry Truman received near-unanimous advice from his top foreign policy advisers—Secretary of War Henry Stimson was the notable exception—that it was time to "get tough" with the Soviets. They were strongly reinforced by Churchill, who was becoming nearly obsessed with the tightening Soviet vise on Central Europe and the looming threat to Turkey, Greece, the Dardanelles, and, as Churchill saw it, to the entire Mediterranean basin. His confidence of "managing" Stalin vanished, Churchill now saw the Soviet Union as an "invincible colossus bound to have her way on every point of the European settlement unless checked by the most determined and concerted action." Truman rejected Churchill's advice that the American armies stake out advanced positions in Eastern Europe, as too direct a contravention of the zonal understandings worked out at Yalta. But he was persuaded by Harriman and the professionals in the State Department that it was time to "lay it on the line" about Poland.

When Molotov visited the President in late April on his way to the United Nations conference in San Francisco, Truman, by his own report, "gave him the straight one-two to the jaw" on keeping the agreements on Poland. "I have never been talked to like that in my life," Molotov blustered—a doubtful statement in view of the supervisory habits of his boss, who once imprisoned Molotov's wife, presumably to encourage loyal service. "Carry out your agreements and you won't be talked to like that," Truman retorted.

The San Francisco Conference did not bode well for future Soviet-American relations. Roosevelt had induced the two leading Republican foreign policy spokesmen, Senators Arthur Vandenberg and John Foster Dulles, to serve as members of the American United Nations delegation in the hope of building bipartisan support for the organization. The strategy backfired when both men were repelled by the rude obstinacy of the Soviets, and the conference nearly broke up over Molotov's insistence that the Lublin Poles receive full recognition and a seat in the General Assembly. Stalin hardly improved the atmosphere by inviting sixteen Polish anti-Communist leaders to Moscow under a promise of safe-conduct and then promptly arresting them. Molotov reassured his horrified Western colleagues that "the guilty ones would be tried." Nearly all received long prison sentences in June, effectively destroying the Polish anti-Communist underground.

The United States was by this time openly organizing an anti-Soviet voting bloc in the General Assembly and enraged Molotov by insisting on a seat for Argentina, despite that country's pro-Nazi record. For the first time, the liberal press in America became alarmed at the possibility of a falling out between the two countries. Walter Lippmann wrote privately, "The issue here has apparently been drawn between the Soviets and ourselves. . . . This should never have happened. It would never have happened, I feel sure, if President Roosevelt were still alive"—a dubious judgment.

From the Soviet standpoint, the lack of progress on economic issues during the spring of 1945 was as frustrating as the Polish deadlock was to the Western Allies. American businessmen were enthusiastic over the prospect of trade with the Soviet Union. Eric Johnston, the president of the U.S. Chamber of Commerce, had a warm personal visit with Stalin, who assured him that Communists would be good customers. (On the whole, Stalin liked American businessmen better than American diplomats. They weren't as confused by principles.) A number of economic theorists, both in the West and the Soviet Union, predicted that the United States would suffer a serious depression after the war if it could not quickly generate massive new trade flows to maintain wartime production levels.

Somewhat to Harriman's surprise, Molotov approached him about the possibility of a large postwar credit shortly before Yalta, promising that a substantial portion would be spent in the United States. The State Department was interested, but cool. George Kennan, for one, consistently opposed loans to Russia on the ground that they would merely speed the "military-industrialization" of the country in directions inimical to the United States. Harriman persuaded Truman that credits should be viewed as "one of our principal levers for influencing political action." To be realistic, Congress was not yet in the open-handed mood of 1947. Even Great Britain received postwar credits only after an arduous negotiation over British economic policy and the system of imperial trading preferences, a humiliation that hastened the death of John Maynard Keynes, the chief British representative.

The truculent style of Soviet diplomacy undercut their case. Molotov could not resist explaining how the logic of capitalism would force the Americans to make the loans to stave off an economic crisis. More important, an influential bloc of conservative Congressmen were digging in their heels against loans without an accounting of the lend-lease aid to Russia, which Stalin refused to give. Roosevelt had basically granted Stalin whatever he asked for in lend-lease, and there was little question that by the end of the war, the Soviets were siphoning off substantial amounts of lend-lease for industrial reconstruction. Anxious to demonstrate his toughness to the conservatives, Truman decided abruptly to cut off all lend-lease aid to the Soviets that could not be identified to a specific military purpose. Whether by misinterpretation or by design, aides in the State Department interpreted the order so rigidly that even ships on the high seas were ordered to return to port, prompting infuriated complaints from Stalin, and a reversal of the order by Truman.

By the end of May, Truman himself had become sufficiently alarmed by the sharp deterioration in relations to dispatch Harry Hopkins to Moscow in a dramatic gesture to restore goodwill. Hopkins was a dying man in 1945, but he was warmly regarded by Stalin, and although Truman told him to "use a baseball bat if necessary" to straighten out Soviet-American issues, it was well known that he had been a major influence on Roosevelt's conciliatory approach at Yalta. His two weeks of personal meetings with Stalin were widely regarded as a signal success. Stalin took a hard line on Poland, but the two men eventually reached an agreement that "four or five of the eighteen or twenty" ministries in the Lublin government would be given to outsiders. It was considerably less than "free and unfettered elections," but it at least fulfilled the Yalta stipulation that the government be broadened. Hopkins also pressed for release of the Polish underground leaders, but Stalin convinced him that there was evidence of "grave crimes" and that he could rely on the fairness of the Soviet judicial system. On his side, Stalin made further concessions on United Nations voting procedures, reiterated his commitment to enter the war against Japan, probably in August, and agreed to a personal meeting with Truman in the summer. Truman was greatly heartened by the talks, and announced that "there has been some very pleasant yielding on the part of the

Russians. . . . If we keep our heads and be patient, we will arrive at a conclusion; because the Russians are just as anxious to get along with us as we are with them." In July, in a major diplomatic triumph for the Soviet Union, the United States officially recognized the Lublin government, much to Churchill's chagrin.

The Potsdam Conference, convened in the summer of 1945 in a suburb of Berlin, was the last of the great exercises of personal diplomacy by the wartime leaders. It was indeed the last time an American President met with Stalin personally. It also marked the end of Churchill's wartime leadership; he was summoned home in the midst of the conference to receive the news that his government had been turned out of office, a development that provoked "gibbering . . . astonishment" on the part of the Russians. If the atmosphere at Yalta had been one of "frank cooperation," that at Potsdam, just six months later, was one of suspicious circling. Truman is often blamed for the change in tone, but if anything, he approached the conference in a more open-minded spirit than his partners. Churchill was in a foul mood over the apparent American acquiescence to Soviet control in Eastern Europe and became almost apoplectic when Truman suggested he might meet with Stalin privately so the dictator wouldn't feel the Americans and British were ganging up on him.

Stalin was at his grabbiest. He wanted recognition of the Communist regimes in Hungary, Rumania, and Bulgaria; he wanted acceptance of his annexation of Czechoslovakia's Carpatho-Ukraine; he wanted to confirm the western Neisse as the boundary of Communist Poland; he wanted a major transfer of German industrial capital; he wanted colonies in Africa, territory in Turkey, bases in the Bosphorus, and a role in the postwar governance of Italy and Japan. In one priceless exchange of after-dinner toasts, Churchill delivered an orotund statement suitable to the summit of world diplomacy, refilled the brandy glasses, and motioned that it was Stalin's turn. After a pause, Stalin said, "If you find it impossible to give us a fortified base in the Marmora, could we not have a base at Dedegeatch?"

The discussions at Potsdam are striking for the degree to which diplomats on both sides had already conceded the principle of a divided postwar world. The Americans insisted, for example, that Russia could collect reparations only after Germany had fed its people, but agreed to avert their eyes while the Soviets looted their own German zone for whatever reparations they could get—"an invasion of the barbarians," Harriman called it. On the other hand, the West would content itself with, although not officially accept, the de facto Polish border staked out by Stalin's troops. "If we fail to reach an agreement, the result will be the same?" Molotov asked bluntly. "Yes," replied James Byrnes, the new American Secretary of State.

But the most significant event of the Potsdam Conference occurred in Alamogordo, New Mexico, when the United States carried out the first successful explosion of an atomic bomb. Truman's major objective coming to Potsdam was to set a firm date for the Soviet entrance into the Pacific War, on the advice from his military that Soviet help was still essential to an early victory. Stalin was willing to join the fighting, because he wanted to stake a claim to territorial buffers on his Asian perimeter. Truman readily confirmed Roosevelt's territorial concessions in China—neither Stalin nor the two presidents evinced much concern for their respective Chinese clients, Mao and Chiang Kai-shek —and a deal was struck on the very first day. "Could go home now" Truman told an aide.

The bomb was exploded shortly thereafter, on July 16, and the following week, Truman received word that it was much more powerful than anyone expected and would be ready for combat use right away. "He was a changed man," Churchill commented. "He told the Russians just where they got on and off and generally bossed this whole meeting." The American contingent began to wonder whether Soviet help in the Far East was so essential after all, and Truman became immensely impatient to end the conference so he could drop the bomb before Stalin got a share of Japan. The atomic bomb was exploded over Hiroshima on August 6, and over Nagasaki on August 8. Soviet troops entered Manchuria on August 9, and overran the province within a week. Japan sued for peace on August 14. The Soviet-American alliance had lost its last vestige of common purpose.

# CHAPTER 2

# The Beginning of the Cold War

### Six Fateful Weeks

American public opinion was still surprisingly favorable toward Russia. Distrust of the Soviet Union was a sentiment restricted primarily to professionals in the State Department, despite all the subsequent charges of "pinkos" and fellow travellers in that organization. Between the wars, the Soviet Union, as a Communist, atheistic country, had a bad press in America; but once the Red Army was joined in the war against Hitler, Russia was accepted almost uncritically as a comrade-in-arms. *Life* magazine, for instance, devoted a full issue to the Soviet Union in 1943. The Russians were "a hell of a people . . . who look like Americans, dress like Americans, and think like Americans." Lenin was "perhaps the greatest man of modern times," and the NKVD was "a national police force similar to the FBI." The *New York Times* proclaimed in 1944, "Marxian thinking in Soviet Russia is out. The capitalist system . . . is back." Douglas MacArthur said that "the hopes of civilization rest on the worthy banners of the courageous Red Army." Reinhold Niebuhr observed that Russia had less liberty but more equality than America, but thought it an open question whether "democracy should be defined primarily in terms of liberty or of equality." Sometimes the enthusiasm was ludicrous. Joseph Davies, Roosevelt's Ambassador to Moscow, rhapsodized about Stalin, "A child would like to sit on his lap, and a dog would sidle up to him." Despite his occasional hard-line outbursts, Truman preferred to think of Stalin as a typical Missouri politician, "more like Tom Pendergast than any man I knew," and speculated that Stalin's hard line on Poland meant that he was in trouble with his Politburo at home, even though he was "a fine man who wanted to do the right thing." As late as the fall of 1945, only 25 percent of Americans thought that Stalin intended to impose Communist governments on Eastern Europe.

The Soviet line seemed to turn harder after the surrender of Japan, perhaps to demonstrate that Russia could not be intimidated by the atomic bomb. Molotov's truculence was the despair of Truman's Secretary of State, James ("Jimmie") Byrnes, a politician of southern Irish descent, an Anglophobe, and a natural mediator and conciliator. Molotov refused to make even face-saving gestures in the direction of Eastern European elections at a Foreign Ministers' meeting in London in September, and his language was unusually abusive, even by the back-alley standards of Soviet diplomacy. The conference broke up without a communiqué and with Molotov and Byrnes absolutely at loggerheads. Byrnes, who had come to London with high hopes for settling most of the postwar issues, complained bitterly that "The Russians are welching on all the agreements reached at Potsdam and Yalta." And he warned, "We were facing a new Russia, totally different from the Russia we dealt with a year ago."

Byrnes quickly recovered his optimism and pressed for another Foreign Ministers' conference to repair the damage done in London; but this time, Byrnes insisted that the meeting be held in Moscow, where he could appeal directly to Stalin's moderating influence to keep Molotov in line. As an added inducement to the Soviets, Byrnes brought an idea for sharing atomic technology that Truman had floated in October. The Moscow talks, in December 1945, by Byrnes's lights, turned out to be a great success. In a private meeting, Stalin agreed to open up two ministries to non-Communists in Rumania and one in Bulgaria, the same order of compromise he had made with Hopkins over Poland. Byrnes quickly agreed that the United States would recognize the Rumanian and Bulgarian governments and accepted that the Soviet Union would have an advisory voice in the government for Japan. With these issues out of the way, an agreement was easily reached on the principle of international cooperation in the development of atomic energy.

An elated Byrnes returned home to find that he had completely missed a sharp negative swing in attitudes toward the Soviet Union. Congress was openly hostile toward the atomic-sharing proposals, and Senator Arthur Vandenberg, the symbol of Republican bipartisanship in foreign policy, but with a large Polish voting constituency, served notice that he was fed up with continued "appeasement" of Stalin. Truman thought Byrnes had exceeded his instructions, was irritated that his Secretary had announced the agreements before clearing them with the White House, and was upset that Byrnes had proceeded so hastily with the notion of atomic sharing—he was still refining a proposal for his 1946 State of the Union address. Public opinion was undergoing an abrupt reversal: a new poll showed that 71 percent of the people disapproved of Soviet foreign policy and only 3 percent approved. The Republicans were clearly intending to make policy toward the Soviets a major issue in the 1946 congressional elections, and Truman had no intention of holding the fortunes of his party hostage to Stalin's good behavior.

There then ensued an extraordinary series of events during barely a six-week period in February and March of 1946 that may reasonably be pinpointed, if any particular time can be, as the actual beginning of the Cold War. On February 9, Stalin made his "election" speech at the Bolshoi Theater. The sudden change of tone was stark and ominous. The war was no longer a victory for "Russia," the ancient motherland Stalin had so successfully evoked during the war, but for the "Soviet system." Russia's allies were nowhere mentioned. Nazism and fascism were conspicuously labelled as late developments of "monopoly capitalism," the source of all wars. The foreign press had been disappointed, Stalin said, in their expectation that the Soviet system would collapse; instead, it had proved "a form of organization superior to all others." Agricultural collectivization and rapid industrialization had demonstrated their worth. But forced growth would continue, at a threefold pace, for only then "can we regard our country as guaranteed against all eventualities." In particular, the Soviet Union would "in the near future . . . overtake and surpass the achievements of science beyond the boundaries of our country"—a pointed reference, most Western analysts assumed, to nuclear technology.

The speech shocked even American liberals. Eric Sevareid wrote, "If you can brush aside Stalin's speech . . . you are a braver man than I am." William O. Douglas called it a "the Declaration of World War III." Even Walter Lippmann was momentarily shaken; he declared that the Soviet Union was seeking "military superiority," requiring a "mighty upsurge of national economy" on the part of the West. (*Business Week* said that Lippmann "had gone berserk and virtually declared war on Russia.")

Three days later, the Soviets announced a new government in North Korea, formed on the Soviet model and composed entirely of Communists. News from the North was blacked out, travellers from the South were being arrested, and there were reports of large Soviet troop movements South.

Just a few days later, on February 16, news broke in the United States—it had first been bruited in a Drew Pearson column on February 3—that a Soviet defector in Canada, Igor Gouzenko, had revealed the presence of a far-flung network of Soviet spies. Canada had made twenty-two arrests for espionage. Klaus Fuchs, a British physicist working on atomic energy projects for the National Research Council of Canada, later confessed to having passed a description of the American plutonium bomb to the Soviet Union in June 1945, the month before Truman's revelation at Potsdam. Small wonder that Stalin had reacted so calmly.

During the same week, J. Edgar Hoover held meetings with Treasury and State Department officials to discuss investigations of the loyalty of Harry Dexter White, an Assistant Secretary of the Treasury, and Alger Hiss, a key aide in State. Interestingly, given the loyalty hysteria just a few years later, the Attorney General, Tom Clark, recommended that White be made American director of the International Monetary Fund, but be "surrounded by people who . . . were not security risks."

On February 21, the Joint Chiefs forwarded to the President a bleak assessment of the postwar world, stating for the first time that, "from a military point of view, the consolidation and development of the power of Russia is the greatest threat to the United States in the foreseeable future." Continued Soviet expansion in Asia, the Middle East, or in Europe would inevitably lead to clashes, either with the United States directly or with Great Britain, in which the United States would necessarily become involved. The United States could no longer count on its "fortunate geographic position" for its security; modern weapons meant that "neither geography nor allies will render a nation immune from sudden and paralyzing attack, should an aggressor arise." The chiefs had little faith in the ability of the United Nations to maintain peace; their paper was a plea for maintaining a military establishment consistent with the country's commitments. The nature of modern—atomic—war meant that "our long term potential . . . owing to the length of time required for mobilization . . . might not be sufficient to avert disaster."

The very next day, George Kennan's famous "Long Telegram"—later elaborated into the even more famous "Mr. X" article in *Foreign Affairs*—arrived in Washington. Kennan tells in his *Memoirs* how he was bedridden in the Moscow Embassy with sinus trouble and toothaches, and depressed over the naivete of Washington policymakers, when he received a message that reduced us all to a new level of despair—despair not with the Soviet government, but with our own. It was a telegram informing us that the Russians were evidencing an unwillingness to adhere to the World Bank and the International Monetary Fund . . . in tones of bland innocence came the anguished cry of bewilderment. . . . How did one explain such behavior on the part of the Soviet government? What lay behind it.

The more I thought about this message, the more it seemed to be obvious that this was "it." For eighteen long months I had done little else but pluck people's sleeves, trying to make them understand the nature of the phenomenon with which we in the Moscow Embassy were daily confronted . . . it had been to all intents and purposes like talking to a stone. . . . Now, by God, they would have it.

Kennan unburdened himself with an 8,000-word telegram that explored the sources of Soviet conduct, the nature of the regime, their attitudes and behavior in international affairs, and guidelines for American dealings with them. World communism, he said, was a "malignant parasite," and the Marxist doctrine of the Soviets was but a "figleaf of their moral and intellectual respectability." The Soviet rulers were in reality "only the last of that long succession of cruel and wasteful Russian rulers who have relentlessly forced country on to ever new heights of military power in order to guarantee external security of their internally weak regimes." He warned that "increase of the military and police power of the Russian state . . . isolation of the Russian population from outside world, and . . . fluid and constant pressure to extend limits of Russian police power . . . are together the natural and instinctive urges of Russian rulers." Official Soviet policy in much of the world would be "directed toward weakening of power and influence and contacts of advanced Western nations," and on a "subterranean plane" their mischief would be carried out by "an inner central core of Communist parties in other countries . . . in reality working closely together as an underground operating directorate of world communism, a concealed Comintern, tightly coordinated and directed from Moscow." These underground efforts would attempt "To undermine general political and strategic potential of major western powers. Efforts will be made . . . to disrupt national self-confidence, to hamstring measures of national defense, to increase social and industrial unrest, to stimulate all forms of disunity."

But while Kennan expected Soviet influence in the world to be wholly "negative and destructive," he did not expect war, for he stressed that

Soviet power, unlike that of Hitlerite Germany, is neither schematic nor adventuristic. It does not work by fixed plans. It does not take unnecessary risks. Impervious to the logic of reason, it is highly sensitive to logic of force. For this reason it can easily withdraw—and usually does—when strong resistance is encountered at any point. Thus, if the adversary has sufficient force and makes clear his readiness to use it, he rarely has to do so.

The timing was perfect. Kennan himself concedes that, "six months earlier [the telegram] would probably have been received in the Department of State with raised eyebrows and lips pursed in disapproval. Six months later, it would probably have sounded redundant, a sort of preaching to the convinced." As it was, the effect was "sensational." The President read it. It was required reading in the State Department. Forrestal had it reproduced and sent to "hundreds, if not thousands" of armed services officers. In modern jargon, a "paradigm shift" in the way the country regarded the Soviet Union was under way.

Kennan's telegram articulated the paradigm that would govern American policymaking for the next forty years. Within weeks of the "Long Telegram," Frank Roberts, the British chargé in Moscow, sent a series of dispatches to the Foreign Office offering similar views; these were apparently sent on his own motion and drafted quite independently of the "Long Telegram," although Roberts knew Kennan well and had been influenced by his views.

Five days after Kennan's telegram arrived in Washington, Vandenberg delivered a major foreign policy address that hammered at the question, "What is Russia up to now? . . . We ask it in Manchuria. We ask it in Eastern Europe and the Dardanelles. . . . We ask it in the Baltic and the Balkans. We ask it in Poland. We ask it in Japan. We ask it sometimes even in connection with events in our own United States." On the very next day, Byrnes himself, his political antennae back in tune, delivered a strong speech signalling a new tough attitude toward the Soviet Union and effectively repudiating the agreements he had reached in Moscow two months before. (The speech was inevitably, and unfairly, dubbed "The Second Vandenberg Concerto" by the press; but Byrnes had probably written his first.) The United States wished to be friends with Russia, he announced, "but will not and . . . cannot stand aloof if force or the threat of force is used contrary to the purposes and principles of the [United Nations] Charter." He listed maintaining troops in other countries, delaying peace treaties, and stealing property without reparations agreements as practices the United States would no longer tolerate.

Less than a week later, on March 5, Churchill shocked the American public with his famous commencement address at Fulton, Missouri: "From Stettin in the Baltic, to Trieste in the Adriatic, an iron curtain has descended across the Continent. Behind that line lie all the capitals of the ancient states of central and eastern Europe." *Time* called the speech a "magnificent trial balloon" for the administration's new policy. Truman had arranged the speaking engagement—Fulton was in his home state—accompanied Churchill there by train, and probably read the speech during the trip. He introduced Churchill and conspicuously applauded at the finish. He seems to have underestimated the impression the speech would make, however, for he wrote privately a few days later to his mother and sister that "I am not ready to endorse Mr. Churchill's speech." Criticism in the United States centered as much on Churchill's proposal for a new Anglo-American alliance as on his anti-Soviet theme. But Walter Lippmann thought Churchill was saying that "it was important to fight the Russians sometime in the next five years."

That same month, the United States gave substance to its new harder-line policy by forcing Stalin to back down in Iran. Both British and Soviet troops had occupied Iran during the war and had made an agreement, several times confirmed, that they would withdraw by March 2. Great Britain honored the deadline. The Soviet Union did not, and there immediately began to unfold the same sequence of events that had become so depressingly familiar in Eastern Europe. Officials with pro-Western sympathies began to be drummed out of the Iranian government. The Soviet Union announced that its troops were necessary to protect Iranian oil fields from sabotage. The Iranian Communists, the Tudeh Party, took control in the north, and Moscow suggested that the north become autonomous. Moscow began to insist that Iranian oil resources be brought under the control of a joint Soviet-Iranian company, 51 percent owned by the Soviets. (American and British companies participated in similar consortia.)

The Americans and British both reacted by sending stiff notes; the issue was troops, they insisted, not oil rights. When there was no response, Byrnes steadily escalated, implicitly threatening the use of force. Tempers flared to the point where Andrei Gromyko, the Soviet United Nations delegate, stalked out of a Security Council meeting, but, more or less as Kennan had predicted, the Soviet Union backed down. Its troops were withdrawn from Iran, the separatist Tudeh regime in the north was turned out of office, and Iran returned to the Western orbit. Another staring contest later in the summer over Turkey had the same result. Stalin, frustrated at Potsdam in his desire for a base on the Bosphorus, decided to offer Turkey his fraternal assistance in the defense of the Dardanelles. While Ankara pondered the offer, Soviet troops massed on the Turkish border. Truman dispatched a stiff note to Moscow, and ordered a contingent of the American fleet to the Turkish Straits. Stalin immediately backed away.

Washington, and Harry Truman, were still not ready for a final break. Stalin's mind, of course, is not known. Truman's view seems to have been that the United States was engaged in some rough-shouldered jostling with an obstreperous and untrustworthy ally, not that the two nations were moving toward an inevitable war. The series of confrontations and revelations in the winter and early spring, and growing opposition from key members of Congress, from the military, and from Churchill, did not deter him from pressing his State of the Union proposal to turn over the development of atomic energy to the United Nations. The idea was entrusted to an expert panel under the chairmanship of David Lilienthal, with the close involvement of Dean Acheson. The panel made detailed recommendations on March 28, over the strong dissents of General Leslie Groves, the director of the Manhattan Project, and Vannevar Bush. The plan, an unusually well-drafted and thoughtful one, called for an international authority for mining uranium, developing, owning, and leasing nuclear material, and manufacturing and controlling all nuclear weapons. (Inconceivable as it seems forty years later, it was assumed that the United Nations might need nuclear weapons to keep recalcitrant states in line.) Nations, companies, and research institutions could use nuclear materials as needed, but only under strict supervision.

There is almost no possibility that the Soviet Union could have accepted such an intrusion on its nuclear plans. Even Robert Oppenheimer, a key draftsman of the proposal, conceded that "the plan was entirely incompatible with the Russian system." In any event, the proposal quickly foundered on United Nations politics. Byrnes appointed Bernard Baruch to head the American nuclear disarmament delegation to the United Nations as a sop to conservatives. Baruch insisted that the plan be revised to eliminate the Security Council veto in nuclear matters. It was not, on the merits, an unreasonable proposal; the Soviets had already shown their willingness to obstruct United Nations business and could easily use the veto to defeat nuclear inspections. But Baruch was touching a Soviet sore point, and the amendment virtually guaranteed that the plan would be stillborn. Baruch's meddling is sometimes blamed for derailing a genuine opportunity to denationalize nuclear weapons, but Soviet-American relations were deteriorating so rapidly in 1946 and 1947, no proposal requiring the slightest reliance on the good intentions of either side had even the faintest prospects of success.

## The Truman Doctrine

The Truman Doctrine, announced in the spring of 1947, was in form a declaration that the United States would oppose Communist subversion throughout the world. Rhetoric aside, however, it was really intended to serve notice that the United States would step into the shoes of British imperial administrators and ensure continued Western access to the Mediterranean and the Middle East. In retrospect, at least, it is clear that by 1947, whatever his commitment to Marxist-Leninist concepts of world proletarian revolution, Stalin was pursuing a classically expansionist Czarist foreign policy. The war had sounded the knell for the British Empire; even the polemical exertions of a Winston Churchill could not obscure that. In the time-honored pattern of imperial succession, Stalin expected to fill the power vacuum created by the departing British in the Middle East and the eastern Mediterranean littoral and realize Catherine the Great's dream of bringing its warm water ports and raw material resources under Russian sway. Rather unexpectedly, in view of the strong isolationist current in American statecraft, Harry Truman announced that the United States stood ready to block Russia's way. By its unequivocal acceptance of the role of a world power, the Truman Doctrine was as much a watershed in American politics as Roosevelt's entrance into the war.

It was the crisis in Greece in the winter of 1947, the third apparent confrontation with Stalin in less than a year, that spurred Truman's declaration. Greece was óne of the countries that Churchill, in his notorious "division of the spoils" conversation with Stalin, had marked as "90 percent" within the British sphere of influence. In the wake of the Nazi evacuation of Greece in 1944, the British Army, in concert with the royalist Greek government, had been actively engaged in putting down bands of Communist insurgents, many of whom, as Stalin continually reminded Churchill at Yalta, had been in the forefront of the partisan activity against the Nazis. By 1947, the royalist cause was looking increasingly hopeless. The insurgency, with critical support from the Yugoslavs and the Albanians, had already virtually supplanted the official government in the mountainous north. The royalist government was incompetent, the economy was sinking into chaos, and Great Britain, exhausted by the war, was rapidly running out of resources. In February 1948, the British government informed Washington that it would withdraw from Greece in six weeks. At least a quarter of a billion dollars in aid would be needed to stem the insurgency. Would Washington care to try?

There was virtually no dissent among Truman's advisers that the United States should supply the requested aid. George Kennan, who took over that week as chief of Policy Planning in the State Department, and who, along with Bohlen, expressed strong reservations about the sweeping language of the Truman Doctrine, strongly supported intervention in Greece. As he explained it at the time: "if nothing were done to stiffen the backs of the non-Communist elements in Greece at this juncture, the Communist elements would soon succeed in seizing power and establishing a totalitarian dictatorship along the lines already visible in other Balkan countries . . . [with the] most unfortunate strategic consequences from the standpoint of any military adversary of the Soviet Union."

Kennan and his staff adjudged that Turkey, which at the time seemed well positioned to resist Communist subversion, would be much more vulnerable if Greece were in Communist hands. A Communist Greece and Turkey inevitably raised questions about an increasingly shaky Italy. It was arguably the first formulation of what later became known as the "domino theory" of Communist subversion.

The consensus so quickly reached at the State Department was a professional one, among men who had been brought up to admire the British tradition of balance-of-power politics, who thought naturally in terms of power vacuums and strategic positioning, and who viewed diplomacy as a long-term process of testing and nudging for marginal, cumulative advantages. It was a view radically at variance with that of most of the American people and their representatives in Congress who conceived of America's traditional policy of isolationism as a refuge from precisely the decadent, Old World, diplomatic notions that led to two devastating global wars in thirty years. Truman, although he was no foreign policy sophisticate, was generally in tune with the State Department's vision of an expanded American world role. The problem was to convince a Congress increasingly restive about "pouring money down foreign ratholes" that America should care who was temporarily in charge in Greece, or for that matter, Turkey or Iran.

George Marshall, Truman's new Secretary of State, put the case for

Greek aid to a delegation of congressional leaders that Truman called to the White House and, in Dean Acheson's words, "most unusually, and most unhappily, flubbed his opening statement." Marshall essentially presented the State Department argument without embellishment, and the Congressmen, including the internationalist Vandenberg, were simply not impressed. Acheson, Marshall's Undersecretary, then sprang to the rescue of his chief and painted an apocalyptic picture of the consequences of inaction: "Soviet pressure on the Straits, on Iran, and on northern Greece had brought the Balkans to the point where a highly possible Soviet breakthrough might open three continents to Soviet penetration. Like apples in a barrel infected by one rotten one, the corruption of Greece would infect Iran and all to the east. It would also carry the infection to Africa through Asia Minor and Egypt and to Europe to Italy and France."

The congressmen were stunned. After a silence, Vandenberg addressed Truman: if he was willing to come to Congress himself and ask for aid in just those terms, telling the public just what Acheson had said, then "we're with you," and he, Vandenberg, would personally support the President's program.

Truman took Vandenberg's advice. His message asking for aid to Greece and Turkey, delivered to Congress on March 12, posed the issue as "communism vs. democracy":

One way of life is based upon the will of the majority, and is distinguished by free institutions, representative government, free elections, guaranties of individual liberty, freedom of speech and religion, and freedom from political oppression.

The second way of life is based upon the will of a minority forcibly imposed upon the majority. It relies upon terror and oppression, a controlled press and radio, fixed elections, and the suppression of personal freedoms.

I believe it must be the policy of the United States to support free people who are resisting attempted subjugation by armed minorities or by outside pressures.

The "two ways of life" contrasted in Truman's message were not an unreasonable description of the differences between Stalin's Russia and the United States. Nor were they an unfair rendering of the barbarities Stalin was inflicting on his hapless Eastern European satellites. The problem was that outside of the industrial nations of Western Europe, few, if any, of the countries the United States wished to support, including Greece, Turkey, and Iran, were the models of Western democracy

Truman was proferring as the alternative to Stalinism. In the global jockeying with the Soviet Union, the choice would often come down to one between friendly and unfriendly dictators.

A second American misconception, although it was based on a genuine misunderstanding, was the notion that the Communist insurgency in Greece was orchestrated from the Kremlin. In fact, it was more the result of Yugoslav free-lancing than of Soviet scheming. Stalin's communism, as Kennan had shrewdly analyzed, was neither "schematic nor adventuristic." He was willing to test Western tolerance as he had in Iran and Turkey but he was not ready to risk a war. According to Milovan Djilas, he scornfully upbraided the Quixotic Yugoslavs: "What, do you think that Great Britain and the United States—the United States, the most powerful state in the world—will permit you to break their line of communication in the Mediterranean? Nonsense." It was a judgment that was eventually proved correct after two more years of bloody fighting. The Yugoslavs could fairly complain, however, that Stalin's refusal to supply the partisans was as decisive as American support for the other side.

Acheson did his best to dispel the messianic tone of Truman's address in the congressional hearings that followed but to little avail. The notion of an ideological struggle caught the imagination of the public and became fundamental Cold War doctrine. Thenceforward, American statesmen had to turn hypocritical handsprings to demonstrate to the Congress and the public that each strategically located little dictator, however sleazy, was a true friend of democracy. Ironically, Acheson was himself caught in the backlash of the ideological confrontation in 1949 when the administration withdrew support from the incompetent and repressive Chinese Kuomintang regime on the grounds that mere anticommunism did not justify American intervention.

## The Marshall Plan

There was one last scene to be played out before the wartime alliance between the United States and the Soviet Union lapsed into official enmity. The "Marshall Plan" for aid to war-torn Europe was first bruited by the Secretary of State at a Harvard commencement address in June 1947. It was to be the crowning adornment of American postwar foreign policy, possibly the most successful and far-sighted initiative in the history of American international relations. It also provided the last slender thread of opportunity for an American-Soviet reconciliation. Neither country was prepared to grasp it.

American motivations for the Marshall Plan were a complex blend of anticommunism, economic self-interest, and genuine altruism. The revisionists of the 1960s and 1970s tended greatly to exaggerate the economic motivations. American businessmen had feared a recession in 1945 and 1946, but those fears had receded by 1947, and economists were more worried about inflation. Substantial credit creation to finance aid to Europe, by the conventional analysis of the day, would only worsen inflation. Most analysts were reasonably confident that the American prosperity could weather a collapse in Europe—the export surplus with Europe, for example, accounted for only about 2 percent of American GNP. Averell Harriman and Herbert Hoover, in fact, wanted to build up the German steel industry explicitly to *avoid* tying the American economy to European export markets. At the same time, as Adam Ulam writes, the strain of altruism in American policymaking roused the "most nightmarish suspicions" in the Soviet Union. To the brooding and fearful men in the Politburo, it was inconceivable that capitalists would give away billions of dollars without some sinister purpose, which they assumed was the military conquest of the Soviet Union with European mercenary armies. The Soviet fears may have been paranoid, but they were correct in divining that the anti-Communist impulse in American policy was now at least as strong as the altruistic.

Marshall conceived of a massive rehabilitation effort when he toured Europe in April 1947 and was sobered and shaken by what he saw. The European economies had enjoyed a brief recovery the previous year—production reached prewar levels in some countries—but the upturn merely depleted the last remnants of their devastated capital stock. The 1946 harvest was poor, and industrial production plummeted the following winter. In large parts of Europe, particularly Germany, a listless and debilitated population was literally starving.

Marshall's European trip also marked his first visit with Stalin in his new role as Secretary of State. Like so many American statesmen, he had gone to Moscow convinced that he could "work with" the Soviet dictator; and, like so many others, he was at first charmed by Stalin's affability, in such welcome contrast to Molotov's blunt obstructionism. But as the discussions dragged on, Marshall finally came to the "chilling" realization that Stalin had little interest in reaching an early German settlement; Soviet policy would be better served by letting matters drift. As Bohlen remembered: "Stalin's seeming indifference to what was happening in Germany made a deep impression on Marshall. . . . Economic conditions were bad. . . . Unemployment was widespread.

Millions were on short rations. There was danger of epidemics. This was the kind of crisis Communism thrived on. All the way back to Washington, Marshall talked of the importance of finding some initiative to prevent the complete breakdown of Western Europe."

The principles that Marshall laid down in his Harvard speech were that the United States would finance reconstruction, not relief; that the program would be open to all nations—both the Soviet Union and Germany could participate; and that the United States would not propose a program; aid would be available only for a reconstruction program developed cooperatively by all the participating nations. He proferred both a club and a carrot to the Soviet Union. The club was that the United States was prepared to proceed with the rehabilitation of the western zones of Germany, effectively ending the search for an agreement with Moscow on a German peace treaty and making the question of German reparations a dead issue. The carrot was that substantial aid would be available to the Soviet Union, but at the price of lifting the veil of secrecy that shrouded its economy and introducing some leavening of free-market principles.

The early signals from Moscow were all negative. *Pravda* linked the Marshall Plan to the "bloodstain[ed]" Truman Doctrine, which had "contributed to bitter economic conflicts in France," and was aligned with the "black forces of reaction and oppression in Italy and other lands." With the Marshall Plan, Washington had moved "From retail purchase of several European countries . . . [to] wholesale purchase of the whole European continent." When Molotov arrived at the opening of Marshall Plan negotiations in Paris with more than a hundred technicians, he proceeded to lecture the Europeans and the Americans about the coming depression in the United States. He scoffed at the European ability to draw up an effective plan—but even if they did, he promised, the American depression would foreclose the possibility of aid.

Both the Americans and the Soviets had ample reason to suspect each other of bad faith. The Americans were alert to Stalin's desire to maintain Western Europe and Germany in a weakened condition. Molotov's skills as an obstructionist were infamous, and it was feared that if he stayed in Paris, he would bring the discussions to a grinding halt. There was also real concern that Congress would not approve an aid program that included large grants to the dictatorship that was grinding Eastern Europe under its heel. But the Americans also had Machiavellian reasons for offering the program to the Soviets. As the French Foreign Minister, Georges Bidault, told an American diplomat:

"Molotov clearly does not want this business to succeed but on the other hand his hungry satellites are smacking their lips in the expectation of getting some of your money. He is obviously embarrassed." A successful program threatened a split in the Communist ranks. It was a dangerous gamble, for the entire program of European reconstruction was at stake. When Molotov, his forehead swelling red with indignation, made his final speech and stalked out of the Paris negotiations, there was an almost audible sigh of relief in Washington.

Events moved rapidly through the remainder of 1947 and early 1948. Stalin cracked down hard on the Eastern European governments that had volunteered for Marshall aid. The Czechs and the Rumanians abjectly retracted their initial enthusiastic expressions of interest; Imre Nagy's government was turned out of office in Hungary, and Nagy himself expelled from the Party.

In July, George Kennan's famous "X" article, "The Sources of Soviet Conduct," based substantially on his "Long Telegram" of the previous year, and enunciating for the first time the doctrine of "containment" of the Soviet Union, appeared in *Foreign Affairs*. It became, arguably, the most famous article on international relations in American history, was reprinted in the *Reader's Digest*, excerpted in the Luce publications, and widely summarized in the popular press. Walter Lippmann published an almost equally famous rebuttal in a series of columns that gave the Cold War its name. Lippmann attacked, probably unfairly, the breadth of the commitment he understood Kennan to be proposing, and its excessive military bias, but he did not question the fundamental clash of interests between the United States and the Soviet Union.

Sixteen European nations reached agreement on a five-year $20 billion aid program in September. Truman called Congress into special session in November and requested an emergency interim aid package of $595 million. It passed in less than a month. A week later, Truman recommended a four-year European Recovery Program with a price tag of $17 billion (substantially more than the annual defense budget) and requested that Congress act before April 1, 1948. George Marshall embarked on a nationwide tour to drum up support for the aid. To the Republican Congress, even to the internationalist Vandenberg, the request was enormous, and the demand for a four-and-a-half-year authorization unprecedented. At first, Marshall couched his arguments in primarily economic terms—the health of the West depended on European recovery. But as the deadline for Congressional action neared, he increasingly sounded the anti-Communist note: "This is a world-wide struggle between freedom and tyranny, between the self-rule of the many as opposed to the dictatorship of the ruthless few." And he gave a stern warning to the Italians that if they voted Communist in the 1948 elections, they would have no hope of Marshall aid.

The same month Truman's Marshall aid request went to Congress, the Soviet Union announced the formation of the Communist Information Bureau, or Cominform, reeking of the old Communist International, and charged with coordinating Communist activity throughout the world. At the first meeting, Moscow's representative, Andrei Zhdanov, delivered a blistering speech that described the world as divided into two camps, one seeking war and led by the imperialistic United States, the other led by the Soviet Union and fighting for socialist freedom, democracy, and peace. Disruption of the Marshall Plan was laid down as the first task of the European Communist parties. Jacques Duclos, the French Communist leader, left the meeting in tears, but dutifully followed Moscow's bidding. The Italian leader, Palmiro Togliatti, made a similar humiliating recantation. The American Communist leader, Earl Browder, was harshly denounced for seeking alliances with other left progressive parties. Throughout the fall and early winter, Western Europe was virtually paralyzed by Communist strikes against basic industries. There was widespread famine, fighting in the streets, and the sulfurous smell of anarchy in the air. Most of the European Communist parties announced that if war came between the West and the Soviet Union, they would not fight against Russian troops.

The "spring crisis" of 1948 succeeded in sweeping away the last lingering vestiges of isolationism in the Congress. A Communist putsch in Czechoslovakia, carried out with lightning speed on February 24, exposed the ugly reality of Stalinist power in Eastern Europe. The coup stemmed from the original unanimous decision of the Czech cabinet—Communist and non-Communist alike—to participate in the Marshall Plan. Jan Masaryk, the popular Foreign Minister, a non-Communist and son of Tomas Masaryk, the revered founder of the modern Czech state, was summoned to Moscow and ordered to reverse his country's stand. ("I went to Moscow the Foreign Minister of a sovereign state, and I came back the stooge of Stalin. *Finis Bohemiae.*") After some months of debate, the twelve non-Communist ministers resigned in protest, calling upon the aged president, Edvard Beneš, to form a new government. In the midst of the cabinet crisis, Valerian Zorin, Molotov's deputy, arrived in Prague and delivered Beneš an ultimatum: turn the government over to the Communists—only he and Masaryk would be allowed to retain office—or face an invasion. Weakened by two strokes, Beneš, who ten years before had succumbed to British and French pressure and delivered his country to Hitler at Munich, capitulated again and named a Communist cabinet. Within a day of the coup, secret police swept through the city arresting thousands of non-Communists. Tens of thousands of non-Communist government workers were evicted from their offices, often bodily; bands of goons wrecked the offices of all the non-Communist political parties; and the non-Communist leadership that had not been arrested was forced underground.

On March 5, General Lucius Clay, the commander of American Occupation Forces in Europe, wired home reporting "a subtle change in Soviet attitude." Whereas he had previously felt that war was highly unlikely, he now had the feeling that "it may come with dramatic suddenness."* On March 8, the U.S. Embassy in Nanking reported that in view of a sudden string of Communist victories, a complete rout of the Nationalist Chinese government by the Communists now appeared inevitable. On March 10, news came from Czechoslovakia that Masaryk had committed suicide. Rumors began to circulate immediately that he had been planning an escape from the country and had been murdered.† On March 12, Ernest Bevin, the Socialist Foreign Secretary of Great Britain, requested that the United States provide military assistance so Western Europe could defend itself against the Soviet Union. On March 16, the Central Intelligence Agency reported to Truman that it could confirm only that "war was not likely within sixty days." On March 17, Truman sent a special message to Congress requesting re-enactment of the draft. On April 1, the Soviet Union began to interfere

---

*This was a sharp change from Clay's previous position that the Soviet Union would not fight if directly challenged, a position which he maintained throughout the subsequent Berlin Blockade. There is circumstantial evidence that Clay sent the telegram at the request of the Army Chief of Intelligence, General Chamberlain, to support increased military appropriations—a serious charge made first by the editor of Clay's papers.

†There is substantial circumstantial evidence that Masaryk was indeed murdered. An inquest was begun at the time of his death, but the official who pressed it was shortly also the victim of a "suicide." During the "Prague Spring" of 1968, the Dubcek government opened an inquiry into Masaryk's death and communicated a considerable amount of information to the West. The inquiry was cut short by the Soviet invasion and the removal of all records to Moscow. The evidence arguing that Masaryk was murdered includes the following: He had in fact indicated his intention to flee the country. The hotel window through which he was alleged to have jumped was one of the most awkward windows to climb through. The position of the body on the ground and its distance from the hotel indicated that it had been hurled forcefully from the window. The room was in disarray, with much broken glass, as from a scuffle. There was a pillow in the bathtub that, conjecturally, was used to smother Masaryk before he was thrown from the window. There were certain physical signs, such as excrement on the broken window, that are consistent with death by suffocation, but not by suicide.

with Western train traffic into Berlin. On April 3, the President signed the Marshall Plan into law, passed in substantially the form and amount he had requested and almost precisely on schedule. Stalin had succeeded, where decades of diplomacy had failed, in unifying Western Europe and cementing relations between the United States and the Old World.

The success of the Marshall Plan exceeded even the most optimistic dreams of its sponsors. The contours of European recovery and the German "economic miracle" were already visible by the end of 1948. But the wartime alliance with the Soviet Union had irrevocably given way to the Cold War. Henceforth, East and West would glare balefully at each other behind their respective glacis along a line running through the very heart of Europe.

In retrospect, it is difficult to see how it could have been otherwise. Stalin, to be sure, had legitimate security concerns on his western borders; history had taught the Russians that they had much to fear from a strong Germany. Stalin also had a reasonable claim to reparations for the damage to his ravaged country—although by some calculations, the value of the goods looted from Poland and the eastern zones of Germany exceeded the reparation amounts mentioned at Yalta. But the French also had legitimate security concerns about the Germans, and so did the British. The difference was that both countries understood, however hesitatingly in the case of the French, that, for the salvation of them all, the Germans needed to be brought back into the common European cultural and commercial system. The xenophobic Soviets could hardly be expected to share such a concern for Germany, or indeed for the revival of European culture and commerce—objects of their scorn both before and after the war.

More important, Stalin's security requirements were without limit. The French were also enormously worried about the possibility of a remilitarized Germany, but their security concerns were weighed on a scale with other values and other fears. Stalin's were absolute. He could not be satisfied with dominating the foreign policy of a constitutional Polish government, for example, a concession Roosevelt and Churchill were quite prepared to grant. He needed to control the country totally, and would scruple at nothing to do so. The desire for absolute security is necessarily insatiable. Whether Stalin ever had a plan for conquering Western Europe is not clear, although there is defector evidence that plans were once made for an occupation of

France. But the unending drive for greater security, for broader buffer zones, is at some point indistinguishable from the aggrandizing impulse of an expansionist power.

Western statesmen could hardly be expected to make fine distinctions between defensive and offensive aggrandizements. Hitler was wont to justify his outward thrusts on the basis of German security needs. It was still less than a decade since the West had so grievously misjudged the military impulses driving Nazi Germany and Tojo's Japan, and so tragically underestimated their military power. Kennan was probably right that Stalinist Russia was "neither schematic nor adventuristic," but policy makers needed better assurances than that. Stalin, on the other hand, had much less reason to misinterpret Western intentions. If he was puzzled by Western motivations, it was not for lack of information. The British government was thoroughly penetrated with his agents, and during the tensest periods in 1945–46, including the period of the confrontation over Iran, the Soviet agent Donald Maclean, then acting head of chancery at the British Embassy in Washington, served as a key communication link between the Americans and the British, and was privy to almost every important evolving policy. At one point, when the two countries were attempting to develop a unified negotiating position on troop withdrawals from Austria, the British communications were coordinated by Maclean and the American ones by Alger Hiss, who was probably a Soviet agent as well.

American statesmen of the period made their share of mistakes, as legions of revisionist historians have documented. But as Kennan commented, it would have required Western statesmen who were "paragons of detachment, self-confidence, broad-mindedness, and tolerance" to maintain the alliance after the close of the war. Indeed, it might fairly be argued that the leading American statesmen of the day, the Marshalls, the Kennans, the Bohlens, the Achesons, the Harrimans, were as good as, or better than, any comparable group since the founding of the Republic. All were men of vision and broad sympathies, steeped in history and culture, not a rigid ideologue or crass self-seeker among them. Marshall, indeed, by the common consent of his contemporaries and historians, was one of the great men of American history. A happier resolution of Soviet-Western differences was simply beyond their powers.

CHAPTER 3

# "An Action Short of War"

### The Snows of Russia and the Cliffs of Dover

By the spring of 1948, Western statesmen were, for the first time, openly admitting the possibility of a shooting war with the Soviet Union. The consensus was still, as Clay put it, that "the Soviet Union does not want war"; but Stalin was pressing his program of subversive expansion so aggressively that all of continental Europe felt under threat. In the ten years since his infamous pact with Hitler, Stalin had extended his domination to include, by one quasi-official count, the Baltic states—Latvia, Estonia, Lithuania, and Bessarabia—Finland, Poland, Czechoslovakia, Yugoslavia, Bulgaria, Hungary, Rumania, Albania, Sinkiang, Outer Mongolia, Manchuria, and North Korea. East Germany seemed already lost, and only resolute British and American opposition had prevented the list from including Greece, Turkey, and Iran. Even George Kennan, who generally downplayed the Soviet military threat, feared that the Communists were on the verge of "an actual seizure of power by violent means in France and Italy." Ernest Bevin's anxious request for American military assistance was prompted by Stalin's ominous gestures against Norway. The extension of Stalin's power, in short, was already vastly greater than Hitler's had been in 1938, and no end was in sight. Sitting amid the rubble that remained of industrial Europe, barely two years after fighting a devastating global war to stop totalitarian aggression, Western statesmen might well be cautious as they sniffed the aggressive designs of a restless new power.

There is little question that Stalin was arming as fast as his war-torn economy would permit by 1948, although the precise extent of his power is still conjectural. (A relatively detailed assessment of Soviet military capabilities is possible only for the early 1950s, and is given in Chapter 5.) In Stalin's eyes, the buildup was probably entirely defensive. He was moving as rapidly as he could to build his own atomic bomb—one scholar has called his postwar atomic effort the "greatest crash military program in the regime's history"—was rebuilding his tactical air force to defend against American air attacks on his atomic facilities, which he considered likely as soon as he exploded his first weapon, and was constructing a forward defense of his western front so he could meet the anticipated American-European attack well away from his boundaries.

Certainly, there were statements and stirrings enough from the West to feed his paranoia. The American press was making increasingly explicit references to the possibility of war, and high officials like General Groves were speculating on the contingency of a nuclear attack on Russia in classified documents that the spy Maclean was well positioned to pass on to Moscow. The American eagerness to rehabilitate Germany and Japan, Russia's traditional enemies—forgetting the alliance of convenience in 1939—fuelled Stalin's suspicions. His doctrine, in any case, held that peaceful coexistence was impossible. Lenin had written that "a series of the most frightful collisions [with the capitalists] is . . . inevitable."—"Clear, one would think," Stalin had noted in the margin next to this passage. Djilas recalls Stalin "almost in a transport" at a dinner at the end of the war, hitching up his pants like a boxer and crying out: "The war will soon be over. We shall recover in fifteen or twenty years, and then we'll have another go at it."

In the West, military leaders were for the most part absolutely terrified at the prospect of a land war with the Soviet Union. Recent scholarship tends to regard their fear as grossly exaggerated, although, given the state of information on Russia at the time, it is difficult to argue that it was unreasonable. In the first place, Western intelligence on the Soviet Union was execrable; there was no way of knowing for sure whether the secrecy in which Stalin had shrouded his country concealed weaknesses or war preparations. Truman did not create a unified intelligence agency until 1946, and the capabilities of the first group were considered "something of a joke." Roosevelt had actually instructed the military intelligence agencies not to spy on the Russians during the war, although the order seems to have been disregarded after 1943. British intelligence was little better. Churchill created a specialist Soviet unit in 1944, but, bizarrely, until 1947 it was under the supervision of H. A. R. "Kim" Philby, another of Stalin's agents.

The consensus Western estimate in the late 1940s was that the Soviets had about 4 million men under arms—some estimates were as high as 5.6 million—compared to a wartime peak of about 12 million. The actual size of the Soviet military in 1948, however, according to Nikita Khrushchev in 1960, was only 2.8 million, a figure now accepted by most scholars. (Khrushchev actually may have been cooking the numbers just a bit. He was trying to show how rapidly Soviet troop strength had built up during the Korean War and how sharp his own subsequent force reductions had been. Significantly, his figures for the early 1950s were as surprisingly high as his 1948 figures were surprisingly low.) The main source of uncertainty was that until the early 1950s, Western intelligence agencies had reasonably accurate counts only of Soviet divisions, not their level of manning. The count of 175 to 200 divisions in 1948, down from the wartime peak of 600, was roughly right, but many, perhaps most, were maintained only at skeletal manning levels. Approximately 2.8 million troops, if that is the right number for the 1948 Soviet military establishment, was not enough to attack Europe, since Stalin probably needed that many just to keep order in the satellites. And the logistic capability to support a *blitzkrieg* war of attack and maneuver, the kind of battle the Western military expected, was almost certainly lacking. Soviet troops were a tatterdemalion lot at the end of the war, depending almost entirely on horse transport for artillery and supplies, and maneuvering for the most part without benefit of radio communications.

Casually dismissing the 1948 Soviet military threat to Europe from the vantage point of thirty or forty years' hindsight, however, is much too glib. Whatever the state of Stalin's divisions at home, the thirty divisions in Eastern Europe, and another thirty on the western Russian border, within easy jumping-off range of Europe, were all at or near wartime manning complements. More important, if hostilities flared, Stalin was in a far better position to reinforce his cadres than the West was. And too much can be made of Russian logistic incapacities. By the end of the war, Russia's war production rate was second only to America's—despite losing 80,000 airplanes in the first months of the war, for example, the Russians had completely rebuilt their air force by 1944 and enjoyed clear air superiority over the Germans in the Battle of Berlin. Stalin's troops couldn't move as fast as Eisenhower's did, but the ponderous Russian war machine had still managed to grind up the Wehrmacht over hundreds of thousands of square kilometers during the summer and fall of 1944. Western correspondents did not think to deride Russian horse transport when they wrote of Stalin's "whirlwind offensive" to the Elbe.

If Russian power was uncertain, the weaknesses of the West were glaring. The American demobilization had been headlong. United States strength stood at 1.4 million men in 1948, barely 10 percent of the wartime peak, with the majority on the American continent, and the rest scattered all across the globe. There was strong resistance even to that level of manning. "Bring Daddy Home" clubs had sprung up around the country, protesting mothers were mailing baby shoes to their congressmen, and there had been sporadic rioting among American troops in Europe. The total Western strength in Europe was a patchwork of slightly more than four partially manned British divisions, two French, and two American. (Marshall estimated the total American effectives at about one and a third divisions.) West Germany was completely disarmed, and Italy was for all practical purposes defenseless. There was only slight rhetorical excess in Churchill's statement that "There was nothing between the white snows of Russia and the white cliffs of Dover" to stop Stalin's troops if he but chose to give the signal. Less poetically, when Omar Bradley was asked what the Soviets needed to reach the channel, he replied, "Shoes!"

The American military began to develop contingency war plans as tensions rose throughout 1948. It was taken for granted that a Soviet assault on central Europe would be cataclysmic. The planners assumed that the Soviets would mount parallel attacks through Germany to France and through the Balkans to Italy, strike at the Iranian and Arabian oil fields, and invade northern China. The Western strategy would be to fight a retreating action through France and Italy, secure North America from air attacks, and prevent an invasion of Great Britain or Japan. It was assumed that within six months all of continental Europe would be lost and the Mediterranean would be a Soviet lake. The offensive response would be an all-out American atomic assault on the Soviet Union's seventy leading industrial and population centers, accompanied by atomic and conventional bombing attacks on Soviet troop formations in Europe. If the bombing was successful, the planners guessed, the Soviet offensive would run down in about three months. It would then take another nine months for the Americans and British to build up invasion forces for what was expected to be a prolonged and bloody slog to win back the European continent and the Middle East.

None of the services except the Air Force evinced much confidence that the strategy would work. They were not certain that American political leaders would authorize the all-out use of nuclear weapons, and they were worried that their nuclear advantage might not last. Despite alleged American smugness over its atomic monopoly, the documents from 1948 and 1949 evince real, and, as it turned out, justified concern that the Soviets had already achieved fission technology. The American military had profound respect for Soviet defense capabilities, and conceded the Soviets numerical superiority in aircraft; they were also fairly certain that their maps of Soviet industrial centers were not accurate enough for effective bombing.

Most important, although it is not clear which military leaders were in on the secret (the President wasn't), America's atomic stockpile was too small for its war strategy. There were actually fewer than fifty bombs available, many of which were unusable. In 1948, it still took a long time to develop and assemble nuclear weapons, and the Manhattan Project scientists had scattered after the war. The "Sandstone" tests that pointed the way to build lighter, easier-to-make weapons were conducted only in the spring. But without ready supplies of bombs and a rapid response, the entire nuclear strategy would fail—no one could drop an atomic bomb on Soviet troops already occupying Paris. The American planners also fully appreciated the stolid bravery displayed by the Russian people at battles like Stalingrad; they worried that atomic attacks might rally the Soviet citizenry behind their government and actually prolong the war. Finally, the planning documents are almost plaintive in their insistence that the object of any war would be a reasonable negotiated settlement, *not* an unconditional Soviet surrender: the military had little stomach for Normandy-type invasions against the Red Army.

Few American political and military leaders, however, actually expected a war to start with a surprise Soviet attack. Even John Foster Dulles, among the coldest of the cold warriors, was confident that the Soviets would not intentionally start a war. The fear was that Stalin's aggressive policies would touch off a conflagration that neither side wanted. It was easy to construct scenarios that were only too plausible. Palmiro Togliatti had warned publicly that if the Communists failed to win control of Italy democratically, they would seize it by violence. Truman's cabinet had a worried discussion in 1947—how to respond, for example, if the Italian Communists started riots in one of their northern urban strongholds and a Communist mayor requested help from the neighboring Yugoslavs? What if they tried to create a rump state in northern Italy? Clay posed a similar scenario in opposing American troop withdrawals from Germany. With Americans safely across the Atlantic, he expected the Communists to foment riots and strikes, and then call for "fraternal assistance" from Soviet troops waiting across the border in Poland. Truman's major fear during the tension in Berlin was "the risk that a trigger-happy Russian pilot or a hotheaded Communist tank commander might create an incident that would ignite the powder keg." Robert Lovett, Marshall's Undersecretary at State, thought the Soviet leaders' heads were "full of bubbles." Marshall was of the same view, and was afraid that, because of the low state of American readiness, the Soviets might underestimate Western power or the speed with which the United States could return to a war footing if it came to a showdown.

Again, these were not unreasonable fears. The period from the founding of the Cominform in 1947 to the start of the Berlin Blockade is sometimes known as the *Zhdanovshchina* because of the unrelieved truculence of the Soviet foreign policy line laid down by Cominform boss Andrei Zhdanov. It was a time when the Soviet Union systematically consolidated its military grip on Eastern Europe and tightened political repression in the satellites, ultimately provoking the break with Tito; it was the period of the coup in Czechoslovakia and the death of Masaryk; it was a time of ever-more threatening calls for violent revolution by Communist leaders in the West. We have Djilas's testimony on the state of Stalin's mind. At a banquet for the Yugoslavs in 1948, Stalin lamented not having occupied Finland. "We were too concerned about the Americans, and they wouldn't have lifted a finger." In fact, two years later Stalin made just such a grievous underestimate of the American willingness to fight when he consented to the invasion of South Korea. Most dramatically, however, 1948 was the time of the direct military challenge laid down to the West by the blockade of Berlin.

## The Berlin Blockade

The crisis in Berlin grew out of the continued inability of the Western powers and the Soviet Union to reach an accord on the future of Germany. Despite the sheen of agreement at Potsdam, and the confusions and vacillations on both sides, it was becoming clear that events were pressing inevitably toward a divided Germany. The actual diplomatic initiatives, however, were all on the western side. As early as 1946, George Kennan pointed out how rapidly Stalin was consolidating his grip in the Eastern zone and warned that a unified Germany might facilitate his takeover of the entire country. Later that year, the Americans and British agreed to an administrative merger of their two zones—creating "Bizonia"—a move that infuriated Stalin. By the time Marshall became Secretary of State the following year, Soviet bad faith on Germany was taken as axiomatic. In two abortive Foreign Minister meetings in 1947, Marshall quickly broke off the discussions when it appeared that Molotov had no intention of reaching an early agreement on unification. In early 1948, with the French finally willing to risk a break with Stalin and merge their zone with Bizonia, the Western Allies set in motion the machinery to create a separate West German state.

But if Stalin was content to leave the diplomatic initiatives to the West, it was because his interests were best served by waiting. By 1948, the Sovietization of East Germany had already progressed to the point where it would have been a major obstacle to reunification. Businesses had been reorganized into government cooperatives with a majority of stock owned by the Soviet Union. Agriculture was being collectivized on the Stalinist model. The natural flows of commerce with the West were being redirected toward the East. There was no free press, and local government bodies and trade union councils were firmly in Communist hands. The GULAG, the Soviet labor camp administration, had set up operations throughout the country, and a "people's police" was systematically rooting out all vestiges of opposition to Communist rule in the name of denazification.

All of the tensions came to a focus on Berlin. The city was a postwar anomaly. Located 110 miles within the Soviet zone, it did not fall within Soviet jurisdiction, but was divided into four occupation sectors, administered jointly by the "Kommandatura," a council of the four occupation military commanders. Since Kommandatura decisions had to be unanimous, a state of continuous confrontation between the Soviets and the West developed almost from the beginning. At the same time, the Soviet military openly intimidated the non-Communist political parties in Berlin, denied them newsprint, and broke up their meetings. Communist goon squads beat or sometimes kidnapped non-Communist Party leaders. Elections that went against the Communists, in one case by a 10–1 majority, were simply declared null by the Soviet commander. At one point, because the populace, even in the Russian sector, refused to vote Communist, and the Soviet commander refused to recognize non-Communist officeholders, Berlin was without a mayor for a year and a half. Pressures on non-Communist teachers and student leaders at the University of Berlin, located in the eastern sector, were so intense that the students held full-scale demonstrations to force the western authorities to create a "Free University" in the western sectors.

The key responsibility for managing the Western response to Stalin's roughhouse tactics fell on General Lucius Clay, the American Military Governor for Germany. Cut in the MacArthur mold of the American military proconsul, Clay was imaginative, combative, brilliant, and willful. His command of the details of the occupation administration, even on such technical subjects as currency reform, overawed his nominal military superiors and State Department officials in Washington. On close policy calls, Clay almost always got his way, simply because no one was in a position to dispute him. At the beginning of his administration in Germany, Clay had been confident he would get along well with the Russians—"They know what they *want* and it is always easier to do business with those who know their own desires"—and he had emphatically disputed the analysis of Soviet behavior in Kennan's "Long Telegram." But by 1948, he had become thoroughly disgusted with Soviet duplicity and the heavy-handedness of their occupation policies, a view completely shared by Robert D. Murphy, Clay's assistant and liaison from the State Department.

Clay's insistent remonstrances from Germany—he thought the country was on the brink of starvation—were a major factor in the aggressive diplomatic line adopted by Marshall. The key to recovery, Clay and Marshall agreed, was currency reform. The German mark was trading at less than one five-hundredth of its face value, bringing commerce to a grinding halt; without a sound currency there was little hope that Marshall Plan aid could be effective. The Soviets generally refused to discuss currency reform until there had been a settlement on reparations, or if they did discuss it, insisted on independent issuing authority in the eastern zone. Clay had little reason to trust the Soviets on monetary matters. He had given them a set of occupation currency plates in 1945, and they had promptly flooded the country with new currency to "pay for" the stripping of capital equipment. The worthless currency ultimately had to be redeemed by the Americans for dollars.

In the spring of 1948—only weeks after the ominous coup in Czechoslovakia—the Western powers declared their intention to proceed with the political and economic integration of their three zones. In response, Clay received a note from General Mikhail Dratvin, the Soviet commander in Berlin, stating that as of April 1, the Soviet Union would insist on boarding and inspecting all military traffic destined for Berlin—the first step in the spring "creeping blockade." Dratvin's note said that the step was being taken to "further the expansion of such traffic," and to avoid "sowing distrust in the mutual relations of the occupation authorities."

Clay recommended a tough response—an armed truck convoy to force the blockade, because he was confident the Soviets would back down—but was overruled by Washington, and authorized only to test the blockade with trains. The convoys were instructed to show identification to Soviet officers, but not to permit them on board. The train guards could prevent a Soviet boarding with force, if necessary, but were not to use their weapons unless fired upon. Three trains were dispatched to Berlin on midnight, March 31. But when two of them refused the Soviets access (one commander apparently lost his nerve), the Soviets simply switched them to sidings, where they sat for several days until they were ignominiously withdrawn. In the meantime, the State Department set a brigade of lawyers to work squirreling out the Western Allies' legal rights of access to Berlin, and discovered to their shock that, save for the air corridors, there were no written agreements at all. Everything had been worked out orally between Clay and Marshal Zhukov at the end of the war.

Over the next several weeks, the confrontation gradually fizzled into anticlimax as the mid-command levels on both sides evolved an unofficial modus vivendi. There was no more military train traffic into Berlin, but truck traffic continued to flow. The truck troops would show their ID to Soviet inspectors and open the back of the truck so inspectors could peer inside, but refused to unload the trucks or permit the inspectors to enter them. After several uncertain standoffs—no one was in a hurry to be shot—the partial blockade settled into the realm of minor irritant. Significantly, Clay also began an airlift, the so-called baby airlift, to increase the store of supplies in Berlin. At first the Soviets buzzed and harassed the airlift planes, but after a fatal collision between a Soviet fighter and a British transport on April 5, the air harassment tactics ceased.

The Americans attempted a diplomatic initiative on April 20. Bohlen and Kennan at the State Department argued that things had been going rather badly for Stalin in Europe, despite the Czech coup. The evidence was already overwhelming that the Marshall Plan would be a spectacular success; the Communists had just been decisively defeated in the Italian elections in March; and the split between Stalin and Yugoslavia's Tito had suddenly become both open and embittered. The State Department decided that Ambassador Walter Bedell Smith in Moscow should inquire orally of Molotov whether the time was propitious for serious discussions on Germany. Molotov promptly published an edited version of Smith's questions, making it appear that the United States had proposed bilateral negotiations for the settlement of Europe. The British and French, particularly the French, were outraged, and the Americans seriously embarrassed, not least because the American press interpreted Molotov's remarks as a major Soviet peace initiative. When the diplomatic flutterings died down, the Americans were even more convinced of Soviet bad faith.

On June 1, the Western Allies agreed to proceed with currency reform in the western zones, *excluding* Berlin—the first concrete step toward establishing a functioning government for West Germany. The announcement was withheld for more than two weeks to permit the French Assembly to ratify the decision—a nail-biting period for the Americans, and particularly for Clay and Murphy, who spent most of their time propping up the slippery French resolve. The French held firm, and the currency reform was announced on June 18, to take effect on June 20, dates set by Clay, who had been delegated the responsibility for timing the moves. General Vasily Sokolovsky, Dratvin's superior in Germany, issued a strong protest, then announced on June 21 that the Soviet Union would proceed with currency reform in its own zone, including all of Berlin. (The Soviet currency reform was a fascinating exercise in stalinist monetary principles. The new eastmarks were exchanged for old marks at a ratio of 1:1 for card-carrying Communists; at progressively lower rates for bourgeoisie, kulaks, and other undesirables; and were not available at all to "Nazi" or "Fascist" elements.)

After consultations with the British and French commanders, but without advance notice to Washington, Clay responded by extending the new western currency to the three Allied sectors in Berlin. It was a striking illustration of Clay's independence and his central role in determining the pace of events—Army Secretary Kenneth Royall somewhat plaintively asked him to send a full summary of his actions to Washington. The next day, Sokolovsky announced that because of "technical problems," no traffic of any kind would be permitted to enter West Berlin and that there would be a complete cutoff of electrical power to the Allied sectors. The blockade of Berlin had begun.

The seriousness of the situation dawned only slowly on official Washington. The western sectors of Berlin contained 2 million people, isolated 110 miles within the Soviet zone, cut off by the blockade from power, food, and medical supplies. There was not even a consensus that Berlin was worth defending. As Royall reminded Clay, currency reform seemed a poor pretext for a war. Clay's proposals for an armed convoy to challenge the blockade were turned down firmly. The Soviets had an overwhelming fifteen-to-one troop advantage in Germany, and Bradley, the Army Chief of Staff, worried that a convoy could easily be cut off and isolated, just by destroying bridges. The Joint Chiefs argued that, if there was to be a war with the Soviet Union, the West should withdraw as quickly as possible to more defensible lines.

But while Washington agonized, Clay was rapidly limiting its options. On the first afternoon of the blockade, Colonel Frank Howley, Clay's commander in Berlin, stated flatly in a radio broadcast: "We are not getting out of Berlin. I don't know the answer to the present problem—not yet—but this much I do know. The American people will not stand by and allow the German people to starve." Clay was similarly emphatic when he told reporters that the Soviet Union "cannot drive us out by an action short of war as far as we are concerned."

Clay had already come up with the answer, although no one realized it at the time. He and his advisers had explored the possibility of a major airlift with the American Air Force commander in Europe, General Curtis LeMay, during the partial blockade in April. They speculated that they could airlift some 700 tons of supplies a day, far short of the 3,500 tons Berlin required, but perhaps enough to provide some breathing space. The British commander, General Sir Brian Robertson, quickly agreed to place his transports at Clay's disposal, but before making a recommendation to Washington, Clay first tested the idea with Ernst Reuter, the Berlin Socialist leader—whose election as mayor Sokolovsky had refused to ratify in 1946—and his young assistant Willy Brandt. Reuter doubted that an airlift would accomplish much, but told Clay that Berliners were in no mood to buckle under Soviet pressure: "Do what you are able to do; we shall do what we feel to be our duty. Berlin will make all necessary sacrifices and offer resistance—come what may." Clay recalled Reuter's statement as "the most dramatic moment" of the entire crisis.

The airlift appealed to Truman's activist temperament, and at a cabinet meeting on June 26, he ordered all available transport to be put at Clay's disposal. But air supply was still viewed as a temporary expedient, and the meeting adjourned without coming to any final decisions on the American posture. The 27th was a Sunday, and Forrestal, Royall, and Lovett had a hand-wringing meeting in the Pentagon where they were unable to decide on any course of action. The military position in Berlin was untenable, they agreed; but a humiliating exit could undermine the Western alliance and open the way for a Soviet takeover of all Europe. When they began to present their uncertainties to Truman the next day—as an admiring Forrestal recorded in his diary—he cut them short. As far as staying in Berlin was concerned, "there was no discussion on that point, we were going to stay, period." It was one of the momentous decisions of Truman's presidency, and a striking example of his decisiveness in a crisis.

Clay, LeMay, and Robertson quickly raised their estimate of the airlift's capacity to 2,000 tons a day, and by mid-July, when Clay returned to Washington for consultations, they were already averaging 250 flights and 2,500 tons a day. At the July meetings, Truman somewhat reluctantly ruled out the use of force, although sixty B-29 "atomic bombers" were dispatched to bases in England as a symbol of American seriousness. (Photographers and reporters were denied access to the planes, ostensibly so they could not photograph the special bomb bays required for atomic weapons. In fact, the "atomic bombers" had never been outfitted with atomic bomb bays, and had no atomic weapons at their disposal.) Truman also finally settled on the airlift as the basic American response, authorized Clay to build another airfield in West Berlin, and ordered the Air Force to shift all of their available transports to Clay, including the big new C-54s that they had been jealously holding back from Europe.

Ironically, throughout the discussions, it was Clay's civilian advisers who pressed the most forceful responses; at one point, Murphy considered resigning over Washington's refusal to permit an armed convoy probe. It was the Air Force that was most opposed to the airlift—they were afraid it would strip their capacities in the rest of the world; and it was the Joint Chiefs who most strongly opposed the use of force—they thought they needed eighteen months to return to a war footing.

Throughout the summer, Stalin seemed content to delay diplomacy and wait for bad weather to ground the airlift and crack the Berliners. An American diplomatic initiative in late July was met with the response that Molotov was "on vacation." After several inquiries, Stalin finally agreed to a meeting in Moscow, where Ambassador Smith found him "literally dripping with sweet reasonableness."At one point, in a late evening meeting with Smith, Stalin leaned back in his chair, lit a cigarette, and asked, "Would you like to settle the matter tonight?" He proposed that if the United States agreed to the introduction of east-marks into Berlin, he would lift the blockade, and would drop his demand that the Western Allies stop planning for a separate West German state, although it was his "insistent wish."

Marshall was predisposed to accept the offer, over Clay's objections, but on the condition that there be some form of quadripartite control over the issue of Berlin eastmarks. When this was communicated to Molotov, he responded with a draft agreement that was much more narrow and demanding than Stalin's offer had appeared to be. Smith appealed back to Stalin, who magnanimously confirmed his earlier offer, but suggested that the details be worked out in the military occupation authority. Negotiations were duly held with Sokolovsky, but after several fruitless sessions, the Western Allies realized that they were engaged in a charade—Sokolovsky had no instructions remotely resembling the terms Stalin had appeared to offer so generously in Moscow. In his diary, Forrestal recorded a conversation with Lovett in which they wondered with astonishment whether Stalin had simply been lying to them. It was too much to contemplate. Forrestal fell back on the Harry Truman theory that Stalin was just another machine politician. Stalin and Molotov had tried to cut a deal in Moscow, Forrestal surmised, but had taken it to the Politburo and "lost their shirts."

The Soviets steadily increased the propaganda barrage in Berlin. The Communist press published stories almost daily that the airlift was a failure and that the Americans were preparing to evacuate. At one point a group of Soviet officers drove slowly and ostentatiously through the American barracks area, as if appraising the quarters. For a period, the Communist press even referred to the "Anglo-American blockade." Stories were regularly published about the bulging food bins in East Berlin, and doggerel verse mocked the "dried potato" diet in the West. East Berlin authorities announced that the abundance of coal in the eastern sector might create a storage crisis during the winter. Free food was offered to all West Berliners who would simply come to the eastern sector and register; fewer than 1 percent took up the offer.

But by mid-September, it was slowly becoming clear that the Berliners would hold firm and that the airlift might break the blockade. Clay was already brimming with confidence. The airlift was turning into the kind of technical exercise in which the Americans excelled. LeMay and the Air Force commanders were working to achieve a "steady even rhythm" of flights, and tonnage was approaching 4,500 a day, enough to sustain the city through the winter. The morale of the Berliners was extraordinary. Two hundred and fifty thousand people jammed into the Reichstag Square on September 9 to hear their Socialist leaders denounce the Communists. "In the shadow of Russian imperialism, the Communist are trying to carry out a *coup d'état* in Berlin," Reuter thundered. His Socialist co-chairman, Franz Neumann, denounced the

East German puppet government: "The concentration camps are still the same, but now the hammer and sickle waves over them instead of the swastika."

In the municipal elections in the western sectors later that month, 84 percent of the registered voters cast their vote for the non-Communist parties. The spectacle of the airlift, and the enormous expenditure of resources that it represented, seemed to be drawing the alliance together and softening some of the lingering hatreds of the war. When a transport crashed in September, killing two American pilots, anonymous Berliners erected a plaque on the site that read: "Once we were enemies, and yet you gave your lives for us."

Clay's main worry in the fall was that Washington would have less staying power than his Berliners. The Joint Chiefs were increasingly unhappy about the airlift and were resisting Clay's requests for more planes. Ambassador Smith, a former general, stated flatly that "from a military point of view, [the Berlin position] makes no sense whatever." The State Department was pressing to involve the United Nations in a negotiated solution, and the diplomatic stamina of the British and French was shaky at best. Truman was deeply involved in his famous "whistlestop" presidential campaign and had little time to focus on Berlin. Clay's anxieties finally eased in October when Truman returned to Washington long enough to give the Joint Chiefs a flat order to provide all the planes Clay asked for. The American position hardened for good in late November when the Communists carried out a putsch in the Russian sector of the city. All non-Communist officials and administrators were expelled from the city government and the City Assembly, and a new Communist government proclaimed its intention to merge East Berlin with the Communist regime in East Germany. When a United Nations committee recommended two months later that the eastmark be accepted throughout Berlin, Clay was able to argue, quite correctly, that a divided city administration made the compromise impossible.

There were a few anxious moments in the winter, as one stretch of bad weather permitted only fifteen flying days out of thirty. But as the weather improved, it was obvious to the whole world that the Soviets had come out clear losers in a test of nerve and resources with America. The airlift was supplying 10,000 tons a day, far more than Berlin imported even before the blockade. On Air Force Day, April 16, the airlift triumphantly established a new record of 12,490 tons. There was even enough surplus carrying capacity to fly in 5,000 tons of heavy machinery to rebuild a hydroelectric power station that had been dismantled by the Soviets. In March, West Berlin's papers trumpeted the names of Soviet officials who had been seen in the western sector furtively trading their eastmarks at black market rates to buy western goods. The sheer spectacle of the airlift—the enormous planes taking off and landing only minutes apart, hour after hour, all day and all night, month after month—had become one of the wonders of the world. It was an awesome demonstration of the exuberant technical capacity of the United States, and a stark warning of its ability to project power anywhere in the world.

Stalin finally signalled that he was ready to back down. In answer to a question from a Western reporter at the end of January, he said he would be willing to end the blockade if the West ended its own retaliatory restrictions of shipments to the Soviet zone. Bohlen noticed that for the first time Stalin had not mentioned the currency problem. A cautious period of soundings followed. Philip Jessup, an American U.N. official, approached the Soviet representative, Jacob Malik, on February 15 and asked if Stalin's omission was "accidental." Malik said he didn't know but would check. A month later, he told Jessup that the omission "was not accidental." The British and French were very wary; it sounded like one more effort to divide the Allies. The three Western governments agreed to be firm: no western concessions would be offered on the formation of the West German government or the circulation of Western currency in Berlin.

Stalin, after several probes, yielded on all points. The face-saving formula was that Western trade restrictions would be dropped when the blockade ended and that the Western governments would participate in a four-power Foreign Ministers' meeting before forming a separate government in West Germany. The Soviet Union dropped its blockade on May 12, 1949. Clay returned home a hero, after being acclaimed by Reuter in an emotional speech in the Reichstag, "The memory of General Clay will never fade in Berlin . . . we will never forget what he has done for us."

# CHAPTER 4

# From Berlin to the Yalu

## The Shambles of Stalin's Foreign Policy

"Why," Winston Churchill asked in the spring of 1949, have the Russians "deliberately acted for three long years so as to unite the free world against them." Thanks to Stalin's "harsh external pressures," "unities and associations are being established . . . throughout the free world with a speed and reality which would not have been achieved perhaps for generations." Stalin might well have pondered Churchill's words, for all of the combinations of Western power he had sought so diligently to prevent were coming to pass. Under the spur of the Berlin Blockade, the various non-Communist parties in West Germany had ceased their squabbling long enough to agree to an American-sponsored constitution and to set a definite timetable for holding elections and establishing a new government. For supporting the blockade, the influence of the Communists in West Germany had dropped to near-zero. Rubbing it in, the Basic Law authorizing the West German elections was signed on May 23, the day of the opening of the Foreign Ministers' conference requested by Stalin as a condition for ending the blockade. (The Western Allies had promised not to take final steps toward a West German government *before* the opening of the meeting. Andrei Vyshinsky, the new Soviet Foreign Minister, pretended not to notice.)

For the first time since the founding of the Republic, breaking with the solemn admonition of George Washington, the United States entered into a mutual defense treaty with foreign governments—the North Atlantic Treaty, at this point a treaty, not yet a defense organization—along with Great Britain, France, the Benelux countries, Greece, Turkey, Spain, Portugal, and Canada. The treaty was ratified by the American Senate by an 82–13 majority in July 1949, and was followed by a billion-dollar military assistance program for Europe and a $5.4 billion increase in appropriations for the Marshall Plan.

Economic recovery was everywhere apparent in Western Europe. The effect of the currency reform in West Germany had been magical: output increased by more than 60 percent between the spring of 1948 and the spring of 1949. In dreary contrast to the budding prosperity in the West, living standards in the satellites seemed actually to be dropping, particularly in East Germany where the pressures to bring the country into line with Stalinist economic theory were the harshest. It was at least partly in reaction to Stalin's heavy-handed economic exploitation of the satellites that the Yugoslavs risked their break with the Soviets in 1948. The economic revival of the West was fraught with implications far beyond the strategic and political. Loyal Communists were waiting for the collapse of capitalism with all the wide-eyed confidence of early Christians scanning the horizon for the Second Coming. It would be hard to maintain discipline in the ranks if the Marxist paradise were just a millenarian dream. Stalin, in his inimitably direct way, dealt with the problem by forcing an abject recantation from one leading Soviet economist, Eugene Varga, who had theorized that state planning might permit a protracted prosperity in the West, and executing another, Nikolai Voznesensky, who speculated along similar lines.

Kremlinologists have woven subtle purpose into Stalin's foreign policy throughout early 1949, but to all appearances, Soviet behavior was confused and floundering. At about the same time that Stalin first signalled he might back down on Berlin, for example, the dean of the French Communists, Marcel Cachin, surprised the French Assembly by extolling the benefits of peaceful coexistence; then flew to Italy, where he and Togliatti made conciliatory speeches on the desirability of achieving communism by democratic means, belying everything they had said during the previous two years. The statements obviously had the approval of Moscow, and Western statesmen began to gear themselves for a full-scale peace offensive. Barely a month later, the French Communist leader Maurice Thorez made the extraordinary statement, for no apparent reason, that if Soviet troops invaded Paris, the French Communists would fight on the Soviet side. Once again, the statement had obviously been approved by Moscow, for it was immediately reprinted in the Cominform newspapers throughout the world. Predictably, it caused a storm of protest in France: there were calls in the Assembly to indict Thorez for treason, a number of Communists were arrested for espionage, General de Gaulle fulminated that the Communists really *were* planning an invasion of Western Europe, and there was a sharp drop in support for the Party among the French public.

After Thorez's statement, Communist policy took an ominous turn. There were a series of violent strikes in France and Italy, the worst since the struggle against the Marshall Plan the previous year. The Soviets carried out a number of menacing troop movements along the Yugoslav border and there was a sudden spate of border incidents with Iran. Radio Moscow said that the Thorez statement was a warning to "the warmongers" that "the working class will carry out its duty of international proletarian solidarity," and an official Soviet publication in East Germany said that if peace efforts should fail, "the Soviet Army in the course of pursuing the imperialist aggressor naturally will be compelled to march into the territory of some West European states."

A series of purges in the satellites beginning in 1948 and 1949 recalled the bad old days of the 1930s. Glimpsed through the murky gloom that swirled around Soviet decision making, the purges appeared to be mere flailing, causing some Western experts, Kennan among them, to wonder if Stalin was insane. Wladislaw Gomulka, an old Stalinist and former General Secretary of the Polish Communist Party, was demoted and then imprisoned. Traicho Kostov, deputy prime minister of Bulgaria and a militant Zhdanovist, was executed for treason, after repudiating a confession that he was a CIA agent. General Koci Xoxe, former deputy prime minister of Albania, was executed on charges of being a Titoist. Lazslo Rajk, the Hungarian Minister of the Interior, was executed on charges of being *both* a CIA agent and a Titoist.

The tempo of the purges increased almost until Stalin's death—Rudolf Slansky, the deputy prime minister and former Party General Secretary in Czechoslavakia, and Vladimir Clementis, the Czech Foreign Minister, were executed in 1951 and 1952, and the purges may have reached as many as a fourth of all East European Party members.* The crackdown in the satellites was paralleled by an ugly upsurge of official anti-Semitism in the Soviet Union itself, in the form of a cam-

*One explanation for the purges is that Georgi Malenkov and Lavrenti Beria, who had been eclipsed by Zhdanov during the latter's ascendancy in 1947 and 1948, were making a comeback, and Stalin was letting them fight it out with Zhdanov's followers. (Zhdanov had died, of natural causes apparently, in August 1948; Stalin later insisted that he had been murdered by Jewish doctors.) Most of the prominent East European victims were known to have been close to Zhdanov, and the economist Vosnesensky may have had the same problem. The Malenkov-Beria/Zhdanov theory of the purges stems from Khrushchev, who, in 1957, could not be considered a trustworthy source on Malenkov and Beria. Kostov and Rajk were rehabilitated during the de-Stalinization period, and it was admitted that their confessions were extracted by torture.

paign against "homeless cosmopolitanism"—all worrying signs that Stalin might be girding for a final confrontation with the West.

Soviet tactics shifted sharply again in mid-1949. Molotov made a speech that seemed to soften slightly the Zhdanov "two camps" thesis. Word went out through the Cominform organs in the summer that national parties were to concentrate on the peace movement, with the goal of separating the peace-loving peoples of the world from their warmongering leaders. Malenkov followed with a major address in the fall, downplaying the possibility of war, and placing emphasis once again on the peace movement. Vyshinsky's performance at the Foreign Minister's conference in May was distinctly lackluster, with none of the obstructionist verve Western statesmen had come to expect of Molotov. He contented himself with bland requests to return to four-power control over Germany, with a Soviet veto, reparations, and Soviet participation in the administration of the Ruhr. He could not have expected the proposals to be taken seriously, and they weren't.

The cohesion and confidence of the West was now at its highest point since the war. A line had been drawn across Europe, and Soviet expansion had been brought to a halt. The West had faced down Stalin in Berlin, proving that the alliance could act together in a crisis and, perhaps most important, that Stalin was not willing to risk a war. Full economic recovery in Western Europe was now just a matter of time, and similar steps were being taken to rehabilitate Japan. Cracks were already showing in Stalin's empire, and the disgraceful behavior of the Communist regimes in the satellites, and their visible lack of economic progress, were serving as the most effective inoculation of the European masses against the appeals of Marxist revolutionaries. A western military alliance was in place; France, Great Britain, and the United States had all increased their defense budgets; and discussions were under way to integrate their military resources in Europe. Although Kennan's "X" article had been published only two years before, the doctrine of containment it recommended, so far at least, it might fairly be claimed, was already enjoying real success.

## The Battle Over American Defense Spending

Revisionist historians trace the rise of the American "national security state" to the period 1948–49, when the American military and American industry, particularly the airframe industry, seized upon the Soviet challenge in Europe to militarize American foreign policy. That there were powerful pressures is beyond question. But Harry Truman was determined to resist them; and until the spring of 1950, his administration was wracked by a continuing controversy over the scale and purpose of military spending that strained relations within the cabinet, spilled over into congressional hearings, created bitter rivalries between the services, and at one point led to a brief, but direct and public, confrontation between the highest echelons of the military leadership and their civilian controllers.

For all his recent assertiveness in foreign policy, Truman's primary agenda as he began his second term was a domestic one: full employment, national health insurance, an improved social security system, and regional development programs like the TVA. The line in his inaugural address that had drawn the greatest applause was one that he had penciled in himself, that he would give America a "Fair Deal." Truman had approved a $3 billion military supplemental appropriation—on top of an approved budget of $10.5 billion—during the "spring war scare" just before the Berlin crisis, but he was determined to hold the line the next fiscal year. As the administration began to work on its budget during the summer, he told Forrestal, his Secretary of Defense, to keep his request to $14.4 billion, essentially enough to maintain current programs with modest improvements.

Truman's military spending ceiling threw down the gauntlet to a host of interests—the aircraft industry, defense-minded congressmen, the service chiefs themselves—who were building a coalition in favor of a much stronger military establishment. The case of the pro-defense lobby was a strong one: The United States was in no position to fight a land war in Europe and arguably did not really have the atomic air strike capability to win a war against a determined Soviet Union. Recent events in Europe were all too reminiscent of 1938—if there was any lesson from Munich, it was that expansionist dictatorships needed to be stopped in their tracks early and forcefully. The United States had made precisely such a commitment in enunciating the Truman Doctrine; it now had the responsibility to acquire a military capability consistent with its rhetoric.

Truman does not seem to have questioned any of these propositions. He was simply not prepared to base American policy on the supposition of war. His stance was powerfully reinforced by Marshall, who thought that collective security, and the rehabilitation of Europe, both economically and militarily, was the best way to prevent a war. Perhaps surprisingly for a career military man, Marshall also insisted that intensive preparation for war might itself increase the danger that war would actually break out.

The first trumpet flourish from the pro-defense forces was sounded in early 1948, with the publication of the Finletter Report, a report of a presidential commission charged with reviewing American air defense policy and chaired by Thomas Finletter, a lawyer who was later to become Secretary of the Air Force. The Finletter Report's posture was both alarmist and unabashedly pro-Air Force. Although the United States was presently secure, because no other country had the capacity to produce atomic weapons "in quantity," the report assumed that "a hostile power"—it never mentioned the Soviet Union by name—would be able to mount "direct attacks on the United States mainland" by early 1953. The attacks would be atomic ones, would come without warning, and could be deterred only by creating and maintaining the ability "to retaliate with the utmost violence." The report proposed a 70-squadron Air Force, the long-time impossible dream of the Air Force generals, an increase of about 2,000 planes. The recommendations also included a major Air Force modernization program, with particular emphasis on the new heavy long-range bomber, the B-36, and a huge buildup in the air fleet reserves. To achieve the report's objectives by 1953 would require a national industrial policy aimed at maintaining the airframe industry at virtually war production levels and a doubling of the defense budget, with almost all of the increase targeted for the Air Force.

As the Air Force took the spending offensive, the Navy reacted with undisguised alarm. Public and congressional pressure for a stronger air arm, coupled with the administration's determination to hold the spending line—the Admirals feared—would scuttle their most cherished projects, particularly a long-planned new generation of supercarriers. The administration's emphasis on nuclear weapons put the Navy at a distinct disadvantage, because atomic bombs were still too heavy to be delivered by carrier-based aircraft. The ensuing melee quite literally drove Forrestal to a mental breakdown and provoked some of the most unseemly confrontations between the services on public record. At one point, the Navy accused the Air Force of advocating an "immoral" strategy, since the brunt of atomic attacks would inevitably fall on civilians. The Air Force riposte was that any weapon is immoral if it is "too big for your service to deliver."

The Joint Chiefs took the Air Force's seventy-squadron target as a starting point, made commensurate increases in the other services, and submitted a $35 billion budget request to Forrestal in the spring. Forrestal spent weeks of fruitless negotiations with the chiefs, but ran into a stone wall of non-cooperation from the military and open rebellion from his politically ambitious Air Force Secretary, Stuart Syming-ton. Despairing of a compromise, Forrestal finally developed his own budget of $16.9 billion, but was turned down firmly by Truman—$14.4 billion was the number, and that would be that.

Forrestal was a man on a rack. As Secretary of the Navy, he had fought the creation of the office of Defense Secretary, and had helped ensure that its executive authority was weak, little more than an arbiter among the services. He genuinely believed in the necessity for a stronger defense; actual paranoia about the Soviet Union was one of the symptoms of his mental deterioration. But at the same time, as a former Wall Street investment banker, he admired the President's "hard-money" stance, and was personally convinced that a budget much bigger than the one Truman had authorized would "wreck the econ-omy."

Forrestal finally secured some nominal service support for his own compromise budget and pressed his case hard through the summer and fall. But as so often in the Truman administration, the swing vote was held by Marshall. Forrestal secured a showdown meeting between him-self, the President, and Marshall in late 1948, hoping to enlist Marshall in his cause. Marshall refused to support higher defense spending—the European recovery program was too important; this, it should be re-called, was at the height of the crisis in Berlin, and well before the airlift had met the test of winter flying weather. For a man whose career, personal life, and mental health were in ruins, Forrestal took his defeat with remarkable graciousness. "In the person of Harry Truman," he said in a speech in December, "I have seen the most rock-like example of civilian control that the world has ever witnessed."

Pressures for more military spending eased briefly with the success of the Berlin airlift, but the controversy broke out anew in 1949. In January, Chinese Communist forces swarmed across the Yangtze River, signalling the beginning of the end for the Nationlist regime. In the spring, the Communists captured Chiang's last stronghold, the city of Nanking, put the last remnants of his army to disorderly flight, and quelled any lingering hopes that the country might fend off a complete Communist takeover. Much more frightening, in September, an Ameri-can reconnaissance plane picked up unmistakable evidence that the Soviet Union had exploded an atomic weapon. Truman still insisted that the Soviet Union did not have the technology to mass-produce bombs, but it was clear that America's confident assumption of its own safety was a thing of the past.

The fall of China precipitated what Acheson, who succeeded Mar-

shall as Truman's Secretary of State, called "the attack of the primi-
tives." A strong right-wing group of senators and congressmen, the
so-called China Lobby—William Knowland and Richard Nixon of California, Walter Judd of Minnesota, Styles Bridges of New Hampshire,
Own Brewster of Maine, Homer Capehart of Indiana, Karl Mundt of
South Dakota—was coalescing around the belief that America's sudden
insecurity stemmed from Roosevelt and his left-wing advisers "selling
the country down the river" at Yalta. The group had an almost mystical
conception of American relations with China (Judd had been a medical
missionary there) and close ties to the strong anti-Communist movement that was developing within the American Catholic Church in
response to Stalin's religious repression in Eastern Europe.

Acheson fanned the flames with the release of the "China White
Paper" in August, one of the more remarkable documents in American
diplomatic history. Intended almost as a lawyer's brief in defense of
American policy in China, it is a book-length narrative of the dishonesty
and corruption of the Kuomintang regime, a devastating commentary
on the cowardice and incapacities of the Nationalist Army under
Chiang's leadership, and a powerful argument against wasting American resources in a hopeless cause. In a long section that was certain to
infuriate the China Lobby, the report chronicles Marshall's year-long
effort to mediate between the Nationalists and Communists in 1945 and
1946, and leaves the clear impression that Marshall gradually came to
regard Zhou Enlai and the Communist negotiators as by far the more
reliable and capable of the parties. Perhaps more important, the China
White Paper is a repudiation of the literal language of the Truman
Doctrine. The rhetoric in 1947, Acheson seemed to be saying, that the
United States would resist Communist encroachments "everywhere"
really meant "primarily Europe," or other limited cases where the
regimes under pressure both merited support and were ensured a good
chance of success with American aid.

The furor on the right intensified in early 1950 with the perjury
conviction of Alger Hiss. The Hiss case sprang from the revelations by
Whittaker Chambers, a former Communist, that Hiss had passed him
confidential papers while in a high position at the State Department,
culminating in the dramatic episode when Chambers led House investigators to a pumpkin patch where he had concealed a microfilm of
secret documents allegedly passed to him by Hiss. Hiss's brother, Donald—more than once confused with Alger by Acheson's attackers—had
been Acheson's executive assistant at the State Department and his law

partner, and Alger and Acheson were friends, if not close friends. On the day after Hiss's conviction, Acheson, with his patrician's sense of personal loyalty, made one of the more impolitic statements on public record with the gratuitous comment to a press conference that "I shall never turn my back on Alger Hiss." The thunderous outburst from the right that greeted Acheson's remark was but the lowering prelude of what was to come. A few weeks later, at a Lincoln's Day speech in Wheeling, West Virginia, Senator Joseph McCarthy made his famous claim that he had a list of 57 (or 205, the record is confused) Communists in the State Department, and launched the movement that ripped at the country's political fabric for the next half decade.

The fall of China, the Hiss case, Stalin's atomic explosion, and the McCarthyist onslaught are the essential context for understanding the boldness of Truman's decision to *reduce* defense spending in the fiscal year that was to begin in July 1950. As in the 1948 battle, Truman was motivated by his conviction that war was not imminent, by his fear of big budget deficits, and by the priority he assigned to his domestic programs. At the start of his second term, he replaced Forrestal at Defense with Louis Johnson, a huge bull of a man, with presidential ambitions and solid military credentials—he was one of the founders of the American Legion. Johnson was even more of a hard-money man than Forrestal, was dogmatically convinced of the necessity for economy in government, and believed that he would advance his own career by trimming the mammoth defense establishment. He and Truman announced that their budget target for the next fiscal year would be $13.5 billion, requiring a reduction of some 45,000 armed forces personnel, and that they hoped to make even deeper cuts the following year, with a target budget of $10.5 billion. To make matters worse from the services' standpoint, Johnson set out to save money right away by impounding part of Symington's appropriation and cancelling construction of the *United States,* the Navy's beloved supercarrier, and its major hope of competing against the Air Force in the battle to be the service of choice in the new era of overseas force projection. Actual military spending that year, in fact, measured as a percent of Gross National Product, was, at about 4 percent, the lowest during the entire postwar period to the present day.

The war between Johnson and the services broke into the open in the fall of 1949 with the "Revolt of the Admirals," precipitated through the unlikely agency of Captain John Crommelin, one of six career naval officer brothers (two of whom had died in the war) who was assigned as an aide to the Joint Chiefs of Staff in Washington. Acting entirely on his own, Crommelin released a statement to reporters in September charging that the Navy was being "nibbled to death" and its morale destroyed by Johnson's economy policies. The naval brass reacted by promoting Crommelin to deputy chief of naval personnel, a post previously held by a rear admiral, and were reversed the same day by the Secretary of the Navy, Francis Matthews, a loyal administration placeman. Two weeks later, Crommelin, by now determined to press his one-man war, delivered to the wire services copies of confidential letters endorsing his statements by three of the highest-ranking naval officers, Admirals Gerald Bogan, commander of the First Task Fleet in the Pacific, Arthur Radford, commander in chief of the Pacific Fleet, and Louis Denfield, chief of naval operations.

Crommelin's new revelations were a sensation in Washington, and Congress immediately scheduled an investigation. Matthews led off the administration testimony by declaring that all was well in the Navy, and was promptly repudiated by a long parade of admirals, culminating in testimony by Denfield that accused the administration of adopting "an unsound concept of war," of imposing "arbitrary reductions that impair or even eliminate essential naval functions," of "illogical, damaging, and dangerous" favoritism toward the Air Force, and of attempting to "relegate the navy to a convoy or antisubmarine service." The hearings ended with the administration bloodied, but with its economy flag still waving. The Navy undercut its own case by attacking the other services, prompting Omar Bradley to testify that the admirals were "'fancy dans' who won't hit the line with all they have on every play unless they can call the signals." The controversy died down when Congress recessed in late October, and Truman forced Denfield to retire, replacing him with Forrest Sherman, commander of the Sixth Fleet, and one of the few top naval officers who had not appeared to testify against the administration.

The controversy over defense spending puts into perspective the celebrated document, NSC-68, that was produced by a joint State and Defense Department working team in 1950, and which is usually taken, as one scholar put it, as "the official imprimatur" for a policy of "confrontation with the Soviet Union." NSC-68 is nothing less than a call to arms. Intended as a sweeping reassessment of American foreign policy, it presents a demonic picture of the Soviet Union, almost a caricature of the 1950s view of the Cold War. The Soviet Union, it says, is seeking "to bring the free world under its dominion by the methods of the cold war. . . . Every institution of our society is an instrument which it is sought to stultify and turn against our purposes." The document argues that "there is no way to make ourselves inoffensive to the Soviet Union except by complete submission to its will" and warns that the current defense spending policies were rendering the American military "less and less effective as a war deterrent," and could lead to "disaster." The document compares the warmaking potential of the United States and the Soviet Union and concludes that the Soviet Union could outspend America because of its greater ability to harness its economy in service of the state, making the essentially economic argument—one that was being advanced strongly within the Council of Economic Advisers by Leon Keyserling, one of the early Keynesians—that the United States could greatly expand the scale of military spending without economic damage.

However accurately NSC-68 reflected subsequent American policy, it appears to have been on the *losing* side of the policy debate in Washington in the spring of 1950. The document was drafted primarily by Paul Nitze, who had succeeded Kennan as chief of Policy Planning at the State Department, and who supplied most of the momentum for pushing it through the bureaucracy. Nitze and Acheson seized the opportunity to draft a sweeping new policy statement when Truman asked for a background paper on the desirability of building a thermonuclear bomb. (There was a concern that an H-bomb program would steal too many resources from atomic weapon production.) Acheson admitted to having set out to write a tract to "bludgeon the mass mind of 'top government,'" although Nitze recalls no such intention. The project was opposed within the State Department both by Kennan, who thought sweeping policy assessments were useless, and "big war" planning simply wrong, and by Bohlen, who thought it a mistake to so overstate the Soviet threat. It was opposed most violently within the administration by, ironically, the Secretary of Defense, who—quite correctly—saw it as just one more attempt to endrun his economy program. When the document was finished, Johnson and Acheson were barely on speaking terms.

In the short run, Johnson appears to have won the argument. Truman read NSC-68 in April and asked for its cost; when told that it implied doubling annual defense expenditures, his interest noticeably flagged. Senator Walter George, the key Democrat on both the Finance Committee and the Armed Services Committee, had a similar reaction. Technically, the document was assigned to a study committee charged with developing its cost implications further. Nitze believes that it would have had some effect on the new defense budget, but concedes that Truman was "rather ambivalent"; he recalls being "very much disturbed" in the late spring when Truman told Arthur Krock that he was still planning to stick with his original defense budget.

NSC-68 had practically no influence on the defense budget hearings in April and May, which, compared to the pyrotechnics in the fall, were relatively uneventful. The military had no stomach for more public confrontations. Although they privately let it be known that they preferred a defense appropriation of $18 billion, they supported their civilian chiefs at the public hearings. Bradley, the new chairman of the Joint Chiefs, testified that the health of the economy had priority over military requirements: "So if we came here and recommended to you a $30,000,000,000 to $40,000,000,000 budget for defense, I think we would be doing a disservice and that maybe you should get a new Chairman of the Joint Chiefs of Staff." By the first week of June, the House had passed a defense appropriation bill of $13.8 billion, up slightly from Truman's and Johnson's request for $13.5 billion. The Senate had not yet acted on June 24, when Communist mortars and artillery suddenly shattered the silence of an early Korean Sunday morning, and North Korean troops began pouring across the 38th parallel. Without that attack, one careful historian of NSC-68 has said, the document's "value would very probably have been only historical."

## The Korean War

From virtually any point of view, the Korean War was an unmitigated disaster. There were almost 2 million casualties, including a half million Korean civilians and 100,000 Americans killed or wounded. The Soviet Union found itself at the end of the war confronted with a vastly more powerful American military presence on its eastern rim, the loss of any opportunity to influence developments in Japan, and compromised relations with its huge new ally to the south, Communist China. The Chinese gained marginal benefits in the form of new military respect throughout Asia and a more equal relationship with the Soviet Union, but at the price of normalized relations with the United States, the loss of any hope of recovering Taiwan from the Nationalists, huge losses of wealth and manpower, and a serious delay in their national reconstruction program. For the Americans, any confidence that Communist expansion was being successfully contained was rudely dashed, all of Truman's hopes for his domestic programs were sacrificed to a vastly accelerated rearmament effort, the Republican right-wing image of a diabolical world Communist conspiracy seemed dramatically confirmed, and the country was laid open to the repressive excesses of the McCarthy era.

Like Berlin, Korea was one of the unresolved remnants of the war. The Soviet Union had entered North Korea two days after the Japanese surrender, and the Americans—with little choice in the matter, since the nearest American troops were 600 miles away in Okinawa—agreed that they could disarm the Japanese north of the 38th parallel. The Americans had promised an independent and unified Korea in 1943, and Stalin endorsed that objective at both Yalta and Potsdam. When the war ended, however, Stalin refused to withdraw his troops, concentrating instead on building a Communist state in the North under Kim Il-Sung. Under American prodding, a United Nations commission canvassed the possibility of nationwide elections in 1947, but were refused access to the North. In response, the Americans and their closest allies recognized the nominally democratic, and very shaky, regime of Syngman Rhee, a Chiang-like figure, as the legitimate government of South Korea in 1948.

The American military regarded both Rhee and Korea as liabilities, and recommended in 1947 that American troops be withdrawn. Rhee was still supplied with American arms but was not permitted tanks and assault aircraft, because the Americans were afraid he would attack the North. The impression that the Americans had effectively written off Korea was reinforced when both the American commander in the Far East, Douglas MacArthur, and Acheson made separate declarations in the year before the war that Korea was not within the American defensive perimeter in the Pacific.

The attack from the North was not planned by Stalin, but was clearly launched with his approval. In view of the tight grip Stalin kept on his satellites, it is inconceivable that he would have permitted Kim to use his Soviet-supplied armory without prior consultation. Kim visited Moscow twice just before the attacks, and we have Khrushchev's testimony that Kim assured Stalin "the first poke would touch off an internal explosion in South Korea." Stalin, Khrushchev says, was worried about a possible American response but Kim convinced him that the war would be over before the Americans could react. Before giving Kim his head, Stalin apparently also checked with Mao, who endorsed the project. From Stalin's standpoint, he had little to lose from "unleashing Kim" and perhaps much to gain. It was already clear that the Americans and the Japanese were proceeding toward a separate peace treaty aimed at making Japan a firm military and commercial ally of the United States. A Sovietized Korea only 100 miles away might shock the Japanese into neutralism, and at worst, would serve to draw American attention and resources away from its reconstruction programs in Europe.

Events came within a whisker of bearing out Kim's assurances. The South Korean defenses crumbled under the first artillery barrage, and within two hours, the North Koreans, spearheading their attacks with about one hundred fifty Soviet tanks, were thrusting deep into southern territory on three separate salients and mounting amphibious assaults all along the east coast. When MacArthur made his first personal inspection four days later, he reported the South Koreans in utter confusion, having lost or abandoned their equipment, and with no capacity for united action. A few more weeks at most, and the war would be over.

The American reaction was so sharp and so unhesitating that it caught the Soviets completely by surprise, and their diplomatic actions over the next several weeks were fumbling and bewildered. Within the first few days of the attack, Truman had pushed resolutions through the United Nations Security Council authorizing member—that is, American—air and sea strikes in support of Rhee, and even before MacArthur's gloomy assessment from the front, the use of ground combat troops. The Soviets could have vetoed the resolutions, but they were boycotting the Council over its failure to seat Communist China, and lacked the self-possession to end the boycott in time. (A veto would not have stopped the American action. State Department lawyers and the British had already found language in the U.N. Charter that plausibly authorized unilateral intervention.)

In response to an American note, amidst the usual denunciations, the Soviets gave a clear message that they didn't intend to fight in Korea, and in the first several weeks after the attack seemed to float ideas for ending the conflict, most of them involving the recognition of Communist China. The Americans were in no mood to bargain. Acheson wrote to Bevin on July 10: "It is imperative that the Soviets not be paid any price whatever for calling off an attack that they never should have started."

The American performance, and particularly MacArthur's, in the first months of the crisis was splendid. In MacArthur's own words:

My directives were to establish a beachhead in the neighborhood of Pusan [on the southeast coast of the country]. . . .

I was reminded at the time that my resource for the time being was practically limited to what I had and that I must regard the security of Japan as a fundamental and basic policy. . . .

I managed to throw in a part of two battalions of infantry, who put up a magnificent resistance before they were destroyed—a resistance which resulted, perhaps, in one of the most vital successes that we had.

The enemy undoubtedly could not understand that we would make such an effort with such small force. . . . Instead of rushing rapidly forward to Pusan, which [the enemy] could have reached within a week, without the slightest difficulty, he stopped to deploy his artillery across the Han River.

By that time I had brought forward the rest of the Twenty-fourth Division under General Dean. I gave him orders to delay the advance of the enemy. . . . He fought a very desperate series of isolated combats in which both he, and a large part of that division, were destroyed.

By that time we had landed the Twenty-Fifth Division at Pusan, and it was moving forward by rail. And we had landed the First Cavalry Division on the east coast, and they moved over and formed a line of battle. I do not think that the history of war will show a more magnificent effort against what should have been overwhelming odds as those two divisions displayed.

By that time the Eighth Army Command had moved over under a very indomitable leader, General Walker. From that time on, I never had the slightest doubt about our ability to hold a beachhead. And on July 19, . . . I predicted that we would not be driven into the sea.

It was one of the few occasions of his life when MacArthur was guilty of understatement. The first contingent of American troops, only 500 strong, held off a North Korean column estimated to be six miles long and led by tanks. General Dean's 7,000 men engaged more than 80,000 North Koreans. Whole battalions and regiments were completely wiped out. Dean himself, after his division was destroyed, his shoulder broken, eluded capture for more than a month behind enemy lines before he was taken prisoner.

Only weeks after he had secured the perimeter around Pusan, MacArthur launched one of the most daringly conceived and brilliantly executed amphibious operations in military history, a surprise nighttime assault at Inchon on the rocky and inhospitable west central Korean seacoast, two hundred miles behind the North Korean lines. MacArthur's military superiors were unanimously opposed to the operation. "If every possible geographic and naval handicap were listed— Inchon has 'em all," Admiral Sherman summed up the view of the Joint

Chiefs. The tides were among the highest in the world. Because of the extreme tidal fluctuations, there were only four possible dates for a landing through the fall—MacArthur characteristically chose the earliest one. The landing force would have only some three hours in the early morning darkness to fight their way past a heavily fortified island before ebb tide bogged them down in mud, and only another three hours in the afternoon to bring up supplies and troops to secure the beachhead. MacArthur overbore all the objectors, citing Wolfe's scaling of the heights at Quebec, the incalculable value of surprise, and the necessity for a quick victory—"I can almost hear the ticking of the second hand of destiny. We must act now or we will die."

MacArthur's assault took the North Korean garrisons by complete surprise. The beach was secured by eight o'clock on the morning of the 15th, and by the afternoon, the troops and equipment of the Tenth Corps under Major General Edward Almond were pouring in to cut the North Korean supply lines. Seoul, eighteen miles inland, was taken a week later, and the next day the Eighth Army smashed its way out of the Pusan Perimeter. The North Korean army, which just one week before had been in confident control of almost the entire country, suddenly found itself in disorderly retreat, in hostile territory cut off from any supplies, pounded from the sea and the air, and trapped between two powerful advancing armies. It was a total rout. Vanguards of the Eighth Army and Tenth Corps linked up on the 26th, at almost the same spot where American troops had first come under fire eighty-three days earlier. Within another two weeks, South Korea was virtually cleared of enemy troops, with an estimated 25,000 North Korean soldiers managing to straggle home through the American lines.

It is tempting to speculate how different events might have been if the Americans, having secured their original objective in such spectacular fashion, had stopped there. Stalin would have received a severe bloody nose in Asia, little more than a year after a similar setback in Europe. Truman would have demonstrated for the second time in two years that a firm, but limited, response was sufficient to contain Communist aggression. The seeming invincibility of American power and its ability to react suddenly to events almost anywhere in the world would have been strikingly confirmed. Although the American overseas military establishment would surely have been strengthened as a consequence, the headlong American rearmament that actually ensued might have been avoided.

It was not to be. Virtually the only voice in the government that suggested stopping at the 38th parallel was George Kennan's. An ambiguous Soviet peace feeler in October was brushed aside. After years of frustration with Stalin's steady encroachments in Eastern Europe, the Americans and their major allies were almost unanimous in the conviction that Kim's troops must not escape to sanctuary and that Korea would not be a repeat of Poland—the long-delayed nationwide elections would finally be held without Soviet obstruction. Trygve Lie, the U.N. Secretary General, supported the move across the parallel, and the General Assembly endorsed the action on October 7.

Washington's enthusiasm for pressing ahead in Korea was only slightly dampened by worries about Soviet or Chinese intervention. The Chinese, it was known, were massing troops in Manchuria, and Zhou Enlai, the Chinese premier, began to issue increasingly explicit warnings in September. But the State Department was not disposed to take Zhou seriously. They didn't trust his intermediary, the Indian Ambassador in Peking; they had a low regard for Chinese fighting capabilities, based on the experience with Chiang; and most important, Acheson and his advisers, particularly Dean Rusk, who was in charge of the Far Eastern desk, obstinately refused to understand the growing Chinese alarm at the American buildup in Asia. Truman might make soothing noises about America's limited objectives, but the Chinese could read the papers, and could hardly fail to be impressed by MacArthur's open campaign for military cooperation with Chiang, the China Lobby's mounting crusade to roll back Asian communism, or Senator Knowland's demands for a Manchurian "buffer zone" to protect the new Korean state.

The Joint Chiefs sent orders to MacArthur on September 27 that his objective was the "destruction of the North Korean Armed Forces," but warned him against provoking the Soviets or Chinese, and instructed him to use only Korean troops on the borders of Manchuria. South Korean units were already moving north by the time the orders arrived. On September 29, MacArthur filed his plan for subduing the North. For the sake of speed, he proposed to split his small force into two isolated wings moving north on either side of the Taebaek mountains, leaving a fifty-mile gap in his center. The plan raised eyebrows, but none of the Chiefs was willing to challenge the genius of Inchon. On the 30th, Marshall, who, aging and ailing though he was, had been recalled from retirement to replace Johnson at Defense, sent MacArthur a message that he should "feel unhampered tactically and strategically to proceed north of the 38th parallel." The message has been the subject of much controversy, because MacArthur chose to interpret it as superseding the carefully drawn order from the Chiefs. But it is clear that Marshall had no such intention: the United Nations was debating a Korean resolution that week, and Marshall merely wanted to reassure MacArthur that he needn't wait for the conclusion of the debate before moving.

Fresh from his imperial reign in Japan, MacArthur seems to have been determined to show the world how to deal with Asians. Washington, he insisted, "underestimate the Oriental mentality. . . . They do not grant that it is in the pattern of the Oriental psychology to respect and follow aggressive, resolute, and dynamic leadership [and] to quickly turn on a leadership characterized by timidity and vacillation." When an Army spokesman told the press in October that American troops would stop 40 miles south of Manchuria, consistent with the Joint Chiefs' orders, MacArthur's headquarters immediately contradicted him. Three days later, when Truman said at a press conference that it was "his understanding" that only South Korean troops would approach the Manchurian border at the Yalu River, MacArthur immediately contradicted *him:* "The mission of the United Nations forces," he said flatly, "is to clear Korea." On the 24th, MacArthur sent his field commanders instructions that they should employ all available troops, not just Koreans, in the advance to the Yalu. When the Joint Chiefs received a copy of the order, they informed MacArthur that he was in violation of their order of September 27. MacArthur replied that he was acting out of "military necessity"; the chiefs dithered and backed off.

The first Chinese troops were encountered on the 26th by South Korean units pushing close to hydroelectric installations on the Yalu. Correspondents at the front reported heavy fighting—one South Korean regiment was almost completely lost—but MacArthur's headquarters in Tokyo denied the stories. ("Investigation showed that the report was based on the reports of two prisoners of war . . .") By the first week of November, reports were flooding in of Chinese pressing south along every available road, and several South Korean units were badly chewed up by Chinese cavalry astride Mongolian ponies, attacking to the sound of Wild West bugle calls. Tokyo still insisted there were no Chinese, but conceded that some Manchurian-bred Koreans may have been repatriated by the Communists. By the 5th, Chinese involvement was no longer deniable, and MacArthur suddenly announced that he was facing "a new and fresh army . . . backed up by the possibility of large alien reserves and adequate supplies within easy reach," and that the Chinese had "committed one of the most offensive acts of international lawlessness of historic record." Two days later MacArthur decided on a reconnaissance probe to test the new enemy's intentions. To his surprise, the Chinese broke off contact and disappeared back across the Yalu—"a phantom that casts no shadow," one commentator said.

If Chinese attacks in October were intended as a warning, they had the desired effect. The British were thoroughly alarmed, and there was a burst of activity in the United Nations to find grounds for a negotiated settlement. On November 24, the Joint Chiefs sent MacArthur a message suggesting—not quite ordering—a variety of means to contain the conflict by leaving a North Korean or a neutralized buffer zone between his troops and Manchuria. They were too late. MacArthur was determined to head off any lack of resolve. A buffer zone was "an immoral proposition," he told an aide; it would be "the greatest defeat of the free world in recent times." On the same day the Chiefs sent their message, MacArthur flew to Korea and announced the "home by Christmas offensive," an all-out race to the Yalu to "close the vise," secure the entire country, and win the war.

Inchon was a high-risk gamble by a daring commander; the November offensive was just reckless. MacArthur's 40,000 troops were badly disposed in two isolated wings unable to support one another. His intelligence had told him that there were 40,000 North Korean guerrillas massing in the mountains to exploit the division in his lines. He knew there were hundreds of thousands of Chinese in front of him who had announced and demonstrated their willingness to fight. He knew that winter conditions in the North Korean mountains would soon be desperate, with temperatures ranging to 40 degrees below zero Fahrenheit. He launched the attack anyway, apparently counting on his own invincibility, his knowledge of "Oriental psychology," and most important, the willingness of the United States to launch an atomic attack on Manchuria to carry him through. He was wrong on all counts. The Chinese entered the war in force on the 26th, drove a wedge between MacArthur's lines, and began to roll up his flanks. On the 28th, MacArthur cabled the Joint Chiefs that "we face an entirely new war."

The hapless Chinese that MacArthur had conjured only a few weeks before had magically transmuted into supermen. On December 3, he cabled Washington that the enemy was "fresh, competently organized, splendidly trained and equipped, and apparently in peak condition for actual operations." Barely a week after he launched his great offensive, he recommended evacuating the entire country. Although MacArthur's admirers staunchly insist that his withdrawal from the Yalu was a great feat of generalship, it is hard to escape the conclusion that he simply panicked. The Eighth Army in the west made a brief fighting retreat before MacArthur broke contact with the enemy and headed pell-mell for the south. The Tenth Corps, isolated on the east wing, fought their way through the mountains, were nearly surrounded several times, and for three perilous days were mortally exposed on the beaches of the port city of Hungnam until they were evacuated in heavy weather and rough seas. The Chinese took Pyongyang and Inchon almost immediately, crossed the 38th parallel early in the new year, occupied Seoul on January 4, and by mid-January had driven the Americans all the way back to the original Pusan Perimeter. Embittered at the failure of Washington to launch a full-scale war against China, MacArthur turned his Korean command over to Matthew Ridgeway ("It's all yours, Matt, do what you want with it. You've got a completely free hand.") and went sulkily back to Tokyo, where he fulminated publicly against U.S. policy until Truman dismissed him in April.

Truman, Marshall, and Acheson, with Kennan in agreement, quickly decided that evacuation was out of the question. The long-term consequences of an outright American defeat in Asia were almost too dreadful to contemplate. But so was any thought of using atomic weapons. American allies panicked when a press conference reporter drew Truman into speculations on the use of the atom bomb in Korea, and Truman quickly promised the British that there would be no consideration of their use without prior consultation.

Ridgeway eased the decision to stay by a masterly demonstration of limited war generalship during the dark winter and early spring of 1951. Taking over a shattered, demoralized, and disorganized command, he quickly restored morale, reorganized his troops into fighting units, and consolidated defensible lines. At the same time, the Chinese were experiencing serious supply problems. (Stalin, always the hard bargainer, made Mao pay market prices for whatever he received, although he had given Kim much higher-quality equipment for free just the year before. By 1953, the Chinese regime was canvassing schoolchildren for donations to pay for Soviet planes and trucks. Mao never forgave it.) As the Chinese drive ran out of steam, Ridgeway began to fight his way back to the parallel in careful stages, recapturing Seoul in March. Then, as the Chinese massed for an end-the-war assault of their own in May, he launched a textbook preemptive counteroffensive that decimated the Chinese forces in the South; by the first anniversary of the war, Ridgeway had, for all practical purposes, restored the *status quo ante* in Korea, and so bloodied the Chinese that they made no serious challenge to the stalemate that dragged on for two more dispiriting years.

Truman's defense budget was one of the earliest casualties of Korea. He declared a national emergency on December 16, and something like a war hysteria gripped the United States. Serious statesmen took it for granted that the Soviet Union had accelerated its plans for world conquest, and would shortly make a move in Europe. Atmospheric disturbances over Canada early in December were interpreted to be Soviet bombers on an attack pattern against the American mainland. Hanson Baldwin, no rabid partisan, summed up the consensus on America's predicament in 1950:

The economy program, inaugurated by Louis Johnson when he took office as Secretary of Defense in the Spring of 1949, was in considerable part responsible . . . [for] the weaknesses in our military policies and military organizations. . . . Yet . . . a major part of that blame rests also upon the American people. . . . Lack of discipline, inadequate unit esprit, a will-to-fight-and-to-die that was often inferior to the enemy's—these are the country's as well as the service's failures. They must now be pitilessly and immediately remedied."

Baldwin's language is extreme, but American heroics in the early days of the war could not obscure how thinly stretched American military resources were. In Nitze's phrase, Korea demonstrated the "terrible risk" that Truman and Johnson had taken with their rigid military economy program. MacArthur had less than a division's worth of effectives in Japan; the first combat team sent to Korea was scraped together from cooks, orderlies, and assorted other non-combat personnel. With only a slight change in luck, the North Koreans would have run him off the peninsula completely in the first weeks, making a subsequent invasion a much more daunting enterprise, with incalculable implications for the future of Japan and all of East Asia. Atomic power was a poor substitute for soldiers in marginal areas like Korea.

But the nearly hysterical atmosphere following MacArthur's rout from the Yalu would not allow a measured response. Truman submitted two separate supplemental defense budget requests in 1950 that taken together were twice his original budget. The defense budget for the fiscal year that began in June 1951 was $53 billion, well over three times the budget Johnson and Truman submitted the previous year, and far more than even the highest estimates in NSC-68. From that point, the world contest with the Soviet Union would be defined primarily in terms of arms.

# PART II

---

# SUPERIORITY AND DOUBT

------------------------------------------------------------

# CHAPTER 5

# In Stalin's Wake

## Two Successions

Within weeks of each other, in early 1953, the United States and the Soviet Union changed governments. Dwight Eisenhower took his oath of office on January 20. It was a chill and overcast day, but just as the new President began to deliver his inaugural address, the clouds lifted and a bright burst of sunshine warmed and cheered the crowds. "Eisenhower luck," the insiders nodded knowingly to each other.

Eisenhower became President by a landslide victory over the Democratic nominee, Adlai Stevenson. The Roosevelt coalition had ruled the country for twenty years, and Truman's administration seemed tired and devoid of new ideas. The persistent whiff of scandals that surrounded Truman's last years in office and the prolonged and bloody stalemate in Korea were forceful arguments for change. Eisenhower, a prime architect of the victory in Europe, an experienced internationalist, on a first-name basis with most of the great statesmen of the world, a commander who had promised to "go to Korea," a man of the center, of great personal vitality and magnetism, possessed of an infectious grin and the enviable ability to impress friend and enemy alike with his sincerity and candor, was the obvious choice. In retrospect, it is difficult to understand why most newspapers on election eve still thought the race was too close to call.

Barely six weeks later, at a dacha on the outskirts of Moscow, a small group of frightened and suspicious men—Malenkov, Voroshilov, Beria, Kaganovich, Khrushchev, Bulganin—gathered around the bedside of Joseph Stalin and for two days watched him die. Officially, Stalin died of a stroke. It is entirely possible that he was murdered by his successors. Certainly his death was a deliverance; for the signs were mounting that the old man was planning another bloodletting in the Soviet hierarchy, and that at least some of the men sitting solemnly in deathwatch were to be among his victims.

Lavrenti Beria, the former head of the secret police, who had replaced the hated Yezhov at the end of the Great Purge in 1938, was in the most immediate danger. He had lost his long-time control of the state security apparatus, and his ally, Rudolf Slansky, who had supervised the recent purges in Eastern Europe, had himself just been executed. He knew that no one had ever been removed as Minister for State Security and lived. Molotov, too, still on the edge of the center of power, had reason to be frightened: he had dared to defy Stalin by abstaining on a vote to exile his wife to Siberia. But even Georgi Malenkov, the porcine *apparatchik* who ruled over Party affairs, and who was Stalin's heir-apparent, could not rest easily. At the Nineteenth Party Congress in October, Stalin seemed to build up Khrushchev in opposition to Malenkov, and unnerved all of the ruling elite by enormously expanding the official inner circle with some twenty relatively unknown men of dubious political affiliation.

The purge machinery began to move into gear in January, when Stalin announced that nine doctors, seven of them Jews, had been arrested for conspiring to poison key Soviet leaders and for having murdered Zhdanov. *Izvestia* proclaimed a massive Zionist conspiracy organized by the American Secret Service and demanded that enemies of the state be "squashed like disgusting vermin." Khrushchev nervously scanned the *Izvestia* article and, to his alarm, found that his own name was conspicuously absent from the list of the doctors' targets, although one of the arrested doctors had treated him only months before. In February, there were a series of arrests in Georgia, Beria's stronghold; most of the accused were his political protégés. Then on March 3, providentially—or so it would seem—Stalin suffered his stroke.

The transition was not a smooth one. The Bolshevik leaders, George Kennan said, had since the Revolution existed "in something very close to a complete moral vacuum." Boris Nicolaevsky has speculated on the psychological impact of Stalin's Great Terror on "those Communists who had participated in the campaigns [as all of the new leadership had] and, instead of going mad, had become professional bureaucrats for whom terror was henceforth a normal method of administration." Put less fastidiously, the new leadership had been trained as thugs. The first months of the transition were not unlike a transfer of power among Mafia chieftains.

On the day of Stalin's death, Beria filled the streets of Moscow with tanks and state security troops armed with flamethrowers. He and Malenkov had arranged to rule as a duumvirate as they sat in vigil at Stalin's bedside: Malenkov would be in charge of the government and the Party, while Beria would gather into his hands the entire secret police and state security apparatus.* Malenkov immediately orchestrated massive rallies and poster parades in an unconvincing and unsuccessful attempt to transfer the old Stalinist hagiolatry to himself. He was cut down to size ten days later at a Central Committee meeting, in which he "voluntarily" relinquished his Party post to concentrate on his government job as president of the Council of Ministers.† Khrushchev, still not an apparent contender for power, became the senior member of the Party Secretariat—the same job in which Stalin built his power base—although he did not yet have the title of First Secretary, and he was required to relinquish his job as Moscow Party leader, which some regarded as the more powerful post.

Within a few weeks, it was clear that Beria was making a bid for the supreme power. Surprisingly enough, almost as if he was running a political campaign, he began to orchestrate a program of adroit liberalization, including the release from prison and rehabilitation of those who—at least in the view of the other members of the power elite—would help him curry favor with the masses. There was also the persistent, but to this day unsubstantiated, rumor that he made private overtures to the West offering the possibility of a major settlement in Germany.

Khrushchev tells the story of Beria's downfall in his memoirs, giving himself the key role in convincing the others that Beria was a threat to them all. Remarkably—Khrushchev's version is absolutely straight-faced—as soon as they agreed that Beria was not acting like a "true Communist," they jumped to the conclusion that he had been an English spy since 1919, and hideous revelations began to tumble out. Their erstwhile comrade was in fact "a beast," who as secret police chief had strangled his victims with his own hands and who had raped "more than a hundred girls and women," including the seventh-grade stepdaugh-

*The two secret police ministries, the MVD (formerly NKVD), which was responsible for internal security, and the MGB (formerly NKGB), which included foreign espionage and security, had been separated in 1943, partly in reaction to the excesses of Beria's predecessor, the psychopathic Yezhov. Beria's reuniting of the two ministries, to veterans of the Terror, was truly ominous.

†A brief description of the Soviet political and governmental system is included in the notes to this chapter.

ter of Malenkov's chief bodyguard. Officially, Khrushchev tells us that Beria was criticized and relieved of his duties in June and held for a secret trial in the fall. But in moments of relaxation he regaled foreign visitors with a more lurid version: that at a climactic Praesidium meeting, he and his comrades cross-examined Beria for four hours, then left him alone in the room—the very room in which his visitor was sitting, Khrushchev on one occasion emphasized—while they withdrew to deliberate. They decided he was certainly guilty, but that there was insufficient evidence to convict him, so they returned to the room and shot him on the spot. "But," Khrushchev would insist piously, "we felt much easier when, some time after his condemnation, we received sufficient and irrefutable evidence of his guilt."

The execution of Beria and six of his closest comrades was not announced until December. *Pravda* said Beria was guilty of being a "rabid enemy of the Soviet people," of "profound moral degeneration . . . terroristic murder . . . and exterminating honorable cadres," who plotted to "seize power and liquidate the Soviet system" in order to "restore capitalism and the domination of the bourgeoisie." A short while later, subscribers to the *Great Soviet Encyclopedia* received an article on the "Bering Sea," and were instructed to cut out with a razor blade the article and photograph on "Beria, L." and paste in the new one, which was just the right size.

It was four years before the transition was complete. The last of Beria's henchmen was executed at the end of 1954, but by that time Khrushchev and Malenkov were already locked in a struggle for power. Nikita Khrushchev, bull-necked, bullet-headed, uneducated, but with vast energy and vitality, a peasant wit, and a rough-and-ready shrewdness, had the enormous advantage over Malenkov that he had actually ruled 40 million people as Stalin's viceroy in the Ukraine, and had supervised the war on the Eastern front, while Malenkov's supple mind and quick intelligence were wasted in fetid Party intrigues in Moscow.

Khrushchev's hands were as bloody as any. He had been on the scene immediately after Kirov's assassination to assist in the cover-up, and he professed to have "always liked" Yagoda, Stalin's first purgemaster. Khrushchev had run a series of violent purges of his own in the Ukraine after the fall of Yezhov, and after the Nazi-Soviet Pact, he supervised the deportation, or more accurately, the death march, of a million eastern Poles. The massacre of the Polish officers at Katyn Forest occurred within his jurisdiction. His saving grace was that he had the natural politician's flair for the common touch and human contact, and actually travelled throughout his jurisdictions, talked to people, and seemed to listen; as he matured as a leader, he seemed to identify with the Soviet people in a way that the bloodless sycophants Stalin had gathered around him in Moscow never could.

Khrushchev emerged ascendant in 1955; Malenkov simply admitted his failings—being too interested in consumer goods and insufficiently militant against the United States, although these were pretexts merely—and resigned his position as head of the government. The bloodless transfer of power was a watershed in Soviet history. Malenkov and Molotov fought a stubborn rearguard action until 1957 when, after the hair's-breadth failure of a concerted attempt to unseat Khrushchev, the "anti-Party" group was purged from the ruling elite. Malenkov was dispatched to run a power station in Siberia, while Molotov was granted the opportunity to hone his diplomatic talents as Ambassador to Outer Mongolia.

## The American Defense Buildup

The new rulers of the Soviet Union faced a dramatically altered world military balance as a result of the enormous American buildup that accompanied the Korean War. Between 1950 and 1953, the annual rate of American defense spending roughly quadrupled, and with the draft reinstated, the number of Americans in uniform tripled to 3.6 million men, not quite a third, that is, of peak World War II levels, and not far from the best contemporary estimates of Soviet strength. The United States now fielded a twenty-division Army, with eight divisions in Korea, five in Europe, and the remainder in reserve at home.* During the same period, the Air Force doubled, from 48 wings to 96, with a target of 143 wings in two more years. The battle between the Air Force and the Navy had long since ended, with both services getting essentially everything they wanted. The huge ten-engine B-36 long-range bomber was in production, as was the *Forrestal,* the first of a new class of 76,000-ton supercarriers, five times bigger than any ship the Soviet Union could put to sea. Up to $100 billion had been spent on new equipment. The entire front-line fighter command had been converted to jets, and the F-86 Saberjet, the "fastest fighter in the world" and the workhorse American plane in Korea, enjoyed a 13:1 kill ratio over its nearest competitor, the Soviet MiG-15. Tanks were rolling off the pro-

*A note on military organizational terminology is included in the notes to this chapter.

duction line at a rate that replaced all the losses since the start of the Korean War every six weeks.

Western Europe had also been temporarily jolted into a serious defense commitment; between 1950 and 1953, the European NATO countries spent $32 billion of their own money upgrading their defenses, in addition to $12 billion of American military assistance funds. Some of the most absurd deficiencies had been patched over: in 1950, for example, it took twelve hours for Western forces in Oslo, a major outpost, to place a call to NATO headquarters in Paris, and the calls had to be routed through Soviet operators; by 1953, at least, there were secure phone connections. The gaps in capability were still pervasive, but the Europeans could now plausibly claim to field twenty-five infantry divisions, all of them grossly understrength and underequipped, with another twenty-five divisions in reserve. It was still far less than the promises regularly extorted by the Americans, and not nearly enough to withstand a serious Soviet ground offensive, but at least the Soviets could no longer count on a walkover to the Channel. In addition to the buildup in Europe, practically any country located on a possible point of friction with the Soviet Union, some 45 countries in all, was receiving a flood of American World War II surplus materiel—8 million tons of it by 1953, including 4,000 planes, 550 naval vessels, 27,000 tanks and combat vehicles, 25,000 artillery pieces, and more than 1 million rifles and machine guns.

The American buildup was strategically shapeless, more of a spasm than the expression of a coherent military world view, but it was overwhelmingly massive. It is a tribute to the iron will and relentless determination of Joseph Stalin that his inheritors did not have to cringe before this suddenly burgeoning might. The vast program of forced modernization and upgrading that Stalin had set in motion almost from the day the war ended in 1945—making up with single-minded dedication for the Soviet Union's inferiority in wealth and technological base—had bequeathed a military machine that was the second most powerful in the world and in certain key respects even superior to that of the United States.

## The Soviet War Machine

Soviet military doctrine in the early 1950s insisted that wars were won or lost by armies fighting on the ground. The leadership feared the consequences of an American nuclear attack on their homeland, but did not believe it could be decisive. Soviet doctrine taught that wars were decided by "permanently operating" or "fundamental" factors: the stability of the rear; the morale of the army; the quantity and quality of divisions and armaments; and the organizing ability of commanders. Atomic weapons, it was conceded, could wreak devastating terror among civilian populations, but were thought to be of little use against soldiers moving rapidly in the field—any other doctrine, of course, would have been a counsel of despair, for the Soviets could not match the American atomic delivery capability. In a future war, doctrine taught, there would be a fearsome exchange of nuclear strikes with the United States, but Soviet civilian morale would hold, their armies would defeat the West on the ground, and they would take control of Western Europe, vastly extending the reach of communism, and quickly replacing their losses with Western Europe's industrial capacity—an "improved World War II" strategy, one analyst has called it. All recent experience—the staying power exhibited by the Soviet population against the Germans, and the inability of the United States to use its nuclear capabilities in Korea—seemed to confirm the essential soundness of the view.

The infantry was the heart of the Soviet military system—Stalin called artillery the "God of War"—but Soviet commanders were acutely aware that their troops had performed badly against the first wave of German attacks in 1941. The years after the war, sometimes called a period of "Stalinist stagnation," seem rather to have been devoted to a thorough revamping of organizational and strategic concepts. The threadbare 600-division, horse-drawn Red Army of 1945 had been honed down to 175 divisions, all of them motorized, and at least 65 of them armored. Equipment had improved dramatically. Radios were standard equipment, and the number of armored vehicles per unit had quadrupled, most of them new. Weapons were simple but robust. The new standard-issue machine gun, for instance, was easy to repair in the field and was designed to achieve a high volume of fire at the price of accuracy, precisely the weapon to put into the hands of unsophisticated soldiers who were apt to be poor shots. Soviet training methods were harsh but realistic, given the low educational levels of most Soviet draftees; almost all recruits needed driving lessons, for instance. Western observers were grudging admirers of the toughness of the Soviet foot soldiers.

The most striking evolution was in the tank forces. Before the Terror had snuffed out any instinct to innovate, Soviet tank strategists had been among the first to develop the concept of the armored unit as an independent striking force—the principle exploited by Guderian's *Panzers*. Stalin personally squashed such thinking in 1939 when he decreed that tanks were to be dispersed among infantry units and used solely to support foot soldiers. He thereby dispossessed the Russians of one of their major military advantages over the Germans, for they had four times as many tanks, and better ones. The success of the *blitzkrieg* assaults demonstrated the enormity of his error, but too late. The German drive caught the Russian tank forces in the middle of a frantic reorganization and destroyed them as an effective fighting force in a matter of weeks. It was well into 1943 before the Soviet tank arm was rebuilt, and it was not until the very end of the war that Soviet commanders could manage the 50- to 100-mile-per-day forays that were routine for the *Panzers*.

By 1953, the tank divisions had developed into the Red Army's elite force, designed as an independent striking arm of great speed and mobility, able to mount massive and complex night exercises in Eastern Europe. The tanks themselves were outstanding. The main battle tank, the T-54, was a lineal descendant of the famous World War II T-34, originally engineered from purchased American designs, that so astonished the Germans that they seriously considered using the T-34 as a model for a new generation of *Panzers*. (Bronze replicas of T-34s are scattered through village squares in Eastern Europe as a symbol of the liberation from the Nazis.) The Soviet tanks were the fastest in the world, with very heavy firepower; characteristically, their greatest weakness was the lack of attention for the safety and comfort of the crews. There were two types of armored division: "tank" divisions, which were heavy units of about 250 tanks and two regiments of motorized artillery designed to break through enemy defenses; and "mechanized," later called "motor rifle" divisions, with fewer, but lighter and faster, tanks, and approximately three regiments of motorized riflemen, designed to exploit the initial breakthrough and penetrate deep behind enemy lines. The total force of tanks and armored vehicles, at about 25,000, was the largest in the world. Ominously, as far as Western Europeans were concerned, three of the five Soviet Armies poised in East Germany consisted entirely of tank and mechanized divisions.

The Soviet Air Force chiefs were as forward thinking as the tank commanders, and were among the first to take seriously the concept of an independent long-range aerial striking force developed by the Italian air strategist Giulio Douhet and the American Billy Mitchell in the 1920s and 1930s—and were as firmly squelched by Stalin. The air mission, in Stalinist doctrine, was to support the infantry: to clear the skies of enemy aircraft during an advance, and to serve as a form of extended artillery to soften up enemy lines before an assault.* The Soviet Air Force, too, was caught shamefully off guard by the German advance: by noon of the first day of the Nazi attack in 1941, the Luftwaffe destroyed more than 1,200 first-line aircraft sitting undefended on exposed airfields.

The recovery of the Soviet Air Force during World War II, after the enormous losses in the early days of the fighting, was a prodigious feat, and producing a pool of competent pilots was something of a miracle in itself, given the backwardness of the Soviet labor force. At the same time, the Soviets managed to maintain a generally high standard of design, and benefited from the capture of the Heinkel and Junker installations along with a number of advanced Messerschmitt at the end of the war. The authoritative *Jane's* annual called the MiG-15—the mainstay of the Communist forces in the Korean War—"one of the world's best jet fighters." It was only a shade slower than the F-86, had a tighter turning radius, a faster climb rate, and was a particularly formidable competitor at altitudes over 35,000 feet.

Still, *Jane's* almost certainly overrated the plane. It was less stable in flight than the F-86 and was an erratic shooting platform. The Soviets also had trouble with the complex fire-control mechanisms required for high-speed jet aircraft and were much less advanced in night and all-weather technology. The MiG-15's lopsided 1:13 kill disadvantage against the F-86 during the Korean War cannot be explained solely by the inexperience of the Chinese and North Korean pilots. (American planes' margin of superiority over Soviet models have been of roughly the same magnitude in almost every engagement since, including those between India and Pakistan, in which the pilot factor should have been at a minimum.) The Soviet Air Force was rounded out with the Il-28 light attack jet bomber, usually considered the equivalent of its Western counterparts, with the single major exception that the American attack bombers operated from carriers, a capability the Soviets entirely lacked.

The Soviets still lagged far behind the United States in strategic

---

*Tukachevsky's espousal of a long-range air doctrine was apparently a factor contributing to his execution. In the turbid, quasi-medieval world of Communist ideology, everything was related: Stalin was not shooting his best officers simply because he disagreed with them on the merits. Long-range striking forces, whether of tanks, planes, or ships, at some level of abstraction, were inconsistent with Stalin's doctrine of defending "socialism in one country" and more compatible with an internationalist view of the Communist mission, which of course was one of the ostensible issues in the murderous dispute with Trotsky.

airpower. They began work on their first rudimentary long-range bombing capability at the end of the war under the direction of the grand old man of Soviet aircraft design, Andrei Tupolev. Tupolev represents a remarkable triumph of technical genius over adversity. Imprisoned during the purges, but hurriedly sought out in the first dark days after the German attack, he gathered the leading lights of Soviet aeronautics from throughout the GULAG to work on aircraft designs as their concentration camp assignment—the so-called *Tupolevskaya Sharaga.* After his release and rehabilitation, in an outstanding feat of engineering analysis and organization, he worked from three downed B-29s—the Americans refused to sell B-29s to Stalin—to create, in less than a year, a production version of the Tu-4* bomber, a B-29 clone, that was the mainstay of the Soviet heavy bomber force for the next decade.

Despite Tupolev's labors, there was nothing in the Soviet arsenal in 1953 to match the 10,000-mile range B-36. Their "long-range" air arm (the word "strategic" connoted that airpower could be decisive, which Soviet doctrine denied) still consisted entirely of the propeller-driven Tu-4, which would have been effective against targets in Europe, but was obviously no threat to America. The Tu-16, a medium-range, twin-engine jet bomber, dubbed "Badger" by NATO, began to enter service about 1954 and proved to be the workhouse of the Soviet long-range air force for the next twenty-five years. The first models had a range of perhaps 4,000 miles at a top speed of 600 mph and a bomb load of 4–5 tons. It was theoretically possible for Tu-16s to reach America from Arctic bases with mid-air refuelling; but the Soviets had no experience with refuelling technology, and the necessity to refuel over NATO (Canadian) territory made such an operation totally impractical.

The 1954 and 1955 air shows in Moscow created a stir in the West by unveiling two long-rumored new bombers, the Mya-4 "Bison" and the Tu-95 "Bear," both with 6,000–8,000-mile ranges. Neither plane was ever a significant factor in the military balance. Contemporary intelligence grossly exaggerated the number of Bears and Bisons in service, but the best recent estimates are that only 150–200 planes of both types were produced through the 1950s, with most of those rele-

---

*In an uncharacteristic personal touch, Soviet letter designations for aircraft signify the names of their designers, or after their deaths, the design bureaus bearing their names. Thus, the "Tu-" series are Tupolev's; the "MiG-" series of fighters are the work of Artem Mikoyan and Mikhail Gorevich; the "Il-" planes are Sergei Ilyushin's, and so on. The American designations are more prosaic: "F" is for fighter; "B" for bomber; "FB" for fighter-bomber; "C" for cargo; and "A" for attack bombers.

gated to tanker and reconnaissance service. The Bear in particular is an example of dead-end technology. Its eight 18½-foot propellers were an engineering marvel, but propeller-driven aircraft could never achieve the speeds necessary for effectiveness in modern warfare. (So long as modern warfare demanded speed and penetration capabilities from aircraft, that is: thirty years later, the Bear found new life as a cruise missile carrier.) It appears that sometime either shortly before or after Stalin's death, the Soviet Union decided to make a drastic shift of resources away from long-range bomber development in order to concentrate instead on rockets.

The navy was the stepchild of the Soviet armed forces. Soviet admirals had coveted a "blue-water," or deep ocean, capability in the 1930s, but had been as firmly disabused of their innovations as the tank commanders and air force generals. As one scholar put it in the mid-1950s, the Soviets "do not contest for command of the seas." Stalin's naval strategy was strictly defensive; it was based, as Khrushchev's reforming admiral, Sergei Gorshkov, sneered, "on the illusion of inveigling the enemy to contest the Soviet fleet within mined Soviet waters within range of coastal artillery." The only branch of naval warfare in which the Soviets were at all advanced was in submarines. They actually had more high-quality submarines than the Germans did in 1941, and in the first half of the 1950s, the long-range "Whiskey" and "Zulu"-class submarines were being turned out at a wartime production rate. About 1950, the Soviets also embarked on their first program of oceangoing combat vessels, the *Sverdlov*-class cruiser, displacing 15,000 tons, but lightly armed for its size. Khrushchev scoffed that the ship was "only suitable for taking statesmen about the world on good-will missions" and cancelled the program when it was about halfway completed.

In matters of strategy, Soviet military doctrine was conservative in the extreme. The basic approach was Clausewitzian—Lenin was a great admirer of the German—and emphasized the traditional dogmas: concentration of forces; secrecy and rapidity of attack; seeking numerical superiority at the point of conflict; maintaining the offensive as the aggressor; and moving quickly to the counteroffensive on defense. If anything, Soviet commanders tended to follow the classic principles blindly. In World War II, as if trying to disprove the maxim that "it is impossible to be too strong at the decisive point," Soviet commanders typically threw so many men into battle that they clogged their approaches, confused their logistics, and lost ability to maneuver. The Germans admired Russian bravery, but found their officers "bullheaded . . . repeating their attacks again and again. This was due to the way their leaders lived in fear of being considered lacking in determination if they broke off their attacks"—a striking assessment from commanders who suffered under the demands emanating from their Fuehrer's Eagle's Nest.

The key problem for Russian strategists from the days of the Czars was how to defend such a vast land frontier. Fixed-line defenses, particularly after the experience of the French in 1940, were out of the question. The obvious Clausewitzian solution was to position the Soviet "defensive" armies to strike at the heart of the enemy forces *before* they crossed the border. The difficulty, of course, and one that has bedevilled Cold War relations ever since, is that such a "defensive" strategy looked very aggressive to West Europeans, the more so since, before 1952 at least, there were no armies to speak of pointed at the Soviets. Defensive considerations were probably foremost in Stalin's mind as he positioned his forces on his western borders; but no one could be sure that offensive notions were not also flickering through the dictator's mind.

Finally, despite the scorn that the Soviets heaped on the American preoccupation with nuclear weapons, their own nuclear program was under way well before the war and continued to receive the highest priority that a mortally wounded economy could muster. Soviet scientists were working on uranium chain reactions in 1938, and their first atomic explosion was achieved only four years after the Americans'— another remarkable testament to the potential of a relentlessly driven command economy. The Soviets immediately pressed development of a hydrogen bomb; contrary to the widespread impression that their thermonuclear program was merely a reaction to the American one, the Soviets were actually ahead in thermonuclear weapons technology at least until the middle 1950s.

Thermonuclear explosions are created by placing two elements under such immense pressure that they fuse into a new form and release a burst of excess atomic energy. The first successful American thermonuclear blast, in late 1952, demonstrated the principle with two isotopes of hydrogen, deuterium and tritium. The experiment required the two isotopes to be stored in liquid form at a temperature just above absolute zero, necessitating a cooling installation that was two stories high and weighed 65 tons. The fusion pressure was achieved by blowing up the apparatus with an atomic bomb, generating an instantaneous temperature increase to 100 million degrees. The device that vaporized a coral atoll in the Eniwetok island chain and left a mile-deep hole in the ocean floor, in other words, was really a giant booby-trapped refrigerator, in no sense a usable bomb.

Analysis of the radioactive debris from the first Soviet thermonuclear blast only nine months later, however, showed that the Soviet team, led by Andrei Sakharov, had achieved fusion with a relatively stable compound of deuterium and lithium that did not require refrigeration. A year and a half after that, the Soviet Union increased their technical lead by achieving the first thermonuclear airburst, demonstrating conclusively that they were first to possess a thermonuclear bomb that could be dropped from an airplane—in theory at least, a deliverable weapon.

Even leaving aside the rapid Soviet progress in nuclear weapon technology, the asymmetry of forces presented major strategic problems for the United States. The doctrine of "containment"—or the necessity for "the adroit and vigilant application of counter-force" "at every point where [the Russians] show signs of encroaching upon the interests of a peaceful and stable world," whatever George Kennan hoped to convey when he penned those words—had, explicitly or not, become fundamental American strategy. The problem, however, was that the Soviet forces were so much stronger at most points of likely conflict. The Eisenhower administration took office, therefore, committed to a sweeping review of the entire American military force structure.

CHAPTER 6

# Eisenhower

George Kennan summed up the contemporary appraisal of Dwight Eisenhower: the President was "the nation's number one Boy Scout," presumably innocent of books, a tool of his powerful cabinet, "helpless and pathetic" in the company of the wealthy businessmen with whom he surrounded himself, and, perhaps most damning, plain lazy. "Dwight Eisenhower's difficulties," Kennan opined, "lay not in the absence of intellectual powers but in the unwillingness to employ them except on the rarest of occasions," and he remarked on Eisenhower's "curious combination of qualities—this reluctance to exert authority, this intellectual evasiveness, this dislike of discussing serious things except in the most formal governmental context, this tendency to seek refuge in the emptiest inanities of popular sport. . . . [I]t is my impression that he was a man who, given the high office he occupied, could have done a great deal more than he did."

Kennan, according to a new, and sharply revised, appreciation of Eisenhower among historians of the period, could not have been more wrong. Detailed research in primary sources—White House internal memoranda, minutes of cabinet and National Security Council meetings—reveals an almost totally different picture. Eisenhower was a strong President who, particularly in matters of foreign policy and national security, kept his underlings on a short leash. (Kennan's complaints stand up better in matters of domestic policy; Eisenhower was notoriously reluctant to speak out against Senator McCarthy or to act against racial segregation.) In foreign policy, it appears, Eisenhower consciously chose to cultivate the impression that John Foster Dulles was in control. It allowed him greater freedom of action and permitted him to pamper the tender ego of his subordinate. Dulles, in fact, was in touch with Eisenhower virtually every day of his wide-ranging travels away from Washington and seems to have cleared almost every word he said with the President. Far from determining policy, on certain key issues—the settlement of the armistice in Korea, for instance—he was almost utterly without influence. " . . . there's only one man I know who has seen *more* of the world and talked with more people and *knows* more than [Dulles] does," Eisenhower once remarked to a confidante, "—and that's me."

Eisenhower was an internationalist. His hero was George Marshall. His foreign policy was much closer to the Truman administration's than to old guard Republican isolationism. His stated reason for opposing Robert Taft for the Republican nomination was to preserve the country from "Fortress America" policies. He was a hard-line anti-Communist, but no adventurist. While he supported the intervention in Korea, he gave short shrift to MacArthur's apocalyptic proposals for clearing Asia of communism. He somewhat tentatively tried out Dulles's ideas for a "liberation" of Eastern Europe during the campaign, but stressed that he favored a Communist "roll-back" only if it could be accomplished by peaceful means. Characteristically, when he visited Korea after the election, he did not permit the American commander, Mark Clark, to present his plan for carrying the war to China and would not even see Rhee. He spent his time inspecting positions at the front and decided that the war was unwinnable and should be terminated as quickly as possible.

He was the most unmilitaristic of presidents. His farewell warning in 1960 against a "military-industrial complex" is famous. Less well known is the consistency and determination with which he opposed the threat of an unwarranted accretion of military influence and power in American life. It was perhaps the single most abiding theme of his presidency—one he hammered at repeatedly from his very first days in office. Eisenhower's greatest fear, as he wrote to a friend in 1956, was that "some day there is going to a man sitting in my present chair who has not been raised in the military services and who will have little understanding of where slashes in their estimates can be made with little or no damage. . . . If that should happen while we still have the state of tension that now exists in the world, I shudder to think of what could happen in this country."

Eisenhower's major quarrel with the Truman administration was that its military buildup was creating an increasingly powerful and centralized state, one that was already consuming too much of the country's resources. Truman's strategic testament, NSC-141, drafted in the twilight of his administration by Acheson, Lovett, and Harriman, called for annual military spending increases in the $7–9 billion range. It ran directly counter to Eisenhower's conservative vision of America—as a peaceful country where people were free to pursue their private interests with only the most limited government interference and the lightest burden of taxation. His priorities were to end the war in Korea, drastically reduce military spending, balance the budget, and cut taxes. They were priorities shared by neither Dulles nor the new Defense Secretary, Charles Wilson, the former chairman of General Motors, "the most outspoken, self-confident, bluntest, and ill-informed" member of the cabinet. Dulles, in particular, was strongly opposed to negotiating in Korea "until we have shown—before all Asia—our clear superiority by giving the Chinese one hell of a licking." Eisenhower's only major cabinet ally on defense cuts was George Humphrey, the arch-conservative Treasury Secretary, who preached the evils of budget deficits as incessantly and as fervently as Dulles inveighed against communism. If anything, Humphrey's nightmares were the more lurid, and his devils loomed even more ominously: "You *have* to get Korea *out of the way*," he fulminated, "and after that you have to . . . figure out a *completely new military posture*. . . . We have to . . . us[e] a meat ax."

Upon taking office, Eisenhower's primary objective was to end the Korean War. Stalin's death in March appeared to present new opportunities. Eisenhower delivered a "peace" speech in April, over Dulles's objections, that made a worldwide impression, not so much for its new ideas but for his obvious sincerity:

The cost of one modern heavy bomber is this: a modern brick school in more than thirty cities. It is two electric power plants, each serving a town of sixty thousand population. It is two fine, fully-equipped hospitals. We pay for a single fighter plane with a half million bushels of wheat. We pay for a single destroyer with new homes that could have housed more than eight thousand people. This is not a way of life at all, in any true sense . . . it is humanity hanging from a cross of iron.

When the Chinese indicated that they were willing to resume negotiations for a military armistice in Korea, Eisenhower seized the opportunity, again over the objections of Dulles, which were by now increasingly shrill. Negotiating an armistice with forces in place meant that, for all practical purposes, the United States was accepting the division of the country at the 38th parallel, which Dulles, and probably most Republican congressmen, thought shameful.

But while Eisenhower was willing to concede on unification, he dropped broad hints that he would use atomic weapons against the Chinese if the armistice talks were prolonged. In June, Zhou Enlai produced a proposal that addressed the single key issue the Americans had insisted on for two years: the right not to repatriate captured Communists who wanted asylum in the South. Rhee, who had been excluded from the talks, immediately tried to sabotage a settlement by releasing 25,000 prisoners in contravention of the agreements under discussion; but after a last-minute arm-twisting session, he acquiesced, and the armistice was initialled in July. For long afterward, Eisenhower regarded ending the three bloody years of fighting in Korea as his greatest presidential achievement. He was unquestionably right: no other American enjoyed both the popularity and the military prestige to carry off a settlement that could arguably be regarded as the country's first ever military loss.

### The "New Look"

With the war ended, Eisenhower could concentrate on revamping the country's military posture, an exercise the press inevitably dubbed the "New Look." The new strategy had already begun to take shape during the voyage home from his pre-inaugural trip to Korea. With him were Admiral Arthur Radford, Eisenhower's choice as the next chairman of the Joint Chiefs, and Dulles. Radford was concerned that American forces were overextended; Dulles had for some years been arguing what was essentially the Air Force strategy—greater reliance on atomic weapons and long-range striking power to get one's way in the world. It was a strategy that had been pushed hard by the British air commander, Sir John Slessor, and somewhat apologetically adopted by Churchill on his return to office in 1951, on the reasonable ground that postwar England could afford no other. And it was perhaps the only strategy that would allow America the pretense of maintaining its global military commitments; for as the British case showed, with the war scares of 1948 and 1950 fading rapidly in memory, the other NATO countries had neither the will nor the capacity to live up to the ambitious conventional force objectives they had set for themselves.

Shortly after he took office, Eisenhower appointed a working group and divided it into task forces to debate three separate policy alternatives: (1) a continuation of the Truman administration's containment policy; (2) "drawing a line around the globe" and threatening atomic destruction if the Communists crossed the line—essentially the Radford-Dulles recommendation; and (3) going all-out for "liberation" of Communist regimes outside the Soviet Union, or essentially the policy of the militantly anti-Communist Republicans and the China Lobby. When the group finished its work in May, it recommended "Option 1½," in effect attempting to maintain the basic objectives of containment, but doing so more economically, through primary reliance on air and naval power, backed up by the threat of atomic warfare. It was the recommendation Eisenhower wanted, for it allowed him to continue the broad lines of Marshall's policies in Europe, but would still permit deep cuts in American standing forces.

"Massive retaliation," as the new strategy became known, is irrevocably associated with the name of John Foster Dulles. Although the military implications of the new doctrine were worked out primarily by Radford and the Joint Chiefs during 1953, and Eisenhower outlined his thinking at a number of press conferences and meetings with Congress, the policy shift was officially announced by Dulles in a famous speech before the Council on Foreign Relations in January 1954.

The United States, Dulles said, would no longer rely on local forces to deter aggression, but on its own "massive retaliatory power." Equally important, to recapture the initiative in the Cold War, it would no longer allow the Soviet Union to select the time and places of conflict to its own advantage, as presumably it did in Korea; henceforth, the United States would—in a key phrase pencilled in by Eisenhower himself—"depend primarily upon a great capacity to retaliate instantly, by means and at places of our own choosing." The obvious implication, although Dulles did not say it, was that a Soviet proxy war in a Third World country might precipitate an atomic attack on the Soviet Union itself. If this created uncertainty in the minds of adversaries and allies, so much the better. As Eisenhower put it at a press conference, the beauty of the policy was that no one could "undertake to say exactly what we would do under all that variety of circumstances."

A firestorm of controversy greeted Dulles's speech. *The Washington Post,* the *New York Times,* James Reston, and Walter Lippmann, among others, variously denounced "massive retaliation" as immoral or impractical, or both. Dulles attempted to meet some of the criticisms in a definitive statement of the new policy in the April issue of *Foreign Affairs.* Local defense was still "important," he emphasized, and he insisted, without convincing his critics, that the new defense posture was "not intended to rely wholly on large-scale strategic bombing as the sole means to deter and counter aggression." In July, *Foreign Affairs* carried the quasi-official Democratic response, penned by Averill Harriman. The article is fascinating because it sounds essentially all the themes that John Kennedy hammered at in his 1960 campaign.

"One of the outstanding characteristics of American policy over the last year and a half," Harriman charged, "has been what might be called the short-cut approach, a studied effort to find new-looking and more comfortable ways to reduce our defense burdens," proving his point by citing Eisenhower's unwillingness to intervene on France's side in Indochina earlier in the year. Or, as Henry Kissinger argued in a critical 1955 article, "massive retaliation" limited American flexibility to deal with "brush-fire" conflicts of the kind that erupted in Korea: "An all-or-nothing military policy . . . makes for a paralysis of diplomacy." Harriman also lamented the administration's insistence on subordinating military strategy to economic policy. Soviet military planning, he warned, was "explicitly based on the assumption stated by Stalin and Malenkov in 1952, that the free world will not be able to maintain in the years ahead, a rate of economic growth comparable to that which will be forced in the Soviet bloc. . . ." Assuming that a healthy economy would be an adequate safeguard against disaster might be fatal.

The "massive retaliation" policy that Harriman and Kissinger attacked, and, in fairness, that Dulles seemed to announce in the January speech, was a caricature of the administration's actual posture. In the first place, Eisenhower never placed sole reliance on nuclear weapons. His conventional force budgets were almost triple those of Truman's in the pre-Korean War years, and his military manpower goals were about twice as high. At the same time, as is detailed in the next chapter, he embarked on a massive research and development program for weapon systems of all kinds, both conventional and nuclear, that formed the backbone of the American defense establishment for most of the two decades after his presidency ended.

His key policy objective, as he repeated again and again at press conferences and interviews, was to forge a "long haul" defense strategy, one that could be sustained year after year without violent swings between retreat and commitment, one that was sufficient for American security, but not too heavy a drain on the civilian economy. Caricaturing Truman's defense policies as unfairly as Harriman had caricatured his own, he ridiculed the fact that NSC-68 had identified mid-1954 as a "year of maximum danger," or the likely point by which the Soviets would have enough atomic weapons to mount a surprise attack on America. "Anybody who bases his defense on his ability to predict the day and hour of attack [which, of course, Truman's planners did not pretend to do] is crazy," he scoffed at a press conference. "If you are going on the defensive you have got to get a level of preparation you can sustain over the years." (The Soviets, in fact, may have had *no* operational atomic weapons as late as 1953. It is even more certain that, even if they had the bombs, they did not have the ability to deliver them against America.)

In Eisenhower's mind, the words "by means and at places of our own choosing" were as important as the "massive" in the articulation of the new strategy. The Korean War had demonstrated that, absent immediate and palpable danger, the country did not have the stomach for drawn-out wars in distant lands. If "containment," at least as it was then understood in Washington, was to be successful, the United States had to find some means other than its own ground forces to deter the Communists from "nibbling" at the Western perimeters. Building up the local forces of American allies was one such method, as Truman had done in Greece, and as Dulles had emphasized in his April article. Attacking the Soviets with conventional forces at *their* weak points might be another. Nuclear intimidation, clearly, was a third, and one that was likely to be particularly effective so long as the United States enjoyed an enormous strategic advantage over the Soviets, as Eisenhower was rightly convinced it did.

Eisenhower voiced, again and again, his own mistrust of a military strategy based solely on nuclear power. One day, for example, when Dulles was arguing the advantages of nuclear weapons, he snapped out: "any notion that 'the bomb' is a cheap way to solve things is awfully wrong. . . . It is cold comfort for any citizen of Western Europe to be assured that—after . . . he is pushing up daisies—someone still alive will drop a bomb on the Kremlin."

And in 1954, when the National Security Council staff drafted recommendations for "sterilizing" atomic strikes in Indochina, he dismissed them impatiently: "You boys must be crazy. We can't use those awful things against Asians for the second time in less than ten years. My God." His view of the role of nuclear weapons in a major confrontation with the Soviets, in fact, sounds virtually identical to that of Truman's planners: "our objectives in the first phase of such a global war would have to be to avert disaster, as we, in turn, released our nuclear stockpile on the aggressor. After that we would have time to go on and win"—presumably with conventional forces.

There were, of course, substantial grounds for criticizing the new policy. Most obviously, it effectively abandoned the forward defense of Europe, or the NATO goal of building sufficient conventional forces to stop a Soviet invasion on Germany's frontiers. Under the new dispensation, the role of conventional forces was reduced merely to that of a "tripwire": the Soviets were put on notice, in effect, that an attack on NATO conventional forces would trigger the climactic nuclear shootout. Eisenhower could argue, of course, that the shift was merely facing up to the facts, for there was no hope of NATO meeting its conventional buildup targets. Indeed, by their behavior, the Europeans clearly demonstrated that they preferred living under the American nuclear umbrella to spending on their own defense.

The new strategy also broke with existing policy by specifically endorsing American first use of nuclear weapons. NSC-68 had been more coy: in order to keep the Soviets guessing, it had strongly opposed *renouncing* first use, but had stopped short of actually recommending it. There was now no doubt where the United States stood; as the official strategy statement, NSC 162/2, put it, the military "could plan on using nuclear weapons, tactical as well as strategic, whenever their use would be desirable from a military standpoint."

Quite a different criticism was that the new policy *expanded* American commitments by globalizing containment. It is the same criticism that Lippmann had levelled against Kennan's "X" article, and a valid one. The article spoke in global terms—"at every point where [the Russians] show signs of encroaching upon the interests of a peaceful . . . world." Although Kennan has been much criticized for his later attempts to correct the obvious meaning of these words, his contemporary papers show fairly conclusively that he never intended "containment" to apply to the old colonial jurisdictions of England and France. But whatever Kennan's original intent, global containment was part of the policy consensus of both parties by 1953. Harriman's sharpest criticism of "massive retaliation" after all, was that Eisenhower had chosen *not* to intervene in Indochina.*

*"Containment," of course, has always been more of a slogan than a detailed doctrine. One of the few early attempts to define its content was Acheson's tracing of a line through the Pacific that *excluded* Korea. It is important to note, as well, that the world had changed dramatically since Kennan wrote the original article in 1947. Kennan, like Churchill, assumed that a reunified and rearmed Germany would form the primary bulwark against Soviet expansion in Europe, and that conventional weapons would be the

For the most part, Eisenhower was blandly untroubled by the attacks on his defense policies. Paradoxically, his confidence stemmed from his conviction that *no one* could identify precisely the right policies in advance of an actual war. In particular, he had little respect for the elaborately spun-out war planning exercises that were just beginning to become fashionable in Washington. " . . . no commander—no nation—ever had . . . all the forces, of all the kinds, that might be considered desirable," he wrote. He told his budget director, Joseph Dodge, to ignore the military's "wailing about the missions they have to accomplish," and said he was "damn tired of Air Force sales programs." "In 1946," he told worried congressmen, "they argued that if we can have seventy groups, we'll guarantee security for ever and ever and ever." Now they were asking for "this trick figure of 141. They sell it. Then you have to abide by it or you're treasonous." He thought the notion that the military generals were best positioned to plan the country's defenses was "bunk." "I've served with those people who know all the answers," he reminded the congressmen. The fear that the United States was in great danger from the Soviet Union was "rot," and the possibility of a disabling Russian air strike against America was "pure rot." Put simply, Eisenhower did not believe that the country was on the verge of a war with the Soviet Union, and he was not willing to turn the country's institutions upside down in order to prepare for one.

When he took office, Eisenhower planned to trim Truman's defense budget for the 1954 fiscal year (that began in June 1953) from $45 billion down to $41 billion, then revised the number again down to $36 billion, with the hope of reaching a steady state in the $30–33 billion range. The Joint Chiefs, with the exception of Radford, were much too enmeshed in their intramural struggles to cooperate in a defense cutback, and Wilson, to Eisenhower's profound disappointment, turned out to be the most useless of cabinet members. (At one point, Eisenhower actually sat down himself and wrote out replies to the chiefs' requests for more spending.) When the service chiefs professed themselves unable to cut their budgets below $42 billion and still "ensure the safety" of the United States, Wilson threw up his hands in despair. Radford then took over and, virtually on his own, produced what Eisen-

---

primary military instrument of containment. The actual conditions of a divided Germany, continued military weakness in Europe, and the emergence of two, and only two, strong nuclear states, invalidated many of the article's key assumptions. Significantly, although Kennan also excluded Korea from the reach of his "containment," he supported the intervention there on the grounds of protecting Japan. The reach, even of Kennan's containment, that is, depended entirely on the circumstances.

hower had asked for, a budget under $36 billion with deep cuts in all the services but the Air Force.

Privately, the chiefs—particularly Matthew Ridgeway, the Army Chief of Staff—were outraged at Radford's budget and his high-handed methods. But Eisenhower made support of the budget a straightforward question of loyalty. He told Wilson that the military were to keep their mouths shut if they didn't like his policies: "I will not have anybody in Defense who wants to sell the idea of a larger and larger force in being." Ridgeway stoically testified at the spring congressional hearings that he "accepted" the President's budget, allowing congressmen to believe that he agreed with it. But in the following year he publicly broke with the administration over its policies toward the Army, and after he retired, infuriated Eisenhower by charging, in effect, that Radford had lied in 1953 when he told Congress that the chiefs had "recommended" and "supported" the budget proposals. Ridgeway insisted that he had never agreed with Radford's plans and had not even participated in their formulation; he had "accepted" them only because the President had made it plain that he had no choice in the matter.

By the mid-point of his first term, Eisenhower had reduced the total military establishment from 3.5 million men to about 2.75 million. The Army bore the brunt of the cutbacks, with both its manpower and its budget slashed by about a third. The troops in Korea had been reduced to essentially garrison levels, and the divisions stationed in Europe had been "skeletonized," to use Eisenhower's own phrase. The cuts in the Navy were somewhat smaller—in the 15 percent range—and the Air Force had actually grown slightly. For the most part, the cutbacks were in personnel rather than procurement, although there were some stretchouts of weapons programs. A major new program was started to build a radar early warning system across the northern reaches of Canada and Alaska. The admirals were allowed to retain their cherished supercarrier program. The Air Force was deploying its new medium-range B-47 jet bomber in Europe and, particularly after the Soviet Union unveiled its own long-range Bear and Bison bombers, was accelerating production of the long-range B-52.

There was only a slight slackening of the Truman administration's pace of adding one new nuclear weapon each day—although the United States now had well over 2,000 operational nuclear bombs of all types and sizes, vastly more than the Soviet Union—and Eisenhower pressed the development of Strategic Air Command delivery capability around the Soviet periphery. By 1955, American bombers could strike virtually any target in Russia from bases in Norway, Iceland, Great Britain, Germany, Turkey, Greece, Japan, Guam, and Okinawa, while the carrier-based attack bombers of the Sixth Fleet in the Mediterranean and the Seventh Fleet in the Pacific were beginning to be equipped to carry atomic bombs. For the first time as well, after much soul-searching within the administration and with much anxiety over possible reactions among allies and the public, nuclear weapons were being quietly distributed to the far-flung bomber commands.

Recently declassified summaries of briefings by General Curtis LeMay, the head of the Strategic Air Command, in the first years of the Eisenhower administration show that the Americans intended to, and had the capability to, reduce the Soviet Union to "a smoking radiating ruin at the end of two hours" if it came to all-out war. LeMay's strategy was the simplest possible: If it came to a crisis, he would unleash almost 1,000 B-36s and B-47s against the Soviet Union, each carrying at least one atomic bomb. And the briefing transcript made it plain that, as LeMay put it, while "I am not advocating a preventive war . . . if the US is pushed in the corner far enough we would not hesitate to strike first." Whatever else the doctrine of "massive retaliation" may have been, its nuclear component was far more than an empty bluff.

## The "New Look" and the Arms Race

The central thread of Eisenhower's military strategy was that the superiority of American technology, particularly in nuclear weapons and delivery systems, would allow him to limit the size of the military establishment. But much to his chagrin, a technology-based strategy perversely reinforced the growing "military-industrial complex" he so abhorred, and ultimately came to threaten his entire vision of American society. At the same time, worried doubts that the Defense Department was even capable of managing a technological strategy were already cropping up in Wilson's first semi-annual reports. Electronic fire-control systems for new Navy jet fighters, for example, were turning out to be much harder to build than anticipated, and Wilson lamented that a B-52 prototype required 3 million engineering research hours, or twenty times more than for a new World War II heavy bomber.

Most alarming was the headlong rush by both the Americans and the Soviet Union to develop and deploy thermonuclear weapons, regardless of the potential consequences for the entire world. It was the essentially thoughtless character of the quest that was so frightening.

Robert Oppenheimer had originally opposed the development of the hydrogen bomb, partly for technical reasons—producing the necessary tritium appeared to require prodigal amounts of plutonium, which was in short supply and was essential for the atomic weapons program—but also on moral grounds. Once Edward Teller produced an elegant solution to Oppenheimer's technical objections, however, his doubts at least temporarily evaporated. As Oppenheimer himself put it, "when you see something that is technically sweet, you go ahead and do it. . . ."

The first inklings of the macabre consequences of "going ahead and doing it" came in 1954. Early in the morning of March 1, Shinzo Suzuki, a seaman on board a Japanese fishing boat, the *Lucky Dragon,* raced to the cabin to tell his shipmates that the "sun was rising in the west." Rushing to the deck, the seamen saw a majestically blooming fireball turn from dazzling white to yellow to blood red to flaming orange. Minutes later, a giant shockwave tossed the ship like a chip, and after a few hours, the sky darkened, there was a drizzle, and a light silvery-gray ash slowly settled over the boat. When the sky cleared, the fishermen swept away the ash, hosed down their ship, and eventually went about their business. Two weeks later, when the fishing boat returned to Japan, all twenty-three of the fishermen were seriously ill, exhibiting the classic symptoms of radiation poisoning—low white blood cell counts, nausea, fever, bleeding gums. One of them, Aikichi Kobayama, a thirty-nine-year-old radioman, would eventually die.

The United States had already reported that a number of American seamen and Marshall Islanders who resided near the Pacific testing site had received excessive doses of radiation, but that none of the cases was serious. Radiation poisoning had become known to the world in the aftermath of the Hiroshima and Nagasaki explosions, but the effects had been strictly local, limited to people within just a few miles of the blast. The dosages received by the Americans and Pacific Islanders did not seem radically at variance with the experience in 1945, but the case of the Japanese fishermen was quite different. They had been 85 miles from Bikini atoll where the bomb exploded, well outside the official danger zone.

It gradually became clear, particularly through the efforts of scientists like the physicist Ralph Lapp, the geneticist Hermann Muller, and the chemist Linus Pauling, that the dangers of thermonuclear weapons were of a different order of magnitude than any that had gone before. The device used in the March 1 test, codenamed BRAVO, was so powerful—at 15 megatons, or with the equivalent explosive force of 15 million tons of TNT, it was one of the biggest explosions of the entire nuclear age—that it pulverized millions of tons of earth and Pacific coral and sucked them up into a huge and highly radioactive dust cloud that slowly drifted clear around the world. Depending on wind conditions and the type of explosion, the dust cloud was capable of administering lethal doses of radiation within an area from 10,000 to 100,000 square miles surrounding the original detonation. An alarmed public suddenly realized that both the United States and the Soviet Union had weapons with the capability of killing essentially everybody in any of the world's largest metropolises.

The facts were even more sinister than they first appeared. BRAVO was a peculiarly "dirty" device. When two of the Japanese fishermen who had appeared cured of the radiation poisoning in the spring, including Kobayama, sickened again in late summer, scientists were puzzled to find high levels of strontium-90 in their bodies. Strontium-90 is one of the most lethal of all byproducts of a nuclear explosion. With a half-life of twenty-eight years, it has an affinity for calcium and had become embedded in the bones of the two unfortunate fishermen, where it continued to emit deadly radiation. A radioactive dust cloud containing strontium-90, in addition to irradiating anyone in its path, would theoretically be capable of contaminating milk and other food supplies almost anywhere in the world.

Strontium-90, however, was not an element that would normally be associated with a fusion explosion. Scientists soon deduced that, in order to increase the power of BRAVO, the weapons builders had wrapped the fusion bomb in a casing of uranium 238, the abundantly available natural form of uranium. Although uranium 238 is normally too stable for use in atomic reactions, when subjected to the force of a thermonuclear explosion, it will undergo a violent chain reaction, producing a fission-fusion-fission explosion of incredible power. The power of the explosion can be increased virtually without limit by the simple expedient of layering on more uranium 238, but at the price of spewing enormous amounts of deadly strontium-90 into the atmosphere.

For most of the next ten years, as the Soviet Union and the United States vied with each other in exploding enormous bombs in the race to develop ever more compact and usable weapons, the world lived under the cloud of a possible radioactive disaster. Not much was known about the actual effects of excessive radioactivity; and the most serious potential consequences were of a nature that could require many years to reveal themselves. Official spokesmen issued soothing words about the minuscule probabilities that the tests would cause serious harm to anyone, but the possibilities of slow contamination, worldwide leukemia, an epidemic of stillbirths, or a population of genetic monstrosities, loomed in ghastly prospect before the entire civilized world.

A second consequence of the American emphasis on nuclear warfare, and the widely publicized hydrogen bomb tests through the middle of the decade, was that the country whipped itself into a near-hysteria over the one threat that the Soviet Union was *least* capable of mounting, a surprise nuclear attack on the American mainland. The administration's own attitude toward the Soviet nuclear threat was at best inconsistent. Eisenhower himself seems not to have taken the possibility of a Soviet nuclear strike seriously, and Charles Wilson testified before Congress in May 1953 that the Soviets were concentrating on building a purely defensive air force. But at virtually the same time, Wilson was proclaiming in his first report to Congress: "For the first time in our history, a potential enemy has the long-range bombers and atomic bombs needed to launch a devastating aerial assault upon the United States," which was simply not true. The Air Force Secretary, Donald Quarles, warned of the Soviets' "independent long-range component with thousands of advanced jet fighters [which, by definition, were quite irrelevant to a "long-range component"] and high-performance jet bombers." The Department underscored its misinformation by attempting to mount a massive civil defense effort. Children in schoolrooms regularly huddled under their desks to practice fending off the anticipated nuclear blast, and doctors and nurses received detailed posting instructions in the event of an attack. The Department's SKYWATCH program enlisted almost 500,000 civilian volunteers to study the shapes of Soviet planes and to spend long nights peering up at the stars, straining to glimpse the first black silhouette of a Soviet air fleet that never was streaming out of the icy northern skies to destroy America.

Key Democrats, particularly Stuart Symington, the former Air Force Secretary, by now a senator from Missouri, and Henry Jackson of Washington State, "the Senator from Boeing," together with hawkish newspaper columnists like Stewart Alsop, and Air Force and air industry publicists, labored tirelessly to create a "bomber gap" virtually from whole cloth, which served as a favorite party flogging post until it faded before the equally fictitious "missile gap" later in the decade. In 1954, for example, *Aviation Week* and the semi-official *Military Review* wrote of 400 Il-38s, which "compare in size with the eight-engine

B-52," poised on Siberian airfields to strike across the pole at the American continent—which, again, was simply not true. Il-38s were in any case not long-range planes; the articles were probably referring to medium-range Tu-16 Badgers. But the Soviets did not have that many Badgers at the time, and would have had to use them in one-way suicide strikes to reach the United States, since they did not have mid-air refuelling capacity.

The airfields *did* exist, however, and were being rapidly improved—perhaps in anticipation of a future capability, perhaps just wastefully, or perhaps to keep the Americans guessing. Even Robert Oppenheimer, who should have known better, added to the clamor by suggesting in a widely publicized 1953 article that the Air Force could stop only "20 or 30%" of a Soviet air fleet on a bombing run over America—Oppenheimer at the time was enamored of the concept of a huge northern tier early warning radar system. Authoritative sources like the London-based Institute for Strategic Studies continued to overestimate the Soviet long-range bomber fleet by a factor of four through the remainder of the decade.

The "bomber gap" hypothesis received a spectacular boost in July 1955 during the annual Soviet Aviation Day celebration when the eight-engine Bear bomber was displayed for the first time, and Moscow residents were treated to a show of formation drills by apparently hundreds of Bison long-range bombers. The Bison display, "probably one of the most successful peacetime military demonstrations of modern times," as one study called it, "far exceeded" the CIA's current estimates of Soviet capacities. (The CIA suspected, accurately it seems, but could not prove, that the Soviets were simply circling the same small number of planes over and over past the viewing site.) It put the lie to recent statements by administration defense spokesmen, like that of the respected NATO commander Alfred Gruenther, that the Soviets had "no serious delivery capability" for their atomic weapons, and created a near-panic in the West. The *New York Times* editorialized that: "Secretary Wilson was wrong when . . . he reassured Congress that Russia was concentrating on a defensive air force. . . . Once again as in the case of atomic and hydrogen bombs earlier the West has seriously underestimated Soviet development and production capabilities."

The *New Republic*, the standard-bearer of the Stevenson Democrats, and normally no admirer of the military, turned thoroughly alarmist:

The Russians are now flying in formation a long-range jet bomber . . . clearly aimed at the United States. . . . each engine develops a thrust more than double that of any engine produced in the West. [This statement is apparently based on the fact that the Mya-4 Bison had four engines, while the B-52, a far superior plane, had eight.] This came as a shock to American designers. . . . In short, the Soviets have overtaken us in long-range bomber design, are catching up to us in long-range bomber production, and have far surpassed the United States in fighter plane production.

The magazine placed the blame squarely on Eisenhower's frugal management of the Defense Department budget: "an administration of businessmen . . . is accustomed to testing each new engineering design until all the bugs are out of it, before sending it into production." It also offered a significant insight into the direction of Democratic thinking by praising Symington's decision, while he was Truman's Air Force Secretary, to press for production of the B-47 medium-range bomber. Symington put the plane in production, the editors conceded, "before it was ready" and at the eventual cost of "$300 million in design changes," but in so doing, America stole a march on Russia in the medium-range bomber race. And that, presumably, was the kind of aggressive defense policy management required by the modern age.

## Brinkmanship, Geneva, Budapest

Five times in the year and a half after Dulles's "massive retaliation" speech, Radford and Dulles, with the support of the majority of the National Security Council and the Joint Chiefs of Staff, recommended that Eisenhower use nuclear weapons: twice in Vietnam—first as the French defeat loomed and then as it became a certainty after the Battle of Dien Bien Phu; and three times against the Chinese—to forestall their entry into the Vietnam War against the French; to prevent their attacking islands off the coast of Chiang Kai-shek's Formosa (Taiwan); and to force them to release American fliers captured during the Korean War. Five times Eisenhower turned them down.

Eisenhower's refusal to intervene in Vietnam does not place him on the side of the American "doves" of the late 1960s and 1970s. He was a hard-line anti-Communist, a firm believer in a monolithic worldwide Communist conspiracy. He believed that the Communist Vietminh were controlled and directed by the Soviet Union and the Chinese; he believed that America had vital interests in Indochina; and he was among the more fervent preachers of the "domino theory" of Communist subversion. He strongly supported Dulles's efforts to construct a web of anti-Communist alliances with the warlords and jungle satraps of the area—which produced that forlorn and misbegotten caricature of NATO, the Southeast Asia Treaty Organization, or SEATO. And it was Eisenhower who, after the Geneva settlement and the division of the country in 1954, made the open-ended commitment of support to the Catholic ruler of South Vietnam, Ngo Dinh Diem, that was used by the Kennedy administration to justify its military intervention.

But Eisenhower was also a military professional, and he refused to risk American forces in Vietnam—much to the exasperation of Dulles, the Republican China Lobby, and the Cold War Democrats, including Acheson, Harriman, and a young senator named John Kennedy—because his military judgment overrode his anti-Communist instincts. He did not believe that nuclear weapons would be of much use in Vietnam, and he did not believe that America could count on winning a war against jungle guerrillas. "The jungles of Indochina would have swallowed up division after division of United States troops," he later wrote, "who, unaccustomed to this kind of warfare, would have sustained heavy casualties."

The process of reaching a decision in Vietnam was a vintage Eisenhower performance. Through an enveloping fog of ambiguity and contradiction, the barriers to American intervention were raised one more notch at each step; but until the very end, none of the participants— neither the French, nor the allies, nor the Congress, nor even Dulles and Radford—could be sure exactly where the President stood. The conditions that finally emerged were that an American intervention would require the full support and participation of the NATO allies, particularly Great Britain; that Congress would have to authorize the action; and that the French would have to promise not to withdraw until the war was won, but would nevertheless have to submit their forces to American command, renounce their colonial ambitions in Asia, and, for good measure, support German rearmament in Europe. There was no practical possibility of these conditions being met; but, at the same time, they were never stated so rigidly, nor even so clearly, that the Vietminh or the Chinese Communists could be certain that America was *not* preparing to intervene. And, indeed, recent evidence is that the Chinese put considerable pressure on the Vietminh to reach a settlement at Geneva precisely because they were not willing to risk another test of arms with the United States.

Eisenhower's management of the Formosan crisis that ended in the spring of 1955 followed a similar course, although the path to a resolution was even more treacherous because of the strong emotional base of support Chiang enjoyed in the Republican Party. The crisis began in the summer of 1954, when the Chinese Communists renewed their pledge to take Formosa from the Nationalists, and began intermittent shelling of Quemoy and Matsu, two barren islands held by Chiang's forces just a few miles off the Chinese mainland. Dulles and the Joint Chiefs recommended—with Ridgeway dissenting, based on his experience of the relative ineffectiveness of airpower in Korea—that Chiang be authorized to bomb the mainland and that America commit to defend Quemoy and Matsu against a Communist assault. Eisenhower rejected the recommendation ("We're not talking now about a limited, brush-fire war," he lectured Radford. "We're talking about going to the threshold of World War III"); dispatched Dulles to tighten the leash on Chiang; and, to appease his party's right wing, entered into a treaty to defend Formosa, but specifically refused to commit to the defense of Quemoy and Matsu or any of the various other Nationalist-held islands off the Chinese coast.

As the confrontation escalated in early 1955, the country appeared for several months to be on the brink of a major war. The Communists attacked Chiang's forces on the Tachen Islands, about 200 miles from Formosa, in January. Eisenhower used the Seventh Fleet to evacuate the Nationalists, strengthened defenses on Quemoy and Matsu, and then raised the stakes by requesting, and receiving, authorization from Congress to go to war to defend Formosa and "closely related localities." He raised the temperature again in March by specifically announcing his willingness to use nuclear weapons: "I see no reason why they shouldn't be used just exactly as you would use a bullet or anything else."

At the same time, all of Eisenhower's decisions were shrouded in studied ambiguity. He told bemused congressmen who had supported the war resolution that he intended to defend Quemoy and Matsu only if an attack was preliminary to a broader assault on Formosa, but not if it was limited to the islands themselves, and freely conceded that it would be very difficult to tell one from the other. When his press secretary, James Hagerty, advised him to cancel a press conference because reporters wanted to pin him down on using nuclear weapons, he said: "Don't worry, Jim . . . I'll just confuse them," and responded to questions with such incomprehensible ramblings that the press was stunned into silence. Just as the crisis seemed careening toward disaster in mid-March, Eisenhower noted in his diary that it was probably over; and, indeed, a month later Zhou Enlai made a conciliatory statement that paved the way for a conference later in the year and a face-saving pretext for ending the shelling of the offshore islands.

Eisenhower had ample reason to congratulate himself on his handling of the crisis: he had restrained Chiang and avoided war, but had held his party together and made no major concessions to the Communists. Still, his actions have been fiercely criticized. The most frequent criticism—that he abdicated decision making to Dulles—is based on a misreading of Eisenhower's administrative methods. A more substantial one is that the offshore Chinese islands did not justify risking a nuclear confrontation. It is impossible to know, however, how much of a risk Eisenhower was willing to take. Characteristically, he never disclosed whether he was prepared to use nuclear weapons to defend Chiang, not even in his memoirs. But perhaps a clue to his thinking lies in some remarks he made at a moment of extreme tension during the crisis—the Chinese had just announced that, in violation of the rules of war, they had convicted and imprisoned American fliers captured in Korea. When a reporter asked if America would retaliate, the President, with visible emotion, delivered a moving little homily against war. He leaned over and asked if he might "talk a little bit personally."

"A President," he said, "experiences exactly the same resentments, the same anger, the same kind of sense of frustration almost, when things like this occur to other Americans, and his impulse is to lash out." If he did so, he knew, the nation would be "united automatically. There is a real fervor developed throughout the nation that you can feel everywhere you go. There is practically an exhilaration about the affair. . . . an attitude is created to which I am not totally unfamiliar." But then he quoted Robert E. Lee: "It is well that war is so terrible; if it were not so, we would grow too fond of it." He had personally written "letters of condolences, by the hundreds, by the thousands, to bereaved mothers and wives. That is a very sobering experience." War was not to be waged casually, he urged. One should not "go to war in response to emotions of anger and resentment; do it prayerfully."

The year and a half following the resolution of the Formosan crisis was the most tension-free in a decade. The East and West blocs consolidated their positions and began to adjust their policies, in fact if not always in rhetoric, to the new realities of the world. The French, after much backing and filling, finally agreed to a formula for the rearmament of Germany: the Germans were to raise twelve divisions but to place them under NATO, or effectively American, command, and to forswear developing long-range forces or nuclear and chemical weapons. The Soviets responded by forming the Warsaw Pact, essentially completing the division of Europe. The two Germanies, the new borders of Poland, and the Western presence in Berlin were all faits accomplis. Japan, Italy and France were firmly in the Western orbit, just as the countries of Eastern Europe, with the anomalous exception of Yugoslavia, were firmly in the Soviet one. The recent divisions of Korea and Indochina appeared, at least for the moment, to be stabilizing. The Nationalist Chinese were being restrained by the Americans from adventures against the mainland, and China's new rulers were resigned, again at least for the moment, to Chiang's irritating presence in his island strongholds. Aside from some tentative jostling in the Middle East, neither the United States nor the Soviet Union had begun the wholesale courting of developing countries that was to characterize the conduct of the Cold War through the 1960s.

At the same time, Khrushchev badly needed a period of stability. Malenkov had stepped down only in February 1955, and Khrushchev was still in the process of consolidating his own position as first among equals in the collective leadership. Once in power, Khrushchev's natural political instincts convinced him that the leadership could not continue to neglect the long-suffering Soviet consumer. He also seems to have come to an early realization that the American position was essentially defensive: despite Republican fulminations about "liberation," Eisenhower clearly had no intention of launching a war. Further, there was fence-mending to be done within the Communist movement, and not only with the Yugoslavs. Although the intramural squabbles were carefully concealed from the West, the Chinese were already discreetly challenging the Soviet claim to leadership of the worldwide Party. Finally, the Politburo needed time to sort out the thorny issue of de-Stalinization—how far should they carry it, how far could they, how to tell the country and the world.

Hopes built rapidly in the spring of 1955 that the time might be ripe for a settlement of the Cold War. Even Winston Churchill, the original cold warrior, declared, "[Since] Stalin died . . . I have nourished the hope that there is a new outlook in Russia," and strongly urged convening a Big Four "summit" conference, the first since Potsdam. The Soviets responded with unmistakably peaceful overtures. They returned a naval base to Finland that they had captured in the 1939 war. They announced that they were willing to sign a peace treaty with Austria and withdraw their occupation forces on terms that had long since been declared acceptable by the West. They announced their willingness to accept at least limited on-site inspections—a major sticking point in arms control negotiations—as part of a comprehensive nuclear test ban treaty.

The sudden wave of warm feeling emanating from Moscow, within weeks of the war scare over Formosa, caught the administration quite by surprise. Eisenhower quickly agreed to a July summit conference in Geneva, but his internal councils were hopelessly divided, and, for the first time, the administration was on the defensive on the peace issue. Dulles had grave misgivings about a summit meeting, and Eisenhower himself, with his great love of orderly staff work, mistrusted the very idea of personal diplomacy. The Republican Party elders, of course, after a decade of excoriating Yalta, were deeply suspicious of the whole exercise. Eisenhower's response to a surprisingly forthcoming, if imperfect, Soviet inspection proposal was merely churlish: "Are we ready to open up every one of our factories, every place where something might be going on . . .?" Although he sprang his "Open Skies" aerial inspection proposal at Geneva, his approach to actual arms control negotiations was always "picayunish and recalcitrant," in the words of his usually admiring biographer, Stephen Ambrose; and two years later, despite the worldwide concern over atmospheric testing, he refused to accept a testing moratorium. The American nuclear superiority, it appears, was too central an element in the entire "New Look" strategy to be easily bargained away in talks with a nation that both Eisenhower and Dulles viewed as inherently untrustworthy.

Nothing of substance was accomplished at the Geneva summit, but the personal contact was still of enormous value for both sides. It was Khrushchev's first meeting with Western leaders, and he is almost touchingly frank about his anxieties in his memoirs. Stalin had told all of his underlings that when he was gone, "the capitalists will wring your necks like chickens." Khrushchev was nervous about his dress and was embarrassed to arrive in a two-engine plane when the Western leaders all used four-engine planes. And he was astonished to meet Nelson Rockefeller in the flesh—like a Puritan encountering Beelzebub—and to find him "dressed fairly democratically."

For the Western powers, it was their first opportunity to take the measure of the new Soviet leaders. Of greatest importance, perhaps, was the confirmation that the Soviet leaders were not madmen: they appeared to understand the dangers of nuclear war and the necessity for maintaining East-West conflicts within some broad margin of safety.

Almost as important was the discovery that Khrushchev was the real leader—not Bulganin, who had nominally replaced Malenkov as prime minister. Bulganin officially led the delegation, he was the person to whom official statements were addressed, and he delivered the formal responses. After Eisenhower announced his "Open Skies" proposal, Bulganin seemed impressed and responded that the Soviets would consider the proposal very seriously. But at the next recess, over cocktails, Khrushchev told Eisenhower curtly, "I don't agree with [Bulganin]": "espionage" proposals like Eisenhower's were not acceptable. From that point, the American delegation wasted no more time on Bulganin.

For all the lack of progress on specifics, Geneva was a personal triumph for Eisenhower. With the summit atmosphere in danger of souring after the fruitless haggling that characterized most of the sessions, he closed the conference with a moving speech on the intangible accomplishments:

In this final hour of our assembly, it is my judgment that the prospects of a lasting peace with justice, well-being, and broader freedom are brighter. The dangers of the overwhelming tragedy of modern war are less. . . . I came to Geneva because I believe mankind longs for freedom from war and rumors of war. I came here because of my lasting faith in the decent instincts and good sense of the people who populate this world of ours. I shall return home tonight with these convictions unshaken.

The world accepted Eisenhower's judgment. The "spirit of Geneva," as it came to be called, seemed like a ray of subshine after a decade of icy confrontation. The *New Republic,* no admirer of Eisenhower, wrote that: "the personal impact of President Eisenhower was tremendous in Geneva. . . . For the present, Soviet ambitions are unaltered. And yet the new spirit is also very real." Robert Donovan reported that "Eisenhower conveyed a sense of decency and dignity which mocked the picture of his country as an immature nation hellbent for war." Richard Rovere commented: "The man has an absolutely unique ability to convince people that he has no talent for duplicity." The French conservative paper, *Le Monde,* long skeptical of American Cold War leadership, agreed that Eisenhower had "emerged as the kind of leader that humanity needs today." Even the Soviets seemed impressed, and Khrushchev began to suggest cautiously that war with the capitalists was perhaps not inevitable after all, although he had pilloried Malenkov for a similar heresy.

The optimism increased early in the following year as word leaked out from Eastern Europe that Khrushchev had denounced Stalinism and the "cult of personality" in a secret speech at the Twentieth Party Congress in January. By the time the State Department secured a text of the speech in the spring, it was clear that a groundshift was under way in the Soviet Union. At midnight after the close of the Congress, the delegates, numbering in the thousands, were suddenly rousted from their hotels out into the frigid darkness to the Kremlin, where, bleary-eyed and in shock, they sat until early dawn, some weeping openly, some shouting in anguish, as Khrushchev ripped down the edifice of their God, Stalin. He spared them none of the lurid details—except those from his own stewardship of the Terror in Poland and the Ukraine. He lingered mercilessly on the "cries of horror" from the old Bolsheviks lying with broken bodies in Lubyanka Prison, on "the untold number of corpses," the "thousands executed without trial," on the "prolonged torture" and "beatings" of Soviet heroes, on "criminal murder" and the conspiracy against Kirov, on the lying charges against Bukharin, on the psychotic bloodthirst of Yagoda and Yezhev and Beria, on Stalin's cowardice and his panic in face of the German attack, on his petty vanities, on the lies about his role in the Revolution, the lies about his leadership in the war, the lies about the books he had authored—the whole sink of pathology that was Stalin's Russia.

The springtime of hope in 1956 was as brief as it was bright. Khrushchev's de-Stalinization campaign touched off seismic disturbances throughout the satellites, challenges to Soviet power that had been brewing ever since Stalin's death—the summer of 1953 had been marked by large-scale rioting in East Berlin and scattered uprisings throughout the other satellites. In June 1956, there was a major riot by workers in Poznan, in Poland, that was put down only after a full-scale battle with the security police. The Polish Party responded with a frank admission of "unquestionably existing grievances" and installed a reformer, Wladislaw Gomulka, as Party leader. Gomulka, to the warm applause of Tito, responded with a striking speech that contained a wide-ranging indictment of Soviet-style economic practices. He stressed that there were "many roads to socialism," called for "full independence from the Soviet Union," and even invited the Catholic Church to join in the competition to develop new "cooperative forms" of social organization. Soviet divisions in Poland stirred ominously, but after Khrushchev, Kaganovich, Mikoyan, and Molotov made a nervous flying visit to Warsaw, the Politburo apparently decided that a semi-independent Communist Party was better than open revolt, and accepted Gomulka's policies.

In October, the scene shifted to Budapest. On the steely-gray morning of the 6th, 200,000 people, most of them carrying a single carnation, marched silently behind a funeral cortege bearing the bodies of Lazslo Rajk, a former Minister of the Interior, and three of his colleagues, all of whom had been tortured and murdered during the bloody 1949 purges. Matyos Rakosi, the brutal Stalinist Hungarian overlord, a few months before had publicly admitted that Rajk had been framed, giving Hungary, at least for a brief time, "the distinction of being the only country in Eastern Europe with a self-confessed murderer of Communists at the head of the ruling Party."

Militant demonstrations throughout Budapest two weeks later quickly turned ugly. When a crowd swarmed around a huge statue of Stalin in Kossuth Square and began pulling it down, the Hungarian Party, it appears, called for Soviet assistance. There were a number of hand-to-hand clashes with Soviet troops over the next two days, some sporadic rifle fire, some Molotov cocktails (named with wonderful irony) were thrown at Soviet tanks and jeeps, and both sides sustained some injuries. At the same time, there was widespread fraternization and stories of Soviet defections. Moscow, following a conciliatory line, installed Imre Nagy as prime minister. Nagy had led a short-lived reform movement in 1953, and had been twice expelled from the Party by Rakosi.

On the 25th, there was a massacre, the bloodiest single encounter of the Hungarian uprising. After a crowd of several thousand demonstrators in Kossuth Square grew unruly, Soviet troops fired over the heads of the crowd to disperse it, and then raked the square with their machine guns. No one knows precisely how many people were killed or wounded, but it was at least several score, and possibly several hundred.

Mikoyan, Moscow's man on the scene, was outraged that Soviet troops were drawn into the confrontation, and the remaining Hungarian hard-liners were summarily fired and sent off to exile in Moscow. Janos Kadar, a mildly reformist Communist, who had been imprisoned and tortured by Rakosi, was installed as Party leader, and made a conciliatory address to the nation the same afternoon. But it was too late for conciliatory speeches. Revolution was sweeping Hungary. In the countryside, away from the lowering guns of Soviet troops, the Communist government apparatus simply melted away; in town after town, officials handed the keys to town halls to revolutionary councils and walked away from their offices. In Budapest, workers' councils deposed the Party-dominated trade union organizations, and revolutionary councils, led by intellectuals, journalists, and university students, virtually took over the government.

Nagy, a most reluctant revolutionary during the first stages of the crisis, was increasingly swayed by the councils' demands. On October 28, he insisted that the Soviets withdraw their troops from Hungary; on the 30th, he announced that the country had a right to multi-Party democracy; and finally, on the 31st, after a tumultuous session with the leaders of the revolutionary councils, he declared that Hungary would withdraw from the Warsaw Pact. Communist officials in Poland, Czechoslovakia, and East Germany telegraphed Moscow that their countries were on the brink of revolt. The men in the Kremlin were staring into the abyss.

Exactly when the Soviet Politburo decided to intervene in Hungary is not clear. Khrushchev reports that there was bitter division on the issue, and that he was afraid of provoking the United States and NATO—although the Eisenhower administration had gone out of its way to declare that it did not consider Hungary to be a military ally, the early Dulles "liberation" rhetoric notwithstanding. The Politburo's decision was made the easier by the surprise attack on Egypt launched by Israel in concert with Great Britain and France, in an elaborate and star-crossed plot both to deceive the United States and to recover the Suez Canal from Egyptian nationalization. The three countries knew that the United States would oppose the operation, but were betting that Eisenhower, at the climax of his 1956 reelection campaign, would not risk alienating the American Jewish vote, and with turmoil in Eastern Europe, would not hazard a split in NATO. To their shock, Eisenhower condemned the invasion, led the call for withdrawal in the United Nations, and cut off American oil sales to Europe.

The Soviet reaction was gleeful. Khrushchev and Bulganin paraded as the defenders of the rights of small nations, demanded that all the Western powers withdraw from the Middle East, and at one point, after the worst of the crisis was over, threatened a nuclear rocket attack on England and France, the first public declaration of Soviet missile prowess. Eisenhower threatened a counter-retaliation if the Soviets intervened in Egypt, Dulles went to the hospital for emergency cancer surgery, the West hunkered down for a possible nuclear confrontation, and the Soviets had a free hand in Hungary.

In Budapest, the Soviet Ambassador, Yuri Andropov, suddenly dropped his threatening tone and became smoothly reassuring. Nagy inquired anxiously about reports of Soviet troop movements on the border; not to worry, Andropov replied, extra troops were required "to ensure discipline" during the planned Soviet withdrawal. Janos Kadar, Nagy's presumed comrade in arms, mysteriously dropped out of sight sometime during the evening of November 1. The following day, when Nagy again insisted that Soviet troops leave the country, Andropov invited the Hungarian military command to visit the Russian Army Headquarters to help coordinate the withdrawal. They were never heard from again.

Early in the morning of the 4th, Soviet armored contingents began pouring into Budapest and other major cities in overwhelming force. There was no organized resistance, although armed bands continued fighting for some weeks. Several thousand people were killed—there is no precise number—and nearly 200,000 refugees fled to the West. On the day of the invasion, the quisling Kadar, from somewhere in the countryside, proclaimed "a revolutionary worker-peasant government" firmly allied with their Soviet brothers. Nagy took refuge in the Yugoslav Embassy. After Kadar and the Soviets made a solemn undertaking to guarantee Nagy's safe conduct, the Yugoslavs turned him over to the revolutionary government. He was arrested by the Soviets, spirited to a prison outside the country, and duly executed.

The "spirit of Geneva" was interred along with the democratic dreams of the Hungarians. The Politburo's rocket-rattling during the Suez crisis revived the recently muted fears of an East-West confrontation and invigorated the rearmament forces in the United States. The pretensions of the American "liberation" lobby were exposed as empty bombast; indeed, by encouraging the delusions of the freedom fighters, they were accused, with considerable justice, of contributing to the carnage in Hungary—Radio Free Europe, although not actually promising American help, repeatedly broadcast to Budapest the American declaration in the United Nations that "We shall not fail them." A deep chill settled over Eastern Europe. Tito-style independence was once again *non grata* at the Kremlin; even reformists like Gomulka quickly adopted the mien of traditional, conservative communism. Khrushchev, indeed, made unwonted kind remarks about Stalin, and the following year survived by a hair's breadth a hard-line revolt in the Politburo led by Molotov and Malenkov, who had conveniently switched ideologies in keeping with the new freeze in the Cold War.

# CHAPTER 7

# The Technological Imperative

## *Sputnik*

Long before dawn broke over the cluster of concrete bunkers and work towers of Tyuratam, on the chilly Kazakhstan steppes far away from Moscow, on October 4, 1957, a deep peal like thunder came rolling up out of the earth, and a squat and ungainly rocket, the *semyorka,* or "old number seven"—actually a cluster of twenty separate rocket engines, a third as wide as it was tall—lit the night with a burst of flame. It rose steadily off the launching pad, slowly at first, then with gathering speed, until it was a tiny corsage of fire disappearing into the engulfing blackness. Some minutes later, after the radio interference from the blast had cleared, the ground station, with wild jubilation, picked up the steady "beep, beep, beep" of the radio transmitter on board. Sputnik, "the companion," was safely in orbit, soaring 560 miles above the earth's surface, sweeping around the globe at 18,000 miles per hour, beeping in triumph to the entire world, its little transmitter trumpeting the conquests of the new Soviet man and the bursting glory of space-age communism. Underscoring their achievement, the Soviets followed a month later with a 6-ton satellite (most of which was the third-stage rocket, which failed to disengage), complete with life-support monitoring systems and a live dog, Laika, who, it was revealed, would be left to die slowly in space—for a shocked American public the final confirmation, if any was necessary, of the fundamental wickedness of the Soviet regime.

The American press reacted to the Sputnik launchings with a "media riot" which Eisenhower was helpless to quell. When the President said at a press conference that the Sputnik launch "does not rouse my apprehensions, not one iota," the pro-administration *Denver Post* jeered, "Come Off It, Ike, Who Are You Kidding?" *Life* magazine headlined "Arguing the Case for Panic." *Newsweek* entitled an issue "Satellites and Our Safety" and wrote of "extremely accurate . . . bombardment from satellites." The *New Republic* became so shrill about the "Soviet Union's . . . commanding lead in certain vital sectors of the race for world scientific and technological supremacy" and the "explosive potential" of the Soviet economy that it felt constrained to remind its readers: "We're not suggesting that the five-star general in the White House has disarmed us."

It was the great size of the Soviet satellites—the biggest American satellite planned would weigh only about 21 pounds—that so badly shook the confidence of a public already rattled by the "bomber gap" scare two years before. And surprise made the shock all the nastier. Except for a small group of insiders, few people even in the scientific community knew that the Soviets might be first in space. A power that could launch a projectile clear around the globe obviously had the ability, or so it seemed, to fire a missile at the United States whenever it chose. The very next day after the Sputnik launch, *Pravda* pointedly announced an H-bomb explosion "at great height," and sneered that the West would have to adjust its political goals in the face of the new Soviet prowess. A few days later, amid some NATO-USSR jostling over Turkey, Khrushchev warned that "the rockets can begin flying," and chortled that America's long-range bombers should be consigned "to museums." During the celebration of the Revolution's fortieth anniversary in November, there were massive parades and displays of missile launchers in Red Square every night for two weeks.

The press hooting grew to a crescendo in December when America's space entry, the Vanguard, hurriedly made ready with immense hoopla, blew up on its launch pad. Vanguard was "Kaputnik," "Stayputnik," and "Flopnik"; a "Sputnik cocktail" was "two parts vodka and one part sour grapes"; the matron in *The New Yorker* cartoon said to her husband, "Isn't it nice, dear. The Russians have the ICBM and we have the Edsel." The Vanguard debacle confirmed for the world's television watchers that America lagged far behind the Russians in missile and rocket technology. Edward Teller called the Sputnik launch a "greater defeat for America than Pearl Harbor." A Soviet delegate at the United Nations remarked snidely that America might qualify for aid to undeveloped nations. Democratic congressional leaders—Lyndon Johnson, John McCormack, Stuart Symington, Henry Jackson, John Kennedy—were in full cry. The "missile gap" would dominate American politics through the remainder of Eisenhower's administration and, more than any other factor, lent substance to John Kennedy's slogan, in his narrow 1960 electoral victory, that it was time "to get the country moving again."

Eisenhower's handling of the race for space was probably the greatest blunder of his administration. But it is significant both of Eisenhower's presidential style, and the changing character of American politics, that his failures lay almost entirely in the realm of public relations rather than in matters of substance. For there was in fact no missile gap. The United States was already ahead of the Soviet Union, or forging ahead, in almost every area of missile and rocket technology that had any military significance. America had a substantial lead, in most cases amounting to years, in missile guidance, nose cone and re-entry systems, electronics of all kinds, weapons design and weight reduction, propellant technology, and miniaturization. The only area in which Soviets were ahead of the United States was in the throw-weight of its rockets—and that was an indication of the primitiveness, not the advanced character, of its technology. The Soviet Union had to strap together so many rockets to get its payloads off the ground because its rocket engines were very inefficient compared to the American ones, and its scientific payloads and available nuclear warheads were much larger and more cumbersome.

There is no question that the Soviets had been much more consistently attentive than the United States to the military potential of rocketry. Capturing the German rocket scientists was one of Stalin's major military objectives in the closing days of the war. Long before the Red Army reached Peenemünde, however, almost all the important scientists, led by Wernher von Braun, slipped away from their laboratory and made an exhausting trek through Germany to surrender to American troops—introducing themselves to a surprised sentry on a muddy road one rainy day in 1945. Stalin's and Khrushchev's space program was essentially the work of native scientists and engineers, although they may have learned German systems engineering from some second-level captures. The grand old man of Soviet rocketry was Sergei Kornilev, a former test pilot and airplane designer, and a true genius like Tupolev, who managed prodigious accomplishments against enormous odds, doing some of his most important work in the same concentration camp where Tupolev labored. (Eisenhower and Dulles knew better when they churlishly ascribed the Soviet Sputnik success to captured German scientists. They were roundly, and justly, upbraided after the press had checked the facts.)

It is known that as early as 1947 Stalin had great hopes for an intercontinental rocket that could deliver nuclear weapons—"to keep the gentleman shopkeeper in his place"—but contemporary technology and the enormous size of the first atomic bombs made it, for the time being, an impractical dream. But from the very end of the war Soviet scientists worked hard on improving German V-2 technology, and the T-1, a conventionally armed V-2 derivative with a range of perhaps 500 miles, was being deployed as early as 1949. Stalin seems to have kept the rest of the Politburo in the dark about his missile plans—Khrushchev reports that "we gawked as if we were sheep seeing a new gate" when Kornilev gave the leadership a tour after Stalin's death—but the decision to press ahead with a long-range rocket force must have been taken not long after he died. It was probably forced by Khrushchev, quite possibly because of the disappointing performance of the Bear and Bison bombers. In any case, by 1954–55, American tracking stations in Turkey and in the Himalayas were monitoring 1,000-mile-plus test flights of the T-2, the world's first genuine intermediate-range ballistic missile. The T-2 was a liquid-fuelled, two-stage rocket, some 66 feet tall with an eventual maximum range of 1,300 miles. In most essential details, it appears to be the same rocket that Kornilev crowded together to lift aloft his first Sputniks.

Neither Truman nor Eisenhower, by contrast, was interested in pushing for all-out rocket development, and until almost the mid-1950s, the military space and rocket program was confined to a shoestring operation under Von Braun at the Redstone Arsenal in Huntsville, Alabama. It was not until 1953 that Von Braun was able to fly a production-ready, 500-mile-range, V-2 derivative—four years, that is, after the equivalent Soviet T-1. Budget considerations determined the slow early pace of rocket development in both administrations, as the post-Sputnik critics charged, but there were also more substantive reasons. For one thing, the outlandish claims of the pro-rocket faction in the military made them easy targets for the sarcasm of doubters like Truman's science adviser, Vannevar Bush. The military—and again the post-Sputnik press—were fascinated by the possibility of thermonuclear bombardment from orbiting weapons platforms, but the advantages of such systems were far from obvious. Even if a bomb could be dropped accurately from a space station 600 miles above the earth moving at 18,000 miles per hour, it would be in firing position for only a brief moment every ninety minutes or so as it spun around the globe. The earth, as one review concluded, was a far superior shooting platform. Just as important, American strategic bombing requirements could be fully met by the burgeoning fleet of B-47s and B-52s. Planes could deliver much bigger payloads far more accurately than rockets, and—of increasing importance in the scary new world of thermonuclear super-bombs—could be recalled in the event of a false alarm. It was precisely the Soviet Union's lack of a long-range striking force that prompted its interest in rockets in the first place.

Despite his budget worries, however, Eisenhower became intensely interested in space technology as soon as the Soviet intermediate-range missile firings were reported by American intelligence. In 1954, he quietly appointed a panel chaired by Dr. James Killian, the president of the Massachusetts Institute of Technology. The panel included Edwin Land, the inventor of the Polaroid camera, the presidents of Caltech and Williams College, the soon-to-be president of Bell Labs, and forty other scientists and engineers. It offered a sobering, but not alarmist, assessment of Soviet capabilities and estimated, quite accurately, that the buildup in the American long-range bomber fleet would create a substantial American strategic advantage until at least 1960. But it predicted that from 1960 on, the strategic balance would increasingly turn on the availability of long-range missiles (usually called ICBMs for Intercontinental-range Ballistic Missiles), and urged stepped-up development of an American capability. Most important, it stressed the necessity for greatly improved surveillance of Soviet missile developments, with Land, in particular, advocating high-altitude photographic surveillance. The emphasis on surveillance dovetailed with two remarkably prescient RAND reports, written in 1946 and 1950, which speculated that high-altitude photographic satellites might offer an effective way to penetrate the shroud of Soviet military secrecy. (RAND, for Research ANd Development, was established by Donald Douglas of Douglas Aviation in cooperation with the Air Force, and spun off as the first non-profit military "think tank" in 1947.)

Eisenhower adopted virtually the whole of the Killian Report as his own policy. By his own standards, in fact, his spending on missiles was lavish—his budget request in the spring of 1955 contained $500 million for missile research, and a year later, he asked for $1.2 billion. He was astonished, therefore, when first Symington, and then Stevenson in the 1956 campaign, attacked him for not spending enough on missile development. He had expected to be attacked for spending too much. It was not to be the last time that Eisenhower underestimated the powerful symbology of being ahead, or appearing to be ahead, in a missile race.

One of the first concrete outcomes of the Killian recommendations was the U-2 spy plane, a remarkable technical achievement master-minded by Richard Bissell of the CIA, the godfather of the American "spy-in-the-sky" program, and produced at Kelly Johnson's famed "skunk works" at Lockheed. Designed and built in just eighty days, it was a thin, black, spidery affair, with wings almost twice as long as its body, and so light that they drooped on the ground when the plane was sitting on the runway. Its first operational flight was in early 1956: it glided soundlessly and invisibly 16 miles above the Soviet continent, far out of reach of Russian air defenses, photographing a 120-mile wide swath of territory on a line that carried it directly over Moscow and Leningrad. Bissell hoped that the U-2 would fly too high even for Soviet radar, but the very first flight drew a prompt and sharp, but secret, protest—for the Soviets could hardly announce that they were unable to shoot down American spy planes.

Everyone knew that the U-2 was a stopgap measure—Bissell estimated, accurately, that it could fly for perhaps four years before the Soviets would be able to down it. The requirement was clearly for a photographic satellite. The problem, however, as the early RAND reports had pointed out, was that a spy satellite would appear to be an illegal incursion on a country's air space; and there was no doubt that the Soviets would take that position if the subject ever came to a debate at the United Nations. The prerequisite to an American spy satellite program, therefore, would be international agreement that space was the common property of all nations—a substantial modification of the ancient law that a nation's territory extended *usque ad coelum,* or "all the way to the sky."

The administration decided, therefore, about 1955, to make a sharp distinction between its military rocket program, which was kept largely secret, and its space program, which would be presented as a civilian, scientific endeavor, focused on peaceful objectives. Eisenhower announced that America would attempt to launch "small, earth-circling, satellites" for the benefit of "scientists of all nations" as part of the International Geophysical Year, a kind of world's fair of scientific endeavor scheduled for 1957–58. Scientific space launches, providing data to physicists and astronomers all over the world, would, it was hoped, set a strong precedent in favor of international ownership of space. There was a half-hearted attempt to encourage the Soviet Union to join with the United States in a scientific launch, but shortly after the American announcement, Moscow quietly announced that it too would attempt to orbit a satellite during the International Geophysical Year.

The constant stress on the civilian and scientific character of the

American space program effectively disqualified Von Braun's rockets as launch vehicles, even though they were by far the most advanced. Because of the post-Killian boost to rocket funding, Von Braun was ready to launch a satellite in 1956. But, aside from the taint that still attached to an ex-Nazi scientist—it was hardly a decade since his V-2s had terrorized London—the Redstone project was so clearly a military one that it would undercut all of the administration's rhetoric. The choice accordingly fell on the Viking rocket, developed by Martin and the Naval Research Laboratory for the express purpose of scientific research in the upper atmosphere.

The Vanguard project, as the Viking satellite launch program was named, was known to be a risky choice, because the rocket's three upper stages would have to be developed virtually from scratch. But despite the fulminations of Von Braun, and of Nelson Rockefeller, who insisted on the immense symbolic importance of being the first nation in space, the administration was not overly concerned about losing a space race; there was a considerable feeling, in fact, that if the Soviets were first, it would help establish the principle of free overflight for American surveillance satellites. Von Braun continued his work on his powerful new boosters, but he was under strict instructions not to fire anything into orbit, and at one point in 1956 inspectors were dispatched to Redstone to ensure that high-altitude tests of the new Jupiter-C booster did not launch a satellite "by accident." Braun actually launched two rockets powerful enough to orbit a satellite before the Sputnik launch, but, in accord with instructions, neither one contained any payload.

Von Braun had the last laugh. After the Vanguard debacle at the end of 1957, the Jupiter-C was hurriedly pressed into service and launched the "Explorer I" on its first attempt in January of the new year. Vanguard did not get into orbit until March 1958. Although it was not much remarked upon at the time, the first American satellites underscored the big American lead in micro-electronics. Explorer weighed only about 10 pounds, but sent back a wealth of scientific data and discovered the Van Allen radiation belts; the first Vanguard launch established beyond doubt the true shape of the earth.

Eisenhower wearily repeated that there was a great difference between experimental space shots and serviceable ballistic weaponry. Maddeningly, because of the illegal nature of the flights, he kept the U-2 data one of the most closely held secrets of his administration. The U-2 photographs were still fragmentary, but had disclosed nothing resembling ICBM deployment—they had located only two ICBM sites, both of which were clearly test installations—and the Turkish radar installation had picked up a total of only six ICBM tests spaced further and further apart, probably indicating that the Soviets were running into technical problems. (The Air Force insisted that the slowdown in tests proved how smoothly the program was going.) But it should have been obvious that none of the rockets launched by either side would have been of much use in a war. The liquid fuel was both dangerous and difficult to handle, each rocket took a week or more to prepare, the launch failure rate was much higher than could be acceptable in a weapon system, and guidance systems were still unreliable. Yet the "missile gap" seized the imagination of a diverse lobby organizing in opposition to Eisenhower's tight-fisted military spending policies, including important segments of the press, the leaders of the Democratic Party, Southern congressmen like Lister Hill of Alabama who were looking for a national issue that would draw attention from segregation, military spending enthusiasts from the defense industry and both political parties, and an emerging new group of articulate and highly vocal defense intellectuals, working in universities and in think tanks like RAND.

The claims made by the missile gap publicists were altogether fantastic. The *Reporter* magazine, for instance, a normally careful, somewhat left-of-center weekly, reported in 1959 that the Soviet Union had "20,000 ballistic missiles with ranges from 150 to 6,000 miles"; that Khrushchev had secretly reported the completion of a 14,000-mile-range "super-missile"; and that the Soviet Army could fire 1,200-mile-range thermonuclear missiles in salvos of a half-dozen each. *Aviation Week* reported that the Soviets were building fifteen new ICBMs each month, and Joseph Alsop claimed that the United States was behind 100–0 in operational ICBMs, and that by 1961, the Soviet lead would be 1,000–70—implicitly assigning to the Soviets a rate of production several times faster than the most optimistic claims the American military made for its own missile production facilities. The Soviets were widely claimed to enjoy substantial leads in "submarine-launched, solid-propellant ballistic missiles," "computerized early-warning systems," and " 'smart' air-defense interceptor missiles." Asher Lee, a military aviation expert, even claimed that the Soviets had perfected the "Sanger plane,"* a mythical, conventionally powered airplane that

---

*The "Sanger plane" was the brainchild of Dr. Eugen Sanger, a Nazi airplane designer, who was working on the problem of lift-to-drag ratio. At Stalin's insistence. Soviet

could "skip" across the stratosphere halfway around the world, strewing thermonuclear destruction from altitudes of 160 miles. In 1958, John Kennedy intoned that the country's "most pressing technological problem" was the "missile lag," which was "certain to grow for the next five years."

All of these reports were either confabulated from the most fragmentary information filtered through the Iron Curtain or invented from whole cloth. As far as is known, the Soviet Union had *no* operational ICBMs as late as 1960; and only four Soviet missiles had been seen in public, all at the post-Sputnik Red Square celebrations. One of them was the 500-mile-range T-1, and the other three were battlefield launchers with ranges from 10 to 50 miles. There was more or less reliable information that the intermediate-range T-2 was available to the Red Army; that the Soviets had developed a functional surface-to-air missile, on the order of the American Nike-Ajax; and that they were working on the Golem missile, a submarine-towed, surface-launched, intermediate-range rocket, although it was not known whether they had succeeded in developing the solid fuels essential to sea deployment or mastered the guidance systems required for a launch from a heaving ocean surface. They still had an advantage in throw-weight, although the Americans were fast closing the gap, and they were improving their guidance systems. The big rockets and improved guidance allowed the Soviets to score another space first in 1959, when they succeeding in crashing an object—Lunik II—into the moon.

The publicly available information on American missile development, on the other hand, despite Symington's attacks on Eisenhower's tight-fistedness, demonstrated a program that was impressive in breadth, quality, and speed of deployment. Indeed, the late 1950s may have been a golden age of the military-industrial complex—the only period of recent history when it produced outstanding weapons with outstanding efficiency at reasonable costs. The Jupiter intermediate-range missile had achieved its designed range of 1,500 miles in 1957 and was in production for deployment in Europe, shortly to be joined by the Thor, with similar range and payload characteristics. The Titan missile was already being tested at 5,500-mile ranges and would begin deployment in 1959, remaining in the American arsenal until the 1980s. The Atlas rocket, with a unique thin-skinned design that re-

---

designers tinkered with the idea in the late 1940s, but never attempted serious development. The idea was revived in the United States in the late 1950s, as the X-20, or "Dyna-Soar" airplane, but was finally killed in 1963.

quired it to be pressurized at surface atmospheres, a significant metallurgical advance, had achieved thrusts in excess of a million pounds, and would prove to be the workhorse of the American space program for the next decade.

The Navy had received permission to opt out of the Jupiter program in 1956 to develop its own solid-fuelled underwater-launched Polaris missile to be carried by huge, silent, nuclear-powered submarines. The entire program, both submarines and missiles, was on schedule and under budget. The Polaris missile itself was successfully fired from underwater in the spring of 1960—using an ingenious compressed-air system to "pop" it to the surface, where it then ignited and fired like a conventional rocket. The first nuclear-missile-carrying nuclear submarine, the *George Washington,* carrying sixteen 1,200-mile-range thermonuclear-tipped Polaris missiles, was launched in November, and five more Polaris-class submarines were under construction.

The Air Force was adapting the Polaris solid-fuel design to its own Minuteman missile, a relatively cheap and lightweight, but very accurate missile that could be stored underground in silos for years and launched with only minutes of preparation time. The first sketches were made in 1955; the program was funded in 1956; the missile was successfully tested less than two weeks after John Kennedy's inauguration; and full-scale deployment began in 1962. By the end of Eisenhower's presidency, in other words, the entire American strategic "triad"—the submarine-launched Polaris, the silo-based Minuteman and Titan, and the long-range B-52 bomber—was either in place or in the last stages before deployment. Essentially the same weapons would form the heart of the American nuclear posture for the next twenty years.

The American defense establishment had also made huge strides in electronics and miniaturization. American reconnaissance satellites were flying by late 1960, not long after Francis Gary Powers's U-2 was finally downed by the Russians. The SAGE and DEW-line string of radar and sensing devices stretched across the Arctic (relieving the Defense Department's mid-fifties corps of late night sky-watchers). In 1958, two Bomarc missiles, "the only long-range surface-to-air missile yet announced anywhere in the world," according to *Jane's,* were launched by a SAGE ground control unit 1,500 miles away in Canada, and tracked and killed two pilotless drones 100 miles out in the northern Atlantic—a remarkable achievement, considering the still-rudimentary computers that were available in the late 1950s. The 1959 version of the Bomarc had an operating ceiling of 100,000 feet and top speeds of four times the speed of sound, clearly superior to anything possessed by the Soviets, who were still helplessly shaking their fists at the U-2. Thousands of heat-seeking Sidewinder air-to-air missiles, probably the best air-battle weapon America ever made, had been deployed to the air forces of the United States and a number of friendly nations. The Hounddog air-to-surface missile had been installed in European-based B-52s, giving the American bombers a "standoff" nuclear firing capability of 350 miles. Wisely or not, small tactical nuclear weapons had been deployed to NATO forces and could be launched by thousands of Honest John short-range rail-type rocket launchers.

In short, there was neither a missile gap at the end of the Eisenhower presidency, nor any substantial reason for informed observers to believe that there should be, even without the data from the secret radar tracking stations or the U-2 overflights. In addition, well before the 1960 presidential campaign, key congressmen, including particularly Lyndon Johnson, one of the most strident critics of the alleged slow pace of missile development, had all the facts the administration did. The congressional inquiry that followed the downing of Powers's U-2 plane was "thorough, suspicious, and secret." Allen Dulles, head of the CIA, testified for five and a half hours, with ample photographic documentation from previous U-2 flights. It was impossible to demonstrate that the Soviets had *no* ICBMs, but the persistent absence of missile bases in the U-2 photographs made it equally implausible to argue that they had an overwhelming lead.

There was, of course, partisan political advantage to be gained by not listening. George Reedy told Johnson shortly after the Sputnik launch that he could ride the "missile gap" issue all the way to the White House. But, important as it was, political jockeying does not fully explain the avid enthusiasm with which the most influential sectors of society—the media, academia, politicians, leading businessmen—embraced the "missile gap." The late 1950s was a period of restless searching for a "national purpose" on the part of a new technocratic elite that was just beginning to dominate American political discussion. Reports like the Rockefeller Panel's *Goals for Americans* pointed to problems of education, health, social equality, science and technology, military strength, and above all economic growth, that could be solved only by aggressive and centralized technocratic management. Men whose formative experiences had been in World War II, as John Kennedy's had been, had an understandable faith in, and nostalgia for, the power and majesty of large-scale enterprise, harnessing the spirit and will of millions of people in common endeavor.

For the technocratic reformer, the "missile gap" was like a sign from the heavens. It touched all the major themes. The research and engineering development required would be massive, of the same unprecedented scale as the effort to put men in space. Total reform of education would be required to produce the necessary scientists and mathematicians. Whole new industries would need to be created. Centralized, Keynesian-style demand management was a must: the economic growth rates of the Eisenhower era, steady and non-inflationary though they were, would not support such grand visions. As Arthur Schlesinger, Jr., wrote in a Kennedy campaign document, the nation risked falling "farther and farther behind the Soviet Union in ICBMs and the fight for space"; it faced "the deterioration of American education and the quality of American life." Unless America seized the technocratic moment, it would "drift into minor-power status and oblivion." Both social progress and outstanding military hardware alike, it seemed, would be the common product of a brave new technocratic society.

## The Years of High Theory

By the end of the Eisenhower administration, his military policies were under heavy and sustained attack from an entirely new quarter, a small group of "defense intellectuals" centered in the RAND Corporation and in certain key universities, particularly Harvard, Princeton, and Yale. The defense intellectuals proved to be adept polemicists and publicists, with a flair for the eye-catching slogan and the flashy phrase. They were both resourceful and tireless in pressing their views and quickly achieved ready access to the media, to key figures in Congress, and to the administration's opposition in both political parties. By the early 1960s, they had attained such prestige and influence that a foreign correspondent described them as men "who move freely through the corridors of the Pentagon and the State Department rather as the Jesuits through the courts of Madrid and Vienna three centuries ago."

The RAND staff men included men like Bernard Brodie, a Yale historian who was possibly the very first (1946) to state the modern theory of nuclear deterrence; Albert Wohlstetter, a mathematical logician; Thomas Schelling, a Harvard political economist; Herbert Dinerstein, an early "Sovietologist" and military historian; William Kaufmann, a Princeton historian; and the nuclear physicist Herman

Kahn, who had made major contributions to thermonuclear weapons development. Outside of RAND was Klaus Knorr, who had been recruited by Brodie for Princeton's Institute of International Studies, and Henry Kissinger, a young professor of international relations at Harvard, who had become the darling of the New York foreign policy establishment centered in the Council on Foreign Relations. Although the defense intellectuals were generally mistrusted by professional military men, two scholar-generals, Maxwell Taylor and James Gavin, published important books that strongly reinforced their concepts.

If anyone qualified as the patriarch of the defense intellectuals, it was Brodie, and his book, *Strategy in the Missile Age,* became a basic text. Brodie's book is elegant and cultivated, affecting a tone of ironic understatement. (A nuclear weapon dropped on our Korean base at Pusan "could have been very embarrassing for us.") It begins with a long disquisition on the history of military strategy to demonstrate that the strategic judgments of the best professional military men, as opposed to their day-to-day tactical judgments, are almost always wrong. The vast power of nuclear weapons, however, would make virtually any nuclear exchange between the United States and the Soviet Union a strategic one—that is, one capable of settling the outcome of the entire war—or precisely the sort of encounter professional military men are least capable of handling. Therefore the preparation for and management of nuclear war, Brodie argued, required a new type of civilian strategist, combining the best attributes of the scientist and the historian, the economist and the logician. The irrationality of an all-out nuclear war was, after all, no assurance that it might not come to pass; history was full of irrational wars. The side that had prepared most rationally for the cataclysm, however—indeed, that was prepared actually to *fight* a nuclear war most rationally—was not only the most likely to survive, but possibly even to prevail.

Brodie established the basic categories of thinking about nuclear warfare that prevail to this day. His central points are simple and logically unassailable. To the extent that deterrence was a prime concern of policy, the size and killing power of the deterrent force was less important than its survivability. It was not the power of the American forces *before* a Soviet strike that would deter a surprise attack, but their reliable ability to inflict punishing retaliation after the Soviet strike was over.

Equally important, Brodie suggested that there were many conceivable ways of fighting a nuclear war beyond the common picture of both sides unleashing all their destructive forces upon each other's populations. Indeed, the best first-strike strategy would be to attack the other side's *weapons*, not its cities—a *"counterforce"* strategy, in the new jargon. Even if the victim of a counterforce strike retained enough weapons to attack the other's cities, it might still choose to surrender: a last-gasp retaliatory strike would simply elicit a second assault by the aggressor that would wreak almost total destruction on the victim's population and cities. Surrender would be much the more prudent course. Millions of lives, in any case, would hinge on making the correct decisions during the course of a nuclear war, reinforcing the necessity for tight, centralized control over nuclear weapons and a clear theory of how to use them. Ominously, such reasoning also implied that the side that launched a surprise counterforce strike could win a nuclear war with only minimal losses of its own.

Deterrence also required credibility. Even the most powerful nuclear force would not deter if an enemy did not believe that it would be used. Brodie argued that the American "massive retaliation" policy was inherently incredible, since it was inconceivable that America would risk mass death in any circumstances short of the most egregious Soviet assault on the West, such as an all-out attack on Europe. The lack of a credible deterrent posture, he feared, might actually increase the risk of a general nuclear war, since it would induce the Soviets to indulge in ever more risky behavior. Nuclear-based deterrence, therefore, needed to be supplemented by a clear capacity and willingness to fight and win limited wars. Brodie assumed that limited war, in which both sides tacitly agreed to restrict both the means and the geographic boundaries of conflict, as in Korea, might become the characteristic mode of warfare of the latter twentieth century, and it was one that the United States had neither the equipment, the manpower, nor the doctrine to wage effectively. Finally, Brodie concluded, building an effective nuclear deterrence and limited war capability would require much greater defense investment than the United States was then making, but it was one that the country could easily afford.

Brodie's central ideas were extended to the point of parody, although in rather different directions, by Thomas Schelling and Herman Kahn. Schelling was fascinated by John von Neumann's newly invented game theory, which explored the mathematics of weighing and making choices.* Schelling's writings, which were influential in shaping the

---

*The classic illustration of game theory logic is the problem known as the "Prisoner's Dilemma." Assume two prisoners are charged with, and are in fact guilty of, a joint murder. The police are holding them separately so they cannot communicate with each other. An offer is made that the first prisoner to confess and implicate the other will receive a stiff prison sentence, but the other will be executed. If *neither* confesses,

American bombing campaign in Vietnam, focused on the problem of inducing desirable behavior on the part of the enemy and the importance of communicating a proper understanding both of one's actual power and one's willingness to use it. He criticized the Chinese intervention in Korea, for instance, and quite correctly, on the grounds that if the Chinese had intended to deter the American advance, they should have telegraphed their ability and willingness to intervene much more clearly than they did.

In Schelling's hands, nuclear war becomes an extraordinarily bloodless and cerebral affair, an enterprise suitable for tweedy professors smoking pipes. Nuclear war is reduced to a special case of an exercise in game theory, so a nuclear attack on a specific target becomes a "proposal." A successful war in Europe, Schelling argues, would require the skillful and well-controlled bargaining use of nuclears.

In other words, nuclears would not only destroy targets but would signal something. Getting the right signal across would be an important part of the policy. This could imply, for example, deliberate and restrained use earlier than might otherwise seem tactically warranted. . . . Whenever the tactical situation indicates a high likelihood of military necessity for nuclears in the near future, it may be prudent to introduce them deliberately while there is still opportunity to do so with care, selection, and properly associated diplomacy.

In contrast to Schelling, no one could accuse Herman Kahn of being bloodless. Enormously fat, endlessly voluble, with an encyclopedic stream of talk on virtually any subject, he loved to shock lecture audiences with graphic depictions of the aftermath of a nuclear war: "some high percentage of the population is going to become nauseated, and nausea is very contagious. If one man vomits, everybody vomits. It would not be surprising if almost everybody vomits." But still he insisted that nuclear war could be and must be analyzed and discussed rationally, and if need be, fought rationally. He insisted on heavy investments in civil defense programs, for example, precisely because it would make the United States more willing to fight a nuclear war. The essence of a credible deterrent was a perceived willingness to use it—"in order to appear willing, one must *be* willing."

---

however, both will likely go free. The prisoner who applies game theory will confess immediately. Although his confession guarantees a prison sentence, it also preserves his life, and game theory's "minimax" principle suggests that one should always seek to minimize the worst possible outcome, even at the cost of ensuring an undesirable one. It was unsettling, to say the least, to ponder the implications of game theory for nuclear war. Logically, if it would help prevent extinction, a national leader should launch a surprise attack even at the risk of substantial retaliatory casualties.

Kahn was an indefatigable cataloguer and taxonomist. His method was that of exhaustion, listing every conceivable scenario and attempting to evaluate each available option as scientifically and as cold-bloodedly as possible. His major work, *On Thermonuclear War*, created a storm of controversy when it was published in 1960; one critic called it a "moral tract on mass murder: how to plan it, how to commit it, how to get away with it, how to justify it." The spirit of the book is captured by reproducing one of its many tables:

**Table 32. Flexible War Plan for Defender**

| Capabilities of Surviving Forces | Assumed Level of Damage | Action |
| --- | --- | --- |
| Negligible Counterforce Moderate Countervalue | 80–100% | All-out Countervalue |
| Some Counterforce High Countervalue | 40–80% | All-out Counterforce; Some Withholding |
| High Counterforce High Countervalue | 10–40% | Cautious Counterforce; Moderate Withholding |
| More than 90% of capabilities | 0–10% | Temporizing measures or very discriminating Counterforce |

The table suggests that it makes sense to launch an all-out retaliatory strike against an aggressor's cities ("Countervalue") only if his first strike is so successful that it disables almost all of the available retaliatory weapons. Otherwise, the appropriate response is to strike back at the other side's remaining weapons, but not to initiate an exchange of cities. And if the opponent's first strike has been a small one, then only a "discriminating" or "temporizing" nuclear response will be called for. The table implies, in addition, that a nuclear war might extend over a considerable period of time, beginning with cautious counterforce probing, with numerous opportunities to bring the exchange to an end before it spirals out of control.

Kahn's analysis of the nuclear war-fighting process was expanded into another book, *On Escalation,* in which he identified forty-four "rungs" on the escalation ladder, beginning with "Ostensible Crisis" and proceeding grimly through way stations like "Harassing Acts of Violence" (Rung 8), "Large Compound Escalation" (Rung 13), and "Spectacular Show of Force" (Rung 18), to "Demonstration Attack on Zone of Interior" (Rung 26), "Exemplary Attacks on Population" (Rung

29), "Slow-motion Counterforce War" (Rung 34), "Countervalue Salvo" (Rung 40), and, finally, "Spasm or Insensate War."

It is important to attempt to sort out the basic truths, the significant insights, the theoretically arguable but irrelevant musings, and the dangerous foolishness from the defense intellectuals' writings, for all were represented in generous admixture. The basic truth was that an actual or emerging Soviet long-range nuclear delivery capability made the key premises of Eisenhower's military posture outdated. Even stripping out the usual elements of caricature, Eisenhower's policies still relied in substantial measure on nuclear intimidation, and could work effectively only so long as the nuclear balance was grossly one-sided, as it had been during most of the 1950s. Whether the Soviets had a long-range nuclear capability or not, or were five years away from one, it was still time for a major rethinking of the American force structure. Dulles conceded as much before he died, and Eisenhower himself quietly convened an outside task force at the end of his second term to reconsider the right mix of nuclear and conventional power.

An additional key insight was that survivability of nuclear forces was at least as important as absolute striking power. Albert Wohlstetter led a pathbreaking RAND study in the early 1950s which demonstrated that, although forward basing of the American bombing fleet in Europe and Asia shortened attack routes to the Soviet Union, the advantage was offset by the increased vulnerability of the bombers' airfields. The long range of the B-52 allowed the Air Force to relocate its bombers to the continental United States—the few hours' extra flying time to targets was more than compensated for by the assured safety of the deterrent. A similar series of later RAND studies under Wohlstetter and Fred Iklé developed the "fail-safe" procedure—bombers would take off at the first hint of crisis, thereby assuring their safety, but would not proceed to their final target run until receiving a positive order to do so; and the "permissive action link," a remotely coded, combination, multiple-key system of arming nuclear weapons, which greatly reduced the dangers of accidental or unauthorized nuclear detonations.

Other insights were not so obviously useful. At some level of abstraction, for instance, Schelling's point that war is a process of bargaining is true, or even truistic. But the insight is of little help in devising a useful set of signals. Lyndon Johnson's desperate attempts to signal the North Vietnamese through his limited bombing campaign—in fairly strict accord with Schelling's theories—apparently communicated little except the American lack of appetite for more fighting. Interestingly enough, MacArthur insisted that the Chinese warnings in Korea meant that they would *not* attack, since no serious opponent would telegraph his punch. And in any case, real-life signalling problems are much more complicated than simple two-person games. American weapon procurement decisions are often justified as "signals"; but it is rarely obvious whether the intended recipient is the Soviets, the Western Allies, the American voters, or the world in general, all of whom, of course, could interpret a "signal" in unpredictably different ways. The whole concept of nuclear deterrence, as Lawrence Freedman has suggested, since it is "fundamentally a psychological theory," depends on the efficiency of threat communication and the predictability of the opponent's response, "both of which are notoriously difficult to manipulate and control."

Just as frequently, the defense intellectuals' airy theorizing led to dangerous nonsense, like Schelling's notion of "skillful and well-controlled bargaining" with nuclear weapons—a policy suggestion, typically, made despite the dearth of information about nuclear weapons effects. Phenomena like the electromagnetic pulse from a nuclear blast that can disable electronic communications equipment for hundreds, and possibly thousands, of miles had not yet been identified. (See Chapters 15 and 19 for a broader discussion of blast effects and the problem of command and control in nuclear war.) More obviously, as the Soviets mockingly pointed out, in a real war it would be virtually impossible to tell a "counterforce bargaining" strike from the first salvo in an all-out attack. The "clean, surgical" tactical weapons that the defense intellectuals were casually detonating in their war games were almost all bigger than the bombs that destroyed Hiroshima and Nagasaki; and almost all military targets of any consequence throughout Europe and the Soviet Union were located in or near highly urbanized areas. No national leader could be counted upon to endure an atomic attack on a major city without an all-out retaliation. Even Herman Kahn occasionally conceded that it was wholly unlikely that a nuclear exchange could be kept under control.

Henry Kissinger's attempts to forge a coherent doctrine of tactical nuclear war led to a series of embarrassing *volte-faces* over a period of several years: in his 1958 book *Nuclear Weapons and Foreign Policy,* he enthusiastically plumped for the use of tactical nuclears in a European war; shortly thereafter, he argued the reverse position just as fervently; then he finally reversed himself again in the 1960s. Europeans, understandably, were horrified at the very notion of a "controlled" nuclear war. Tactical nuclear doctrine looked like a transparent ploy to allow the United States to fight the Soviet Union at long distance, leaving Europe a smoking ruin for the third time in the century while America escaped unscathed.

Similarly, if it was true, as the defense intellectuals contended, that a perceived American willingness to engage in conventional warfare might decrease Soviet adventurism in marginal trouble spots around the world, it was also possible that an increased capacity to fight limited wars would make limited wars more likely. Admittedly with hindsight, there appears to be a straightline connection between the Kennedy administration's fascination with "counterinsurgency" operations in the service of "flexible response" and the tragic commitment in Vietnam. And, of course, any military engagement between the two superpowers or their proxies vastly increased the risk of a general conflagration.

But even at the theoretical level, serious questions could be raised. One major problem stemmed from the essentially static character of the analysis. A key assumption was that the United States was a rule-constrained power, whereas the Soviet Union was not. The premise was not unreasonable, given the postwar history of Soviet diplomacy, but it led to a troubling chain of reasoning. It followed, for example, that it was the Soviet Union, not the United States, that would be likely to launch a first strike once conditions were favorable. It was crucial, therefore, that the United States develop a substantial second-strike capability, and given the moral asymmetry between the two powers, one that was much larger than the Soviet Union's—massive redundancy was essential to ensure survivability. There was little recognition, however, that the Soviet Union was not likely to accept that it was the morally inferior power or be content with a huge American strategic superiority. From the Soviet point of view, an overwhelmingly large and well-defended American strategic force would appear to be an intolerable counterforce first strike threat; the almost inevitable Soviet attempt to close the strategic gap could create a limitlessly spiralling strategic arms race.*

An even more fundamental theoretical problem was the implicit

*Schelling was one of the few to recognize the problem explicitly, in his *Arms and Influence,* but he convinced himself that the Soviets would accept strategic inferiority, citing, oddly enough, Churchill's unsuccessful attempt in 1912 to induce the Kaiser to accept inferiority in dreadnoughts. Eisenhower also recognized the problem, leading to his impassioned, and exasperated, pleas for a "sufficiency" of nuclear weapons rather than an endless cycle of trump-counter-trump.

premise that political leaders thought the way RAND analysts did. At least two baneful consequences flowed from this assumption. The first was the expectation that, once a stable balance of strategic forces had been achieved, the Soviets in particular would understand that further competitive arming would be to the detriment of *both* sides' security. Michael Mandelbaum has, quite ingeniously, compared this line of reasoning to the classical economist's case for free trade. It can be shown beyond argument that if *every* nation follows free trade policies, all will be better off. But what if *one* nation violates the rules? Quite probably the offending nation will prosper, particularly so long as everyone else abides by the theory. The political temptation to take unilateral advantage is almost overwhelming. Not surprisingly, although almost all the major trading nations in the world proclaim their allegiance to free trade, almost all, the United States included, have erected a variety of trade barriers in the pursuit of one short-term interest or the other. Just so, the United States preached the virtues of mutually stable deterrence even as it built a nuclear striking force vastly greater than the Soviet Union's in the first half of the 1960s; and the Soviet Union made similar protestations of its strategic rectitude while it was on its own rocket-building binge in the late 1960s and the 1970s.

More mischievously, the implicit premise of a game theory model of the great power confrontation was that the Kremlin was ruled by an academician's "rational despot," a kind of disembodied genie who spent his days calculating strategic probability matrices until his computer announced the moment to strike. There was little recognition, as McGeorge Bundy later remarked, that "Political leaders, whether here or in Russia, are cast from a different mold than strategic planners. They see cities and people as part of what they are trying to help—not as targets. . . . The deterrent that might not please a planner is more than deterrent enough for them."

The assumption that Soviet leaders would behave in accord with the hyper-rational canons of the new strategic theory inevitably focused attention on the possibility of a "bolt from the blue" surprise rocket attack. Surprise attack scenarios were the object of an extraordinary amount—an almost hysterical amount—of analytic energy toward the end of the decade. Game theory did not readily recognize degrees of moral or political constraint; there is nothing compassionate, after all, about a chess endgame. If the Soviet Union was classified as a power implacably bent on world domination, a surprise nuclear attack became altogether plausible. Indeed, game theory suggested that it was the right choice to make: the loss of a few million Soviet citizens in an American death-throes counterstrike was a small enough price for world conquest. It was only the smallest step from an analysis that suggested that a great power might benefit from launching a first strike to an argument that the Soviet Union was actually planning to do so.

The "bolt from the blue" scare did not spring, as might be supposed, from a vulgar misinterpretation of what the defense intellectuals were saying. It was the direct conclusion of two immensely influential articles published in *Foreign Affairs* in 1958 and 1959. The first was "The Revolution in Soviet Strategic Thinking" by Herbert Dinerstein, which was quickly expanded into a book, *War and the Soviet Union;* the second, and even more frightening, was Albert Wohlstetter's "The Delicate Balance of Terror." Both "created a huge sensation among the defense intellectuals along the Washington–New York–Cambridge corridor" as one reporter put it. Wohlstetter's article, in particular, was enshrined by Schelling in 1985 as an "intellectual milestone" in the history of strategic theory.

Dinerstein's argument is an interesting example of the contemporary tendency to slide glibly from writing about what the Soviet leaders *would* do if they *could,* to flat statements about present capability. In his book, for example, he writes: "The ballistic missile—when it becomes operational and has, in a satisfactory combination, accuracy, numbers, and reliability—will indeed be a formidable weapon of strategic surprise." But just six pages later, he states baldly, "Thus, it seems reasonable to believe that the Soviet ICBM system is now assigned essentially, although not exclusively, to a first-strike mission." This was not, Dinerstein stressed, a theoretical statement about some remote future: "If the Soviet Union should continue to gain technologically while the NATO alliance made little progress, the Soviet Union would be able to make war without fear of the consequences. . . . By flaunting presumably invincible strength, the Soviet Union could compel piecemeal capitulation of the democracies. This prospect must indeed seem glittering to the Soviet leaders."

The argument in Wohlstetter's "Delicate Balance of Terror" was even more alarmist. Wohlstetter had been a consultant to the Gaither Committee, convened by Eisenhower after the Sputnik launchings to review America's civil defense effort. The panel, which was heavily peopled and supported by the RAND intellectuals, came up with a broad-scale surprise attack protection program, drafted primarily by Nitze, with a price tag of $44 billion. The proposals were based entirely on the assumption that the Soviets would be able to launch a coordinated attack with less than six hours' warning, since the testimony before the committee made it clear that, with five or six hours' notice of a Soviet attack, American forces would be in reasonably good shape. Predictably, Eisenhower displayed almost no interest in the recommendations, not because he was complacent or ignorant, as the RAND intellectuals were quick to assume, but because he thought their ideas were preposterous. Eisenhower understood the limits of large-scale military operations, and was developing good intelligence surveillance of the Soviet Union; the notion of a worldwide coordinated Soviet surprise attack with less than six hours' warning, and with no preceding period of heightened tension or visible preparatory activity, was just too implausible to warrant billions of new expenditure.

"The Delicate Balance of Terror" was dedicated to refuting that notion, to exploding the common assumption "that a general thermonuclear war is extremely unlikely." Wohlstetter's jumping-off point was game theory, and his basic assumption was that the policymaking echelons in the Kremlin were populated with game theorists making the same calculations he was:

Suppose both the United States and the Soviet Union had the power to destroy each other's retaliatory forces and society, given the opportunity to administer the opening blow. The situation would then be something like the old-fashioned Western gun duel. It would be extraordinarily risky for one side not to attempt to destroy the other, or to delay doing so, since it can not only emerge unscathed by striking first but this is the sole way it can hope to emerge at all.

And he assumes the Soviets would be under no moral or political constraints in reaching such an assessment:

Russian casualties in World War II were more than 20,000,000. Yet Russia recovered extremely well from this catastrophe. There are several quite plausible circumstances in the future when the Russians might be quite confident of being able to limit damage to considerably less than this number. . . . Then, striking first, by surprise, would be the sensible choice for them, and from their point of view, the smaller risk.

Wohlstetter details at great length all the reasons why an American retaliatory force might not operate effectively. Warnings of an attack might be misconstrued or communicated improperly. Weapons and warning systems are notoriously unreliable, he warns, and could not be counted upon to work as planned. Even if hardened forces should survive, communications problems might prevent their timely firing. Missiles could not be fired quickly or in a coordinated way ("Countdown procedures for early missiles are liable to interruption"). Much of America's bomber force would have difficulty reaching the Soviet Union because of "operational problems such as coordination with tankers." It would be very difficult to get through modern air defenses. And the low payloads and average inaccuracy of the newer missiles, such as Minuteman and the Polaris, would likely mean poor target destruction results.

Miraculously, none of these problems would bedevil the Soviets, whom Americans persisted in underestimating grievously: "Where the published writings have not simply underestimated Soviet capabilities and the advantages of a first strike, they have in general placed artificial constraints on the Soviet use of the capabilities of the forces attributed to them." And the situation could only grow worse: ". . . we must expect a vast increase in the weight of attack which the Soviets can deliver with little warning and the growth of a significant Russian capability for an essentially warningless attack." Nor would improved surveillance be of much help, for, "not even the most advanced reconnaissance equipment can disclose an intention from 40,000 feet." Indeed, the Soviet ballistic missiles could be expected to work almost perfectly—no "countdown interruptions" here. Concealment and dispersal of American forces, in fact, would be almost hopeless: "In the case of ballistic missiles, the elapsed time from firing to impact on target can be calculated with great accuracy. Although there will be some failures and delays, times of firing can be arranged so that impact on many points is almost simultaneous—on Okinawa and the United Kingdom, for instance, as well as on California and Ohio."

These were not the conclusions of an academic theorist calculating abstract interactions between two idealized states in some idealized future. Wohlstetter and Dinerstein were both privy to vast amounts of classified information; and Khrushchev's bombast notwithstanding, they were as well positioned as anyone to assess the actual balance of Soviet and American strategic capabilities. As certified experts, they were pressing specific, and urgent, policy shifts upon the political leadership and a wide audience of influential opinion makers. They had an obligation, if not to be right, at least to ground their arguments in something more than rumor, speculation, and the enthusiasms of the moment.

The fact was, "intellectual milestone" or not, their articles were precisely and completely wrong. At the time they were writing, the Soviet Union not only did not have a first-strike capability, but had no operational ICBMs at all; was ten years away from possessing an ICBM fleet of any significant consequence; and was at least twenty years away from possessing an ICBM fleet that could even plausibly be said to pose a genuine first-strike counterforce threat. The strategic situation, in fact, was precisely the opposite of what Wohlstetter and Dinerstein said it was. The only superpower that had both the nuclear weapons and the delivery capacity to visit a devastating, unanswerable nuclear strike against the other's homeland was the United States. If there were game theorists resident in the Kremlin, they must have been scared silly. Indeed, in that light, Khrushchev's incessant boasting about Soviet missile prowess acquires a somewhat desperate air.

## The Intellectual as Hero

By the end of the decade, the demands for a full-scale technocratic response rang ever more shrilly. Henry Kissinger's *Necessity for Choice*, based on a series of *Foreign Affairs* articles published in 1958 and 1959, is the *cri de coeur* of the intellectual pining for power, at once poignant, exposed, and fatuous. The book is a self-proclaimed "stirring call to arms," a summons to "heroic" dedication, to "a major national effort" to meet demands "unprecedented in our history and perhaps in the history of any nation." Time is not on our side, insists Kissinger. The Soviet Union is an "implacable" foe determined "to smash the existing framework," while the United States, because "of recent budget levels, ha[s] caused *every* mission to be neglected." At the same time, the Cold War had been transformed—it was no longer "an effort to build defensive systems," but a "contest for the allegiance of humanity." To prevail, the United States must turn to the intellectual. In a long section entitled "The Policymaker and the Intellectual," Kissinger broods over the plight of the "creative" individual who truly understands the deeper meanings in the daily currents of the world, shunted aside by an administration of "pragmatists," or worse, businessmen, forced to function as a kind of retainer or court jester, permitted to work on narrow assignments within the current framework, but never given the responsibility to direct the sweep of events.

Salvation would require "methodological certainty," "above all, the clarification of doctrine" that only the intellectual could achieve. The essential characteristics of Americans—"willingness to compromise," "absence of dogmatism," the lack of a "felt need to push disputes to their logical conclusion"—which Kissinger conceded were "the very qualities which have made for ease of relationships in American society," would have to go. He rejects out of hand George Kennan's warning that an unrestrained response to the Soviet threat would place America's values at risk. Such values were no longer functional in a new and "dangerously vulnerable" world. America needed to reconstruct its world view in terms of "power" and "will": "Certainty in foreign policy . . . derives from the imposition of purpose upon events." The country needed a "heroic effort without the solace of popular acclaim." "A democracy, to be vital, requires leaders willing to stand alone . . . for all innovation spells loneliness." The statesman, therefore, is "like one of the heroes of classical tragedy who has had an intuition of the future, but who cannot transmit it directly to his fellowmen and who cannot validate its truth. . . . Statesmen must act *as if* their intuition were already experience, as if their aspiration were truth."

Kissinger has been occasionally prone to such unrestrained glorification of the role of a "leader," or of his own role in the world; indeed, he has been disarmingly frank about admitting such vanities. He used similar language in the famous interview with Oriana Fallaci in 1972, when he spoke of himself as "the cowboy, who leads the convoy, alone on his horse. . . . This romantic . . . character suits me." The Fallaci interview came at a time when Kissinger's dazzling diplomatic accomplishments might actually have justified some such musings, but they were greeted with catcalls from every side. Not so in the late 1950s, when the dramatic image of the lonely leader, and the thudding and perfervid style of *Necessity for Choice,* were standard rhetoric not only of the defense intellectuals, but of much of the liberal community. Dean Rusk, for example, running hard for Secretary of State in a new administration, insisted on the need for a heroic President, who "after all the advice was in," would "ascend his lonely pinnacle and decide what he must do." And James Tobin, the liberal economist, castigated Eisenhower's insistence on giving precedence to the health of the private economy. His misplaced emphasis, and his "lack of an ideology," had "cost the United States its world leadership and gravely threatened its survival as a nation." The country was "on the brink of a catastrophe, a different and infinitely more serious catastrophe than the internal collapse of 1932." The government had to take charge; control of events could not be abdicated "to the wisdom of corporate management." "Military security," Tobin insisted, "is not achieved by making civilian goods. The way to become strong at producing aircraft is to produce aircraft and to build plants that produce aircraft. The way to have scientists and engineers skilled in missile development is to develop missiles."

The constant theme was the necessity for power, power to marshal and direct the total resources of the economy. Wohlstetter demanded that the country take measures that: *"are* hard, *do* involve sacrifice, *are* affected by great uncertainties and concern matters in which much is altogether unknown and much else must be hedged by secrecy; and, above all, they entail a new image of ourselves in a world of persistent danger. It is by no means *certain* that we shall meet the test." At the Center for the Study of International Affairs at Princeton, Klaus Knorr argued: "What is required is clear enough. . . . To do enough for defense . . . demands from society a huge diversion of effort which its members, naturally enough, prefer to devote to the pursuit of private ends. It means less consumption and more work, less freedom of self-direction . . . in short, it means giving up a great deal of what is worth defending."

The economist Wassilly Leontieff bemoaned that the administration was ignoring the impressive new economic planning tools developed by, *mirabile dictu,* himself. Khrushchev would almost certainly make good on his threat to bury capitalism because "the Soviet economy, directed with determined, ruthless, skill," was using all the new tools, and there was "little doubt that the introduction of scientific planning methods will increase [its] overall productivity . . ." The results were already outstanding: in "key" industries, such as machine tool building, [Soviet] output exceeds that of the United States." (The "economy gap" was an unexamined article of intellectual faith much like the "missile gap"; only occasionally would an unbiased article puzzle over, for example, the absence of tractors on Russian farms.) Indeed, the United States was apparently headed for third-class economic status, for "over twenty countries, not including the Soviet Union and its satellites, are ahead of the United States in modern economic planning techniques." Only the rankest conspiracy prevented Leontieff and his colleagues from taking over the economy in the interest of the nation and the free world: "[C]ertain business circles in the United States have viewed with unconcealed alarm the application of these methods . . . [for] fear that too close and too detailed an understanding of the economic machine and its operation might encourage undesirable attempts to regulate its course."

Herman Kahn weighed in with the promise that, "by 1965, the

Soviet defense budget could easily be twice ours," and warned that since 1956 or 1957, the Russian attitude toward the American military had been "contemptuous." He drummed home the solutions in bold type: **"We Must Take Seriously the Consequences of the Growth of Soviet Power"** and **"We Must Be Willing to Allocate the Necessary Resources."** Klaus Knorr rhapsodized that "the war potential of nations" depended crucially "on administrative skill and morale," and most particularly required "a top authority in which the power to plan and decide major issues is concentrated." The advent of systems analysis and computers, and modern "quantitative management techniques," however, would make centralized direction of the economy more effective than ever before. The average citizen might resent the "huge diversion of effort" required, but Knorr, Kissinger, Kahn, Schelling, Leontieff, Tobin, Wohlstetter and their friends were planning to have the time of their lives.

# CHAPTER 8

# The Failure of Dwight Eisenhower

Anatoly Dobrynin, the long-time Soviet Ambassador to the United States, remarked wistfully to Henry Kissinger in 1972 that their countries had fluffed a golden opportunity to defuse the Cold War in the late 1950s. Kissinger was astonished at Dobrynin's comment—he could recall only unmitigated Soviet truculence—and muses in his *Memoirs* on the inscrutability of the Russian mind. Kissinger's surprise was not unreasonable: between 1957 and 1960 Khrushchev's diplomacy was not only wildly unpredictable, but he frequently resorted to the crudest tactics of bullying and intimidation, mixing the direst threats with the grossest personal insults, to an extent that Western governments found both humiliating and frightening. The truth seems to be, however, that Khrushchev badly wanted and needed a settlement with the West, as Dobrynin said. And erratic as Khrushchev's behavior was, there were ample signs of his true situation, and they were accurately analyzed by a number of Western specialists. The communication problem, in fact, was only partly of Khrushchev's making. A Henry Kissinger who was calling for "heroic dedication" against an "implacable foe" had closed his ears, along with almost all of the other defense intellectuals, the leadership group in Congress, the entire cast of presidential hopefuls, and most of the Washington press corps, to peaceful hints from the Soviet Union. Dwight Eisenhower had not, and for a brief period in late 1959 and early 1960 he thought peace might be within his grasp. Through a combination of bad luck and bad judgment, the moment was irretrievably lost. Eisenhower had dedicated his presidency to limiting the arms buildup and reducing the danger of war, but his efforts, by the end of his administration, met only with frustration and failure.

Khrushchev was a man on a tightrope, a fact that the West was slow to realize, just as it had failed to appreciate the true nature of Stalin's rule. (*Vide* Truman's and Forrestal's image of Stalin as "just another Missouri politician.") As the 1950s drew to a close, Khrushchev's economic program was in serious difficulty, his military policies were meeting open dissent from his Marshals, and he was under sustained, if subdued, attack from a Politburo faction led by the chief Party ideologist, Mikhail Suslov, and the deputy premier, Frol Kozlov—in opposition both to the de-Stalinization campaign and to Khrushchev's penchant for playing fast and loose with received Leninist dogma. Khrushchev's political weakness was evident at the Twenty-first Party Congress in 1959: he lost a key vote on expelling the remnants of the 1957 "anti-Party group," and Suslov made a speech that spoke of Khrushchev's keynote agenda in strikingly lukewarm terms, even questioning, in a veiled way, whether the gathering was an official Congress at all, since it was meeting out of the normal five-year cycle.

Adding to Khrushchev's problems was an increasingly vituperative struggle with the Chinese for the leadership of the world Communist movement. Mao took Khrushchev at his word when he claimed to possess the power to destroy capitalism with the push of a button, and demanded, in effect, that Khrushchev stop bragging and go ahead and do it: " . . . the sacrifices [of nuclear war] would be repaid on the debris of a dead imperialism. The victorious people would create very swiftly a civilization thousands of times higher than the capitalist system and a truly beautiful system for themselves."

Khrushchev—and probably the rest of the Praesidium—was horrified, and promptly reneged on a rash 1957 promise to supply Mao with nuclear weapons. The Chinese remonstrated bitterly that Khrushchev "unilaterally tore up" his agreement "as a presentation gift" to Eisenhower. Khrushchev returned slander with slander: the Chinese were "madmen," "dogmatic left adventurists," and their attacks on the Soviet Union were "disgusting, shameful, gangsterish." By September of 1960, relations had deteriorated to the point where Zhou Enlai actually publicly proposed a treaty between China and the United States—"the countries in Asia and around the Pacific, including the United States, [should] conclude a peace pact of mutual nonaggression to make this region free of nuclear weapons." The West, in general, was slow to appreciate the significance of the Sino-Soviet split, even though the Chinese published their fulminations openly in their Party newspapers, and the intra-Party slanging matches were always eagerly reported by the voluble Italian Communists.

The Soviet Union's economic problems were at the root of Khrushchev's difficulties. Despite his attacks on Malenkov's version of consumer communism in 1955, once he was in power Khrushchev effectively adopted the whole of Malenkov's agenda—trying to increase grain and meat production and shift resources from heavy industry to consumer goods. But by 1959, his hopeful programs were coming almost completely unstuck. The celebrated "virgin lands" project to increase wheat output was turning into an ecological disaster. Vast areas of the steppes had been plowed up and subjected to intense single-crop cultivation. At first, production soared, particularly in 1956 when weather was highly favorable. But by the end of the decade, output was dropping precipitately as the fragile land was drained of its nutrients and wind erosion stripped away millions of tons of topsoil. The meat production program—typical of Khrushchev's sloganeering approach to management—was a catastrophe on a similar scale: foolishly high collective farm quotas caused wholesale slaughter of breeding herds and a near-total collapse of the industry. At the same time, the very high industrial growth rates of the first half of the decade—which are typical of newly industrializing countries—were dropping rapidly as the economy matured. The rigidly centralized state planning apparatus was quite unable to cope, generating simultaneous absurdities of over- and underproduction, while Khrushchev's shoot-from-the-hip decision making continued to make the worst of a bad situation.

In order to release resources for economic growth, Khrushchev adopted a set of military policies that, ironically, closely paralleled Eisenhower's. Although precise year-to-year Soviet spending comparisons are notoriously contentious, the share of the Soviet economy commandeered by the military in the late 1950s was probably lower than at any other time during the entire postwar period. Khrushchev's avowed objective was to shift to a "short-war" strategy, substituting missiles and nuclear firepower for expensive standing forces. From 1955 to 1961, the Soviet military was reduced by some 2.5 to 3.3 million men, or approximately 40 to 50 percent of its 1955 strength. Predictably, the cutbacks met with the same resistance and grumbling from the professional military that Eisenhower encountered—even from Khrushchev's personal friend and hand-picked Defense Minister, Rodion Malinovsky, who, not unlike Matthew Ridgeway, steadfastly insisted that strong conventional forces were an essential adjunct to nuclear power. The professional misgivings stemmed partly from traditional military conservatism, but undoubtedly also from the queasy knowledge that

Khrushchev's claims for Soviet rocket power were still mostly bluff, at least if the major opponent in an upcoming war was to be the United States.

The powerfully conflicting pressures operating on Khrushchev produced violent swings in his foreign policy. Because he desperately needed a conciliation with the United States to justify his military cutbacks, he pointedly refused to back the Chinese in the confrontation over the Taiwan Straits in 1958, and his response to an American intervention in Lebanon the same year was distinctly muted, even though they directly threatened his new client state, Iraq. (See Chapter 11.) But at the same time, he could not afford to appear pusillanimous: it would take substantial foreign policy victories to squelch the sideline sniping of the Chinese and convince his Marshals that his new strategy was based on a sound understanding of Western intentions and reactions.

West Berlin, that long-festering sore point 110 miles inside the Soviet glacis, finally became the focus of Khrushchev's foreign policy— "Berlin," he remarked with characteristic elegance, "is the testicles of the West. Each time I give them a yank, they holler"—and in late 1958 he provoked a crisis that brought the world to sword's point. Khrushchev announced to the stunned Western governments in November that they had six months to reach an agreement with him on Berlin, or he would sign a separate treaty with East Germany and turn the problem over to them. The East Germans, it was made clear, considered Berlin part of their territory and would immediately block Western access to the city.

The brutal tone of Khrushchev's note was as shocking as its substance. The West was staying in Berlin, he fulminated, only "out of feelings of hatred for Communism"; refusal to comply with his terms would bring matters "to the danger point." There was no pretense of diplomatic niceties. "But only madmen," his note said, "can go to the length of unleashing another world war over the preservation of the privileges of occupiers in West Berlin. If such madmen should appear, there is no doubt that straitjackets could be found for them. . . . [A]ny act of aggression against any member state of the Warsaw Pact will be regarded . . . as an act of aggression against them all and will immediately cause appropriate retaliation."

His note was followed in January 1959 by a draft peace treaty: it called for a Western pullout of troops and weapons from Germany; West German withdrawal from NATO; and absorption of Berlin by East Germany. Once again, Khrushchev's accompanying statements seemed to make clear that if the West did not accept his demands within the six-month deadline, there would be war.

There was no possibility of the West acceding to such demands, and Khrushchev must have known it. Nor, it gradually became clear as the deadline wore on, did Khrushchev have any intention of going to war. Anastas Mikoyan visited the United States as Khrushchev's personal emissary in the spring and dropped broad hints that a bargainer "sometimes names a higher price than he expects to get," and Khrushchev began backing away from his deadline soon after he announced it, although the statements from Moscow on this score were usually contradictory, perhaps intentionally so. But Khrushchev clearly did have hopes that he could resolve the German issue; more than that, the possibility that the West Germans would soon have their hands on nuclear weapons made a German settlement a policy imperative.

Western governments grossly underestimated the cold terror that was struck in the hearts of the Soviet leadership by the specter of a nuclear-armed West Germany. NATO ministers, in 1957, had agreed to a formula for the deployment of nuclear warheads in the NATO command. The decision was taken, after much wrangling, during the worst days of the surprise attack panic that followed the Sputnik launchings and in the wake of Bulganin's crude threat to use nuclear weapons against France and England during the Suez crisis. The missiles were to be distributed among the various national armies, but the nuclear warheads would be kept under American control. Once the decision was made, Konrad Adenauer, the West German chancellor, began to insist that it be implemented. Heading off that possibility seems to have been the key aim of Khrushchev's Berlin proposals. Adam Ulam, one of the most careful students of Khrushchev's foreign policy, speculates that he was setting the stage for a deal: if the United States would guarantee a nuclear-free Germany, he would keep atomic weapons away from the Chinese.

Eisenhower and Dulles responded to Khrushchev's threats with bland flexibility—which was all the more surprising to contemporaries, who still assumed Dulles was making policy on his own. (Dulles, in fact, was hospitalized for the last time in the midst of the crisis and died in May.) For the most part, they simply ignored Khrushchev's Berlin deadlines, but "welcomed" the opportunity to begin talks on reunifying Germany. If the Soviets signed a treaty with the East Germans, the United States would treat them as Soviet "agents." (They would be no such thing, Khrushchev retorted.) The United States would insist on free elections as prerequisite to unification, but perhaps there could be an interim "confederacy" before elections were necessary. Dulles drew attention to the Soviet Union's internal economic problems, opined that the Soviet leaders were being gradually forced to loosen their internal controls, and suggested that dictatorships often appeared harder and more unyielding to the outside world than they really were. At the same time, the Americans began flying heavy transport planes outside of the normal Berlin air lanes to remind the Russians of the 1948 blockade.

Eisenhower reiterated that, of course, he was ready to fight over Berlin but insisted that he didn't expect to. "Destruction is not a good police force," he patiently explained to reporters. "Nuclear war doesn't free anyone." He was convinced Khrushchev was bluffing, but didn't want to back him into a corner, so he refused Army Chief of Staff Maxwell Taylor's request to increase the Berlin garrison, although he sent a small but visible number of reinforcements to Europe, and he proceeded with planned cutbacks in the Army—much to the irritation of the defense intellectuals, who saw Berlin as the ideal laboratory for their "flexible response" theories. What would he do with more soldiers, Eisenhower demanded at a press conference; "Does anyone here have an idea? Would you start a ground war?" Dean Acheson wanted a general mobilization:

Now, did you ever stop to think what a general mobilization would mean in a time of tension?" Eisenhower asked John Scali. "Now, if you are going to keep a general mobilization for a long time in countries—democracies—such as ours, well, there is just one thing you have, and that is a garrison state. General mobilizations . . . would be the most disastrous thing we could do.

Both Khrushchev and Eisenhower suffered from fractious allies. The East German leader, Walter Ulbricht, far outdid Khrushchev in bellicosity, making his most outrageous statements whenever Khrushchev appeared in a mood for compromise—prompting speculation on the existence of a Peking-Pankow (the East German capital) axis. On the NATO side, any hint of reasonableness from Washington panicked Adenauer. (Eisenhower was convinced that Adenauer had no interest in German unification, elections, or anything else that might threaten his uncontested control in West Germany.) At the other extreme, Harold Macmillan, the British prime minister, was most prepared to accede to Khrushchev's demands to avoid fighting; while Charles de Gaulle in France took a consistently hard line on Berlin, but was much more worried about an Anglo-American condominium in Europe.

For a time, Khrushchev kept up his barrage of threats. He met a plaintive attempt at mediation by Macmillan with insults, and he stormed at Averell Harriman in Moscow: "If you send in tanks, they will burn. And make no mistake about it. If you want war you can have it, but remember, it will be your war. Our rockets will fly automatically." "Automatically!" chorused the Soviet officials around the conference table. But he quickly dropped his deadline when the United States agreed—much to the irritation of Adenauer and de Gaulle—to begin negotiations in May. Andrei Gromyko, the Soviet Foreign Minister, quite outclassed his western counterparts in the subsequent talks, but despite the numerous small concessions he won, as the summer of 1959 wore on, Khrushchev's position was becoming untenable. It was clear that the outlines of a general German settlement still eluded him, and that Eisenhower, Adenauer, and de Gaulle, if not Macmillan and the Western press, were increasingly unimpressed by his bluster and threats. He wanted to announce another series of troop cuts, but was under severe pressure from the East Germans and the Chinese and from the military and Suslov at home to show some results from all of the flailing.

After a brief and abortive attempt to divide the French and the Germans—wasn't West Germany their "common enemy," he winked at de Gaulle—Khrushchev apparently decided, "in the greatest gamble of his career," to bet his entire stake on reaching a personal agreement with Eisenhower. Eisenhower was extremely mistrustful of summit diplomacy, but after much pressure from his own staff, reluctantly agreed to invite Khrushchev for a goodwill visit to America in September, to be followed by personal conversations. If nothing else, he conceded, Khrushchev would be able to see first-hand that America was not a society on the verge of collapse.

Khrushchev's trip was a travelling circus. His ebullience and boorishness alternately delighted and horrified Americans, although they responded affectionately to the smiling composure of his wife Nina. Khrushchev visited the Lincoln Memorial, was awed and appalled by New York's financial district, got stuck in an elevator in the Waldorf, leered at the chorus girls during the filming of *Can-Can* in Hollywood, chatted with Shirley MacLaine, flew into a fist-pounding rage when he was prevented from visiting Disneyland because of security problems, insisted that the Soviet people had no desire for private cars or houses, and waved his arms in glee when his favorite farmer, Iowan Roswell Garst, pelted the hovering crush of newsmen with corn silage. At the end of his tour, he and Eisenhower withdrew to Camp David for two days of talks that turned out to be both friendly and positive, to the considerable consternation of hard-liners both East and West. The two men agreed to hold a summit meeting; they concurred on the need for a nuclear test ban treaty and progress on disarmament; Khrushchev dropped all deadlines for a Berlin settlement, and Eisenhower admitted that Berlin was an "abnormal" situation that should be resolved. But there was an important clue to Khrushchev's shaky grip on the leadership when, to Eisenhower's irritation, he insisted that the Berlin agreement not be announced until he had returned to Moscow and brought the Praesidium on board.

As the date for the summit, to be held in Paris, neared, and the "Spirit of Camp David" seized the public imagination, Eisenhower allowed himself to hope that he and Khrushchev might achieve real momentum toward a lasting peace. He had no illusions about Paris; he expected hard bargaining, particularly on Berlin. But he thought Khrushchev wanted to reduce military spending as badly as he did, and knew he was worried about the Chinese. As a gesture of his sincerity, against the objections of his military chiefs, the CIA, his science advisers, the Atomic Energy Commission, and almost all of the cabinet and the congressional leadership, the President reversed long-standing American policy and decided to accept a nuclear test ban agreement without verification, taking the risk that the Soviets would conduct covert underground tests. It was a major concession, but he thought the opportunity for progress at the summit was worth it. Macmillan was delighted, and when de Gaulle and Adenauer came to the White House in March and April 1960 to coordinate summit diplomacy, the omens for solid steps to ease world tensions seemed more propitious than ever before.

The summit never even started, to Eisenhower's deep chagrin and bitter disappointment, and he had to blame himself for the failure. Two weeks before he was scheduled to leave for Paris, on May 2, his assistant Andrew Goodpaster called to tell him that a U-2 spy plane, "the black lady of espionage," as the Soviets had come to call it, was missing and presumed down over Soviet territory. It was an eventuality Eisenhower had feared. Khrushchev had implied at Camp David that his new air defense missiles could hit a U-2. Eisenhower had considered ending the flights in February, but acceded to CIA demands that they be continued, partly, it seems, as a sop to the agency after overruling it on the test ban. He allowed about one flight a month and insisted on approving each flight.

As the summit approached, Eisenhower indicated again that he wanted to end the flights. His main asset at the Paris meeting, he said, would be his reputation for honesty: "If one of these aircraft were lost when we were engaged in apparently sincere deliberations, it could be put on display in Moscow and ruin my effectiveness." Bissell argued that the Soviets might be building new missile sites in a remote area that had never been photographed; Soviet weather patterns made the area accessible to U-2 flights for only a few months each spring. Eisenhower acceded again and authorized a flight on April 9. The flight was a success, trailing a wake of Soviet jet fighters topping out miles below and antiaircraft missiles bursting harmlessly far out of range. It photographed half the new territory and disclosed no missile sites.

Bissell wanted one more flight. Allen Dulles, head of the CIA, Thomas Gates, the Secretary of Defense, and the Joint Chiefs of Staff all insisted it was essential. Significantly perhaps, because of the closely held secrecy of the flights, Eisenhower did not solicit a broader spectrum of opinion, particularly from specialists who might have had a better sense of the Soviet point of view. Eisenhower approved it, and when cloud cover intervened, gave an extension to May 1 as the absolutely last day. On May 1, the clouds lifted for the first time in weeks; Francis Gary Powers, a contract CIA pilot, took off from his U-2 base in Peshawar, Pakistan. American radio posts lost contact with his plane as it neared Sverlodsk, 1,300 miles inside Soviet territory, but almost 1,000 miles south of Plesetsk, its ultimate objective. Although it was little consolation when it was finally revealed, the final irony was that Bissell and Dulles had been right: had Powers made it to Plesetsk, he would have photographed the start of construction on the first four operational Soviet ICBM sites.

The U-2 affair, as Michael Beschloss has convincingly argued, is a striking example of the mutual incomprehension that has bedevilled American-Soviet relations. The Americans, with the partial exception of Eisenhower, viewed the U-2 flights as a standard, if technically virtuosic, exercise in espionage. They assumed the Soviets saw the flights the same way, a perception that was reinforced by the fact that Khrushchev never raised the issue at Camp David. (Eisenhower said he would certainly have stopped the flights before the summit if Khrushchev had asked him to. Khrushchev said it was on the tip of his tongue several times to do so, but it would have been just too embarrassing.)

But the Soviets saw the repeated intrusion on their air space as almost an act of war, a point of view that seems never to have occurred to the Americans. (The Soviets were not likely to appreciate, on the other hand, that their obsessive secrecy almost forced such an action.) The American nuclear arsenal was air-delivered; an American plane overflying Moscow could easily have been carrying a thermonuclear bomb—some U-2s, in fact, could carry bombs. The Americans, as well, did not understand the enormous political risks Khrushchev had taken by travelling to the United States, by embracing Eisenhower as his "friend," by dropping his deadline on Berlin, and by announcing another troop cut in advance of the summit.

A number of minor setbacks on the road to the summit had already raised Soviet suspicions and increased Khrushchev's exposure. At Camp David, the two leaders had set late fall 1959 as the summit date, and Khrushchev had announced as much in Moscow. But Eisenhower's problems with the allies, particularly de Gaulle, had forced a delay. They had also planned that Eisenhower would bring his grandchildren to Russia after the summit; but Eisenhower's son refused, in order to shelter the children from publicity, a change that was read in Moscow as a possible sign of cooling friendship. Less subtly, in the weeks before the summit, Richard Nixon, Christian Herter, the new Secretary of State, and Douglas Dillon, his Undersecretary, in order to keep the Republican right wing on reservation, all made tough anti-Soviet speeches.

In such an atmosphere, the April 9 flight looked like a calculated insult. The Americans "knew they were causing us terrible headaches whenever one of these planes took off on a mission," Khrushchev later complained. In October, in fact, he had publicly asked the West to refrain from actions that would "worsen the atmosphere" and "sow the seeds of suspicion." After Khrushchev had invested so much political capital building up Eisenhower's peaceful intentions, Beschloss speculates, the resumption of the flights was making him a "laughingstock."

At the first news of Powers's downing, however, the administration saw little cause for alarm. A routine statement was issued that a weather observation plane may have strayed and crashed over the Soviet border. Eisenhower had been assured that there was little possibility of a crashed U-2 being recovered: the plane was equipped with a self-destruct mechanism that was timed to go off seventy seconds after the pilot ejected. Even if the plane survived, the Soviets seemed to have every incentive to avoid the embarrassment of revealing the story of years of overflights. When the Soviets made no statement for several days, it was assumed the matter would quietly be allowed to die.

But the Soviet silence only masked the fierce debate in the Kremlin.

Khrushchev finally announced in the Supreme Soviet on May 5 that the Russian air defense system had shot down an American spy plane. He then displayed photographs of a wrecked fuselage that was decidedly *not* that of a U-2. Now sure of itself, Washington began issuing indignant denials, at almost the same time as a Soviet diplomat let slip to Llewelyn Thompson, the American Ambassador to the Soviet Union, that the U-2 pilot was safely in custody. Thompson was sure that the indiscretion was an intentional warning, but his alarmed cable arrived in Washington only minutes after the denials went out.

Khrushchev triumphantly, or so it seemed, sprang his trap. He not only had the real plane, he had the pilot, and the pilot was telling everything. (That was not true: Powers subsequently got little credit for the amount of information he managed to withhold.) As it turned out, Powers had not ejected from the U-2; he had bailed out—either because the contract pilots did not trust the CIA's assurances about the self-destruct delay, or because, as Powers insisted, he had gotten caught in a position in the falling plane that made it impossible to eject.

During the next two weeks, Khrushchev staged a carnival of revelations: Powers's silencer pistol, his poison suicide needle, the U-2 film, and finally a full-blown exhibit in Gorky Park. The Americans responded with a series of confusing and contradictory denials, until Eisenhower—perhaps stung by the repeated allegations that he had lost control of his administration—almost on the eve of the summit accepted full blame for the affair.

Khrushchev seemed genuinely shocked at Eisenhower's open admission of complicity, whether because it violated all known rules of statesmanship or would derail his peace plans was never clear. He told de Gaulle at one point that Eisenhower's admission indicated contempt for the Soviets rather than truthfulness. But he still insisted that the summit would proceed, and the statesmen gathered in Paris on schedule. Eisenhower planned to issue an opening statement that he had stopped the U-2 flights, but Khrushchev, uncharacteristically nervous and pale, his hands shaking and one eyebrow twitching, with Malinovsky glowering at his side, cut him off and launched into a red-faced harangue on American perfidy. De Gaulle interrupted and pointed out that a Soviet satellite invaded French air space eighteen times a day. How did he know it did not have a camera? "As God is my witness," Khrushchev expostulated, "my hands are clean and my heart is pure. You don't think I would do a thing like that?"

When he finally finished, he announced that he would publish his remarks. De Gaulle was shocked: there could be no summit if he published such insults. Then there would be no summit, Khrushchev retorted. "You have inconvenienced us," de Gaulle cut in icily.

Even today, there are mysteries surrounding the U-2 affair. It is still not known, for instance, whether Powers was actually shot down by a Soviet missile, or whether his engine "flamed out" in the oxygen-poor upper atmosphere—as U-2 engines were sometimes prone to do—perhaps bringing the plane within reach of Soviet batteries. Nor is it clear why Khrushchev brought everyone to Paris only to break up the meeting. One theory is that he came to the summit intending to go through with it, but was overruled in his absence by the Praesidium, which might account for his unusually agitated demeanor. Or perhaps he really thought he could exact a sufficiently abject apology from Eisenhower that would satisfy his colleagues in the Kremlin.

A successful summit in Paris, of course, would not have ended the friction between the United States and the Soviet Union. The agreements contemplated there were quite modest ones. Eisenhower, and apparently Khrushchev, were looking, not for world peace, but for a way to reduce the pressures building so inexorably in both countries for an upward surge in the intensity of the military competition. The aborted summit had the opposite effect. The circumstances of the breakup were so humiliating, and Khrushchev's subsequent tirades, particularly at the United Nations in the fall—the occasion of the famous shoe-pounding exercise—so unrestrained, that the atmosphere turned markedly more hostile.

Most important, Eisenhower lost control of the arms issue. The nuclear test ban was dead. All of the presidential candidates, including, to his annoyance, Richard Nixon, were demanding major increases in arms spending. The press was increasingly disrespectful: where did he get the right not to spend money Congress appropriated for arms? Why was the Strategic Air Command not on full alert to protect against a Soviet surprise attack? How could he turn down the Air Force's pet B-70 bomber? Why did he put a balanced budget ahead of national security? Eisenhower refused to spend more money on a space race, "a multibillion-dollar project of no immediate value." He would not fund a massive fallout shelter program that Nelson Rockefeller, Henry Luce, and all of his generals were demanding. He was irritated by the big defense contractors' public relations programs: "Almost every magazine you pick up has an advertisement of a Titan missile or an Atlas or what have you . . . [as if] the only thing this country is engaged in is weaponry and missiles." He was infuriated when Nixon and Rockefeller issued a joint statement that "there must be no price ceiling on America's security." Above all, he detested John Kennedy, the most militaristic candidate of them all, and was outraged by the Democratic "missile gap" campaign slogan.

Walter McDougall has placed Eisenhower's arms policies in the broader context of his distrust of the powerful new impulse toward a technocratic state that was building in the land, pressed forward, not only by the defense intellectuals but by the precocious and brilliant young people in almost every field. Toward the end of his administration, Eisenhower warned his cabinet that:

The question is whether free government can continue to exist in the world, in view of the demands made by government and peoples on free economies. . . .

We have got to meet the [Soviet threat] by keeping our economy absolutely healthy. . . . We are the world's banker. If our money goes bad, the whole free world's position will collapse or be badly shaken.

We must get the Federal Government out of every unnecessary activity. We can refuse to do things too rapidly. Humanity has existed for a long time. Suddenly, we seem to have an hysterical approach, in health and welfare programs, in grants to the states, in space research. We want to cure every ill in two years, in five years, by putting in a lot money. To my mind, this is the wrong attack.

In phrases "sagging with future memories," Eisenhower repeatedly warned that "public policy could itself become the captive of a scientific-technological elite." But even Eisenhower could not have envisioned what was to ensue: the failure in Vietnam; the Great Society's experiments in social engineering; runaway world inflation; and, perhaps most damaging in the long term, the revolt, in the wake of such debacles, of so many of society's brightest young people against technology, authority, and reason itself. Eisenhower, of course, had been in both "the rearguard and vanguard" of the change. Although he had fought, largely successfully, to moderate the pace of defense spending, he had supervised the flowering of military technology that was to produce the sudden spurt of American weapons deployment that, for a time at least, would leave the Soviets gasping across a seemingly hopeless weapons "gap" of their own. And, accurate as Eisenhower's premonitions of disaster may have been, he would have been the first to admit that he did not know what to do about it. He placed such uncharacteristic hopes on an agreement with Khrushchev because he feared it might be a last chance to avoid a headlong rush to catastrophe.

Eisenhower's Farewell Address, during his last week in office, was full of foreboding. He warned of the dangers of communism, but pleaded for "the need to maintain balance . . . between the cost [of weapons] and the hoped-for advantage." Because of the Cold War, "we have been compelled to create a permanent armaments industry of vast proportions."

This conjunction of an immense military establishment and a large arms industry is new in the American experience. The total influence—economic, political, even spiritual—is felt in every city, every statehouse, every office of the federal government. . . . In the councils of government, we must guard against the acquisition of unwarranted influence, whether sought of unsought, by the military-industrial complex. The potential for the disastrous rise of misplaced power exists and will persist . . . [and could] endanger our liberties and democratic processes. We should take nothing for granted.

Eisenhower's speech was almost universally acclaimed. His warning on the military-industrial complex was treated as a pearl of wisdom, the distillation of an aging statesman's long experience—a new insight for the press and public to ponder. It was none of those things. It was the same theme he had been hammering at for eight years. The praise his speech received was the measure of his failure. He had not been heeded, his message had not been heard, and America was about to launch a new and vastly more dangerous cycle in the military competition with the Soviet Union.

# PART III

AMERICA AT THE CREST

# CHAPTER 9

# The Summons of the Trumpet

On the steps of the Alte Hofburg, an ugly square building that was the official residence of the president of Austria, on a rainy morning in Vienna in June 1961, surrounded by Austrian police with muzzled Alsatian guard dogs, John Kennedy and Nikita Khrushchev shook hands and posed for photographs in their only meeting of Kennedy's short presidency. After one handshake, Khrushchev started to proceed up the steps, but Kennedy motioned that the photographers probably wanted more pictures, and Khrushchev obliged with a wide grin. As the photographers jockeyed for camera angles a second time, Kennedy stepped back and "bluntly surveyed the Russian from head to toe," as if to assure himself that he could take the Soviet leader's measure.

He didn't. For seventeen hours of talks, lunches, and tête-à-tête walks in the Alte Hofburg gardens, Khrushchev alternately bullied, harangued, and needled the young President, even dispensing lectures on the meaning of the American Revolution. Kennedy was "visibly shaken." As a sympathetic reporter who travelled home from the summit with the President put it: "As hour after hour and point after point passed, Kennedy began to get a great unsettled feeling. Never before when he had sat down to talk with men who disagreed with him had he found, when human suffering or great tragedy might result from the difference, that they would be totally unbending." George Kennan, who counted himself among Kennedy's admirers, was blunter when he reviewed the transcripts of the meetings: "I think [the Russians] thought this is a tongue-tied young man who's not foreceful and who doesn't have ideas of his own. They thought they could get away with something. He was, I thought, strangely tongue-tied in this interview with Khrushchev, and numbers of these typical, characteristic Communist exaggerations and false accusations were simply let to pass . . . instead of being replied to, being rebutted."

Kennedy's discomfiture was not lost on foreign observers. Bruno Kreisky, the Austrian prime minister, remarked that "the President was very gloomy at the airport. He seemed upset and his face had changed. Obviously the meeting did not go well for him." Khrushchev himself adopted a smugly patronizing tone in his memoirs. "I couldn't resist using a little bit of irony to mock what [Kennedy] was suggesting . . . [but] I hadn't meant to upset him." He adds, doubtless with more sincerity, and with the wisdom of a decade's hindsight:

I felt doubly sorry because . . . [the meeting] had aggravated the Cold War. This worried me. If we were thrown back into the Cold War, we would be the ones who would have to pay for it. The Americans would start spending more money on weapons, forcing us to do the same, and . . . impoverish our budget, reduce our economic potential, and lower the standard of living of our people. We knew the pattern only too well from our past experience.

The setback in the face-to-face confrontation in Vienna, so soon after the tragi-farcical Bay of Pigs invasion in April, was the more galling since Kennedy had made regaining the initiative in the Cold War the major issue of his presidential campaign. Indeed, it was arguably his sole theme, as he hammered away at the "missile gap" and the "space gap"; at Eisenhower's apparent complacency in the face of Soviet threats to Berlin, to the Caribbean, and in Southeast Asia; at the inability of the country to produce the scientists and engineers needed to keep up with the Russians; at the steady loss of ground in the economic competition with the Soviet Union and the loss of prestige in the uncommitted nations of the world; at a country grown "soft" in its devotion to private wealth and private pleasures in a hard world where to be unready was to die.

As a Boston Irish Catholic, Kennedy was a strong anti-Communist by disposition, training, and family tradition. But his insistence on the primacy of the competition with the Soviet Union sprang from imperatives imposed from within his own administration and campaign rather than from a set of abstract anti-Communist convictions. Kennedy, in fact, was an ideologue. His ideology, however, was the apolitical creed of the pragmatic technocrats who drew their inspiration from the writings of John Dewey. They were the men who provided the intellectual energy behind the Progressive reform movements in the first thirty years of the century and enjoyed a brief place in the sun during the early days of Franklin Roosevelt's New Deal, and who were flocking from academia, law firms, investment banks, and the media to join Kennedy's New Frontier, brimming with confidence, enthusiasm, and ideas.

The pragmatists' central theme, and the underlying message of Kennedy's entire campaign, was that scientists, engineers, and economists had discovered the answers to most of the problems that bedevilled the country. Eisenhower's sin had been to ignore their achievements, to allow instead the uninformed gropings of atomized decision makers—individual businesses, or school boards, or cities and towns—to dictate the flow of events. In Kennedy's view, Eisenhower failed as a leader because he failed to understand that the President is "the vital center in our whole scheme of government," that it is the President's responsibility to spur the country on by instilling a spirit of discipline, organization, and sacrifice. One of Kennedy's advisers remarked incredulously that Eisenhower even fostered "disagreement as to whether the nation faced a major crisis. In fact, the President used a part of his influence to deflate the nation's sense of urgency . . ." Kennedy, by contrast, wanted to infuse the country with energy and purpose; to recapture a spirit of risk and adventure; to organize some great national endeavor. That was the attraction of the space program: that it would require a total national effort—"the personal pledge," in Kennedy's words, of "every scientist, every engineer, every technician, contractor and civil servant."

But Kennedy's narrow electoral mandate—the election was one of the closest in history—cast doubt on whether the country shared his vision. Why should anyone be willing to "pay any price, bear any burden, meet any hardship"? Did people really believe, as Arthur Schlesinger insisted, that they were in danger of drifting into "oblivion" unless the President exercised "national leadership"? Kennedy's "Presidential problem," as Theodore H. White wrote shortly after the election, was "lack of crisis." And Richard Rovere observed, "President Kennedy is attempting to meet a crisis whose existence he and his associates are almost alone in perceiving."

It was not for lack of insisting. In the weeks before his meeting with Khrushchev, Kennedy hammered at the theme in tones as strident as any that issued from the blackest moods of John Foster Dulles:

Each day the crises multiply. . . . the tide of events is running out and time is not our friend. . . . The tide is unfavorable. The news will get worse before it gets better.

Our way of life is under attack. Those who make themselves our enemy are advancing around the globe. The survival of our friends is in danger.

. . . we face a relentless struggle in every corner of the globe that goes far beyond the clash of arms or even nuclear armaments. . . . [S]ubversion, infiltration, and a host of other tactics steadily advance, picking off vulnerable areas one by one.

Power is the hallmark of this offensive—power and discipline and deceit . . . We dare not fail to see the insidious nature of this new and deeper struggle.

. . . The complacent, the self-indulgent, the soft societies are about to be swept away with the debris of history. Only the strong, only the industrious, only the determined, only the courageous, only the visionary who determine the real nature of the struggle can possibly survive. . . . I am . . . convinced that history will record the fact that the bitter struggle reached a climax in the late 1950s and early 1960s. Let me then make clear as the President of the United States that I am determined upon our system's survival and success, regardless of the cost and regardless of the peril!

The first two years of the new administration brought two crises, over Berlin and Cuba, that were real enough for anyone's appetite. But in their first months in office, Kennedy and his men displayed a positive penchant for crisis-conjuring in almost every foreign arena. Theodore Sorenson includes among his list of early "shattering crises" such less-than-earth-shaking events as the resignation of the president of Brazil, unrest in the Dominican Republic, new Soviet demands at the Geneva arms control talks, fighting between France and Tunisia, and optimistic statements by the Communist forces in Laos. The continued insistence on crises stemmed partly from the fact that Kennedy enjoyed them; they showed him at his best, and he knew it. As a close journalistic observer wrote after the Berlin crisis: "As the crisis grew, Kennedy's own sense seemed sharper. He was brusque, more to the point. He enjoyed finding solutions to problems as they came along and he showed more confidence in himself and his conclusions."

The preoccupation with crisis reinforced the Kennedy strain of *machismo*, made more dangerous by the new President's insecurity in his sudden role as leader of the Western world. Kennedy sometimes seemed to boast about his readiness to fight a nuclear war: he told a reporter, "If Khrushchev wants to rub my nose in the dirt, it's all over." Or as an admiring Sorenson put it, while Kennedy had "no appetite for nuclear war, it was a responsibility he was coolly prepared to meet."

On the new administration's crisis radar the rotund figure of Nikita

Khrushchev showed up as a giant blip glowing on all horizons. If Kennedy welcomed crises, Khrushchev revelled in them. His entire career as Party Chairman was a lurching from one extravaganza to another—the virgin lands program, the "secret speech," Sputnik, the carnival visit to America, his exhibitions at the United Nations, the U-2 affair, his exaggerated claims of missile prowess, the grossly overreaching Five-Year plans, the war of vituperation with China, the posturing and threats to Western Europe. Indeed, it was undoubtedly his "adventurism," as the Chinese phrased it, that led to his final downfall a year after Kennedy's death. Khrushchev's swaggering invective combined with Kennedy's *machismo* was a volatile and almost literally lethal brew. For the first twenty months of Kennedy's administration, the two countries careened jaggedly from confrontation to confrontation until both men, ashen-faced and sobered by the near-catastrophe of the Cuban missile crisis, made a tacit agreement to lower their rhetoric and take a safe step back from the brink.

The chain of confrontation began two weeks before Kennedy's inauguration with Khrushchev's famous announcement of support for "wars of national liberation."* The two parties then jostled at second hand in the Congo, when that hapless country descended into near-chaos following a hasty grant of independence in the summer of 1960. Kennedy, continuing Eisenhower's policy, strongly backed a United Nations force sent to restore order and prevent a breakup of the country, and incidentally to block Soviet arms shipments to Patrice Lumumba's leftist regime. Somewhat surprisingly, the Afro-Asian bloc voted down a Soviet protest in the United Nations—keeping their jury-rigged nations from flying apart was more important than tweaking the colonialists—and the Soviet initiative fizzled with Lumumba's assassination in early 1961.

In April, America's allies were appalled to see the new administration launch an invasion of Cuba and, worse, make a thorough botch of it. B-26s, flying from CIA bases in Central America, made bombing runs over Cuba on the 15th—with the United States denying involvement, much to the subsequent embarrassment of Adlai Stevenson, who in honest ignorance had been defending America's innocence at the United Nations—and a full-scale invasion was launched on the 17th. Castro incredibly left his small air force "sitting ducks . . . lined up in

*Kennedy, and most commentators, took Khrushchev's declaration as a direct challenge, tantamount to a declaration of war in the Third World. In all likelihood, Khrushchev's intended audience was the Chinese, who were threatening to supplant the Soviets as leaders of the Communist movement in Africa and Asia. His rather ambiguous statement was probably a bid to recover his revolutionary stature on the cheap.

a neat row" on an airfield outside Havana, but Kennedy, for reasons that have never been satisfactorily explained, called off a second air strike at the last moment. He reversed himself the next day, much too late to save the little band of invaders being hunted down in noxious coastal swamps by Castro's far superior army and small fleet of jet trainers, firing 20mm. cannon the CIA didn't know they had.

Kennedy shouldered full responsibility for the failure, and his popularity rating soared to an astonishing 80 percent at home; but the international repercussions were serious. The episode exposed the inexperience at every level of the new government and made Kennedy appear reckless and indecisive at the same time. The entire scheme was foredoomed from the start. It had long been telegraphed in the newspapers, and Castro had systematically rounded up every possible guerrilla sympathizer throughout the spring. As Dean Acheson told the President just before the invasion, you didn't need "Price Waterhouse to discover that 1,500 Cubans weren't as good as 25,000 Cubans." In fairness, the operation had been planned during the Eisenhower administration, and with the President's knowledge—although it seems inconceivable that he would have allowed it go forward as it did—and was implemented by Dulles and Bissell, both of whom, after having survived in office after the U-2 affair, resigned over this latest fiasco. But neither Kennedy nor any of his advisers had the self-confidence to speak out against the invasion, and Kennedy's last-minute waffling on the second air strike was a death warrant for the raiders.

The most sinister consequence of the debacle was that Khrushchev probably decided he could bully Kennedy. He had sent a personal warning couched in the strongest terms just before Kennedy called off the air strike. "It is not yet too late," wrote Khrushchev, "to prevent what may be irreparable. The U.S. government can still prevent the flames of war that have been lit by the interventionists in Cuba from growing into a conflagration that it will be impossible to extinguish. . . . As for the Soviet Union, let there be no misunderstanding of our position: We will give the Cuban people and their government every assistance necessary to repulse the armed attack on Cuba."

As Herbert Dinerstein has pointed out, Khrushchev ran a real risk in sending such a note. All previous Soviet rocket-rattling, over Suez and the Taiwan Straits for instance, came after the crises were well over and there was no practical danger of Soviet entanglement. But the Cuban warning was sent when it was still quite possible that the Americans would invade the island, and Khrushchev would have been hard-pressed to back up his threats. The Soviet note, in fact, had little influence on Kennedy's actions; but to an expansive personality like Khrushchev's, it almost certainly would have appeared to have done so.

Another confrontation was brewing in Asia almost simultaneously with the Cuban invasion. Kennedy held a full-dress press conference in late March, complete with pointer and maps, to inform the public about the "grave problems" in Laos, and implicitly threatened intervention— "No one should doubt our resolution." Eisenhower had strongly warned Kennedy that holding Laos was the key to all of Southeast Asia,* and the Western position was deteriorating rapidly. Kennedy had been pushing for a neutralist solution while supporting a right-wing military general. But Khrushchev weighed in with substantial military assistance to the leftist forces, and the neutralists joined forces with the leftists. Extremely cautious in the aftermath of the Bay of Pigs, the Joint Chiefs advised Kennedy that intervention in land-locked Laos was impractical.

The administration was saved further embarrassment in May when the Vietnamese—apparently anxious not to draw the Americans into the Indochinese peninsula—pressured the left coalition to accept a compromise that saved face all around. Kennedy later said, "Thank God the Bay of Pigs happened when it did. Otherwise we'd be in Laos by now and that would be a hundred times worse." The compromise in Laos was the kind of messy resolution that Eisenhower usually regarded as a victory—the United States had not backed down, but there had been no war—yet Kennedy felt bested by Khrushchev once again. It was primarily in reaction to the setback in Laos that he authorized the first dispatch of a Special Forces Group to Vietnam a few weeks later.

June brought the summit meeting in Vienna. Khrushchev insisted on devoting the second day of meetings to Berlin, and at the close of the sessions handed Kennedy an *aide-mémoire* that effectively announced another crisis. Just as in 1958, Khrushchev wanted Western recognition of the East German regime and its right to rule in Berlin with, he assured Kennedy, appropriate guarantees for Western access. Otherwise, at year-end he would hand the problem over to the East Germans, who made no secret of their intent to seal Berlin off from the

*There is a marked contrast between Eisenhower the elder statesman and Eisenhower the President. Perhaps the outstanding hallmark of his administration was his judiciousness in the use of force; once out of office, however, his advice to both Kennedy and Johnson was consistently hawkish in the extreme. Its effects were usually mischievous, the more so since Kennedy had made such a campaign issue out of Eisenhower's fumblings and hated to appear less decisive and forceful than the old general.

West. In typical Khrushchevian fashion, the deadline was announced orally to leave maximum room for maneuver; no date appeared in the *aide-mémoire* itself. On narrow legalities, Khrushchev's case was not unreasonable—he had, after all, already recognized West Germany. But Stalin's attempt to starve out the Berliners was still too fresh in memory, and the police state Walter Ulbricht was building in East Germany too horrific, for the West to countenance the ultimatum.

Before the Americans could reply to the Russian note, Khrushchev published it in *Pravda,* then, bemedalled and decked out in a military uniform, raised the temperature with a strong speech on June 21, the anniversary of Hitler's invasion of Russia: "if you really threaten us with war, we do not fear such a threat; if you unleash a war, this will mean suicide for you." On July 8, he announced a suspension of Soviet military cutbacks and a one-third increase in the defense budget, citing the dangers of Kennedy's rapid arms buildup—"This is how Western powers are replying to the Soviet Union's unilateral reduction of armed forces and military expenditures."

Kennedy trumped him with a blistering speech of his own two weeks later: "I hear it said that West Berlin is militarily untenable. And so was Bastogne. And so, in fact, was Stalingrad. Any dangerous spot is tenable if men—brave men—will make it so. . . . We do not want to fight—but we have fought before." The President asked for a special appropriation of $3.3 billion to increase the Army by 125,000 men, call up the reserves, fund massive procurement of conventional weapons, and, scariest of all, provide $207 million for civil defense. The emerging American decision to defend Berlin with conventional force, in keeping with the new RAND- inspired "flexible response" doctrine, unnerved the Europeans—the West German Foreign Minister said a conventional response "would give me holy terrors"—while the civil defense request touched off a bout of midsummer lunacy in the United States. Businesses sprang up overnight selling survival kits, fallout suits, ration packs, sandbags, periscopes, and other expensive paraphernalia. *Life* magazine published detailed plans for do-it-yourself blast protection, complete with an introductory letter from the President himself. The headline ran: "You Could Be Among the 97% Who Survive If You Follow the Advice in These Pages." Weapon sales boomed, and philosophers and clergymen debated the ethics of shooting the improvident neighbor pounding at the fallout shelter door.

The rhetoric on both sides was almost identical. Dean Acheson had been called in by Kennedy to head a Berlin task force and summarized the problem, in Schlesinger's words: "West Berlin was not a problem but a pretext. Khrushchev's *demarche* had nothing to do with Berlin, Germany, or Europe. His object . . . was not to rectify a local situation, but to test the general American will to resist; his hope was that by making us back down on a sacred commitment, he could shatter our world power and influence. This was a simple conflict of wills." Khrushchev used almost the same words, albeit somewhat more colorfully:

The question of access to West Berlin is for them . . . only a pretext. . . . [The capitalists] would in no time broaden the range of their demands. They would demand the abolition of the socialist system in the German Democratic Republic . . . undertake to wrest from Poland and Czechslovakia the lands that were restored to them . . . [and demand] that the socialist system be abolished in all the countries of the socialist camp. They would like that even now! . . . The imperialists want to test our firmness; they want to do away with our socialist achievements. Your arms are too short, Messrs. Imperialists!

Kennedy's response to the Berlin provocation differed from Eisenhower's mostly in its stridency. Eisenhower downplayed the possibility of war, while insisting he was willing to fight if necessary. Kennedy felt compelled to trumpet his readiness, partly because Khrushchev seemed so obviously to doubt it, and partly to underscore the contrast between a new "activist" presidency and the torpor of the Eisenhower years. The reserve callups and conventional force budget increases were purely symbolic demonstrations of resolve, just as Khrushchev's military budget increase was. (Eisenhower had also responded to the earlier Berlin crisis by increasing European force levels, although in smaller amounts and with relatively little publicity.) The force increases Kennedy asked for were not, in the main, designated for Germany, and none would have arrived in time to be of much help. The increases had been planned anyway for the next budget year, but Kennedy seized upon the crisis to accelerate his funding request.

Posturings aside, the Soviet-American positions were not far apart. Khrushchev and Ulbricht's problem was to plug the refugee leak in Berlin before the East German state melted away before their eyes. More than 2.5 million East Germans had defected to the West through Berlin since 1949—some 15 percent of the entire population and an even greater share of its most productive and ambitious people; 103,000 people defected in the first half of 1961, another 30,000 during the month of July, and 20,000 in the first twelve days of August. The West, on the other hand, save for ceremonial rhetoric, had long since adopted a policy of "mild two-Germanyism," in the words of one scholar. Adenauer, in particular, had no interest in unification negotiations, fearing that a combined East-West Socialist Party could threaten the security of his tenure as chancellor. The West wanted only minimum guarantees of their links to West Berlin, which Khrushchev in fact consistently reiterated that he was quite prepared to give.

Khrushchev cut the Gordian knot on August 13. Pankow simply announced that West Berliners were thenceforth banned from East Berlin, and that East Berliners could visit West Berlin only with "special permission." The new rules explicitly exempted non-Germans, carefully skirting the principle of Western access. East German soldiers, "scruffy, but well-armed"—although it was later revealed that they had no ammunition—began erecting barbed wire at the major crossing points; the actual Wall was constructed throughout the fall. There were several days of anxious waiting, while Western embassies sat gape-jawed. Finally, Dean Rusk, the new Secretary of State, announced lamely that the United States would make "vigorous protest through appropriate channels."

Prodded by an angry Willy Brandt, West Berlin's mayor, Kennedy produced a flurry of symbolism. Lyndon Johnson was dispatched on a fact-finding tour; troop reinforcements were rushed to Germany; an American battle group travelled from the Federal Republic to West Berlin—it was unmolested, as Khrushchev had indicated it would be, although Robert Kennedy *remembered* that "we felt war was very possible then"; and later Lucius Clay was brought out of retirement and sent to command the American garrison. Mikoyan gloated in Geneva: "You may not like the German Democratic Republic . . . but you will have to ask them for a pass if you want to enter Berlin. Without it you cannot get through. No one can fight over this. Only a lunatic can fight over this."

There were still some anxious moments. In September, Ulbricht, apparently acting on his own while Khrushchev was tied up with his Party Congress, refused passage to American diplomats. The Americans returned with a small tank force. Soviet tanks lined up on the other side of the crossing point, and there was an uncomfortable standoff. In his memoirs, Khrushchev says he assured his colleagues that if the Soviet tanks withdrew, the American tanks would be gone in twenty minutes—which is what happened, and the diplomats were allowed to proceed. At his Party Congress in October, Khrushchev dropped his Berlin deadline by simply announcing that there had never been one. Kennedy in turn pressured de Gaulle and Adenauer to accept negotiations, which, at least as far as the original Vienna *aide-mémoire* was concerned, were all Khrushchev had asked for. Adenauer scotched the negotiations the following spring, however, and the entire matter was quietly allowed to drop.

Just as the Berlin crisis eased, Khrushchev announced a massive new series of nuclear tests, breaking the moratorium he and Eisenhower had agreed to in Geneva. The tests, forty in all, had clearly been planned over an extended period, although Khrushchev linked them to American aggressiveness in Europe. The Americans, of course, announced a test series of their own, but a much smaller one. The Soviet weapons tests were enormous, with the biggest in excess of 50 megatons, frequently at high altitudes, and delivered huge amounts of fallout all over the world. Khrushchev's chortling about even bigger weapons in the Soviet arsenal was ghoulish.

Throughout the first part of 1962, the public confrontation was more muted, although Kennedy issued a warning on Laos in the spring and began the steady expansion of the American commitment to Vietnam. Khrushchev's initiation of a personal correspondence with Kennedy, however, seemed a promising sign. Few people noted a series of broad hints in early 1962, both in official Soviet statements and in several pointed claims by Fidel Castro, that there would shortly be a substantive change in the security of Cuba from an American invasion.

The first American press reports of unusual military shipments from the Soviet Union to Cuba came in late August 1962. Exile groups reported that at least 5,000 Soviet and East European technicians had arrived with shiploads of heavy equipment. There were reports of mysterious 40-foot-long crates being unloaded at night under the strictest security precautions. The administration made anxious inquiries, and—relying on assurances by Ambassador Anatoly Dobrynin* and a private communication by Khrushchev that he would not complicate Kennedy's midterm election problems, stated that there was no evidence of "significant offensive capability" on the island in either Soviet or Cuban hands. Kennedy warned, however, that "the gravest issues would arise" if Cuba acquired the ability "to export its aggressive purposes by force or threat of force."

Over the next six weeks, there was an astounding breakdown in

---

*The Kennedys later accused Dobrynin of having lied, but admitted the possibility that, like Stevenson the year before, he had not been kept informed by his government. Dobrynin's reassurances, given to Robert Kennedy, actually appear to be carefully drawn and technically true, although designed to mislead. He said, in effect, that the Soviets did not propose to place missiles in the hands of a third party. Since the missiles were intended at all times to remain under Soviet control, this was a true statement.

American intelligence. The regular schedule of U-2 flights over Cuba was inexplicably suspended, and the CIA steadfastly ignored the mounting alarms being sounded by the Cuban exile groups. In one instance, an enterprising peasant even reported the precise measurements of a Soviet intermediate-range missile being trundled along on a flatbed truck to the launching sites under construction near the town of San Cristobal. The intelligence agencies were used to false alarms from the exile groups and habitually discounted their reports; but in 1962 they were particularly wary of beating drums about a Soviet missile threat. They had been humiliated by the recent exposure of their poor performance during the "missile gap" hysteria, and demoralized by the fiasco at the Bay of Pigs. Since Soviet nuclear missiles had never previously been placed on foreign soil, not even in the East European satellites, the notion that Khrushchev would risk them with so flamboyant and mercurial an ally as Castro seemed utterly fantastic.

The crisis developed swiftly in mid-October. Prodded by a series of detailed revelations about the Cuban buildup by Senator Kenneth Keating (who never revealed the source of his information), U-2 overflights were resumed and returned unmistakable evidence that the Soviets were building launching sites for ground-to-ground nuclear missiles with a range sufficient to mount an attack over most of the American mainland. There was a heated, and at times frantic, internal debate at the White House. Dean Acheson plumped hard for an immediate pre-emptive strike at the missile sites. Robert McNamara, missing the political implications of missile emplacements so close to America's shores, reported that they were of negligible strategic significance. Dean Rusk appears to have argued on all sides of almost every issue. The Joint Chiefs reported cautiously that a so-called surgical strike, at that point the favored option, was unrealistic. A major coordinated air operation would be required to overcome the island's rapidly elaborating air defenses, and substantial Soviet casualties would be unavoidable. Even then, the chiefs would hazard only a 90 percent assurance that they could eliminate the possibility of a retaliatory nuclear strike against the mainland.

The Cuban missile crisis was Kennedy's finest hour. Probably for the first time, he displayed the "cool precision" that his publicists had been promising since the early days of the campaign. Quibbles aside,* he

*There were frequent quibbles: From the left: the risks of Kennedy's brinkmanship were not justified by the stakes; the Turkish missiles should have been quickly volunteered as a trade; Khrushchev had as much right to place missiles in friendly countries as America did. From the right: the invasion option was too readily foresworn; the Turkish missiles were in fact traded in a secret protocol. (The Turkish missiles were removed not

turned the clamor of advice from his frayed and exhausted advisers into a careful course of firmness and restraint. The initial naval "quarantine"—the word was chosen because the more accurate "blockade" was legally an act of war—shifted the onus of aggressive action to the Soviet Union. When construction of the missile sites continued despite the blockade, the United States made unmistakable preparations for a conventional air strike. There was a massive buildup of fighter aircraft and attack bombers in Florida, Marines were transferred from both coasts, substantial units of an armored division were moved to an invasion jumping-off point, and SAC units around the world were put on alert.

Just as the air strike began to appear inevitable, Kennedy received a private letter from Khrushchev that proposed, in a rambling, emotional way, to withdraw the missiles if Kennedy lifted the blockade and promised not to invade Cuba. Khrushchev's letter was followed almost immediately by a second communication, this time from the Soviet government, that offered to withdraw the missiles only in exchange for an equivalent American withdrawal of missiles from Turkey. Ominously, the second letter arrived on the same day as a U-2 plane was shot down over Cuba after a long period of unmolested reconnaissance flights, raising fears that warhawks in the Praesidium had seized control of the bargaining. The administration responded with its "Trollope ploy"—Trollope's lovelorn heroines always interpreted suitors' letters in the light most conducive to marriage. The proposal in the first letter was accepted, while the second was simply ignored, and there was no riposte to the U-2 downing.

A tense weekend followed: Robert Kennedy estimated the invasion would begin on Tuesday at the latest. On Monday, Khrushchev, back in control if he had ever lost the initiative to the Praesidium, responded positively. The missiles would go home. The crisis was over. It was the closest America and the Soviet Union had ever come to an actual nuclear war. For once, the newspaper cliche that the entire world breathed a sigh of relief was not an exaggeration.

Both Khrushchev and Kennedy softened their rhetoric markedly

long afterward, but the missiles were obsolete and the action had been planned before the crisis. It is likely that their retirement was delayed by the crisis, so as not to create the appearance of a bargain.) The criticisms from the right were actually closer to the mark; the intuition that Kennedy would have made further concessions before launching an air attack was recently confirmed by Dean Rusk. Kennedy was prepared to make the Turkish missiles part of an explicit deal, which presumably would have allowed Khrushchev to claim a major victory—with worrisome implications, to say the least, for his subsequent behavior. Khrushchev caved, however, before Kennedy made the offer. Robert Kennedy had previously informed the Soviets that the Turkish missiles were slated for removal, but forbade them to announce it, or treat it, as part of a deal.

after the Cuban missile crisis. Parading a willingness to fight a nuclear war was one thing; actually looking into the abyss was quite another. American-Soviet relations immediately after the crisis were as warm as in the period following Khrushchev's Camp David meetings with Eisenhower. Kennedy's American University speech in June virtually disavowed the rhetoric that had propelled him to office. There was none of the "half-slave, half-free" divisions of the world or the calls to a climactic confrontation with communism. Instead, he cautioned Americans against "only a distorted or desperate view of the other side." In an obvious reference to Cuba, he warned that "nuclear powers must avoid those confrontations which bring an adversary to a choice of either a humiliating retreat or a nuclear war," and concluded: "In short, both the United States and its allies, and the Soviet Union and its allies, have a mutually deep interest in a just and genuine peace and in halting the arms race. Agreements to this end are in the interests of the Soviet Union as well as ours—and even the most hostile nations can be relied upon to accept and keep those treaty obligations, which are in their own interest."

Khrushchev called it the best speech by an American President since Roosevelt. It was published in full in the Soviet Union, and shortly thereafter the Soviets, for the first time in fifteen years, stopped all jamming of Western radio broadcasts.

The most immediate outcome of the sudden change in tone was the Limited Nuclear Test Ban Treaty signed two months later, after a remarkably short negotiation. The treaty finessed the troublesome issue of on-site inspections by simply banning all tests in the atmosphere, in space, or underwater, and underground tests large enough to generate extraterritorial radioactive debris—all tests were banned, that is, that could be monitored from outside national borders. It was to be the only legacy, albeit an important one, of the brief thaw. The burst of good feeling did not outlive the two mens' tenure. Kennedy was killed six weeks after the Senate ratified the test ban treaty, and Khrushchev was deposed a year later. By that time, the war in Vietnam, and the felt Soviet need to improve its military position vis-à-vis the United States, were already beginning to dominate relations.

The military and diplomatic lessons drawn from the Berlin and Cuban confrontations were, as often as not, the wrong ones. Kennedy set a pattern of the command-post President that was followed by almost all subsequent administrations. The defense intellectuals' doctrine had stressed the necessity for centralized management of military forces. They were, of course, undeniably right that the decision to use nuclear weapons must be reserved at the highest levels. But, since Kennedy, presidents and defense secretaries have almost never resisted the temptation to exert microscopic tactical control over troops in the field. At one point during the Berlin crisis, Kennedy maintained direct contact with a young lieutenant probing a highway blockade with a convoy of trucks, giving him detailed instructions on what to say and do. (The lieutenant finally stopped reporting in and made it through to Berlin on his own, to much consternation at the White House.) Control during the Cuban confrontation was even tighter, or at least was thought to be. Apparently unknown to anyone in the White House, American submarine commanders, acting under a broad interpretation of their orders, were hunting down and forcing to the surface Soviet missile submarines operating off both American coasts, disabling a key element in the current Soviet nuclear deterrent "almost as completely as if they had been sunk." In other words, as John Steinbruner concludes: "what might have been to the Soviet Union one of the most compelling U.S. military actions largely escaped [the White House Executive Committee's] attention. One is reminded of Napoleon making intricate maneuvers on the battlefield at Jena unaware of the main battle occurring at Auerstadt."

Superficially as well, both Berlin and Cuba seemed to vindicate the administration's new principle of "flexible response," probably the central departure from the old Eisenhower "massive retaliation" strategy. In fact, it did nothing of the kind, as McNamara himself later quietly acknowledged—although it was to be some years before he publicly backed away from his earlier doctrines. Just as in 1958, there was no question that if Soviet divisions in East Germany decided to overrun West Berlin, they could have done so. At first, McNamara insisted that it was Kennedy's call for conventional reinforcements that deterred the Soviets in Berlin, not American nuclear power. Bernard Brodie—who was apostasizing from all of his teachings of the previous decade—argued to the contrary in a series of scathing articles: it was absurd to claim that the Soviets refrained from moving into West Berlin because they feared American conventional might that was not anywhere near the scene; quite simply, they were afraid of precipitating an all-out nuclear war in which they would have been destroyed.

The irrelevance of "flexible response" doctrine was even clearer in the Cuban missile crisis. As McNamara later testified: "We faced the possibility that night of launching nuclear weapons and Khrushchev knew it, and that is the reason, and the only reason, why he withdrew the weapons." Certainly, the American ability to take out the missiles with an air strike from Florida conferred an enormous local advantage. But Khrushchev held a number of powerful cards of his own if the two sides started playing escalatory poker, like marching on West Berlin, or matching an air strike in Cuba with one on the vulnerable American missiles in Turkey. His reluctance to act could not have been unconnected with the warnings of a "full retaliatory strike" that Kennedy was issuing at the height of the crisis. Virtually all of the American participants leave no doubt that they expected hostilities, however commenced, to eventuate in a full-scale nuclear exchange. It would take a connoisseur's eye indeed to discern other than tonal differences between the American posture over Cuba and that of Eisenhower during, say, the Formosan crisis of 1958. As George Quester remarked: "The declaratory policies which had seemed desirable when a general war was a more abstract question appeared to have lost their appeal when a contest of wills had begun."

The final puzzlement of the Cuban crisis was why Khrushchev had committed such an irrational act. It was Khrushchev's ineptness and lack of predictability, Henry Kissinger later wrote, that was the most frightening aspect of the entire episode. There is no question, of course, that if a policy is to be judged by its success, Khrushchev's decision to place missiles in Cuba was a serious error. He grossly misjudged the probable American response; his humiliating climbdown permitted the Chinese to add the charge of "capitulationist" to their list of indictments; and his embarrassment was undoubtedly a major factor in his downfall two years later.

But it required a stubborn refusal to face strategic facts not to appreciate the problem from Khrushchev's perspective. It was the huge disparity that was opening up between Soviet and American nuclear capabilities that prompted such desperate gambits. By 1962, the American missile buildup was moving ahead at a pace Khrushchev could not hope to match for years. Imperfect a solution as it was, the Cuban missiles helped plug a *genuine* missile gap that any responsible Soviet analyst would have found terrifying.

# CHAPTER 10

# Winning the Arms Race

## *The Search for Rationality*

Before Robert McNamara, no Secretary of Defense had ever attempted to deal explicitly with the question of how much power America needed during a time when it was technically at peace with the Soviet Union. The military buildup at the end of the Truman administration was specifically in response to the war in Korea, and Eisenhower's vague and ambiguous policy of "massive retaliation" was more a rhetorical posture than a strategy. McNamara's greatest strength as an administrator, and arguably his greatest flaw as a strategist, was his intolerance for vagueness and ambiguity. He was the quintessential rationalist, one of the first practitioners of the scientific management techniques that had evolved out of the experience of World War II. After a stint as a professor of statistical control techniques at the Harvard Business School, he joined the Ford Motor Company and rose to company president only weeks before he was fingered by Kennedy's talent scouts. His claim was that he could manage large organizations, not that he was a military expert. Kennedy liked him instantly, and embraced him as possibly the one man in the country who could impose logic and coherence on the sprawling defense establishment and infuse it with the crispness, clarity, and energy that were to be the hallmark of his new administration.

McNamara's affinity with the intellectual critics of the Eisenhower administration was immediate and lasting. The staff at RAND were recruited wholesale. Charles Hitch, a senior RAND economist, became Pentagon comptroller and created the new Office of Systems Analysis, headed by the thirty-year-old Alain Enthoven, a protégé of Wohlstetter. Henry Rowen, another young admirer of Wohlstetter, became deputy to Paul Nitze, the author of NSC-68 and the Gaither Report, who was

179

installed as Assistant Secretary for International Security Affairs. William Kaufmann left RAND to split his time between McNamara's office and a teaching post at MIT. A host of other young analysts—Daniel Ellsberg, Frank Trinkl, Frederick Hoffman—all signed on as full-time staff or regular consultants. Wohlstetter himself refused several offers for a full-time post, but was a frequent adviser, and was awarded the Department of Defense Medal for Distinguished Public Service by McNamara. Thomas Schelling's influence was felt through his long-time associate John McNaughton, who became McNamara's closest adviser on the Vietnam War. As Colin Gray remarked, "the intellectual dominance [of the RAND alumni] in the early 1960s was nearly absolute . . . mere recitation of their names understates their influence."

The influence of the defense intellectuals in McNamara's Pentagon was immense, but it derived from the towering stature of McNamara himself. The force of his personality and intellect hit the Pentagon like a thunderclap. He made no attempt to conceal his lack of awe for the military mind and the service chiefs' experience, and his young associates quickly picked up his tone: "I've fought as many nuclear wars as you have, General," Enthoven once snapped at a beet-faced Air Force commander. McNamara was appalled at the quality of the briefings he received during his first days in office—"Here is an airplane flying fast," an aide parodied the typical military slide presentation. The generals squirmed and sweated as McNamara impatiently pointed out inconsistencies in their data, contradictory slides, factual mistakes, conclusions at variance with their facts, outlandish assumptions. How much power was required to take out Soviet city X? Did the generals realize that was twenty times more than was dropped on Hiroshima, a city the same size? How many nuclear warheads would the generals hope to launch in a war with Russia? Did they realize that the fallout from such a stupendous number of weapons would probably kill most of the people in the world? Did the generals seriously mean it when they said their war plan was to launch everything they had, all at once, against all the countries of the Eastern bloc, the Soviet Union, and China?

The weapons in McNamara's bureaucratic revolution were the analytic techniques developed at RAND and detailed with great particularity in Charles Hitch's book, *The Economics of Defense in the Nuclear Age.* McNamara called them collectively PPBS, for Program Planning and Budgeting System. The trick was to specify the desired American defense posture in terms of missions, then to define the capabilities required to execute each mission in a series of likely scenarios. Mission capabilities had to be specified in terms of *outputs:* the question was not how many planes did the Air Force generals want, but rather how much destructive power or how many troops needed to be delivered to a specified location. McNamara and his analysts would then decide how many ships or planes or missiles would do the job most efficiently and construct their forces accordingly.

PPBS was genuinely revolutionary, not for the light it shed on strategy, but because it radically shifted Pentagon power alignments. Instead of allowing the military departments to define their own force requirements, McNamara and his analysts handed down to the services nine basic missions or programs that their forces were supposed to fulfill. "Strategic Retaliatory Forces," "Continental Defense Forces," "General Purpose Forces," and "Airlift and Sealift" were the four basic combat programs. "Strategic Retaliatory Forces," for example, included the B-47, B-52, and B-58 medium- and long-range bombers, their tankers and base support systems, the Air Force's Atlas, Titan, and Minuteman missiles, the Army's Jupiter, and the Navy's Polaris missile-carrying nuclear submarines.

The system's bureaucratic genius was that all of the new programs cut across the service organizations; at a stroke, the individual service chiefs lost control of force planning. The Air Force, for example, was enamored of its new B-58 bomber—it had just flown for 1,000 miles at 1,000 miles per hour only 500 feet off the ground. But what could it do that a Polaris couldn't do faster and cheaper? B-58 production was discontinued. And the B-70 Mach 2 long-range bomber, the cherished dream of Air Force Chief Curtis LeMay, was just a "manned missile" to McNamara. The Minuteman was much cheaper and invulnerable to enemy air defense systems. The B-70 was scratched, to LeMay's wailing that Khrushchev might as well be Secretary of Defense. The Navy had long been planning a new generation of massive nuclear-powered aircraft carriers. But a new carrier didn't obviously fit any of the missions McNamara had laid down. It was too slow and vulnerable for the "Strategic Retaliatory" mission and too expensive for the limited firepower it would contribute to the "General Purpose" mission. It was summarily cut. If nothing else, McNamara remarked grimly, it would teach the Navy to prepare their presentations properly.

PPBS led to immense centralization of power in the hands of McNamara and the Office of Systems Analysis. The essential requirement, as Hitch put it, was to "bring together in one place and at one time, all the information . . . need[ed] to make sound decisions on the forward program." It was primarily Enthoven's mathematicians and economists who simulated the detailed scenarios that led to the mission definitions: How many targets did the Soviet Union present? How much firepower was needed to eliminate them? How effective were the Soviet defense systems? How many targets would be "hardened"? How many American missiles would fail at launch?

And it was the systems analysts who performed the calculations that supported McNamara's procurement decisions: What was the true cost of a megaton of explosive delivered from an aircraft carrier, taking into account the naval bases, the destroyer escorts, the attack submarines, the interceptor aircraft, the tenders and tankers that a carrier battle group required? How many men could an Air Force transport plane deliver in a week of flights at what cost, compared to the men a transport ship could move in a week's voyage? What were the mission differences for an Air Force fighter bomber and a Navy carrier-based attack bomber? Why did they have two different procurement programs, and how much extra did that cost? Considerations of tradition or sentiment carried little weight. McNamara curtly dismissed the Air Force contention that the air-launched Skybolt missile would prolong the useful life of the manned bomber forces: " . . . the argument is wrong. The appropriate objective for the design of our strategic retaliatory forces is to destroy the required number of targets at a minimum cost; it is not to prolong the lives of particular weapon systems."

The centralization was often carried to extremes. McNamara enjoyed immersing himself in the most trivial decisions—belt-buckle procurement, for instance; he was quite proud of having standardized military belt buckles. Since so many issues flowed to the very top of the Pentagon, the services had to construct highly centralized management structures of their own to handle the decision flow, and worse, people them with a new class of officer who could translate standard decisions into the new quantitative-analytic argot. In the long term, it was a powerful reinforcement to the tendency, already evident at the end of the Eisenhower administration, for the peacetime Pentagon to degenerate into an impossibly convoluted, hopelessly sclerotic, clog. Hitch, oddly, had issued just such a warning shortly before taking office:

the superficial illogicalities of decentralization are more strikingly obvious than the deadening consequences of extreme centralization. . . . Much of the time and energy are consumed attempting to assemble, at the center, the information so readily available "on the firing line"; and since these efforts are never successful, then decisions have to be made on the basis of information that is both incomplete and stale.

Robert McNamara may have been the only man who could have imposed such a procrustean decision structure on an institution as sprawling and uncontainable as the Defense Department. Despite the grumblings of the military brass and their friends on Capitol Hill—the morale of the top officer corps sagged noticeably during McNamara's tenure at Defense—he swept all before him. His appearances before congressional committees were performances of dazzling virtuosity, displaying a sweeping strategic vision and an almost incredible grasp of the smallest details of his budgets and force plans. Kennedy trusted him absolutely, and he was the unrivalled star of the administration. In White House defense councils, his word was almost always final; even Kennedy's turf-conscious personal staff—Theodore Sorenson, Arthur Schlesinger, McGeorge Bundy, Walt Rostow—were great McNamara admirers. Their academic bent (all but Sorenson came from universities) predisposed them to the McNamara/RAND style of analysis, and the decisive break with Eisenhower's administrative methods warmed their political souls.

## Creating a Missile Gap

Eisenhower bequeathed a weapons procurement program aimed at an eventual strategic force of about 1,100 missiles, including 450 Minutemen in silos, 90 mobile Minutemen on rail beds, 255 Atlas and Titan missiles, and 19 Polaris submarines. The programmed force was about two-thirds that recommended by an outside group of consultants convened in 1959, and about two thirds the overall force levels eventually adopted by McNamara, on a much-accelerated procurement schedule. It was also, Eisenhower made clear, about twice as high as he thought necessary. He had originally thought that about 20 to 40 ICBMs would be more than enough to round out a bomber-based deterrent; but, as he was worn down by the post-Sputnik hysteria, the programmed figure kept inching up, first to 100, then 200, and finally to the number in his budget legacy to Kennedy. At each stage of program increase, Eisenhower had sarcastically noted, the military increased its "requirements" to almost precisely double the new programmed level. When McNamara took office, the military requirement statements were even higher, since they had seized upon the opportunity of a Kennedy "spending window" to double their requirements once again. The Air Force was asking for about 3,000 missiles, and there were some requirements estimates as high as 10,000.

The central premise of McNamara's procurement philosophy—or at least his stated premise—was that weapons requirements were a *derived* quantity: requirements flowed from a clearly defined strategy, not the other way round. He set a task force to work revamping Eisenhower's nuclear war plans (known as the Single Integrated Operational Plan, somewhat awkwardly shortened to "SIOP," pronounced "S-eye-Op") and outlined his strategic concepts in a series of confidential memorandums to the President. He developed his argument by identifying three possible strategic defense postures, with two of them presented as unacceptable extremes, and the third as his own recommendation. As he described them in his memorandums to Kennedy, the three basic options were:

"Full First-Strike Capability." The first unacceptable strategic extreme, McNamara wrote, would be to attempt to acquire forces that: " . . . were so large and so effective, in relation to those of the Soviet Union, that we would be able to attack and reduce Soviet retaliatory power to the point at which it could not cause severe damage to U.S. population and industry."

First-strike capability, in McNamara's view, was "almost certainly infeasible," although "it has become clear to me that the Air Force [budget] proposals" were based on just such an objective. Even with an overwhelming weapons advantage, McNamara reasoned, the United States could not be assured of taking out all of the Soviet retaliatory capability. The Soviet Union was improving its submarine-launched missiles, and McNamara assumed they were hardening their land-based missile sites. They were also claiming progress on antimissile defenses. Nor could the United States count on achieving tactical surprise in a first-strike launch; any secrecy breakdown might cause the Soviets to fire everything they had before the American attack arrived. And even if the Soviets completely bungled their defenses, there was enough uncertainty about Soviet missile locations and the accuracy of the American launchers to assume that a few Soviet missiles would survive and be fired at major American cities, causing tens of millions of deaths. "I do not consider this an 'acceptable' level of damage," McNamara wrote.

He also rejected a variant of the first-strike strategy, a "combined" first-strike and "coercive" strategy. America, the theory went, could launch a first strike that would knock out most of the Soviet missiles and military installations, but spare their cities, and thereby "coerce the Soviets into avoiding our cities (by the threat of controlled reprisal) and accepting our peace terms. In this case, we would be counting on our ability to destroy their will, not their ability, to destroy our cities." A coercive strategy, McNamara conceded, might be "a sensible and desirable option" *after* the Soviets had unsuccessfully attempted a first-strike against America, but to assume that a coercive first-strike strategy could protect America against Soviet retaliation would be "foolish."

"Minimum Deterrence Posture." The second unacceptable strategic extreme, "minimum deterrence," was defined by McNamara as "one in which, after a Soviet attack, we would have a capability to retaliate, and with a high degree of assurance be able to destroy most of Soviet urban society, but in which we would not have the capability to counter-attack against Soviet military forces." Such a policy would be dangerous, he argued. It would invite Soviet moves against our Allies "by reducing to a minimum the possibility of U.S. nuclear attack in response to Soviet aggression . . . [and] weaken our ability to deter such attacks." Moreover, should war break out for "accidental or unintended reasons, . . . a capability to counter-attack against high-priority Soviet military targets can make a major contribution to the objectives of limiting damage and terminating the war on acceptable terms."

"Assured Destruction." The third strategic alternative was therefore the only possible choice remaining. The goals of "assured destruction" were: "first, to provide the United States with a secure, protected, retaliatory force able to survive any attack within enemy capabilities and capable of striking back and destroying Soviet urban society, if necessary, in a controlled and deliberate way; and, second, to deny the enemy the prospect of achieving a military victory by attacking our forces."

"Assured destruction" was distinguished from "minimum deterrence" by McNamara's emphasis on the "controlled and deliberate" character of the American retaliatory strike and the necessity of denying a "military victory" to the Soviet Union. McNamara thereby adopted as official policy two of the constants of RAND teaching: the Schelling-Kahn notion of nuclear war as a process of rational bargaining and calculated escalation—the doctrine of "flexible response"—and the Brodie-Kaufmann theories of "counterforce", or the ability to strike at Soviet military targets, not just cities. It was in this context that McNamara argued that a "coercive" strategy—a controlled second strike at Soviet military forces while holding their cities hostage—might be "sensible and desirable." By incorporating "flexible response" and "counterforce" into his "assured destruction" strategy, McNamara was recommending nothing less than a genuine nuclear war-fighting capability. He summarized the strategy in a secret briefing to NATO defense ministers in May 1962, and, using virtually identical language, in a major policy speech in Ann Arbor, Michigan, the following month:

The U.S. has come to the conclusion that, to the extent feasible, basic military strategy in a possible general nuclear war should be approached in much the same way that more conventional military operations have been regarded in the past. That is to say: principal military objectives, in the event of nuclear war stemming from a major attack on the alliance, should be the destruction of the enemy's military forces, not of his civilian population. . . . We are convinced that . . . if, despite all our efforts, nuclear war should occur, our best hope lies in conducting a centrally controlled campaign against all of the enemy's vital nuclear capabilities, while retaining reserve forces, all centrally controlled.

McNamara addressed the issue of the force levels required by his newly clarified doctrine with his customary precision, presenting elaborate charts and graphs depicting all conceivable Soviet military and civilian targets and the mix of American forces that would most efficiently destroy them. The strategic alternatives were carefully ranged under "optimistic," "pessimistic," and "most likely" assumptions regarding Soviet strategy and defenses and American weapons performance. Choosing, as seemed advisable, the "pessimistic" or the "most likely" cases—since the Air Force's "pessimistic" assumptions were often wildly improbable—he produced a hermetically reasoned, five-year rolling schedule of weapons procurement. He clinched his arguments with cost-benefit analysis: that is, once a target had been identified, weapons to destroy it should be accumulated only to the point of diminishing returns, i.e., to the point where the cost of additional weaponry could not be justified by the additional destructiveness delivered against the target. As he expressed it in a memorandum on weapons targeted against Soviet defensive radars and airfields: "Of course, there is an upper limit to the number [of defense suppression targets] it makes sense to attack. For example, if it were necessary to destroy 300 targets in order to permit the bombers to penetrate and destroy 500 other targets, the question would naturally arise as to whether it wouldn't make more sense to direct the whole effort at the destruction of the 500 'primary' targets themselves. Defense suppression can price itself out of the market."

Diminishing returns or not, Congress gave McNamara virtually everything he asked for; and over the next four years, he built an awesome margin of strategic superiority over the Soviet Union. The new Minuteman missile, with a range in excess of 6,000 miles and a megaton-plus payload, became the centerpiece of the American deterrent, building rapidly toward a force of 1,000 deployed in hardened underground silos. The Minuteman's solid fuel could be stored indefinitely and permitted "instant" firing upon receiving an electronic command sequence, which could even be radioed from an airborne command and control aircraft. The rocket force also included 234 Atlas and Titan intercontinental missiles—about two thirds of them in hardened or semi-hardened silos—each with range comparable to the Minuteman's and even greater striking power, but with much slower firing cycles.

The strategic nuclear submarine fleet was programmed at 41 ships, of which 30 had been commissioned by 1965, each with 16 subsurface-launched Polaris missiles, or 480 in all. The newest models of the Polaris had an effective range of 2,500 miles and could reach virtually any Soviet target. The strategic nuclear forces were rounded out by more than 1,100 bombers, half of them always on fifteen-minute ground alert. Six hundred and thirty B-52s were securely based on the American continent but had ample range to reach anywhere in the Soviet Union. A substantial number of the B-52s were also equipped with Hounddog air-to-surface missiles, giving them a standoff thermonuclear firing capacity of 600 miles. The remainder of the bombing force consisted of supersonic B-58s and aging B-47s flying from the Strategic Air Command bases that ringed the Russian continent. In all, the United States could rain more than 5 *billion tons* of TNT-equivalent destructive power upon Soviet cities and military installations.

Against this stunning array of nuclear striking power, the Soviet Union fielded only some 200 intercontinental missiles by 1965. The Soviet force still included a handful of SS-6s—"SS" is a NATO designation for "surface-to-surface" missile—the original Sputnik rocket that had started the "missile gap" scare in the first place. But the primary weapon was a follow-on missile, the SS-7. The SS-7 was more reliable, and easier to launch, and sufficiently accurate at least to hit a city, which the SS-6, with an estimated inaccuracy of about five miles, could not do with any confidence. The SS-7, however, was still inferior in almost every respect to the American rockets; the Soviets were also obviously having a great deal of trouble with their newest missile, the SS-8—only nineteen were ever deployed.

The mainstay of the Soviet missile forces in the mid-1960s was still the medium and intermediate-range SS-4s and 5s targeted on Europe. Introduced in the 1950s, about 700 were deployed by 1966. While they provided a formidable "massive retaliation" capability against Europe, they were far too big and inaccurate to be of much use as a supplement to a conventional attack. The Soviet nuclear option in the early 1960s, basically, was to destroy Europe—which would make little sense, since taking political control of Europe was supposed to be the object of a Soviet offensive—before being destroyed in turn by the United States.

The Soviet long-range bomber force consisted of about 90 propellor-driven Bears, many of which had been relegated to tanker duty, and 130 Bisons—the same planes that panicked American commentators during the "bomber gap" scare of 1954–55. Even in the early 1960s, the Bears and Bisons were obsolete airplanes with little prospect of penetrating American air defenses, although some Bears were being equipped with a standoff missile-firing capability. (The "missile," in keeping with conservative Soviet engineering tradition, actually appeared to be a refitted Sukhoi fighter carried under the Bear's belly. A true Bear-based missile capability was not successfully achieved until the mid-1980s.) The medium-range TU-16 Badger could reach targets in Greenland and Alaska, and in a suicide-strike worst case analysis, possibly in the northernmost United States. The Mach 2 Blinder, the Soviet Air Force's version of Curtis LeMay's beloved B-70, had been introduced in the early 1960s with much fanfare, but never achieved strategic range, presumably because of technical problems.

The Soviets could also claim about 120 additional missiles on 40 submarines, but were just beginning to solve the problems of undersea launchings, and a large number of their submarine missiles still had ranges of only about 400 miles. Much to the surprise of McNamara and his analysts, the Soviets were hardening their missile sites only very slowly and had allowed their air defenses to deteriorate markedly. The great majority of defensive aircraft had no independent target acquisition capability—other than what the pilot could see—and so were heavily dependent on ground radar stations, whose locations were well known and highly vulnerable. McNamara estimated that 70 percent of the Soviet air defense force was obsolete. It was becoming clear as well that Khrushchev's much-touted antimissile missile, which nearly created an "antimissile gap" hysteria around 1963, was just another example of the Chairman's irrepressible penchant for military confabulation.

McNamara's administration of the Pentagon was undeniably

touched with genius. Particularly in the early years, his ability to bend the conflicting demands of the military services into a single coherent budget request was a stupendous administrative accomplishment; and overall Pentagon management, particularly in strategic force procurement, achieved moments of sparkling efficiency. The substantial augmentation of American forces, both nuclear and conventional, during his first years in office was achieved at a surprisingly small increase in costs. McNamara's first four defense budgets—at a remarkably constant $50.7, $51.9, $51.9, and $50.9 billion, before the buildup in Vietnam—were only about 15 percent bigger than the last military budget bequeathed by Eisenhower. (Although the suspicious consistency of the numbers casts doubt on McNamara's oft-repeated claim that he did not plan military requirements on the basis of predetermined budget levels.)

The policies adopted at McNamara's Pentagon, however, as opposed to the efficiency with which he pursued them, are a different matter. Indeed, his central claim, that he was building a force structure derived from a clear and defensible strategic logic, was mostly Wizard-of-Oz flummery, a fact sedulously obscured by the many volumes of self-serving history churned out by his young acolytes. Desmond Ball has assembled a painstaking chronology of the Kennedy administration's major strategic and weapon procurement decisions. Strikingly, almost *all*, including the decision to emphasize the Minuteman, the size of the force, and the pace and schedule of procurement, were taken during the administration's first months in office, mostly in the first *two* months, well before there was anything remotely resembling a "McNamara strategy" that they could have been derived from.

The key strategic decisions, moreover, were taken at a time when the appreciation of the Soviet strategic threat was in a state of rapid flux. In subsequent years, McNamara blamed faulty intelligence for what he conceded was an excessive missile buildup. But, in fact, he quickly learned that there was no "missile gap," and outraged the White House when he let the fact slip at his first press conference. A shocked Pierre Salinger, Kennedy's press secretary, told reporters that McNamara was "absolutely wrong," but after McNamara presented his evidence, the President lamely announced the formation of a "study committee." The Air Force generals, who were frantically insisting that the Soviets had more than 600 missiles targeted at the United States, had a collective fit of apoplexy. They fought a rearguard action through the summer, poring hopefully over the satellite photographs for signs of Soviet missiles. McNamara finally lost patience when they suggested that a medieval tower and a Crimean war memorial might be missile sites in disguise; he forbade any further "missile gap" testimony, and began to centralize the services' independent intelligence-gathering capabilities in his own hands.

By October, at the latest, the great margin of present American strategic superiority was taken for granted throughout the administration, although it had no perceptible impact on force planning. Stuart Symington needled McNamara in 1962 that his missile procurement schedule seemed unaffected by a recent intelligence estimate of Soviet rocket forces thirty times smaller than the one the pre-inauguration planners had worked with. Thomas Schelling forthrightly commented: "The fading of the 'missile gap' did not nearly reverse the decisions it had earlier provoked."

When pressed on the lack of Soviet threat, McNamara usually argued that the presence or absence of a missile gap was irrelevant to force planning, since he wanted to develop a strategic structure that could respond to any plausible range of *possible* Soviet capabilities. There are several problems with such an argument. In the first place, the enemy force, presumably the key variable in the equation, becomes a purely conjectural one, or as James Schlesinger remarked, in a wide-ranging critique, "the subjective starting point" becomes "the royal road to quantitative conclusions." Secondly, McNamara's argument is really one for building a strategic production *capacity*, not for large-scale deployment. But when McNamara entered office, Minuteman factories were already in place that could turn out a missile every day. With a strategic gap already substantially in the United States' favor, there would have been little risk in delaying large-scale missile deployments until the Soviet program became somewhat clearer. Finally, the argument has the autistic flavor of much of the early RAND work. It implies that there is a "right" number of American missiles, irrespective of what the Soviets do, and, of course, completely ignores the possible interactions of American deployments with the Soviets' own force planning.

The Kennedy/McNamara strategic recommendations, in short, were political ones, politically derived, with little relevance to a military strategy. The extensive supporting quantitative analysis was mostly an elaborate rationalization of decisions that had already been taken on other grounds. The numbers didn't even stand up to the cost-benefit criterion. White House staff who were arguing for a smaller buildup got access to the Pentagon's calculations and discovered that diminishing returns set in at about 450 Minutemen, not 1,000 or 1,200 as McNamara was suggesting in 1962. McGeorge Bundy recalls specifically that both Kennedy and McNamara "intellectually agreed that there was no persuasive case" for a missile buildup. The actual Minuteman number, Maxwell Taylor says, was based on a "visceral feeling," and Enthoven concedes that the size of the Polaris force was just "a historical accident."

There appears, in addition, to have been little thought to the impact of such a huge buildup on the Soviet Union. McNamara could advertise his "counterforce" missiles as part of an "assured destruction" strategy, but from the other side of the ramparts they would look very much like a first-strike force, particularly when, as in 1961, the powerful House Appropriations Committee was insisting that American policy should be to "launch an attack *before an aggressor has hit* either us or our allies . . ." (italics in original). As a Pentagon aide summarized a "counterforce" strategy: "if you're going to shoot at missiles, you're talking about a first strike." Bernard Brodie, more than a decade later, commented that those who complained about the "brutal momentum" of the Soviet missile buildup in the 1970s appeared to have forgotten about the one engineered by Kennedy and McNamara.

Clearly, Kennedy was politically obligated to propose *some* increase in American strategic forces. After his militaristic campaign, he would have been a laughingstock if he had not done so. And McNamara, Arthur Schlesinger says, was afraid he would "get murdered" if he proposed less than 950 Minutemen to the Congress, and was also worried about Air Force morale in the wake of the B-70 cancellation. (Desmond Ball, on the other hand, can find little evidence for Congressional, or even industry, pressure behind any *specific* number of missiles; there was substantial uproar, however, about the B-70 cancellation.)

But political pressure does not explain the haste with which basic decisions were taken; nor was there any any need to put procurement on such an accelerated track. Even granting the political necessity for a military buildup, the administration learned almost as soon as it took office—indeed, it knew as much long before—that there was no immediate strategic crisis. The Navy, in fact, protested against the acceleration of the Polaris program, because it would ensure block obsolescence of the fleet, forestall progressive modernization, and lacked strategic justification. The unseemly rush to take such momentous decisions sprang, it seems, almost entirely from Kennedy's anxiety to contrast the "vigor" and "movement" of his new administration with Eisenhower's. The decision to emphasize the Minuteman, for example, was driven by the felt necessity, in McNamara's words, not to "endors[e] previous policy decisions." (The decision to favor the small-payload Minuteman, in fact, sharply limited strategic choices in the 1970s when the Soviets began deploying land-based missiles with many more big warheads than American missiles could carry.)

The accelerated Kennedy/McNamara missile buildup was a momentous decision, arguably one of a handful of turning points in the arms competition between the United States and the Soviet Union. It was a decision, it seems, motivated primarily by political considerations—or, less kindly, by public relations concerns. It greatly aggravated a nuclear force imbalance that was already lopsidedly in favor of the United States, and did so with little regard to any perceived strategic necessity. To the degree that any strategic criterion at all was proposed, it was McNamara's "war-fighting" strategy, but that was actually developed well after the essential decisions were already taken, and, in any case, as will be seen, was soon called into question by McNamara himself. Finally, the great rush to decision and the continual reiteration of a strategic crisis in the face of overwhelming evidence to the contrary, at a time when the administration's language was marked by unusual stridency, could not have been better calculated to alarm the Soviet Union and virtually to ensure a compensatory Russian response.

## The Other Gap

The immense leap in strategic nuclear striking power engineered by Kennedy and McNamara was perfectly consistent, however, with one stream of American military thinking that dated from the very beginnings of the Cold War. A substantial nuclear superiority was essential, defense analysts argued, to counter the great advantage the Soviet Union enjoyed in European theater land forces. The sudden reversal of the "missile gap" was frequently understood in that light—the new American margin of superiority was enormous, but was required to balance overwhelming deficiencies elsewhere. To put the worst face on it, since American willingness actually to *use* its nuclear power would necessarily diminish as Soviet arsenals grew, a number of defense thinkers argued that the Western position was actually deteriorating, strategic superiority or not. Alistair Buchan, the director of London's influential Institute for Strategic Studies, for example, wrote in *Foreign Affairs* in 1962 of "the steady widening of the range and types of challenge which the Soviet Union now feels able to offer to the Atlantic powers. . . . The Soviet threat to European allies is not only formidable, but is becoming steadily more so."

The great Soviet conventional preponderance in Europe plunged Henry Kissinger into despair, leading him to reverse position again in mid-1962 and advocate the use of tactical nuclear weapons in a European land war. (In his Athens speech shortly before, McNamara had said forthrightly, and quite sensibly, that he did not believe it was possible to wage a tactical nuclear war in Europe because of the enormous destructiveness of the weapons and the improbability of controlling their use.) Without the use of nuclear weapons, Kissinger wrote, NATO troops would be able to resist only "minor incursions." Worse, the American nuclear umbrella could no longer be relied upon, despite the Western missile superiority, because of the possibility of a Soviet retaliatory strike—"To pretend that these factors will not reduce any President's readiness to initiate general war would be sheer irresponsibility," he fulminated, and concluded gloomily: "increasingly direct Soviet challenges will be likely."

In actual fact, Soviet conventional power, if not so egregiously exaggerated as Khrushchev's early missile capabilities—Soviet ground forces, after all, were not completely mythical—was grossly overstated. Almost all Western analysts persisted in stating comparisons between Warsaw Pact and NATO forces in Europe in terms of *divisions,* not manpower, long after simple arithmetic should have made plain the absurdity of the standard count of 160 to 175 Soviet divisions. Dividing the number of divisions into the approximate total manpower count for the Red Army produced a "division slice," as it was called, that was impossibly low. The number of effective troops the Soviets could put into the field, in short, was far lower than the customary comparisons had led the world to believe.

The steady decline in Soviet force levels came at a time when McNamara was engineering a substantial American conventional buildup in pursuit of his "2½ war" capability—that is, the capacity to fight, all at the same time, major conventional engagements in Europe and Asia and one "brushfire war" somewhere in the Third World. (This was another piece of flummery. A detailed study of the "2½ war" strategy showed that it required fifty-five Army divisions, not the budgeted sixteen, a conclusion as ridiculous as it was rigorous, and one that, of course, was quickly shelved. Vietnam ended any "2½ war" illusions.) Arguably, by 1963 or 1964 the American military buildup, coupled with Khrushchev's persistent force reductions, had actually shifted the conventional balance to favor the West.

McNamara himself, with his customary clear-headedness, was among the first to challenge the conventional view, in a sweeping reassessment of Soviet non-nuclear capabilities sent to President Johnson in December 1963. "For many years," McNamara wrote, "Soviet and CHICOM forces have been greatly overestimated in western military thinking. This has led to an overestimation of the forces required to stop them and, consequently, to an air of hopelessness about our prospects of winning in a major non-nuclear war. As the discussion below shows, however, our prospects for a successful non-nuclear defense along the Sino-Soviet periphery are better than is commonly supposed."

McNamara's data indicated that the Soviet Union fielded only 115 to 135 divisions, of which perhaps 58 to 75 were combat-ready, with almost all the remainder at "cadre" strength, that is with only officers and noncoms on duty—all much lower numbers than an official National Intelligence Estimate had concluded only the previous month. More important, McNamara continued, the standard U.S. division was 5,000 to 7,000 men bigger than its Soviet counterpart, had 5 to 50 percent more divisional firepower, and twice as much additional firepower available from the corps level. Three times the number of men were assigned to armored cavalry regiments as in a Soviet division, creating a great advantage in mobility; there was much greater lift capacity; and each American division had an average 101 aircraft, including both helicopters and close-support fighters, compared to the Soviet average of only five. In the critical Central European region, NATO forces had a slight overall manpower edge, even counting unreliable satellite troops in the Soviet totals, and an average one-third advantage in firepower.

About the only area where the Soviets had a marked advantage was in the sheer number of tanks, with about half again as many tanks per man as NATO. NATO commanders were also much impressed with the new Soviet T-62 tank, reputed to be lighter, faster, and with more firepower than the best Western tanks, the German Leopard and American M-60. (In fact, as subsequent wars in the Middle East demonstrated conclusively, Western tanks were far superior.) But however formidable the T-62, the large Soviet tank advantage resulted from considered Western tactical decisions, not procurement shortfalls. The Soviets had long favored massed armored assault tactics, while NATO used a different mix of tanks and mechanized infantry in the interest of greater mobility and flexibility, and, in addition, was deploying the first generation of "smart" weapons, like the Shillelagh antitank missile, that raised substantial doubts about the long-term viability of tank forces.

Counting conventions all tended to exaggerate the Soviet forces. Tactical aircraft comparisons, for example, used a "Unit Equipment" method for NATO forces, which excluded aircraft on maintenance, assigned to combat training, or otherwise unavailable. Soviet aircraft, however, were computed on the "Air Order of Battle" method, which included such aircraft. In 1966, McNamara carried out a detailed re-estimate of Soviet tactical air capabilities, long the pride of the Soviet Air Force. The study showed dramatic slippage. Fully half of the Soviet tactical air fleet were classified as "low performance," or "subsonic, low radius/payload" aircraft—mostly Korean War-vintage MiGs—and three quarters of the fleet were air-to-air combat planes, useful, that is, as defensive interceptors only. The old Il-28 tactical bombers were being rapidly retired, but the new all-weather Yakovlev and Sukhoi models were coming on line very slowly. By the time of the 1966 study, NATO had 12,000 tactical aircraft, compared to the Warsaw Pact's 8,000, and 40 percent of the NATO total were multi-purpose, nuclear-capable, supersonic fighter bombers, like the big, twin-engine, Mach 2 Phantoms, with all-weather and night attack capabilities, which the Soviets simply could not match. At the same time, the steady procurement of new non-nuclear ordnance, like the Bullpup air-to-surface missile, created a massive firepower advantage in NATO's favor.

The military chiefs resisted McNamara's reassessments, but their complaints had a half-hearted air. One favorite tactic was to add the Chinese totals to the Warsaw Pact forces. It was difficult, of course, to argue that the Soviets and Chinese were allies, since they were already on the verge of a shooting war by 1963, but the Army insisted that "Communist opportunism makes it logical to expect that the Soviets and CHICOM's would attempt to capitalize on situations created by each other." The Joint Chiefs downplayed the NATO firepower advantage because, they argued with a straight face in a memo demanding more equipment, "in war the moral is to the physical as three is to one."

Arguments that the Soviets could overcome their equipment and manpower disadvantages by surprise assaults against weak points in the

NATO lines began to look increasingly silly. It was settled Soviet/ Clausewitzian doctrine that the attacker needed a three-to-one advantage at the point of assault. Western aerial reconnaissance capabilities would make it extraordinarily risky for the Soviets to attempt to mobilize such an attack by "surprise." Attack scenarios also required the Soviets to meet wholly improbable mobilization schedules. The authoritative *Military Balance* series, for instance, assumed that Soviet cadre divisions could be brought to full strength with "30 days uninterrupted mobilization," which even NATO commanders thought was an absurdity. By this time, indeed, Bernard Brodie was already arguing that the whole strategy of building up conventional forces in pursuit of "flexible response" was a misconception based on a "war-game room" opponent, not "the real Soviet Union . . . with whom we have had prolonged experience," and who "not infrequently blunders but who always shows a deep respect for our strength." The true balance of forces, in short, was such that it would have required an inconceivable breach of an entire command tradition of prudential caution for the Soviets to march their armies westward.

McNamara went public with his new estimates in Congressional testimony in late 1963: "In Central Europe NATO has more men and more combat troops on the ground than does the [Soviet] bloc. It has more on the ground in West Germany than the bloc does in East Germany. It has more and better tactical aircraft, and these planes carry twice the payload twice as far as their Soviet counterparts." There was a lively debate within the defense community throughout 1964, but by the end of the year, the majority opinion seemed to have swung to McNamara's position. Alistair Buchan, for example, cautiously recanted his pessimism of two years before: "The size of the Soviet division has been reduced so that they are about half to two-thirds as strong in firepower as a NATO division. These developments, when combined with permanent vulnerability of lines of communication across Eastern Europe . . . by no means suggest the possibility of a successful Soviet assault against the 26 NATO divisions across the Rhine."

NATO's total absorption with political bickering was the surest sign of its new confidence. Despite McNamara's earnest exhortations for "centrally controlled" and "graduated" nuclear responses, Charles de Gaulle built his own nuclear striking force—*le force de frappe*—because it was inconceivable that France should be dependent for its vital defenses upon a third country. Harold Macmillan, the British prime minister, was politically ravaged when McNamara cancelled the Skybolt missile that would have prolonged the life of Great Britain's aging bomber fleet. (McNamara offered the Hounddog as a substitute. It was probably a better weapon, but its name made the deal impossible.) De Gaulle seized upon this example of British subservience to help justify his veto of their entry into the Common Market. A contrite McNamara tried to save Macmillan's career by approving an independent British Polaris submarine force—which, to de Gaulle's great pleasure, violated every rule laid down for coordinated Western nuclear defenses. Throughout 1963 and 1964, some of the best minds in Europe and America labored over the "Multilateral Force," a Caliban-like conception of a fleet of NATO nuclear missile ships, with a multilingual confusion of crewmen from all the NATO countries. No one seriously pretended that the concept was of any military value, but with the "Soviet threat" now merely an incantation, it was as constructive a way as any for military statesmen to spend their time. Finally, in 1966, de Gaulle sent shock waves through NATO by removing his troops from the unified NATO command. He did not repudiate his treaty obligations in the event of an attack, but refused any longer to submit his force planning to what he regarded as American dictates.

One positive diplomatic outcome, from the American point of view, was that the Europeans, with de Gaulle on the sidelines, finally accepted McNamara's "flexible response" strategy some five years after he first proposed it. When he presented his plans in Athens, the NATO defense ministers had been "incredulous." "Flexible response" appeared just another maneuver, like tactical nuclear warfare, to detach America from Europe's defenses, and to weaken the American nuclear guarantee. The fear of an American "decoupling" had made McNamara's insistence in Athens that Europeans give up their independent nuclear forces even more grating. And, of course, the Europeans, as always, were unwilling to spend more money on conventional arms—the American nuclear guarantee was much cheaper. The revelations that the West already had a substantial margin of conventional superiority, however, allowed the issue to be neatly finessed. Like the man who discovered he had been speaking prose all his life, the NATO ministers, in effect, recognized that "flexible response" was a reasonable policy after all.

By the end of the first Kennedy-Johnson administration, leading defense opinion had concluded not only that the West had clear military superiority over the Soviets but, in effect, that the arms race was over and the West had won. The possibility of actually winning the arms race may have been first bruited by Thomas Schelling: "Perhaps it is not altogether unwise deliberately to plan and communicate a somewhat excessive military buildup ratio relative to the Soviet forces in order to enhance their inducements to moderate their own program." For Walter Lippmann, Schelling's musings were an accomplished fact. He wrote shortly after Kennedy's death that one of the young President's "greatest achievements" was "to convince the Soviet Union that it must perforce and that it can comfortably and honorably live within a balance of power that is decidedly in our favor."

Thomas Wolfe, one of the top Soviet analysts at RAND, similarly concluded in 1964 that the Soviets had "drifted away" from the necessity for military superiority; while J.M. Mackintosh, a leading British Soviet military analyst, decided that the Soviets had "settled down to living with strategic inferiority." As late as 1967, Herman Kahn's Hudson Institute adjudged: "There is reason to believe that the Soviet Union is attempting to match a counterforce strategy of ours with a minimum deterrence position. This may be for reasons of economy, doctrinal trust in our restraint, an inclination not to make major provocations, a hesitance to indulge in an expensive and hopeless arms race, a belief in the efficacy of of secrecy, or for some other reason."

"In any case," the Hudson report added ominously, and not very reassuringly for Soviet readers, "this may represent a mistake on their part."

# CHAPTER 11

# Vietnam Prelude: The Road from Bandung

John Kennedy took office amid an acute consciousness that the central scenes of the Cold War were moving to a much broader stage, one peopled by new and exotic actors, most of whom in fact were at the same time anxiously seeking to thread a path of safety and, if possible, profit through the midst of the East-West confrontation. The representatives of the "non-aligned nations" convened for the first time in April 1955, in the modest little city of Bandung, perched in the highest reaches of the Javanese mountains, amid startling green gorges, brightly flitting cockatoos, and 1,000-foot waterfalls, four hours of heart-stopping train travel from Djakarta. Twenty-nine nations, most of them less than a decade old, were represented.

The Bandung Conference may not have quite "ranked with the Congress of Vienna," as one Western reporter gushed, but it was surely one of the most colorful of world gatherings. Indonesia's President Sukarno was resplendent in white and gold as he welcomed the delegates to the "first international conference of the so-called colored peoples in the history of mankind." Jawaharlal Nehru, the prime minister of India, and the leading spokesman for a "third world" consciousness, appeared in white pyjamas and a long white tunic, with a bright red rose at his breast. V. K. Krishna Menon, Nehru's foreign policy spokesman, all smoldering eyes and burst of gray curls, turned out in a loin cloth and a thin white cotton shirt. Egypt's Gamal Abdel Nasser was glorious in military medals and braid, while Zhou Enlai, whose speeches at the conference were "gentle and . . . infinitely mild," glided quietly in the background in his gray Sun Yat-sen uniform. Arab and black African leaders swirled in their native robes, and in the halls, buttonholing anyone who would listen to their tales of lost territories, stalked His Eminence the Grand Mufti of Jerusalem and His Beatitude the Archbishop of Cyprus.

The delegates' utter dependence on Western technology was poignant counterpoint to their ritualistic denunciations of Western economic imperialism. They arrived in Western airplanes, communicated over Western telephone and speaker systems, aped Western press conference techniques, used hastily installed Western plumbing systems to wash and scent their bodies, and—particularly the delegates from Muslim countries—frequented lunchtime fashion shows of Western lingerie. The official language of the conference was English, and speeches were scheduled in the English alphabetical order of the countries' transliterated names. (Most of the delegates mispronounced Zhou En-lai's name as "Chow," because they were confused by the idiosyncratic Wade-Giles English spelling rendering, "Chou".) Almost all of the press facilities were Western—there were 379 American reporters, someone counted, more than were accredited to the Korean War—and the main newspapers in even the larger countries were dependent on Western news agencies for conference coverage. The delegates soon learned that the best way to get front-page notices in their own countries was to make anti-Communist speeches, because they always got headline treatment from the American wire services.

The Soviet Union was conspicuous at Bandung by its absence— except for a small, dark-suited press delegation that appeared thoroughly confused by the goings-on—although as an Asian power, it arguably had a right to an invitation. Bandung, however, marked a watershed in Soviet policy. Until Bandung, despite the fulminations of John Foster Dulles about the threat of "international Communism," the Soviet Union seems to have had no policy at all, or at best a confused one, toward Asia and Africa. Lenin had insisted dogmatically that only industrialized Europe could provide fertile ground for Communist expansion, and Stalin xenophobically wrote off even the most radical of Third World leaders as "petty-bourgeois nationalists."

Khrushchev, on the other hand, according to Soviet sources, was inspired by Bandung to shift the Kremlin's policy toward forging alliances with the "bourgeois-nationalist" leaders who were emerging in the newly decolonized nations—although Zhou's stylish performance at the conference undoubtedly had a great deal to do with that sudden new insight. Khrushchev signalled the new policy departure when he and Bulganin made a much-publicized visit to India, with side trips to Burma and Afghanistan in the summer of 1955, followed up by a major speech the next year declaring that "the peoples of the East . . . need not go begging to their former oppressors for modern equipment. They can get it from the socialist countries, free of any political or military obligations."

There were at least two discernible strands in Khrushchev's "Third World" policies. On the one hand, flirting with the Indias and Indonesias of the world had its own rewards: it greatly alarmed the Americans, helped underpin the Soviet Union's shaky new conception of itself as a world power, and created occasions for eye-widening travel to exotic climes for Khrushchev and the other bumpkins in the Kremlin, even if the substantive gains from buying steel mills for Nehru were not always clear. A far different prospect, however, was offered in the Middle East. It was possibly the one area of the world that offered an obvious opportunity to strike a serious blow at the West and to advance the power and security of the Soviet Union at the same time. The countries on the southwest border of the Soviet Union—Iran, Iraq, Turkey, and Afghanistan—were the gateway to the Mediterranean and to the Indian Ocean and, just as important, were the barrier states between Russia and the vast oil reserves of Saudi Arabia, Kuwait, and the emirates to the south, already the source of 75% of West Europe's oil supplies and 20% of America's. For at least the full first decade and a half after Stalin's death, the Middle East became virtually the sole focus of Soviet foreign policy outside of Europe. Stripped of ideology, there was, in fact, little difference between Soviet policies in the Middle East in the 1950s and 1960s and those of the nineteenth-century Czars in the days of the "Great Game" between Great Britain and Russia in the Balkans, the Caucasus, and the Khyber. As Palmerston observed in 1835: "Russia pursues the same system of strategy against Persia and Turkey, she creeps down the Black Sea and wants to do the same down the Caspian and to take both Persia and Turkey on each of their flanks."

The West awoke with a shock to the potential for Soviet mischief in the Middle East with the disclosure in September, 1955, that Czechoslovakia, obviously acting at the behest of the Soviets, had entered into a major arms contract with Egypt, on terms far more generous than any available from the West—payments were long-term and were to be made entirely in Egyptian cotton. The arms sale, which was apparently suggested to Nasser by Zhou en route to Bandung, represented a major policy shift for the Soviet Union, with profound implications for the global balance of power. Dulles, with characteristic understatement, called it "the most serious development since Korea, if not since World

War II." At a stroke, the Soviet Union had leaped over the "northern tier" states of Iran, Iraq, Turkey, and Pakistan that Great Britain had painstakingly bound together in the Baghdad Pact as the first line of defense against Soviet incursions; and it had unmistakably announced its presence as a major—and hostile—new player on the international stage. The possibility of war in the Middle East was increased exponentially, and the problem of containing Soviet communism had taken on entirely new dimensions.

The opportunity for the Soviet *démarche* to Egypt was created by the French, who, as so often in the postwar years, played dog-in-the-manger in Western policy circles. Flouting an American-British agreement to limit arms sales to the Middle East, the French entered into a major arms contract with Israel in early 1955 for the delivery of 100 light tanks equipped with Nord antitank missiles (the first of their kind ever to be used in warfare) and 37 Mystère jets, a high-performance plane for its day, heavier and faster than the comparable MiG-15— altogether roughly doubling Israeli military capabilities. The subsequent Soviet arms deliveries to Nasser were much larger, although the Egyptian armory before the Soviet shipments was only slightly smaller than Israel's *after* the French arms sale. Details of the shipments are still obscure, partly because there appear to have been two arms deals, the one announced in 1955, and a later, secret, deal just before the outset of the Suez engagement. Estimates of the total deliveries range from 80 to 200 MiG-15s, 100 to 300 heavy tanks (World War II T-34s and even heavier "Stalin" class IS-111s), 100 to 200 armored personnel carriers, substantial numbers of self-propelled guns, and 30 to 45 Il-28 light bombers. The Il-28s were particularly worrisome because Israel, with only two old B-17s, had no comparable ability to deliver bombs against the Egyptian homeland and feared tying up the greater part of its air force in city defense. There were also rumors of shipments of supersonic MiG-17s, although these were never confirmed.

In the event, the Kremlin's weapons largesse was almost totally wasted by a combination of Egyptian incompetence and Soviet caution. During the fighting over Suez in 1956, most of the pilots for Nasser's new MiGs were either untrained or away at training in Eastern Europe, and Israel cleared the skies of Egyptian aircraft in the first few days of the fighting. The numerically superior Egyptian tank forces were never a factor. Following outmoded Soviet tank doctrine, they assumed static defensive positions in the desert and Israel's light tanks simply ran around them. The Il-28s and apparently all the Soviet technicians in

Cairo were withdrawn by the Soviet Union as soon as the Anglo-French bombardment started, and the French claimed to have caught about half the I1-28s on the ground during a desert refuelling stop and destroyed them.

Despite the publicity generated by Bulganin's rocket-rattling warnings to Great Britain and France, the Arab leadership, according to Muhammed Heikel, a confidant of Nasser, was acutely aware that the Soviet Union was very frightened of drawing the United States into the quarrel and that it was American pressure, not Bulganin's warning, that forced Great Britain to withdraw from the Canal. The Syrian president, Shukrih al-Quwatli, was in Moscow, in fact, during the first Israeli attack and tearfully pleaded for Soviet intervention. Marshal Zhukov spread out a map: "Here is a map. Look at it. How can we intervene?" For all of Eisenhower's irritation at the British and the French, on the other hand, there seems little doubt, based on the records of his meetings with Dulles and his other advisers, that he would have intervened if the Soviets had entered the fighting.

Far from being discouraged by the military inadequacies of their new clients, the Soviets redoubled their efforts. They picked up the tab for the Aswan Dam—Dulles had reneged on an American funding promise when Nasser recognized Red China—and began providing military assistance to Syria, Iraq, and Afghanistan, and, using Nasser as a funnel, became the main source of support to Yemeni rebels fighting against the continued British presence in the port city of Aden, a Western outpost at the entrance of the Red Sea and a key staging post to the Far East. In 1958, the Soviets broadened their arms shipments to include Indonesia, and eventually sent Sukarno more than $1 billion worth of arms—almost all of which was wasted—to use in his successive wars in Sumatra, West Irian, and Malaysia. By 1964, a dozen additional non-aligned nations were receiving Soviet military aid. A cautious estimate is that between 1958 and 1964, the Soviets exported more than $2.7 billion worth of arms, 80 percent of it to non-Communist countries.

During the latter part of the 1950s and the early 1960s, American commentators tended to credit the Soviet Union with extraordinary skill in its diplomatic and military dealings with underdeveloped countries. Soviet "mastery" of the "techniques of gaining control of the civilian population" in an undeveloped country was a typical *Foreign Affairs* formulation. In reality, the Soviets were at least as fumbling and ham-handed as the United States in its worst "ugly American" incarnations and as shamelessly exploited by their Third World dependents.

Nasser was one of the more cynical manipulators of the big powers and joked about writing a manual for dealing with the Kremlin. As Heikel recorded Nasser's rules:

- *Always speak English or French.* Russian leaders insisted on their own translators, but the translators had very poor Arabic and would never admit mistakes.

- *Equating America and Russia is strictly taboo.* Anyone who speaks of "the two superpowers" will be accused of falling victim to Chinese propaganda.

- *Ask for arms or factories, but never for food.* The Soviets were always unable to provide food, which made them "apologetic and embarrassed."

- *Pay attention to your category.* The Soviets loved to categorize. Aid recipients were ranked A, B, or C. "A" countries went right to the Kremlin and got fifty-year loans. "B" countries were referred to committees and got twenty-five-year loans. "C" countries dealt with bureaucrats and rarely got anything.

- *Category signs were unmistakable.* Egypt made "A" status, Nasser knew, when in the same year the ballerina Galina Ulanova visited Cairo; Yevgeny Yevtushenko wrote a poem about the Nile; there was an Egyptian film festival in Moscow; and the Soviet Union gave him a reactor. Of all the signs of favor, ballerina visits were the most important.

The Soviets seem to have been acutely aware of the manipulation and exploitation. Khrushchev was appalled at the luxuries in Sukarno's palace and was shocked to come upon the sybaritic Indonesian president chatting gaily with a naked woman. He finally exploded during a native handicrafts exhibition in Djakarta. He thought his money was going for steel mills and cement factories, he ranted, not for palaces and basket weaving. The inability of the aid to buy permanent allies was as frustrating for the Russians as it was for the Americans. Nasser was the master at extorting money from all sides and managed to keep food shipments flowing from the United States of roughly the same value as the Soviet economic and military assistance. Heikel commented, "Sometimes when I have been in Moscow listening to Gromyko talking about non-alignment I have felt that if I closed my eyes I could have been listening to Dulles."

In dispensing aid and choosing allies, the Soviets displayed an impressive degree of ideological agnosticism—just as the United States courted allies with only the most tenuous commitments to "freedom and democracy." One of the most anti-Semitic of states, the Soviet Union was still among the very first to recognize Israel in 1948, in order to tweak the British, and Soviet arms supplies were a critical factor in Israel's surviving its first war with the Arabs. The Soviet clients in the Middle East repeatedly suppressed the local Communist parties, often brutally, and with Soviet weapons. Khrushchev once refused to shake the hand of the Iraqi strongman Abdel Arif, because it was "stained with the blood of Communists," but he continued to supply him with arms. Nasser openly flaunted his independence. When he helped suppress the Iraqi and Syrian Communist movements in 1958, he said that "the road to Moscow does not lie through Baghdad and Damascus"— the Soviet Union would have to support him no matter how he treated the local parties. In 1959, just after receiving the Soviet commitment to fund Aswan, Nasser made a bitter attack: "the Communists want to dominate [the Middle East] and establish a terrorist, bloody dictatorship [and create] a Red fertile crescent." Unabashed, the Soviet Union made the second-stage Aswan funding commitment the following year, and in 1964, to the shock of Arab Communists, ordered the dissolution of the Egyptian Communist Party.

As often as not, the Soviets found themselves on both sides of so-called national liberation movements. After supplying arms for many years to the Imamate in Yemen, they switched sides when local Republicans overthrew the new Imam in 1962. *Pravda* wrote in the same breath of the "friendly ties" between Yemen and the Soviets since 1928, the "glorious history of struggle against imperialism and colonialism" in Yemen, and "the absolute feudal regime" that was being overthrown. The Soviets supported the Kurdish separatists in Iraq at the same time as they were courting the Iraqi regime and supplied arms to both sides in the long war in the Sudan. A concerted effort to improve relations with Turkey in the early 1960s—*Pravda* denounced Communist demonstrations in Ankara as an "insult [to] the national dignity of Turkey"—foundered on Soviet support for Greek separatists in Cyprus. The Soviets actively courted the Shah in Iran, beginning almost immediately after his overthrow of the leftist Mossadegh government in 1953, and despite his violent repression of the Tudeh Communists and the hostility between the Shah and Nasser. As Alexei Kosygin, the Soviet prime minister, later explained to Nasser's successor, Anwar Sadat:

"You must understand that Iran is our neighbor. The Americans, the British, even the Japanese are there. We can't tell the Shah, 'Go to hell. You are a Shah and we are Communists.' "

The decisiveness of Eisenhower's reaction to the Soviet probes in the Middle East was in marked contrast to his reluctance to intervene against Communist encroachments in China or Vietnam. Trained in military geography, he, even more than Dulles, viewed continued Western control of the Arabian littoral to be of overriding importance. Almost as soon as the British pulled out of Suez in 1956, he announced the "Eisenhower Doctrine," or a formal American commitment to regional stability and anticommunism (to the accompaniment of muted "I told you so's" on the part of British conservatives), managing in the process to offend almost all the Arab leaders by his references to a Middle Eastern "vacuum." The first test came when Jordan's King Hussein, fearful of being swallowed up by Egypt and Syria in 1957, shouted "international communism" and immediately received $10 million in military aid and a visit from the Sixth Fleet. But the convincing demonstration of the American commitment came the following year, when Eisenhower dispatched 14,000 troops to Lebanon, the only time in his entire presidency that he resorted to the direct use of military force.

The critical background events to the intervention in Lebanon were an agreement between Egypt and Syria in early 1958 to join their countries in a United Arab Republic, and the overthrow of the Hashemite monarchy of Nuri Said in Iraq the same year. The formation of the short-lived UAR was the high point of Nasser's semi-mystical, anti-Western, Pan-Arab movement that for a brief time threatened to sweep the entire Middle East, not least of all Lebanon, one of the few countries in the area with decided pro-Western leanings. Violence erupted in Lebanon in May, directed against Camille Chamoun, the conservative Christian president. Chamoun, who was thoroughly corrupt, was attempting to consolidate his power after parliamentary elections, widely believed to be fraudulent, that were highly unfavorable to the left and to the Nasserist Arabs. At the first sign of radical Arab disturbances, Chamoun invoked the Eisenhower Doctrine and appealed to Washington for assistance.

The initial reaction from Eisenhower and Dulles was circumspect. They were willing to send assistance, but only if the appeal was made through the United Nations and if at least one other Arab country associated itself with the request. But the Sixth Fleet was moved closer to Lebanon and quiet preparations were made for a landing. The pro-Nasser military coup in Iraq in July removed any hesitancy. Eisenhower convened a National Security Council meeting, where "he was the most relaxed man in the room," and announced that he had made up his mind on sending troops. To their mutual embarrassment, Eisenhower forgot to ask Dulles his opinion, and when the Secretary somewhat plaintively requested to be heard, he was substantially opposed to the landing.* The congressional leaders were briefed the same afternoon and were almost all opposed. The British prime minister, Harold Macmillan, was informed by telephone, but Eisenhower refused his offer to join in the landing. With no other notice, 1,700 Marines hit the Lebanese beaches the next afternoon, building up to a full divisional equivalent with almost continuous landings of Marines and Army airborne units from Germany through the following weeks. The British supported the American action by landing paratroopers in Jordan to strengthen Hussein.

The crisis in Lebanon was merely a pretext for a show of force in the Middle East. Eisenhower had no particular attachment to Chamoun's regime. Robert Murphy was dispatched to Lebanon at the end of July and quickly forged an arrangement for Chamoun to step down in favor of a neutralist general whom Nasser had declared acceptable even before the American action. Nor there was any evidence of Moscow's involvement in Chamoun's problems, and Eisenhower knew it—although he leaned heavily on the anti-Communist theme in his message to Congress. His real purpose was to send a message to Nasser and to the Soviet Union that the Americans had genuine interests in the Middle East and that they could and would fight to support them. Just as important, he wanted Nasser to know that he could not rely on Soviet support in a crisis.

Sending troops to Lebanon ran substantial risks—it is not clear how American forces would have responded if the landing had been opposed by the Lebanese Army, which at one point was a distinct possibility—but it arguably accomplished all of Eisenhower's objectives. Nasser flew to Moscow almost immediately to seek military reassurances, but Khrushchev, excited and shaken, insisted that he was "not ready for a confrontation." He finally agreed to stage a demonstrative maneuver with Soviet troops near Turkey, "but only a maneuver," and otherwise

---

*The press assumed, as always, that the Lebanese invasion was just another case of Dulles's unrestrained adventurism. A current joke when news of the invasion broke was, "Wait till Eisenhower finds out about this."

limited his response to demanding a four-power summit meeting. His proposal pointedly excluded the Chinese, which infuriated Mao, but at the same time indicated that Khrushchev was serious about talking. The regime in Jordan was perceptibly stabilized, and fears of a Nasserite coup, which would have probably touched off another Arab-Israeli war, subsided. The conservative Arab regimes felt more confident in the face of Nasserism, and Nasser himself began to improve relations with the United States. All the American troops were withdrawn within about three months of the initial landing.

John Kennedy's dispatch of 5,000 combat troops to Thailand during the Laotian crisis of 1961–62 had a number of parallels with Eisenhower's action in Lebanon. American interest in Laos stemmed from its major investment over the years in Thailand as the linchpin of its alliance system in Southeast Asia. Laos was viewed as a critical buffer between Thailand and the Communist regimes in China and North Vietnam. Although the United States had accepted a coalition Laotian regime at Geneva in 1954, it sponsored a rightist coup in 1958 when it became concerned that the government was leaning too far to the left. After an initial burst of energy, the leader of the rightist forces, a young general named Phoumi Nosavan, a cousin of the Thai premier Sarit Thanarat, lapsed into lethargy and irresponsibility. The Communist Pathet Lao, with strong ties to China and North Vietnam, joined forces with the neutralists to mount a military offensive against Phoumi's government. The Soviet Union, by this time actively bidding against the Chinese for influence with the North Vietnamese, supplied substantial military assistance to the left coalition.

The crisis first came to a head shortly after the American debacle at the Bay of Pigs, and Kennedy, to the consternation of the American China Lobby, quickly agreed to support new Geneva talks and a return to a neutralist coalition government. But the Geneva discussions broke down when Phoumi proved intransigent, and new fighting broke out in early 1962, climaxing with the decisive rout of the rightist forces at Nam Tha in March. Nam Tha threw the Thai regime into a panic. There were reportedly 10,000 North Vietnamese troops in northern Laos, supported by a large number of Chinese advisers. Sarit's fears that a left victory in Laos would lead immediately to an assault on the mixed Lao-Thai-Vietnamese ethnic regions of northeastern Thailand were entirely reasonable, and he began preparing for a unilateral Thai intervention into the Laotian fighting. Kennedy's quick dispatch of American troops was intended to stabilize and reassure the Thai regime and slow the Chinese and North Vietnamese intervention in Laos. (In the interest of secrecy, Kennedy did not brief congressional leaders on the troop action until the day the first new forces arrived in Thailand, three days after the decision was taken.) In the best Eisenhower style, Kennedy was intentionally ambiguous about the limitations that would be placed on the American combat forces. At the same time, he cut off aid to Phoumi and exerted all possible pressures to drive him back to the bargaining table.

Like Eisenhower in Lebanon, Kennedy achieved all his near-term objectives. The fighting stopped immediately—scholarly research indicates it may have stopped anyway—and both the Chinese and the Vietnamese cooperated in reaching a new Geneva agreement on a neutralist government in July. The episode was also a high watermark in American-Soviet cooperation. Khrushchev was anxious to discipline the Chinese, whose bellicosity was scoring points with Soviet clients around the world. His loud denunciations of the American action carried a pointed message to Beijing and Hanoi. Don't believe Kennedy's peaceful statements, he warned: "[American troops] arrived with their weapons. They did not come to play golf. They will shoot, and those they shoot will shoot back." Then he added soothingly—and with unwitting prescience—"the Americans may fight fifteen years if they want to, but it will not help." China and Vietnam, if they went to war with America, could count on the full moral support of the Soviet Union, but, the implication was clear, not much else.

The longer-term results of the action in Laos were rather more negative. The American commitment was greatly deepened in a region of little strategic significance, save as a counter in the continuous totting up of square yardage under "Communist" or "democratic" control. The administration seems also not to have understood how much Khrushchev's helpfulness was motivated by his quarrel with the Chinese, and so was unwilling to believe the reports of missiles in Cuba a few months later until it was almost too late to respond. Similarly, Khrushchev's success in bringing the Chinese and Vietnamese to the bargaining table led to a gross overestimate of Soviet ability to dictate subsequent events in Vietnam and much wasted "signalling" and misdirected diplomatic effort. Finally, and most important, the settlement in Laos left Kennedy with a gnawing feeling that Khrushchev had somehow bested him again in the Cold War—the new neutralist government, after all, had a decidedly leftist tinge—and led directly to the expansion of the American commitment to South Vietnam, a country much better suited to military operations than Laos.

The wisdom of hindsight aside, the actions in Lebanon and Laos were reasonable and proportionate responses to the new problem of global Communist containment. Geopolitics could no longer be restricted to Central Europe. Quite apart from ideology, the Soviet Union and China had declared their hostility to Western interests everywhere in the world; their global ambitions needed to be checked by the careful application of force or the threat of force at the vital chokepoints of the Western economic or military system. The case for intervening in Laos was less persuasive, perhaps, than the obvious necessity of maintaining a strong Western presence in the Middle East; but the United States was a Pacific basin power, and the danger of a Soviet-dominated Japan or India was properly a matter for serious concern. It was becoming painfully clear as well in Cuba, as it had long since become clear in Europe, that once Communist regimes were ensconced in power, they were extremely difficult, if not impossible, to dislodge. To be effective, a check to Communist encroachments needed to be early. Finally, it is the judiciousness of the commitments in Lebanon and Laos that recommends them. There was no attempt to impose a "pro-Western" solution, or to pursue "victory" at any cost; but rather a quick and practical acquiesence to a marginally acceptable outcome. The hostile advance was slowed, not stopped, but would proceed thenceforth with a greater degree of caution.

A new global power balance was taking on a roughly permanent shape in the early 1960s. The lines drawn through Central Europe and around Japan were hard; a breach by either side would lead to cataclysmic war. The big power commitment to the Middle East ranked next in importance; the jostling would be forceful and dangerous, but would stop short of drawing the Soviets and the Americans themselves into a direct confrontation. Elsewhere, strong economic linkages were giving the United States a permanent advantage with the rapidly industrializing countries along the Pacific rim; while the Soviet Union, and to a lesser extent, China, had the paramount influence in the larger socialist Asian countries like Indonesia and India,* although the naive replication of Soviet central economic planning systems greatly reduced the potential wealth and importance of such countries to Western com-

*Soviet exertions in India illustrate the lengths the Kremlin will go to achieve paramount influence in a major non-Communist state, although the mutuality of Indo-Soviet interests were also reinforced by the Soviet dispute with China. Through the late 1970s, the Soviets financed 30 percent of India's steel capacity, 70 percent of its oil-extracting equipment, 20 percent of its power, and 80 percent of its metallurgical industry. It was India's largest trading partner until the United States displaced it in 1984, but even then purchased a higher share of Indian exports. The Soviet Union has also furnished about 70 percent of Indian military hardware over the years.

merce. The remaining fringe areas of the world (sub-Saharan Africa, for example) would be contested for, but with a degree of actual exertion—as opposed to rhetoric or the shipment of outmoded military hardware—commensurate with their importance, which was not very much.

The commitment of military advisers to South Vietnam in 1961, therefore, as a demonstration of the reach of American elbows throughout the world, did little violence to the emerging protocols of big power behavior. Insofar as it served to brake Mao's aggressiveness, it was probably not entirely unwelcome to the Kremlin. Insofar as it was limited and judicious, it was in keeping with the marginal importance of the region. In short, it was not the American commitment to Vietnam that so unsettled the world power balance during the subsequent decade, and gave such dramatic impetus to the world arms race, but the utter lack of perspective and proportion with which the commitment was pursued.

CHAPTER **12**

---

# Hubris

### *"Pleikus Are Streetcars"*

Dwight Eisenhower made the original commitment of American money and prestige to Vietnam. John Kennedy militarized the commitment. Lyndon Johnson, acting against all his better instincts, took over the fighting with American combat troops and lost the war, his political career, and the postwar American imperium.

Eisenhower's support of France's war against Ho Chi Minh's Vietminh revolutionaries was at first equivocal and grudging—the payment of blackmail, in effect, to secure French consent for German rearmament. But with the French defeat at Dien Bien Phu in 1954, Vietnam became a key outpost in the *cordon sanitaire* that Eisenhower and Dulles were constructing against the advance of "international Communism." A temporary division of the country was agreed at the 1954 Geneva Conference, and the administration threw its support behind Ngo Dinh Diem as president of an independent South Vietnam. Diem was a pudgy mandarin of considerable national reputation—Ho had offered him a key post in a proposed coalition cabinet—and a Catholic who had spent a number of years in the United States building support among Catholic anti-Communist leaders, including Francis Cardinal Spellman and Senator John Kennedy. Eisenhower wrote Diem a famous letter—it was cited almost as a religious text by subsequent administrations—that promised to "assist the government of Vietnam in developing and maintaining a strong and viable state capable of resisting attempted subversion or aggression through military means." Forgotten almost immediately was the hedge that aid would be conditioned upon "assurances as to the standard of performance . . . in undertaking needed reforms," and the establishment of a government "responsive to the nationalist aspirations of its people."

212

With American connivance, Diem reneged on the Geneva provision requiring national unification elections in 1956, for the simple reason, as a blunt State Department assessment put it, that "Almost any type of election that could conceivably be held in Vietnam in 1956 would, on the basis of present trends, give the Communists a very significant, if not decisive, advantage. . . . [C]onditions of electoral freedom . . . might operate to favor the Communists more than their opponents." To the shock and disappointment of the Communist government in Hanoi, none of the other Geneva conferees—France, Great Britain, China, or the Soviet Union—supported its demand for elections. Moscow, in the midst of one of Khrushchev's periodic campaigns for detente, actually proposed that both Vietnams be represented in the United Nations, a suggestion the Chinese called "just and reasonable." With American support now unconditional, Diem set about imposing a brutal and corrupt dictatorship in South Vietnam, controlled by a nouveau riche, mostly Catholic elite—in a country that was 90 percent Buddhist—whose wealth and power derived solely from the billions in American aid flowing into the country.

There was little Ho could do. His own brutal dictatorship in the North had brought his country to the brink of famine, and he had no resources to intervene. Fearful of losing control of the Vietnamese revolutionary movement, he appears in fact to have discouraged the activities of the Southern National Liberation Front, or the Viet Cong,* at this time a substantially indigenous movement, which was mounting a rapidly expanding guerrilla offensive against the Diem regime.

A principled view of containment would look to both the strategic significance and the political character of a client country. Ideally, American support would be limited to democratic governments in areas critical to the West. In practice, unsavory regimes could be supported in regions of overriding geopolitical importance, like the Middle East; conversely, democratic countries of only marginal strategic value would still warrant some assistance. South Vietnam met neither criterion. The regime was as unsavory as any with which the United States was associated, but the country, if important, was clearly not vital. Some

---

*"Viet Cong" is an originally pejorative shorthand for "Vietnamese Communist" applied to the National Liberation Front by Diem and the Americans, although the movement contained a substantial admixture of Communist and non-Communist elements, and among the Communists, a substantial number that were not followers of Ho. It is used here in the sense it came generally to be used in the war, as a generic term for the South Vietnam-based insurgency, as distinct from the regular North Vietnamese units that began to move south in force beginning about mid-1965.

check against Communist expansion in Asia was appropriate, but the financial and emotional commitment to the rightist regimes in Laos and Vietnam that Eisenhower handed to John Kennedy in 1961 was already straining at the limits of both policy and principle.

It was the enthusiasm with which the Kennedy administration approached containment in Southeast Asia that distinguished it from its predecessor. Guerrilla warfare was a "hot" topic among defense intellectuals, the extreme test of the new strategy of "flexible response"— "precisely the application of their ideas which they could not help but relish," in Bernard Brodie's words. The enthusiasm began at the very top of the administration. Kennedy made a great show of reading Mao's and Ho's handbooks on guerrilla warfare, personally prodded the Army to form Special Forces units, picked out their uniforms, fussed about their footwear, insisted that they wear berets, and designated his brother Robert to head a "Counterinsurgency" task force, a sure sign that the issue was at the very top of the President's agenda. Guerrilla warfare capabilities was a major theme for McNamara. "It is tempting," he said,

to conclude that our conventional forces will leave us free to compete with communism in the peaceful sphere. . . . But we shall have to deal with the problems of "wars of liberation" . . . [in which] the force of world communism operates in the twilight zone between political subversion and quasi-military action. Their military tactics are those of the sniper, the ambush, and the raid. Their political tactics are terror, extortion, and assassination. We must help the people of threatened nations to resist these tactics by appropriate means. . . . Combating guerrilla warfare demands more in ingenuity than in money or manpower. But to meet the range of Communist military challenges calls for unprecedented efforts in men, money, and organization.

Kennedy's chief military advisers on guerrilla warfare were Edwin Lansdale and Maxwell Taylor. Lansdale was a guerrilla warfare expert who had led a successful antiguerrilla campaign in the Philippines and was fresh from directing sabotage expeditions against North Vietnam. For a time, he was Kennedy's first choice for the post of Ambassador to Vietnam. Taylor, who was later chairman of the Joint Chiefs of Staff and Ambassador to Vietnam, had written a book deploring, among other things, Eisenhower's unwillingness to develop a counterinsurgency capability. He testified to a congressional committee with evident excitement on the opportunities in Vietnam for officer training and tactical development: "Here we have a going laboratory where we have subversive insurgency, the Ho Chi Minh doctrine, being applied in all its forms. This has been a challenge, not just for the armed services, but for several of the agencies of the Government, as many of them are involved in South Viet Nam. On the military side, however, we have recognized the importance of this area as a laboratory."

A key early Kennedy adviser, and later Johnson's principal civilian adviser on Vietnam, was Walt Rostow, whose enthusiasm for guerrilla warfare approached the mystical. Rostow was an economist and historian, given to sweeping theories of world development, who believed that his book *Stages of Economic Growth: A Non-Communist Manifesto* offered an alternative doctrine to Marxism for the developing world. He was convinced that the world was entering "The Third Round" of an epochal struggle with communism: the contest with Stalin for the soul of Europe was the first round. The orbiting of Sputnik initiated "the second great Communist offensive of the postwar years." Wars of national liberation were Round Three, and counterinsurgency was the West's sacred mission. As Rostow orated to a class of Green Berets at Fort Bragg: "We are determined to destroy this international disease. This requires, of course, not merely a proper military program of deterrence, but programs of village development, communications and indoctrination. . . . I salute you as I would a group of doctors, teachers, economic planners, agricultural experts, civil servants, or those who are now leading the way in the whole southern half of the globe in fashioning the new nations."

It was not that Kennedy lacked countervailing advice. Charles de Gaulle, his country still strained by the painful extrication from Algeria, made an impassioned personal plea to the young President in 1961:

You will find that engagement in [Vietnam] will become an endless entanglement. Once a nation has been aroused, no foreign power, however strong, can impose its will upon it. You will discover this for yourselves. . . . The people . . . do not want you. The ideology you invoke will make no difference. Indeed . . . it will become identified with your will to power. The Communists will appear as champions of national independence. . . . You will sink step by step into a bottomless military and political quagmire. . . . I tell you this in the name of the West.

But Kennedy's men wanted to try their hand in a real guerrilla fight. As William Kaufmann wrote—in 1964, still proudly—"the multiple option approach facilitated intervention [in Vietnam] because of its emphasis on resources for countering insurgency." Or, as Rostow exhorted:

"We must somehow bring to bear our unexploited counter-guerrilla assets on the Viet-Nam problem: armed helicopters; other Research and Development possibilities; our Special Forces units. It is somehow wrong to be developing these capabilities but not applying them in a crucially active theater. In Knute Rockne's old phrase, we are not saving them for the Junior Prom."

The ensuing story is one of the saddest and most sordid in all of American history. Kennedy dispatched Taylor, Lansdale, and Rostow to Vietnam to help decide a course of action. The recommendations that would emerge from such a team were a foregone conclusion, and even before they left, Kennedy directed the State Department to write a report that: "was to demonstrate wholesale violation of the 1954 accords by the other side, thus supporting whatever counter-breach of the Accords might emerge in the President's own decisions." On their return, Taylor and Rostow argued for a sharp increase in military aid, particularly helicopters, an increase in the American role at all levels of the South Vietnam government, and the introduction of American combat troops, in the guise of flood-control workers. The recommendation for combat troops met strong protests from the State Department, including the Secretary, Dean Rusk, and Averell Harriman. The Joint Chiefs were willing, but the requirements they laid out were huge. (John Kenneth Galbraith wondered how the modern Army would have fared against the Sioux.) Surprisingly, Diem was also opposed to an American combat role. His regime was shaky enough as it was; being clearly labelled an American puppet could be the last straw.

Kennedy finally ruled against combat troops, but directed an increase in military advisers that amounted almost to the same thing. The mission was rapidly expanded from 685 men—the Geneva limit that Eisenhower had scrupulously observed—to 11,000 men by 1962 and 16,000 in 1963. More important, the "advisers" began taking an active part in combat missions, usually piloting the helicopters that took Diem's troops into action—although a Vietnamese was supposed to be at the controls when the helicopters sprayed napalm or chemical defoliants, which were already coming into wide use. The Americans also initiated a "strategic hamlet" program designed to protect loyal villages from Communist infiltration. Given the description of the hamlets by Roger Hilsman, a strong hamlet proponent and a key Kennedy adviser, it is hardly surprising that most peasants had to be forced to live in them: "[There would be] hedgehogs of strategic hamlets spreading out like an oil blot from the sea toward the mountains and the jungle. Plastic identity cards had to be issued, curfews established, and provincial forces trained to set up checkpoints and ambushes during curfew hours. An iron grid of security had to be established to control the movement of both goods and people, of rice and recruits."

Finally, Kennedy ruled out any negotiations. As his own decision memorandum stated:

"If we postpone action in Vietnam to engage in talks with the Communists, we can surely count on a major crisis of nerve in Viet-Nam and throughout Southeast Asia. The image of U.S. unwillingness to confront Communism—induced by the Laos performance—will be regarded as definitely confirmed. There will be panic and disarray. . . . If we negotiate now—while infiltration continues—we shall in fact be judged weaker than in Laos; for in that case we at least first insisted on a cease-fire."

For the next year and a half, the administration deluded itself that the intervention was successful. The false precision that pervaded McNamara's Pentagon supported the self-deception. Highly suspect numbers from Diem's corrupt bureaucracy proved that "two thirds of the populace" was safely and loyally ensconced in 7,205 strategic hamlets by June 1963, while detailed "body counts" of Viet Cong killed in action demonstrated that the insurgency was on the verge of collapse. As one combat adviser, Lt. Col. John Paul Vann, reported in a briefing script that was squelched by the Pentagon: "the number of enemy reported killed . . . is highly misleading. . . . we estimate, and I stress this can only be an estimate, that the *total number of people killed was less than two-thirds of those claimed.* Additionally, *we estimate that from 30% to 40% of the personnel killed were merely bystanders who were unfortunate enough to be in the vicinity of the combat action*" (italics in original).

In fact, the Viet Cong showed an impressive ability to engage and defeat government troops even after the large-scale introduction of helicopters and chemical weapons. Virtually an entire platoon of the government's crack Vietnamese Rangers was wiped out during a routine Delta sweep in October 1962. The following January, at the village of Ap Bac, a Viet Cong battalion fought a government force more than four times its size to a standstill, causing almost 200 casualties, including three American dead, and downing five helicopters, before finally withdrawing through an opening conveniently provided by the cowed attacking force. The American claim that Ap Bac was a "victory" because the village was occupied after the Viet Cong withdrew helped fuel the growing cynicism of the American press corps covering the war.

For the next four years, the band of committed advisers—

McNamara, Rostow, the national security adviser McGeorge Bundy, and later Rusk—clung grimly to their adventure in Vietnam, long after the last shreds of justification had been stripped away. During the summer of 1963, widespread Buddhist protests against Diem's rule, including several spectacular self-immolations by Buddhist bonzes, and a savagely repressive police response, destroyed any illusion that the Diem government represented the "nationalist aspirations of the people." Rather than seize the opportunity for an honorable, if somewhat tarnished, departure, the Kennedy administration resolved to change the regime; in other words, holding South Vietnam—or perhaps more accurately, avoiding the political onus of *not* holding Vietnam—had become the objective, not supporting a free and democratic ally. The resolve for a change increased when it was disclosed that Ngo Dinh Nhu, Diem's influential brother, was putting out feelers to the insurgents on a coalition government. Shortly thereafter, the American mission connived in a military coup in which both brothers were assassinated.

To the administration's great disappointment, the new military junta determined almost immediately that it had no hope of winning the war. The generals, believing that the Viet Cong was still relatively independent of the North, began actively exploring a neutralist solution and "a relationship of peaceful coexistence between Saigon and Hanoi," in the words of the junta's prime minister, Nguyen Ngoc Tho. McNamara expressed his alarm after a brief visit to Saigon shortly after Kennedy's death: "The situation is very disturbing. Current trends, unless reversed in the next 2–3 months, will lead to neutralization at best and more likely to a Communist-controlled state. . . . We should watch the situation very carefully, running scared, hoping for the best, but preparing for more forceful moves if the situation does not show early signs of improvement."

The answer was another military coup only three months later—dubbed "the Pentagon's coup" by South Vietnamese officers because of widespread rumors that the coup was supported or even conceived by the American military command in Saigon, with the approval of the Pentagon. There is considerable circumstantial evidence to support the rumors. The second coup already had an air of desperation. As Paul Harkins, the senior American military officer in Saigon, wired back to Washington: "One thing is for sure with this coup. We've gone through all the eligible officers." Desperation led to absurdities like McNamara's barnstorming political tour of Vietnamese villages with the new junta's leader, Major General Nguyen Khanh, as if a little old-fashioned American politicking and McNamara's few butchered Vietnamese phrases could turn the trick. Desperation also meant an even grimmer American determination to hold the line. McNamara told President Johnson that any sign of an American willingness to negotiate: "would simply mean a Communist takeover in South Vietnam. . . . Only the U.S. presence after 1954 held the South together under far more favorable circumstances, and enabled Diem to refuse to go through with the 1954 provision calling for nationwide 'free' elections in 1956. Even talking about a U.S. withdrawal would undermine any chance of keeping a non-Communist government in South Vietnam, and the rug would be pulled before the negotiations had gone far." Or, as Dean Rusk wrote to the American Embassy in Saigon; "Is there any way we can shake the main body of the [new Vietnamese] leadership by the scruff of the neck and insist that they put aside all bickering and lesser differences in order to concentrate on the defeat of the Viet Cong? . . . Somehow we must change the pace at which people move and I suspect this can only be done with a pervasive intrusion of Americans into their affairs."

Scarcely a year had passed before Khanh, the administration's presumed last best hope, was also found to be negotiating with the Viet Cong through the Buddhist leadership, and was duly deposed. Military regimes were now following upon one another with comic-opera rapidity, and the moral and political basis for American intervention had narrowed to the vanishing point. But Bundy, McNamara, the Joint Chiefs, and Rusk pressed their arguments for aggressive American intervention ever more fiercely upon a reluctant President; until finally, Lyndon Johnson, confronted by a "Macedonian phalanx" of unanimity among his top advisers—all save George Ball, who was second rank— overruled his own better judgment and plunged into the dreaded "land war in Asia" that bitter military experience had made a cardinal principle of avoiding.

The military intervention in Vietnam, and particularly the gradually escalated bombing campaign, as it was conceived and directed by McNamara and Bundy, was a textbook application of the war-fighting theories of Thomas Schelling and the RAND defense intellectuals; and it exposed, to the mocking skull-laughter of 59,000 dead American soldiers, the empty pretension and sheer fraudulence of the entire baroque conception they had been a decade elaborating. The central teaching of the defense intellectuals was that war was a bargaining process, an intricate gavotte of signal and subtle countersignal, a refined calculus by detached rationalists who weighed each thrust and parry in a mathematical scale of outcome and advantage, a teaching—Colin Gray suggests—that appeared to receive striking confirmation in the Cuban missile confrontation. Not so in Vietnam. In Bernard Brodie's caustic summary: "The failure of the civilian strategists in Vietnam . . . is that parts of their theory . . . proved utterly irrelevant, and many of their ideas that were not irrelevant proved false." As Leslie Gelb pointed out, civil wars are almost never settled by bargaining: the great civil wars of the recent past—the American, the Russian, and the Spanish civil wars—ground on until one side or the other was exhausted and defeated, an observation that perhaps should not have escaped the eye of so many political scientists and historians.

The entire American war plan was designed as an appeal to the rationalists who supposedly resided in the Hanoi Politburo, or in Beijing, or in Moscow, to look to their self-interest and offer honorable terms. As soon as the shakiness of Khanh's junta became evident in mid-1964, the administration began looking for some way to "send a message" to both the North and South Vietnamese that America was in for the long haul unless a satisfactory result was achieved. What was needed, in Bundy's words, was an American "commitment which the Vietnamese would interpret as a willingness to raise the military ante and eschew negotiations begun from a position of weakness." The opportunity for such an "irreversible commitment" presented itself just a few weeks later when North Vietnamese torpedo boats attacked, or apparently attacked, American destroyers operating in the Tonkin Gulf off the coast of North Vietnam. The first torpedo boat attack, on August 2, is not in doubt. The second, alleged to have occurred on August 4, was probably a figment of the imaginations of jumpy crewmen. The crewmen's mistake, if it was one, was honest; but there are substantial reasons to believe that either the President intentionally concealed the shakiness of the evidence for the second attack from the Congress or that his top policy advisers concealed it from both him and the Congress. The Tonkin Gulf Resolution, passed almost unanimously in response to the alleged second attack, gave the administration virtually a free hand in pursuing the war by methods and at levels of commitment of its own choosing.

The one-day retaliatory bombing strike that Johnson authorized in the wake of the Tonkin Gulf incidents demonstrably failed either to stiffen the resolve of the South Vietnamese or to slow the Communist campaign. Barely two weeks after the air strikes, there were widespread demonstrations against the government in the South. On Christmas Eve, the Viet Cong bombed the American officers' billet in the heart of Saigon, killing two Americans and wounding thirty-eight. Early in 1965, at the town of Binh Gia, just 40 miles north of Saigon, two of the best government battalions, with ample armor and firepower, were decisively defeated by a much smaller Viet Cong unit and saved from utter disaster only by a last-minute swarm of American "adviser"-piloted helicopters, at the cost of sixteen American casualties and four lost helicopters.

The political atmosphere in South Vietnam was seething. The populace, almost all the politicians, and probably most of the military were sick of the war, and there was real danger that the United States would be invited to leave. The overwhelming reaction from Johnson's advisers was not that the position was hopeless, but that America was still sending the wrong signals. As Bundy wrote in a long memorandum to the President:

The underlying difficulties in Saigon arise from the spreading conviction there that the future is without hope for anti-Communists. . . . Our best friends have become somewhat discouraged by our own inactivity in face of major attacks on our own installations. The Vietnamese know as well as we do that the Viet Cong are gaining in the countryside. Meanwhile, they see the enormous power of the United States withheld, and they get little sense of firm and active U.S. policy. They feel we are unwilling to take serious risks.

The necessary "firm and active" commitment, the President's advisers argued, again almost to a man, could be demonstrated only by an American bombing assault on the North. The call for forceful action intensified in February 1965, when the Viet Cong attacked an American air base at Pleiku in the central highlands, killing eight Americans, wounding 126, destroying ten airplanes and damaging numerous others. In Bundy's famous phrase, "Pleikus are streetcars"—when one comes along, you get on it.

Johnson, who had steadfastly resisted additional bombing of the North since the previous August, finally authorized the "Flaming Dart" series of reprisal strikes against the North, but only in response to specific provocations from the Viet Cong. It was not what his advisers wanted. Bundy, Taylor, and McNamara were pressing for a sustained bombing campaign, "a measured, controlled sequence of actions"; or in the words of John McNaughton, McNamara's chief assistant on Vietnam, and a long-time friend of Schelling, "Progressive squeeze-and-talk. Present policies plus an orchestration of communications with Hanoi and a crescendo of additional military moves against infiltration targets, first in Laos and then in the DRV [North Vietnam], and then against other targets in North Vietnam. The scenario would be designed to give the U.S. the option at any point to proceed or not, to escalate or not, and to quicken the pace or not."

Johnson held out for three weeks, partly because Khanh, whose loyalties were now in doubt, would not clearly support the bombing. But on March 1, with Khanh safely overthrown and a new government headed by Air Marshal Nguyen Cao Ky, a bombing enthusiast, the "Rolling Thunder" program of sustained bombing was launched against the North. Rolling Thunder was intended as a precise application of Schelling's theories of "compellence bombing." It was to be surgically directed and gradually escalated—or de-escalated—depending on the military actions of the Viet Cong and their presumed masters in the North. Henry Cabot Lodge, who entered his second tour of duty as ambassador in the summer, summarized Rolling Thunder's subtleties: "If you lay the whole country waste, it is quite likely you will introduce a mood of fatalism in the Viet Cong. Also there will be nobody left in North Viet Nam on whom to put pressure. . . . What we are interested in here is not destroying Ho Chi Minh (as his successor will probably be worse than he is), but getting him to change his behavior."

It was quickly apparent that the bombing was a failure; if anything, the tempo of insurgent activity quickened. The only puzzle is why the President's advisers expected otherwise. In the first place, the White House knew that Ho was not in complete control of the Viet Cong—the first unmistakably North Vietnamese troops in the South were identified only in April 1965. Just as important, the concept of "surgical" bombing strikes was a self-delusion. High-altitude B-52 carpet-bombing attacks were necessarily imprecise, and the interpretation of bombing results occasioned bitter interbureaucratic disputes between the military and the civilian analysts in the CIA and the Pentagon, particularly after Ho dispersed his limited industrial capacity throughout the countryside. Further, the diplomatic semaphores between Ho and the United States were inherently ambiguous, "like sending smoke signals in a high wind," in the words of one Pentagon official. Several times when Johnson ordered bombing pauses to encourage negotiations, there was a visible stepup of activity on the supply routes to the insurgents, and then maddeningly, just as the bombing resumed again, Ho sent a signal—always a clouded one—that he was interested in talking.

Conversely, one of the few times that Ho seemed to respond positively to a bombing halt, during the Operation Marigold diplomatic assault of 1966, the opportunity was aborted by an untimely bombing resumption, either because of military bloody-mindedness or, more likely, the inability to maintain the required fine degree of coordination.

The daily spectacle of Lyndon Johnson and Robert McNamara meticulously choosing each day's bombing targets pinpoints the central confusion. Picking bombing targets gave an illusion of control, but virtually none of the information necessary for intelligent target-picking could possibly be available in Washington. Cables from the front were necessarily fragmentary and inaccurate. Local military or civilian conditions could not be reliably understood at 10,000 miles remove. And there was no information at all on the state of mind of Ho or the North Vietnamese Politburo. It was the same illusion that said that numerical body counts—*because* they were numerical, and therefore precise—conveyed more information than the reports from the correspondents at the front who were insisting that the war had been lost long ago.

With Rolling Thunder an obvious failure only weeks after it was begun, McNamara and Bundy began to press aggressively for the next decisive and fateful step: an American takeover of the ground war in the South. No one, except Rostow and some of the military, argued for an invasion of the North: 50,000 Chinese troops had entered the northern parts of the country, pointedly making no effort to conceal their presence from American intelligence—the language of "signals" could hardly have been clearer. McNamara's private assessment, prepared by McNaughton, was that with "200,000–400,000+" American troops, there was a 50 percent chance of winning the war in three years and a 70 percent chance of achieving a Laos-type compromise; but that at the present level of American troop commitment, which had crept up to 75,000, there was only a 30 percent chance of winning by 1968 and a 40 percent chance of achieving a face-saving compromise. As far as is known, he did not present this estimate to the President, perhaps because the huge manpower increase seemed to buy such marginal improvements. McNaughton's statistical presentation also demonstrated how radically American war aims had shifted during two years of steady escalation. They were now "70%—To preserve national honor as a guarantor . . . 20%—To keep SVN (and their adjacent) territory from hostile expansive hands . . . 10%—To answer the call of a friend." Since the feckless commitment to Vietnam had placed American reputation and honor at such risk, in other words, it was now necessary to risk even more to save them.

Johnson fully appreciated the significance of the move. He asked McNamara to make a personal visit to Vietnam before making his recommendation, and then scheduled a series of meetings over most of a week in late July 1965, with a wide and shifting cast of advisers encompassing the inner circle, a broader representation of the military chiefs and service secretaries, and a number of outsiders, including John McCloy, Omar Bradley, Arthur Dean, and Clark Clifford. McNamara presented a bleakly accurate assessment of the situation in the South:

The situation in South Vietnam is worse than a year ago (when it was worse than the year before that) . . . [The government controlled] fewer and fewer people in less and less territory . . . a hard VC push was on to dismember the nation and maul the army. . . . [Government] desertions are at a high rate, and the force build-up has slipped badly. . . . There are no signs that [the bombing attacks] have throttled the inflow of supplies for the VC or can throttle the flow while their material needs are as low as they are. . . . Nor have our air attacks in North Vietnam produced tangible evidence of willingness on the part of Hanoi to come to the conference table in a reasonable mood. . . . [South Vietnam is] not capable of successfully resisting the VC initiatives without more active assistance from more US/third country ground forces than those thus far committed.

McNamara recommended an additional 100,000 American troops, with another 100,000 to follow in 1966, to take over both the direction and the fighting of the war. "Isn't this going off the diving board?" the President asked:

Do all of you think the Congress and the people will go along with 600,000 people and billions of dollars 10,000 miles away?

*Stanley Resor* [*Secretary of the Army*]: Gallup poll shows people are basically behind our commitment.

*President:* But if you make a commitment to jump off a building and you find out how high it is you may withdraw the commitment."

George Ball, with only Clifford and later Senate Majority Leader Mike Mansfield in support, made a powerful dissent:

We cannot win, Mr. President, This war will be long and protracted. The most we can hope for is a messy conclusion. There remains the great danger of intrusion by the Chinese. But the biggest problem is the problem of the long war. . . . I think we have all underestimated the seriousness of this situation. It is like giving cobalt treatment to a terminal cancer case. I think a long, protracted war will disclose our weakness not our strength. The least harmful way to cut losses in SVN is to let the government decide it doesn't want us to stay there. . . . I have no illusions that after we were asked to leave South Vietnam, that country would soon come under Hanoi control. . . .

*President:* But, George, wouldn't all these countries say that Uncle Sam was a paper tiger, wouldn't we lose credibility breaking the word of three presidents? . . .

*Ball:* No, sir. The worst blow would be that the mightiest power on earth is unable to defeat a handful of guerrillas."

The dissenters were lonely voices. General Earle Wheeler, chairman of the Joint Chiefs, was brimming with confidence: "North Vietnam may reinforce their forces, but they can't match us on a buildup. From a military point of view, we can handle, if we are determined to do so, China and North Vietnam." Lodge painted the failure to intervene in apocalyptic terms, but was as confident as Wheeler in the outcome of an American intervention: "I feel there is greater threat to start World War III if we don't go in. Can't we see the similarity to our own indolence at Munich? I simply can't be as pessimistic as Ball. We have great seaports in Vietnam. We don't need to fight on roads. We have the sea. Let us visualize meeting the VC on our own terms. . . . The procedures for this are known." McNamara thought the intervention could be handled economically: "$12 billion in 1966. . . . It would not require wage and price controls in my judgment. The price index ought not go up more than one point or two."

The President announced his decision to Americanize the fighting and send 100,000 additional troops on July 28, 1965. The tide was not turned. By the end of 1966, American troops in Vietnam exceeded 385,000, and by mid-1967, 425,000, although William Westmoreland, the American commander in Vietnam, was already asking for 671,000. When McNamara left the Pentagon in 1968, his elegantly rationalized world in ruins, and Lyndon Johnson retired, virtually in shame, from the presidency, the total forces committed to the losing struggle in Southeast Asia, including the men in Thailand and stationed in the Seventh Fleet, exceeded 650,000. By the time the last Americans were airlifted off the roof of the Saigon Embassy in 1975, some 200,000 Americans had been wounded and 59,000 killed. There is no way to calculate the injuries and deaths suffered by the Southeast Asians.

## Imbalance of Power

As the American commitment to Vietnam deepened, the Kremlin's initial complacence slowly gave way to mounting alarm. For opinion makers in the United States, Vietnam may have been a frustrating demonstration of the massive ineffectiveness of military power; but to the conservatives in the Soviet military, who had never accepted Khrushchev's belief in the "doctrinal restraint" of the United States, the rapid American buildup in conventional forces, coupled with its frightening lead in missiles and nuclear weapons, was a deeply dangerous development. By 1968, with 3.5 million men on active duty, the American armed forces were almost a half million men bigger than the Soviet Union's, and for possibly the only time in the twentieth century, the United States even enjoyed a slight edge in infantry troops. The American buildup was the more disturbing for its apparent effortlessness. A force of 650,000 men, the most powerfully armed, richly equipped, and lavishly supplied in the history of warfare, was being maintained 10,000 miles from home without full mobilization, during a time when domestic spending programs of all kinds were being rapidly expanded.

The size, the reach, and the speed of the American buildup were alarming enough. But the United States was also making huge strides in precisely the capabilities that forward-looking Soviet and American military analysts had long pinpointed as the secret to victory in Europe. A decade before, Western military writers had begun to theorize about fighting a war of rapid maneuver on the European front after both sides had resorted to tactical nuclear weapons. As one prominent analysis put it:

The atomic weapon is countered in military operations by movement, cover, concealment, and dispersion. . . . Atomic warfare emphasizes the value of rapid manoeuvre as a defensive measure also. Static lines, once located, may be broken by multiple heavy-burst atomic strikes, followed immediately by fast-moving attack. A defence characterized by rapid sharp blows against the flanks and rear of the attacker's advancing divisions or armies results in a kaleidoscope of unexpected situations in which the slower reactions of the Soviet forces are likely to place them at a disadvantage.

The advent of the Kennedy-McNamara strategy of "flexible response" focused renewed attention on rapid-maneuver warfare. The Soviet military was clearly thinking along similar lines, despite Khrushchev's preference for his own version of massive retaliation. As Malinovsky boasted in 1961: "The Ground Forces . . . can wage active highly maneuverable combat actions at unprecedentedly high tempos to a great operational depth in conditions of use by the enemy of nuclear weapons."

The original Taylor-Lansdale idea of building a worldwide counterinsurgency capability within the American military was only distantly related to the new theories of maneuver warfare. But counterinsurgency's sudden fashion was seized upon by a small core of Army enthusiasts who were pressing radical new concepts of infantry mobility, built around the armored helicopter. For years, despite the attention it received in theoretical military journals, and the support of mavericks like General James Gavin, air mobility doctrine had been firmly squelched by the Pentagon brass. The old-line tank and infantry commanders were more interested in developing faster and longer-range armored vehicles, while the Air Force was violently suspicious of any hint of Army encroachment on its close-support air combat role, although close-support tactics had long been the stepchild of the more glamorous nuclear attack mission. The air mobility advocates managed to convince McNamara's civilian analysts to sponsor a head-to-head test with the Air Force, in which integrated helicopter units decisively outperformed units supported with traditional Air Force tactics. The first air-mobile division was activated by McNamara just eight days before William Westmoreland made his formal 1965 request that American troops take over a combat role in Vietnam, and the new division was included in the very first dispatch of combat troops.

The role of the combat helicopter evolved with extraordinary rapidity. When the first units were sent to Vietnam, the helicopter was still viewed primarily as an observation tool and troop carrier. The first "Huey" helicopters (the Bell UH-1) were armed troop carrier escorts; but by 1968, with the appearance of the third-generation Huey, the HueyCobra, with 75 percent more firepower than its predecessors, the helicopter had effected a minor revolution in infantry tactics. In the words of the editors of *Jane's:* "The armed helicopter, pioneered by the Bell UH-1 and HueyCobra, is now firmly established as an essential and formidable weapon for close support duties." Or as an enthusiastic commander put it, the helicopter "extended the infantry unit's area of control at least threefold. A commander could react to opportunities quicker, delay his decision, or even change his plans en route. He could pile on, block escape routes, extract, or surprise."

The HueyCobras were awesome fighting machines. Fifty-three feet long from nose to rotor tip, they could skim the treetops at more than 200 miles per hour, like swarms of evil-looking steel locusts, spewing destructive fire in any direction. The HueyCobra's basic armament was a six-barrel 7.62mm. "minigun," with firing settings of 800 and 4,000 rounds per minute, and a 40 mm. grenade launcher with 300 rounds.

Exterior mounts allowed room for two more miniguns, twin pods of 2.75-inch high-explosive rocket launchers with seventy-six rockets—the equivalent firepower of a 105mm. howitzer—and three antitank "TOW"* missiles. The guns and launchers were designed to have a wide radius of fire ahead of and around the hovering helicopter and above to protect against enemy aircraft. Basic jungle assault tactics called for circling fire at the low minigun firing setting, using full fire once the enemy was flushed and engaged. With tracer bullets on night attacks, the high-fire setting probed into the darkness of the jungle like a solid finger of flame.

Helicopters were used to spot the enemy—"Nighthawk" infrared-equipped Hueys could pinpoint troops at night—to ferry troops to battle, to lay down aerial artillery barrages ahead of the advancing infantry, or even to carry huge banks of searchlights in night assaults. Huge "Flying Crane" helicopters forced remote skirmishes into forms the Americans were familiar with. Bizarre hailstorms of machinery would appear dangling incongruously from chains in the sky—bulldozers for clearing trees; 155mm. howitzers; radar installations that were bounced from terrain feature to terrain feature; specially-adapted M113 armored personnel carriers (a cross between an armored jeep and a lightly protected tank); and the M551 "General Sheridan" airborne assault vehicle—literally a light tank, with a 152mm. gun, that could be carried to battle by a helicopter.†

Soviet commanders, who had not led troops in battle for twenty years, could only have envied the opportunity to test men, equipment, and tactics under fire. The Army experimented with new formations for advancing tank and infantry platoons to maximize the weight of outward-directed fire. Howitzers were redesigned so crews could accomplish "speed-shifts," sweeping the huge guns to cover a 360° radius in minutes, a task that previously would have taken almost an hour with a much larger crew. Rapid fuel air drops with flexible rubber drums that could absorb a long fall without breaking, and new stream-bridging

---

*"TOW" stands for "Tube-launched, Optically tracked, Wire-guided." The TOW antitank missile is connected to the launching mechanism by a thin filament of wire. After launching, as the gunner tracks a moving target through a sight, the missile changes direction to maintain its target fix.

†It is no denigration of the formidable combat capabilities of the armed helicopter to say that the Army has been forced to rely too exclusively on the helicopter for air close support. Particularly against armored enemy troops, helicopters are quite vulnerable to return fire. Fixed-wing air support, however, must come from the Air Force, which has never given the mission top priority. The overemphasis on the helicopter stems from the fact that it is the only air weapon which the Army fully controls.

tactics and equipment presaged an "area" war in Europe, conceived as a rapidly shifting battlefield without fixed lines, in which troops pounced from weak spot to weak spot in the enemy alignments, attacking as often from the rear as from the front or the flanks. It was quickly discovered that taking away the cannons from the F-4 Phantom—a splendid airplane—made it vulnerable in a dogfight, and that the F-111, McNamara's troubled TFX, was unreliable to the point of uselessness. Bullpup air-to-ground missiles, the standard Navy and Air Force attack weapon, with a conventional warhead explosive equivalent of 250 pounds of TNT, barely dented the massive steel and stone Thanh Hoa railroad bridge in North Vietnam in two years of attacks. When the bombing campaign against the North was briefly resumed in 1972, however, laser-guided "smart" bombs took out the span in a single strike.

From the Soviet standpoint, the great danger of the burgeoning American military capability was the international behavior it would induce. The arms race between the United States and the Soviet Union has never been, as it often is simplistically portrayed, a straightforward process of action and reaction whereby one side, usually the United States, invents a weapon and the other side reproduces it. But on a deeper level, an action–reaction logic unquestionably drives the competition. An actual or perceived preponderance of warmaking capability on one side or the other generates a more expansively aggressive posture in the international arena, one that the other side feels impelled to counteract. The Johnson administration understood, for example, how profoundly threatening the rapid buildup in Vietnam would appear to the Soviet Union and China. Only America's overwhelming military superiority allowed it to pursue the adventure with so little heed to their sensibilities. One telling incident betokens the sense of American confidence. The 1965 "Flaming Dart" bombing campaign was launched against the North while Alexei Kosygin, the Soviet prime minister, was in Hanoi on a state visit that was widely assumed by the CIA and American press to be an attempt to defuse the looming confrontation. The refusal to delay the bombing campaign for just a few days was a gratuitous and unmistakable insult, of the kind that only a country supremely sure of its power would dare administer.

If the world had lingering doubts of the second-rank military status of the Soviet Union, they were effectively dispelled by the 1967 six-day desert war between Israel and Egypt, Syria, and Jordan. In just a few days, Israel, using French fighter planes and British and American tanks, and with only relatively light losses of its own, destroyed a military machine twice as big that had been painstakingly built up by the Soviet Union since the Suez War at a cost of more than $1 billion. To make matters worse, much of the Arab equipment was the best the Soviets had to offer. About half of Egypt's 1,200 tanks were T-54s and T-55s, the same tanks that were the mainstay of the Soviet and satellite forces in Europe. The Arab air forces consisted substantially of late-model MiG-21 interceptors and MiG-19 ground attack planes, and a contingent of TU-16 "Badger" bombers, again the same equipment the Soviets used.

Although it was cold comfort for the Soviets, the apparent ease of the Israeli victory was hardly a true indicator of the East-West balance. Either because of Arab fecklessness or poor Soviet advice, the Egyptian Air Force was left conveniently clustered at vulnerable airports as war fever mounted. In their lightning pre-emptive strike on the morning of June 5, the Israelis destroyed more than 300 of the 500 Egyptian planes, and a few hours later effectively eliminated the smaller Syrian, Jordanian, and Iraqi air forces. In the first stages of the strike, Israel reportedly left only twelve planes behind for home defense. Had Syria and Jordan displayed the slightest initiative and scrambled their air forces before the second Israeli strike, or had the Egyptian Air Force been able to get off the ground, Israel would have been quite vulnerable.

As the battle shifted to the ground over the next several days, the Arab tank forces, with their air cover destroyed, were helpless against Israeli air strikes in the open expanses of the desert. Two thirds of the Israeli air strikes were directed against Arab ground forces and the great majority of the 500-odd Arab tanks lost were hit from the air. Once again, the Israelis proved vastly superior in every area of logistics and tactics. Israeli ground crews turned around fighter planes in seven minutes, while Egyptian crews took up to two hours. Israeli tank gunners were far more accurate and could sustain much higher rates of fire than the Egyptians. With Arab command and control in disarray, the stolid Russian three-echelon defensive formations left the Arab armored forces in a stationary mass that was easily enveloped by the slashing Israeli advance and trapped in enfilading fire from all sides.

To their Third World clients, the Soviet diplomatic performance during the Six-Day War was as significant as the ease of the Israeli victory. The initial Soviet protests against the Israeli attack were the minimum that form required, and Kosygin's request to Johnson to restrain the Israelis was polite and unthreatening. During the fighting,

Johnson twice used the "hotline" between Moscow and Washington to convey messages to the Arab leaders about American actions on the periphery of the battle. The Russians dutifully relayed the messages, making them appear, in Heikel's words, "dupes of the Americans or too frightened to be able to come to the help of their friends." Most important, the Soviets refused to resupply the Arab losses during the fighting. Additional planes could have made a major difference, since the Israeli pre-emptive attack on the Arab airfields had left the Arab flight crews intact. Logistics problems may have entered into the Soviet decision, although there were reports of Soviet supply ships turning back from within sight of Alexandria. In the view of a disgusted Nasser, the Soviets "were frozen into immobility by their fear of a confrontation with America."

The tone and threatening content of the Soviet protests escalated sharply in the last stages of the war, as the Israeli forces advanced virtually without opposition. But, as with the late-stage threats during the Suez War, the tough talk came only after the key elements of a cease-fire were already in place. General Wheeler, chairman of the Joint Chiefs, is reported to have advised: "We have nothing to fear from Soviet action. The Soviets have no large mobile units to put into action at once in the Middle Eastern war. They have alerted their paratrooper divisions, but they know how dangerous it would be to put them into action."

The Soviets' uneasy sense of their own supineness might be gleaned from the extraordinary Central Committee meeting that was held immediately after the war to endorse "the speedy, resolute actions by the Soviet Union . . . in stopping the military operations in the Middle East." Significantly, the same meeting took pains to criticize "the slander campaign and splitting activities of Mao Tse-tung's group aimed at disuniting the anti-imperialist forces and undermining the trust between the peoples of the Arab states and the peoples of the socialist countries." It is easy to imagine what Mao was saying about the courage of his socialist brothers in Moscow. And it is easy to imagine that, to the new leadership in the Kremlin, a continuation of the enormous arms gap between the United States and the Soviet Union would be intolerable. Steps had been in train for some time, in fact, to rectify the imbalance.

# PART IV.

---------------------------------------------------------------

# THE SHIFTING BALANCE

CHAPTER 13

---

# Decisions in the Kremlin

Nikita Khrushchev expressly ordered the launching of the Soviet satellite Vokshod I in October 1964 to coincide with the anniversary of the Russian Revolution. Vokshod was the kind of space spectacular he loved—it carried three cosmonauts to one-up the two-man American Gemini series—and *Pravda* gave it the full treatment: "Sorry Apollo! . . . the so-called system of free enterprise is turning out to be powerless in competition with socialism." Khrushchev was on a short holiday in the Crimea on the date of the launch, the 12th, but was kept abreast by phone. Naturally, he planned to fly home in time to meet the cosmonauts at the end of their "glorious" flight. But the Praesidium unexpectedly requested that he return early, and, mysteriously, the Vokshod flight was ended after only a single day in space. When one of the cosmonauts complained, Sergei Korolev, still directing the space program, reputedly replied, "There are more things in heaven and earth, Horatio, than are dreamt of in your philosophies." The Central Committee, it was announced two days later, had "acceded to the plea of N. S. Khrushchev" and released him from his duties on account of his health. By that time, Khrushchev had already been escorted by KGB men to a retirement home in the countryside where, according to his grandson, he sat in a chair and wept for months. His life was not in danger, but the leadership was taking no chances that the wily old politician would pull another countercoup, as he had against Malenkov and Molotov in 1957.

With a nice touch of irony, the Praesidium plucked from Khrushchev's own litany of Stalin's sins and accused him of too "personal" a rule—although they themselves immediately dampened the anti-Stalinist rhetoric and slowly restored some of the old trappings, if not quite

the methods, of Stalin's day. The "Praesidium of the Central Committee," a name with democratic, or at least participatory, overtones, was
changed back to the traditional and authoritarian "Politburo," and the
powerful Party Secretariat, which had been abolished on Stalin's death,
was reinstituted.

Khrushchev had tested his colleagues' patience sorely. His ambitious
economic schemes were almost all shameful failures. The Party's claim
to the leadership of the Communist movement had been dissipated in
the vituperative slanging match with the Chinese. Foreign policy toward NATO and the West was a shambles. His nuclear brinkmanship
had jangled aging nerves. The backdown in Cuba was still a stinging
humiliation. Finally, there was a continuous, and exhausting, battle
between Khrushchev and the Soviet military. Running through almost
all of the economic and foreign policy disputes was an increasingly
bitter debate over military priorities that pitted Khrushchev's "mod-
ernists" against the old-line military conservatives, the new breed of
consumer-goods economic moderates against the "steeleaters" in the
Red Army and their allies in heavy industry.

The fundamental dispute between Khrushchev and the army leaders centered on his own version of "massive retaliation," the strategy
that, ironically, was so discredited in the United States. Khrushchev
evolved his new strategy throughout the 1950s, but gave it a definitive
formulation in a watershed speech to the Supreme Soviet in January
1960. Wars between the great powers, he declared, would in the future
be fought with nuclear rockets; and the new weapons were so powerful
that the first days of the war would be the decisive ones. No state,
Khrushchev implied, could expect to win such a war: "The state which
suffers the attack, if, of course, we are speaking of a sufficiently large
state, will always have the possibility of giving a proper rebuff to the
aggressor." As a consequence, Khrushchev announced, he would ele-
vate the Strategic Rocket Forces to a fifth branch of the military services and would accelerate his policy of conventional force reductions,
with a manpower target of 2.4 million men by 1964, down from 3.6
million in 1960, or a cutback of one third. Manpower cuts would not
reduce fighting effectiveness, he stressed, for they would be more than
made up by the increase in "nuclear firepower." To the Marshals, particularly the powerful heads of the Ground Forces, Khrushchev's new
strategy looked like buying a defense system on the cheap, much as
Eisenhower's "New Look" perturbed the professional military in the
United States.

There is no definite information on Khrushchev's missile deployment plans. Understanding the planning behind actual Soviet deployments is difficult enough; interpretations of plans that were *not* implemented are necessarily conjectural. Michael MccGwire, of the Brookings Institute, however, has developed an ingenious reconstruction which suggests that Khrushchev's original rocket plans called for "area coverage" against the United States. SAC bases and critical military installations were located throughout the major American conurbations; by mapping the country on a grid and targeting a giant warhead at the center of each grid, the United States would be destroyed both as a military threat and as a functioning society. Since American military targets at the time were all still "soft" targets, "area" targeting not only made military sense, but would get maximum mileage out of the big, inaccurate Soviet rockets.

Policy, as always, would have been pre-emptive—that is, if a crisis reached the point where war was inevitable, the Soviets would do their best to launch first. There is little point in characterizing such a rocket strategy as either "counterforce" or "countercity." It is hardly distinguishable, in fact, from the similarly pre-emptive "smoking radiating ruin" strategy of Curtis LeMay in the early 1950s—except for the mode of delivery, and of course for the fact that the actual *capability* to execute such a strategy was still only a gleam in Khrushchev's eye. The huge Soviet atmospheric tests in 1961, before the Cuban missile crisis, were precursors of the very large missiles that began to make their appearance in the second half of the 1960s, and are consistent with an area-targeting strategy.

MccGwire conjectures that another round of even bigger missiles was planned, building to a force of perhaps 1,200 land-based missiles sometime in the early 1970s. The specific number programmed is entirely speculative, but MccGwire calculates that an "area" strategy would need about that many. It is a number, in addition, not greatly different from the number of nuclear bombers LeMay disposed of. Everything we know about Soviet thinking, or military thinking in general, indicates that if missiles were to be the heart of the Soviet forces, they would have eventually deployed enough to make the post-launch United States at least as uninhabitable, indeed as unrecognizable, a place as LeMay would have left the Soviet Union.

Despite a core of enthusiasts among younger officers, Khrushchev's new strategy apparently met with widespread military opposition. Marshal Zhukov was sacked as Defense Minister in 1957, only months after helping Khrushchev retain power, at least partly because he and his general staff ridiculed "one-weapon strategies" as the "arbitrary fabrications of bourgeois military theorists," insisting that nuclear weapons "only supplement the old forms of armament" and that "the significance of men on the battlefield not only does not decrease but increases all the more" with nuclear weapons. The criticism was muted for a time by the grossly exaggerated American claims for Soviet missile prowess, and the impressive string of diplomatic and public relations successes from Khrushchev's rocket-rattling; but by 1961, the unease was serious enough to surface even through the elaborately orchestrated ritual of Party Congress speeches.

Khrushchev's opening address to the October Congress once again stressed the radically different nature of modern war and the Soviet Union's "undisputable superiority in nuclear and rocket arms"—signalling his intention to continue the troop reductions, which had been suspended during the summer's Berlin crisis. But in a speech delivered on the very same day, Rodion Malinovsky, the Soviet Defense Minister, appeared to take issue with Khrushchev by insisting on the importance of "multi-million-man armies," and arguing that modern wars could be won "only by the joint action of all the services of the Armed Forces." Malinovsky went out of his way to acknowledge the primary place of nuclear weapons, but the difference in emphasis was plain, and was the more striking because Malinovsky was Khrushchev's close friend and hand-picked successor to Zhukov. The clinching argument was that it was precisely this strategy that the United States seemed to be adopting with its conventional force buildup in Europe. As Marshal Rotmistrov put it, "the bourgeois in practice are following the course of creating multi-million-man armies."

The Soviet Marshals' worries could hardly have been soothed by American revelations of the insubstantiality of Khrushchev's missile boasts. Honest men could differ over the relative merits of conventional and nuclear weapons; it was quite another thing to base a nation's entire strategy on a fiction. After Khrushchev's proclamation of nuclear superiority at the Party Congress, Roswell Gilpatric, McNamara's deputy at Defense, made a widely publicized reply, laying out the two countries' respective nuclear striking forces in considerable detail and showing that American *second-strike* forces, under worst-case assumptions, would be bigger than anything the Soviets could launch in a surprise first strike. During the Berlin crisis, Kennedy's negotiators pointedly showed Andrei Gromyko satellite photographs of Soviet missile sites. The implication was thudding: if it came to a nuclear exchange, the

Soviet Union would have no chance. McNamara's flat assertion, in early 1962, that the United States was "fully capable" of destroying "virtually any Soviet targets it chose" must have chilled the Marshals' spines.* Malinovsky's riposte betrayed his nervousness: "Such boasting is to say the least reckless. Let us go so far as to grant that our forces are equal. We are prepared to agree to that in order not to fan war psychosis."

The debate on military strategy within the Soviet Union was an unusually extensive one, ranging over all the new questions introduced by nuclear weapons: the changed nature of modern war, the proper roles of nuclear and conventional power, and the most sensible strategic posture vis-à-vis the United States. To a unique degree, Western analysts were able to follow the discussions in considerable detail, particularly through an extraordinary volume, *Military Strategy*, published in the Soviet Union in 1962. The book was a wide-ranging survey of current Soviet military doctrine, written by a panel of military officers under the chairmanship of Marshal Sokolovsky— General Clay's opposite number during the Berlin airlift. The essays in the Sokolovsky volume explicitly address the debates on military policy or as often implicitly reveal them by failing to reach a consistent point of view on key issues. The Sokolovsky volume itself then became a subject of published debate within the Soviet Union, and a second edition was shortly issued "clarifying" controversial points. Most extraordinarily, the editors engaged in a kind of de facto arm's-length discussion with Western military experts by attempting to address in their second edition various "misinterpretations" of their work by Western scholars.

To a great extent, the book appears to be an attempt to reach a middle ground between Khrushchev's radical new approach to military strategy and the massed-force approach of the unreformed land-army troglodytes. Although many issues were left unresolved, certain key points stood out:

● The West was enormously powerful and growing stronger.

● Any war between the great powers would inevitably be a nuclear one, causing immense damage to both sides. The American hope of limiting an engagement in Europe with "flexible response" tactics was wistful and foolish.

*Most analysts assume that the Marshals were willing to play along with Khrushchev's bluffing as long as it worked, or at least as long as the real facts weren't public. It is entirely probable, of course, that all but a handful didn't know the true facts. Recall how Stalin kept his entire Politburo in the dark about his new missiles.

- A war would be won, however, only by a ground battle, carried out in the aftermath of a nuclear exchange.

- But there was considerable uncertainty how such a ground battle would eventuate, how many troops would be needed, and how the Soviet Union would engage in a final battle with the United States.

For a Western reader numbed by the sodden formulas of Soviet Party rhetoric, the Sokolovsky book is striking for its relative lack of cant, its realism, and its bleak assessment of the strategic position of the Soviet Union in the mid-1960s. The book paints the consequences of another war in apocalyptic tones, and scorns the Western analysts who have attempted "to draw a veil over the horrors of a future nuclear war." A new war would be "a war of world coalitions, the extreme solution to the historical problem." It would:

"threaten the nations of the world with terrible disasters—the deaths of many hundreds of millions of people and the destruction and devastation of cities."

There would be "no 'quiet areas' where medical treatment could be given."

"The entire territory of the country will be subject to enemy nuclear strikes and, in this sense, will become a military theater."

Losses "will be six to eight times as great as in the past war"; "60–85% of aircraft" and "30–40% of troops" will be lost in the first weeks.

The long section on Western military potential must have been thoroughly alarming to a reader lulled by Khrushchev's repeated proclamations of Soviet superiority. The list of new American weapons continued for page after page—mostly drawn from public Western sources—accurately specifying the capabilities and deployment patterns of the Minuteman and the Polaris missiles, the long-range nuclear bomber force, the standoff air-to-surface missiles, the enormous striking power of the carrier fleet, the new high-performance tactical aircraft, the rapid buildup in conventional manpower and equipment. The United States and Western Europe were also credited with having achieved impressive unity of command through NATO and a degree of success in integrating weapons systems and procurement that must have amused McNamara.

If the exposition of Western military power was respectful, the book's review of Western economic potential was awestruck. Once again, for page after page, the book detailed the enormous output of the NATO countries, especially the huge growth in steel, capital equipment, and energy production, with particular emphasis on the burgeoning economic might of West Germany. The section is all the more striking for the absence of conventional slogans on the superiority of socialism, or references to Khrushchev's claims that Russia would "bury" the West. The only solace the book offered to the Soviet reader worried by this daunting array of Western power was the bland assurance that his own country's "Strategic Missile Forces now have so many launchers, missiles and nuclear warheads, that they can completely carry out their missions."

The book's analysis of the McNamara-RAND "flexible response" strategy—documented with liberal quotations from McNamara's Ann Arbor speech and congressional testimony—was both reasoned and compelling. Abstract logic aside, the Sokolovsky authors argued, so many prime Soviet military targets were so intermingled with Soviet cities that it would be impossible to distinguish an American "counterforce" strike from a "countercity" attack—a contradiction, in fact, that deeply troubled McNamara. The same situation, of course, obtained in Europe and to a lesser extent in the United States. If NATO was serious about flexible response, it would relocate its own military targets away from urban centers. But such a move would be extremely provocative, the book suggested, for the Soviets would have to view it as a first step in preparing for war. Hammering the point home, the authors argued, quite correctly, that with the possible exception of the Minuteman, the present arsenals of nuclear rockets were not accurate enough for a counterforce strategy. Data on launch performance and target locations were much too imperfect; the surprise essential for a counterforce attack was probably impossible; and the civil defense arrangements the strategy would require were lacking.

The Sokolovsky editors found the American theories of graduated nuclear escalation utterly implausible. The only conceivable scenario for a great power nuclear war, they insisted, was an all-out "spasm" exchange. The elaborate American distinctions between "strategic" and "tactical" nuclear weapons were not persuasive to the Marshals; once the nuclear "firebreak" was passed, escalation would be rapid and uncontrollable. It is hard to argue that their view was not the more realistic one: a substantial body of opinion in Western Europe held a similar opinion of the Hiroshima-size "tactical" weapons in the American arsenal. McNamara himself had expressed grave doubts about the usefulness of tactical nuclear weapons, although not yet publicly. Even Bernard Brodie, by 1963 at least, had disavowed his earlier views on controlled escalation, partly because it was clear that the Soviets wouldn't play:

Everything we know about Soviet military thinking indicates rejection of those refinements of military thought that have now become commonplace in this country, concerning, for example, distinctions between limited war and general war, between "controlled" and "uncontrolled" strategic targeting, and between nuclear and non-nuclear tactical operations. . . . [V]iolence between great opponents is inherently difficult to control, and cannot be controlled unilaterally. . . . Once hostilities begin, the level of violence has in modern times tended always to go up.

The Soviets did not altogether reject the concept of "flexible response," however. There were glimmers throughout the book that it might be possible to contain a purely *conventional* confrontation between the great powers—that is, if the use of "tactical" nuclears was avoided. Standard Soviet doctrine held that *any* war between the great powers—as distinguished from wars between proxies—would inevitably become nuclear. But at one point the Sokolovsky volume says only that the danger of escalation would be "high," although most frequently the book restates the fundamentalist view: "any armed conflict [will] develop, inevitably, into a general war if the nuclear powers are drawn into it."

It was not until the latter half of the 1960s that the Sokolovsky volume's hints of a purely conventional strategy began to command serious attention within the Soviet military, prompting a decade-long upgrade of Soviet conventional forces in Europe. As the Soviet forces grew, the possibility of *winning* a conventional war became increasingly plausible. Since all the natural advantages in a European war rest with the Soviet Union—at least so long as the distant United States is the mainstay of the defense—the Soviet conventional force buildup, as will be seen later, forced the West, ironically, to fall back once again on a policy indistinguishable from the earlier "massive retaliation" in order to deter a Soviet assault. The "flexible response" doctrine came full circle, with the flexibility on the Soviet side, and the new stalemate established at a much higher level of potential violence.

The grimness of the Soviet view of war pervades the Sokolovsky volume. It is strikingly different from the prevalent Western view. Unlike the West, the Soviets did not assume that the inevitability of an all-out nuclear exchange obviated the need for strong conventional forces. Despite the great importance Soviet doctrine assigned to the first nuclear salvos, they insisted that these would not *end* a war. Wars would still be won only by conventional troops fighting "broken-backed" battles in the aftermath of the nuclear exchange. Understanding the nature of the battle once the missiles had been launched was identified as a key doctrinal problem. (This is not the same as Western "graduated escalation"; the Soviets were exploring the nature of battle after an *all-out* strike.) By contrast, the leading Western strategists, who were not for the most part military men, thought in terms of *preventing* a war, or at least an all-out salvo. There was nothing further to do after a "spasm" launch except run for a bunker. The Soviet military would have retorted that they had no such luxury; their job was to fight whatever war they needed to, and fight it so as to ensure the best possible outcome for the Soviet Union.

The details of the conventional force strategy, however, were shrouded in confusion. The Sokolovsky authors admitted that doctrine was in a state of flux: "It must be kept in mind, however, that trends in the development of armed forces are not constant." In particular, they struggled with the practical problems of keeping conventional forces in fighting readiness during the first-stage nuclear salvos, since "the technical and material basis for waging a long war can be shattered at the very outset." Mobilization after the outbreak of a nuclear exchange was fraught with difficulties, but—accepting Khrushchev's Eisenhower-like worries about bleeding the peacetime economy—"to maintain armed forces on a [fully mobilized] basis is not within the economic capability of any, even the strongest, state." Finally, the implications of a conventional conclusion to a war against the United States were mind-boggling. After much pointed criticism in Soviet military journals, the second Sokolovsky edition waffled considerably on its insistence that a war could be won only by capturing the enemy's "military bases" and occupying "strategically important regions." There was, obviously, no way the Soviet Army could accomplish any such thing against the United States.

Just as Americans tended to interpret Soviet force deployments through the games theory analytic filter, the Soviets saw American moves through their own strategic lenses. Since Khrushchev's Marshals insisted on the inevitability of nuclear escalation and preached the necessity for strong conventional "finishing forces," the West's buildup of conventional and nuclear weapons in name of "flexible response" would have appeared deeply sinister. The Marshals might mock McNamara's theories of graduated escalation as "some sort of suggestion to the Soviet Union on 'rules' for the conduct of nuclear exchange," but it required only a modicum of military paranoia to see the coordinated buildup as preparation for a preventive war. The Sokolovsky authors noted particularly the "high level of combat-readiness" of Western forces and their "constant combat alert" (which was, in fact, at a much higher level than the Soviets'), and concluded that "the Pentagon is preparing a surprise nuclear attack against the U.S.S.R. and the other socialist countries."

Persuasive evidence of an American first-strike intention, ironically, was found in the writings of none other than Albert Wohlstetter and Bernard Brodie, and the drumfire of congressional testimony that insisted on the enormous advantage accruing to the nuclear attacker. More important than rhetoric, of course, was the rapid proliferation of highly accurate Minuteman missiles, an apparently ideal first-strike weapon. The mainstay of the Soviet rocket forces in the first half of the 1960s, the SS-7 (the follow-on to the first Soviet ICBM, the SS-6), could not be launched rapidly enough to evade a surprise Minuteman strike. It would be difficult for a Communist to argue that the Marshals' fears were unreasonable. The Americans, of course, consistently denied any surprise attack intentions, but similar Soviet denials in the 1950s were hardly persuasive to the RAND analysts, who constructed their own paranoia out of a much scantier set of Soviet references and a wholly fictional set of Soviet capabilities.

At the same time, the Minuteman's relative invulnerability in its hardened silos dashed any hopes Khrushchev may have had of achieving a strategic standoff by multiplying big, inaccurate missiles. "Area" targeting would leave the Minuteman unscathed, so a pre-emptive strategy was out of the question. An improvisatory scramble ensued through the remainder of the decade. The first priority was to match the Minutemen in numbers as rapidly as possible, with whatever missiles were readily available. But work was also well under way by 1965 on the accurate, multiple-warhead SS-17, SS-18, and SS-19 missiles that, when they were eventually targeted against Minuteman silos in the latter 1970s, created the flurry of anxiety in the West that the Minuteman in turn had suddenly become vulnerable to a Soviet first strike.

The interactions between the American and Soviet force buildups in the 1960s illustrate the complex dynamics of the arms race. Clearly, decisions were taken with a view toward what was happening on the other side, but there was no simple "action–reaction" mechanism operating. The forces driving each country's buildup were complex in the extreme, including at various times exaggerated perceptions of the other side's power; worst-case assumptions about each other's intentions; purely internal political considerations (in both countries); and more or less exogenous technological developments. Two constants stand out: neither side increased its armaments *solely* because of actions by the other. Khrushchev, it seems, would have eventually built a large missile force, regardless of what Kennedy and McNamara did. But neither side would allow itself to be definitively trumped. If the United States built a powerful missile-striking fleet, the Soviet Union would strive to deploy one even more powerful, and as rapidly as possible. If American missile deployments had only marginal effect on the size of the eventual Soviet fleet, they did influence its operational characteristics, and made it infinitely more dangerous as a result.

It is the mounting pressure from the Soviet military that makes Khrushchev's flailings in Berlin, and more specifically in Cuba, comprehensible. He desperately needed political victories to support a shift of resources from the military to the consumer economy. But the shifting balance of military power made political victories extremely unlikely— certainly none could be gained by bombast and bullying. Moving missiles to Cuba, if it had succeeded, would have been a brilliant counterploy. For the first time, Soviet nuclear weapons would have had a clear capability of reaching American cities, and Khrushchev's blusters about the mutual dangers of nuclear war would have had some substance, greatly strengthening his position against the Marshals and his credibility in insisting on a European settlement.

Khrushchev was apparently forced to accept substantial conventional force increases after the failure in Cuba. He reasserted himself, however, the following year, announcing a 4 percent cut in the military budget in the spring of 1963. At the end of that year, with Malinovsky parroting his claims for a "fundamentally new," "fantastic" weapon, Khrushchev announced that he would press ahead with troop reductions to the 2.4 million level, inviting the United States to limit their forces to the same number. Then, in September 1964, Khrushchev sacked Marshal Chuikov, the army chief of staff, for writing that the West, presumably unlike the Soviets, had abandoned "one-sided" theories of war. Most Western analysts assumed that the old man—he was now seventy-one—was once again firmly in control. But Khrushchev's string had already played out. The final straw may have been a plan to muzzle the conservative faction in the Praesidium by holding meetings before the full Central Committee. In any case, when the conservatives moved against him a month later, the Khrushchev loyalists in the military, including Malinovsky, had either moved into opposition or adopted a position of aloof neutrality. The "Great Debate" was over, Khrushchev was moping in his country farmhouse, and the traditional military view of the Cold War would once again move center stage.

# CHAPTER 14:

# "Mad Momentum"—ABMs, SS-9s, MIRVs

In September 1967, Robert McNamara delivered an extraordinary speech to a United Press International luncheon in San Francisco. He meditated bleakly on the "mad momentum" of the arms race between the United States and the Soviet Union and virtually apologized for the vast American missile buildup in the early 1960s, although as Lawrence Freedman remarked, he indulged in "a little rewriting of history" in doing so: ". . . the blunt fact remains that if we had had more accurate information about planned Soviet strategic forces, we simply would not have needed to build as large a nuclear arsenal as we have today." McNamara went on to warn that there was barely time to halt the "action-reaction phenomenon that fuels an arms race," and made an impassioned argument that the pursuit of strategic advantage by either of the great powers would be "foolish and futile," a "profitless waste of resources."

He pleaded that the world had a golden, but fleeting, opportunity to achieve a stable nuclear balance. The key was for both the Soviet Union and the United States to accept the strategic stalemate posture he called "assured destruction," or "an actual [and] credible capability . . . to inflict unacceptable damage upon any single aggressor or combination of aggressors at any time during the course of a strategic nuclear exchange—even after absorbing a surprise first strike."

The "assured destruction" balance would persist, he promised, so long as neither side sought a "first-strike capability," or the ability to ensure "the elimination of the attacked nation's retaliatory second-strike force." He assured his listeners that there was no possibility of the Soviet Union attaining such a capability because of an American weapon superiority of "at least three or four to one." But at the same time, as if to convince Soviet Pentagon-watchers, he insisted that the vast American arsenal did not threaten the Soviets' own assured-destruction forces: "We do not possess a first-strike capability against the Soviet Union for precisely the same reason that they do not possess it against us. Quite simply, we have both built up our second-strike capability—in effect, retaliatory power—to the point that a first-strike capability on either side is unattainable."

Any attempt to break the "assured destruction" standoff would merely touch off another arms spiral that "in the end . . . would provide neither the Soviets nor us with any greater relative nuclear capability." But if both sides were content to remain safely sheltered behind their second-strike deterrents, the whole world could be spared the perils and expense of a pointless race for nuclear domination.

McNamara's speech is still a canonical statement of American arms control theory, and the classic exposition of the "action–reaction" dynamic of the arms race. A great portion of the speech was devoted to an exposition of the futility of attempting to build an antimissile defense, or ABM* system, to defend American cities against Soviet missiles, as many in Congress were urging. It was precisely the kind of escalatory step to be avoided, McNamara insisted. There was no way to create an "impenetrable shield" in any case, and the attempt would merely ensure that the Soviets would react by building many more missiles to protect their retaliatory capability. Seeking safety by multiplying weapons or defensive systems, McNamara warned, was fruitless: the inevitable counterefforts merely multiplied the dangers to *both* sides.

Most extraordinarily, then, at the conclusion of a speech of unusual force and eloquence, McNamara astonished his listeners and delighted congressional hawks—and, not incidentally, opened a window on the tenseness of the strategic weapons debate within the administration—by announcing that the United States would begin building an ABM system anyway, but only a "thin" one, one that would not be effective against Soviet missiles, but which might be useful against some future Chinese nuclear capability.

There was a counterpoint of gloomy fatalism in McNamara's speech. Perhaps the true picture of man's history, he speculated, is one of

*ABM stands for "Anti-Ballistic Missile." It is one of the small number of military acronyms that have been so widely used that they have virtually become proper nouns. More recently, ABM appears to have been supplanted by BMD for Ballistic Missile Defense.

"persistent outbreaks of warfare, wearily put aside from time to time for periods of exhaustion and recovery that parade under the name of peace." For McNamara knew, even as he delivered the speech, that the entire premise of his nuclear strategy was coming unstuck, and that the world was about to witness a vast upward spiral in the size and lethality of the strategic arsenals of both the United States and the Soviet Union. The passion with which he pressed his case against a blind pursuit of nuclear superiority, in short, was that of the man who knows that he has already lost the argument.

McNamara's San Francisco speech was remarkable for the clarity with which he adumbrated the seismic shifts that were about to take place in the nuclear power balance between the United States and the Soviet Union. First, of course, McNamara announced that America would deploy an ABM system. Despite his success in constraining the program's initial size, he had obviously lost a long, personal, rearguard struggle against missile defenses. The crossed logic of his speech—the powerful argument against an ABM, followed by an announcement of its deployment—merely reflected the messiness of the final compromise. The second new development McNamara only hinted at, when he spoke of the ability to overwhelm defensive systems with multiple warheads. It had been announced earlier in the year that the United States was fitting some missiles with multiple warheads to confuse Soviet missile defenses. It was not revealed until several months later, however, that the United States had successfully achieved "MIRV"* technology, or the ability to attack many separate targets with a single rocket, by launching "a spacecraft that can drop off thermonuclear warheads city by city as it flies over enemy territory," as the Pentagon, with only slight hyperbole, described the new technology in December. At a stroke, the attacking power of the American missile fleet was multiplied manyfold.

The clue to the third, and for Americans the most disturbing, new arms race development was that in San Francisco McNamara did not stress the American lead in numbers and quality of *missiles,* as he usually did, but shifted the comparison to the number of deliverable *warheads* instead. Although it was still a closely held secret, he was

*MIRV stands for *M*ultiple *I*ndependently targeted *R*e-entry *V*ehicles. Like ABM, MIRV has entered the language as a useful word, and an admirably flexible one, that serves as a noun (referring either to the warheads or the missiles), a verb, and a participle. Not all multiple-warhead missiles were MIRVs; the Polaris A3 missile, which was already deployed at this time, released three separate warheads to increase the lethal radius, or "footprint," of the missile, but the three warheads could not be separately aimed.

forced to do so because of rapidly accumulating evidence that the Soviet Union, after years of slow development of its missile forces, was suddenly building new intercontinental missiles at an alarming rate. It was no longer true, as McNamara had repeatedly assured the Congress, that the Soviets were "not catching up or planning to catch up" in a missile race. They were not only threatening to catch up; they were already on the verge of passing the United States in the number of deployed missile launchers and the sheer weight of destructive mega-tonnage that they carried.

## ABM Deployment

The anti-Chinese justification for McNamara's ABM system was embar-rassingly lame. Critics like Senators Henry Jackson and Richard Russell hailed it as a first step in creating an "overall defense" and scoffed at the strained anti-Chinese argument. "The Chinese are not completely crazy," Russell snorted. "I don't like people to think that I am being kidded by this talk of a defense against a Chinese nuclear attack." The Soviets were no more likely to be impressed with the anti-Chinese argument than hard-line senators. For most of the long period of con-struction and testing, it would be impossible for them to distinguish a "thin" system from the first stages of one directed against themselves— although McNamara insisted that "the Russians are sophisticated enough to see the distinction." For a brief time he also tried to argue that a "thin" system would provide "further defense of our Minuteman sites." But sophisticated critics understood that the requirements of missile silo defense were quite different from those for cities, and one system would not easily satisfy both. Even worse, floating the idea of silo defense created a storm of protest in NATO—Europeans regularly pa-nicked at the thought that American defenses might once again suc-ceed in limiting a world war to the Eurasian land mass.

It was the Soviet Union's obvious and persistent emphasis on devel-oping and deploying antimissile defenses that doomed McNamara's long battle against an American ABM. Defense has always been a preoc-cupation of the Soviet military. The conservative Soviet Marshals were never as convinced as Khrushchev that ballistic rockets and nuclear warheads had changed the rules of war. And just as they insisted on forcing nuclear war-fighting doctrine into a traditional military frame-work—nuclear strikes would be just one aspect of a coordinated "multi-million man" army offensive—they refused to believe that any weapon, no matter how radical the advance, could not be met by a stout defense. The first Soviet ABM research may have commenced shortly after the war; the CIA began monitoring a Soviet ABM test site at Sary Shagan as early as 1958; and the last successful U-2 flight, in April 1960, returned the first photographs of the ABM testing grounds. By late 1961 there was no doubt that the Soviets were actually building an ABM defense in the vicinity of Leningrad. At that year's Party Congress, Malinovsky announced that "the problem of destroying missiles in flight has been successfully solved," and, shortly thereafter, Khrushchev made his famous boast that Soviet defense rockets could "hit a fly in outer space."

McNamara always treated Soviet ABM developments with great seriousness, although he was inclined to be more skeptical of their actual technological capabilities than the conservative congressmen who began raising the alarm in 1963. It was the fear of falling behind in an ABM race, in fact, that was the major conservative objection to Kennedy's and Khrushchev's Nuclear Test Ban Treaty. For his part, McNamara worried that a successful Soviet ABM system would strike at the very heart of his theories of nuclear deterrence. If either side could defend its cities against the other's missiles, there would no longer be a stable "assured destruction" balance of terror. McNamara certainly understood, however, although he tended to blur the distinction in public, that his objections applied only to ABM defenses for cities. By his own "assured destruction" logic, defenses for missile silos would tend to *increase* the stability of the nuclear balance by protecting the retaliatory striking forces essential for a credible counterstrike capability.

The Soviet Union's Leningrad missile defense system grew to some thirty half-finished launch sites by late 1962, and McNamara estimated that it would be "capable, under favorable conditions, of engaging an ICBM re-entry vehicle" in "the 1963–1964 time period." Almost immediately, however, Moscow apparently decided that the system was a failure, and work was abruptly halted. But then, after a brief pause, the CIA began to pick up signs of *two* new Soviet systems, one around Moscow and another near Tallinn, the capital city of Estonia. The Soviet military parades in 1963 and 1964 displayed two different missiles purporting to be antimissile weapons but, maddeningly, both were kept sheathed in canisters.

The nature of the Tallinn system was one of the most hotly disputed intelligence issues of the middle 1960s. The missile, dubbed the "Gryphon," had been developed at Sary Shagan, but its size was more suited to an atmospheric, anti-aircraft weapon, and several close observers at the Moscow parades claimed to have seen a pointed, aerodynamic nose and stubby wings. McNamara did not rule out that it was an antimissile system, but he became increasingly dubious as deployment continued. The Soviets were pressing ahead with the Tallinn defenses at a feverish pace, however, and on a huge scale. By mid-1965, launch site foundations were being sunk in a giant arc from Archangel to Riga, clear across the transpolar attack route of the American Minutemen, and in roughly the right position for a forward "area defense" of the major Soviet metropolitan areas. The American military pointed out that if the Tallinn deployment was intended to combat aircraft, its configuration would be "incredibly stupid." The Soviets presumably understood that American bombing doctrine called for ground-hugging attack patterns; but the Tallinn launch platforms and radars were positioned for a high-altitude intercept, which implied that missiles were targets. (Tallinn was planned, however, before McNamara cancelled the B-70, which *was* a high-altitude bomber, although the deployment moved into high gear long after the cancellation.)

As if determined to confirm the military's fears, the Soviets gave wide publicity to a film purporting to show a Tallinn missile intercepting an ICBM, and issued a spate of high-level military statements emphasizing the importance of ABMs and boasting of the Soviet Union's "impregnable defenses." An article by General Nikolai Talensky, a Russian military theoretician who was much respected in the West, extolling the virtues of ABM defenses, was reprinted in an influential American periodical, the *Bulletin of the Atomic Scientists*. (Khrushchev's successors, apparently, were similarly uninhibited about exaggerating their weapons' capabilities.) It was only over the strong dissent of the military that McNamara and the CIA finally concluded in 1966 that Tallinn was an antiaircraft system—its slow, mechanically rotated radars could not possibly track missiles—however "incredibly stupid" or useless that might be. (Tallinn deployments continued for a full decade more, to the mystification of Western analysts. The system still has no discernible purpose. It may some day be converted to an antitactical missile defense, although it was still not suited to such a mission in the mid-1980s. It may be merely a monument to the power of bureaucracies in the absence of political checks and balances.)

McNamara and the CIA agreed with the military chiefs, however, that the second Soviet defense system, the one under construction around Moscow, was indeed a true ABM. The system was many times smaller than Tallinn and comprised only eight launch sites. But the missile, the "Galosh," was huge, even bigger than the Minuteman, and clearly an "exo-atmospheric" weapon—one designed to attack incoming missiles above the atmosphere. Its very large nuclear warhead, presumably, would compensate for a limited ability to "close" with an incoming warhead. More important, the radar installations were clearly designed for an antimissile mission—with a series of "phased-array" radars, (called the "Dog House," "Hen House," and "Cat House" radars by the CIA), designed to pick up missiles early in their flight, track them on the way in, and follow the Galosh after launch. McNamara and the CIA had their doubts about the actual capability of the system, but the Soviet intent was clear.*

For all of the formidable energy McNamara threw into his battle against an American ABM, by 1966 he had become increasingly isolated on the issue. The pressures from the military committees of the Congress were severe, and with the exception of the Air Force—they wanted more missiles, not defenses—the Joint Chiefs were enthusiastic. Even McNamara's own staff was split. Alain Enthoven, for one, thought that American forces were overweighted toward offense, and that some investment in defense would be worthwhile. McNamara's best anti-ABM argument was that it would always be cheaper to multiply warheads than to build defenses. America's program to equip its missiles with multiple warheads, or MIRVs, had already generated enormous momentum of its own by the mid-1960s, but there can be no question that it received important impetus from the Soviet ABM drive. It is both ironic and indicative of the antipathy McNamara felt toward ABM systems—one aide reports that he saw them "in some sense as a symbol of the arms race"—that, to counter the ABM pressure, he was willing to accelerate the deployment of MIRVs, although by so doing, he vastly multiplied what he already regarded as the excessive power of America's missile fleet.

*"Phased-array" radar was a brand-new technology in the mid-1960s, one that is still making rapid strides. Instead of a rotating radar dish, the radar consists of a large stationary array of small electronic antennae, each of which emits its own beam with its own "phase," or timing of the sequence of the peaks and troughs in the wave of the emitted beam. By aligning the peaks and troughs of the waves from adjoining emitters, the beam can be focused in any direction or made to sweep back and forth across the sky in millionths of a second. With a high-speed computer to interpret the data, a single, modern, phased-array radar can track hundreds of incoming objects at the same time. A phased-array radar is an essential component of an ABM system. The Soviets had almost certainly not mastered this technology in the 1960s. The configuration of the Moscow radars indicated that they could track only one or two objects at a time.

With McNamara and the defense chiefs at loggerheads, the ABM decision defaulted to the President. Lyndon Johnson, a practitioner of balance-of-power politics all his life, was instinctively wary of backing a civilian secretary against the united opposition of the military and the key congressional chairmen, particularly now that McNamara's reputation for omnicompetence was so badly frayed by the stalemate in Vietnam. He knew that the military chiefs were spoiling to take McNamara on, and the ABM presented them with an ideal issue. But Johnson would still not overrule McNamara lightly, and the two men reached a compromise at the beginning of 1967. The President announced that the administration would continue ABM research and development, but would defer deployment for a year, in the hope that the Soviets would be willing to discuss an ABM moratorium. At the same time Johnson wrote to the Soviet premier, Alexei Kosygin, frankly outlining his predicament:

I think you must realize that following deployment by you of an anti-ballistic missile system I face great pressures from the Members of Congress and from public opinion not only to deploy defensive systems in this country, but also to increase greatly our capabilities to penetrate any defensive systems which you might establish. . . . We would thus have incurred on both sides colossal costs without substantially enhancing the security of our own peoples or contributing to the prospects for a stable peace in the world.

Kosygin was willing to talk, but he threw cold water on any idea of curbing defensive systems. As if to sharpen McNamara's disappointment, Kosygin seemed to go out of his way to issue a thinly veiled personal attack on the Secretary himself at a press conference in London in February, when he was reported to have said:

I think that a defensive system, which prevents attack, is not a cause of the arms race but represents a factor preventing the death of people. Some persons reason thus: Which is cheaper, to have offensive weapons that can destroy cities and entire states or to have defensive weapons that can prevent this destruction? At present the theory is current in some places that one should develop whichever system is cheaper. Such "theoreticians" argue also about how much it costs to kill a person, $500,000 or $100,000. . . . I understand that I am not answering the question [about an ABM treaty] but you can draw appropriate conclusions yourselves.

A fascinating sidelight on the episode is that Kosygin's apparently negative remarks were a mistranslation by *The Times* of London of what he really said. Much later, Soviet experts found that a tape of his press conference showed his actual remarks to have been much less negative. But several days after the press conference, with presumably ample time for reflection, the Soviets printed the mistranslation in *Pravda* as their official version of the press conference.

McNamara got to plead his case directly in June. Kosygin came to the United States to speak at the United Nations and suggested that he and Johnson might meet in New York. Johnson suggested Camp David as an alternative, and when Kosygin demurred, proposed instead to meet in the little New Jersey college town of Glassboro, midway between New York and Washington. It was sad comment on the near-breakdown in domestic political order that Johnson was afraid of the demonstrations and violence that might attend a New York meeting. With only a day's notice, an invading army of helicopters, limousines, press trucks, television reporters, and secret service men deposited tons of cable, teletypes, secure phone lines, and the other paraphernalia of travelling heads of state on the campus of Glassboro State College, and Johnson and Kosygin retired for two days of talks at "Hollybush," the home of the college president.

The agenda was inevitably dominated by the Middle East—Kosygin was still smarting from the Soviet humiliation in the Six-Day War—but McNamara was invited to join the conversations on the second day to plead his case against an ABM. He made "a long, detailed, and impassioned presentation" on the dangers of a new arms spiral, but, Johnson says, Kosygin "had a block" on the issue. McNamara had had his day in court; the San Francisco speech some ten weeks later was his official announcement both that America would deploy an ABM system, and that he himself had grave misgivings about the decision.

## The Development of MIRVs

Although in his San Francisco speech McNamara focused his formidable forensic energies on the ABM decision, he hinted at a second major new development that was of much greater strategic significance: the decision to equip the American strategic missile force with multiple, independently targeted warheads. Since each MIRVed missile had the capability of attacking separate and widely dispersed targets with great accuracy, the striking power of the American fleet was vastly multiplied at a stroke. The new Minuteman III carried three MIRV warheads, and the new Poseidon missile, the successor to the submarine-launched Polaris, could carry as many as fourteen. In a stark demonstration of the "action–reaction" dynamic, McNamara justified the decision by pointing to the Soviet ABM. MIRVed missiles were essential to defeat defenses and retain "assured destruction" retaliatory capability.

Senator Edward Brooke of Massachusetts sponsored a resolution in early 1970, signed by forty-three other senators, to halt MIRV deployment, making essentially the argument McNamara had made against the ABM: that MIRVs would force the Soviets to increase their defenses or deploy MIRVs of their own. The senators' alarm was far too late; MIRV was already an accomplished fact by 1970. Even McNamara's pointing at Soviet ABMs to justify his MIRVs in 1967 has all the elements of an after-the-fact rationalization. The MIRV, in fact, was a key step in the history of strategic weaponry, almost on a par with the development of the ballistic missile. Missiles brought any part of the globe within ready reach of a great power's nuclear forces. The MIRV facilitated the vast proliferation of those forces, and provided the last few hundred meters of accuracy necessary to attack another country's hardened missile silos—calling into question McNamara's long-sought objective of "assured destruction" stability. But the most striking aspect of the history of the MIRV, given its great importance in the history of the Soviet-American arms race, is the chilling inevitability of its development. Until very late in the day, there was very little controversy surrounding the MIRV; indeed, there appears to have been very little contemporary awareness even that a major step was being taken.

It was the smoothness of the MIRV development that made it so uncontroversial for so long. Building ballistic missiles with accurate, independently targetable warheads was a stunning technological achievement, one that required substantial separate breakthroughs in computerized guidance systems, rocket engine design, electronic systems miniaturization, and the explosive yield-to-weight ratios of nuclear payloads. But even more striking than the substantive scientific and engineering advances is the apparent effortlessness of the achievement. The MIRV program was under budget and ahead of schedule virtually its entire development cycle. It may have been a sense of the awesome technological inevitability of the MIRVs that McNamara had in mind when he spoke in San Francisco about "the mad momentum intrinsic to the development of all nuclear weaponry."

The MIRVed missile, instead of launching a warhead into space as an ordinary missile does, launches a "bus" that has its own engine and on-board computer along with an assortment of warheads. It was the MIRVed bus that the Pentagon referred to in its first announcement as the "spacecraft that . . . flies across enemy territory." After the bus is launched into its ballistic, or free-fall, trajectory and the booster rocket has disengaged, the on-board computer tracks its flight path and releases its cargo of warheads, using its own small rocket thrusters to maneuver into position for each release. The bus's fuel supply limits the dispersion of the separate targets to perhaps 100–300 miles, but that is more than enough for "cross-targeting" warheads from two widely separated MIRVed missiles on the same target—thus substantially increasing the likelihood of a kill by reducing the effect of random malfunctions in a single missile. Even more important, although the small nozzle thrusters on the bus can affect its trajectory only fractionally, the opportunity for post-boost trajectory correction was a last crucial step in developing missiles accurate enough for a true counterforce strategy.

Interest in MIRVed missiles dated from the very earliest stages of the American missile program. Several major companies, in fact—GE, Thiokol, and Autonetics—began MIRV research with their own funds about 1958. Defense profits were high, and the lead times imposed by the military rocket programs were increasingly urgent, so the companies were investing to "keep an eye on the future," as one of them put it. At about the same time, RAND analysts became concerned about the great size of the early Russian space rockets; they feared that big rockets could be used to launch many small warheads at American targets, and recommended an active program of MIRV research to keep abreast. Both the early Soviet and the American space programs experimented with multiple-satellite launches, demonstrating to weapons analysts that MIRV technology was in principle feasible. The persistent Soviet experiments with multiple-payload space launches indicate that, although their MIRV program lagged the Americans' by a good margin, early development probably began in parallel.

The concept of a MIRVed missile attracted McNamara's favorable attention at the very beginning of his tenure in the Pentagon. The "war-fighting" counterforce strategy he announced in 1962 dramatically increased the number of priority Soviet targets, and MIRVs were the most cost-effective way to achieve the necessary multiplication of American firepower. To the number-crunchers that Hitch and Enthoven had recruited to the Pentagon, MIRV was the ideal weapons program—much more effective payload could be purchased at a fraction of the cost of building new missile launchers. Rather to McNamara's chagrin, MIRV soon turned into an essential spending lid when the Air Force's enthusiasm for his notions of counterforce warfare turned out to be unbridled; it was possibly the only idea of McNamara's that they ever liked. As the military gleefully totted up new lists of essential Soviet targets and the correspondingly essential new American weapons requirements, MIRV was a readily available fallback to help McNamara stave off an endless multiplication of Minuteman silos and new bomber programs.

The Air Force resisted MIRVs for a bit—much like the Soviets, they would have preferred more and bigger rockets with the biggest possible warheads—but the smoothness and swiftness of the MIRV technical development and the high accuracy of test shots overcame their objections. The Navy was pro-MIRV from the beginning. Polaris had been deemed too inaccurate for a counterforce role, but the Poseidon's promise of a ten- to fourteenfold increase in submarine warheads together with substantial accuracy improvements offered the hope of challenging the Air Force for a counterforce war role. President Johnson jumped on the bandwagon during his 1964 campaign against Senator Barry Goldwater. Goldwater was an Air Force Reserve officer, and along with respected conservative critics like Hanson Baldwin, pressed the administration for its lack of new weapons development and the cancellation of the B-70 bomber and Skybolt missile. Hints of "major improvements in missile payloads," clearly referring to MIRVs, was the best response Johnson had.

The clincher for MIRV, of course, was the apparent Soviet progress on ABM defenses in the mid-1960s. Loading up a missile warhead with decoys and "chaff" to confuse Soviet radar was an obvious response to an ABM, and one that was available with the earliest technology. The Polaris A3 missile, deployed in 1964, went a step further by including three separate warheads that were released simultaneously during the ballistic trajectory. But only the very wide warhead dispersion of the MIRV "bus" system appeared certain to avoid a blast from the big nuclear warheads that the Soviets were deploying on their Moscow ABM. When McNamara went public on the MIRV in 1967, and during his subsequent congressional testimony, he justified it principally by the threat of the Soviet ABM, the standard interpretation of the "action–reaction" school. MIRV was indeed a valid response to an ABM threat, but the MIRV program was proceeding so rapidly and so smoothly that it is hard to conceive of any way in which it could have been derailed, whether the Soviets had ever deployed an ABM or not.

## The Soviet Missile Buildup

At the outset of his tenure at Defense, despite the quick disappearance of the "missile gap," McNamara's estimate of Soviet intentions was quite cautious. His official mid-range projection was that the Soviets would build 750 ICBMs by 1965 and 1,000 by 1967*—a missile fleet of roughly the same order of magnitude, that is, as he was planning for the United States. At the same time, he stressed the importance of not allowing the Soviets to attain a large missile superiority. A superior Soviet force, he wrote, would be a threat to America's land-based missiles, could worsen the outcomes of a war, and "would be likely to have a very unfavorable impact on Soviet aggressiveness in the cold war."

The consensus estimate of Soviet intentions was significantly reduced the following year: in late 1963, McNamara's median estimate was only 600 Soviet ICBMs by mid-1967, a 40 percent reduction. The so-called median estimate, in fact, was the National Intelligence Estimate's "high" projection. It was a mid-range estimate only when compared to the Air Force's guess of 800 Soviet ICBMs by mid-1967, which itself was sharply down from the previous year's Air Force estimate of 1,500. In 1963, McNamara's estimate was further reduced to 325–525 Soviet ICBMs by 1967, a projection that was essentially unchanged with his 1964 prediction of "400–700 Soviet launchers by the early 1970s." In mid-1964, he made a congressional presentation on the steady decline in the estimates and showed the congressmen the 1959, 1960, and 1961 consensus intelligence estimates for the 1963 Soviet ICBM fleet. Compared with the actual number of about 100, all of the estimates, of course, were grossly overstated. By 1965, McNamara was convinced, as he put it flatly, that the Soviets "have decided that they have lost the quantitative [nuclear] race, and they are not actively seeking to engage us in that conflict. . . . There is no indication that they are catching up or planning to catch up."

In an interview the same year, McNamara confirmed that "there was no indication" that the Soviets would engage in a missile race.

*These projections do not include submarine-launched missiles. McNamara's estimates in these years consistently assumed a Soviet submarine missile fleet in the 200–400 range. As he noted in 1963, however, contemporary Soviet submarine missiles had a range of only 350 miles, while the new generation under test had a range only twice that. The submarine missile fleet also contained a number of even shorter-range cruise missiles which seemed designed for an antishipping mission. Soviet submarines could theoretically attack American coastal cities with their missiles; but since the fleet was composed almost entirely of highly vulnerable and easily tracked diesel-powered vessels, and since the coordination and communication difficulties of a submarine missile attack were severe, it did not pose a genuinely credible threat at the time.

While he conceded intelligence predictions could always be wrong, he stressed that "the possibility of error is materially less than it has been at many times in the past because of the improvement in our intelligence collection methods." By 1966, even the Air Force's estimates were dipping down toward the consensus range, and the Pentagon's Posture Statement reaffirmed that "There does not appear to be any Soviet attempt to match us in sheer numbers of ICBMs."

When signs of imminent deployment of a huge new Soviet missile appeared in 1964, it was not a matter of great concern. The intelligence agencies had been tracking the development of the new missile, the SS-9, for some time. The SS-9 rocket booster was enormous; with sufficient thrust to carry a 25-megaton warhead, it dwarfed America's 1- to 2-megaton Polaris, Minuteman I, and new Minuteman II. But the reports that the Soviets were building forty-two hardened SS-9 silos fit neatly with McNamara's theories of "assured destruction." The new hardened silos would give the Soviets more confidence of riding out an American attack, and the new missile's storable liquid fuel would allow it to react almost as fast as the solid-fuelled Minuteman. Paradoxically, a quick-reacting Soviet missile would actually improve the stability of the strategic balance, because the Soviets would have more time to assess American intentions in a crisis.

Even the great size of the warhead was perversely reassuring. American strategic doctrine pointed to a secure, second-strike, counter-city missile force as the essential ingredient for stable mutual deterrence. A missile as huge as the SS-9 fit the theory because it seemed useful primarily as a "city-busting" terror weapon. McNamara assumed the Soviets would deploy about 100 SS-9s in hardened silos and target them on the 100 or so American cities of significant size.

The confidence McNamara had in his projections was just beginning to collapse at the time of his San Francisco speech, as it gradually became clear that American intelligence was losing a game of frantic catch-up with the actual pace of Soviet missile deployment. The appearance of a new missile, the SS-11, in 1965 was a rude surprise. In fact, it had been developed in a marine missile design bureau and was pressed into service without a full cycle of tests. The appearance of the SS-11, however, could still be accommodated within existing theory. With a 1- to 2-megaton warhead and an accuracy of 1 to 1.5 nautical miles, the SS-11 was neither as powerful nor as accurate as the SS-9. It looked like an economy weapon to replace the SS-7s and SS-8s and fill in the Soviet retaliatory forces behind the SS-9s.

But comfortable theorizing about Soviet intentions was swept away as the breakneck pace of SS-9 and SS-11 deployment continued year after year. Operational Soviet ICBMs doubled in a single year—from 292 in 1966 to 570 in 1967—and jumped another 288 missiles the next year. At first the intelligence agencies fell back on the assumption that the Soviets were looking for "parity" with the American missile force, relying primarily on the SS-11. But by 1969, the Soviets were fielding more than 1,000 ICBMs, by 1970 1,300, and by 1971 1,500, or a full 500 more than the American Minuteman force. Worse, the SS-9 deployments had jumped past 225, and large numbers of huge new silos were being dug at what appeared to be a frantic rate—nothing less than an all-out run for superiority.

To conservatives, the persistent underforecasting of Soviet intentions appeared as sinister as the deployments themselves. By the end of McNamara's tenure at Defense, the intelligence estimates were running so far behind the pace of deployment that they sometimes undershot the actual Soviet outturn *in the same year* as the estimate. The Soviets had deployed 750 ICBMs by the end of 1967, for instance, against a 1966 estimate of 420–476 and a 1967 estimate of 423–484. In 1968, the Soviets passed the "high" intelligence estimate completed at the end of 1967—for 764 Soviet ICBMs—in a matter of weeks; the Soviet ICBM force grew to 858 by midsummer, 900 by September, and almost 950 by year end. The performance in estimating submarine-launched* missiles was hardly better. The mid-range projection for missiles deployed in 1971 was 101 when estimated in 1966, 200 in 1967, 302 in 1968, 350 in 1969, and 363 in 1970, against the actual deployment of 376.

Albert Wohlstetter published a scathing critique of the intelligence agencies' performance that became almost as celebrated as his "Delicate Balance of Terror" article. Wohlstetter reported, with some relish, that the years of *under*estimating Soviet intentions far exceeded the much-publicized period of overestimation during the "missile gap" era. Of fifty-one National Intelligence Estimates of Soviet missile deployments made between 1962 and 1969, the "low" end of the estimate was too low all fifty-one times; the "median" estimates were too low forty-

---

*The submarine-launched missiles in these estimates include only the newer missiles—the SS-N-5 and SS-N-6—deployed on nuclear submarines, and launched from beneath the surface, not the short-range, primarily surface-launched weapons on diesel vessels. (See prior note on p. 261.) The SS-N-5 was deployed in 1964, had a range of about 750 miles and a one-megaton warhead. The SS-N-6, deployed in 1969, was of about the same size, but with a range of 1,750 miles.

nine times out of fifty-one; and even the "high" estimates were lower than the actual outcomes forty-two times out of fifty-one. Wohlstetter's most devastating criticism was that the estimators did not seem to learn from repeated underestimates. Because of the substantial lead-times for installing new missiles—for testing, production, silo construction, and the like—estimates for the immediate following year should have been accurate, but, particularly during McNamara's last years in office, they were consistently wide of the mark. It was nothing less, Wohlstetter insisted, than a dangerous and potentially tragic case of intelligence judgment overborne by dogmatic insistence on a highly suspect "assured destruction" theory.

Wohlstetter's central point is indisputable, although the details of his argument were slanted and unfair. It is not true that McNamara and the CIA persistently underestimated Soviet nuclear capabilities. McNamara consistently *over*estimated Soviet ABM prowess and progress toward MIRVed rockets, for example. Moreover, since Wohlstetter concentrated his analysis on missile launchers and gross nuclear megatonnage rather than on accurately deliverable warheads, his analysis tended to exaggerate the effect of the huge new Soviet rocket boosters. The American policy preference for small, accurate nuclear weapons was properly a measure of its continuing technological lead over the Soviet Union, not an index of disadvantage. The competition in space had by this time demonstrated that the United States could launch much larger effective payloads than the Soviets when there was a demonstrable need for them.

Finally, a substantial portion, but not all, of the difference between McNamara's estimates and the actual outcomes stemmed from McNamara's assumption that the Soviets would retire the 223 outmoded SS-6s, SS-7s and SS-8s in their rocket arsenal. The SS-6s were essentially the old, clumsy Sputnik rockets and would be virtually useless in a war. The SS-7s and SS-8s were better weapons but were very difficult to maintain. They used a non-storable liquid fuel, so each launch was time-consuming and quite dangerous for the rocket crews. Most important, from McNamara's point of view, they were by and large not hardened, and the belated steps the Soviets had taken to protect them had only made matters worse. Clusters of three (there were reports of as many as eight) SS-7s were bunkered in semi-hardened underground silos that would have greatly complicated a launch. The missiles had to be raised and fired one at a time, and it would have taken as much as eight hours to prepare and launch each weapon. Even worse, the silo was insufficiently hardened to withstand a Minuteman strike, but the clustered deployment meant that a single American warhead could now take out at least three of the Soviet main-line missiles.

In the event, however, the Soviets retired only the four SS-6s, leaving the SS-7 and SS-8 fleet intact for many years after the American military would have scrapped it. If the 219 SS-7 and SS-8 missiles are eliminated from the CIA/McNamara estimates given above, their numbers come much closer to the mark at least through the early 1970s; although, at the same time, it is hard to justify ignoring the SS-7s and SS-8s, particularly as the Soviets showed no disposition to deactivate them year after year.

Stripped of exaggerations and distortions, however, Wohlstetter's central contention was still highly damaging to McNamara's view of the strategic balance. In the late 1960s it was not correct to assume, if it ever was, that Soviet nuclear strategy was premised on the same "assured destruction" doctrine as the declared American posture. Wohlstetter hit the heart of the matter when he charged that the assumption of shared nuclear doctrine conditioned McNamara and the CIA to make gross misestimates of Soviet intentions. In the treacherous new world of proliferating nuclear arsenals, fundamental misconceptions about an opponent could be extremely dangerous.

Wohlstetter, however, carries the argument a step further than the data will bear. The implication of his article is that there are two possible, mutually exclusive, strategic postures: a "minimum deterrence" posture, which he appears to equate with McNamara's "assured destruction" position, and a "war-fighting" or "counterforce" nuclear posture, foreshadowing a debate that flared into much greater prominence a few years later (see Chapter 19). If the Soviets were not satisfied with a "minimum deterrence" posture, therefore, they were, by definition, seeking a "war-fighting" or "counterforce" capability.

Several points are relevant. In the first place, although McNamara can be fairly taxed with not clearly defining the requirements of "assured destruction," or, worse, changing the requirements to fit the force dispositions of the moment, his "assured destruction" was always something considerably more than "minimum deterrence," as Wohlstetter himself at one point acknowledges. In particular, his shift away from his 1962 "war-fighting" stance to a more passive deterrent policy, although hailed by arms controllers, was always more rhetorical than real. During the entire period, American *targeting* doctrine never changed from its counterforce emphasis on Soviet military targets, as the Soviets were certainly aware. And it could hardly have escaped the Soviets' attention that McNamara made his most impassioned plea for "assured destruction" stability at precisely the time that the United States was revolutionizing the strategic balance with MIRVs; McNamara's "assured destruction" stability, in short, looked suspiciously like American superiority.

Arguably, with accurate American warheads proliferating rapidly, the Soviets needed a very large number of missiles to ensure a survivable deterrent. Indeed, because of the great risks involved, there will always be a tendency on both sides to define "assured destruction" or "minimum deterrence" requirements robustly—robustly enough to appear like a good margin of superiority to the other side. It was one thing for McNamara to assure the Soviets in San Francisco that an ICBM force of several hundred missiles was all they needed to deter the United States; it was quite another for the Soviets to take so supine a view of their own requirements. The strategic deployments of *both* sides, in short, were inherently ambiguous, a fact that has bedevilled assessments of the strategic balance since the inception of the American-Soviet arms competition.

It may never be known for certain whether the Soviets ever, at any time, adopted American nuclear doctrine as their own policy. But it is almost certain that Wohlstetter is correct that the slow pace of the Soviet missile buildup in the early 1960s was determined more by technological backwardness than by a comfortable acceptance of a "minimum deterrence" posture, as McNamara had defined it. The projections of a permanently small Soviet missile force were compounded equally of bad intelligence and wishful thinking. By 1970, in any case, the Soviet Union's missile deployments were forcing a radical reexamination of the true nature of the balance in strategic weaponry.

## Intelligence Melee

When Richard Nixon, his foreign policy adviser, Henry Kissinger, and Melvin Laird, the new Secretary of Defense, took over the direction of American arms policy in 1969, strategic theory was in disarray. The military and congressional conservatives were in an uproar as the evidence of the huge Soviet missile buildup continued to pour in from all sides. At the same time, the congressional "doves," who controlled the power balance in the Senate Foreign Relations Committee, were, if anything, outshrilling the conservatives. Disgusted with the continued savagery in Vietnam, key Senators from both parties like William Fulbright, Frank Church, Edward Brooke, Jacob Javits, and at one point even Stuart Symington, along with major liberal newspapers like the *New York Times, Washington Post,* and *Christian Science Monitor,* had adopted a sharply antimilitarist stance. They were pressing hard for an arms agreement with the Soviet Union at almost any cost, and were emphatically opposed to any further American arms deployments, whether of MIRVed missiles, ABM systems, or even new bombers and fighter planes. The actual deployment of McNamara's "thin" ABM system, meanwhile, with construction getting under way around thirteen American cities, was running into an increasingly ugly series of demonstrations and protests, in keeping with the expressive political style of the times.

Nixon's and Kissinger's view of the strategic arms race was decidedly undoctrinaire. They trusted neither the Soviet Union nor abstract theories of stability and deterrence, although Nixon's proclaimed objective of nuclear "sufficiency" was interpreted by hopeful arms controllers as a Republican version of McNamara's "assured destruction" formula. Kissinger was less interested in weapons deployments or the arcana of strategic doctrine for their own sake than as counters in the intricate game of world power balance politics; in particular, he viewed any diplomatic dialogue with the Soviet Union as an opportunity to isolate the North Vietnamese and hasten a settlement of that corrosive conflict. Both men took a cautious view toward arms limitation talks, which McNamara had almost succeeded in getting started just before he left office. But they were ready to explore the possibilities with the Soviets so long as they would not appear as supplicants. Kissinger decided with the President's concurrence that an ABM system was essential to the American bargaining posture to offset the Soviets' own ABM systems and their emerging lead in missile launchers. They quickly agreed with Laird to change the name of McNamara's ABM from "Sentinel" to "Safeguard" and to shift the deployment from cities to Minuteman sites, starting with Grand Forks, North Dakota, safely out of the reach of antiwar protestors. It was Laird's job to sell the system to Congress.

Laird was a long-time Midwestern congressman and a former member of the House Armed Services Committee, universally respected for his political skills and native shrewdness rather than for his knowledge of defense issues. As a politician with a populist touch, he had little stomach for the war in Vietnam, but was almost as mistrustful of the

Soviet Union as he was of the young civilian analysts McNamara had left behind in the Pentagon. Blunt and aggressive, with a bullet-shaped bald head that cartoonists loved to portray in the shape of a missile warhead, he took up the cudgels on behalf of the administration's Safeguard ABM with a gleeful ferocity that touched off a full-scale donnybrook between the administration and the military on the one side and the CIA, most defense analysts, the arms control lobby, and a near-majority of the Congress on the other.

Laird made a brief attempt to base his ABM argument on alleged Soviet progress with their Moscow and Tallinn systems. But the Moscow system, which everyone agreed was an ABM, had made hardly any progress, and there was by now a clear consensus that the Tallinn system, which the Soviets were still throwing up at a frantic pace (it would eventually consist of 1,800 launch sites) was configured against aircraft. Laird floated the possibility that the Soviets might be planning a rapid upgrade of Tallinn once the system was in place, but the idea was too implausible to sell to a skeptical Congress. (During the brief period that Laird floated the "SAM* upgrading" question, he made it such a catchword that wags wondered whether "Sam Upgrading" was a new member of the National Security Council.)

The rapid pace of Soviet SS-9 deployment was a much more ominous development, and Laird decided to base his ABM case on the threat the big new missiles posed to America's defenses. He and John Foster, the head of weapons development at the Pentagon, argued, with steadily increasing fervor, that as Soviet technology improved, the huge size of the missiles would allow them to carry enough warheads to pose a real threat to American Minuteman silos—perhaps as early as 1973, according to Foster. They justified the sudden alarm by pointing to Soviet tests of a new SS-9 with three warheads, known as the SS-9 "triplet," that began in the summer of 1968. The tests had prompted a bitter debate on whether the Soviets had actually succeeded in building a MIRV, or whether the "triplet" was merely a multiple warhead, like the Polaris A3. (In fact, it was somewhere between the two; the three warheads were released separately, but apparently without additional post-boost course adjustment.) Foster insisted that the debate was irrelevant. Air Force analysts had noted that the triangular "footprint" of the SS-9 triplet came quite close to matching the silo deployment pattern in Minuteman fields; it was therefore the "functional equivalent" of a MIRV, whether or not the warheads were independently

*SAM stands for Surface-to-Air-Missile.

targetable. Moreover, the orientation of the radio antennae at the SS-9 launch sites—SS-9s were guided by ground-based radio signals during their initial boost stage—indicated a trajectory aimed at American Minuteman installations.

Once the Soviets had deployed 420 SS-9 triplets, Foster argued, which was expected about 1973, they could target a warhead against each Minuteman silo and still have 260 left over for a second-wave attack on any silos that survived the first volley. Eighty percent firing reliability, which he confidently expected the Soviets to have, and an average warhead accuracy within about a quarter mile of the silo target, would be all that was required. Indeed, if they could achieve a .15 mile accuracy with the single-warhead SS-11, they could launch at least two warheads against each Minuteman silo in the first strike and have plenty left over to deter any thoughts of American retaliation.

Laird rode Foster's theory hard, much to the embarrassment of the CIA, for Laird continually misquoted them to make it appear that they agreed. The agency thought Foster was talking nonsense: neither the SS-9 nor the SS-11 was nearly as accurate as Foster was claiming—a .15 mile accuracy for the SS-11 would have required a six- to ten-fold accuracy improvement, which was preposterous—and an attempt to take out three separate missile silos with a triplet warhead lacking independent guidance would be unimaginably reckless. But Laird warned the Congress that "with the large tonnage the Soviets have, they are going for a first-strike capability. There is no question about that," and he pounded home that if the Soviets improved SS-11 accuracy, "the serviceability of our Minuteman force as presently deployed would be virtually nil by the mid- to late-1970s." Even America's submarine-launched missiles might be useless. Rapid Soviet progress in ABM deployment could counter the Polaris, he insisted, and "we cannot preclude the possibility that the Soviet Union in the next few years may devise some weapon, technique, or tactic, which could critically increase the vulnerability of those submarines."

(Interestingly enough, during this period neither Laird nor Foster, nor any other spoksman, expressed concern that the Soviets would target the Minuteman Launch Control Centers. As will be discussed later, the American command and control system was much more vulnerable than its missiles. The 1,000 Minutemen were controlled by only 100 Launch Control Centers, which were much "softer" than the silos themselves. There are some retrospective indications that the Soviets understood this. Pre-emptive targeting of the SS-9s against the Minuteman control centers would have given the Soviets a formidable counterforce capability. Launching against the control centers, of course, would still be a wholly desperate act, since the Soviet military would have to assume that the Americans had alternative communication capabilities, which was arguably, if only arguably, true. The prospects for success could hardly entice a surprise "bolt-from-the-blue" strike, but it was still the most plausible second-best strategy for the Soviets if the two countries had come to the brink of a nuclear war.)

Laird's warnings became even shriller as a parade of technical witnesses, many of whom were philosophically predisposed toward antimissile defenses for Minuteman silos, told the Congress that the administration's ABM system was a technological turkey. McNamara's "Sentinel" system was designed to defend cities; shifting its mission to "hard-point" defense raised wholly new problems that a simple name change could not eradicate. The most fundamental issue was the radar. The basic requirement of a city defense system was that *no* missile could get through. A single 1-megaton-plus blast would utterly destroy any city, so there was no point in hardening the radar system. If it was taken out by a missile, the rest of the city would have already gone with it.

Defending Minuteman silos posed exactly the opposite requirements. The silos were hardened, so it could be assumed that if only *some* attacking missiles got through, enough Minutemen would survive to launch a counterstrike. It was essential, then, that the radar be the most invulnerable element in the defense, since it would have to remain operative during repeated attacks, some of which might be successful. But the "Safeguard" radars were the softest part of the entire system and clearly unsuitable for their new mission.

There were other awkward problems. The Safeguard's defensive configuration, for example, was the right size for a typical city, but too small to cover an entire Minuteman field and too big for efficient protection of a single missile wing. Even worse, the long-range weapon in the Safeguard system, the Spartan missile, designed for exo-atmospheric interception, carried an enormous 5-megaton warhead, one of the biggest in the American arsenal. (A second, much smaller high-acceleration missile, the Sprint, was designed to attack anything that got past the Spartan.) But a 5-megaton high-altitude blast would wipe out any electronic systems for hundreds, possibly thousands, of miles, and effectively blind the Safeguard radars to any subsequent shots. It was clear that, despite all of Laird's stumping, the ABM could not be sold on the merits.

The administration, of course, and particularly Kissinger, were no more interested in *building* ABMs than the congressional doves. Kissinger sensed, quite correctly, that he needed the ABM as a "bargaining chip" for arms talks. In the final analysis, a vote for Safeguard came down to a question of party loyalty and old-fashioned horse trading. The antimilitarist mood in the Congress was so strong that, even with the administration pulling out all the political stops, Safeguard squeaked through the Senate only by virtue of a tie-breaking vote by Vice-President Spiro Agnew. If nothing else, the episode illuminates the great difficulties imposed by the open American political system for any administration hoping to play bluff poker in arms bargaining with the Soviets.

Perhaps the most significant aspect of Laird's battle for the ABM was that he became thereby the first major official spokesman for the "Minuteman vulnerability" problem. The worry about the safety of the Minuteman resurfaced with each Soviet technological improvement during the succeeding decade, until it provided important impetus for the Reagan administration's defense buildup in the early 1980s. In its refined form, which is rather more subtle than Laird's customary version, it was essentially a restatement of the game theory "coercive strategy" that McNamara bruited in 1962, but with American-Soviet roles reversed. If the Soviets could launch a successful first strike on American Minuteman silos, it could be argued, the American President would face the dreadful decision of launching his remaining submarine-based missiles against Soviet cities in the certain knowledge that the Soviets would utterly destroy urban America in retaliation. The better course would be to retire from the field without further casualties; in other words, bow to Soviet coercion and allow them to work their political designs wherever they chose. A successful first strike on the Minutemen, in short, would mean that the Soviets had won a nuclear war.

The question of land-based missile vulnerability was central to the strategic debate of the 1970s. To understand the issues involved, and to evaluate the plausibility of the arguments, it is essential first to understand the basic technology and capabilities of long-range nuclear missiles.

# CHAPTER 15

# The Technology of Long-Range Destruction

Destroying an enemy military target, particularly a hardened target, like a missile silo, with a long-range nuclear weapon is an extraordinarily complex undertaking. The target must be precisely located and mapped. The missile must fire reliably and on schedule, and must deliver a warhead to the target with sufficient accuracy. The warhead must detonate precisely on time: the attack plan may call for detonation just before the warhead strikes the target, for example, or may even require the warhead to tunnel into the ground before detonating. The physics of the blast must behave as the technologists predicted, and the target's defenses—the resistance of a missile's concrete silo, for example—must have been correctly divined. Since the nuclear plans of the United States and the Soviet Union assume follow-on strikes to back up first-wave missiles that malfunction or otherwise fail to get through, the attacker must receive accurate information on the results of the first assault and be able to retarget his reserve weapons very rapidly. The requirements of a retaliatory strike are even more daunting, of course—that is, if it is not simply to be an all-out "spasm" launch of all surviving weapons against the other side's population—for there is the additional problem of sending precise commands to launch crews, some of them under distant oceans, during the electronic maelstrom that will follow a nuclear attack of any size at all. All of these issues are essential to understanding the reality of "first-strike" scenarios of any kind. This chapter, therefore, will break the chronological course of the narrative to summarize the unclassified literature on the performance of nuclear rockets. The issues of command and control of nuclear forces are more directly relevant to "flexible response" and "war-fighting" nuclear theories and are treated in Chapter 19.

### Ballistic Missiles

The central fact about long-range missiles is that they are *ballistic* weapons (from the Greek word *ballein*, "to throw"), meaning that they are hurled into space by their rocket booster and travel virtually the whole of their flight path in a state of free fall, like an artillery shell. The boost phase of a missile launch, then—which may involve one, two, or even three different rocket engines, each one igniting in turn, then disengaging and falling away as its fuel is exhausted—may be likened to the barrel of a huge howitzer. The boost phase typically lasts some two to three minutes and carries the missile about 100 miles to a point above the earth's atmosphere. As the last booster rocket disengages, it will have thrown the warhead or re-entry vehicle into a ballistic trajectory at a speed in excess of 7,000 miles per hour and on a trajectory heading toward its target some 8,000 miles distant. The warhead will then arch majestically over the earth in a stupendous 1,000-mile high, twenty-five-minute long flight path, until it hurtles back into the atmosphere at speeds approaching 15,000 miles per hour. Since any errors at the outset of the flight will be vastly magnified by the time the warhead begins re-entry, the boost phase is by far the most critical stage of the launch. A velocity miscalculation of *one tenth* of a mile per hour at the point of release will cause a target miss of about 500 meters, or too wide of the mark to take out a hardened missile silo. Building the guidance systems to place a warhead within a few hundred meters of its target on the other side of the world is one of the most dazzling technological feats of the modern era.

American designers successfully solved the boost-phase control problem in the late 1950s by developing "on-board inertial guidance" systems that were the basis of missile guidance technology for the next twenty-five years. The scientific concepts involved are relatively straightforward. If the launch acceleration, the angle of the acceleration, and the elapsed boost time are known at every moment, the basic formulas of Newtonian physics can be applied to calculate the precise flight path of the missile at every point. The instrumentation required is similarly straightforward: an accurate clock and accelerometers (devices that measure the inertial resistance of test masses to acceleration) oriented in each of the three basic directions permit measurement of the angle and acceleration of the flight path. As the rocket is launched, the data from the clock and the accelerometers are constantly fed into a high-speed on-board computer that measures the deviation from the planned trajectory and continuously recalculates the angle of release and terminal velocity required to make up for the accumulating errors. The computer will time the precise instant to cut off the main engine and adjust the angle of the rocket by firing small nozzle thrusters. Typically, the main portion of the boost-phase flight path is nearly straight up, to clear the heavy, low-level atmosphere as quickly as possible; the nozzle thrusters then turn the rocket in a graceful curve to the ballistic trajectory that will carry it to its target. The great advantage of the MIRV "bus," of course, was to create the possibility of a further small but crucial correction in the ballistic trajectory in the "post-boost" phase of flight after the initial launch.

Building accurate missiles in the early 1960s, like the Minuteman I, with an accuracy in the half-mile range, involved a staggering series of technical breakthroughs: "whole new branches of knowledge, including the development of new materials, detailed models of their stability and behavior, new types of bearings with essentially zero friction and incredibly long life, new advances in the stability of electronics, and highly specialized methods for production, assembly, and calibration. One expert described [the new] current instruments as 'almost unreal.' "

The miniaturization achieved to package a highly sophisticated computer within severe missile weight constraints was remarkable for its day. But substantial advances were required in even the most mundane technologies, like ball-bearing manufacture. The gyroscopes in a missile guidance system that stabilize the accelerometers at the proper angles require highly precise and reliable ball bearings. The tiniest error, on the order of millionths of a degree, in the accelerometer's orientation will feed incorrect flight information to the computer and cause an unacceptably large error in the flight path. A gyroscope is essentially a spinning wheel that, because of the law of conservation of angular momentum, resists change in its angle of orientation; measuring the resistance measures the change in orientation. The gyroscopes in the Minuteman, for example, spin at thousands of revolutions per minute, and because the Minuteman missiles are kept in a constant state of readiness, are kept spinning by their electric motors for tens of thousands of hours between replacements.

Machining gyroscope bearings with the necessary durability and exquisite precision to maintain virtually perfect alignment for such extended periods was an extraordinary technical accomplishment. Indeed, a major criticism of the period of detente between the United

States and the Soviet Union levelled by conservative critics in the late 1970s was that the United States allowed its European allies to transfer advanced ball-bearing technology to the Soviet Union, which was used to achieve substantial upgrades in Soviet missile accuracy.* The MX missile, which began production in 1983, employs an essentially new approach to the inertial guidance problem built around a sphere floating in a gas-filled chamber.

Precise and reliable inertial guidance systems, of course, were only part of the solution. Substantial advances were required in mapping and measuring the earth's gravitational and magnetic field. The guidance system's accelerometers, for example, measure only the *change* in acceleration from some initial state. The computer must know the starting location and gravitational state precisely in order to calculate the flight path correctly. The difficulty of measuring the precise starting point is the major obstacle to developing highly accurate submarine-launched missiles or mobile land-based missiles.† And even after a perfect launch, gravitational and magnetic anomalies along a missile's flight path can degrade its accuracy significantly unless they are properly accounted for in the trajectory computation. Finally, the target's location must be known. In the beginning of the missile era, there was considerable uncertainty regarding the precise location of significant Soviet targets, including major industrial installations, until satellites had accurately mapped the entire country. Maps readily available from the United States Geological Survey locate most major American industrial installations with accuracies of about 100 feet.

The final crucial stage in a missile's flight is re-entry. The great heat generated by a high-speed re-entry could burn up a warhead or destroy its delicate fuzing mechanisms. Early nose cones had a blunt shape and re-entered the earth's atmosphere at a low angle so they would slow down quickly in the lighter outer atmosphere. But a slow re-entry meant that winds and other atmospheric disturbances could easily dis-

---

*It is difficult to assess the validity of such charges. Conservative critics of detente were also predisposed to attribute high levels of accuracy to Soviet missiles well before the alleged technology transfer; Soviet missiles, that is, were either substantially less accurate than many critics of detente claimed, or the ball-bearing technology was no longer so strategically significant.

†The submarine launch problem persisted into the 1980s. The newest generation of American submarine-launched missiles, the Trident II D-5, scheduled for deployment in 1988, will use the NAVSTAR satellite guidance system. During the missile's boost phase, it will take a fix on satellites in stationary orbit and recalibrate its initial launching position accordingly. The Trident II D-5, it is claimed, will have accuracies that rival those of any land-based missile. The positioning problem for mobile land-based missiles is solved by moving them among a series of precisely calibrated launch sites.

rupt their trajectories; and if the re-entry angle was even slightly too high, the warhead could "sail" far off course. A major breakthrough came with the invention of the "ablative" nose cone for the first MIRVed Minuteman. The warheads were shielded with newly invented materials that burn away, or "ablate," to carry off the heat buildup. The nose cones could then be designed for the most direct and rapid descent possible, virtually eliminating the importance of target site winds. Part of the technical challenge, of course, was to ensure that the shielding burnt off in a precisely regular pattern; otherwise the change in warhead shape would throw it off course. Progress in warhead design has required substantial breakthroughs in the theory of fluid dynamics and the mathematics of turbulence.

Efforts in the 1980s focused on developing maneuverable warheads. At least two different kinds, using varieties of fins, are "on the shelf," and a further type has been deployed on the intermediate-range Pershing II missile. Work is also proceeding on a maneuverable re-entry vehicle for the Trident II D-5—the warhead itself reportedly will have some intelligence to allow it either to avoid missile defenses or home in on a target. Analysts are generally dubious about the effectiveness of such devices. The high re-entry speed of a ballistic warhead builds up a powerful field of electrical interference—around ICBMs more so than around shorter-range weapons, such as the Pershing II. Operating homing or defensive maneuvering devices through such a field presents daunting technical problems.

In the first few years of the missile era, there was roughly a fourfold improvement in the accuracy of American missiles. Until then, indeed, the Air Force's preference for the manned bomber was strategically well founded. The first generations of deployed American ICBMs, like the Atlas, had accuracies on the order of two miles, limiting their usefulness to terror weapons against large metropolitan areas. The Atlas E, the first all-inertially guided missile, apparently came close to a one-mile accuracy, and the American Titan I achieved two thirds of a mile accuracy in 1961. With the deployment of the Minuteman I missile in 1962, with an accuracy possibly as good as a half-mile, the United States possessed a weapon that could, with assurance, be pinpointed against industrial plants or military bases, and which posed a genuine threat to the poorly protected Soviet missile sites. All American missiles from that point, including the underwater-launched Polaris, had average accuracies of one mile or less. (For reasons explained below, however, all estimates of missile accuracies can only be approximations.)

The first Soviet intercontinental missile, the SS-6, essentially the Sputnik missile, reportedly had an average accuracy of only about five miles; it was far too clumsy an instrument to be a practical weapon, and only four were ever deployed. The follow-on missile, the SS-7, and a variant, the SS-8, became the mainstay of the Soviet intercontinental rocket forces until 1966. It is highly unlikely that the SS-7 or SS-8 achieved accuracies of one mile. The clinching evidence of Soviet backwardness is that, as late as 1967, radio signals were still being used to direct the booster phase of the newest model SS-9s. Part of the evidence of an SS-9 threat to the American Minuteman fields, it will be recalled, was the orientation of the ground-based guidance antennae. Ground-based guidance is far more unreliable than a self-contained on-board system because of the problem of signal delay and the possibility of interference; during a war, no radio-based system could work if there had been a nuclear blast anywhere in the vicinity, even within quite large distances. The electronic miniaturization necessary for on-board guidance, presumably, still eluded the Soviets in the late 1960s, which adds perspective to the SS-9 scare at the outset of the Nixon administration. The prolonged Soviet campaign to buy Western ball-bearing technology was a further indication of guidance system problems, although their technology improved rapidly during the remainder of the decade.

Delivering a warhead accurately, of course, is only part of the problem entailed in destroying a military target. The warhead must detonate on schedule, and the detonation must have the effects that the weapon's designers predicted.

## The Effects of Nuclear Explosions

A nuclear explosion releases a small portion of the binding energy that holds particles together in the nucleus of the atom. The released energy takes the form of electromagnetic waves—mostly very active gamma rays that quickly cool to X-rays, visible light, and ordinary heat—and as kinetic energy propelling subatomic particles, mostly neutrons, like so many billions of tiny bullets.* For most military purposes, two effects are crucial. The first is the enormous pulse of electromagnetic energy.

*It is basically the hail of particles that causes radiation sickness. The particles destroy the machinery inside the cell that controls cell reproduction. The cells can repair themselves up to a point, but the repair process takes time. If the cells are short-lived ones, like those that line the stomach and intestine, they can withstand less damage because they have less repair potential. That is why vomiting and diarrhea are characteristic symptoms of radiation sickness.

The pulse from a ground burst will destroy any unprotected electrical or communication system for 10–15 miles around. Even more spectacularly, the pulse from a single large-megaton burst high above the atmosphere in the middle of the United States, since its initial propagation would be unimpeded by air molecules, would very likely cause a nationwide blackout and blow out unprotected generators, computers, or communication facilities anywhere in the country.

The second and more important effect is the shock wave. As the air molecules surrounding the explosion absorb the sudden burst of radiation, they are heated to millions of degrees in a few billionths of a second. Since the air is heated much faster than it can expand, it builds up an immense pressure that blasts out in the form of a wall of hot wind moving at more than 100,000 miles an hour. The force of the shock wave is measured in terms of its "overpressure," or the pounds of pressure per square inch (psi) in excess of normal atmospheric pressure. An overpressure of 3 psi will level most wood frame houses, and an overpressure of 5 psi will knock down a brick wall. A 1-megaton bomb, or a bomb having the explosive equivalent of 1 million tons of TNT—fifty times bigger than the Hiroshima bomb—would be likely to generate overpressures of at least 5 psi in a great circle up to 10 miles in diameter. Obviously, a 1-megaton explosion will flatten any city center and wreak dreadful damage over a much wider area as people are trapped in wooden houses, killed by flying glass, electrocuted by fallen power lines, or incinerated in the ferocious firestorm that will spring up in the wake of the initial blast of superheated air.

The effects of a nuclear explosion against a hardened military target, like a missile silo, however, are not nearly so certain, and present a number of imponderables for both the defender and the attacker. The Minuteman missiles, for example, are encased in concrete silos 25 meters underground. The concrete walls and thick concrete lid (blown away by an explosive device when the missile is ready to fire) are designed to protect the missile from the damaging effects of the electromagnetic pulse and the shock wave's overpressure. There is a special shock-resistant floor under the silo and the missile is suspended in a network of shock absorbers. The electronics in the warhead are heavily shielded, and the electronic systems are designed to cut quickly off and then back on at the occurrence of a damaging electrical pulse.

The silos were originally designed to withstand overpressures of 300 psi, but an extensive refitting program during the 1970s, precipitated in part by the SS-9 scare, upgraded them to an average hardness of

2,000 psi, while the lids were reshaped to deflect debris that might accumulate from an attacking blast. (The theoretical maximum hardness of a concrete silo is not much higher than 2,000 psi. Various sources have claimed much higher hardening levels for Soviet silos, but such claims should be viewed with skepticism. The United States had planned a "superhardened" silo, to about 5,000 psi, for its new MX missile in the early 1980s, but quietly dropped its development.)

It is quite literally impossible to estimate with any certainty the effects of an explosion on a missile silo, for the simple reason that very little is known about the effects of large nuclear explosions. A quarter century has passed since either the United States or the Soviet Union conducted an atmospheric test, and those tests were mostly aimed at creating big explosions with lighter warheads; no one had yet thought much about hardening silos. There are virtually no data at all on overpressures in the 2,000 psi range, and even at lower overpressures, the data are quite sparse and show variations from the mean of as much as 50 percent. Theoretical calculations, in fact, indicate that the duration of the shock wave may be more important than its raw power, but there are no empirical data relating duration to destructiveness in large blasts. Virtually all the operative assumptions on overpressure and shock wave characteristics are merely extrapolations from mathematical models.

Blast effects will also vary widely depending on the timing of a blast: a low air burst, i.e, split seconds before the bomb actually hits the target, generates a shock wave as much as 40 percent more powerful than a surface blast. A successful subsurface blast, on the other hand, will generate the maximum seismic damage against a missile silo. The propagation of the seismic wave, however, will depend critically on local geology; indeed, the power of the wave can depend crucially on the level of the local water table on the day of the strike. The catalogue of possible effects here leaves out the variety of injuries that the flux of electromagnetic energy can inflict on the delicate guidance system and electronic circuits of the missile. The official position of the Defense Department is that the overpressure measure states the lower limit of resistance. That is, a silo hardened to 2,000 psi can resist successfully any other effects of a blast generating less than 2,000 psi of overpressure. But, obviously, since no missile silo has ever actually been exposed to such a blast, such assurances cannot be given with any certainty. In short, an attacker can have no great confidence that a 2,000-psi blast would put much of a dent in a hardened silo; but a defender can have no greater certainty that his missiles could ride out attacks that were even much less severe.

From the attacker's standpoint, the precise profile of the blast is less important than its location. The raw energy released by a blast increases roughly proportionally to the size of the weapon. But the rate of shock wave dissipation is disproportionately rapid: so much so that it negates much of the increase in destructive energy. The bigger the bomb, that is, the more thoroughly it will vaporize whatever is in its immediate vicinity; but each increase in a bomb's size will add proportionately less and less extra destructive radius to its shock wave. The precise formula is that the killing power of a nuclear weapon increases proportionate to the two-thirds power of its yield. The two-thirds power rule means that an increase in the size of a bomb from 1-megaton to 25 megatons will increase its destructive power only about eight and a half times; and a thousandfold increase in a bomb's power will increase its destructiveness by only a hundred times. Increasing the size of a bomb, in other words, is a very inefficient way to increase its effectiveness; beyond a certain point, in fact, the improvement is hardly worth the effort.

The concentration of energy at the center of the explosion, on the other hand, means that improving the *accuracy* of a missile will dramatically increase its killing effectiveness. Missile accuracy is measured by a value known as "circular error probable," or CEP. CEP reflects the statistical fact that the impact points of a volley of warheads launched at a target will form a circular scatter pattern around the target. The radius of the circle around the target that includes half of the warhead impact points is the CEP. To say that a missile has a CEP of one mile, therefore, means that half the warheads launched by that type of missile, absent other sources of error, may be expected to land within one mile of the target. Weapons technologists quickly discovered that CEP reductions produced about five times better probability of a target kill than comparable increases in warhead yield.*

To take a specific example, in an attack against a Minuteman silo, a 1-megaton warhead would have to impact within about 350 meters of the target to generate 2,000 psi of overpressure on the silo. If the missile was only half as accurate, however, with a CEP in the 700–750 meter range, the warhead would have to be increased to 10 megatons to generate the same amount of overpressure on the silo. Reducing the CEP by a factor of two is as effective as multiplying the yield by ten.

*A more detailed statement of the yield/accuracy/lethality relation appears in the notes to this chapter.

More accurate missiles, in short, have far more strategic significance than bigger warheads. The debate about the possible counterforce capabilities of either the Soviet Union or the United States, then, turns first of all on the question of missile accuracy.

Even with only 300-psi overpressure protection for Minuteman silos, and despite the huge SS-9 warheads, in the early 1970s there was almost no possibility that the Soviet SS-9s or SS-11s were accurate enough to pose a plausible threat to America's land-based missile silos— although, as mentioned, they could have threatened the still relatively unprotected Launch Control Centers. The situation began to change dramatically in the middle of the decade when the Soviets rapidly introduced new generations of far more potent weapons, the SS-17, 18, and 19. Estimating the CEPs of Soviet missiles is an uncertain undertaking, and estimates tend to vary with the politics of the estimator. (Satellite tracking shows precisely where a Soviet test missile landed, but never where the Soviets intended it to land.) But at the plausible lower ranges of CEP estimates, both the big, single-shot, 20-megaton SS-18, and the newest MIRVed SS-19, with an average of six 560-kiloton warheads, should have more than enough killing power to take out a fully hardened Minuteman silo.

The first version of America's three-warhead Minuteman III missile, which created such a controversy when deployment began in the early 1970s, would have been quite effective against the contemporary Soviet SS-9 and SS-11 sites; but, with its relatively small 170-kiloton warhead, it may not have been quite accurate enough to take out a silo fully hardened to the American 2,000-psi level. (Though there were enough conflicting claims that a conservative Soviet defense official would have had to assume that it *could* attack a fully hardened silo.) With the installation of an improved re-entry vehicle, the Mark 12A, beginning in 1980, however, the power of each Minuteman III warhead was doubled, and claimed CEPs were reduced to the 200-250-meter range, or more than enough to generate the overpressures to kill the hardest silos. The remaining Minuteman IIs, slightly less than half the fleet, have a bigger single warhead of 1.2 megatons, but a wider CEP rating; they can plausibly deliver a 2,000-psi overpressure blast against a hard target, but with a rather greater range of uncertainty compared to the upgraded Minuteman III.

The relation between missile accuracy and warhead size, finally, casts perspective on the tendency to frame the later debate on Minuteman vulnerability in terms of the very large throw-weight of Soviet missiles. As Jan Lodal pointed out in 1976, the size of a warhead was relevant only over a very narrow range of accuracy. When a missile's CEP is in excess of a quarter mile or so, *no* warhead is big enough to assure a hard-silo kill; on the other hand, when CEPs dip below 100 meters, almost *any* nuclear warhead will do the job. In the 1980s, a cruise missile, with only a 50-kiloton warhead but a thirty-meter CEP, could generate almost 175,000 psi of overpressure on its target, many times more than required for the hardest silo. The example of the cruise also demonstrates the futility of investing in silo hardening much above the 2,000-psi level.

To return to Melvin's Laird's concerns for American missile vulnerability at the end of the 1960s: based solely on the destructive power and accuracy of Soviet missiles, Minuteman silos, while not yet in danger, would appear to have been well on their way toward becoming so. But accuracy and throw-weight are still far from the whole story, for estimating the likely success of a pre-emptive counterforce strike involves much more than estimating the theoretical killing power of a single missile.

## Uncertainties of a Ballistic Missile Strike

Estimating the likely success of a 2,000-plus warhead attack against 1,000 or more hardened missile silos poses entirely new areas of uncertainty that far transcend even the complex questions of missile accuracy and payload effectiveness. Would the missiles all work? Would they be accurate enough under operational conditions? Could the launches be coordinated to take out substantially all the other side's weapons at the same time? The discussion in this section will focus on the technical achievability of a successful counterforce missile launch, completely omitting the political considerations. It proceeds, therefore, on the wholly unrealistic assumption that a first strike would be launched totally by surprise during a time of relative peace, the "bolt from the blue" that Albert Wohlstetter anticipated in 1959. In real life, of course, particularly since Soviet missile forces are usually kept in a low state of readiness, there would have to be a considerable period of preparation—sending nuclear submarines to sea, for instance—that could hardly escape American intelligence. If the strike was preceded by a deepening period of political crisis, moreover, American missiles would presumably be in a high state of alert. The early warning systems across Canada and Alaska routinely pick up false signals of Soviet missile launches and as routinely ignore them. The Soviets obviously could not count on such complacency during a crisis: the whole point of the strike would be defeated if a substantial number of American missiles "launched on warning" as soon as the signs of a large enemy missile strike appeared on the radar screens.

Omitting all considerations of political plausibility, a key issue is the basic question of missile reliability. The United States, for example, has *never* successfully fired a missile from an operational silo. Four attempts have been made over the years, under a variety of constraining conditions, before the effort was abandoned because of the potential risk to civilians. (The Air Force points to the safety constraints as part of the problem; in one case, the missile was tethered.) In each instance, the launch problem was easily identifiable and quickly fixed, but the experience raises considerable doubt about the possibility of a large-scale launch with split-second timing, doubt that is reinforced by the hundreds of tiny problems that bedevil space rocket launches. The Soviet Union, it is known, has conducted a small number of tests from military silos, but like the United States, has accumulated by far the greatest part of its test experience on special test ranges. Reliability problems stemming from random malfunctions can be substantially reduced, but hardly eliminated, by cross-targeting two warheads from different missiles on the same silo. In theory, they could be reduced further by cross-targeting three warheads, but until the mid-1980s, neither the Soviet Union nor the United States had sufficient surplus hard-target warheads to do so. The small reliability improvement from the third warhead, moreover, is bought at a large cost: at some point, the attacker would be expending more warheads than he was disabling. In effect, he would be disarming himself.

Testing procedures for American missiles appear to be as rigorous and fair as possible, but necessarily fall short of wartime conditions. The standard protocol is to select a missile at random and, before removing it from the silo, to test all procedures and circuits for bringing the weapon to alert status. Testing the launch circuitry, however, presents a good example of the problem of test realism, since there is only a simulated launch. One Pentagon analyst has commented: "You can't go down a launch countdown sequence without going through with it. You end up taking irreversible steps. But if you don't do those, you don't have a real countdown."

The next step is to ship the missile to the Vandenberg Air Force Base in California, where its warhead is replaced with equipment to monitor the flight and to destroy the missile if the flight goes awry. The guidance system is recalibrated for the test flight to the Kwajalein Lagoon in the Pacific, a distance of about 5,000 miles. Launch is delayed for fifteen days after calibration—real-life guidance systems are calibrated every thirty days, so an unexpected launch would occur, on average, after fifteen days. The Air Force insists that there is no "gold-plating" or other intentional interference with the effort to get the most realistic test results possible. (Defense critics are often skeptical of such claims.) It may be assumed that Soviet testing goes to equal lengths to ensure meaningful results.

There are still a number of problems with interpreting the test results. For one thing, the frequency of testing is relatively low. A new American weapon gets about twenty-five tests, and an additional five to ten tests per year after deployment. But because of the continuing process of model changes and component upgrades, the actual number of total tests for identical models is closer to the six–twelve range. Soviet test frequency is probably even lower. A second concern is that the Kwajalein test range is shorter than the average American wartime missile trajectory would be, and, of course, wartime trajectories would include a wide variety of distances. The Soviet Siberian test range is almost 1,000 miles shorter still, although the Soviets occasionally conduct long-range tests in the Pacific. The accumulation of guidance errors, of course, is a direct function of the distance travelled. The Kwajalein test target, in addition, is one of the calmest atmospheric areas in the world, so it may understate a warhead's susceptibility to re-entry turbulence.

Perhaps most important, and one of the most controversial topics among weapons professionals, is the possibility that systematic biases in missile guidance calibrations will be undetectable by normal testing. In a strict mathematical sense, CEP is a measure of dispersion around an average landing point, *not* around a predetermined target. A 250-meter CEP, that is, means that half of all missiles fired will land within a circle with a 250-meter radius. It requires a technological leap of faith to be confident that the center of the circle will be *precisely the target that is being aimed at.* The possibility of systematic bias arises primarily because both the United States and the Soviet Union have always fired their missiles along test ranges where every gravitational and magnetic anomaly has been exhaustively tracked, mapped, and calibrated for decades. The transpolar attack routes that would be used in an actual war obviously have different gravitational and magnetic characteristics, different atmospheric conditions, and different trajectories from the test ranges; and there is no way of knowing whether the guidance calibrations have left key differences systematically unaccounted for. *Systematic* errors of this sort present a much more serious problem than random missile malfunctions because they would affect every missile launched. And, obviously, since surprise is such a critical factor in a first strike, there is no way to fire a test shot to check whether serious systematic guidance errors exist.

Pentagon spokesmen have, in the main, tended to belittle the bias problem. Dr. Seymour Zeiberg, a key missile development official, testified in 1979, for example:

We were never able to find factual evidence of that kind of concern. . . . there is no hidden phenomena that we are not modelling. . . . there is no known bias in [Minuteman tests] that we know about. Every now and then, because of some trouble with one flight, you find something, but it gets unraveled in the post-flight analysis. We don't have a bias in the Minuteman that is concerning us.

Or, as he put it later in an interview with James Fallows, "There are no unknowns. There are no surprises."

Other weapons scientists are not so certain. Richard Garwin, for example, a physicist with considerable weapons testing experience, has said that: "every time you fire a new-model missile over the same range, or the same missile over a slightly different range, the bias changes. Sometimes it is greater, sometimes it is smaller, but it has never been calculated beforehand." And J. B. Walsh, a former director of missile testing and development, said in 1976:

The problem with increased accuracy is your confidence in that accuracy . . . I have concern about uncertainties and factors that might have been left out, biases in the system, for example. I might be able to fire 10 RVs [re-entry vehicles] from 10 separate missiles and land in exactly the same spot, except that the spot is removed by a fraction of a mile from the target. And it is very difficult to find that kind of error or to know that it exists.

There is no question that the range of possible bias has been steadily reduced in recent years as satellite mapping technology has permitted ever more precise calibrations—satellites *do* fly over the transpolar routes. A recent estimate, however, primarily on theoretical grounds, indicates that a minimum expected bias in a first shot on a new range would be about 100 meters, given a fairly strong set of assumptions about the guidance system. An error of that size is very small along a 5,000-mile flight path, but is still enough to degrade significantly the certainty of a Minuteman taking out a 2,000-psi silo. Estimating the bias in Soviet weapons, of course, is even more speculative than estimating their accuracy. But there is no reason to believe that their guidance systems are more advanced than the Americans'; indeed, the history of the technological arms race and the persistent Soviet emphasis on large payloads would imply that they have substantially greater problems.

Finally, there is the enormous problem of timing the launches, even assuming that the launchers work with a high degree of reliability. The problem is much more complicated than simply firing in a sequence that will assure that all the missiles complete their different trajectories at the same time. For one thing, a successful attack will require the ability to retarget missiles in a second salvo based on the success of the first attack. For the second salvo to arrive on time—that is, before the defender retaliates—the retargeting decision will have to be based on flight data from the boost phase, and carried out within minutes. The refitted Minuteman III is claimed to have such a retargeting capability, at least in theory; but there is considerable doubt as to whether the Soviets have achieved it.

A much more difficult timing problem arises from the possibility of warhead "fratricide." American Minuteman silos are spaced between two and six miles from each other. A nuclear explosion over one silo will engulf the entire missile field in electromagnetic pandemonium, create spectacular atmospheric turbulence, and, depending on the height of the burst, raise a huge umbrella of hundreds of tons of particulate matter and other debris. Any one, or all, of these effects would be enough to destroy the shielding or the fuzing mechanisms of an incoming warhead or throw it substantially off course. At the speed of warhead re-entry, for example, a floating pebble-sized particle would have the impact of a bullet. More important, the precise character of all these effects, and countless others, is essentially unpredictable.

To avoid fratricide, it is usually assumed that a Soviet attack on Minuteman fields would have to follow a "rollback" pattern. Since the warheads would be arriving from the north, they would attack the southernmost silos first, rolling up the silos northward in rapid succession, so no warhead had to fly through a previous blast pattern. The attacking time window is quite small, since the attacks will have to be completed in the few minutes it will take for the first blast effects to spread across the entire missile field. The requirements of timing and patterning precision increase exponentially if two warheads from different missiles are cross-targeted on each silo, which should be considered the normal case; the difficulties of a three-warhead attack would be exponentially greater still. Various exotic attack patterns have been proposed to surmount the problem, such as firing a one-warhead per silo salvo, then "pinning down" the remaining Minutemen with high-altitude blasts—on the theory that the Minuteman warheads couldn't survive a launch through the electromagnetic pulse—and timing a second salvo to arrive just as the effects of the high-altitude blasts dissipate. But there is a point where speculation becomes fantasy.

The last plausible first-strike capability—in the sense of a pre-emptive silencing of the other side's land-based missiles—possessed by either side belonged to the United States about 1966, when 854 Minuteman I missiles, 54 Titan IIs, and 496 single-warhead Polaris were faced off against 219 poorly protected and slow-reacting SS-7s and 8s and the four antique SS-6s. The rapid Soviet missile buildup outran American first-strike abilities within another year or two, but the subsequent Soviet launcher advantage was never enough to shift the balance the other way until the very recent past, when the missile balance shifted sufficiently to create at least plausible doubts about the survivability of the Minuteman silos. But even assuming the most robust Soviet capabilities, introducing relatively modest levels of uncertainty about missile reliability, guidance system bias, reprogramming capabilities, fratricide, and blast and silo hardness interactions quickly reduces the statistical probability of a hard silo kill from the 90 percent-plus range to something closer to 50 percent. Fifty percent uncertainty is far too much. A first strike that risked leaving half the Minutemen undamaged, with some half billion tons of TNT equivalent striking power, obviously would achieve nothing except to hasten the ultimate holocaust. James Schlesinger, who succeeded Melvin Laird as Defense Secretary, after reviewing the unknowable elements in a counterforce strike, put it forcefully:

I believe there is some misunderstanding about the degree of reliability and accuracy of missiles. . . . We can never know what degrees of accuracy would be achieved in the real world. . . . We know that and the Soviets know it, and that is one of the reasons I can publicly state that neither side can achieve a high-confidence first-strike capability. I want the President of the United States to know that for all future years, and I want the Soviet leadership to know that for all future years.

The "window of vulnerability" concern that surfaced from time to time throughout the 1970s and most prominently during the 1980 presidential campaign was not, on the basis of this analysis, a realistic fear. Schlesinger's statement quoted above, however, may place rather too much reliance on the inherent limitations of technology. The record of "window of vulnerability" false alarms is not, by itself, assurance that a first-strike capability is in principle unattainable. Even the more routine modern weapons were almost unthinkable a generation ago. The gargantuan technological leaps that have been accomplished within the past thirty years suggest rather a substantial probability that the technical problems of an assured first-strike capability will eventually be solved. The phenomenal improvements in weapon accuracy that are emerging in the 1980s, indeed, point ineluctably in that direction.

# CHAPTER 16

# SALT and the Shifting Military Balance

### Agreement in Moscow

Leaving the Kremlin on a late afternoon in May 1972, the General Secretary of the Central Committee of the Communist Party of the Soviet Union, Leonid Brezhnev, to the horror and alarm of Henry Kissinger and American Secret Service agents, kidnapped the President of the United States. Brezhnev "physically propell[ed]" Richard Nixon into a huge ZIL limousine and set off at breakneck speed through the streets of Moscow to a dacha outside the city, with Kissinger and the Secret Service men in ineffectual pursuit. By the time the President's retainers arrived at the dacha, Brezhnev and Nixon were already soaring down the Moscow River in a hydrofoil. Kissinger commandeered another hydrofoil to follow, he recalls, while "Far behind, wallowing uncomfortably in our wake, was a conventional vessel loaded with the same Secret Service agents who had now seen their charge abducted a second time by the wily Soviet leader, this time by water."

Returning from the river, the party adjourned to a conference room in the dacha, where the Soviet leadership triumvirate, Brezhnev, Alexei Kosygin (the premier) and Nikolai Podgorny (president of the Supreme Soviet)* berated Nixon for three hours over American policies in Vietnam. Brezhnev, a rough-humored bear of a man, spoke gruffly, emo-

---

*President of the Supreme Soviet is an almost purely honorary title. By protocol, however, Podgorny would pair off with Nixon for official toasts at Moscow banquets. Podgorny got his presidential title when he lost out in the succession struggles of 1966. Up until the Moscow summit, the Americans had always assumed that Kosygin—or (who, as Premier, was the official head of the government—or) was the *de facto* leader. Strictly speaking, as head of the Party, Brezhnev had no official role vis-à-vis foreign governments. Although it was clear at Moscow that Brezhnev was *primus inter pares*—it was he, not Kosygin, who signed the SALT agreements—it was equally clear that fundamental decisions were taken by the collective leadership. It would be several more years before Brezhnev established himself as the unchallenged Soviet ruler.

tionally, even crudely. Kosygin was analytic and tough, but "glacially correct." Podgorny was bland. It no longer surprised the Americans that Brezhnev spoke first. A new piece of information from the Moscow summit was that Brezhnev, not Kosygin, was the real power in the Kremlin, much as Eisenhower learned at Geneva that it was Khrushchev who was really in charge.

Their lectures over, as if "the Soviet leaders . . . were speaking for the record," the mood suddenly brightened, and the party adjourned to a huge meal that continued past midnight, with much jesting about the Americans' incapacity for hard liquor. After the last toast was downed in the early morning, Kosygin announced that Andrei Gromyko, the Soviet Foreign Minister, would join the party with another official so Gromyko and Kissinger could retire and negotiate the details of an arms limitation treaty. The new official appearing "out of the blue," whom the Americans had never heard of, was Leonid Smirnov, a brilliant man in Kissinger's appraisal, and one of the Soviet Union's leading experts on nuclear weapons and strategic missiles.

The negotiation of the first Strategic Arms Limitation Treaty, or SALT I as it quickly came to be called, between the United States and the Soviet Union was surely one the more disorderly of diplomatic undertakings, even apart from the unruly proceedings in Brezhnev's dacha. There were in fact two negotiations proceeding quite separately from each other, an official one that had been meeting regularly at Helsinki and Vienna for almost three years, and the *real* one, which was concluded at the Moscow summit. The parallel negotiation had been started by Henry Kissinger more than a year before, with elaborate secrecy precautions, through the "backchannel" he had created with Anatoly Dobrynin, the long-time Soviet Ambassador to the United States. Secret negotiations, which the Soviets clearly preferred, could obviously proceed with a minimum of posturing and without the frequent destructive press leaks that so enraged Kissinger and Nixon (at one critical point in the Vienna talks, the *New York Times* announced in advance both the opening and the fallback positions of the American team), but the separate processes led to more than a few diplomatic pratfalls. The same point was often resolved simultaneously, but slightly differently, by the two sets of negotiators; and, much to Kissinger's irritation, Vladimir Semenov, the head of the official Soviet team, who *was* in on the secret, several times initiated talks with Gerard Smith, the chief of the American delegation, on topics that had already been settled in the backchannel, as if to test how much Smith really knew.

Smith and his boss, Secretary of State William Rogers, were not informed about the backchannel negotiations until Dobrynin and Kissinger had made a major breakthrough in the talks—it was an awkward moment, Kissinger concedes—but the two separate sets of talks continued in parallel right through to the end. One consequence was that the American technical experts were all in Helsinki when Kissinger was facing off against Smirnov on the detailed restrictions on each side's weapons.

Negotiating highly sensitive issues with the obsessively secretive Russians was a bizarre experience in itself. The Soviet civilian negotiators were completely ignorant of their own military capabilities, and until the last days of the Moscow summit, all data on Soviet weapons were provided by the Americans. When the American delegates began to discuss Soviet weapons characteristics at Helsinki, the Soviet military representatives took them aside and anxiously pleaded that they not reveal state secrets in front of the Soviet civilians. Even in Moscow, Smirnov became visibly upset when Kissinger began talking about Soviet weapons in front of Gromyko. The final confusion came on the last day of the summit. An agreement was reached at the Kremlin, and identical instructions in Russian and English were sent to the two official teams; but the American instructions were delayed by the elaborate Moscow-to-Washington-to-Helsinki secure communication system, so the much-abused Smith was forced to arrive in Moscow late for the signing, clutching an official text which he had barely had time to read, and which, he complained bitterly, he was not sure he understood.

Disorderly or not, the Moscow summit was the climax of a two-year period of American diplomacy marked by rare imagination, boldness, and sustained success. Kissinger's dramatic secret visit to China the year before, and Nixon's successful summit with Zhou Enlai in Beijing, had radically reshuffled the "correlation of world forces," and strongly prodded the Soviet Union to reorder its relations with the United States. The separate agreements with Moscow and Beijing also greatly added to the pressure on the North Vietnamese to reach a settlement which Nixon and Kissinger could consider "honorable," and which was in fact achieved, if only temporarily and only after considerably more violence, early in 1973. The Moscow summit itself dramatized that the Soviet Politburo valued its relations with America above its fraternal obligations to Hanoi. North Vietnam had launched a major military offensive in the weeks leading up to the summit, and Nixon ordered a tough response, including mining and bombing attacks on the Haiphong and Hanoi harbors that caused a number of Soviet casualties.

Nixon, despite the outcry from his domestic critics, in effect challenged the Kremlin to declare their priorities. He won the gamble; indeed, he probably came to Moscow in a stronger bargaining position than ever. At the same time, Kissinger skillfully played upon the Kremlin's desire to capitalize on West Germany's new *Ostpolitik* both to increase the pressures toward a SALT agreement and to engineer, finally, a four-power treaty on Berlin, in which the Soviet Union at last undertook minimal guarantees on Western access to the city. On both substance and procedure, there is much to criticize in Nixon's and Kissinger's diplomatic performance, but measured by the accomplishments of preceding and succeeding administrations, it was extraordinary. The period of the Marshall Plan is the only one that immediately suggests itself for comparable constructive achievement.

The Moscow SALT agreement was the high point of a long struggle, stretching back more than twenty-five years to the abortive Baruch Plan, to place some limits on the growth of nuclear arsenals. Previous substantive accomplishments had been few and far between. A test ban treaty was in prospect before the collapse of the Paris summit in 1960, and a partial treaty was finally achieved after John Kennedy delivered his American University speech in the sober aftermath of the Cuban missile crisis. Kennedy and Khrushchev also agreed to establish a permanent "hot line" between Moscow and Washington, which was of considerable usefulness during the 1967 Six-Day War in the Middle East.

Lyndon Johnson was anxious to continue the Kennedy-Khrushchev detente, both to leave a genuine legacy of peace and to deflect the growing domestic criticism of the war in Vietnam. He pressed a variety of treaties upon the Kremlin and managed to secure a ban on military weapons in outer space in early 1967—neither side had plans for any— and the Nuclear Non-Proliferation Treaty the following year. The impetus for a non-proliferation agreement came largely from the Soviets, who had become almost as paranoid about Chinese nuclear technology as they had always been about West Germany's. China, of course, along with France and India, refused to sign the treaty. Soviet Sinophobia surfaced continually during the SALT negotiations, most notably in a bizarre proposal—delivered to Gerard Smith during an opera performance in Vienna—that the United States and the Soviet Union agree to come to each other's assistance in the event of a Chinese nuclear attack.

The groundwork for the SALT agreement itself was one of Robert McNamara's proudest legacies. He lobbied ceaselessly for arms limitation during his last year in office, and despite Kosygin's coldness in

Glassboro, the Soviet position appeared to change slowly through the following year. Suddenly in the late summer of 1968, to Johnson's delight, a burst of quiet diplomacy produced an agreement to hold an arms summit in Moscow in the fall. Perhaps the Americans should have suspected Soviet ulterior motives, for on the day the summit was to be announced, Soviet tanks rolled into Czechoslovakia to begin the brutal suppression of the "Prague Spring," accompanied by Brezhnev's alarming statement that ". . . the sovereignty of individual socialist countries cannot be counterposed to the interests of world socialism or the world revolutionary movement."

A frustrated Johnson, whose fondest dream was to leave office as an architect of peace, had no choice but to cancel the planned summit. Portentously, that same week saw the first test of the Soviet SS-9 "triplet" warhead and the first successful tests of the American MIRVed Minutemen and Poseidon. Johnson made one last futile, and probably foolish, attempt after the presidential election in November. A feeler to the Kremlin seemed to receive a positive reply, but a sharp warning came from the Hotel Pierre, headquarters of Nixon's transition staff, that the new administration would not be bound by anything Johnson negotiated during the presidential interregnum.

By the time Nixon and Kissinger began to examine seriously the possibility of an arms treaty in mid-1969, there had been a drastic realignment of Soviet and American bargaining positions. When McNamara floated the idea of an arms treaty in 1967, the United States still enjoyed a massive lead in strategic weaponry, and was anxious to forestall further development of the Soviet ABM. Two years later, the Soviet Union was zooming past the United States in the number of deployed missiles, but was making worried inquiries of its own about an ABM treaty. It was the Soviet flip-flop on the ABM that made SALT possible. Soviet motivations will never be known for certain, but in all likelihood they realized they were doomed to lose an ABM race. Huge offensive rockets could make up for their slow progress in electronic miniaturization, and large warheads would partially compensate for guidance system deficiencies. But antimissile systems required the most sophisticated technologies—such as advanced, computerized, phased-array radars and the high-acceleration Sprint short-range interceptor, that the Soviets were unable to achieve for many years.

A straightforward counterforce calculus also demonstrates a considerable Soviet stake in heading off the American ABM. If the United States had defended its MIRVed Minutemen with an ABM system, the

Soviet Union would have had to build a much bigger missile force than it actually did to achieve an effective counterforce standoff by the late 1970s. Because the American ABM system was originally developed as a city defense, Americans tended to discount heavily any system with less than a 90 percent-plus effectiveness. But in a counterforce nuclear exchange, which Soviet doctrine had always envisaged, an effectiveness as low as 50 percent could make a substantial difference to the outcome. With a reasonably effective ABM system, it required only a slight exaggeration of the likely accuracy of the first Minuteman and Poseidon MIRVs to argue that the United States would win a counterforce exchange. If Soviet analysts were only half as likely as their American counterparts to overestimate both the prowess of the other side and its propensity for a "bolt-from-the-blue" surprise attack, the ABM-MIRV combination would have looked sinister in the extreme.

Nixon and Kissinger reserved judgment on arms talks for several months, despite strong pressure from the Soviets, the media, and the liberal wing of the Congress, while they elaborated their intricately unfolding scheme of triangular diplomacy. But once they decided to press ahead, they faced a series of major hurdles, only one of which was raised by the Soviets. They had to convince the Soviet Union to cap its offensive missile deployments in exchange for an ABM treaty. They had to convince the American military and potential critics on the right that a mutual freeze on missile deployments would not place the United States at a substantial strategic disadvantage. They had to convince critics on the left, including the growing arms control community and most of the national media, that McNamara's objective of an ABM treaty was no longer sufficient; because of the dramatic change in relative strategic power, it was essential to link an ABM treaty with a ceiling on offensive deployments. Finally, they had to convince the Congress to authorize an American ABM, despite the impressive array of technical objections, in order to maintain the Soviet interest in striking a bargain.

The evolution of the American bargaining position through 1970 involved a series of marked role reversals. The State Department's arms control agency, which typically tended to minimize Soviet offensive capabilities, constructed a horrific picture of a near-future Soviet attack in order to prove the uselessness of any kind of an American ABM system. The Air Force, anxious to preserve the Minuteman's central position in American nuclear strategy, for the first time in almost thirty years began to play down the Soviet threat. The Pentagon's civilian systems analysts came up with a more hard-line position than the Joint Chiefs by imagining a "technologically feasible" Soviet attack. Finally Kissinger, in one of the bureaucratic *coups de main* he made famous, seized control of the agenda by creating the innocently named "Verification Panel" under his own chairmanship. Thenceforth all SALT technical appraisals flowed through his own panel or one of its numerous subcommittees, each chaired by a close aide. By mid-1970, the Verification Panel had forged the essential intragovernmental consensus. The Joint Chiefs agreed, with Laird writhing uncomfortably, that the current and immediately deployable Soviet missiles did not yet threaten America's counterforce capabilities. The State Department's arms controllers agreed, with equal reluctance, that a Minuteman defensive system would substantially improve America's bargaining posture, whatever they thought of its strategic merits. And even Laird conceded that a so-called hard-site defense was not yet technically ready, if by no means completely out of reach.

Orchestrating a unified arms limitation stance with the Congress and the influential media was a harder problem, made more complicated by the administration's own internal confusion. For example, one of the ABM options Kissinger had distilled out of the welter of conflicting recommendations in the Verification Panel called for symmetrical ABM deployments around Moscow and Washington. It was the one option that Moscow was likely to accept—which they did with alacrity—and the one option, it became clear to everyone's intense embarrassment, that Congress would never approve. In the superheated atmosphere of the early 1970s, starting an ABM system around Washington would have been political suicide. The discomfited American team was later forced to withdraw its own proposal, to the accompaniment of politely subdued raspberries from the Soviets. It was not, Kissinger concedes, "the proudest hour of the Nixon administration."

The American MIRV program readily survived congressional hesitations—its momentum had been building for so long that it could not be easily derailed—leaving ABM deployment as the main focus of the jockeying between the administration and its critics. Even after a limited ABM authorization scraped through the Congress, there was intense pressure to agree to an ABM-only treaty, which the Soviets badly wanted, without any movement on the American objective of limiting offensive weapons. Herbert Scoville, the doyen of the arms control community, roundly condemned "President Nixon's refusal to negotiate an 'ABM-only' limitation as a first stage of an arms limitation agreement," while George Kistiakowsky and George Rathjens, both of whom frequently spoke for the scientific community on public policy issues, warned that missiles were being multiplied only through fear of defensive systems. If an ABM treaty was signed, they predicted, the United States could halt its MIRV deployments, and the Soviets would follow suit. In the Senate, Frank Church, Hubert Humphrey, George McGovern, Edmund Muskie, Harold Hughes, William Proxmire, and even Stuart Symington all joined in the call for an ABM-only treaty, while William Fulbright attacked the whole "bargaining chip" concept as "fallacious." The *New York Times* outdid even the Democratic doves by proposing that the administration link an ABM-only treaty with a unilateral abandonment of its MIRVs.

An apparent slowdown in the feverish pace of Soviet missile silo construction in early 1971 was eagerly seized upon as a "signal" to end the arms race. Hubert Humphrey promptly urged a freeze of the American ABM and MIRV. "At no cost to ourselves, and with absolute guarantee of our own security," Humphrey orated, "we can stop our part of the nuclear arms race in response to actions already taken by the Soviet Union." But after a brief lull, Soviet silo construction resumed at an even faster pace, excavating new silos that were bigger than ever. When Henry Jackson suggested—undoubtedly based on leaked information from the Pentagon—that the new silos were intended for a huge new follow-on to the SS-9, as was in fact the case, he was berated by the once-militant *New Republic:* "The tone and timing of Jackson's statement is strikingly similar to John F. Kennedy's illusory missile-gap of 1960. These Soviet activities are subject to many different interpretations. . . . Focusing on the worst possible interpretation, exaggerating and even distorting facts, serves only to foster hysteria."

Ironically, as the pressure for unilateral American action reached a peak, Dobrynin and Kissinger quietly agreed in May 1971 on the essential breakthrough: an ABM settlement would be inextricably linked with a freeze on offensive weapons. At one of the surprise press conferences he so dearly loved, Nixon made the cryptic announcement that put his critics to rout. The essential outlines of the eventual SALT agreement were all in place. ABM deployment would be sharply limited for both sides. The Soviet Union would keep its lead in missile launchers, but would bring its breakneck construction program to a halt and accept some sublimits on the heavy missiles that so alarmed the Pentagon.

There was to be a year's hard bargaining before the signing ceremony at the Kremlin.* The Soviets made a number of concessions. They agreed to ignore English and French nuclear forces. They agreed not to count American forward-based nuclear forces in Europe, such as the carrier-based Phantom fighter bombers, even though they could reach the Soviet Union. The American strategic bomber force was exempted from the negotiations. And, most difficult of all, and a point that was not resolved until Nixon and Brezhnev had a staring contest in the Kremlin, they agreed to limits on their submarine-launched missile program.

The Americans made perhaps fewer concessions, but arguably more important ones. They agreed to a substantial numerical advantage in Soviet missile launchers and permitted the Soviets to escape any meaningful definition of a "heavy" missile, a point that was later to be a source of much contention. Both sides tacitly agreed to ignore the problem of MIRVs for the time being. The Americans were unwilling to bargain away their one area of clear strategic advantage; a MIRV agreement would be very hard to verify; and the Soviets, much to the disappointment of the American arms control lobby, showed almost no interest in the issue. They would bargain about MIRVs only after they had mastered the technology themselves, at which time, of course, their advantage in heavy launchers would take on vastly greater significance. As Kissinger himself remarked in 1974, "I wish I had thought through the implications of MIRVed worlds more thoughtfully in 1969 and 1970 than I did. What conclusions I might have come to, I don't know."

The SALT agreement itself was actually two separate treaties. The first governed ABM deployment; it was of unlimited duration, but either party had the right to withdraw upon six months' notice. The second treaty limited offensive weapons. It was an "Interim Agreement" for a period of five years only, and specifically contemplated a continuing process of "active follow-on negotiations" toward a more permanent treaty. Verification would be by "national technical means," the euphemism for satellite photography. Both treaties were accompanied by a number of "Agreed Statements," "Common Understandings," and "Unilateral Declarations"—in descending order of consensus and binding authority. A "Standing Consultative Committee" was established to review compliance issues and suggest amendments and refinements in the treaty language.

*The breakthroughs in the Kissinger-Dobrynin backchannel should not obscure the detailed hard work accomplished by Smith's team, who negotiated virtually all of the language of the treaties, with the exception of the items left for Moscow. Not least of their accomplishments was to educate the Soviet negotiators in the intricacies of the arms balance. Largely because of McNamara's groundwork, the American team was far better prepared than its Soviet counterpart.

The key provisions of the ABM treaty were:

- ABM sites would be limited to two each, one centered on the national capital and one centered on an ICBM complex; each could contain no more than 100 launchers and interceptor missiles and a specified number of radars and radar complexes. [In effect, the United States could continue the Safeguard system it was building in North Dakota, and keep the Washington option in reserve, while the Soviets could proceed with their Moscow system.] A 1974 protocol signed at Nixon's second Moscow summit reduced the permitted sites to only one each. The Soviets chose to defend Moscow, while the United States decided to drop its ABM completely.

- Both parties agreed not "to develop, test or deploy ABM systems or components which are sea-based, air-based, space-based, or mobile land-based."

- Missiles, launchers, or radars other than those specified in the treaty could not be given ABM capabilities or tested "in an ABM mode," in order to put to rest the "SAM upgrade" worry.

- Radars "for early warning of strategic ballistic missile attack" could not be deployed "except at locations along the periphery of [a Party's] national territory and oriented outward." Radars were the most visible component of an antimissile system; limiting their deployment would assure ready verification of treaty adherence.

Since it was well known that both sides had begun research on lasers and other directed-energy weapons language was included to cover the so-called exotic ABM technologies. The language is unfortunately ambiguous, and, as will be seen, became of considerable, controversial importance in defining the permissible limits of the Reagan administration's "Star Wars" program a decade later.

The key provisions of the Interim Agreement on offensive weapons were:

- No construction of land-based ICBMs could be started after July 1, 1972. By a "Common Understanding," however, both sides agreed to observe the standstill from the date of the signing. The Soviets were left with 1,618 land-based launchers to the United States' 1,054.

- Missile launchers for "light ICBMs," or for missiles deployed prior to 1964, could not be converted into launchers for "heavy ICBMs of types deployed after that time." The Americans hoped the provision would prevent the Soviets from converting their "light" SS-11 launchers or their pre-1964 SS-7s and SS-8s into launchers for the SS-9 or the new SS-9 follow-on. The effect of the provision was to create a sublimit of 313 Soviet SS-9-type missiles, which appeared to pose the greatest threat to the Minuteman.

- An "Agreed Statement" specified that in the process of modernizing existing missile silos, which was permitted, the dimensions of a silo could not be "significantly increased." A "Common Understanding" defined "significantly increased" as an increase "greater than 10–15 percent of the present dimensions of land-based ICBM launchers." To the United States, this provision was an important control on the Soviet heavy missile sublimit.

- The Soviets were allowed a maximum of 950 missile tubes on 62 modern submarines, while the United States was permitted 710 tubes on 44 submarines. But the Soviets could move to their full complement of 950 launchers from their then-current baseline of 740 launchers only by trading in older missiles, either from obsolete diesel submarines or from their old land-based missile fleet. The United States had to perform a similar trade-in to move from its baseline of 656 submarine launchers to the full 710.

- The parties agreed not to interfere with the "national technical means of verification" used by each other, or to use "deliberate concealment measures which impede verification . . . of compliance with the provisions of this Interim Agreement."

The Soviet Union appended one "Unilateral Statement": that it would have the right to increase its quota of submarine-launched missiles if there was any increase in the submarine-launched missiles of other NATO countries; the United States registered its official disagreement with the Soviet position. The United States made seven "Unilateral Statements," including particularly that

- It regretted the Soviet unwillingness to limit mobile land-based ICBMs and would consider their deployment "inconsistent" with the treaty.

- It regretted the Soviet unwillingness to define a "heavy" missile, but stipulated that it would consider a heavy missile to be any missile with a volume "significantly greater" than the largest light missile in either arsenal. The implication was that "significantly greater" carried the same connotation as in the limitation on silo dimensions—i.e., 10-15 percent.

SALT was far from a perfect agreement, and it came under heavy criticism during the ensuing decade, particularly as the Soviets exploited virtually every ambiguity in the two treaties' language to their maximum advantage. Hindsight, however, should not detract from the significance of the SALT achievement. Heading off an ABM race was an accomplishment in itself, and was generally accepted as such, although the agreement was made the easier by the grave technical doubts that both sides harbored about their ABM systems.

The feature of the agreement that received the brunt of contemporary criticism—the unequal limits on offensive weapons—merely recognized reality. The Soviet Union already had half again more launchers than the United States, and had huge new construction programs on the drawing boards, while the United States had frozen the basic outlines of its strategic forces for some years, and had virtually no new weapons in the pipeline, save for the continued modernization of the Minutemen. Capping the gross number of Soviet weapons was not the millennium, but it was better than nothing. To move to the full ceiling on modern submarine-launched weapons, the Soviets would be required to dismantle 210 older missiles, while the United States had to dismantle only 54—the superannuated Titans, which had long been scheduled for retirement. The only giveup for the United States, in the final analysis, was an ABM system that the administration had little confidence in, and that the Congress would almost certainly not have authorized in any case.

The essential fairness of the treaties is obliquely confirmed by the gleanings of contemporary Kremlinologists, who detected a distinct undercurrent of reservations from the Soviet military and the hard-line elements in the Politburo. Soviet satisfaction with SALT, in fact, appears to have been based much more on achieving the long-sought recognition as a strategic equal of the United States than from any specific provisions of the treaties themselves. Probably as reasonable an assessment as any was offered by then-Congressman Gerald Ford to his Michigan constituents: "What it all comes down to is this. We did not give anything away, and we slowed the Soviet momentum in the nuclear arms race."

On the merits, SALT I was a modest step toward limiting the upward spiral of nuclear arsenals. More important, it indicated that the

United States and the Soviet Union could discuss weighty matters with wary respect and reach reasonable mutual accommodations. But that is all it meant. The subsequent decade would dash the expansive hopes of SALT's most enthusiastic supporters. SALT did *not* mean an end to the arms race. It did *not* mean that the Soviet Union had accepted a simplistic version of "assured destruction" strategic theory. It did *not* signify the end of the dangerous competition between the United States and the Soviet Union for power and influence throughout the rest of the world. And, most emphatically, it did *not* mean that the Soviet Union was about to reduce its effort to match or surpass the United States in the power of its military establishment.

## The Rusting American Military Machine

Richard Nixon must surely rank, in the popular mind, among the more militaristic of postwar presidents, but during the height of detente in the aftermath of the SALT treaty, he presided over the sharpest decline in military spending since Truman's budget cuts before the Korean War. In the last full budget year of the Nixon/Ford administration, defense outlays dipped to 5.9 percent of GNP and less than 27 percent of the federal budget outlays. By contrast, in Dwight Eisenhower's last full fiscal year, defense spending accounted for more than 53 percent of the federal budget and about 10 percent of GNP, and in the 1964 fiscal year, the year just before the burst of spending for Vietnam, defense still commanded 8.8 percent of GNP and 45 percent of the federal budget, despite the very rapid growth of the economy and the sharp expansion of new domestic programs.

The decline in defense spending was a real one. Constant-dollar military spending in 1964, the year before the beginning of the Vietnam buildup, was about 20 percent higher than in 1975, and in 1968, at the Vietnam War's peak, it was 50 percent higher. The spending squeeze was even worse than constant-dollar budget comparisons indicate, for the cuts came at a time when the real cost of the military establishment was rising sharply, driven by rapid inflation in military pay. New federal pay comparability standards and Nixon's shift to an all-volunteer force in 1970—which ended the campus anti-Vietnam protests as if by magic—drove military pay up 42 percent between 1968 and 1975, even though total manpower was cut by almost a fifth. The cost of each soldier, in other words, went up by about 75 percent. The huge increase in payroll costs meant that spending for all other purposes, primarily maintenance and procurement, was cut almost in half in constant dollar terms.

The spending cuts affected almost every aspect of the military structure. The number of men under arms dipped to less than 2.2 million in 1975, down from from 2.7 million in 1964 and 3.5 million during the Vietnam War. American troops in Europe had been cut from 430,000 in the early 1960s to about 300,000. The situation was even worse than it appeared on paper: Gen. Andrew Goodpaster, who was NATO commander from 1969 to 1974, estimated that his "cutting edge" forces—tank troops, engineers, and artillery troops—were usually 35–40 percent under authorized strength. Naval surface combat ships had been cut in half, from almost 1,000 in 1964 to less than 500. At home, at a time when the Soviets were beginning to pay renewed attention to long-range bombers, the United States had essentially no air defense system. Its antiaircraft missiles had all been dismantled, and its interceptor forces comprised a grand total of 331 planes, of which only 20 were relatively modern F-4s.

The budget declines came on top of the investment distortions caused by the strains of Vietnam. A series of studies by the General Accounting Office showed that the U.S. Air Force squadrons in Europe were in a poor state of readiness, with high equipment outages and severe shortages of spare parts, that reserve equipment and the vital "pre-positioned" combat materiel in Europe were in disarray, and that supplies of all kinds required to sustain combat were dangerously low. At the same time, basic equipment was getting older. The newest American tank, the M-60, and the mainstay fighter bomber for both the Navy and the Air force, the F-4 Phantom, were both 1950s designs, while the bomber fleet was dependent on the increasingly venerable B-52 and the unreliable FB-111.

Military procurement and staffing predilections just made matters worse. Part of the reason that combat divisions' "tooth-to-tail" ratios were dipping so low was a refusal to reduce officer corps proportionately to the reduction in front-line troops, compounded by grade creep and a proliferation of headquarters units. The pressure on readiness and spare parts budgets was made much worse by the services' insistence on procuring only the most complex, technically advanced, and expensive equipment. American troops were making do with the M-60 tank because its follow-on model, the MBT-70, was a thoroughly unworkable machine that was finally cancelled by Congress as "over-sophisticated, unnecessarily complex, and too expensive." The price of the new F-15 fighter for the Air Force, billed as the ultimate "air superiority" plane, had risen to more than $12 million each, or 30 percent more than had been estimated just the previous year.

The Navy was, if anything, even more profligate. At a time when it was railing against the decline in surface combatants, it focused almost all its procurement planning and lobbying energies on billion-dollar behemoths like the *Nimitz*-class carrier. Its F-14 airplane, designed to replace the carrier-based Phantoms and budgeted at about $20 million per unit at the time, was, and still is, the most expensive fighter plane ever built; buying the F-14 on the Navy's recommended schedule would have cost $8 billion, which was simply out of the question. In theory, at least, the plane possessed fabulous avionics and electronic target acquisition systems capable, for instance, of tracking and destroying a low-flying cruise missile from a high altitude at night during a rainstorm. But for rest of the decade at least, the F-14's capabilities remained in large part theoretical, since about half the planes tended to be out of service at any one time—a situation that was greatly exacerbated by the sharp decline in education and intelligence of the average military recruit following the shift to an all-volunteer force.*

The sharp dip in American military investment cannot be blamed on SALT: there was nothing in the SALT Treaty that prohibited investment in conventional forces or even the modernizing of strategic weaponry. But the United States was rudderless and disillusioned in the aftermath of Vietnam and Watergate, and in the midst of one of its periodic antimilitaristic mood swings, the very antithesis of the attitude in the first years of John Kennedy's presidency barely more than a decade before. To the extent SALT or the Soviet-American detente was relevant, they merely reinforced a prevailing opinion that it was time for sharp reductions in the military establishment almost as a matter of principle.

No such inhibitions were operating in the Soviet Union. During the entire period of compression of American defense spending, the Soviet Union was expanding the breadth, the depth, and the capabilities of its

*The issue of weapons complexity will be treated in more detail in Chapter 20. Suffice it to say here that it is a complex one that is too often oversimplified by journalistic and congressional defense critics. A Defense Science Board report in 1981, for example, pointed to the lack of spare parts rather than equipment complexity as the main reason for the high F-14 downtimes; the services had apparently deliberately decided to spend for new equipment rather than spare parts on the assumption that maintenance could be taken care of later. The services can certainly be taken to task for risking most of their investment dollar on equipment they knew would not be usable, but that is a separate issue from the question of appropriate weapon technologies.

military machine at a pace and on a scale not seen since the days of Stalin. It was an armament program that cut across all elements of the Soviet force structure—its Strategic Rocket Forces, the Ground Forces, its Tactical and Long-range air arms, and the Navy. It was accompanied, moreover, by an active program of antimissile research and testing, antisatellite weapons testing, considerable attention to hardening command and control links with missile forces, new work on "directed-energy" weapons—that is, lasers, X-rays, radio-frequency or other "beam"-type weapons—and a visibly stepped-up program of civil defense.

## The Shifting Missile Balance

The continued growth and improvement in the Soviet strategic missile programs drew the most attention. At the production peak in the 1970s, about six new ICBMs were rolling out of Soviet missile factories each week, distributed among four brand-new missile types. The monster SS-18, the follow-on missile to the big SS-9s, with about a 40 percent greater throw-weight, was deployed in four versions between 1974 and 1979—two with single warheads in the 20–24-megaton range, one with eight 900-kiloton warheads, and one with ten 500-kiloton warheads. More important than the sheer size of the weapon was the reported CEP of less than a quarter mile; there was little question of its ability to attack a Minuteman Launch Control Center, although its capability against a fully hardened silo was probably still marginal.

The SS-18 had long been expected, but its sister weapon, the SS-19, deployed in two versions between 1974 and 1976, was more disturbing because it was a replacement for the "light" SS-11 and was deployed in modified SS-11 silos. It had a volume some 50 percent larger than the SS-11, and a throw-weight seven times as great, apparently making a mockery of the SALT I "Agreed Statement" and "Common Understanding" which provided that silo dimensions could not be "significantly increased" and defined "significant" as "10–15 percent of the present dimensions" of the silos. The SS-11 silos were made to fit the SS-19s by extending them 15 percent in *both* width and depth, so that the actual size of the SS-19 was about halfway between the "light" SS-11 and the "heavy" SS-9. The SS-19 was produced in a single-shot 10-megaton warhead version with an estimated quarter-mile CEP and a 560-kiloton six-warhead MIRV version with a reported CEP of .15 nautical miles—or an accuracy that rivalled the Minuteman IIIs. At least in the MIRVed version, the SS-19 was a plausible threat to hardened silos. Parallel to the SS-19, a third missile, the SS-17, of about the same size, was also deployed in modified SS-11 silos. It came in a single-shot 6-megaton version, and a 750-kiloton four-warhead MIRV version, both with estimated CEPs in the quarter-mile range. The fourth weapon, the SS-16, a mobile ICBM, was in production, but the Soviets withheld its final testing and deployment as a bargaining chip for a SALT II agreement.

The SS-19 deployment, as much as any other factor, was responsible for undercutting American confidence in the "SALT process." The Soviet insistence that a 50 percent increase in silo dimensions did not violate the Moscow agreements looked like the dangerous pettifoggery of an unworthy bargaining partner. But the issue is not so black and white. Gerard Smith, Raymond Garthoff, and Paul Nitze all confirm that the Soviets had been forthright throughout the SALT negotiations that the SS-17 and SS-19 were nearing deployment, that they were about 50 percent bigger than the SS-11, and that they could not be bargained away. They had also, Garthoff says, expressed a willingness to limit *visible* silo dimension increases to the 10–15 percent range, since deeper silos of that width would accommodate their new missiles. The final agreement was left to the Moscow meeting, which the professional negotiators did not attend.

There is little doubt that Kissinger knew about the new missiles and knew that the Soviets had insisted on keeping them. What is not clear is whether, in the flurry of last-minute trading, he was confused by the 10–15 percent language—Brezhnev apparently was at one point—into thinking that the Soviets were making a genuine concession, or whether he was engaging in some last-minute cosmetology to facilitate congressional approval. In fairness to Kissinger, the counterforce implications of the powerful, highly accurate, MIRVed SS-19 did not become clear until rather later. During the period of the SALT negotiations, the Americans were almost obsessively focused on limiting the big SS-9s and SS-18s; Kissinger also later conceded that he had not understood the significance of the lighter, but accurate, Soviet MIRVs.

By the end of the decade, the Soviet land-based missile force had grown to 1,398 launchers, of which 620, or about 45 percent, had been deployed within the previous five years. It was a missile fleet that was far bigger and more destructive than the American Minutemen and Titans. The American fleet,—discounting the 54 big-warhead Titans, which were being deactivated—disposed of 450 Minuteman IIs with single-shot 1.2-megaton warheads and 550 Minuteman IIIs, with the three-warhead 170-kiloton Mark 12 MIRV. The Minuteman IIs were not quite accurate enough to attack a hardened Soviet silo, while the warheads on the Minuteman III had only a marginal hard-silo capability; indeed, Nixon had specifically undertaken to the Congress that the Minutemen would *not* be able to attack Soviet silos as the price of the Minuteman III budget appropriation. (Nixon's statement was almost certainly posturing. The Mark 12 MIRVs were the best the United States could fit on the small-payload Minuteman in the 1970s, but the incident is revealing of the two countries' approach to the "spirit of detente.")

By contrast, all of the Soviet warheads were a half-megaton or larger, and almost 3,500 warheads were on modern MIRVed missiles that were approaching hard-target kill accuracies. The Americans doubled the yield of each Minuteman III warhead with the Mark 12A Minuteman III upgrade between 1980 and 1983, but the total of 1,650 accurate warheads was still only about half as many as would be necessary for a two-on-one counterforce strike against Soviet missile silos. In short, if the two countries were to find themselves once again in an eyeball-to-eyeball confrontation like the Cuban missile crisis, the implied threat of an American first strike against Soviet missiles would carry little weight, since it was literally impossible at the beginning of the 1980s; a Soviet first strike, on the other hand, if still wildly improbable, was slowly becoming more plausible.*

The Soviets had made similar progress in submarine missiles. By the end of the decade, they had filled their SALT I quota of 950 modern nuclear submarine missiles—compared to the 710 permitted to the United States—deployed primarily on the Yankee-class and newer Delta-class nuclear submarines. A new submarine, the Typhoon, comparable in size to new *Ohio*-class Trident submarines fielded by the Americans, was under construction. Soviet submarines were still substantially inferior, both in range and noise suppression capabilities, to the American models, but they had made enormous strides; as recently as 1970, over half the Soviet submarine missile fleet was still diesel-powered. The newest Soviet submarine missile, the SS-N-18, surprisingly, had a 5,000-kilometer range, or longer than that of the new American Trident C-4s. A long-range missile reduced the importance of sub-

*For a more detailed calculation of relative Soviet/American first-strike capabilities at the end of the 1970s, see the notes to this chapter.

marine technology, since it could be launched from relatively safe waters. The Soviets were also fielding a new supersonic bomber, the TU-26 Backfire, that was arguably, if just barely, of strategic range, although it was almost certainly intended as an antishipping weapon.

Overall, the United States still had a substantial, if rapidly declining, lead in strategic warheads at the end of the 1970s—some 9,200 to 5,875 for the Soviets. But almost half the American inventory was accounted for by the large number of Poseidon warheads, which, at 40–50 kilotons apiece, were the smallest in the strategic arsenals of either side and useful only against softer targets. The new Trident C-4 missiles carried eight 100-kiloton warheads, but they were just entering service at the end of the decade. An additional 2,000-odd nuclear weapons were carried by manned bombers, which could not be brought into play during the very first hours of a nuclear confrontation, and which in any case were much more vulnerable to defensive systems than missiles. The United States, in theory at least, could launch or drop many more nuclear weapons—although with much less firepower—than the Soviet Union could over the course of a prolonged nuclear exchange. The Soviets, on the other hand, could launch vastly greater nuclear destructive power at the very outset of a war, when presumably it would have the greatest effect.

## The Shifting Conventional Balance

The improvements in the Soviet Strategic Rocket Forces were matched by a broad-scale upgrade of general purpose forces. The Soviets increased their combat divisions by about thirty, back to the 175-division figure that prevailed before Khrushchev's cutbacks in the 1950s, and made across-the-board upgrades in combat readiness and manning levels. Almost all the new divisions were deployed on the Chinese front, where there had been a series of fierce clashes in 1968 and 1969 resulting in hundreds, perhaps thousands, of casualties. Impressively, however, at the same time that they were arming on the Chinese border, the Soviets strengthened their manpower on the European front by about 20 percent, and brought all their divisions in Eastern Europe to "Category One" or combat-ready status. The force level of a motorized rifle division in Germany, for example, was increased from 9,000 to 11,000 and tank divisions were increased from 10,500 to 13,500.*

*There are widely varying estimates on the total size of the Soviet military manpower establishment, largely because of the difficulty in counting reserve, internal security, and

More impressive than the manpower increases was the sustained Soviet commitment to implementing the "combined arms" doctrine Malinovsky had so futilely preached against Khrushchev's "massive retaliation" strategy. Soviet force deployment throughout the 1960s had underscored their primary reliance on missile striking power. The combat divisions in Central Europe were, as always, in offensive dispositions, and on the surface at least appeared to be impressively mobile; but severe deficiencies in logistics and supplies made it plain, as McNamara pointed out in the mid-1960s, that the Soviets did not truly have the ability to sustain an offensive.

By the mid-1970s, Soviet divisions in Europe presented a far more formidable picture. All the divisions were fully mechanized—NATO still had several traditional infantry divisions—and the mix of tank and motorized rifle divisions was designed for a fluid, mobile attack, with rapid exploitation of breakthroughs at a number of points along a shifting front. The tanks in a typical motorized rifle division had been increased from 188 to 266, or just short of a tank division's, and troops would move in new classes of armored personnel carriers—particularly the widely admired BMP-76, which disposed of its own cannons and antitank missiles that crews could fire from protected positions on the move, in contrast to the Western M-113s, which required that the crews dismount to use their weapons.

The fire-suppression capabilities of the new divisions were also impressive, and obviously geared to support a rapid-advance style of attack. The heavy artillery pieces had been increased by about 50 percent; each division carried more than 700 multiple-tube rocket launchers, a sixfold increase, and a wide array of nuclear-tipped short and medium-range missiles—the 25–50-kilometer FROGs, the newer SCUD-B, with a 125-kilometer range, and the longer-range "Scaleboard." The increases in firepower and mobility were matched by much improved supply capabilities and, for the first time, assignments of a reasonable number of troops to support and logistics duties, although support manning ratios were still far below the bloated Western standards.

The increase in ground mobility and firepower was paralleled by a

---

headquarters support troops. The annual estimates in the *Military Balance* series grew slowly from about 3.3 million men in the early 1970s to 3.75 million by the end of the decade, with a sharp re-estimate upward to more than 5 million in 1983, and 5.3 million in 1985, due to a recount of headquarters and support troops. Collins gives a 4.8 million figure for the end of the decade, or more than twice the size of the American military establishment.

sustained investment in improved air support. The swing-wing Sukhoi 17, and the heavier Sukhoi 24, a slightly downsized Soviet version of the F-111—"the first modern Soviet fighter to be developed specifically as a fighter-bomber for the ground-attack mission"—were designed as deep interdiction attack planes against NATO airfields and supply lines. Drawing from the American experience in Vietnam, the Soviets also began to deploy a series of helicopter transports and gunships, including a HueyCobra copy, the M-24 "Hind,"* capable of aerial antitank attacks. In all, by 1976, the five Soviet armies in East Germany alone disposed of ten tank divisions and ten motorized rifle divisions, with 370,000 men, 7,000 tanks, 2,400 armored personnel carriers, and 175 helicopters, supported by an air army division with more than 900 combat aircraft. It was an impressive force, one that even the most charitably disposed would be hard-pressed to consider "defensive," and which prompted Western analysts to conclude the Soviets were building a capacity to carry a conventional battle to Europe so rapidly that the West would be precluded from using its nuclear weapons.

At the same time as the Soviets were upgrading their missile, ground, and tactical air forces, they were also making dramatic improvements in their naval capabilities, in a sharp break with traditional practice, which had always confined the naval mission to defense of the home waters. The Soviet naval buildup has been often misunderstood or misrepresented in the West. The Soviets did not attempt to match, and certainly not to overmatch, the American fleet. The two countries' naval missions are quite different. The U.S. Navy, in addition to its strategic missile role, is the central cog in the American power projection machinery. The United States has been for the past forty years a global, status quo power, with a military strategy—all shifting "doctrines" notwithstanding—aimed at containing the expansion of Communist power in distant parts of the world. The carrier fleet is a floating striking force that can be deployed anywhere. Its large amphibious landing capability can get Marines or other infantry into battle quickly on faraway shores. The mission of controlling the major sealanes is essential to supplying American or Allied troops once hostilities begin.

*NATO's nomenclature for Soviet aircraft must surely rank as one of the grossest excesses of the arms race. The names follow the letter designations used for American planes—thus "Bison," "Bear," and "Badger" are bombers, a "B-" series in American usage. The names for Soviet fighters include such abominations as "Fishbed," "Flogger," "Fishpot," and "Fiddler." "Hind," of course, is for "H-" or "helicopter" and is perhaps barely tolerable; but the prize goes to the Soviet Ka-25 utility helicopter, designated "Hormone."

For the Soviet Navy, power projection is a subsidiary mission, although occasionally an important one. The Soviets' new Alligator marine landing ships were a notable presence during the Mideast and African crises of the 1970s. But it is meaningless to compare the new Soviet *Kiev*-class carriers, which began to appear in the latter part of the decade, with a modern American aircraft carrier in the *Nimitz* or *Enterprise* class. The *Kievs*—four were deployed by the mid-1980s— displace about 37,000 tons and carry some 14 short-range V/STOL (vertical/short takeoff and landing) fighters and an assortment of helicopters. The American nuclear-powered carriers, on the other hand, displace about 90,000 tons and dispose of about 90 airplanes, including several types of nuclear bombers.

The prime mission of the Soviet fleet, and one that it seems admirably designed to execute, is simply to disrupt the American one, or as fleet Admiral Gorshkov put it: "to bind the hands of the imperialists [and] deprive them of the possibility of interfering unhindered in the affairs of the people." The Soviet emphasis, therefore, was on relatively small and fast guided-missile ships, like the nuclear-powered, 28,000-ton *Kirov* cruiser, which made its appearance at the end of the decade. The power of seaborne cruise missiles against surface ships was displayed when Egyptians sank the Israeli destroyer *Elath* in the 1967 war with a relatively old-fashioned Soviet Styx missile, and was demonstrated even more dramatically in the 1980s in the Falklands War and in the Persian Gulf. The power to disrupt the American naval mission was greatly enhanced, in addition, by the advent of the long-range supersonic Backfire bomber.

The shift in the balance was relatively subtle. There was still no question, for example, when the Sixth Fleet faced off against a Soviet Mediterranean task force during the 1973 Yom Kippur War, that the Americans would have prevailed in a fight. But victory might have carried a heavy price. The Soviets had deployed their ships well and disposed of heavy antiship missile ordnance. As the Admiral of the American Fleet put it, "Our forces were targeted for instant attack from multiple points." It was a power shift that was, if anything, even more disorienting than the shift in the balance of ground forces or strategic rockets, since American military planning had simply assumed free and unfettered access to the world's waterways almost as a matter of right for so many years.

It is important to place the Soviet military buildup in perspective without either belittling or exaggerating it. The changing balance did *not* mean that the Soviet Union had achieved military superiority over the West. The great advantage in missile throw-weight and warhead availability that the Soviets would enjoy at the outset of a nuclear exchange, for example, did *not* mean that they had achieved a first-strike capability, despite the flurry of "window of vulnerability" anxieties in the early 1980s.

Nor did the shift in the conventional balance mean the Soviets had the ability to overrun Europe. Soviet readiness standards, for instance, were much lower than NATO's, and most of the Soviet "Category One" divisions would not have met NATO's own tests for combat readiness. The Soviets had a staggering numerical advantage in certain weapons classes like tanks—in 1974, for instance, the number of medium tanks actually deployed in active U.S. Army divisions was only 2,600, compared to a Soviet figure of 30,700—but that was partly reflective of deliberate strategic choices. The NATO countries had no interest in overrunning Eastern Europe, and so were inclined to invest more heavily in tank defenses than in tanks. And the Soviet numerical superiority often concealed serious weapon deficiencies. The mainstay of the Soviet tank force into the 1980s was still the T-62, and its variant, the T-64. But the Yom Kippur War and analysis of captured models showed them to be seriously deficient in combat radius, staying power, firing rate, and firing range. Their vulnerable exterior gas tanks ignited easily in battle, and they were very difficult to repair. The Soviets, indeed, probably intended to treat their T-62s as readily discarded disposables, but a cautious Soviet general would have suffered restless nightmares of his deep-thrust strategy choking to a stop on a clanking pile of broken-down tanks.

The celebrated case of Viktor Belenko's MiG-25 Foxbat also points up the Western tendency to exaggerate Soviet weapons prowess. The Foxbat was proclaimed "probably the best interceptor in production in the world today" by the American Air Force in the mid-1970s, until Belenko, in pursuit of a million-dollar bounty offered by the CIA, landed his aircraft in Japan in 1976. It was a far more primitive machine than Western analysts had expected. Its electronic systems were still heavily dependent on vacuum-tube technology; the fuselage was mostly steel, with titanium (the standard American fuselage material) only at heat-stress points, making the plane much heavier and slower-accelerating than expected; its range and its ability to achieve and maintain rated top speeds also were much less than assumed. The reality of the MiG-25 and the T-62 cast doubt on the breadth of the gap between the "two tiers" of the Soviet economy, the one producing shoddy tractors and consumer goods and the other splendid military weapons. It did not mean that Soviet military power was not formidable; Lenin, indeed, remarked that "quantity is a most impressive form of quality."* But it did mean that statements like this one from a prominent American naval analyst: "[Soviet] surface warships [are] of ultra-modern design— ships that have dazzled the West by their design efficiency, their fire-power, and their propulsion and electronic systems..." should be taken with a healthy dose of skepticism.

The growing perception of the scale of the Soviet buildup received impressive confirmation in late 1976, when it was revealed that the CIA, in a radical revision, had doubled its estimates of the Soviet defense effort for the previous decade. (The CIA revisions are often confused with the so-called Team B exercise in competitive intelligence assessment at the end of the Ford administration—see Chapter 18. The two exercises were quite separate, but reinforced each other's impact on the public consciousness.) It is important to understand what the CIA revisions meant, for they engendered enormous confusion. The CIA did not revise its estimates of Soviet defense *output,* but its estimates of Soviet defense *effort.*

Before the CIA revisions, there were essentially three methods for calculating Soviet defense spending, all of them designed to facilitate comparisons between the American and Soviet defense programs, and all of them unsatisfactory. One was to estimate the dollar cost of the Soviet defense establishment—what it would cost Americans to match the Soviet program. By imposing an American pay scale on the huge Soviet manpower establishment, dollar costing tended grossly to exaggerate Soviet spending. The opposite solution, ruble costing, had the opposite problem: the ruble price of high-technology equipment in the American inventory was essentially infinite—there was no way Russians could buy it or make it, no matter how many rubles they spent. The third method, working from official Soviet budget data, was least satisfactory of all, since the numbers were so obviously false.

The 1976 revisions were based on an essentially new analytic method developed by William T. Lee, a former CIA analyst who spe-

*The Russian stress on quantitative superiority seems to be a constant, dating from the time of the czars. It is worth recalling, for example, that at the outbreak of World War II, the Soviets had more tanks than the rest of world combined, the biggest air force in the world, and twice as many submarines as Germany. Understanding that Russia has always tried to to overawe its neighbors with the size of its arsenals, however, does not make the trait a more endearing one.

cialized in Soviet economic data. Its adoption by the CIA marked a considerable personal victory for Lee. He had long been convinced that the current methods were seriously misleading and had waged a long, one-man campaign for a new approach that sparked considerable controversy within the defense and intelligence community. Lee's method neatly finessed the dollar-ruble exchange problem by making a painstaking sector-by-sector analysis of Soviet output and calculating the proportion of each sector, and cumulatively, the proportion of Soviet national wealth devoted to defense. Regardless of the pricing unit used, Lee's analysis showed that since the early 1960s, the Soviets had been devoting 11–13 percent of their national output to defense, or twice as much as the 5–6 percent estimate produced by the conventional methods. Lee was *not* saying, however, that Soviet military capabilities were twice as great as previously supposed. He took it more or less for granted, in fact, that the CIA's estimate of deployed Soviet forces was about right—it was almost impossible to keep major weapons systems or combat units secret. The import of the new analysis was rather that the Soviet military establishment, in terms of real economic burden, *cost twice as much as previously supposed.*

It was a conclusion with two main corollaries. The first and most comforting was that the Soviet defense industry was far less efficient than the West had assumed. The second was more disturbing for what it revealed about Soviet intentions. Clearly, the Soviet Union was taking the arms race much more seriously than the West had previously understood, and was deliberately undergoing substantial economic privation in order to press forward on its armament programs. It followed either that the Soviets thought that war was much more likely than the West did, or that they still believed that military power, whether or not it was actually used, would play a much greater role in settling international disputes than the "spirit of detente" would seem to imply.*

The gradual revelation of the Soviet military programs jolted an American public and political leadership lulled by the comfortable and widespread assumption that a new era of detente reduced the necessity for competitive arming. In fact, there had been an immense shift in the

---

*There were further implications, as well, which had significant influence on the policies later adopted by the Reagan administration. If the present levels of defense spending already imposed such a heavy burden on the Soviet economy, it followed that if the West ratcheted up the level of arms spending another notch or two, which it could still well afford to do, the Soviet Union would be forced either to accept the reality of its second-class power status or become more forthcoming in arms control negotiations. The tougher line on technology trade was also designed to increase the burden of the Soviet defense effort.

power balance, no less important because it was a *relative* change, rather than an actual shift to Soviet superiority. The Soviet Navy was still no match for America's, but for the first time it had become a significant factor in American planning. NATO could still withstand a surprise Soviet conventional attack in Europe, even assuming one was possible, but the clear superiority of the 1960s was gone, and there were serious questions about how long NATO could hold off a Soviet offensive before resorting to nuclear weapons. If Soviet missiles performed with the reliability NATO planners assumed, they would have a clear advantage in an initial nuclear exchange, although the value of such an advantage, of course, was the subject of much dispute. And if the West still did not come off too badly in terms of absolute comparisons, the trend in relative power was not one that could be allowed to continue. As Brookings analysts, who in general did not take an alarmist view of Soviet capabilities, put it in 1977, "the sheer pace and range of change of Soviet strategic development" provided ample grounds for worry.

The alarm raised by some conservative critics of detente was doubtless excessive, but liberals who adopted a dismissive attitude toward the Soviet weapon programs were guilty of serious inconsistencies. As Robert Tucker pointed out, the standard liberal critique of the American military establishment was that arms buildups *induced* aggressive behavior, as the adventure in Vietnam demonstrated—the more reason to worry about the Soviet Union, whose leaders labored under far fewer institutional constraints. Nor was the long record of Soviet caution in military affairs necessarily a comfort, for it was feckless to assume that the West's customary military superiority was *not* a factor in that caution. The increasingly bold resort to force by the Soviet Union throughout the 1970s, in fact, culminating with the invasion of Afghanistan, testified perhaps that Soviet caution was a sometime trait.

# PART V.

THE JAGGED COURSE

# CHAPTER 17

# The Bear Stretches

## Global Reach

In the early afternoon of the high Jewish holy day of Yom Kippur, October 6, 1973, the dry Sinai desert air was split by a thunderous barrage of Egyptian artillery trained on the sparsely manned Israeli fortifications on the opposite side of the Suez Canal. As the Israeli answering guns fell silent, the Canal's quiet waters suddenly beetled with thousands of dinghies and small barges, as more than 8,000 Egyptian infantry swarmed across to string pontoon bridges for the armored divisions massed on the Egyptian side. Some 250 miles away on the Golan Heights, at almost the same instant the Egyptians first opened fire, Syria launched an all-out attack with more than 900 tanks supported by another massive artillery barrage and MiG-17 fighter bombers.

By the end of the first day of fighting, the Egyptians and the Syrians had swept away virtually the entire cease-fire line established at the end of the 1967 war. Egyptian forces occupied a line some three to six miles deep into the Sinai along the entire length of the Canal; and at some points on the Golan Heights Syria had established salients 15 miles deep.

The attack took the Israelis almost completely by surprise, but did not at first shake their confidence. No one doubted that the Israeli counterattack would overwhelm the Arab attackers despite the huge Arab advantage in men and numbers of weapons; even the Soviet Union, probably anxious for the vast stocks of arms it had delivered to its clients, pressed the Egyptian president, Anwar al-Sadat, to preserve his victory by requesting a cease-fire as soon as he crossed the Canal.

But the first days of fighting held a series of rude shocks for the Israelis. On the very first afternoon, Soviet SA-6 surface-to-air missiles, the most sophisticated battlefield antiaircraft weapon in the Russian inventory, and new rapid-fire antiaircraft guns ("It was like flying through hail," one Israeli pilot said) downed thirty American-built A-4 Skyhawks—subsonic attack bombers—or almost a fifth of the Skyhawk fleet, and even more distressingly, several F-4E Phantoms. Losing Phantoms was deeply disturbing, for with fewer than a hundred of the planes, the Israelis had enjoyed total dominance of the air in the sporadic fighting since the 1967 war, roaming freely and attacking distant Arab targets virtually at will, despite the two-to-one Arab advantage in combat aircraft.*

The first encounters on the ground were just as sobering. On the third day of the war, an Israeli armored brigade with sixty tanks broke through the Egyptian lines and headed for the Canal. But the Egyptians, instead of scattering as they always had, held their ground and raked the Israelis with new Soviet "Sagger" antitank guided missiles.† After quickly losing thirty-four tanks, the brigade was forced into a humiliating surrender. Like the SA-6s, the Saggers profoundly shook the self-assurance of the Israelis. As one tank commander said, "suddenly you see a single man holding onto a stick standing 2,000 yards ahead of you. You cannot believe that this single man has the power to destroy the huge tank, but in a few seconds the tank is a wreck." By October 10, the *New York Times* noted with surprise that Israeli reports from the front were "noticeably lacking in confident predictions of victory."

The Yom Kippur war was a severe and early test of Nixon and Kissinger's new architecture of detente. At the summit meeting in the United States the previous June, a scheduled follow-up to the Moscow SALT summit, Brezhnev and Nixon had signed an agreement "on the Prevention of Nuclear War" in which they undertook to "act in such a manner as to prevent the development of situations capable of causing a dangerous exacerbation of their relations." At the close of the summit, Brezhnev made a forty-seven-minute television address to the

*For details on the extraordinary mismatch between Soviet and American planes in the 1973 war, see the notes to this chapter.

†The Sagger was a wire-guided weapon like the American TOW. The Israelis knew the Arabs had the weapon but had not properly briefed their tank commanders. The weapon's effectiveness was sharply reduced when the Israelis advanced with good infantry support and air cover, for the defender had to stand in the open and keep the moving tank in his sights for about ten seconds after he launched his missile. The Egyptian Sagger crews reportedly fired up to 30,000 practice rounds per man in the year leading up to the October War and went to combat with the promise that after they had fired their supply of missiles they could go home.

American people in which he spoke warmly of Nixon and the new "trend for peace and detente" between their two countries. But the fine words and bright ceremonies were shadowed by the growing specter of an American constitutional crisis. John Dean began his testimony to the Ervin Committee the very week of Brezhnev's visit, and it was probably only at the American summit that the Soviets began to realize that the Watergate investigations, which they must have found utterly incomprehensible, were a genuine threat to Nixon's authority. At the same time, Soviet words on preventing confrontations seemed belied by their increasingly unrestrained arms shipments to Egypt and Syria. And Brezhnev's behavior on the final night of the summit—he insisted, in a gross breach of courtesy, on arousing Nixon from sleep to present demands on the Middle East—carried an ominous edge.

Israeli counterattacks on both the Egyptian and Syrian fronts on the second and third days of the war were repulsed by the Arab SA-6s and the Saggers. The Israelis regrouped, concentrated their forces against the Syrians, and mounted a ferocious counterattack on the Golan Heights. For almost two days, a series of grim and bloody infantry engagements pushed the Syrians back foot-by-foot, while some 60,000 Egyptian troops were allowed to pour across the Canal virtually unimpeded. On the 10th, the SA-6 installations on the Heights fell silent, apparently because the Syrians ran out of missiles. With sudden control of air, the Israelis wreaked havoc in the Syrian lines with savage bombing attacks. Within hours the entire Golan front had collapsed, and the Syrians were in disorderly flight before a broad and deep Israeli offensive rolling through open country toward Damascus. The United States immediately proposed a cease-fire in place—Egypt would have gained in the Sinai, and Israel would have gained on the Golan. The Soviet response was an Arab resupply airlift from Kiev and Budapest. It was a major step, "historically the first massive resupplying by the USSR of any non-Communist combatant engaged in full hostilities." Except for some clandestine shipments of previously purchased spare parts—the Soviets had continued comparable small shipments to the Arab belligerents—the United States had so far refused Israeli requests for more arms in the hope that the war would quickly grind to an exhausted stalemate.

The Israeli breakthrough, the new American cease-fire proposal, and the first news of the Soviet airlift all came on the 10th; back in the United States the same day, Vice-President Spiro Agnew admitted he had taken bribes—money in brown paper bags—and resigned his office.

On the 11th, Kissinger interrupted urgent consultations with the Israelis and the Soviets to receive Agnew's resignation. Under the Succession Act of 1792, such unpleasant duties were the responsibility of the Secretary of State. In Theodore H. White's words, the press reaction was one of "... fury that Agnew, their chief public enemy, had been snatched out of reach, had been spared the shame and public guillotining of impeachment. Now that pent-up wrath focused on the President."

On the 12th, Kissinger's protest against the Soviet resupply effort (it was up to eighty-four planeloads a day) was met with a thinly veiled threat that "The Soviet Union will of course take measures which it will deem necessary to defend its ships and other means of transportation." Kissinger responded curtly that "any Soviet military intervention— regardless of pretext would be met by American force." They were brave words, for it was the same day that Congress passed the War Powers Act—intended as a pointed rebuke to the administration— limiting executive powers to commit troops without congressional approval. Publicly, Kissinger was restrained. He actively tried to "discourage speculation" about the Soviet airlift, and at a press conference on the 13th argued somewhat lamely that the spirit of detente had indeed modified Soviet behavior: they were "less provocative, less incendiary, and less geared to military threats" than in previous crises.

Nixon ordered an American airlift to Israel on the 13th, when an attempt to mount a resupply attempt with contract carriers quickly proved inadequate, and only after furious arguments between Kissinger and Defense Secretary James Schlesinger—not entirely unreasonably, the services have always been cautious about intruding upon hostilities without the forces for a full-scale battle. With both sides amply supplied, there was no hope of a cease-fire until there was a resolution on the battlefield. New supplies of armor and SA-6s allowed the Syrians to stabilize a defensive line between the Golan Heights and Damascus, and Israeli air attacks on Syrian ports and cities seemed only to stiffen Syrian resolve. The Israelis broke off their Syrian offensive and began to shift their forces back to the Suez front. In the meantime, Egypt had been busy consolidating its positions in the Sinai and, unwisely as it turned out, transporting virtually all of its armor to the Israeli side of the Canal.

Egypt mounted a major armored assault into the Sinai on the 14th, apparently in response to urgent requests from Syria's president, Haifez al-Assad, to help relieve the Israeli pressure on Damascus. The assault was as unexpected as it was costly for the Arabs, for it pulled the

Egyptian armor out of the effective range of the SA-6 batteries on the west side of the Suez. The Israeli armor rolled out to meet the Egyptian offensive, and the two armies, each with at least 1,000 tanks, clashed in one of the great tank battles of history, one comparable to the massive armored engagements of World War II. Israel scored an overwhelming victory, destroying more than 500 Egyptian tanks in a single day at the cost of only 30 of its own, and decisively regained the initiative in the war.*

The next day, a brilliantly daring armored maneuver under Ariel Sharon exploited an opening between the Egyptian Second and Third armies and forced a crossing of the Canal; in three days of fierce fighting, the Israelis steadily widened the gap in the Egyptian lines. By the 18th, Sharon's wedge on the Canal was a floodgate, and Egypt's armies in the Sinai were in mortal peril. Several hundred Israeli tanks were roaming freely on the Egyptian side, taking out the SA-6 batteries one by one, and restoring undisputed control of the air to the Israeli Sky-hawks and Phantoms. The Egyptian armies' supply lines were almost closed—in the desert fresh water is more important than ammunition—and their escape route to Cairo in danger of being cut off. Kosygin was already in the Egyptian capital pleading with Sadat to accept a cease-fire.

It was only on the 19th that Sadat finally understood that the war was lost, and the Kremlin immediately requested that Kissinger fly to Moscow. The banner headline in the *New York Times* that day was: "Nixon to Keep Tapes Despite Ruling." Kissinger departed for Moscow on the 20th, the same day that John Dean pleaded guilty and began to tell all to the Watergate investigators. On the evening of the 21st, a Saturday, Nixon ordered the firing of the Special Prosecutor, Archibald Cox, and accepted the resignations of his Attorney General and Deputy Attorney General, Elliott Richardson and William Ruckelshaus, for refusing to comply. The next day the Egyptians, almost certainly with Soviet assistance, fired several short-range (125 miles) Scud missiles at Israeli troops from deep inside Egypt, presumably as a warning that Israeli cities were not invulnerable if the war escalated further. By

*The early successes of the SA-6s and the Saggers obscured the surprisingly poor performance of the Soviet tanks, particularly the new T-62s, which turned out to overheat much too quickly for effective desert operations. The evidence is that tank performance in the October War caused considerable concern among the Soviet Marshals, the more so since Israel's tanks (the American M-48 and M-60, and the British Centurion) were considered to be dated designs, not nearly of the quality of the German Leopard, which was entering service in the NATO forces in large numbers.

Monday, the 23rd, Kissinger and the Soviets had agreed to a cease-fire formulation that was acceptable to all sides in the Middle East, the same day that a clamor for Nixon's impeachment arose from both sides of the aisle in the Congress. To the editorial writers and columnists of the country's major newspapers, the President had become an object of loathing, something almost reptilian. The *New York Times* announced that resignation was the "one last great service Mr. Nixon can perform for his country." Resignation would not satisfy *The Washington Post*. It wanted to savor Nixon's agony—to watch him writhe through the slow process of impeachment, for the sake of its "exorcising" benefits. Stewart Alsop wrote that the President was an "ass."

The cease-fire broke down in a matter of hours. Which side was first responsible for the violations is not clear, but the Israelis, angry and vengeful after their humiliation during the first days of the war, and with total victory almost in their grasp, moved aggressively to complete their encirclement of the Egyptian forces. Nixon and Kissinger responded coolly to Soviet demands for joint intervention to enforce the cease-fire; at this point they were not above enjoying the Soviet panic, after Moscow's considerable contribution to prolonging the war. But on the 24th, Brezhnev wrote possibly the sharpest note ever sent to an American president by a Soviet leader. It was addressed "Mr. President" rather than the usual "My Dear Mr. President." The key paragraph read: "I will say it straight, that if you find it impossible to act with us in this matter, we should be faced with the necessity urgently to consider the question of taking appropriate steps unilaterally. Israel cannot be permitted to get away with the violations." The note concluded, "I value our relationship."

Brezhnev's note carried greater menace than any of Khrushchev's "rockets will fly" tirades. Khrushchev's blusters usually were timed to come safely after, if sometimes just after, the resolution of a crisis. Brezhnev made his threat at the tensest moment in the war, when he knew that an introduction of Soviet troops carried a real risk of provoking a direct clash with American arms. More important, in contrast to previous Soviet threats in third-country conflicts, the Soviets now had the capacity to carry out their threats. They had already demonstrated their new airlift abilities, and had built up a significant naval presence of some eighty-four ships in the Mediterranean, including Alligator-class landing vessels for Soviet sea infantry. The Soviet naval detachments did not dispose of firepower at all comparable to the Sixth Fleet's, but were carefully, and obviously, maneuvering for position in the event of a confrontation.

There were further ominous, if ambiguous, signs. The Soviet Union had recalled most of its transport planes over the two previous days— perhaps because the cease-fire had ended the necessity for further airlift, or perhaps, the Pentagon worried, because they were being reassembled to pick up Soviet troops. Unconfirmed reports said that three of seven Soviet airborne divisions had been placed on full alert. As one careful analyst of the episode has put it: Brezhnev's note was "a credible threat, adroitly employed as an instrument of diplomatic pressure."

Kissinger's first reaction was to match the threatening display of the Soviets. Just before midnight of the 24th, after a late night meeting of the National Security Council, the alert status of American forces worldwide was moved a notch higher, to "DefCon III," the highest alert status for forces in peacetime, and the third rung on a five-step alert ladder, one below "Readiness for Combat." It was not a wartime alert status; in the main, for example, leaves were not cancelled. But officers in the Strategic Air Command underground control center in Nebraska soberly took their places in the balcony overlooking a blinking computer spitting out current data on Soviet targets and targeting conditions, while EC-135 airborne missile command posts warmed up on the runway. All the crews in the Minuteman sites shifted to a slightly more hair-trigger firing posture. B-52s taxied to their takeoff points on SAC airfields, and at least some crews spent the night in their cockpits. To be sure the Soviets got the message, Kissinger and Schlesinger ordered two additional carrier groups to the Eastern Mediterranean.

What effect the alert had in the Soviet Union is not known, but the scorn with which it was dismissed two days later may indicate that it was taken very seriously indeed. On balance, however, and mutual theatrics aside, the Soviets came out on top in the exchange of threats. Kissinger did exactly what they wanted him to do: warn the Israelis that the Soviets were about to intervene and that Israel might face them on its own if it didn't behave. "Unless Israel abided by the cease-fire," Moshe Dayan says they were told, "the United States would not stand in the way of the Soviet Union." The American communication of the Soviet threat effectively ended the war. On the 26th, Israel allowed the resupply of the Egyptian troops in the Sinai, and the cease-fire, with a United Nations peace-keeping force to monitor it, took hold across both fronts.

The events of the alert are most significant as a demonstration of Nixon's weakening grip on executive authority. At Kissinger's press conference the next day—news of the alert had leaked almost immediately—he said that the decision was taken by "the President at a special National Security Council meeting at 3 A.M.," implying, if not directly stating, that the President was physically present at the NSC meeting. He was not; it is quite likely that he did not even know of the alert until that morning. Nixon had gone to bed early the previous evening distraught at the crescendo of demands for his impeachment, and Kissinger and Alexander Haig, Nixon's chief of staff, agreed not to wake him when they received Brezhnev's note.

From that point, decisions were taken by Kissinger and Schlesinger in telephone consultation with Haig, who gave the impression, probably a fiction, that he was consulting with Nixon at each step. The press did not question Nixon's involvement, but suspected that the alert was merely a ploy to distract attention from Nixon's Watergate problems. Kissinger responded angrily: "It is a symptom of what is happening in our country that it could even be suggested that the United States would alert its forces for domestic reasons." But James Reston, in a *New York Times* column conceding the substantial reasons for the alert, still wondered "how long the American people are going to be dragged along the brink by a jumpy government they no longer trust."

The alert had a number of fascinating sidelights. It appears actually to have gone into effect at 11:25 P.M. It is not clear why Kissinger said 3 A.M.; possibly because it was more plausible that Haig had awakened the President by that point. It seems quite certain that Kissinger and Schlesinger did not order the alert for domestic reasons, as Kissinger's and Nixon's critics have occasionally charged. A more serious question relates to the use of alerts to demonstrate resolve. As Scott Sagan has recently argued, political leaders, including the Secretary of Defense, cannot possibly understand all the operational details of an alert, many of which greatly increase the risk of impetuous or accidental war. The most dangerous aspects of the alert—Minuteman firing command consoles are placed at the elbows of the crews, for example, intelligence-gathering facilities are shifted to track signs of incoming missiles, the command and control readiness is heightened to make a launch-on-warning possible—would be invisible to the Soviets in any case. Dispatching the additional ships to the eastern Mediterranean, the most visible military step of all, was not, obviously, standard practice in a Defcon III alert, but was taken more as an afterthought to make sure the Soviet Union understood what was going on.

The behavior of the Soviet Union during the Yom Kippur War was a dash of cold water on enthusiasts of detente. But the new relation between the United States and the Soviet Union did seem in fact to have real, if limited, value in moderating the conflict. The central demonstration, however, was that detente did not mean an end to interests. When the Soviet leadership made statements like "In conditions of detente the front lines of ideological conflict do not become silent. On the contrary they become wider and deeper," they were serving notice that they did not intend to forsake their traditional foreign policy objectives for the sake of the new American relationship. Nixon and Kissinger were saying very much the same thing, and acting accordingly. There is reason to believe, for example, that the American destabilization of Salvador Allende's Marxist regime in Chile a few months before the Yom Kippur War led to severe questioning of the wisdom of detente from the hard-liners in the Kremlin.

That detente should do little more than moderate the pursuit of self-interest should hardly have come as a surprise. The Soviet Union could no more desert its Arab clients than the United States could desert Israel. Cultivating client states in the Middle East had been a consistent Russian objective since the time of the czars. The Arab states were, in addition, shining examples of new, "progressive," socialist regimes. The fact that the West's ravenous demand for oil made it increasingly dependent on Middle Eastern supplies only added flavor to long-standing policy. Given the intensity of Soviet interests, their resupply of the devastated Arab military machines after the 1967 war was a foregone conclusion. The new rounds of arms shipments, however, were in the main both reluctant and restrained, despite the desperate importunings and shameless manipulations of Nasser and Sadat, and their repeated accusations, echoed clamorously by the Chinese, that the Soviets were afraid of the United States. It was not until Sadat took the dramatic step of expelling Soviet advisers and virtually breaking relations in 1972 that the Soviets began to supply arms in volumes that came close to satisfying bellicose Arab appetites. And even then, except for the Scud missiles, which were kept under Soviet control, they refused the modern bombers or fighter escorts the Arabs so badly wanted for deep-strike attacks on the Israeli interior.

The evidence for Soviet connivance in planning the Arab attacks is ambiguous,* and competent analysts have come down on both sides of

*The argument centers around questions like: Did Sadat and Brezhnev hold a secret meeting in Bulgaria on September 21? There is circumstantial evidence that they did. And if they did, did they discuss war plans, or did Sadat merely test for possible Soviet objections? Did the shift of a Soviet intelligence satellite over the battle area at the start of the war indicate Soviet complicity, or simply a lack of information? How much pre-

the question. It is fairly certain that the Soviets were informed of the impending assault several days in advance; they did not—obviously could not—warn the United States, as a scrupulously legalistic interpretation of the obligations of detente might have required. But they did evacuate Soviet dependents on October 3, a step unprecedented in previous Soviet practice, which may have been intended as a signal that hostilities were about to begin. In any case, there was ample intelligence of Arab troop movements in Israel and the West. The intelligence was ignored because everyone believed that an Arab attack would be irrational. Kissinger freely admits that he totally misunderstood Sadat's war objectives, which were to unblock the frozen territorial status quo and to restore a semblance of Arab military self-respect—both of which he achieved, if only by the margin of a nick-of-time cease-fire.

Regardless of Soviet intentions at the outset of the crisis, the Yom Kippur War was a watershed in the postwar relations of the superpowers. The close consultations between Kissinger and Dobrynin throughout the war and the peremptory summons of Kissinger to Moscow to settle the cease-fire were unmistakable signs of a new equality, if not actually a condominium, in the disposition of world affairs. Most important, the fact that the Soviet Union could credibly threaten unilateral action in an area of historic U.S. interest was a clear message that it would no longer quail before American power, as Nasser accused it of doing in 1967. At the cost of an immense diversion of economic resources the Soviet leadership had, in the decade after Khrushchev, built the conventional firepower, the airlift and sealift, and the nuclear striking power to contest the United States throughout the globe.

In the immediate aftermath of the war, however, Soviet fortunes in the Middle East and North Africa took a decidedly downward turn. Sadat, who never confused loyalty and interest, was in touch with the United States even before the cease-fire—since American diplomacy and pressure would be essential to getting back some of Egypt's lost territories. Kissinger rose to the occasion with a dazzling display of diplomatic virtuosity, and personally mediated two separate disengagement agreements in the winter and spring of 1974, one between Israel and Egypt and another between Israel and Syria (three more fractious diplomatic hagglers could hardly be imagined), setting the stage for the

planning did the Kiev-Budapest airlift require? Dobrynin later insisted that the Soviets had issued many veiled warnings to the United States between June and September, but that they fell on deaf ears.

complete expulsion of Soviet influence from Egypt the next year and the Camp David peace treaty between Egypt and Israel in 1977. The year 1974, indeed, was one in which Marxist curses must have showered down upon the heads of Arab ingrates. Not long after Kissinger stole the diplomatic show in the Middle East, the Soviets were expelled from their North African port of Berbera in Somalia by President Siad Barre, despite having lavished some $300 million worth of arms to further Barre's irredentist designs on the Ogaden Desert. And at about the same time, a Soviet-inspired coup against Col. Jaafar al-Numeiry, the military ruler of the Sudan, fizzled ignominiously, costing the Soviet Union both the affections of another long-time client, if an insufficiently radical one, and another valuable point of military pressure in the Persian Gulf.

But Kissinger's extravaganzas in the Middle East were the last reapings of his and Nixon's extraordinarily fertile diplomacy. A harbinger of the collapse of American authority came at what should have been a high point in Kissinger's career, when he returned from Tel Aviv in May 1974, flushed and triumphant with the Syrian disengagement agreement. As he met, beaming, with the press, one of the very first questions was whether he expected to be indicted for perjury. In such an atmosphere, Kissinger and Nixon's brand of diplomacy could not possibly be sustained. Their statecraft was of an Old World variety, like that plied by the nineteenth-century diplomats Kissinger so admired. It was an essentially virtuosic enterprise, one that required an executive like the "world statesman" Kissinger had eulogized in his early writings who could dispose of international relations with a far freer hand than the Congress or the media were prepared to accord to Richard Nixon.

Kissinger once described his diplomatic style as "existential," meaning a continuous process of pushing and edging to secure American interests, without expectation of clear victories or final answers, merely a dogged pursuit of small advantages amid frequent setbacks, because that is what statesmen *do*. It was a diplomacy that required closed doors, quiet agreements, and a ready, if rarely used, ability to resort to force. Above all, it required a shared sense of national purpose and commitment, much as all classes of British society endorsed their nation's civilizing mission in the nineteenth century. Americans had occasionally, in previous decades, shared such a sense of international purpose, most certainly, for example, during the era of the Marshall Plan; and they had been been willing to grant the necessary broad delegations of judgment and authority to their leaders, most recently during the first swaggering days of the New Frontier. But their reservoirs of trust and goodwill had been fecklessly dissipated by Kennedy's and Johnson's antiguerrilla adventures, Spiro Agnew's venality, and Richard Nixon's dark schemings, rendered in amber on the Oval Office tapes. Now, with military vainglory punctured by the humiliation in Vietnam, and economic self-confidence shattered by the OPEC oil price shock, the country was withdrawing into a mood of sour and suspicious isolationism, guilt-ridden, recriminating, and rudderless.

As the forces that were engulfing his presidency lashed angrily about Richard Nixon in the late spring of 1974, he took frantic and broken-winged flight with a grand tour of the Middle Eastern capitals and another Moscow summit in June. It was a poignant and pathetic exercise, the mortally wounded President once more inhaling the heady air at the summits of world diplomacy like an elixir, touching the scenes of his greatest triumphs as if they were talismans that could restore his powers. Brezhnev entertained Nixon cordially, even with a certain gentleness. Little of substance was accomplished; everyone understood that the summit was merely the playing out of a last, sad ceremony. The kindness the Soviet leadership showed to Nixon, of course, did not indicate a softening of their ambitions in world affairs. America's constitutional crisis was of its own doing; as Khrushchev remarked to Kennedy at Vienna, "Americans could not expect the Soviet Union to sit, so to speak, with its arms folded."

Six months later, the armies of North Vietnam were on the move southward, not flitting, guerrilla-style, on secret jungle trails, but marching in gleaming armored panoply, propelled by a swelling stream of arms from the Soviet Union. In the words of the North Vietnamese commander, Gen. Van Tien Dung, he enjoyed local superiority of "5.5 of our troops for each enemy soldier. As for tanks and armored vehicles, the ratio was 1.2 to 1. In heavy artillery, the ratio was 2.1 to 1. . . . Cadres of the front staff . . . could not draw maps fast enough to keep up with the advance of our forces."

It had been clear from the very first days of the 1973 cease-fire agreement that only the threat of renewed American bombing kept the North Vietnamese on their side of the 29th parallel.* As the North

*When the necessity for intervention confronted Congressional leaders in 1975, they pleaded ignorance of Nixon's commitments, calling them "secret, illegitimate agreements." It was the sheerest hypocrisy. The promises were about as public and explicit as such commitments can be, absent a formal military treaty. The North, in fact, had begun to mass troops for an assault on the South almost as soon as the cease-fire agreement was signed, and was deterred only by the constant repetition of bombing threats. Nixon's commitments to Thieu and his power to make them were explicitly acknowledged by such anti-Nixon and anti-entanglement partisans as the *New York Times* ("The President massed its troops in January, the new American President, Gerald Ford, was told by congressional leaders that they would not approve any aid, of any kind. By March, 300,000 Northern troops were moving through the central highlands, opening their way with rocket and artillery attacks on roads clogged with hundreds of thousands of fleeing civilians.

The House of Representatives and the Senate Democratic caucus confirmed their opposition to aid by 5–1 majorities. Lawyers at the State Department pondered whether evacuation assistance for loyal Vietnamese would violate the War Powers Act, while Kissinger fumed helplessly that the United States could "not abandon friends in one part of the world without jeopardizing the security of friends everywhere."

Fifteen Northern divisions encircled Saigon in April, as Ford blustered that the abandonment of South Vietnam did not mean that "United States commitments will not be honored worldwide." On April 23, he announced that the commitment to Vietnam was "finished as far as America was concerned." The Thieu government resigned shortly thereafter, and Gen. Duong Van Minh surrendered unconditionally on April 30.

On the roof of the American Embassy compound in Saigon, on the last day, Marine guards beat back the clawings of the unwisely loyal with pistols and rifle butts, as an elderly couple lay impaled and bleeding on the barbed wire guarding the evacuating helicopters. The departing helicopters needed fighter cover to fend off attacks from maddened, and doomed, South Vietnamese pilots. It was a most shameful ending to a star-crossed and shameful adventure. Detente, however, survived; Kissinger reported lamely that the Soviet Union had been of "some help" in the evacuation.

## The End of Detente

Four years after the fall of Saigon, in September 1979, *Pravda* reported that, "in view of the state of his health," their client, President Nur Mohammed Taraki of Afghanistan, had requested that "he be released

---

left little doubt that he regarded resumption of bombing and harbor mining as a viable option against North Vietnam. Hanoi's leaders recently tried to test Mr. Nixon's resolve on the cease-fire terms . . . and when they saw the administration's firmness, they returned to the agreed upon schedule"—March 17, 1973) and the *Washington Post* ("We do not doubt at all that, if he chose, the President could resume the bombing . . . nor do we know of anyone else who doubts it. . . . He is in an enviable position to conduct his Vietnam policy on the merits alone."—March 18, 1973.) Legally, of course, the War Powers Act, as Kissinger reluctantly acknowledged, superseded a commitment that did not have the force of law. But for Congressional leaders to insist that they knew of no such commitments when they passed the Act, and had not, therefore, repudiated an American guarantee was a craven pretense.

from his party and state offices" and that his duties be assumed by his colleague, Hafizullah Amin. Taraki's health, in fact, was very poor, having been mortally compromised by gunshot wounds inflicted by his fellow Communist Amin, who had himself only recently escaped Taraki's attempt at similar ministrations. Amin, however, had even less success in convincing his fractious countrymen of the virtues of communism than Taraki; and in late December, after Soviet troops had massed on the Russo-Afghan border for some days, the Kremlin piously reported that, "at the request of the government of friendly Afghanistan," it would supply fraternal assistance to help Afghanistan maintain "its independence."

Soviet airborne troops quickly secured the Kabul airport, and by the 27th at least 6,000 Soviet soldiers were in the capital. Amin's status shifted abruptly from "Comrade" to "bloodthirsty agent of American imperialism . . . murderer, charlatan of history," and he received the same medical treatment from his Soviet friends that he had meted out to Taraki. Babrak Karmal, the third Communist leader in four months, but one more to the Kremlin's liking, was flown in from Czechoslovakia to take charge. Jimmy Carter called Leonid Brezhnev on the "hotline" to insist that the Soviets withdraw, but Brezhnev patiently explained the obligations of a good neighbor policy. By late January 1980, in an impressive demonstration of Soviet logistic capabilities, there were more than 80,000 Soviet troops in Afghanistan, fanning out through the mountainous countryside to carry the Marxist gospel to the skeptical *mujadaheen.*

Jimmy Carter's hapless protests against the invasion drew mostly snickers. Afghanistan was the low point of a decidedly unhappy period for the foreign policy of the United States. There were at least six more violent seizures of power by radical pro-Communist regimes throughout Asia and Africa in the four years after the fall of Saigon. The list includes the Pathet Lao takeover in Laos, shortly after the American withdrawal from Vietnam; the MPLA's victory in Angola in 1975–76; Col. Mengistu Haile-Mariam's seizure of power in Ethiopia after the "red terror" of 1977; the takeover by Nur Mohammed Taraki in Afghanistan in 1978; the coup in South Yemen, sweeping non-Communist leftists out of the government in 1978; and North Vietnam's conquest of Cambodia in 1979. In addition there were abortive Communist coup attempts in Somalia and the Sudan, and Communists from South Yemen were apparently responsible for the murder of Col. Ahmed al-Qashini of North Yemen in 1978. At the same time, Soviet support for radical regimes like that of Libya, and of the terrorist organizations spawned by the unrest in the Middle East, became ever more unrestrained.

The final blow before the Afghanistan invasion came with the abdication of the Shah of Iran in early 1979, and the quick descent of that country, long the bulwark of the American presence in the Middle East, into anarchy. The Shah shuttled from capital to capital seeking asylum, a continuing embarrassment to the United States, his erstwhile ally and supporter; at the same time, the top ranks of the Iranian officer corps, who were encouraged by their American mentors to stay at their posts and work with the new regime, were systematically executed. In November 1979, a mob of Muslim radicals took over the American Embassy in Teheran, making its residents hostage with the public approval of Ayatollah Khomeini, the leader of the new Iranian theocracy. The Soviet Union could not resist gloating: "One must not . . . forget about those activities of the US vis-à-vis Iran that can in no sense be reconciled with [international] law or morals."

The invasion of Afghanistan six weeks later merely underscored the administration's helplessness. Humiliated and frustrated by the obsessive media attention to the embassy hostages, Carter approved an ill-fated rescue attempt in April 1980, and then withdrew into the seclusion of his Rose Garden to concentrate on the hostage negotiations. From that lonely vantage point he watched sourly as Ted Kennedy savaged him and his policies in the Democratic primaries and America's allies busily undercut his various boycotts of Soviet Olympic Games, wheat sales, and trade agreements. His defeat in November—when he suffered the worst electoral humiliation ever inflicted upon a sitting President—was a relief and a release.

The decline of American power and prestige was in inverse proportion to the rise of the Soviets'. It appears that about the time of the Yom Kippur War, the Soviet Politburo, perhaps stung by the recurrent defections of Sadat, made a conscious decision to reorient its policies in the Third World away from Khrushchev's favored "bourgeois nationalists" toward radical "Marxist-Leninist Vanguard Parties," like those of the Colonels Mengistu and Qaddafi in Ethiopia and Libya. The new policy built on the obvious compatibility between such regimes and the Kremlin: radical military leaders were naturally attracted to the Soviet command-based economic system; Soviet military and economic assistance came without tiresome nattering about rights and elections; and the Soviet leadership itself, unburdened by official and unofficial consciences like the American Congress and press, readily turned a blind eye to local horrors such as Mengistu's use of famine as a weapon in Eritrea and the Ogaden.

The new policy was announced in official Communist organs and pursued through the rest of the decade with considerable diligence, if not consistency—relations were also cultivated with other major states, like Syria and India, that clearly did not fit the same description. Colin Legum, a specialist in Soviet African policies, points to several distinct threads. First, the price of open-handed aid to radical regimes was, in most cases, Soviet access to air or naval bases. Secondly, greatest attention was paid to the regimes that would help shift the balance of power in the Middle East and the southern NATO flank, the traditional objectives of Soviet, and indeed, Russian, foreign policy. And finally, particularly in the Middle East and the Horn of Africa, instead of pursuing a grand scheme of subversion, the Soviets displayed an impressive ability to sustain a policy of ". . . persistent, aggressive opportunism [based on] a steady recognition of the strategic significance of the region and a determination to expand influence in it by whatever action is likely to be effective when openings develop."

The sheer aggressiveness of the Soviet interventions in Angola and Ethiopia marked a whole new departure in itself. The warring sides in Angola were three vaguely Marxist factions that, after loosely cooperating in guerrilla warfare against the Portuguese colonial regime, fell out with each other upon the Portuguese withdrawal, supporting their military pretensions with small amounts of aid from, variously, the CIA, the Chinese, and the Soviets. The Soviets, however, were the first outside power to ship military equipment in significant volumes and, sometime in early 1975, began lavishing MiG-17 and MiG-21 fighters, T-34 and T-54/55 tanks, armored troop carriers, and large quantities of bazookas, rockets, machine guns and rifles upon Augustinho Neto's MPLA, probably the best organized of the three warring factions. Neto's troops were on the verge of consolidating control over the entire country when they were put to flight by an invasion of 1,500–2,000 South Africans.

By late November 1975, the South Africans, combined with the other two factions, Jonas Savimbi's UNITA and Holden Roberto's FNLA, were threatening the MPLA's power base in the capital city of Luanda; the MPLA itself, its fortunes turned upside down, was facing a retreat to a guerrilla existence in the forests. The Soviet Union responded with a massive increase in the volume of aid and an airlift of

Cuban troops, their first appearance as a kind of Soviet Foreign Legion. As the Cuban contingent built rapidly to some 20,000 highly professional troops, a Soviet naval contingent, including an Alligator troop landing ship with Soviet sea infantry, steamed to the Angolan coast to discourage other third-party interventions. They need hardly have bothered, for the U.S. Congress cut off all aid to UNITA/FNLA at almost the same time. Vastly outnumbered, the South Africans withdrew, leaving a clear field to the Cubans and the MPLA. A decade later, there are still some 23,000 Cubans serving in Angola, the FNLA has effectively disbanded, but Savimbi's UNITA still presses a guerrilla campaign from the southern jungles, once more with limited American assistance.

The ready availability of Cuban infantry, willing and eager to fight in the immiserated countries on the clashing edges of the Eastern and Western imperiums, vastly expanded the practical reach of Soviet power. Cuban troops conveniently finessed the long-standing Soviet reluctance to use their own soldiers in foreign combat; they blended much better with local populations than the brusque and overbearing Russians; and they assured that expensive shipments of military equipment would be put to good use, instead of being wasted by Third World clients with no experience of modern machinery or weapons. The arrangement also perfectly suited the evolving relationship between Castro and the Soviet Union. Soviet transport and money advanced Castro's aspirations to the military and spiritual leadership of the radical "non-aligned" nations, while Cuban mercenaries were modest enough recompense to the Soviets for the continuing drain of welfare payments to the little island.

Emboldened by the success in Angola, the Soviets intervened even more massively in the fighting between Ethiopia and Somalia in the Horn of Africa the following year. The Soviets had long provided military assistance to Somalia, one of the few racially homogeneous nations in Africa, to support its claims to the ethnic Somali areas of the Ogaden Desert. Aid to the Somalis allowed the Soviets to establish a military and naval presence in the strategically important Horn, and together with aid to Eritrean separatists funnelled through the Sudan, put pressure on Haile Selassie's pro-Western Ethiopia. Selassie was overthrown in 1974; Somalia put frantic pressure on the Soviets for more weapons to take advantage of the ensuing chaos, and finally expelled them when they responded with insufficient alacrity.

The Soviets, meanwhile, had been cultivating radical elements in Ethiopia, particularly Colonel Mengistu, who took control of the

Dergue, the Ethiopian ruling military council, after a bloody shootout in 1977. As Ethiopia descended into near-anarchy, Somalia seized the occasion to march on the Ogaden. Mengistu appealed for help, and the Soviets came in with both feet, airlifting some $2 billion worth of military equipment and perhaps 15,000 Cuban troops, treating the world to the spectacle of a clash between two Soviet-supplied and trained armies that was finally won only by the intervention of a third. The United States declared an arms embargo on both sides, and the Somalis were routed by the Cubans. The Cubans remained in Ethiopia as a kind of permanent force of Mengistu palace janissaries; they have been used to suppress local dissent, to enforce a Stalinist-style collectivization of agriculture, and to help put down the continuing insurgency in Eritrea, which, of course, was also originally sponsored and armed by the Soviets.

The scale of the Soviet interventions in Africa can be measured by the relative flows of arms shipments from the Soviet Union and from the United States and its allies. Between 1973 and 1980, the United States transferred 290 tanks, armored vehicles, and self-propelled artillery pieces to Africa; other allies, primarily France, shipped 1,040; while the Soviets sent 6,980. The figures for planes and helicopters are: United States, 50; other allies, 560; and Soviet Union, 670; for surface-to-air missiles, United States, none; Western Europe, 200; and Soviet Union, 1,960. Dollar estimates of Soviet aid are, of course, imprecise, but it was most likely in excess of $4 billion.

The actual value of the Soviet inroads in Asia and Africa has been much disputed, not least by the Soviets themselves in the mid-1980s, as their radical client states began to appear as much self-serving nationalists as any of the Soviets' more "bourgeois" clients, and as unreliable in the pursuit of Soviet interests as their appetite for money and arms was insatiable. But appearances count for much in international relations, and to most of the world, the pattern of Soviet behavior— from the Yom Kippur War through the sponsorship of Hanoi's imperial thrust in Southeast Asia, the intervention in Angola, the battle for the Ogaden, to the invasion of Afghanistan—appeared to trace a rising curve of confident, and violent, assertion of Soviet power, a forceful shouldering for strategic position, untrammeled by ideological scruple and with increasingly unrestrained resort to weapons assistance and troops.

The contrast to the dithering inaction, or sometimes bland inattention, of the United States could not have been more striking. The overthrow of Selassie, for instance, occurred during the worst paroxysms of the Watergate crisis, when the authority of American foreign policy was heavily dependent on the personal stature of Henry Kissinger, who happened at the time to be preoccupied with a Greek-Turkish confrontation over Cyprus. Arguably more important than the cutoff of American aid to Angola was the fact that the case for aid was never really argued. Congress prohibited assistance to the MPLA opposition, at the height of the Soviet/Cuban intervention, as an almost purely reflex action, born out of the revulsion for the experience in Vietnam—"we will now have no new Gulf of Tonkin Resolution," exulted Senator Alan Cranston, one of the architects of the cutoff, although no one had proposed sending troops. The high-minded moralizing of Jimmy Carter about human rights in areas of the world that had never displayed the slightest interest in Western concepts of democracy and freedom merely underscored the impression of American isolation and ineptitude. As Donald Zagoria remarked: "One shudders to think of what might have been the American response to seven communist takeovers in Asia and Africa at the height of the cold war . . . But the lack of response today—indeed, the lack of comprehension—is just as frightening!"

There were a number of casualties of the Afghanistan invasion besides the hapless Amin. Carter bowed to the inevitable and, a week after the invasion, requested the Senate to postpone "indefinitely" consideration of the second installment of the Strategic Arms Limitation Treaty, or SALT II, which he and Brezhnev had signed in June 1979, after more than six years of excruciating negotiations. The treaty's chances of ratification in the Senate, in fact, had never been more than marginal, even before the Soviet invasion. The shelving of the SALT II Treaty marked the official, if belated and largely unmourned, interment of the policy of detente with the Soviet Union that Nixon and Kissinger had crafted so painstakingly a decade before.

# CHAPTER 18

# Arms Control Revisited

## The Demise of SALT

The treaty that Carter and Brezhnev signed in Vienna in 1979 was, technically, a considerable improvement over SALT I. In contrast to the earlier agreement, SALT II provided that both sides would have the same number of intercontinental-range missile launchers—2,250 after January 1, 1981—and specifically included a sublimit of 1,320 on MIRVed missiles, with additional MIRV sublimits on land-based missiles and submarine-launched missiles. There were a number of other useful provisions. Each country agreed to test and deploy only one new type of "light" intercontinental missile; the United States could proceed with its MX, but the Soviets would have to choose between some four new designs on their drawing boards. The number of warheads on a MIRVed missile could be no greater than the maximum number previously tested, eliminating the worry that the big SS-18s might be equipped with forty or more warheads, but at the same time preserving the right of the MX to carry ten. "Counting rules" facilitated MIRV warhead verification—any weapon that had been tested with MIRVs was assumed to be MIRVed with the highest number of warheads ever tested. (An exception was made for the Minuteman III, which had once been tested with seven warheads, but which everyone knew was deployed with only three.) The ambiguity surrounding the definition of "heavy" and "light" missiles was resolved by simply bowing to the inevitable and accepting that the Soviet SS-19 was a "light" missile, as was the MX. An ambiguous limitation on the encryption of telemetric test data improved verification procedures slightly. And for the first time, the Soviet Union produced an official count of its own intercontinental nuclear forces. (The SALT I negotiators had relied almost solely on American data for both sides' forces.)

The treaty skirted gingerly around two new weapons, the Soviet Tu-26 "Backfire" bomber and the American cruise missile. The Backfire was a high-performance, supersonic, medium-to-long-range bomber. The Americans insisted that, with refuelling, it could attack targets on the American mainland, a contention that the Soviets strenuously denied. The cruise was a pilotless, "air-breathing," nuclear-armed drone—it flew through the atmosphere with conventional jet engines at subsonic speeds—a technology that dated from the German World War II V-1 rocket. An advanced new turbofan engine allowed a very small cruise missile to achieve a considerable effective range; but, most important, a revolutionary new guidance system kept the missile on course by comparing the terrain features of its overflight with an on-board map.* Flying at very low altitudes, and with on-board radar-jamming capability, a cruise would be invisible to Soviet air defense systems, but could deliver its payload with extreme accuracy—with an average error (CEP) generally assumed to be about 30 meters, and possibly as low as 10.

The deal that was finally struck took literally years of haggling. The Backfire would not count as a strategic launcher, but Brezhnev gave Carter a letter confirming that the Backfire could not reach the United States, and agreed to limit production to thirty a month. In fact, Backfire deployments make it clear that it is intended primarily as an antishipping weapon, and, indeed, it poses a formidable threat to the American carrier fleet. The Americans agreed that heavy bombers carrying cruise missiles with ranges in excess of 600 kilometers—the Air Force's cruises had a range of about 2,500 kilometers—would count as MIRVs, and that no bomber would carry more than twenty missiles. The United States also agreed not to deploy long-range ground- and sea-launched cruises until 1982, which it would have been unable to do in any case. (Treaty agreements on cruise ranges are relatively meaningless; there is no way to tell by aerial inspection how far a cruise can fly. On the other hand, stated cruise ranges are misleading. In war, a cruise would follow a zigzag attack pattern that would greatly limit its effective range.) There was some nice reciprocity in the cruise and MIRV sublimits. The limit on air-launched cruises meant little to the Soviets, since their program was still several years behind the American one; but an additional sublimit provided that within the total allowance of 1,320 MIRVed launchers, only 1,200 could be submarine-launched and land-based launchers—a

*For the cruise guidance system, see the notes to this chapter.

limitation that constrained only the Soviet Union, since there were no American plans for that many missiles.

The text of the SALT II Treaty spoke volumes for the state of Soviet-American relations. It is much longer than SALT I, much more detailed and technical, much more concerned with being "cheat-proof"; it reflects none of the goodwill and high hopes that characterized the 1972 Moscow summit, but reads more like a narrow contract between two parties that neither like nor trust each other. On its own merits, purely as an exercise in technical treaty-drafting, SALT II was, as the Joint Chiefs put it in their endorsement, a "modest but useful" step. But that was about the most that could be said for it, and the treaty contained plenty of ammunition for hostile critics, such as a House Armed Services Committee panel that called it "a cosmetic domestic political symbol, which neither limits strategic arms, enhances security, deters war, nor maintains the strategic balance."

Even to its strongest supporters, the treaty was a disappointment. In basic outline, aside from the numerous loophole-closing technical paragraphs, it was patterned after the agreement worked out by Kissinger, Ford, and Brezhnev during the 1974 Vladivostok "mini-summit," although at slightly lower force levels. The Vladivostok terms were tailored to the demands of a growing hawkish wing in the Senate, led by Senator Henry Jackson and his influential staff member, Richard Perle (later a key defense policy official in the Reagan administration). By the end of the Ford adminstration, Kissinger no longer had the prestige to convert an understanding into a treaty. Jackson allied with liberals like Adlai Stevenson, Jr., to make progress on arms negotiations subject to detailed Soviet commitments on Jewish emigration—as if the Soviet Union needed a treaty more than the United States—and persistently undercut the undertakings on trade credits and tariff barriers that Kissinger viewed as central threads in his rapidly unravelling fabric of detente. Jimmy Carter made a vain attempt at the outset of his administration to refocus SALT toward deep mutual cuts in strategic forces, in response to Henry Jackson's insistence that only sharp reductions would represent "real" arms control. But the initiative was so badly bungled— it was premature, ill-thought-through, and announced in a manner almost calculated to infuriate the Russians—that it took at least a year to repair the damage and get the negotiations back on track.

The basic achievement at Vladivostok was a common ceiling on launchers and MIRVed missiles, as Jackson had demanded. But the price of the common ceiling was that the weapon allowances were set so high that they imposed little constraint on either side. The land-based MIRV limit in SALT II, for example, permitted the Soviets to add another 1,300 or so hard-target capable warheads to their missile fleet.* The treaty's terms were in fact so broad that its supporters could argue accurately, however incongruously and uncomfortably, that it accommodated *every* aspect of an eight-point defense buildup advocated by the conservative lobbying group, the Committee on the Present Danger—ranging from speeded-up MX deployment and more cruise missiles to better command and control systems. If it was true, as the Joint Chiefs stressed, that "there's nothing we'd do differently" whether or not the treaty was ratified, the question naturally arose as to the value of any treaty at all. Senator Edmund Muskie, a liberal predisposed in favor of SALT, worried publicly that SALT II might actually accelerate the arms race. Indeed, as the prolonged congressional hearings focused attention on the growing capabilities of the Soviet missile fleet, the lagging American MX program picked up new steam, and Defense Department officials began to speak gleefully of a SALT defense spending "windfall."

The issue of Soviet "cheating" on SALT I trapped supporters of the treaty in another double-bind. Despite the frequent allegations to the contrary, it is not in general true that the Soviets violated the explicit terms of the SALT I agreement.† But it *is* true that their deployments

*SALT II backers argued that the Soviets had to cut their missile fleet by 250 to meet the SALT II guidelines. That was technically true, but the missiles scheduled to be cut were mostly the old, and long since useless, SS-7s and SS-8s. (Whereas the Americans tended to invent exotic new weapons to use as SALT "bargaining chips," the Soviets simply never decommissioned old ones, accumulating their bargaining chips much more cheaply.) At the time the agreement was signed, the Soviets had 608 land-based MIRVed missiles. The sublimit of 820, assuming it was filled out with six-warhead SS-19s, would have added 1,272 accurate new warheads to their inventory, replacing 212 much less capable SS-11s. The value of setting some upper limit on Soviet deployments, as SALT II unarguably did, depended on whether one believed that, in the absence of SALT, the Soviets would have continued to build, or whether one believed that the SALT limits represented about the level the Soviets planned to build to anyway.

†The first clear-cut violation occurred in December 1975: the Soviets began sea trials of new missile-launching submarines without completely dismantling an equivalent number (fifty-one) of old SS-7s and 8s—although they had removed the warheads. After vigorous American protests, the Soviets conceded the violation, pleading difficult winter weather conditions at the Siberian launch sites, and completed the dismantling in the spring. Other controversial areas related to the use of SAM radars during ABM tests (were they "in an ABM" mode?); the construction of a number of command and control silos (they looked like launch silos, but the CIA concluded that they probably weren't); and the SS-20 missile (it didn't have intercontinental range, but it used the first two stages of the mobile SS-16, which the Americans, but not the SALT I agreement, said was forbidden). Later, in the mid-1980s, the construction of the large Krasnoyarsk phased-array radar well away from the coast clearly violates the ABM Treaty restriction that phased-array radars can be deployed only on national perimeters as early warning systems.

pressed the language of the agreement to its absolute limit. Supporters of SALT II were obliged to defend Soviet behavior as part of their defense of the SALT process itself; but that required the admission that the provisions of SALT I were so broad as to be almost meaningless. The SS-19 silos, for example, were some 53 percent bigger in volume than those for the SS-11; it was embarrassing to argue that they still fit within the 15 percent size increase criterion laid down in SALT I because the precise language didn't *clearly* prohibit a 15 percent increase in length *and* diameter. If the choice was only between broadly gauged but meaningless agreements, or narrowly drawn ones that exercised little restraint, both conservatives and liberals could reasonably ask, was SALT really worth all the trouble?

A more subtle, and more telling, conservative argument, one made most forcefully by former Naval Chief of Staff Admiral Elmo Zumwalt, was that the Soviets violated the SALT I agreements *as they were explained to the Congress.* Or as James Schlesinger put it: "if they have not violated the letter of the agreement, they have clearly violated what we said would be a violation of the agreement in our unilateral statements, so they have failed to meet our expectations." In other words, the "spirit of SALT," as Colin Gray wrote, "was wholly a Western invention." Some commentators, like the editorialist of *Aviation Week and Space Technology,* saw more than mere naivete at work, scoring the "legal and technical incompetence" of the American negotiating team and a "deliberate policy of secrecy and deception" on the part of Kissinger.

The bone in the conservative craw was that, whatever their source, inflated American expectations of SALT I were a major factor in the continued real-dollar reductions in defense budgets from 1972 until 1978, a time when Soviet power was expanding rapidly. Kissinger himself admitted as much in 1979:

I am conscience-bound to point out that—against all previous hopes—the SALT process does not seem to have slowed down the Soviet strategic competition, and in some sense may have accelerated it. The Soviets worked hard and

Building it inland probably saved money by increasing its effective coverage, even though it violated the letter of the treaty. The Soviets, however, have a good case that the American upgrading of an old radar at Flyingdales in England to a phased-array type violates the same provision. In general, it is fair to say that the Soviet military read the agreements like legal documents, without attaching independent political value to the "SALT process"; they interpret them, in short, much as the American military would do if there were no oversight from the arms control lobby in the Congress and the executive branch.

successfully to enhance the first strike capabilities of their land-based ICBMs despite our restraint and within the limits of SALT. . . . SALT may have had a perverse effect on the willingness [of American leaders] to face fully the relentless Soviet buildup.

Kissinger even retracted his famous "What in the name of God is strategic superiority?" statement: "My statement reflected fatigue and exasperation, not analysis. But if we opt out of the race unilaterally, we will probably be faced eventually with a younger group of Soviet leaders who will figure out what can be done with strategic superiority."

Finally, and perhaps most disconcertingly, with the steady advance of technology it was no longer obvious that the basic SALT logic still made sense. SALT, paradoxically, might actually increase instability. A fundamental premise of the SALT I agreement was that limits on missile launchers, particularly "heavy" launchers, would act as an effective constraint on either side's developing a first-strike capability. But the Soviets packed so many warheads on their missiles that they were approaching a first-strike capability against America's land-based ICBMs anyway. The American MX, in turn, if 200 were deployed as originally planned, with ten extremely accurate warheads each, would provide similar coverage of the Soviet land-based fleet.* The conundrum was that as long as the limits focused on launchers, both sides had an incentive to stuff more warheads on each missile; but as warheads proliferated on single missiles, the missiles themselves became more valuable, and more time-urgent, targets—targets, that is, that would *attract* a first strike. SALT II did limit warheads on missiles, but the limits were far too high to change the trend toward greater instability.

The cruise missile turned SALT strategic concepts even more topsy-turvy. Cruise missiles are very small—20 feet long, 27 inches wide—and very cheap—only about $2 million each. A cruise missile's guidance system comes into play only in the last stages of its flight, in contrast to a ballistic missile, where the first moments of the launch are crucial; as a result, a cruise can be fired from any kind of platform—a truck, a plane, or a ship, stationary or not makes little difference. They are therefore easy to conceal and highly mobile; and, particularly if they are procured in large numbers and dispersed throughout the countryside or on ships or planes, they are invulnerable to an enemy first strike. At the same time, their small size, low flight pattern, and electronic countermeasure capabilities virtually assure their ability to penetrate Soviet

*For this calculation, see the notes to this chapter.

air defenses, particularly in a large-scale launch; but their slow speed makes them almost useless as first-strike weapons themselves.* Cruises, in short, are the veritable shmoos of the weapons world, a highly accurate, highly reliable, second-strike weapon, devoid of first-strike temptations, the long-sought ideal of "assured destruction" theory. But, confusingly, a central imperative of the SALT process is to improve weapon countability, by *limiting* proliferation and *preventing* concealment and dispersion—in short, increasing the vulnerability of the cruise to a first strike, and negating all the features that make it so attractive to arms controllers.

All the contradictions in SALT theory came together in the search for an MX basing mode. The MX was a response to the emerging Soviet ability to threaten American land-based silos. It was originally designed as a mobile missile in order to counter the accuracy of newer Soviet warheads against fixed silos. But the counting imperative in SALT forbade mobile missiles. The administration accordingly fell back on a variety of "shell game" basing plans, each of which required shuttling the missiles from one launch site to another, in such a way as to facilitate their counting by Soviet satellites, creating at the same time enough uncertainty about their location to discourage a Soviet first-strike attempt. One plan was a "vertical basing" scheme, involving 4,600 hardened silos, and million-pound, 100-foot high "transporter-erectors," 200 in all—giant machines that could lumber from silo to silo, lifting missiles up and placing them down, in a solemn twenty-four-hour-a-day ritual.

The military liked vertical basing because it required less area, and the underground silos were easier to harden. But SALT I had set a precedent for counting silos as launchers, whether they were empty or not, which seemed to preclude their use. Arms controllers, and eventually the Carter administration, came to favor "horizontal basing" or a "race-track" scheme, in which the missiles were moved by huge transporters, either by road or rail, among thousands of above-ground hardened garages, with special portholes (at a cost of $1.5 billion) so Soviet satellites could look into the garages and verify that they were empty.

It was strategic and arms control theory run amok. Any of the basing schemes would have taken years to build, at costs probably hugely in

*The Soviets occasionally claim that the cruise could be a first-strike weapon, since "we don't know it's coming until it explodes . . . [in judging] a first-strike threat, we care about warning time, not flight time." But, in fact, the long atmospheric flight-time would make the timing problem of a surprise first strike impossible to solve, even theoretically. And it is inconceivable that a thousand or so cruises would not be detected long before they reached the Soviet Union, whether or not the Soviets could shoot very many of them down.

excess of $50 billion, and would have consumed tens of thousands of square miles of Western land. By one calculation, the water needed to mix the necessary millions of tons of concrete would have totally disrupted Western state water supplies. All the plans, it should have been obvious, were non-starters; and it is almost inconceivable that any of them, once started, could ever have been finished. The plans, however, created unwonted political alliances. Conservatives were willing to vote for exotic basing schemes, since they had based their case for the MX on the vulnerability of the Minuteman. They would have preferred simply a mobile missile, but understood that any basing mode that clearly violated SALT could not pass the Congress. Those on the congressional left, on the other hand, supported the basing schemes because they knew that deployment of the MX would be the minimum price of a new SALT treaty; but they hoped that if the MX was tied to a hugely expensive basing scheme, the program might eventually collapse of its own weight.

As the awkward alliances behind the various MX basing schemes came unstuck, one by one, amid mutual recriminations and charges of bad faith, the program remained an embarrassing loose end when the Carter administration left office. The new administration, after some embarrassing to-ing and fro-ing of its own, announced—illogically, in light of the campaign clamor about Minuteman vulnerability—that it would deploy 200 MXs in Minuteman silos, presumably as a demonstration of American war-fighting resolve. The issue was eventually buried by a presidential study group, the Scowcroft Commission, which, amid some hooting from the left, let it be known that the "window of vulnerability" that had fuelled the Reagan forces' rise to power was more theoretical than real, and the matter was quietly allowed to drop.

### The Dual-Track and START: Breaking Off Arms Control

Jimmy Carter's tortuous road to a SALT agreement was watched nervously by his European allies, and, in the case of Helmut Schmidt, the West German chancellor, watched suspiciously. Schmidt had good reason not to trust Carter. Early in his administration, Carter had taken the lead in alerting the alliance to the dangers of the growing conventional imbalance in Europe, exacting an equivocal promise that the NATO countries would increase their defense expenditures by 3 percent a year in real terms, as the United States had committed to do. One of the key American programs was the "enhanced radiation weapon" or the "neutron bomb," a munition touted by the Defense Department as a response to the overwhelming armored superiority of the Warsaw Pact.

Despite its exaggerated reputation as a "capitalist" weapon that would kill people without destroying property, the neutron bomb was hardly a radical development. The basic idea was to channel a greater portion of a nuclear explosion's energy into the release of high-energy particles rather than into heat and blast effects—the opposite of the overall trend of postwar weapon development, which was to maximize blast and minimize radioactive fallout. (The Hiroshima bomb, arguably, was an "enhanced-radiation" weapon, since the ratio of fallout to blast was much greater than with modern warheads.) The weapon—not a bomb at all, but an artillery munition—would produce roughly the same radiation as a standard 10-kiloton warhead with only a 1-kiloton explosion, offering greater possibilities for attacking a massed tank formation without wreaking quite as much destruction on Central European towns and villages.

Regardless of its military merits, the neutron bomb proposal evoked demonstrations and protests from antinuclear groups across the continent, working a particular embarrassment on socialist governments like Schmidt's, which harbored strong pacifist constituencies. The Carter administration at first made deployment of the neutron bomb a test of alliance loyalty; then just after Schmidt had enforced party discipline on the issue, at considerable political cost, Carter changed his mind and cancelled the weapon. Schmidt was justifiably outraged, and publicly questioned not only Carter's judgment and consistency, but the reliability of the American guarantee to defend Europe.

Tensions in the alliance, like those resulting from the neutron bomb incident, bring to the fore the underlying neurotic pattern of the American-European military relation. When the United States is building up its nuclear forces in one of its periodic rearmament cycles, the Europeans invariably flutter anxiously about American "brinkmanship" and pursue independent "peace" policies with the Soviet Union. When the Americans and Soviets appear to be nearing agreement on arms control, on the other hand, Europeans agonize about "decoupling"— worried that an American-Soviet nuclear accommodation will leave them defenseless against the conventional power of the Warsaw Pact. The common thread is that the Europeans fear the consequences of a conventional war in Europe, but are unwilling to invest in conventional armaments to the extent necessary to deter it with some assurance, preferring instead to shelter beneath the American nuclear umbrella. As neuroses go, it is a functional one, for while it entails frequent bouts of anxiety and intra-alliance recrimination, it has allowed the Europeans to expend much less of their national product on military establishments than the United States does.*

Progress on SALT and worries about American steadfastness led Schmidt and other defense-conscious Europeans to pay greater attention to the growing Soviet capability in so-called Long-range Theater Nuclear Forces. The Soviets had mounted an aggressive program to replace their 1950s-vintage SS-4 and 5 medium- and intermediate-range missiles with their new SS-20, a mobile, three-warhead, reloadable weapon that could cover targets anywhere in Europe from launching sites in western Russia. The 500 SS-4s and 5s west of the Urals were so old, so cumbersome, and so inaccurate that they had little effect on perceptions of the military balance. The SS-20s, on the other hand, were solid-fuel, quick-strike weapons, with an accuracy in the 300-meter range. When the replacement program was completed, the Soviets would be able to blanket Western European airfields, supply depots, and troop concentrations with nuclear strikes in the first minutes of a battle. SS-20 deployment began in 1977, with 160 missiles (480 warheads) in place by 1979, and 423 (1,269 warheads) by 1985. About a fifth of the fleet was deployed east of the Urals against China.

NATO forces, it was argued, had no comparable weapons. The fifty-six F-111 nuclear bombers based in Great Britain would take hours to reach the Soviet Union, and nuclear-capable F-4s had insufficient range

---

*Some representative spending for various years:

### % GNP Allocated to Military Budget

| Country | 1975 | 1979 | 1983 |
|---|---|---|---|
| West Germany | 3.7 | 3.3 | 3.4 |
| France | 3.9 | 3.9 | 4.2 |
| Italy | 2.6 | 2.4 | 2.8 |
| Netherlands | 3.6 | 3.4 | 3.3 |
| Great Britain | 4.9 | 4.9 | 5.5 |
| United States | 5.9 | 5.2 | 7.4 |

George Kennan, for one, has excoriated the "flabbiness" and "lack of vigor" in Western European civilization that leads it to prefer a continued state of anxiety to looking after its own defenses. He points out, as have a growing number of commentators, that Western Europe is bigger, stronger, and richer than the Soviet Union. If there is a conventional force imbalance, it is by Western Europe's choice. The British willingness to bear rather more of their share of the military burden than the other allies helps reinforce the "special relationship" between the United States and the United Kingdom.

for a round-trip attack. The great majority of NATO's battlefield nuclear weapons were short-range artillery munitions, of doubtful utility in any kind of war. The only medium-range missiles were the 180 Pershings in Germany (108 of them American, the remainder German, but with warheads under American control); but they were almost as old as the Soviet SS-4s and 5s, and couldn't reach the Soviet Union in any case. If the Russians could take out Europe's defenses with a quick SS-20 strike, Europeans contended, the war would be effectively over. With Europe in ruins, no American President would risk national suicide by launching a retaliatory strike merely for the sake of posthumous alliance solidarity.

The American military were unimpressed with Europe's fears. In the first place, the alliance had long since opted for a sea-based rather than a land-based deterrent. Great Britain had 202 Polaris warheads on 4 submarines, the French had 80 submarine-launched missiles, and the United States had assigned NATO 3 Poseidon submarines with another 480 warheads—so an SS-20 attack would by no means destroy NATO's retaliatory capabilities. It was absurd, in any case, to expect the Soviets to lay down a blanket attack on American bases in Europe without anticipating an American strategic retaliation. Putting more land-based missiles in Europe, in the military view, would just complicate control problems and, not incidentally, require greater allied participation in formulating nuclear strategy. Finally, the SS-20 actually had little effect on the military balance anyway, for the Soviets had years before compensated for the incapacities of their SS-4s and 5s by targetting a large, but unknown, number of SS-11 ICBMs on Western Europe. If the Soviets were truly in a suicidal mood, the SS-11s were quick-reacting and accurate enough to destroy NATO's European military infrastructure in a surprise first strike.

The Carter administration finally decided, with a notable lack of enthusiasm, that the shaky state of alliance relations required some response to the SS-20. As Carter's national security adviser, Zbigniew Brzezinski, who was the key policymaker on the issue, conceded: "I was personally never persuaded that we needed TNF [Theater Nuclear Forces, i.e., new land-based European missiles] for military reasons. I was persuaded reluctantly that we needed it to obtain European support for SALT."

The decision was to employ 572 missiles*—108 Pershing IIs with the

*American planners had apparently concluded that the right number of missiles was between 200 and 600; anything less would have been too insignificant, and anything more

remainder ground-based cruises. Once the decision was taken, European enthusiasm predictably cooled: it was one thing to complain in the abstract, quite another to accept an actual deployment. But the American military had by this time climbed on the "Euromissile" bandwagon, and Carter was determined to push the weapon through. He was increasingly exasperated by Soviet international behavior, and anxious to adopt a harder-line stance for the upcoming presidential election. Euromissiles fit well with Presidential Directive 59—the Carter administration's own version of McNamara's original nuclear war-fighting policy, due to be announced the following summer—and countered some of the criticisms of the growing ranks of strategists who were alarmed about the steadily growing Soviet nuclear edge. Two weeks before the Afghanistan invasion, in December 1979, the decision was rammed through NATO, but only on the condition of the "dual track." During the time between the decision and the actual deployment, the United States committed to try to trade away the Euromissiles for substantial reductions in Soviet SS-20 deployments.

The Euromissile deployment decision greatly alarmed the Soviets, and they showed it by their behavior: a mixture of cajolery and clumsy political pressure on the Europeans until the Euromissile deployment actually began in 1983. Their concern focused on the Pershing II—despite the name, a totally different missile from the earlier Pershings. It is a solid-fuelled, mobile, truck-launched missile, with a single low-yield (5–50-kiloton) warhead, and a 1,000-mile range. In a nuclear alert, it can be rapidly dispersed to wooded areas and requires only about a 6-foot-wide clear overhead space for a launch. It is the first, and to date the only, American ballistic missile with a maneuverable, terminally guided warhead. The warhead is designed to tilt up as it re-enters the atmosphere, in order to slow itself down and reduce atmospheric electrical interference. When it has slowed sufficiently, at about 20,000 meters, it tilts back down and exposes its radar nose. The radar performs a circular area scan every two seconds (it is a "doughnut" scan; it does not see the area directly beneath it), correlates the readings with target area maps stored in its memory, and glides to its target with

---

too provocative. The 108 Pershings replaced only the old American Pershings, since it was decided, out of concern for Soviet sensitivities, not to upgrade the German Pershings. Since the missiles had the same name, if they had little else in common, it would appear a normal upgrade. Cruises come in "flights" of sixteen, grouped in units of four flights each for command purposes; 464 was therefore the largest number of cruises that could be logically deployed while keeping the total of the two systems below 600. It was decided to propose a high number in the expectation that the Europeans would argue it down. Surprisingly, the number was accepted with little comment.

movable fins. With the Pershing's claimed 20–45 meter CEP, and an eight-minute flight time to the western Soviet Union, Soviet defense planners insist (with some justification, although the claim requires exaggerating the Pershing's range) that it is a first-strike strategic weapon, one that could black out the Soviet command and control apparatus just before a massive MX and Minuteman counterforce strike. (The Soviets were not much consoled by the virtual certainty that the Pershing II terminal guidance system didn't work. It failed almost all its tests before deployment. Without the enormous political pressure behind the Euromissiles, it may not have been deployed at all.)

Key officials in the new Reagan administration viewed the Euromissiles with scorn. Richard Perle, an Assistant Secretary of Defense, and probably the most influential arms control policymaker, thought the Euromissiles were "a lousy decision if there ever was one . . . a hell of a price tag for a marginal military fix." Moreover, they illustrated perfectly his long-standing objections to arms control as it was officially practiced. America agreed to the Euromissiles in order to drum up European support for SALT—"a classic example of how so-called arms control, far from controlling arms, has had the effect of driving the deployment of new weapons." Any thought of dropping the whole idea, however, as Perle would have preferred, was quickly scotched by the State Department. The Euromissiles had become the focus of the entire American-European relation; another flip-flop would have looked too much like Carter.

The policy finally adopted was the so-called zero option—no Euromissiles if the Soviets deactivated all their SS-20s. It was, in the view of the most knowledgeable arms control observers, a bad faith proposal: as Raymond Garthoff wrote, it "killed the prospect for serious negotiation and agreement," and may indeed have been put forward "for that very reason." Paul Nitze, the chief American negotiator on the Euromissiles, tried "singlehandedly to save the administration from itself," in the words of the historian of the Euromissile negotiations, and, going beyond his instructions, worked out his famous "walk in the woods" deal with his opposite number in Geneva, Yuli Kvitsinsky. Nitze's package would have required deep cuts in the SS-20 forces but not to zero. The final version permitted 75 European SS-20 launchers and 90 in Asia against no new Pershings and 75 cruise launchers (with 4 missiles each) for the United States; both sides, in addition, would have been permitted 150 medium-range nuclear-capable aircraft. It was, in most considered judgments, an excellent deal. It was quickly rejected by the

Reagan administration, however, and apparently, although more ambiguously, it was rejected by the Politburo as well. Euromissile deployment would proceed.

The new administration had even less interest in following up on SALT. SALT II was a campaign issue for Reagan, and there was no way he could endorse it. (SALT II supporters point to the fact that he abided by it anyway, at least through 1986. Whether that demonstrates the essential soundness or essential meaninglessness of the treaty is not clear.) After some embarrassing groping for policy, Reagan finally, only in 1982, announced his START plan—Strategic Arms Reduction Talks—proposing deep cuts in both sides' land-based missiles arsenals, a proposal almost calculated to be unacceptable to the Soviets. The arms control picture was further clouded by his surprise announcement, a year later, of the "Star Wars" program—officially, the Strategic Defense Initiative. When Euromissile deployment actually began at the end of 1983, only after yet another heavy-handed and unsuccessful Soviet political campaign in Europe, the Soviet negotiators walked out of both sets of talks. Arms control, for the time being at least, was dead.

The Reagan administration's initial lack of interest in arms control negotiations was based on more than an instinctive distrust of the Russians, for by the late 1970s, traditional arms control theory in the United States was under heavy attack from a new, and powerful, wing of strategic opinion.

# CHAPTER 19

# Images of War

### War-fighting Doctrine and "Assured Destruction"

In the mid-1970s, a new generation of defense intellectuals—Richard Pipes, Colin Gray, Fritz Ermath, Benjamin Lambeth, Edward Luttwack—supported by grizzled veterans of the doctrinal wars like Albert Wohlstetter and Paul Nitze, were pointing to fundamental flaws in American nuclear doctrine that, they claimed, had caused the United States dangerously to misconceive the nature of the Soviet threat. The debate revolved around a single question: *Why* was the Soviet Union spending so much money on new arms and armies? The question was answered by Richard Pipes in one of the half dozen or so most influential articles of the postwar period—"Why the Soviet Union Thinks It Can Fight and Win a Nuclear War," in *Commentary* magazine in the summer of 1977. Pipes, a Harvard professor and Soviet expert, was a prominent member of the Committee on the Present Danger, organized in 1976 by distinguished "cold warriors," like Nitze, Eugene V. Rostow, Clare Booth Luce, Norman Podhoretz, and Charles E. Walker, and had been chairman, the year before, of the Team B group in the celebrated exercise in competitive intelligence assessment created by CIA director George Bush at the end of the Ford administration.

The "Team B" analysts were outside experts—including such weighty figures as Nitze, Daniel O. Graham, former head of the Defense Intelligence Agency, and Thomas W. Wolfe of RAND—organized to challenge the conventional CIA analysis (Team A's) that the Soviet military buildup was merely a quest for "parity" in weapons with the United States. By all accounts, the outsiders overwhelmed the CIA professionals. According to one participant, "we just licked them on a

348

great number of points." And another was quoted: "Sometimes we left them speechless. We had men of great prestige, some of them with memories going back twenty-five years or more, and they made devastating critiques of agency estimates."

Pipes's *Commentary* article, like the Team B analysis, contended that Soviet military deployments reflected a "war-fighting" military doctrine, or a set of strategic preferences that were in sharp contrast with the American search for stable mutual deterrence. Soviet objectives, wrote Pipes, were "not deterrence, but victory; not sufficiency in weapons, but superiority; not retaliation, but offensive action." Soviet political leaders, to be sure, invoked the unthinkable horrors of nuclear war as ritualistically as their American counterparts; but that was a "commodity for export." True doctrine was to be found in Soviet *military* writings. For at least the previous twenty years or so, ever since the official recognition of the importance of nuclear striking forces, they had sounded a small number of consistent themes, which Pipes listed as: *pre-emption,* that is, a first strike at the moment a political crisis is about to erupt into war; *quantitative superiority* in arms; *counterforce targeting; combined arms operations;* and *defense.*

The major Soviet military texts, in fact, amply support Pipes's claim. While American writings tend to be defensive, or even apologetic, about temporary weapons superiorities, Soviet writings revel in them, to the point of telling broad fibs. The third edition of Sokolovsky's *Military Strategy* (1968), for example, bragged:

The Soviet Union was the first in the world to create the hydrogen bomb and the intercontinental ballistic missile, and also a number of new kinds of rocket armaments which are new in principle. . . . By the admission of competent American specialists, our superiority in total nuclear might of strategic rocket weapons is very considerable. [It was, of course, patently untrue that the Soviets had superior nuclear arms in the late 1960s.]

The Sokolovsky editors go on:

The question arises of what, under these conditions [the availability of nuclear-armed rockets] constitutes the main military-strategic goal of the war: the defeat of the enemy's armed forces, as was the case in the past, or the annihilation and destruction of objectives in the enemy interior and the disorganization of the latter?

The theory of Soviet military strategy gives the following answer to this question: both of these goals should be achieved simultaneously . . .

Mass nuclear rocket-strikes will be of decisive importance for the attainment of goals in future world war. The infliction of these assaults will be the main, decisive method of waging war.

Armed combat in ground theaters of military operations will also take place differently. . . . [Nuclear rocket strikes] will lead to the formation of numerous zones of continuous destruction, devastation, and radioactive contamination. Great possibilities are created for waging extensive maneuverable offensive operations with the aid of high-mobile mechanized troops. Trench warfare . . . has been replaced by rapid, maneuverable fighting operations carried out simultaneously or consecutively in individual regions at different depths of the zone of military operations.

The Sokolovsky themes of massed counterforce nuclear attacks closely integrated with conventional arms operations were a constant in Soviet military writings. As another important military text, *Scientific-Technical Progress and the Revolution in Military Affairs,* under the editorship of Col. Gen. N.A. Lomov, put it in 1973:

Strikes by strategic missiles against major enemy installations will create favorable conditions for conducting offensive operations by the Land Forces to a great depth and at a pace significantly exceeding the pace of a troop offensive during the operations of the last war. . . .

The new conditions have altered the role of maneuver in the offensive, as well as its goals and content. At present, a maneuver may be carried out not only for the purpose of placing one's troops in an advantageous position vis-à-vis the enemy, but also for carrying out such missions as the rapid use of the results of fire and above all of nuclear strikes for rapidly advancing in depth; the shifting of efforts to a new axis; the crossing or bypassing of areas of radioactive contamination and fire regions; the replacement of units and formations which have been put out of commission by enemy nuclear strikes.

And a third text, published in 1975, stressed: "But while weapons of mass destruction should not be underrrated, neither should they be overrated, viewed as some kind of *mystical force detached from society.* . . . nuclear weapons, just as other weapons, constitute a means of implementing policy." [italics in original]

The focus on war-fighting capabilities explained the continued Soviet emphasis on defense. All three Sokolovsky volumes, for example, insist that

An extremely important type of strategic operations is the protection of territory of the country from nuclear attacks by the enemy, using PVO [antiair], PRO [antimissile], and PKO [antispace defense]. Without the effective conduct of these operations, successful conduct of a modern war and assurance of the normal vital activities of the country are impossible. These operations are intended to repel enemy air and rocket attacks and to annihilate his aircraft and rockets in flight, to prevent them from reaching the most important administrative-political centers, economic regions and objectives, groups of rocket troops, aviation, the navy, regions of reserve mobilization, and other objectives.

Marshal Grechko confirmed the continuing emphasis on defense shortly after the ABM Treaty was signed in 1972: "At the same time," he said in September, [the treaty] does not place any limits on carrying out research and development work directed toward solving the problems of defense of the country against nuclear/missile attack."

Finally, the Soviet emphasis on war fighting, counterforce, and defense was underscored by the ambiguous position adopted by the most authoritative sources on surprise and "pre-emptive" nuclear attacks. Although Soviet political leaders ostentatiously adopted a policy of "no-first-use" of nuclear weapons,* their military writings were not nearly so categorical. The Sokolovsky editors, for example, stressed that *"the initial period of the war will be of decisive importance for the outcome of the entire war.* In this regard the main problem is the development of methods for reliably *repelling a surprise nuclear attack* as well as methods of frustrating the aggressive designs of the enemy by the timely infliction of a shattering blow upon him." [italics in original]

The "timely infliction of a shattering blow" to "frustrate aggressive designs" implies a pre-emptive attack, like Israel's against Egypt in 1973, that is, *before* the Western powers had launched nuclear weapons. If there was any doubt, the Soviet Defense Minister D. F. Ustinov clarified Brezhnev's ringing endorsement of "no-first-use" in the late 1970s as follows:

Washington and the other NATO capitals should clearly realize that the Soviet Union, in renouncing the first use of nuclear weapons, is also denying the first use of nuclear weapons to all those who are hatching plans for a nuclear attack and counting on a victory in a nuclear war. The state of the military potentials and military technological capabilities of the sides is such that the imperialist

---

*"First use" is not the same as a "first-strike" policy. "First-strike" implies an intercontinental surprise or pre-emptive attack against the other side's central strategic forces—its ICBMs and bombers. "First use" is used by NATO to imply battlefield use of nuclear weapons against the other side's conventional military formations, airfields, etc. NATO has always insisted on its right to resort to nuclear weapons to defend Europe in the event conventional defenses fail under the weight of a massive Soviet attack. The threat of "first use" is viewed as a key deterrent to quantitatively superior Soviet armies. Soviet propaganda blurs the issue of a surprise intercontinental "first-strike" with the NATO "first use" policy. The issue remains a controversial one.

forces will not succeed in attaining military superiority *either at the stage of preparations for nuclear war or at the moment when they try to start such a war.* [italics in original]

Pipes and his colleagues were not preaching a new discovery; Soviet military writings were well known in the West. Rather, they were railing at the refusal of Western arms control theorists to take the Soviets seriously. Twenty years of civilian arms theorizing, in the "managerial" and arms control tradition, Colin Gray wrote in a bitter article, had sapped American military power and saddled the armed forces with leaders unable to think of a nuclear war as a real war, as the Soviets were obviously doing. By their inaction, successive administrations had lost strategic superiority over the Soviets, "welcomed" the loss for its presumed "benign effects" on Soviet policy, frozen the new inferiority into place through SALT, and constructed theories of "stability" to justify their folly. They had refused to comprehend the Soviet Union as a "unique adversary," and had failed to recognize Soviet military superiority until it was almost too late to reverse.

The central villain in the loss of American superiority, in the eyes of the conservative defense intellectuals, was Robert McNamara—the McNamara of 1967 and the San Francisco speech, that is, rather than the McNamara who had laid out the first "war-fighting" nuclear strategy in Ann Arbor in 1962. In his San Francisco speech, McNamara had set out three principles that had become the fixed stars in the doctrinal firmament of American arms control theory. The first was the contention that, in McNamara's words, "substantial numerical superiority in weapons does not effectively translate into diplomatic control or political leverage." The second was the nuclear strategy of "assured destruction." And the third was the assumption that the arms race was governed by an "action–reaction" cycle.

Pipes, Nitze, Gray, and other analysts challenged directly the notion that nuclear superiority did not translate into actual power. As an empirical proposition, they argued, McNamara's statement was simply not true. It was perhaps understandable that McNamara, at the peak of his frustration with the failures in Vietnam, and accustomed to the easy sway of American arms, as in Cuba in 1962 or in the Middle East in 1967, should be dismissive of the fruits of power. But it was not reasonable to expect the Soviet Union, after the long years of watching the United States have its own way in the world, to be similarly scornful of military strength. Indeed, Nitze insisted, the Soviets believed that "superior capability provided a unique and vital tool for pressure in a confrontation situation." The rise of the Soviet Union to global power tracked closely with its accretion of nuclear arsenals. But, the conservative defense intellectuals noted despairingly, even so confirmed a practitioner of *realpolitik* as Henry Kissinger implicitly accepted McNamara's contention with his famous rhetorical question at a press conference: "What in the name of God is strategic superiority?" (Kissinger's subsequent retraction of that statement was much less noted.)

The widespread assumption of the limited utility of nuclear power was the inevitable consequence, the conservative theorists argued, of McNamara's doctrine of "assured destruction." "Assured destruction" set quantitatively limited objectives for the nuclear arsenal; buildups beyond that point were necessarily devalued, regardless of what the Soviets did. McNamara, in fact, came to embrace an "assured destruction" doctrine only slowly and ambiguously. In Ann Arbor in 1962, and in his secret NATO speech in Athens the month before, McNamara was the first American defense official to unveil a "war-fighting" nuclear strategy, the new "strategy of controlled response," in which "military strategy in a general nuclear war" was "approached in much the same way that more conventional military operations have been regarded in the past." He had moved virtually full circle toward "assured destruction" by 1967, however, and had long since instructed the Air Force not to gear its budget requests to war-fighting requirements. In actual fact, however, McNamara never referred to "assured destruction" as a "strategy"; he viewed it rather as a force-sizing criterion, or "a management tool to help in structuring the strategic forces," a minimum *capability* for American nuclear forces. The phrase "strategy of assured destruction" seems rather to be the coinage of arms control theorists, like Herbert Scoville, who enthusiastically adopted McNamara's doctrine as a polemical device in arguing for restraints on American nuclear arsenals.

The precise complaint of the defense intellectuals, however, was that "assured destruction" was either not a strategy at all—but merely an operations researcher's measuring rod, "rigidified . . . and quantified," devoid of strategic content—or if it was intended as a strategy, it was a most inadequate one. In the words of Benjamin Lambeth, "assured destruction" was "an antithesis of strategy. Unlike any strategy that ever preceded it through the history of armed conflict, it ceased to be useful precisely where military strategy is supposed to come into effect: at the edge of war."

In either case, they argued, it was a most inadequate basis for deter-mining the use and disposition of American nuclear power. Fred Iklé wrote that the entire premise of "assured destruction" was that the Soviets would act "crazy" and that America would then act "vengefully crazy." There was no "rational despot" of the games theorist's dreams sitting in the Kremlin waiting for the "opportune, mathematical mo-ment" to strike. Indeed, nuclear war, if it started, would probably start irrationally, just as the Japanese attack on Pearl Harbor was "irrational." But "assured destruction" allowed only for a "swift and massive" American response against Soviet cities that would kill tens of millions of Russians. It included no concept of how a war might start, how it should be waged, and how it might be brought to a close. Indeed, it had all the doctrinal inadequacies of Eisenhower's "massive retaliation" strategy, with the added disadvantage that it encouraged a complacent acceptance of Soviet superiority.

McNamara's final sin, also in his San Francisco speech, was to en-shrine the notion of an arms race driven by an "action–reaction" cycle. The conservative defense intellectuals conceded that Soviet and Ameri-can military deployments and strategies interacted with each other—or else the whole notion of an "arms race" made no sense at all—but the precise nature of the interaction, they insisted, was "muffled, lagged, and very complex." Specifically, there was only the shakiest of empirical evidence for the arms control argument that American weapons de-ployments invariably evoked equal and offsetting deployments by the Soviet Union. Nitze pointed out, for instance, that the MIRV–ABM interaction demonstrated anything one pleased. The possibility of So-viet ABM defenses arguably hastened the American MIRV, which, ar-guably, *reduced* Soviet interest in missile defenses. The fact that superior technology permitted the United States to be the first to de-ploy accurate rocket guidance systems and MIRVed re-entry vehicles did not demonstrate that those deployments induced the Soviet pro-grams; both sides, in fact, probably began work at about the same time, just as they had on the hydrogen bomb.

The asymmetries in the deployments of the two sides made interac-tions very difficult to trace. Massive Soviet tank deployments, for in-stance, were more likely to induce deployment of Western antitank weapons than an offsetting buildup of tanks; American naval deploy-ments might lead to increased Soviet interest in land-based aircraft like the Backfire. Finally, Lee's researches called into question even the assumption that the long-term Soviet military buildup was a reaction to the Cuban missile crisis. His data, in fact, give Soviet defense spending an eerily autonomous air. As measured by the defense burden on the Soviet economy, the buildup may have begun as early as 1959 or 1960, and appears to have continued at a relatively constant pace for the next fifteen years, virtually unaffected—in terms of scale, that is, rather than specific inter-service allocations—by external developments.

In a real sense, McNamara is a victim of both his supporters and his critics. Whatever the defects of pure "assured destruction" or "action–reaction" formulations, it is doubtful that he ever held them. While it is true that an influential wing of liberal opinion tended to adopt extremely simplistic views of the arms race—witness the Senate debates on MIRVs and ABMs in the early 1970s—it is difficult to demonstrate that such views were ever the dominant factor in defense policymaking.

It is simply not true, for example, that McNamara ever "discarded" a strategy of counterforce in favor of "assured destruction," as Scoville enthusiastically claimed, or as his critics charged. Counterforce, or the capability for "damage-limiting" strikes against Soviet military assets, was a central feature of even his last military posture statements; and it was always the primary targeting criterion in American attack planning, if only for the reason that by the end of McNamara's tenure, the United States had far more nuclear weapons than could be usefully launched against Soviet cities.

To be sure, with his increasing emphasis on "assured destruction" rhetoric, McNamara created much of the confusion about actual American policy; but there was more than a trace of disingenuousness in his shift. The public disaffection with the Vietnam War had made war-fighting doctrines very unpopular by 1967. As George Ball wrote in 1971: ". . . all public officials have learned to talk only about deterrence and city attacks. No war-fighting. . . . Too many critics can make too much trouble . . . so public officials have run for cover. That included me when I was one of them. But the targeting philosophy, the options and the order of choice remain unchanged from the McNamara [1962] speech."

Certainly, despite his rhetoric on "action–reaction cycles," McNamara's actual procurement recommendations, like the Poseidon and Minuteman III MIRV programs, continued to multiply American counterforce capabilities.* The conservative criticism that is on target

*To prevent confusion on the "counterforce" point: by the late 1970s, the counterforce debate had come to focus on fully hardened missile silos, which neither the Poseidon nor the first Minuteman IIIs could reliably attack. When McNamara recommended the

is only the relatively narrow one that his strict cost-effectiveness requirements implied a slower procurement schedule than the military would have liked and, at least in theory, imposed a weapons acquisition criterion that had little to do with a war-fighting strategy.

The valid accusation against McNamara—and the strand of truth linking enthusiasts like Scoville and critics like Iklé—is that in his last years in office, he had clearly ceased to *believe* in the nuclear war-fighting doctrines he and his intellectuals had brought to the Pentagon. But the same charge could not be laid against his successors: for the original 1962 McNamara strategy of "controlled response" was reconfirmed, refined, and considerably developed by both the Nixon/Ford and Carter administrations. James Schlesinger, a former RAND analyst himself, took the lead in defining nuclear policy as Secretary of Defense in the Nixon/Ford years. Henry Kissinger, who had a continuing interest in tactical nuclear policy in Europe—he had been on all sides of the issue over the years—played the catalytic role in putting the topic on Nixon's agenda. When Schlesinger's refinements were put into effect, Nixon specifically noted that "These decisions do not constitute a major new departure in US nuclear strategy; rather, they are an elaboration of existing policy."

The nuclear weapons policy guidance signed by Schlesinger in March 1974 did contain a number of important departures, both of rhetoric and substance. "Assured destruction" was explicitly dropped as the dominant force-planning criterion—although the concept continued to provide a ready strawman for hawkish policy theorists. In addition, Schlesinger expressly disavowed Nixon's earlier vague commitment to Congress that America would eschew "hard-silo" kill capabilities: the new policy specifically embraced heavier and more accurate missiles—leading to the deployment of the bigger Mark 12A warheads and improved guidance systems for the Minuteman III in the 1980s, the new Trident family of submarine-launched missiles, and, ultimately, to the controversial MX missile. It was a shift that the *New York Times*, with an eye on previous declaratory, as opposed to actual, policy, called "one of the most basic and controversial changes in strategic doctrine in the last twenty years."

Most important, Schlesinger stressed the necessity for a greater

---

programs in the mid-1960s, however, Soviet missiles were, by and large, not hardened. Weapons like the Poseidon, moreover, retained a counterforce role against Soviet airfields and military installations into the 1980s. Military spokesmen were quite explicit on the "war-fighting" role envisioned for the Poseidon and Minuteman III.

number of limited nuclear options. It was the search for more plausible limited war options, in fact, that impelled the pursuit of greater accuracy. Schlesinger's main criticism of McNamara's 1962 plan was that, without a more careful selection of targets and more precisely accurate weapons, the Soviets would be unable to distinguish a limited counterforce strike from the first salvo in an all-out spasm war, the same objection made by the Sokolovsky volume. Schlesinger did not shrink from the criticism that plausible limited nuclear options could make nuclear war more likely: "A deterrent strategy that one would be unwilling to implement *under duress,*" he retorted, "provides a rather porous deterrent." Nor was he worried that his stance might alarm the Soviets: "It is not our objective to give them reassurance. In order to have deterrence, we must have a credible threat."

In spite of some expectations to the contrary, the Carter administration, after an extensive review, reconfirmed the McNamara/Schlesinger nuclear weapons policy with only minor modifications. Defense Secretary Harold Brown outlined American nuclear posture in 1980 in language that would have fit comfortably with McNamara's Athens and Ann Arbor speeches:

Deterrence remains . . . our fundamental strategic objective. But deterrence must restrain a far wider range of threats than just massive attacks on U.S. cities. . . .

In our analysis and planning, we are necessarily giving greater attention to how a nuclear war would actually be fought by both sides if deterrence fails. . . . [T]his focus helps us achieve deterrence and peace, by ensuring that our ability to retaliate is fully credible. . . .

. . . our plans and capabilities [must] be structured to put more stress on being able to employ strategic nuclear forces selectively, as well as by all-out retaliation in response to massive attacks on the United States. . . . if [the Soviets choose] some intermediate level of aggression, we could, by selective, large (but still less than maximum) nuclear attacks, exact an unacceptably high price in the things the Soviet leaders appear to value most—political and military control, military force, both nuclear and conventional, and the industrial capability to sustain a war.

The conservative defense intellectuals were, by and large, still not convinced. Harold Brown—suspiciously enough, himself once a close aide to McNamara—was occasionally given to statements like: "I am not persuaded that the right way to deal with a major Soviet damage-limiting program would be by imitating it," and he used phrases like "unacceptable damage," which was the same term McNamara used in establishing his "assured destruction" criterion. Colin Gray asked plaintively, "Why must it be assumed that the damage-limitation path would be self-defeating?," ignoring the fact that Brown was just then engaged in creating an extensive damage-limiting set of nuclear options. Even after the Reagan administration had developed greatly elaborated nuclear war-fighting plans in the early 1980s—under Fred Iklé's direction, no less—vastly expanding the Soviet target list and the range of limited nuclear options, Albert Wohlstetter continued to inveigh against "assured destruction," and argued strenuously that the United States was still not taking nuclear "war-fighting" doctrine seriously: "It would be most unwise", Wohlstetter wrote, "to base policy on the widespread belief that the Soviets have never indicated any willingness to consider seriously the possibility of controlling nuclear operations . . ." The "war-fighting" reluctance persisted, he lamented, "in spite of the continuing revolutionary changes in technology, improving the United States' ability to destroy military targets effectively while reducing the collateral damage . . ."

Why the obsessive condemnation of "assured destruction" by critics like Gray and Wohlstetter long after it was explicitly disavowed as the official American nuclear weapons policy? The conservative critics, it would appear, fear that the United States does not have the *nerve* to fight a nuclear war. Policy is still really driven, the "war-fighting" advocates suspect, by a deeply rooted "assured destruction" bias—all presidentially blessed "Nuclear Weapons Employment Policy" directives to the contrary. The elaborate war-fighting scenarios, they fear, mask a lurking hope that the mere possibility of holocaust will deter both sides from *any* use of nuclear weapons. And if Americans cannot wage a nuclear war with the same grim éclat that Soviet planners are alleged to possess, Colin Gray warns, the Western world is doomed:

Appropriate preliminary judgment is to the effect that if the United States would find civilian casualties in excess of, say, 1 or 5 million intolerable . . . whereas the Soviet state took a more brutally instrumental view of the expendability of, say, 10 or 20 (or more) million of its "citizens"—then the "Western world," really, would be out of business. The bedrock of U.S. security guarantees . . . would crumble at the first serious test. U.S. [nuclear] strategy would be a bluff: the United States could be "outbid" in its willingness to accept domestic damage at a rather modest level of nuclear violence.

In short, if the Western world is convinced, regardless of its stated "damage-limiting" nuclear policy, that in real life any nuclear war, even a limited one, would be tantamount to suicide, and if the Soviet Union does not share that belief, the West will be condemned always to back down before Soviet power.

The defense intellectuals' charges cannot, and should not, be lightly dismissed. A declared American policy of "damage limitation" need be no more reflective of the true state of nuclear doctrine than the declared policy of "assured destruction" was a decade ago. Evaluating their concerns, however, requires a closer look at the realism behind nuclear war-fighting doctrines of any kind.

## Nuclear War Fighting and Reality

The concept of a limited nuclear war and its attendant doctrines of "flexible response" and "controlled escalation" occupies a time-honored place in American strategic theory, dating from the very earliest speculations of Bernard Brodie, Herman Kahn, Thomas Schelling, and Wohlstetter. As we have seen, it has provided the central logic of American nuclear weapons policy for the last quarter century. It is premised on the wholly admirable assumption that rationality is to be preferred to irrationality; or as Paul Bracken phrased it, that "Nuclear war would not be a contest between two missile farms that happened to have countries and leaders stuck to them." And it is founded on the unshakable belief that, doctrine notwithstanding, Soviet leaders would be forced to follow essentially the same "rules of the game" as Americans, for the simple reason that the rules are not of national origin, but are implicit in the exigencies of a crisis—or as Schlesinger insisted: "when the existential circumstances arise, political leaders on both sides will be under powerful pressure to continue to be sensible."

Schlesinger's statement, however, contains the central dilemma of any nuclear war-fighting strategy. It presumes, implicitly, that acting "sensibly" requires that both sides *moderate* their use of nuclears. It assumes that if either side initiates the use of nuclear weapons in some measured, controlled way, the other side will understand that its best interests lie in responding in kind. Schlesinger's premise, however, is hardly obvious. Albert Wohlstetter's 1959 article, "The Delicate Balance of Terror," the classic exposition of the "war-fighting" impulse, in fact, makes precisely the opposite argument. If either side believes, as the Soviets insist they do, that any use of nuclear weapons is likely quickly to get out of hand, that side, arguably, would be better off launching a massive counterforce salvo the moment the nuclear "firebreak" is passed. "Acting sensibly," that is, may mean one thing to a

RAND analyst or a Kremlin war games specialist, and quite another to a Soviet general or an American SAC commander. Basing policy on such subjective speculation would seem a very dangerous game indeed.

But the uncertainties of nuclear war fighting are not merely intellectual ones. For twenty-five years, strategists have been elaborating the most abstruse and difficult strategic theories, while the military has been accumulating the most complex and sophisticated nuclear warfighting technologies. The awesome potency of the nuclear arsenals, however, is in stark contrast to the simple, brute, and shocking fact that the United States *has never had* and, indeed, *continues not to have,* any plausibly reliable capacity for fighting a limited nuclear war, and is not likely to obtain one within the foreseeable future. For the entire period that Schlesinger was developing and defending his refinements on "flexible response," the American capacity to carry out an "assured destruction" response was at best highly dubious, not only because of major deficiencies in systems designed to warn of nuclear attacks and communicate instructions to American retaliatory forces, but because of difficult, and perhaps insoluble problems relating to the time and information available to decision makers and the inherent contradictions between the powerful controls designed to prevent the accidental discharge of nuclear weapons and those designed to ensure that weapons are fired on order. Clearly, there would have been *some* response to a Soviet attack, and, doubtless, its effects would have been awful; but, far from the controlled escalation favored by the academic strategists, the responding strike would have been merely a paroxysm of random and indiscriminate violence. The discussion that follows can highlight only some of the more serious problems.

The essential premise of all nuclear doctrine, whether of the "warfighting" or "assured destruction" variety, is the necessity for tight central control over nuclear forces—usually assumed in the United States to be exercised by the President himself. Since John Kennedy created the image of the command-post President during the Cuban missile crisis, top civilian leaders have never shrunk from exerting the closest control over military forces, down to the level of individual combat units. Lyndon Johnson, for example, communicated directly with local commanders in Vietnam; President Ford gave orders directly to the on-the-scene forces during the 1975 *Mayaguez* incident; and Ford's last Secretary of Defense, Donald Rumsfield, one story has it, maintained voice contact with the boatswain's mate in charge of a landing craft evacuating Americans during the 1976 Lebanon crisis.

(Military professionals have always chafed under such direct interventions. The Lebanon commanders reportedly changed ships so they couldn't receive Rumsfield's messages.)

There is no question that, under conditions of a nuclear war, the instinct toward tight control would become stronger than ever. The Soviet Union, it appears, exercises even tighter control over its nuclear forces than the Americans do, since an additional layer of KGB oversight must be introduced into the normal military chain of command. The principle of tight central control, however, implies that all information must flow immediately to the President or the delegated central command authority, and that decisions of extraordinary import must be made in a very few, possibly semi-delirious, minutes.

The most commonly assumed nuclear confrontation involves a Soviet first strike against American Minuteman silos. If the Soviets did attempt such an attack, the infrared signature of their launches would be detected by American reconnaissance satellites, and the boost vehicles would be tracked through the first three or four minutes of flight. It may be assumed that such tracking capability has been in place since the late 1960s, although in all likelihood there have been serious gaps in coverage from time to time. Since ballistic missiles tend to launch straight up through the atmosphere, however, satellite tracking will convey little reliable information regarding a missile's probable trajectory. The intelligence consensus is that the Soviets have designated a number of their "strategic" missile inventory for use against European theater targets, so the mere fact of launch, particularly if a conventional war is already under way, will not unambiguously indicate either a "limited" theater attack or the first salvo of a counterforce launch against the United States itself.

The incoming missiles would be picked up ten minutes later by missile early warning systems in Alaska and Greenland, by two new phased-array radar systems on the East and West coasts of the United States, by the antimissile phased-array radar associated with the deactivated "Safeguard" ABM site in North Dakota, and by other ancillary systems.* With the exception of the two phased-array radar systems,

*For reference, the radar systems are usually referred to as: "BMEWS" for Ballistic Missile Early Warning System, the main 1960s-vintage system; "PAVE PAWS" for Perimeter Acquisition Vehicle Entry Phased-Array Warning System, for the two phased-array systems; and "PARCS" for Perimeter Acquisition Radar Attack Characterization System, for the ABM radar. Under certain alert conditions, an additional phased-array system, the "Cobra Dane" installation on the Aleutians, normally used for intelligence purposes, will convert to a ballistic missile warning system.

which were installed only in the 1980s, and the ABM radar, the warning systems—as of the mid-1980s—were of 1960s vintage and geared to track single, large, incoming missiles rather than a large number of much smaller MIRV warheads; they could report little information except that Soviet missiles were on their way, and would leave wide gaps in coverage against submarine missile launches. The two new phased-array systems improved the ability to pick up submarine-launched missiles, but only the ABM radar has the ability to track large numbers of MIRVs or to provide reliable impact predictions. There are a number of gaps in the ABM radar's coverage, however, and it could be readily taken out by a submarine-launched missile arriving from its blind side before it ever picked up any ICBM MIRVs.

Even the most plausible limited-war scenarios tend to overestimate the time and the information that a President will have available to him. Assume, for example, that a President, with ample time for consideration, had initiated the nuclear exchange with a limited strike in connection with a conventional war in Europe (the problems inherent in issuing such an order will be discussed below). A subsequent satellite detection of infrared plumes from Soviet launches still might indicate anything from a full-scale attack on the United States to a counter-escalation in Europe. And by the time the early warning radars unambiguously confirmed that at least *some* missiles were heading toward the American mainland, less than fifteen minutes—perhaps only eight if submarine missiles were used—would remain before impact. And while it is unlikely that all the warning systems would send a completely false message of a Soviet attack or completely miss an actual attack, the multiple overlapping systems *are*, in fact, likely to send conflicting signals, requiring interpretation under extreme pressure. Misinterpreting a limited Soviet attack might trigger a catastrophic full-scale launch; while the opposite error would invite disaster. And how to interpret a submarine missile launch against a radar site? Civilian theorists might opine confidently that it was obviously the first step in a full-scale counterforce attack, but could, or should, a President then let fly with everything he has? As one high-ranking Air Force general put it, "There is just not enough time to do anything."

To make matters worse, decisions may have to be taken as the President and other command authorities are scrambling to aircraft or hardened shelters. There have been a number of such mobilization exercises; not surprisingly, they have usually been chaotic. And the more "flexible" the response options, of course, the less likely it is that any national command authority will understand their full implications. The Reagan administration has vastly multiplied the list of possible Soviet targets, and modern computers can instantaneously generate thousands of attack-option "menus." But even if the President—Richard Nixon, Gerald Ford, Jimmy Carter, Ronald Reagan—could choose the "right" option from the welter of possible choices, it is far from clear that military commands can execute such finely discriminated strategies. Indeed, it is far more likely that both the implementation and the "signal" to the Soviets will be confused. The discouraging history of "signalling" in Vietnam has been blissfully ignored by the "war-fighting" intellectuals.

The principle of central control itself can seriously conflict with war-fighting requirements. The conventional perception is that only the President can order the use of a nuclear weapon; but substantially greater delegation is essential in wartime to prevent the possibility that a "decapitating" strike—against Washington, D.C., for instance—would disable the entire command structure. More important, the vulnerabilities of the nuclear weapon command and control system are such that a single central authority almost certainly could *not* maintain reliable communications with individual units in wartime. Without substantial delegation of launch authority, in other words, there is serious danger of a major Soviet attack being answered either not at all, or ineffectively. But substantial delegation invalidates the entire principle of controlled escalation, and, of course, vastly increases the danger of the accidental or the feckless launch that would evoke an all-out spasm response from the Soviets. Delegation, in short, presents excruciating decisions for which there are no reliable guides.

The practical limitations of the nuclear command and control system have, for the most part, been simply ignored by "nuclear war-fighting" theorists.* The decision to launch a Minuteman missile, for example, is communicated from high authority to a hundred Launch Control Centers, each controlling ten missiles. Two officers in the control center must execute a specified procedure—inserting a twelve-digit coded key into a command box—to execute a command to a silo,

---

*In military jargon, command and control systems are known as "C³" or "C³I" (pronounced "see-three-eye") systems, for Communications, Command, Control, and Intelligence. Until recently, their development has lagged far behind weapons technology, probably because as a joint project of all the services they have usually lacked for a bureaucratic home, and so were consistently short-changed at budget-cutting time, as choices were made between favored service weapon systems and C³I systems that served only a vague common good.

where another two-man crew must perform a similar procedure to launch the missile. The attack order from higher authority, however, would be communicated to the control center via leased commercial lines that are quite vulnerable both to the blast effects and to the electromagnetic pulse that would result from nuclear explosions. The backup systems—radio spectrum antennae—are even more vulnerable. (A high-altitude nuclear blast, it will be recalled, will generate a powerful burst of electromagnetic energy that could disable unprotected electronic systems across the entire country.)* The control centers themselves are apparently less able to withstand nuclear blasts than the silos, so an attack on a single control center might effectively disable ten missiles. Conservative planning requires the assumption that the Launch Control Centers themselves or their communication systems would be out of commission in the very first minutes of a nuclear attack.

Missile submarine communications present even more difficult problems. Primary communication to submarines is via fixed, land-based, radio-spectrum, Very Low Frequency (VLF) transmitters.† Since VLF signals penetrate only a few meters into the seawater, submarines on active patrol trail either a long antenna wire on the surface, or more safely but less reliably, an antenna buoy just under the surface. Depending on the nature of the patrol, the submarine may be in contact on a continuing basis or only intermittently, since the trailing antenna is the piece of equipment most readily detectable by Soviet

*Minuteman silos themselves were hardened against electromagnetic pulse (EMP) during the 1970s, and additional protection was provided to the Launch Control Centers. A Defense Science Board report released in 1976, however, concluded that "the effects of EMP on the enormously complex leased telephone circuits are not (and, in our opinion, cannot be) understood well enough to assess with reasonable confidence the extent of their vulnerability to EMP." There are further vulnerabilities. A solar storm in 1972 shut down portions of a key AT&T nationwide trunk line because of esoteric "magneto-hydrodynamic effects." A high-altitude nuclear blast would creat such effects at magnitudes many multiples of the solar storm's.

†VLF is a "clumsy" frequency, requiring very tall and very vulnerable transmitting towers. It is used because it has an effective range of some 10,000 kilometers, which makes it, in addition to its water-penetration, capability, an ideal medium for communicating with distant submarines. Backup Extremely Low Frequency (ELF) systems exist and are being further developed, but they are equally vulnerable to attack (one antenna, buried in Michigan, is 56 miles long); they have the advantage that their signals are transmitted worldwide, and can be picked up by submarines several hundred feet below the surface. Their major disadvantage is that communications in the *basso profundissimo* part of the spectrum is very slow. A single "bit," that is, merely an "on" or an "off" signal, takes about 100 seconds to transmit because of the great length of the ELF wave; a simple three-number message would require minutes, and a normal message could take several days. One possibility may be to broadcast a continuous signal that, if it stops, orders submarines, particularly missile submarines, to position themselves for more detailed instructions on other frequencies.

antisubmarine warfare forces. The shore-based VLF transmitters are obviously easily targeted, very difficult to harden, and in any case, well known to the Soviets, so it must be assumed that they would be attacked and put out of commission at the very start of hostilities, probably by short-trajectory offshore submarine-launched missiles.

With no ground-based communication systems able to survive the early stages of a nuclear attack, American command instructions would have to be communicated entirely by airborne control posts and relay stations. McNamara created the airborne system that, in main outline, has served as the essential command and control nerve center until the present day. The basic principle is that, in a crisis, a squadron of EC-135 communications and reconnaissance aircraft—recently supplemented by several more modern "jumbo jet" E-4s—would fly randomized circular flight patterns within signal range of the Minuteman fields and bomber "fail-safe" points. One aircraft, the "Looking Glass" command post, is, in fact, airborne at all times. Two aircraft are designated as "National Emergency Airborne Command Posts," one of which, in all probability, would carry either the President or the Vice-President. The planes could communicate with each other over UHF (Ultra High Frequency) radio bands or over backup LF (Low Frequency) wavelengths, which are less susceptible to nuclear ionization effects, and could send LF or UHF signals to missile Launch Control Centers, or UHF instructions direct to Minuteman silos. The Navy, at the same time, created a similar system of so-called TACAMO (for "Take Charge and Move Out") aircraft, that can relay signals from shore-based transmitters, or the central airborne command posts, to nuclear submarines from their own on-board VLF transmitters.

Throughout the entire decade of the 1970s and well into the present day, there has been no basis for anyone to assume that the airborne command system would work. In the first place, a serious Soviet attack would have a good chance of catching all the planes but the "Looking Glass" on the ground. Normal readiness places the EC-135s on fifteen-minute alert. They require nine minutes to start their engines and take off, leaving only six minutes for crew scrambling. New upgraded command planes, E-4 jumbo jets, require a minute or two longer warm-up. The *longest* Soviet submarine-launched missile trajectory would require about fifteen minutes to target; and even if the planes did get airborne within the fifteen-minute standard, they would still need an additional two minutes to fly outside a blast's lethal range.

Assuming the planes got airborne, they would be extremely vulnerable to nuclear blast effects. Throughout the 1970s, *none* of the EC-135s was hardened against electromagnetic pulse, which would in all likelihood burn out all of their communication systems. Even in the mid-1980s, only the two E-4 National Emergency Command Posts were hardened against electromagnetic pulse. On the heroic assumption that the communication equipment survived, however, a nuclear environment would probably black out all but the LF and VLF transmissions. But to transmit on those band widths, the planes must trail copper wire antennae, up to two miles long, which can make handling and maneuvering difficult, even in weather much milder than the catastrophic conditions that are likely to obtain anywhere near an area of nuclear attacks. Lost antennae are apparently not uncommon on routine flights, and trailing antennae, in addition, would be efficient collectors of high-voltage bursts of energy. To complicate matters, the TACAMO planes must execute a tight circling maneuver to maintain their antennae in a vertical position in order to assure that their VLF signals penetrate the ocean.

It is highly questionable, in short, that the essential unbroken communication link from the Emergency Command Post through the relays of EC-135s, on to bomber deployments and missile fields, and to nuclear submarines through the TACAMO planes, could be maintained in conditions remotely like those that would obtain in wartime. The TACAMO capability, in particular, for most of the period since its creation has been more theoretical than real. On-station standards were generally not met, the planes themselves were propeller-driven with limited range, they still have no airborne refuelling ability, and, amazingly, for part of the 1970s their radio equipment was apparently incompatible with that of the central command post EC-135s.

The nature of the airborne command post system also points up the problems of command system endurance. It is not reasonable to expect the airborne control system, with all the problems of atmospheric turbulence, electromagnetic pulses, and drifting particulate matter, to endure for more than a few hours, even if some planes, with refuelling, could be kept aloft for considerably longer. Dust ingestion, for example, disabled several planes flying near the vicinity of the Mount St. Helen's volcanic eruption. Lethal radioactivity could also pose a danger to crews, since the airborne launch control planes would have to fly within 150 miles of Minuteman fields in order to send a UHF signal.

All the elements in the system, in fact, conspire toward a rapid decision on a maximum launch—"use them or lose them." The bombers heading toward their fail-safe points, for instance, would outdistance the radios on the airborne control centers after about 400 miles. There is a backup system—the Emergency Rocket Command System—consisting of Minutemen with UHF transmitters instead of warheads. In theory, an airborne command post could launch a communications rocket, and use it to relay a UHF message to distant bombers. The actual reliability of such a system is highly problematic and, in any case, an emergency communications rocket would have a life of only twenty minutes or so. Submarines are under much less time pressure, but they *would* be under pressure to launch all their missiles at once, since a launch would make them easily detectable by, say, prowling Backfires. Since a single Trident launch would involve 192 separate warheads, it would place sharp constraints on the options available to targeters, even assuming that command and control could be maintained.

The serious deficiencies in command and control system do not mean that at any time in the 1970s the uncertainties of a Soviet "decapitating" first strike would have been appreciably less than those involved in a first strike against missile silos. The targeting requirements, in fact, would still have been quite demanding. Severe disruption of the American command structure would not, in all likelihood, have meant that the Soviets would have escaped retaliation—although that is by no means absolutely certain—but simply that the war would have proceeded in ways that were overwhelmingly governed by random chance.

Systems would presumably function better if the nuclear exchange began from a "fully generated" alert status. Casual invocation of alert conditions, however, ignores the serious potential interactions of a joint Soviet-American alert. Although American forces have gone on alert status many times in the postwar period, the Soviets have never done so, so there is no experience of interactive effects. For example, some 80 percent of Soviet missile submarines remain in port during peacetime. In a situation of high alert, they could be expected to "surge" to their sea-based patrol stations. The U.S. Navy would have a powerful incentive to interdict their passage through the several dangerous chokepoints that obstruct their access to open water. The Soviets would have a similar interest in pre-empting the dispersal of ground-launched cruise missiles in Europe. Alert conditions, moreover, degrade rapidly after a very few days, because of the suspension of normal maintenance operations and simple fatigue. Command aircraft, for instance, cannot stay aloft indefinitely. Readiness will quickly "gravitate toward an equilibrium point that is far below initial optimum level." Commanders will become alarmed as their war-fighting capabilities deteriorate. The conditions of alert themselves, in short, will create enormous pressures toward hostilities.

Limited-war theorists occasionally argue that second-strike scenarios provide a less realistic test case for "flexible response" than the use of nuclear weapons to supplement conventional warfare—in effect, the Soviet "combined arms" principle. But the problems associated with the use of "tactical" or "battlefield" nuclear weapons—against a massed armored assault, for example—may well prove insuperable. In the first place, authorization must be received from the American central command authority, most probably with the consent of the relevant NATO power, which would have a strong interest in not initiating a nuclear exchange on its own territory. The procedure is designed to take twenty-four hours from the initial battlefield request, and recent exercises indicate that it may actually take up to sixty, by which time a fluid battlefield situation is likely to have changed dramatically. As one analyst put it: "the operational requirements of bottom-up release border on the impossible."

The complicated procedures for the release of battlefield weapons, of course, could be circumvented by a determined American President. In a crisis, he could order deep strikes against Soviet military targets and troop formations with medium-range missiles like the Pershing II or with deep interdiction aircraft. He would be taking an enormous risk, for Soviet military writings have insisted for thirty years that any nuclear weapon fired against the Soviet homeland would signal the start of general nuclear war. With good reason, they do not regard such weapons as the Pershing IIs or forward-based nuclear bombers as "tactical." There could well be, in other words, only a single "rung" on the "flexible response" escalation ladder.

The decision-making process itself could have significant effects on the course of a war. Nuclear weapons for battlefield use are stored in special supply depots behind forward defensive lines and would have to be transported to the front lines if their use was being considered. If a commander had *any* thought of using nuclear weapons, he would be obliged to request authorization at the very earliest possible time. But the dispersal of the weapons would almost certainly be observed by the Soviets, and could well provoke a pre-emptive attack. In addition, large numbers of key NATO weapon systems—the major artillery units, the F-4, F-15, and F-111 fighter bombers—are dual-capable, that is, they can deploy both conventional and nuclear weapons. Under the pressure of a severe attack, a local commander would be torn between committing his dual-capable forces with conventional weapons, or withholding them for possible nuclear use and perhaps jeapordizing his position as a result. And finally, since NATO's fundamental strategy is a defensive one, on NATO territory, the sheer destructive power of nuclear weapons, even "small" ones in the 1–10-kiloton range, presents enormous moral and military problems in so densely populated an area as Europe. Fallout effects could be lethally unpredictable, electromagnetic pulse could disrupt all military communications, and soldiers could suffer retinal burns, or "flash blindness," tens of kilometers from a blast, perhaps as much as 30 or 40 kilometers away if pupils were distended at night in clear weather.

Wohlstetter insists that neither the "BOOB" ("bolt-out of-the-blue") attack scenario nor the limited exchange growing out of conventional warfare in Europe is the most plausible tactical nuclear scenario. (His use of the pejorative "BOOB" presumably signifies that he is denying paternity.) He postulates a Soviet attack on northwest Iran, and assumes that they might use nuclear weapons to prevent NATO troop concentrations in remote bases in, say, Turkey, with little risk of collateral damage. Other analysts have suggested that NATO might use nuclear demolition charges to prevent Soviet passage through key Iranian mountain passes. Both scenarios, however, appear to beg the question. If nuclear weapons could be reliably confined to remote areas, where they would have few, if any, collateral effects—where they could be safely substituted for conventional weapons, in other words—the command, control, and response problem would be comparatively simple. But isolated use scenarios have a strange air of unreality. Michael Howard asks the question, *"What is it about?"* The use of a nuclear weapon, he argues, and the catastrophic risks that such use entails, must bear some relation to a political objective. Survival of the West might qualify as such an objective; slowing troop movements in Iranian mountains almost assuredly does not, particularly since the same task could be accomplished by conventional weapons without the risk of incinerating the world.

Undersecretary of Defense David Packard (1969–72) made a valiant but unavailing effort to address the stark deficiencies in the American command and control apparatus, but the problem did not receive sustained attention until the end of the Carter administration, and was made a high-priority effort by the new Reagan administration. Virtually all components of the system are being upgraded, with particular attention to better earth-based and satellite-based early warning systems, but it will be years before all the essential repairs are accomplished. And the central contradictions will persist. Extreme hardness can be purchased only at the cost of flexibility. The principles of negative and positive controls will continue to compete for priority. Long lists of flexible choices will be irrelevant in face of the very limited information available to decision makers. The essential telephone circuits will continue to be vulnerable, and the system of airborne controls will continue to be seriously deficient. The priority in protecting communications will remain outward from the command center; post-attack or post-decision assessments will continue to present entirely different orders of difficulty. The principle of "assured destruction" will gain rather greater assurance, but the country will emphatically not have the capability to fight a "protracted" limited nuclear war. As a leading scholar of the command and control apparatus concluded after a thorough review in 1985: "the existing command structure cannot begin to support a doctrine of extended nuclear flexible response. . . . the technological and procedural foundations of such a structure have scarcely been defined, much less conceived. . . . procurement of such a structure has not been funded, is bound to be costly, and would compete with force modernization for scarce resources."

What is to be made, then, of the extended Soviet writings on "combined arms" assaults? In the first place, "quote-mongering" does not always make the best analysis; an enormous body of authoritative Soviet literature arguing the uncontrollability of nuclear war can be offset against the "combined arms" theorists. By the same token, the same type of "combined arms" and counterforce writings can be found in NATO journals. Military men, and Melvin Laird, have hedged on official American statements on pre-emption just as Soviet military leaders have. In the 1950s, Curtis LeMay did not even hedge: "If I see that the Russians are amassing their planes for an attack, I'm going to knock the shit out of them before they take off the ground." Immediately after signing the ABM Treaty, American leaders made essentially the same statements on preserving defensive options as Marshal Grechko did, and, particularly since President Reagan's "Star Wars" speech, are pressing ahead very aggressively indeed. It is interesting also that Lomov, in the text quoted earlier, cites the results of *NATO* exercises to demonstrate the feasibility of atomic maneuver warfare, and Sokolovsky's discussion of nuclear "war fighting" is based on extensive citations of Western authors. Moreover, authorities like the Sokolovsky and Lomov editors generally do not speak of nuclear war as a *limited* war; they deride the very notion. Rather, they steadfastly insist that the introduction of nuclear weapons will quickly escalate into an all-out exchange; they merely insist that all branches of the services will continue to play important roles during such an exchange. The American Army and Navy have long argued along similar lines.

Wohlstetter is inclined to insist that the Soviets have already solved the command and control problem. They have, indeed, paid considerable attention to creating thousands of hardened shelters for their political leadership, which they clearly value more than the U.S. public does its own. In addition, they have created impressively hardened cable links radiating outward from Moscow to their missile complexes, and have always paid diligent attention to early warning capabilities. All of these systems improve the Soviet capacity to ride out a surprise attack, but they do not solve the central dilemmas of protracted nuclear war. Soviet intelligence from *outside* their national borders, from Europe during a conventional war, for example, is likely to be rather inferior. Wohlstetter is impressed with low-orbit Soviet observation satellites, which he concedes have a high failure rate and require frequent replacement. But this, he insists, gives them "substantial flexibility"— presumably rather like the T-62 tank. Other Western analysts view the Soviet satellites as merely unreliable. The much-touted Soviet civil defense procedures were tested during the Chernobyl nuclear power plant disaster, which, of course, did not remotely approach the conditions of a nuclear war; by all accounts, they quickly degenerated into chaos.

John Van Oudenaren, in an excellent analysis, suggests that Soviet doctrinal writings are rarely confined by their own incapacities. In contrast to the West, where contradictions between theory and capabilities are exhaustively analyzed and debated, contradictions between Soviet theory and practice tend simply to be incorporated unresolved into doctrine. A pervasive inconsistency between ideals and actuality is inherent in the very concept of a Marxist state, or any other millenarian system. "War-fighting" rhetoric in Soviet military writings, therefore, is hardly proof that the Soviets have solved the central dilemmas of nuclear war, however it may accurately reflect their aspirations. Khrushchev made the most outlandish claims for his rocket forces long before he possessed any; and the Sokolovsky editors were writing confidently about Soviet antimissile defenses in 1962 as if they actually existed. The Sokolovsky editors, in fact, state baldly that "military theory must outstrip the development of the means for armed conflict."

There is no question that the Soviet military has been less constrained by its political leadership in the accumulation of nuclear weapons than the American military has been. Throughout the 1970s and into the present day, if it came to a nuclear war, the Soviet Union could, in gross terms, launch considerably more firepower faster, both at Europe and the United States, than the United States could muster in return. But both countries would still be destroyed as functioning societies. Donald Hansen, in a wide-ranging critique of the prominent "war-fighting" theories, puts the issue this way: "With due respect to Gray and Nitze, the issue is not whether the English language can be employed to produce a suitable definition of strategic superiority but, rather, whether the definition can be brought into some plausible array of connections with [the real world]."

"Metaphysicians," Bertrand Russell once remarked, "like savages, are apt to imagine a magical connection between words and things." The higher realms of nuclear theology in the United States have indeed suffered from such tendencies. The assumption of liberal theorists in the United States that Western nuclear doctrine was the only possible one—that the discrepancies between Soviet and Western writings merely reflected Russian backwardness, as if Soviet defense writers were a species of slightly retarded RAND analysts—was fair game for conservative critics of liberal arms control theory. Consider, for example, Arthur Schlesinger's supercilious comment that Soviet diplomats were "ignorant of the higher calculus of deterrence"; or Herbert Scoville's confident, and quite erroneous, predictions that a "self-denying" American policy to eschew accurate missiles would evoke imitative behavior by the Soviets.

But the deficiencies of liberal "assured destruction" theory do not prove the reasonableness or the feasibility of nuclear war fighting. Military men, as opposed to theorists and intellectuals, of course, must grope toward provision for worst cases. American generals and Soviet Marshals are paid, after all, to think about fighting wars: what if the Soviets *have* deluded themselves that they can win a nuclear war? It is the task of political leaders to keep such efforts in perspective and under control. The hardest lesson for theorists, however, may be that there are no answers, despite the plethora of intellectually appealing and deductively rigorous nuclear eschatologies. The most plausible strategy—something like "assured destruction"—may be a wholly unsatisfactory one, indeed, as Fred Iklé charges, even somewhat crazy. But the most intellectualy satisfying strategies may be wholly implausible.

# CHAPTER 20

# Rearming America

## The Spending Window

As David Stockman tells it, it was mostly a mistake. In the first hectic weeks of the new Reagan administration, the young congressman-turned-budget director visited Caspar Weinberger, the new Defense Secretary, to patch together a "defense plug" number for a new federal budget. There was no question that defense spending would go up—it was a campaign commitment; the only question was by how much. Reagan had variously pledged 5 percent and 8–9 percent real growth in defense, and Stockman and Weinberger quickly agreed to split the difference at 7 percent.

It was some weeks later that Stockman realized that his increase came on top of a Carter lame-duck budget that already provided big defense spending boosts, plus a congressional "get-well" package after the failed Iranian rescue attempt, plus another Reagan "get-well" package upon taking office. Taken together, they added up to a 15 percent real increase *before* the new 7 percent was tacked on. But Weinberger was already running with the numbers and selling them hard, complete with cartoon presentations for the President contrasting a muscular American fighting man—his budget—with the bespectacled little wimp that would result from any cuts. Congress was in no mood to resist; Gallup polls showed that a clear majority of the American public wanted a stronger defense. By any standard, the military budget increases approved during Reagan's first term were enormous. During his first five years in office, military outlays grew, in real terms, by 50 percent. The military's share of total federal outlays grew from 23.2 percent to 27.6 percent during the same period, and its share of GNP from 5.7 percent to 7.4 percent. Total spending, corrected for inflation, rose by a cumulative amount of $330 billion.

373

The Reagan buildup was the third great American defense spending spasm in the postwar period. A constant-dollar chart of American military outlays since World War II presents a fairly level, if undulating, plain, broken by three great volcanic upwellings. The first, and the biggest, is in 1950 at the outbreak of the Korean War; the second begins in the early 1960s with the Kennedy-McNamara buildup and crests with the height of the involvement in Vietnam; and the final mountain, slightly larger than Kennedy's, marks the great upsurge in spending in 1981–85. The Reagan buildup is also the only one that begins and ends entirely during a time of peace—our "only peacetime war," one correspondent called it.

Like the earlier Kennedy buildup, the Reagan defense program invented few new weapons; most of the money was spent on buying hardware developed during the previous decade. Military investment had been badly squeezed throughout the 1970s, and well over half of the new spending ($190 billion out of $330 billion) went for procurement and research and development, with a large share of the remainder—again like Kennedy's—devoted to improving the readiness of conventional forces, particularly the Navy and the forces in Europe.

It is the disorderliness of the Reagan buildup, however, that distinguishes it from Kennedy's and McNamara's. The 1960s spending splurge began relatively slowly in 1962, then soared higher with the expanding involvement in Vietnam. Reagan's spending surge was concentrated very heavily in his first two full fiscal years, until Congress, frightened by looming budget deficits, began to rebel in 1983, and finally brought the buildup to "a shuddering halt" in 1985. The early rush to make the most of the spending window surprised even seasoned Pentagon bureaucrats: "It was kind of a unique situation. . . . Suddenly money was available . . . they just dusted off the old plans. Under Carter's zero-based bugeting, they had priority bands—band one, band two, band three. There was a lot of crap from band five and six that got funded."

Every military buildup in history has been accompanied by waste and fraud, and Reagan's was no exception: its pell-mell character virtually ensured scandal, and the continuing stream of stories about $600 toilet seats, $900 coffee pots, and $100 hammers undercut much of the consensus supporting a stronger defense. Even Weinberger—transmuted from his days as the feared Nixon budget-cutter, "Cap the Knife," into a relentless salesman and sloganeer—conceded the possibility in 1984 that "the Department has paid exorbitant prices for spare parts."

But waste and fraud do not explain the pervasive disappointment among even defense-minded commentators that set in midway through the great upsurge in spending. As Edward Luttwack expressed it: "Vast sums of money and the true dedication of many have gone into the upkeep of American military power, only to yield to pervasive failure in the conduct of war and an unfavorable balance of strength for safeguarding the peace."

Or, in the words of Richard Stubbings, a long-time federal defense analyst:

there is increasing controversy over the extent to which our real defense capabilities have improved. Many experts, on all sides of the political spectrum have criticized the inefficiency of the recent defense buildup. . . . Today, four years into the Reagan buildup, our force structure is almost exactly the same. Moreover, force increases planned for the future . . . are quite small. . . . None of the services has seen a major increase in the rate of procurement. . . . long-standing readiness problems remain despite substantial added funding for readiness-related areas.

Or, finally, according to a *Wall Street Journal* columnist: "The real crisis in defense is not defense input, but the downward spiral in defense output. What America really 'can't afford' is to keep paying more and more for defense while getting less and less of it."

The poor performance of Reagan's and Weinberger's Pentagon is often exaggerated; there have in fact been significant accomplishments. The quality and morale of existing forces has increased substantially. The percent of high school graduates recruited has improved, retentions are up, and shortages of skilled maintenance and engineering personnel are much less severe than they were in the 1970s. (The improvement in recruiting success, of course, received a major assist from the severe 1981–82 recession.) The money spent on readiness and spare parts has had a clear impact. The combat readiness of major weapon systems, like the Air Force's tactical fighters, is much better, flying time has improved, fuel and ammunition are much more available, prepositioned stocks of equipment are in much better shape, and performance has improved, by some accounts dramatically, in large-scale NATO exercises. There have been major, if largely invisible, investments in the nuclear command and control structure, long an area of shameful neglect. Critics of the Reagan-Weinberger defense budgets, in short, often conveniently overlook the severity of the deficits caused by almost ten years of flat or falling real defense budgets combined with steadily rising military salaries and pensions.

Still, after giving all possible credit to the genuine accomplishments of the Reagan-Weinberger defense buildup, the fact remains that the huge upsurge in spending has purchased a very modest increment in fighting capabilities, far less than might reasonably be expected from a 50 percent real increase in outlays. Total men and women under arms, for example, have increased very marginally from 2,050,000 to only 2,150,000, although there has been some strengthening of reserve forces. Between 1980 and 1985, the number of tanks available to the Army went up by about 2,000, all of them the highly capable new M-1 Abrams; but the production rate of new tanks was only about 800 per year, or one fourth the Soviet tank production rate in 1984. Similarly, the Pentagon's master plan calls for 6,900 new Bradley armored fighting vehicles over a ten-year period; the Soviets, in the meantime, by the Pentagon's own figures, have been producing armored fighting vehicles at the rate of 4,500 in a *single* year.

Tactical air forces increased slightly, from 3,200 in 1980 to 4,000 planes in 1985, and older models were steadily retired, but the rate of aircraft procurement has actually *dropped* since the late 1970s, and because of the shorter production lines, unit costs are up sharply. The Rapid Deployment Force, a top national priority since the late 1970s, was still "forming" in 1985; and the new infantry light division that would be its backbone was being created entirely by drawing down troops from other division establishments. By 1985, the first of 100 B-1B long-range penetrating bombers was finally entering service after at least ten years of controversy—twenty, if its parent, the B-70, is included—but the planes have been plagued with technical difficulties after so many designs and redesigns, and the program is a pallid contrast to the 750 B-52s procured in the 1950s—200 in 1958 alone. The MX missile also finally appears to be on track, with 50 being deployed; but, again, it is not much to show for fifteen years of work, particularly when compared with the original Minuteman's five-year development cycle and peak 300-per-year production rate. There are also reports of guidance systems problems with the first deployed MXs. Most telling, and most disappointing in many ways, after all the emphasis on "readiness" improvement, a congressional investigation in March 1983,—having conceded that some substantial progress had been made—concluded that the Army still did *"not have the men and material to sustain combat operations in a major contingency."* (italics in the original)

The defense-minded critics, in short, have ample grounds for their disappointment. Truman's and Kennedy's military buildups, whatever their wisdom, produced quantum leaps—order of magnitude changes—in military capabilities. The Reagan spending surge, although comparable in real terms to both of its predecessors, appears to have accomplished only marginal force improvements. With events still unfolding rapidly it is, of course, much too soon for definitive judgments; still, in searching for reasons for the apparently poor performance of the Reagan Pentagon, at least three factors stand out. The first is the increasing sclerosis of the Pentagon's weapons acquisition process. The second is in the realm of policy: the enormously expensive and potentially dangerous procurement tilt toward the surface Navy. The third, and most pervasive, is the continuing impact of technology in shaping the instruments and methods of war.

The brief golden age, the classical period, of the military-industrial complex was in the 1950s. It is extraordinary to consider, thirty years later, how much the American military machine is still grounded in designs, concepts, and actual weapons dating from a short five- to seven-year flowering of military technology during the Eisenhower era: the hardened, silo-based, Minuteman missile; the nuclear-powered missile-launching submarine; accurate ballistic missile inertial guidance systems; the long-range penetrating bomber, still primarily the B-52; the F-4 Phantom, the archetype of the powerful jet fighter bomber that has dominated air combat ever since (design began in the mid-1950s, the first flight was in 1958, production continued until 1979, with more than 5,000 still deployed throughout the world); the Sidewinder homing air-to-air missile; radar-and infrared-guided surface antiaircraft missiles; the M-60 tank, only now being slowly displaced by the M-1; the M-113 armored personnel carrier; the list goes on and on.

The genuine breakthroughs in the last twenty-five years, by contrast, make a very short list indeed: certainly the cruise missile guidance system, although the cruise itself is a 1950s weapon dating from the Regulus and Snark missiles; the MIRVed missile, although again development groundwork was well under way in the 1950s; and perhaps look-down radar. Other major developments are more in the nature of embellishments and footnotes to the basic 1950s systems and concepts. Inertial guidance systems have gained the crucial last few hundred meters of accuracy; *Ohio*-class Trident missile submarines are bigger, more powerful, and can cruise faster and deeper than the original Polaris missile submarines; the NAVSTAR satellites may greatly improve submarine missile accuracy, although the system is not yet proven; precision-guided weapons have progressed enormously, although their performance under the exacting conditions of actual warfare is still open to large questions.

The declining ability of the Pentagon to design and procure new weapons was already evident during McNamara's tenure. His controversial F-111 (TFX) fighter bomber, for example, has never been a successful plane. Only 240 were ever deployed; it never played the dual-purpose Air Force/Navy carrier attack-bomber role envisioned for it; and it had to be withdrawn from service in Vietnam because of its poor performance. The Nixon/Ford administrations did not buy any major new weapon systems, although they began the long development cycles of the F-15s, F-16s, and F-14s, the MX missile, and the Trident submarines. The F-14 illustrates the contradictory pulls in the procurement process. The plane is an extraordinarily expensive aircraft—up to $40 million in 1985 dollars, depending on how the costs of continuing development and weapon systems are allocated. The F-14, when it is working, is apparently a superb airplane. Its great expense stems in good part from the problem of designing a large and heavy aircraft that could serve as an agile air combat fighter—lack of agility was the F-4's only shortcoming. The F-14's large size and weight was essential because it was intended as a platform for the new Phoenix missile, an all-weather, 80-mile radius, air-to-air target-seeking weapon, with supporting radar able to track a large number of different targets at one time and to foil sophisticated electronic countermeasures.

The point of all this capability is to defend against barrage missile attacks from Soviet Backfires, one of the most dangerous threats to the surface fleet. The Phoenix, however, has been a trouble-plagued weapon; part way through its initial deployment an entirely new model was put into production to solve serious reliability problems. More important, at $1 million-plus per missile, the Navy has bought relatively few Phoenixes and been quite wary of testing them, certainly never in a barrage counterattack against a simulated massive air assault on a carrier fleet, the mission they were designed to perform. But unless the Phoenix is a reliable, well-tested weapon, and in good supply, the expensive capabilities of the F-14 are substantially wasted.

To make matters worse, recognizing that the enormous cost of the F-14 was a severe constraint on force modernization, the Navy designed another fighter/attack plane, the F/A-18, to form the low end of a modern "high-low" carrier fighter mix, just as the Air Force developed the lower cost F-16 to supplement its expensive F-15. But because the plane was not ready for production until the procurement budget was already squeezed, it is being delivered only in small production runs—eighty-four a year most recently—raising its unit cost to about $30 million, which makes it one of the most expensive planes in the American inventory. Less capability is being purchased at almost a comparable price, and the procurement squeeze continues.

The saga of the A-6E Intruder is a similar sad tale. The A-6E is a subsonic carrier-based attack bomber, another weapon that dates from the Eisenhower era, that was refitted in the late 1970s with complex electronic equipment to allow it to attack targets at night and in bad weather. But the electronics made it very expensive to produce, so only a few planes were purchased—twelve in 1981 and 1982, eight in 1983, and six in 1984, when production was discontinued. The short production lines made the planes much more expensive than planned—nearly $40 million per unit in 1984, or almost the same as for an F-14, for a thoroughly modest capability. Ironically, when the U.S. Navy wanted to make a show of force over Lebanon in 1983, it sent these enormously expensive planes in a *daylight* attack, in which one was shot down and its pilot captured by Syrian troops using the simplest, visually-aimed, antiaircraft weapons.

The recent effort to expand airlift and sealift capability is another case in point. Military lift capability has not kept pace over the years with the enormous consumption of materiel in modern war, despite the addition of the huge C-5 Galaxy transport planes that performed so spectacularly in the 1973 Yom Kippur War. The C-5 is an enormous airplane—in theory, only seventeen of them could have handled the entire Berlin airlift. But airplanes, even the biggest ones, do not have a lot of carrying capability. The C-5 will carry only about 100 tons fully loaded, *or* a single M-1 tank, *or* 343 soldiers. In any war in Europe or the Middle East lasting more than a few weeks, sealift will be the only way to keep troops supplied. It would take twenty C-5s working nonstop for a month to deliver about the same equipment to Europe as can be carried on one modern sealift ship. And once a war is more than a week or so old—three weeks in the Middle East—the ships are, paradoxically, faster than planes. One Navy sealift ship, in 1984, delivered 268 tanks, 661 trucks and trailers, and tons of other materiel to Europe in eleven days and, at top speed, could have made the trip in five; the entire fleet of 70 C-5s could not carry that much in five days. But sealift had been allowed to deteriorate to a shocking extent: the cargo ships operated by the Military Sealift Command were reduced from sixty-nine in 1970 to just *four* in 1979, and the number of ships available in reserve from the Merchant Marine and private carriers had declined almost as alarmingly.

Weinberger gave lift capability a high priority, but an instructive donnybrook immediately broke out over how to supply it. The Air Force and the Pentagon professionals wanted an entirely new cargo plane, the C-X, for "Cargo Experimental," unfazed by the fact that it would take seven to ten years to deploy. Lockheed, the C-5's builder, and in serious financial trouble, fought a hard and ultimately victorious battle for a modified C-5. Boeing's offer to supply refitted 747s, only slightly smaller than the C-5, at one fourth the cost and with immediate availability, was simply brushed aside—it was not a "military" plane. The Navy, in the meantime, completed a Carter initiative to purchase eight fast new cargo ships from private shippers, then quietly let the matter drop; the Navy has always preferred buying glamorous instruments like carriers and F-14s over tending cargo.

Defense analysts have estimated that a conventional war in Europe will require about 800,000 tons of supplies in the first thirty days. The fifty new C-5s on order will cost about $11 billion; they could carry perhaps 70,000 tons across the Atlantic in a month. The eight new ships cost less than $1 billion; they could transport about 160,000 tons in the same time period. Forty ships, at a cost, presumably, of about $5 billion, or less than half the price of the C-5s, would do the whole job. Some different mix of ships and planes seems clearly to have been called for—and, "military" planes or no, four 747s have to be a better deal than one C-5 at the same price. The nation, in short, has made some progress toward solving its military lift problems; but it has spent enormous amounts of money to do so, and, in the end, has purchased only relatively marginal improvements.

Procurement horror stories can be multiplied at depressing length. The Bradley fighting vehicle is seven times more expensive than the M-113 armored personnel carrier it is replacing. It is so expensive because it is designed to function almost like a tank; troops will remain inside the Bradley while using their weapons. But it is not really a tank; its armor is aluminum, and is too light to withstand Soviet armor-piercing shells. By concentrating troops inside the Bradley, vulnerability and casualties may well be increased. The Army's Patriot air defense system, with a total system price in excess of $10 billion, has suffered repeated delays, and unit costs have almost doubled in five years. The consequence, of course, is stretched-out production and fewer weapons—only 440 missiles were on order in 1985, hardly enough to make much difference in an all-out conventional war in Europe. The Sergeant York antiaircraft gun, the only weapon that Weinberger ever cancelled, burnt up $4 billion before it was scrapped. But, although the Bradley and the Sergeant York indicate the difficulties and failures of the procurement process, they do *not* prove the futility, as sometimes seems to be alleged, of investing in high-technology weapons. The right level of technology is a many-sided issue that will be treated separately below.

Weinberger might be forgiven his failure to solve the procurement conundrum; after all, no other Secretary of Defense has managed to do so. There are grounds, as well, for defending the free-for-all spending surge. There has always been a spastic pattern to American military investment. Weinberger had ample reason to assume that the spending window would slam shut in just a few years—leaving aside the question of whether the appearance of recklessness hastened its closing. Far less defensible, however, is the decision to concentrate resources on the Navy.

## The Wide Blue Oceans

Of roughly $90 billion in new funds allocated to the theater forces in the Reagan administration's first three years, considerably more than half was devoted to the Navy. John Lehman, the dynamic young Secretary of the Navy who held office during the first six years of the Reagan administration, managed to sell the concept of the 600-ship Navy, up from 475 in the late 1970s, organized around 15 carrier groups—an increase of three—and including in addition a major procurement program of the huge *Los Angeles*-class, cruise-missile-capable, nuclear attack submarines, being purchased at a rate of four per year at a unit cost of about $750 million. In all, the Navy grew by some 75 ships between 1980 and 1986, and procurement will need to continue at almost the same pace well into the 1990s to achieve the cherished 600-ship goal. It is, in Weinberger's words, "the most significant force expansion proposed by the Administration."

The centerpiece of the Weinberger naval program is the increase in carrier task groups, enormous floating conurbations, each centered on a massive aircraft carrier. The modern *Nimitz*-class nuclear-propelled carrier is 1,000 feet long and displaces 90,000 tons. It deploys some ninety airplanes: F-14 fighters, F-4 or F/A-18 fighter/attack planes, A-6 and A-7 nuclear-capable attack bombers, at least two early warning aircraft, antisubmarine patrol airplanes and helicopters, and a variety of aerial refuelling, transport, and other utility planes. Like a queen bee, it is surrounded by a swarm of smaller combat and utility ships, typically including two frigates, two cruisers, and two destroyers—armed with a variety of cruise missiles, antiaircraft surface to-air missiles, and antisubmarine warfare gear—and a fast 52,000-ton cargo ship to keep the convoy fed and supplied. At least one of the cruisers will be an *Aegis*-class ship, stuffed with electronic equipment designed to pick up attacking planes or missiles and manage the deployment of the carrier group's defensive weapons.

All of these ships and planes are very expensive. By itself, a *Nimitz*-class carrier costs about $3.5 billion, and the cost of its aircraft pushes the total over $5 billion. The supporting warships run from $200 million to $700 million, and the Aegis electronic warfare cruisers cost about $1 billion each. The entire group of combat ships, combat and patrol aircraft, and tender and utility ships costs perhaps $18 billion, employs some 8,000 people, and costs upward of $1 billion a year to operate.

For all its awesome majesty, a modern carrier group actually disposes of astonishingly little offensive striking power. Of the ninety planes on the carrier, only about thirty-four to thirty-six are attack planes—typically ten to twelve A-6s and twenty-four A-7s; all the rest, and the most expensive ones to boot, like the F-14, and all the elaborate antisubmarine and antiaircraft systems, are there *to defend the carrier.* About 95 percent of the enormous cost of the carrier group, that is, is devoted just to buying and defending a floating airport for some three dozen offensive war planes. F-111 bombers had to fly from England to participate in the air attack on Libya in 1986 because the entire Sixth Fleet in the Mediterranean could not muster enough offensive planes for two simultaneous attacks on a poorly defended, backward desert country.

The Navy is forced to spend such huge amounts of money and weaponry to protect its carriers, clearly, because carriers are so hugely expensive in the first place, and because in an era of long-range radar and long-distance missile-launching aircraft, any 1,000-foot chunk of floating metal is desperately vulnerable. Defenses are therefore the first order of business—the loss of a carrier would be an unthinkable catastrophe, an unbearable humiliation—and protective systems are layered and lavished upon the carrier group with unstinting prodigality. In such fashion, the modern carrier group is slowly evolving toward a splendid solipsism, plying the seas in isolated grandeur, ever more invulnerable and ever more harmless, its own final cause and final end, the realization in the modern world of the Hegelian *nous,* the ultimate self-regarding system.

The Navy, of course, has developed a military doctrine to support its procurement of large surface ships. It is the "maritime strategy," and it envisions, briefly, that upon the outbreak of a conventional war in Europe, American attack submarines will take on Soviet nuclear missile and attack submarines in their home ports, in the Barents Sea, for example, off the northern Eurasian coast where a great portion of the Soviet surface and submarine fleet is based. Carrier-based bombers will then attack the military bases and airfields that protect the Soviet fleet; and, finally, the Soviet hope of a breakthrough on the Central European front will be foiled by "horizontal escalation"—amphibious troop landings on the presumably now-undefended peripheries of the Soviet Union, diverting Soviet resources and allowing NATO ground forces time to regroup and counterattack.

The strategy has all the earmarks of a desperate improvisation to justify yearned-for weapon systems—mere "idle talk," William Kaufmann calls it. The assumptions that underlie it range from the risky to the wildly implausible. The American submarines attacking Soviet submarines in their home ports would have to traverse treacherous mine barriers and would be the target of intensive attack by all the Soviet Union's formidable shore-based antisubmarine warfare facilities. A carrier fleet steaming toward the Soviet Union would be under attack by Backfire bombers for at least two days before it could attack Soviet air bases itself. A land-based defensive air establishment would have enormous advantages over one precariously based at sea. And even if the strategy were utterly successful, the light division or so that plausibly could be landed on distant Soviet shores could hardly have a major effect on a land war in Europe in any case.

The central problem with a surface ship strategy is the vulnerability of large ships to antiship missiles, like the garden-variety Exocet, a French missile that is now in the inventories of at least eighteen countries. The Exocet can be launched from a plane, a helicopter, or a ship. It is powered by a two-stage solid-fuel rocket, with a 25–40-mile range. After launch, it uses a radio altimeter to dive to just a few feet above the ocean surface—making it very difficult to detect by look-down radar—and skims along under inertial guidance at about 650 miles per hour. Near the end of its flight, it rises slightly above the horizon for a fast radar scan, then locks its homing radar on the closest ship. Since the homing radar lock, which exposes it to ship defensive radars, is delayed until the last seconds of its flight, only the fastest defensive systems have time to react. Four out of six Exocets fired by the Argentinians in the 1982 Falklands War hit a target, and one knocked out the British destroyer HMS *Sheffield.* More recently, in the spring of 1987, an Iraqi Exocet utterly disabled the spanking-new American Perry-class frigate *Stark,* a ship that cost about a thousand times more than the missile that put it out of action.

The *Stark* episode illustrates some of the things that can go wrong with ship defense. An AWACS early warning message did not get to the *Stark* on time; the ship's radars didn't pick up the missile; its Phalanx defense system, an anti-missile gun that screens a ship in a 3,000-round-a-minute hailstorm of machine-gun bullets, was not turned on—it usually isn't, because it fires automatically when an object moves across its field of vision. Even if the Phalanx had been turned on, John Lehman admitted, it has only a two out of three chance of knocking down an Exocet anyway. And there are far more capable antiship missiles in the Soviet inventory than the Exocet—missiles that are faster, that are much more invisible to ship defensive systems, that are less easily foiled by countermeasures.

The Navy pooh-poohs the problem, insisting that its giant carriers are invulnerable behind their layered defensive screens: early warning aircraft; F-14s; Harpoon antiship cruise missiles; Talos, Terrier, Tartar, and new "Standard 1" and "Standard 2" SAMs with both long-range and close-in and high- and low-altitude capabilities; a wide range of antisubmarine air and sea patrols, missiles, and attack submarines; electronic countermeasures to confuse attacking missiles; and close-in missile defenses, including both fast-reacting antimissile missiles like the Sparrow and the Phalanx machine gun. Backfire attacks, the Navy even boasts, are to be welcomed; they will deplete the Soviet Backfire capability just as Japanese air attacks depleted the Japanese Air Force in World War II.

The Navy is correct that the vulnerability of ships in isolation, like the *Sheffield* and the *Stark,* is not a true measure of the vulnerability of an alerted carrier fleet. But even assuming that all of a carrier's defensive systems work as well as the Navy claims, they almost certainly could not withstand a determined barrage attack. A carrier can launch only 24 Phoenix-armed F-14s (assuming they are 100 percent combat-ready, which is unlikely) and each can carry 8 missiles at most, or 192 altogether. A determined attacker, as the Soviets would be if a carrier fleet steamed toward the North Sea in a conventional war, could quickly exhaust the F-14s, particularly by using drones to stimulate missile launchings. Once the perimeter is breached, defense system reaction times become very demanding; supersonic aircraft and missiles cover distances of 100 miles or more in just a few minutes, and electronic countermeasures reduce reaction times even further.

Close-in defensive tactics that depend on screening fire, like that of the Phalanx, can also be quickly overwhelmed—a Phalanx magazine holds only 989 bullets, requiring reload after only twenty seconds of fire. Finally, if all other attacks fail, a low-yield underwater nuclear warhead burst would destroy a surface fleet; and the use of tactical nuclear warheads at sea, while not devoid of escalatory risk, is least likely to provoke a strategic retaliatory response, since collateral damage and injury to civilians will be minimal to nil. The Navy's surface strategy, in short, falls by the weight of internal contradiction. It is beyond the realm of plausibility that a surface fleet's defensive systems could successfully resist a determined, coordinated, barrage attack, particularly one operating with the benefit of shore-based supplies and reinforcements. But even if it could, the massive investment in defensive systems cannot be justifed by the relatively puny offensive power that a surface fleet disposes.

There are crucial roles for the Navy in any future war. Protecting sealane supply routes and clearing the seas of Soviet submarines will be essential for a successful outcome in a protracted conventional encounter. Carriers will always be needed to project power to Third World countries, at least so long as the United States plays its global power-balancing role. In addition, carrier fleets will be, should be, expensive. It has long been a central theme of American naval policy to reduce reliance on third-country bases. One of the reasons the Soviet Union has gone to such lengths to secure base rights in Southeast Asia, in Ethiopia and Somalia, and, it would appear, eventually in Angola, is because its fleets cannot long sustain themselves on the open ocean as the American fleets can. Third-party bases are cheaper in the short run than operating self-sufficient surface fleets—if the costs of the inevitable aid/ blackmail are excluded—but power projection is then always hostage to the good offices of distant and unreliable allies.

Further, the vulnerability of the small British carriers in the Falklands War exposes the penny-wise policy of a poorly defended fleet; if a country invests in carriers, they should be powerful and well-protected enough to make a difference. The issue is not whether the United

States needs carriers; the issue is whether the *marginal* military investment dollar should be so disproportionately devoted to them—why wouldn't a dozen carriers, or even fewer, be more than enough? Finally, and to make matters much worse, the administration has not even invested its naval dollars wisely. By attempting to build a fleet that can combat the Soviet Union, it has produced a fleet that is ill-equipped for precisely the missions a naval power is most likely to be called upon to perform. The vulnerability of the American fleet to the simplest mines in the Persian Gulf—as this book goes to press, American warships are still safely escorting reflagged Kuwaiti tankers, but with no great display of confidence—perfectly illustrates the misallocation of resources. Minesweepers, a low-glamour investment, are in very short supply.

The thoughtlessness with which the Reagan administration has embraced the current grandeur-dosed naval strategy has caused an enormous drain of military resources into weapon systems that add little offensive capabilities and that impose enormous operations and maintenance costs. The burgeoning fleet will require hugely expensive investments in ever-more elaborate defenses as Soviet counternaval capabilities improve, and will continue to distort military investment patterns till the end of the century.

Finally, there is a third reason the nation has seen so little visible return from the upsurge in military spending during the 1980s, one that is quite outside any particular administration's control. It is, simply, the ever-deeper reach, and ever-greater power, of modern technology in shaping the contours of a future war.

## Technology and the Shape of War

When General Mark Clark's Fifth Army fought its way, mile by grim mile, up the Italian peninsula in the spring of 1944 against stubbornly resisting German infantry and *Panzer* units, its route was paved by a classic air interdiction campaign, "Operation Strangle." A detailed statistical study of the American air campaign shows that, on average, about 2,500 fighter bombers and bombers—P-47s and 51s, B-25s and 26s—participated in the air battle. Each plane was able to fly about two sorties every three days and carried, on average, 2,500 pounds of bombs per sortie. The total force destroyed or disabled about sixty to seventy German tanks or other major military vehicles each day. It required twenty to thirty sorties to take out a bridge over a minor river.

A modern air interdiction campaign in a conventional war in

Europe, by contrast, might involve at most a hundred aircraft, able to fly one to three sorties per day—the speed and range of modern warplanes greatly multiplies sortie rates. If they were a mix of F-4s, A-7s, and A-10s, they would carry some combination of gravity bombs—between 1,600–9,000 pounds each—and precision-guided munitions, perhaps three to six each, and would have a fighting radius at least double that of the 1944 striking force. Depending on combat conditions, 100 modern planes should be able to destroy 300–800 Soviet tanks per day, using precision-guided antitank weapons. A river bridge attack should require only a single sortie with laser-guided bombs.

Almost simultaneously with Clark's Italian campaign, off the Mariana Islands in the western Pacific in June 1944, Naval Task Force 58, under command of Admiral Marc Mitscher, broke the back of the Japanese Navy in the Battle of the Philippines Sea. The task force consisted of 112 ships, including 14 carriers, fielding almost 1,000 airplanes. In 1985, the entire American Navy had only about 1,350 planes, or barely a third more than the number in Mitscher's task force; but the three dozen attack planes on a modern Nimitz-class carrier dispose of approximately the same weight of munitions as Mitscher's 416 attack bombers. Merely comparing weight of munitions, however, conveys little sense of the vast differences between a World War II–vintage fleet and a modern carrier task group. An old-fashioned naval fleet would be destroyed by a carrier group's antiship missiles and torpedos long before it even sensed the carrier's presence, much less had the opportunity to employ its weapons.

Technology, in short, is irresistibly reshaping modern warfare. Wars will be fought by fewer and fewer vastly more destructive and vastly more expensive weapons. The arithmetic is inescapable. The cost of a tactical airplane has gone up ten times faster than the Air Force's budget over the past thirty years, and the unit costs of other weapons have outrun their services' budgets at a comparable rate. With some lag, the same phenomenon is evident in the Soviet forces. The trend applies equally to offensive and defensive weapons. The only certain result is that the rate of weapon systems attrition in modern war will be enormously high. The successive wars in the Middle East provide only the faintest premonitory glimpse of the speed and destructiveness that would characterize an all-out clash between NATO and the Soviet Union.

Tactical aircraft, again, demonstrate the leapfrogging cycle. A typical World War II air attack was mounted with large numbers of airplanes of relatively modest destructive power. Antiaircraft defenses, particularly flak-type defenses, were successful if they achieved low, but steady, rates of enemy aircraft attrition. But in modern warfare, the cost of *not* intercepting an attacking aircraft is very much greater, particularly if the plane might be carrying nuclear weapons. High-reliability defensive installations assume much greater importance, and it becomes cost-effective to spend very large amounts of money throwing up virtually impenetrable defensive screens. Since NATO tactics in Europe accord a significant role to deep-strike nuclear-capable attack planes like the F-4, the F-15, and the F-111, the Soviet Union has invested heavily in multilayered area defenses, much as the American Navy has invested in ship defenses against the anticipated Soviet air attacks.

More recently, NATO's cruise missiles are forcing the Soviets to revise their defenses to combat attackers with "small radar cross-sections" that are harder to track than the generally large NATO planes. The SA-10 and SA-12, the Soviets' newest SAMs, appear to be such weapons. In all, the Soviets field some 4,600 SAM launchers and 11,500 other antiaircraft batteries. Conversely, until the late 1970s, NATO made minimal investments in air defense, since Soviet aircraft in Europe and western Russia were almost all short-range interceptors, useful only in a defensive role. But since the Soviets have begun to deploy planes like the Su-24, a swing-winged replica of the F-111, NATO has been forced to field costly defense systems like the Patriot missile, which, in theory at least, could successfully engage supersonic, low-altitude, penetrating fighter bombers. (One Air Force general said that the main military contribution of the F-111 is that "the damnfool Russians went out and copied it.")

Technology, in addition, drives toward central direction of the course of battle. Modern aircraft are too expensive, too scarce, and too lethal to be allowed to wander aimlessly in search of targets; for the same reasons, it would be feckless to leave defensive interceptions to chance encounters. A modern defensive array will include high-altitude radar patrols—like the American AWACS planes and the Soviet Il-76 "Mainstay"—designed to detect invading aircraft at great distances and to direct interceptors armed with air-to-air guided missiles. If the attackers breach the fighter defenses, they must evade homing missiles from long-range fixed SAM batteries, then from shorter-range mobile SAMs, and finally from close-in, hand-held missile launchers. As both attacker and defender improve their capabilities, the interacting complexity of tactical air systems increases dramatically. Offensive forces invest in low-level, high-speed, radar-evading avionics, and add radar jamming and other electronic evasive measures; defenders deploy look-down radars, electronic counter-countermeasures, and "smarter," more reliable missiles.

Defensive systems eventually reach a point where it no longer pays the offense to rely on conventional airplanes, and attackers shift to "standoff" weapons—missiles launched either from planes or from ground batteries outside a defensive system's range. Jimmy Carter's decision to cancel the B-1 bomber in favor of outfitting B-52s with cruise missiles was grounded in just such logic. Tactical aircraft, however, still have a number of advantages over missiles. For all their great acquisition and maintenance expense, modern airplanes, shot for shot, still deliver munitions more cheaply than missiles do, simply because they are reusable. (Perhaps surprisingly, however, missiles are generally more accurate than gravity-delivered bombs.) More important, for the time being at least, missiles can be employed only against fixed targets; the great value of tactical airpower is the ability to deliver ordnance against a large number of rapidly shifting targets, like Soviet tank formations or reinforcing troop echelons moving to the front. The Soviet Union's long reliance on missiles for deep strikes in Europe would have severely hampered its ability to support its forces in a conventional war. It was not until they began to deploy longer-range, bigger, and more powerful tactical airplanes on the NATO model in the 1970s that Soviet combined arms doctrine moved beyond mere rhetoric. Interestingly, they are also working on a new bomber, the "Black-jack," which appears to be similar to the B-1. A successful deployment of a B-1-type fleet of bombers would require a radical reordering of American air defenses.

As technology has reshaped the instruments of war, it has reshaped the tactics. The great efficiency of modern defensive systems, for example, drives tactical airpower commanders to devote significant resources to "defense suppression": opposing defenses must be disabled before other targets can be attacked. The Israeli campaign in the Bekaa Valley in Lebanon in 1982 was the classic demonstration. The approaches to Beirut were thickly defended by layered Soviet SAM batteries that had been painstakingly built up over a period of some years, with perimeter defenses supplied by substantial numbers of MiG-21 and MiG-23 interceptors. The Israelis managed their offensive with Grumman E-2C radar planes, high above and to the rear of the fighting, each capable of tracking 155 targets at one time and spotting Soviet interceptors as they took off from their airfields.

The first attacking wave consisted of camera-carrying pilotless drones able to scan 115 square miles from a 1,000-meter altitude and transmit real-time photos of areas 40-50 meters across. The E-2Cs picked up the radar signature of SAM launchers locking onto the drones and directed anti-SAM rocket strikes. F-4s with "Shrike" anti-SAM homing missiles attacked deeper SAM batteries as the Israeli lines rolled past the range of their ground-based rockets. Follow-on drones recorded the damage, and the E-2Cs directed further anti-SAM missile strikes or precision-guided antipersonnel cluster bomb attacks, thoroughly nasty weapons that spray a shower of deadly razor-like fragments over a wide radius to kill ground crews and prevent SAM battery repair. One report had it that Israeli defense officials could watch the unfolding battle on television monitors in their offices.

Israeli electronic countermeasures also effectively disabled the Syrian interceptor force. As soon as the MiGs took off from their airfields, Israeli jamming cut their contact with their ground control; without central target acquisition, the Syrian pilots were continually under attack by Israeli planes approaching from unexpected directions. And as their SAM batteries were silenced, the Syrian MiGs had no chance against the powerful American F-15s and F-16s leading the second-wave Israeli strike. The entire defensive array—*all* the SAMs and all the airfields—was eliminated in a single day. The Syrians lost eighty-one MiGs, most of them to Sidewinder air-to-air missiles; the Israelis lost either a single plane, or, as the Syrians insisted, three. With Israeli fighters roaming the skies at will, and their own air cover gone, Syrian armored resistance collapsed almost as swiftly.

It is not possible to blame the continued overwhelming successes of the Israelis against enormous numerical odds purely on Arab incompetence, as critics of American high-technology weapons are sometimes wont to do. The Soviets, after all, have been training the Syrians for twenty years. Either Arabs are in fact uneducable—which sounds racist—or Western weapons confer an enormous fighting edge; one suspects that the Soviets incline more toward the latter view. No Western military analyst, of course, believes that Soviet air defenses could be penetrated as easily as Syria's. They are even more densely arrayed, and presumably less susceptible to jamming. The planes, however, are substantially the same; in the mid-1980s, almost all Soviet interceptors were still MiG-21s and MiG-23s.*

*Perhaps significantly, American air tacticians do not employ drones as readily as the Israelis; tend to lead with airplanes, as in Lebanon in 1983; and design fancier drones than

The Bekaa Valley campaign illustrates another fact of modern war: the great uncertainties of the "come as you are" battle. Previous wars, stretching over months or years, always afforded the opportunity for both the offense and the defense to test each other's tactics and capabilities and make the subtle adjustments that are the difference between success and failure. The Soviets and the Syrians apparently believed that they had built an impenetrable defensive screen in Lebanon; and it is entirely possible that, with time to make the appropriate adjustments, their defenses might have withstood the Israeli onslaught. The enormous speed, range, and firepower of modern weapon systems, however, allows no time for "tuning" tactics. The Soviets and Syrians guessed wrong about the nature of the Israeli assault, and a day later the war was effectively over.

The same sequence of technological trump-countertrump is reshaping armored warfare. The vulnerability of massed tank formations to battlefield nuclear weapons has caused both NATO and Soviet armored doctrine to emphasize widely dispersed operations and very rapid maneuvers. Logistics and communication problems are thereby vastly complicated. The fuel requirements for modern high-speed operations are at least six times greater than in World War II, and high rates of fire make the modern tank a prodigal consumer of ammunition. The huge increase in logistics and supplies expenditure is already reaching the point of diminishing return, for there are major limitations on the maneuvering speed of even the most modern tank divisions. Patton's Third Army, in its famous march across France, covered only about 15 miles a day; modern tanks are somewhat faster, but speeds have not changed drastically. In any case, the pounding from prolonged rapid movement can take a heavy toll on crews, and must be a particular problem for Soviet crews, who endure poor suspension systems. Pushing such heavy vehicles across rough terrain inevitably means a high rate of breakdown—on average, about every 100–200 miles. Soviet tank endurance, by many reports, is particularly poor. Modern tank divisions also must haul mobile SAM launchers for their own safety, but SAMs take time to set up and contain delicate components that travel poorly over rough terrain.

The threat of modern antitank weapons constrains armored maneuvers even further: in Marshal Grechko's words, "Tanks have become more vulnerable and the use of them on the battlefield more

necessary. American high-technology weapons without Israeli tactical genius might not prove so effective.

complicated." Antitank weapons use either high-velocity, heavy, armor-penetrating shells—"kinetic-energy" rounds; or so-called shaped charges—high explosive rounds fired from rockets that focus the energy of the charge into piercing the tank's armor. Only artillery or tank cannon have the muzzle velocity to defeat a tank's armor with kinetic energy rounds. Tanks themselves, in fact, are among the most effective antitank weapons. But except in desert warfare, commanders usually prefer not to engage in tank duels; the armored division is far more useful slashing through "soft" defenses. Tank defenses therefore have been dominated by rocket-assisted, shaped-charge weapons, like the famous World War II bazooka and its modern hand-held descendants, the American Viper and the Soviet RPG-7 rocket.

To be truly effective, an antitank rocket must have longer range than a tank's cannon—lightly protected infantrymen within a tank's firing range cannot slug it out for very long; and it must also be highly accurate—anything less than a direct hit will have little effect. Both requirements have spurred the development of antitank guided missiles, like those that so disconcerted the Israelis in 1973. The best modern antitank guided missiles can achieve devastating rates of attrition against most modern tanks, particularly in open areas. But current models have their limitations. They take a relatively long time to reach their targets and can be confused by evasive action—moving behind a clump of trees, for instance—by smoke screens, or just by battlefield dust. Most TOW-type wire-guided weapons, still the most common, require the launching infantryman to maintain visual contact with the moving tank to score a hit, leaving him highly vulnerable to supporting infantry fire. Antitank launchers also have a much lower rate of fire than tank cannon; a determined attacker, like the Soviet Union, who is willing to absorb early losses, could probably overwhelm most antitank defensive emplacements.

It is to combat precisely these deficiencies in antitank weapons that the military is procuring large and expensive systems like the Bradley armored vehicle and the Apache (AH-64) helicopter. They offer some protection to their crews against supporting infantry fire, if not against tank cannon, and can carry bigger and more complicated antitank missiles with greater range, accuracy, and rates of fire. But their cost is also rising rapidly, to the point where antitank weapon systems may cost a quarter, a half, or in some cases almost as much as the tank itself. Armored personnel carriers and helicopters are necessarily more vulnerable than tanks because their armor is much lighter. There is a concern, indeed, that by allowing crews to operate their weapons from inside the vehicles, as both the Soviet and the newer NATO armored personnel carriers do, crews will actually be more vulnerable than if they had dismounted and dispersed. The vulnerability of crews in personnel carriers, however, should be more of a problem for the Soviets than for NATO. NATO defenders will be more often fighting from fixed defensive conditions, using armored vehicles only to speed troops between defensive emplacements to weak points in the defense. The attacker's troops, on the other hand, particularly in the favored Soviet *blitzkrieg*-style attack, will be much more dependent on their armor for protection, since they would be fighting on the move. The Soviets have recently voiced public worries about the actual usefulness of their enormous fleet of armored personnel carriers.

The newest focus of Western tank defenses is the family of precision-guided submunitions being developed under NATO's "Emerging Technologies" program. Gen. Bernard P. Rogers, NATO commander for most of the 1980s, along with a number of Western analysts, believes that in an attack on Europe, the Soviets will employ an "echeloned" offensive—that is, once penetration has been achieved anywhere on the front, highly mobile armored "Operational Maneuver Groups" will attack in successive waves to complete and exploit the breakthrough. The Soviets' echeloned system of organization, it is felt, partially explains the low support ratios in their divisional structure: units will be expected to fight only for relatively short periods of time, after which they will be replaced by entirely fresh, self-supporting divisions. In response, Rogers has enunciated a "Deep Strike" strategy, or a strategy of "Follow-on Forces Attack," adopted by NATO in late 1984. Similar to the Army's "Airland Battle" doctrine, a "Follow-on Forces" strategy will concentrate on disrupting the Soviet rear and interrupting the flow of fresh manpower and supplies with deep interdiction attacks.*

The key weapons in a "Deep Strike" will be new generations of so-called Assault Breaker weapons. Short-range air- or ground-launched missiles currently in testing can carry up to 600 miniature, precision-guided antitank submunitions. As a missile approaches an armored formation, it scatters its submunitions in all directions; each one then locks in on any tank or large vehicle in the vicinity, using a variety of infrared,

---

*It is, to say the least, a controversial strategy, particularly in Germany. The emphasis on follow-on forces implies that the defensive lines might bend while waiting for the interdiction attacks to take their toll. Germans, of course, have little enthusiasm for defensive maneuvers that concede territory. References to the arguments pro and con "Deep Strike" are given in the notes.

microwave, or heat-seeking homing technologies. In some versions, the missile is directed by an airplane spotter or a drone. Others are "fire and forget" weapons: they are simply launched in the general direction of Soviet formations, 50 miles or more away, and will seek out the tanks with on-board search and homing apparatus. It is not at all clear how effectively or how rapidly such weapons will achieve operational status, but even the promise of their success—Soviet planners, of course, are *obliged* to assume that they will work—raises serious questions about the usefulness of the huge advantage in Soviet armor, built up at such great expense over the past decades.

Analysts usually assume that defensive weapons will consistently maintain an advantage over the tank, for the simple reason that tanks are so big and so expensive that their rate of technological adjustment will necessarily be slower than that for antitank weapons. But that does not mean that the defense will always and everywhere have the edge. In mid-1987, there have been reports that the Soviets have successfully adapted Israeli "reactive" armor to their newest generation of tanks. "Reactive" armor actually covers the tank armor with a thin screen of explosive that detonates on contact, dissipating the focused armor-piercing charge of an antitank missile, although it affords no greater protection against kinetic-energy rounds. Since Western defenses are heavily dependent on antitank guided missiles, successful deployment of large numbers of Soviet "reactive" armored tanks would require a substantial readjustment either in NATO tactics or weapons. It is not known, as this book goes to press, how effective the new Soviet armor will be, how widespread its deployment, or how long it will take for the West to devise countermeasures.

Examples of technological interactions can be multiplied. Submarine and antisubmarine warfare shows the same leapfrogging pattern as tank armor and antitank missiles, or aircraft and aircraft defenses. The key technologies are noise reduction for the stalking attack submarine or lurking missile submarine on the one hand, and very high speed computers to interpret the confusing flux of acoustical signals received from the ambient ocean on the other. The United States has maintained a consistent lead over the Soviet Union in all aspects of submarine and antisubmarine technology, which the Soviets have struggled to close by all available means. The exportation in 1987 by a Japanese and a Norwegian company of propeller noise-reduction technology—computer-controlled milling machines, accurate to the millionth of the inch to reduce propeller turbulence and hence noise—

was, by all reports, a major Soviet breakthrough. There is no evidence that the Soviets are even close to mastering the technology to produce the very small, on-board, parallel-processor "supercomputers" necessary to track the new generations of very quiet submarines. But faster, quieter Soviet submarines are better able to elude, and in some cases, outrun, older American torpedos. Inevitably, the newest torpedos must be bigger, faster, with more fuel, and the self-contained intelligence necessary to track a rapidly evading target.

An appreciation of the impact of technology on modern war is the essential context for evaluating both the Reagan–Weinberger rearmament program and the continuing controversy over American weapons procurement policy. There is indeed much to criticize, as should be clear from previous sections of this book. But criticisms of particular procurement decisions, however justified, do not add up to a case against advanced technology. Nor are *numbers* of weapons deployed necessarily the key measure of performance, although there is a tendency for many defense critics to argue in favor of larger numbers of simpler weapons because of the numerical superiority the Soviets enjoy in most weapon categories. As Seymour Deitchmann has pointed out, *producibility* is only one criterion for weapon selection; *usefulness in war* is far more important. The Navy could purchase far simpler and cheaper fighters than the F-14; the critical question is whether a lighter, less complex fighter would be of any use against a Backfire attack, the threat the F-14 is designed to combat. The absurdly high kill ratios scored by Western planes and tanks in the Middle East demonstrate the limits of numerical superiority against well-conceived, integrated tactical execution with technologically superior weapons.

Nor is it clear that more advanced weapons are always more difficult to service and maintain, as is frequently alleged. Function for function, solid-state components are more reliable and longer-lasting, and much simpler and easier to replace than older technology; it is usually the add-on functions that cause the problems. Solid-state technology, however, does change logistics requirements dramatically because spare parts assume crucial importance. If a black box breaks, a new one has merely to be slipped into its place; but if a new black box is not available, there is nothing that a mechanically inclined fighter-jockey can do with a screwdriver to get his plane flying again—except perhaps to cannibalize his buddy's equipment, which apparently was becoming standard practice in the late 1970s. The excessive out-of-service times of the newest generations of aircraft appear to have been substantially related to spare parts availability. To further complicate matters, black box repair must be centralized, because the sophisticated testing machinery required cannot be spread around air bases, even if the technically trained staff were available. Central repair depots might make highly inviting targets in a conventional war.

New capabilities often work unreliably, particularly when they are first introduced. It seems clear that a main purpose of the 1986 bombing attack on Libya was to kill the Libyan leader, Colonel Qaddafi. Bombing a single house or tent in a night raid from a supersonic airplane is an extraordinary feat, but the advanced laser-guided bombing systems of the attacking F-111s laid down the bombs in a tight pattern within yards of where Qaddafi was living. Qaddafi survived, it seems, only because four of the nine attacking F-111s aborted their missions when their laser guidance systems malfunctioned; a fifth plane, apparently because of pilot error, dropped its bombs far off course. The very concept of attacking a single house would have been unthinkable just a few years ago, but in a micro-precise world, micro-malfunctions loom large.

The Soviet Union has always demonstrated far more respect for American technical prowess than domestic military critics, and with good reason. Repeatedly, throughout the history of the arms race, the United States has risen from its military slumbers and altered the power balance with breathtaking speed and ease. The creation of a powerful, long-distance, strategic bombing force in the late 1950s, the rapid deployment of the Minuteman and Polaris missiles, the sudden multiplication of warheads with MIRV technology in the 1970s—it is this history that prompts the Soviets to pay such serious attention to President Reagan's "Star Wars" space-based missile defense program. Marshal Nikolai Ogarkov was relieved of his duties as chief of staff by the Soviet leader, Konstantin Chernenko, in 1984 for speaking out too aggressively on the need for greater Soviet investment in defense, and pounding away at the need to counter Western weapons based on "new physical principles." Indeed, despite the arguments by critics from the right that the Western technological edge has been steadily eroding, the opposite is more likely the case. The Soviets have made impressive strides in the last decades, but, to a great extent, their progress stems from sheer developmental doggedness. As technology leaps ahead faster and faster, mere perseverance pays fewer and fewer dividends. The long-time Soviet emphasis on heavy industry, while a great advantage in turning out tanks, will be of little use in developing the smaller, "smarter," and more flexible weapons that may well be the mainstays of the next generation's armories. "Star Wars" is so unsettling for the Soviets because it drives home how badly they lag in computers and software, electro-optical sensors, guidance and navigation, micro-electronics, robotics, signal processing, and telecommunications, all key technologies in the brave world of future war.

But accepting the emphasis on high technology, the Reagan/Weinberger program is still vulnerable to serious criticism on several grounds. The first is the failure to distinguish consistently between weapons *systems* and weapons *platforms*. With the march of technology, systems are steadily assuming greater importance than platforms; it is its missiles that have made the Soviet Navy a force to be reckoned with on the world's oceans, not the speed or size of its cruisers and frigates. The central error of the American Navy's procurement program has been to pour so much wealth and technology into purchasing and protecting weapons platforms like the carrier, without a clear idea of their function in war. And Jimmy Carter was almost certainly right that the B-52 was as good a platform for a cruise missile as the B-1. The B-1, of course, is a more flexible platform, that will be able to carry its weapon systems closer to their targets faster, but $300 million an airplane is a high price to pay for such marginally improved capability. The advent of precision-guided munitions will degrade the importance of weapons platforms even further; in the foreseeable future, conceivably, low-cost missiles or drones, functioning as submunitions carriers, but without the necessity for sophisticated cruise-type guidance technology, will be able to substitute for expensive deep-strike aircraft even in missions against mobile forces.

The second major error is the failure to recognize the difficulties introduced by *concurrent* technical developments. The development of the B-1B bomber, a relatively straightforward undertaking, illustrates the problem. The development plan attempted to learn from all the highly publicized mistakes of previous weapons programs: Congress funded a multi-year development program to facilitate planning and coordination; the Secretary of Defense personally reviewed progress milestones on a biweekly basis; the Air Force provided general contractor oversight itself to avoid creating impenetrable layers of contractor bureaucracies; the technologies employed were mostly off-the-shelf, ones that had been developed during the original 1970s B-1 program, and were generally less demanding than those already operational in advanced fighters and fighter bombers.

The program has not been a success; as of 1987, the B-1B was over budget, far behind schedule, and with significantly less range, payload, maneuverability, and antiradar capability than planned. An investigating subcommittee identified concurrency as the key problem. Too many new pieces of hardware were being introduced all at the same time. In some instances, designs were still being changed during production, so a single squadron of B-1Bs might incorporate several different generations of equipment, creating logistic and spare part nightmares. It was discovered during flight testing that the offensive and defensive radar systems on the B-1B, developed by different contractors, interfere with each other. With hindsight, all the problems seem obvious; the path to a foolproof development process, however, is hardly so obvious.

The history of the B-1B is useful perspective for considering the "Star Wars" project, which in some ways has come to symbolize the administration's entire approach to technological warfare.

### Astra et Aspera

On March 23, 1983, Ronald Reagan made a televised "address to the nation" devoted to the topic of defense. As most presidential defense speeches do, it reviewed the poor state of repair of the military establishment when he took office, the nature of the Soviet threat, the accomplishments of his administration, and the necessity of securing intact the defense budget then being considered by the Congress. What was extraordinary was the throwaway at the end of the speech, inserted at the insistence of the President himself over the objections of most of his aides. Reagan announced his frustration and horror with the whole notion of "mutual assured destruction." "I have become more and more deeply convinced that the human spirit must be capable of rising above dealing with other nations . . . by threatening their existence." "What if," the President asked rhetorically, "free people could live secure in the knowledge that their security did not rest upon the threat of instant United States retaliation to deter a Soviet attack . . ."

Of such random sentiments are great national enterprises born. The President did not propose a specific program, merely a research commitment, recognizing that any truly effective defensive system would require "years, probably decades, of effort on many fronts." And so the "Star Wars" program began—arguably the most controversial, and to the Soviet Union, the most alarming, American military initiative in decades.

"Star Wars" is of complex parentage. The focus on nuclear "war-fighting" theory in the late 1970s renewed interest in defense. In an "assured destruction" environment, missile defenses are destabilizing, since they threaten the usefulness of the other side's deterrent. If missiles are built to be *used,* however—rather than, as "assured destruction" theory implies, built *not* to be used—then defenses, both of missiles and people, become an integral, indeed essential, part of an overall military capability. The suspicion that the Soviet Union was pursuing a "war-fighting" nuclear strategy bred exaggerated claims of the progress of their defensive research. Gen. George Keegan, former head of Air Force Intelligence and a prominent member of the Committee on the Present Danger, said flatly in 1977 that the Soviet Union would have "technically and scientifically solved the problem of the ballistic missile threat" and would have tested such a defense by 1980. Exaggerated claims of Soviet prowess spawned exaggerated expectations of American technology. Gen. Daniel O. Graham, founder of the "High Frontier" lobby for space-based defenses, insisted in a widely publicized book that outer-space "beam" weapons could defend American cities for less than $13 billion, while only $4 billion would buy a near leakproof defense for American missile silos.

But, judging by the tone of his "Star Wars" address, Reagan also drew inspiration from quite different sources. Freeman Dyson, a scientist-humanist, in his influential book *Weapons and Hope* charges that the very notion of "assured destruction" is "morally repugnant and politically sterile," as must be any national doctrine requiring "the deployment of nuclear weapons in quantities so large as to obliterate any conceivable just cause in which they might be used." As a staging ground toward his vision of a non-nuclear world, Dyson suggests that, "In principle, the substitution of non-nuclear ABM systems for offensive nuclear missiles would be, like the substitution of precision-guided munitions for tactical nuclear weapons in Europe, a giant step for mankind in the direction of sanity."

And he continues, in phrases redolent of Reagan's own speech:

Defense is not technically sweet. The primal sin of scientists and politicians alike has been to run after weapons which are technically sweet. Why must arms controllers fall into the same trap? Nobody can possibly foresee the state of the world ten years ahead, let alone fifty. If a defensively oriented world is an end worth striving for, and if we pursue it diligently with all the available means, especially with moral and political as well as technical means, we have a good chance of success.

The "Star Wars" program born of such diverse impulses is surely one of the most extraordinary of military undertakings. By 1987, research and development funding had risen to about $6 billion annually. The research centers on four main areas: kinetic-energy weapons, or projectiles hurled into the path of an oncoming missile or warhead; directed energy weapons, including optical lasers, charged-particle beams (electrons or protons), neutral-particle beams (neutrons, neutral hydrogen atoms, and gamma rays), and X-ray lasers; surveillance, acquisition, tracking, and kill assessment—SATKA in the jargon; and battle management and command and control systems. Interestingly enough, the terms of reference of the research preclude the use of nuclear warheads, so that ABM missiles like the Spartan developed under McNamara's original ABM program are out of bounds, because they rely on nuclear blasts to kill their targets. (Nuclear bombs, however, are permitted as a *power source*. Edward Teller has great hopes for the X-ray laser, which will be created by focusing the X-ray output of a small fission bomb. The space platform housing the bomb, of course, will be destroyed by the explosion, but the apparatus will focus the pulse of energy in the last microsecond before it disintegrates. The idea, to put it mildly, is far-fetched.)

The central concept is of a "layered" defense, with a specific defensive array employed at each stage of a hostile missile's flight. "Layered" defenses have the advantage of multiplying kill ratios—a four-stage defense, for example, that is 50 percent effective at each stage, would kill some 94 percent of all the attacking warheads and missiles. *Boost-phase* defensive systems would detect Soviet missile launches by their infrared plumes and direct, probably, chemical laser beams to disable the rocket just above the atmosphere. Lasers or some other beam weapons are necessary because of the very short reaction times required. Soviet missile boost phases last from two to five minutes, and with new generations of "fast-burn" boosters could be reduced to about fifty seconds. The second, but even more difficult kill opportunity arises during the *bus phase*, after the rocket has disengaged and the bus is maneuvering to release its MIRVed warheads.

*Mid-course* defense, after the bus has released its contents, is arguably the most difficult because of the problem of discriminating real warheads from chaff and decoys. Since there is no atmosphere in outer space, extremely light objects, like balloons, can assume the same shape and projectile path as a warhead. A full-scale MIRVed missile attack could release hundreds of thousands of decoys to confuse the defense.

The mid-course kill opportunity lasts the longest, however, some fifteen minutes. *Terminal-phase* defenses using lasers or kinetic-energy weapons will detect the remaining warheads for a last-ditch intercept as the atmosphere strips away the light decoys and chaff. (There will be no heavy decoys, since there is no point launching heavy objects that do not carry explosives.)

One of the problems with assessing the "Star Wars" program is that its mission is not yet clearly defined. In its early stages, the intention, apparently sincerely held by the President, was to create a nearly "leak-proof" city defense. But city defense, to put it bluntly, is impossible at any time well into the next century. Too many breakthroughs are required in too many technologies. No one has ever written a computer program of the scale, complexity, and perfection needed for a city defense system. No one has ever built a laser mirror of the size and precision required for space-based laser interceptors, much less put one into space. No one has ever built particle-beam weapons of the required power. (A charged particle-beam at missile kill levels of energy could reasonably require a half-ton of fuel for a two-tenths of a second burst.) By one recent careful assessment, prepared by a study group of the American Physical Society, *all* of the technologies involved in an effective "beam" weapon defense would need improvement of at least two, and for some, four or more orders of magnitude before they could even be seriously considered. (An order of magnitude is a power of ten; two orders of magnitude means a hundredfold improvement; three orders of magnitude, a thousandfold.) A decade's research would be required, the study group concluded, before the technical knowledge would be available for even an informed decision. And even if the physics were understood, the engineering required to launch and maintain the hundreds of enormous space platforms, with mirrors, sensors, computers, fuel, and weapons systems, seems out of all reasonable proportion, particularly considering the recent difficulties in launching relatively simple communications satellites in the wake of the space shuttle Challenger disaster. Such pretensions do not even qualify as hubris; they are merely foolish.

By 1986, however, the "Star Wars" research had shifted drastically toward early deployment options of laser and kinetic weapon "point" defenses, with both space-based and ground-based components, designed to protect missile silos. It is well within the capabilities of American technology, particularly if the non-nuclear constraint is removed, to build an updated version of missile silo defense systems that could plausibly have, say, a 50 percent effectiveness against an attacker, more than enough to degrade significantly a presumed Soviet first-strike capability. The feasibility of so-called point defenses does not mean that they are necessarily the best way of defending missile sites. Investing in smaller, rail-mobile missiles, like the projected "Midgetman" may buy as much protection at a much lower price.

It is not hard to see, amid all the scoffing in America, why the Soviets view the "Star Wars" program as such a sinister development. Plausibly, continued full-bore research will permit an American silo defense "breakout"; if the United States is reasonably confident that its missiles would survive a hostile pre-emptive launch, while the Soviets' could not, it might once more gain "escalation dominance," the same sense of superiority in an eyeball-to-eyeball confrontation that forced the Soviets to back down in Cuba. But the Soviets harbor worse nightmares. There is a very thin line between defensive and offensive systems. Space platforms that can attack missiles leaving their launch pads could attack military assets of all kinds. "Mid-course" warhead defenses could just as easily, indeed much more easily, attack Soviet satellites for military communications, early warning, and battle management. "Star Wars," indeed, may produce the essential technology to create, once again, a clear American first-strike capability against the Soviet Union. And perhaps worst and most certain of all, "Star Wars" will move the arms competition onto an entirely new plane, threatening the instant obsolescence of the bristling arsenals the Soviets have accumulated at such costs and at such pains over the last thirty years.

"Star Wars," perhaps, stands as a fitting monument and symbol of forty years of arms competition. It is huge, dangerous, ambiguous, fiercely expensive, born of uncertain and complicated intentions, some of them undoubtedly peaceable, and with a gathering technological momentum that will engulf its original motivations, whatever and however various they may have been.

# PART VI.

FORTY YEARS AFTER

# CHAPTER 21

# New Opportunities?

In bright blue weather in early December, 1987, the red flag of the Soviet Union, incredibly enough, snapped in the breeze over Ronald Reagan's White House. In a whirlwind, three-day summit, Reagan, and the Soviet General Secretary, Mikhail Gorbachev, signed an "INF" or Intermediate-range Nuclear Force treaty, eliminating all land-based nuclear missiles with a range between 500 and 5,100 kilometers. Both sides expressed hopes of negotiating significant reductions in long-range missiles at a 1988 summit in Moscow. By postwar standards, the INF Treaty is a most extraordinary agreement. The Soviet Union, essentially accepting Reagan's "zero-zero" option, will destroy all of its SS-20 missiles and will remove several hundred modern SS-12/22 and SS-23 shorter-range missiles in Eastern Europe. In return, the Americans will scrap the new European ground-launched cruise missiles and Pershing IIs, and the West Germans, in a separate agreement, will give up the seventy-two American-controlled nuclear warheads for their obsolescent Pershing Is. Overall, the Soviets will lose almost 1,600 modern warheads and NATO about 450. More important, each side is removing modern nuclear forces that the other considered extremely threatening—the SS-20s reinforced the impression of Soviet "war-fighting" propensities, while the Pershing IIs looked like a quick-strike weapon against Soviet command centers. It will be the first arms agreement to accomplish such a feat.

Throughout the entire INF bargaining process, the Soviets were uncommonly obliging. To secure the agreement, they dropped an early demand that the French destroy their eighteen modern single warhead intermediate-range missiles; they recanted their insistence that the treaty be linked to limitations on the "Star Wars" program; they quickly

405

assented to the Western demand that their new shorter-range missiles be included in the bargain; and they accepted a degree of on-site inspection to verify treaty compliance that, by Soviet standards, is quite obtrusive. During most of 1986 and 1987, in fact, the Soviets were accepting Western demands with such unwonted alacrity that allied statesmen were thoroughly, almost comically, confused; the more suspicious brooded that by accepting *Western* proposals so eagerly, the Soviets would gain a substantial military advantage by "denuclearizing" Europe. (The concern, although not entirely unfounded, is at least overstated. Prior to Helmut Schmidt's raising the issue in 1977, recall, the American military was quite content to have its European nuclear deterrent rely primarily on submarine missiles and attack bombers.)

The INF agreement follows upon a very cordial Geneva summit meeting in the fall of 1985 between Reagan and Gorbachev, and the astonishing "pre-summit" in Reykjavik, Iceland, a year later, where the Soviet leader came armed with a set of surprise proposals that would have imposed drastic cuts on the nuclear arsenals of both sides. For one surreal moment, Reagan and Gorbachev actually talked about eliminating all nuclear weapons within ten years. No agreements were reached at Reykjavik because of the American unwillingness to throw the "Star Wars" program into the package; it would, in any case, have been entirely inappropriate for the Americans to make far-reaching agreements with so little advance preparation. But now it appears quite probable that an arrangement to make substantial cuts in long-range missile forces can be concluded before the end of the Reagan presidency.

Gorbachev pressed the all-fronts public relations push through the summer and fall of 1987. American scientists were invited to observe nuclear tests on Soviet soil to demonstrate that a comprehensive test ban would be verifiable. A delegation of American congressmen was permitted to tour the controversial, half-finished, Krasnoyarsk radar site. (The radar's location clearly violates the ABM Treaty, but the visit confirmed that it is not an ABM "battle management" radar, as some conservatives had feared, but only an early warning radar, and probably not a very good one at that.) An American military team was allowed to visit a Soviet chemical weapons installation, again on Russian territory, to gather data for a possible chemical weapons ban. On other global issues, the Soviets have been more than usually cooperative at the United Nations in working for some resolution of the long war between Iran and Iraq; have made plain their willingness to withdraw from Afghanistan if a face-saving formula can be found (shades of Lyndon Johnson); and have shown signs of being more circumspect, and stingier, in their aid to the Marxist Sandinista regime in Nicaragua. Under the new Gorbachev policy of *Glasnost* (openness), dissidents and social critics are being given unprecedented, although far from total, license to speak their minds; a long list of political prisoners has been freed; and there has been a noticeable easing of emigration policies.

In mid-September, Gorbachev gave an extraordinary speech to mark the opening of the United Nations General Assembly. Throughout the entire text, there was hardly a word of criticism for the United States, and certainly none of the unrestrained vituperation that is the normal argot of Soviet official statements; at one point, indeed, he virtually apologized for using the word "adversaries" to describe the NATO and Warsaw Pact blocs. He proposed comprehensive restrictions on all varieties of weapons, including, significantly, conventional weapons in Europe, and in tones that were almost Rooseveltian, suggested a peace-keeping and arms-limiting role for the United Nations quite out of keeping with standard Soviet attitudes:

[Regarding] inter-state conflicts . . . it could be possible . . . to set up under the United Nations Organisation a multilateral centre for lessening the danger of war [including] . . . a direct communication line between the United Nations headquarters and the capitals of the countries that are permanent members of the Security Council. . . . [A] mechanism could be set up under the aegis of the United Nations Organisation for extensive international verification of compliance with agreements to lessen international tension, limit armaments, and of monitoring the military situation in conflict areas. . . . We are arriving at the conclusion that wider use should be made of the institution of the United Nations military observers and peace-keeping forces in disengaging the troops of warring sides, observing ceasefire and armistice agreements.

The speech concluded with a wide-ranging survey of problems requiring global cooperative solutions—Third World debt, international resource development, AIDS, ecology—and contained statements as uncharacteristic of standard Soviet rhetoric as this one: "They say that one thorn of experience is worth more than a whole wood of instruction. For us, Chernobyl became such a thorn . . ." Reinforcing the new cooperative image, the Soviets announced a few weeks later that they would pay all their arrears to the United Nations, including their share of peace-keeping operations that they had opposed.

There is danger, of course, that American political opinion, so prone to fickle extremes, will overreact to the sudden burst of good behavior on the part of Moscow. The "Gorbymania" that accompanied the Washington Summit indicates that it already has. The leaders of the Soviet Union are hardly born-again Wilsonians. But it would be equally foolish to ignore the possibility that large-scale changes may be afoot. It appears, in fact, that the invasion of Afghanistan in 1979, the military act that finally succeeded in mobilizing Western governments against Soviet military expansionism, was a high point of Soviet power and self-confidence—in much the same way, perhaps, as the American buildup in Vietnam presaged a painful, decade-long decline.

The Soviet Union in the 1980s has been a deeply troubled society. Before the accession of Gorbachev in early 1985, the country drifted ineffectually under a leadership that was aged, decrepit, or ill. Brezhnev's incapacity was patent as early as his Vienna SALT II summit with Jimmy Carter. Yuri Andropov, who succeeded him in 1982, gave brief promise of vigorous leadership, but suffered renal failure, it appears, shortly after taking power, and died little more than a year later. Andropov's successor, the wheezing, emphysemic Konstantin Chernenko, was never more than a caretaker, and died after a reign even shorter than Andropov's. Beset by suddenly looming problems, the old men in the Politburo appeared frightened and confused. The Eastern European empire was in crisis. The war in Afghanistan was going badly. Policy in the Third World was an expensive tatter. The country's economy was in evident decline. The enormous level of military investment was an increasingly painful drain. Relations with the United States were poisonous, touching a nadir of sorts with the shooting down of the strayed Korean Air Lines jumbo passenger jet in 1983. Worse, after the sharp Western recession at the start of the decade, the United States was enjoying soaring economic growth, rearming rapidly, and capturing its public's imagination with some flamboyant, if quite cautious, displays of military muscle.

The "Solidarity" labor movement crisis in Poland, beginning in the summer of 1980, exposed the rot at the core of the Soviet imperial system. With Soviet approval, the Polish Party had attempted to import rapid economic growth in the 1970s by financing purchases of Western technology with Western bank credits. In the heady days of the Eurodollar boom, when Western banks were enthusiastically "recycling petrodollars," lenders beat a path to Warsaw, and by 1981 Poland's hard currency debt rose to $27 billion. But the sclerotic Stalinist central planning apparatus proved quite unable to cope, and the technology imports, as often as not, sat uncrated in airports and warehouses. The rapid inflation in commodity import prices in the latter part of the decade squeezed cruelly at a time when rising interest rates were increasing the strain of foreign debt. In the struggle to service its loans and sustain the forced industrialization program, the government engineered a drastic shift of investment resources away from agriculture. By the time Lech Walesa, the hero of the fledgling Solidarity labor movement, led his fellow shipworkers off their jobs in Gdansk in mid-1980, Poland was an economic basket case. The agricultural sector was in utter collapse. Wages and prices were hopelessly out of balance. Rationing was in effect for most basic food items in the major cities. Bribery, hoarding, and corruption were rife. A smarmy new class of Communist millionaires was a visible scandal. National income *fell* 2.3 percent in 1979, 4 percent in 1980, and a staggering 15 percent in 1981.

The enormous popular rallying behind Solidarity and the Catholic Church underscored the great divide between the official Communist ruling party and the Polish people. For more than a year, as events in Poland careened out of control, the Soviets massed troops on the Polish borders, hovering nervously on the brink of intervention. The dithering demonstrated the limits of military power even within the borders of the Soviet land empire. The Poles, unlike the Czechs in 1968, it seemed clear, would fight if invaded. If the Polish Army turned against the Soviet invaders, it might have required a million or more troops to subdue the country, and at least another 300,000 troops to garrison it. Soviet lines in Central Europe would be dangerously thinned; and the Marshals would have even more cause to worry that a mutinous vassal would disrupt their rear in an encounter with NATO. Almost as bad, a Soviet-pacified Poland would expect to be fed, at a time when the Soviet economy was foundering in swamps of its own making. In the event, Soviet intervention was forestalled by the "internal invasion" of Gen. Wojciech Jaruzelski, the recently elected Party leader, in December 1981. Jaruzelski declared martial law, outlawed the independent trade unions, and set about the possibly hopeless task of reconstructing the Polish economy without violating the quirky ideological scruples of its primitive neighbor to the East.

The Soviet indecision at the time of the Polish crisis betrayed much more than military uncertainty. The Soviet Union in the 1980s is confronted with the brute fact that the Marxist-Leninist economic experiment is a resounding failure. The Politburo, in moments of quiet candor, must be aware that it is in no position to dictate economic principles to anyone, least of all to countries, like most of the Eastern European bloc, that have higher standards of living than the Soviet Union. Economic failure in the pragmatic West usually leads to a change in governments, occasionally to a wholesale reordering of policies along socialist or free enterprise lines. Economic failure in the Soviet Union, however, has almost theological implications. The whole point of the Soviet state, after all, the dialectical object of the entire ramshackle apparatus of Communist ideology, is to create a superior economic order. The basis for the legitimacy of one-Party rule, the justification for the substantial limitations on the personal freedom of Soviet citizens, the sole excuse for seven decades of secrecy and police terror, has been the great common enterprise of constructing a successful socialist, and eventually Communist, state. If that mission is an obvious failure, the earth beneath the Party's feet must tremble.

The economic outlook that confronted Mikhail Gorbachev when he assumed the Party leadership in 1985 was one of unrelieved bleakness. The central problem is the slowing rate of Soviet economic growth from a bullish 5+ percent in the 1960s, to the 3.5 percent range in the 1970s, to 2 percent or less in the 1980s. Soviet growth rates in the 1980s are not much slower than those in Western Europe, although considerably slower than those of the United States and Japan since 1982. But the Soviets must do much more than stay even with the West, for matching Western growth rates will ensure only that the East-West wealth gap will continue to expand. (Assume that both America and Russia doubled their real output—from roughly $4 trillion to $8 trillion for the United States and from roughly $2 trillion to $4 trillion for the Soviet Union— the wealth gap would also double, from $2 trillion to $4 trillion.) If the United States managed an average real growth rate of 2.5 percent for the next fifteen years, hardly an heroic aspiration, the Soviets would have to grow at an annual rate of about 7.35 percent, or almost three times as fast, to catch up, and 4.4 percent, or nearly twice as fast, to keep the wealth gap at its current size. Those are daunting targets.

Growth rates of any kind, however, will not come easily. At least partly because of the heavy drain of military spending, which has absorbed 13–14 percent—by some estimates as much as 17 percent—of national product in recent years, the Soviet Union has long been starving its industrial sector of investment resources. From the figures that are available, it appears that for the last fifteen years or so, the rate of Soviet capital equipment replacement has been considerably less than half that in the United States, and slower still than the replacement rate in Western Europe and Japan. Even the notoriously obsolete American steel industry is much more modern than the Soviets'. In 1980, 58 percent of Soviet steel output relied on the old open-hearth method of production, compared to only 12 percent in the United States. (Japan has no open-hearth mills at all.) To make matters worse, the cheap energy sources that maintained the Soviet economy and were a prime source of hard currency earnings throughout the 1970s are drying up. Oil production is trending downward and is becoming much more expensive—more than half of Soviet oil production now comes from wells in the forbidding western Siberian permafrost. The decline in world oil prices has reduced the value of oil exports at the same time as the volume of exports is dropping. A forced-draft effort to replace fossil fuels with nuclear energy came a cropper with the disaster at Chernobyl.

The shortfall of investment in infrastructure is even greater than in basic industries. Astoundingly, in 1981 the state of Texas had more miles of paved roads than the entire Soviet Union, and total Soviet concrete and asphalt highway miles had actually *declined* by 5 percent since 1965. Both France and West Germany had more telephones than the Soviet Union; the total stock of passenger cars was only about a single year's production in America or Japan; the United States had six times as many trucks and buses; and, because of rapidly deteriorating capital equipment and rolling stock, the growth rate in railroad freight traffic declined precipitately throughout the 1970s. The lack of an efficient transportation and communications system—truck parks, repair shops, service stations, spare parts distribution centers, telephone dispatching networks—creates snarls and bottlenecks that make the actual economic picture much worse than statistical comparisons suggest, for a great deal of the production that shows up in official output reports is simply wasted. The Soviet Union, for example, is the largest producer of chemical fertilizer in the world, but Soviet sources themselves concede that perhaps a third of fertilizer output is lost each year because of lack of storage and handling facilities on the collective farms; similarly, in a country desperately striving to become self-sufficient in agriculture, some 20–25 percent of the annual harvest is allowed to spoil because of lack of a proper refrigeration, storage, and transport system.

The central difficulty, of course, is the inability of a rigidly centralized economic management system to allocate resources efficiently in a complex, modern economy. Lenin's aphorism that "Communism equals socialism plus electricity" may have made sense in the 1920s and

1930s: as long as growth depended on building dams and steel mills, modernization could proceed by central economic *ukase*. (There are arguments on both sides of the question; the rate of industrialization, indeed, may have been faster under the czars.) But in the modern era, no central authority has the knowledge, the resources, or the wisdom to manage economic and technological development as directly and in the detail that Communist governments attempt to do.

The evidence of resource misallocation is everywhere. The machine tool inventory is twice as high as in the United States, but industrial output is only two thirds as much. Steel production is 50 percent higher than in America or Japan, but steel is still a production bottleneck. The system is using too much machinery, or too much steel, or wasting it, or the tools and steel are of poor quality, or, most likely, all of the above. Most striking is the low level of labor force productivity—"They pretend to pay us and we pretend to work." The Soviet labor force is 30 percent larger than America's but produces only half the output. Industrial output per worker is some 55 percent of the American level, and agricultural output only about 10 percent, with some 30 million farm workers to America's 3 million. The persisting failure to solve the agricultural production and distribution problem has been the bane of Soviet planners and Party leaders ever since Stalin's rural collectivization. Simply throwing money at the problem has not worked. Agriculture consumes about 27 percent of total domestic investment, but the country still has to direct the great portion of its scarce hard currency resources to import food. Gorbachev's own career barely survived the poor harvests of the early 1980s when he was the responsible agriculture minister.

Perhaps most important, economic and military competitiveness will increasingly depend on successful incorporation of new electronic and opto-electronic technologies, where the gap between the Soviet Union and the West is large and growing. The United States, for example, has perhaps twenty-five times more computers than the Soviet Union. Some analysts have questioned whether it is *possible* for the Soviets to develop a computer-literate society, given the inbred suspicion of free access to information—the paranoid addiction to secrecy requires even copying machines to be closely controlled. The notion of ready access to computerized data bases, even if there were a communication and computer network infrastructure in place, would be anathema. The centers of technological innovation in the West, moreover, have been small-scale entrepreneurial ventures, like those populating

California's Silicon Valley or the "Route 128" technology companies in Massachusetts. There is nothing remotely comparable in the Soviet Union, and it is hard to see how the rigid Soviet resource allocation system can substitute.

The pressure of economic constraints began to bear on the military sector about 1977, according to revised CIA estimates made in 1983 and released publicly in 1985. Ironically enough, that is, the slowdown began at just about the point where Western alarm at the prolonged Soviet buildup had grown sufficiently to generate an offsetting response. Such estimates can be accurate only within very broad ranges, but according to the new data, although Soviet military outlays continued to grow in real terms, the rate of increase dropped almost in half, from about 4 percent per year to about 2 percent after 1977. The CIA traces the slowdown to Soviet problems in assimilating advanced weapons technologies and production bottlenecks in the general economy—suggesting that, despite its privileged claim on resources, the Soviet military may not be as insulated from trends in the general economy as Western analysts have traditionally believed.

What has happened since 1983 is less clear. Official Soviet military budgets have only rhetorical significance; but for what it is worth, the official military budget was frozen from 1981 to 1984, increased sharply in 1985, and was frozen again in 1986. The strategic missile program, however, after a substantial pause, seemed once again to be moving into high gear in 1986. Gorbachev must be under pressure to increase arms spending in response to the Reagan rearmament program, and it is entirely plausible that, economic problems or no, the Soviets have ratcheted up their overall level of defense spending once more. The relentless Soviet determination not to be bested in the arms race, no matter what the cost, has been a constant of recent history, but the strain must be increasing.

There is also considerable evidence, although the picture is still quite blurry, that the Soviet Union's economic problems are generating second thoughts about the expansionist policies followed in the Third World during the latter years of Brezhnev's regime—and particularly the policy of associating primarily with radical "Marxist-Leninist Vanguard Parties." The annual cost of military and economic aid to its Third World clients roughly tripled, measured in constant dollars, during the 1970s, totalling perhaps $40 billion a year by the end of the decade. Even Brezhnev admitted at the Party Congress in 1981, however, that Soviet economic constraints were limiting its flexibility in the Third

World. Nor is there evidence that the radical client states are proving more loyal than the previous generation of "bourgeois-nationalists." The Communist rulers of Mozambique, for example, have worried publicly about becoming a model of "poor socialism." The Soviets permitted considerable published debate on the issue around the time of Brezhnev's death, and Andropov may have been considering substantial policy revisions; at one point he stressed that the proper Soviet global mission was to be an effective model of socialist economic development. Third World policy has not been a major theme for Gorbachev, but he was a protégé of Andropov, and in his first policy speech after assuming office, he made the less than ringing declaration that the Soviet Union's "sympathies" were firmly with their Third World friends.

Staggering as the task of repairing the Soviet Union's economy may be, Gorbachev has thrown himself into it with a flair and energy that rivals Khrushchev's, and with considerably greater consistency and purpose. In his first year in power, he ran noisy but essentially cautious campaigns against drunkenness, corruption, and shoddy workmanship, while concentrating on placing his own loyalists in positions of power in the Central Committee and the Politburo. Through most of 1987, however, as *Glasnost* has given way to *Glasnost II* and *Perestroika* (restructuring) to *Perestroika II*, he seems to be bruiting much more radical changes. Gorbachev, and the band of renegade economists in his train, like Professor Nikolai Shmelev and the doughty Mrs. Tatyana Zaslavskaya, apparently accept that price signals are essential allocators in a complex economy, and that market pricing requires a freer and more efficient flow of information of all kinds than has ever been permitted in the Soviet Union. Shmelev, for example, clearly with Gorbachev's blessing, has been publishing such un-Communist statements as "[There is] no more effective measure of work than profit."

Individual initiative is the central theme of the economic reforms Gorbachev is pushing through a reluctant Politburo. The new law on state enterprises is intended to free factory production of restrictive central quotas by 1991, and to make factory managers responsible for gearing output to their customers' needs. After 1988, wage increases in the 37,000 largest enterprises are supposed to depend on the level of earnings. The multilayered state planning apparatus is supposed to be drastically streamlined, and devoted primarily to long-range planning. The rules for opening small service businesses have already been loosened—although they are still ridiculously confining—and farmers are being given greater opportunities to cultivate and sell their own crops. As early as the late 1970s, Gorbachev was drawing attention to the fact that the Soviet Union's private farm plots, some 3 percent of the total land under cultivation, produce about a quarter of farm output. Nor can he have failed to notice the enormous increase in Chinese food output that materialized almost miraculously after Deng Xiaoping privatized—in fact, if not in theory—Chinese agriculture.

The great promise of a Gorbachev-driven reform movement, if his rhetoric can be taken at face value, is a Soviet Union that is less of an outcast nation, a participant in the normal interstitial transactions of industrialized society, and with a much greater stake in preserving, rather than disrupting, the orderly functioning of trade and commerce—with a joint stake with the West in controlling international terrorism, for instance. For reasons that are argued in Chapter 23, some such shift of perspective and interests is probably a prerequisite to achieving a gradual move away from armed confrontation with the United States. The risk, of course, is that a Soviet Union with an advanced electronics industry might be a much more formidable military opponent; the opposite danger, however, is that a declining society may be the more tempted to lash out in military adventures—even old-fashioned nuclear missiles could still destroy most of the Western world.

Gloomily enough, it is difficult to see how Gorbachev can succeed. Certain of his key reforms are fraught with internal contradictions. He seems, for example, to intend free market pricing only for selected commodities and products, leaving central authority in place for most others, a course that is probably doomed to failure. If raw materials prices are set by a central ministry irrespective of the costs of production, the misallocation of resources and investment will continue, although tracing the problem might be the more confusing. Even more important, Gorbachev has stressed that he intends to shift economic decision making toward market mechanisms without reducing the ultimate power of the Party—to achieve, as Seweryn Bialer has suggested, microlevel democracy combined with macrolevel Party dictatorship, two concepts that may be wholly incompatible, as the military rulers of South Korea discovered.

Even the modest reforms Gorbachev has proposed thus far have already met with strenuous opposition. Zhores Medvedev speculates that he was strongly opposed for the leadership after Andropov's death, and much of the opposition continues. The months-long delay in approving the new law on state enterprises almost certainly stemmed from difficulties in the Central Committee and the Politburo. Power, prestige, and wealth in the Soviet Union derive from membership in the Party and bureaucratic elite, the Communist *nomenklatura,* and its detailed control over the most trivial aspects of daily living. So mightily entrenched a bureaucracy cannot be expected to immolate itself happily on the altar of economic reform.

It is not even clear that the average Soviet citizen is anxious to see the economy unleashed, at least not if it means production-linked wages or the possibility of being fired. Coveting VCRs is one thing; giving up the cradle-to-grave security of the modern Soviet state, drab though it may be, may be quite another. The test will come when Gorbachev ends food subsidies—he has been hinting at substantial increases in food prices through the summer of 1987. The disruptions in Poland began when the Party raised food prices. Just as important, many Communists actually *believe* in Communist ideology. Ideologists, like the second-ranking Party leader Yegor Ligachev, will not easily swallow the social disruption and inequalities that will be the inevitable consequence of a profit-based economic system. Successful as the Dengist reforms have been in China, at least by Western criteria, old-line Communists have been appalled at the rise in crime, sexual license, pornography, vulgar displays of wealth, and all the other seamier aspects of a rapidly growing commercial society—and Deng has been duly forced to moderate the pace of change. Conservative revulsion at the "excesses" of *Glasnost* is already apparent in the Soviet Union.

*Perestroika* and *glasnost* also have unknown implications for Soviet domination over Eastern Europe. The more progressive East European states, including Jaruzelski's Poland, have nominally embraced Gorbachev's reforms. But countries like Poland, Hungary, and Rumania have long operated on rules as liberal as those Gorbachev is trying to force through in Russia. *Perestroika* and *glasnost* in the satellites will inevitably mean much more liberalization than Soviet leaders may be willing to accept. Reformist factions in Eastern Europe are already using Gorbachev's rhetoric as a weapon against their own governments. The crowd of East German youths chanting Gorbachev's name in front of the Berlin Wall in the summer of 1987 must have sent a premonitory shudder through the Soviet leadership. Loosening the reins in Moscow, as Khrushchev discovered in 1956, causes revolution in the satellites. The same risks obtain even at home; the last year has seen unaccustomed stirrings in the Baltic republics and among dispossessed Soviet Tartars.

His chances of success aside, Gorbachev has, it appears, ushered in an almost unique period of opportunity for East-West relations. He has a more direct interest in slowing the pace of military investment than any Soviet leader has had for a long time. Coincidentally, public sector spending in the United States is under severe strain as well, if for different reasons. Conjunctions of the planets producing a mutual interest in a permanent easing of the superpower confrontation have been rare events indeed. The Soviet Union has not been transformed; Gorbachev has yet to demonstrate fully his bona fides, or even his full control over his government. But the change in atmosphere is too great to be dismissed out of hand; cautious, flexible, consistent—in short, wise—statesmanship is called for. That may be a task as daunting for the United States as Gorbachev's grapple with the demon of the Soviet bureaucracy.

# CHAPTER 22

# The Military Balance, 1987

The arms race between the United States and the Soviet Union began within just a few years after the end of World War II. Over the next forty years, both countries spent on their military establishments— estimates of this sort are necessarily approximate—perhaps $15 trillion in 1985 dollars, or the equivalent of four to five years' worth of total output of the entire American economy. The totals would be much higher if the expenditures of the members of their respective alliance systems were included as well. If such enormous outlays are measured against the objective of preventing a nuclear holocaust—a plausible argument can be made that the maintenance of two roughly equivalent arsenals has indeed accomplished such an objective—it is a small enough price. But if such outlays are measured against the achievement of any other conceivable political or military objective, it is remarkable how little has been accomplished.

The fruits of the forty years' labor is that the two sides were, in 1987, approximately at a standoff, arguably where they were at the end of the war. In the late 1940s, it was widely understood by knowledgeable observers that the Soviet Union could, if it chose, overrun continental Europe with its tank and infantry forces. It was also widely understood that the United States could, if it chose, devastate the Soviet Union with nuclear bomber attacks. Neither of these generally accepted propositions was quite true; but the perception of a rough, mutually deterring, if highly asymmetric, standoff prevailed nonetheless.

The asymmetries between the two military establishments are still pronounced forty years later, although much less so. Both sides now unquestionably have the ability to devastate the homeland of the other, and neither side could have great confidence of winning a conventional war in Europe, or certainly not the degree of confidence conducive to military adventurism. As a feat of national organization and commitment, the achievement of relative military equality with the United States by the Soviet Union is much the more imposing: throughout the postwar period, the Soviet leaders had at their disposal only about half the national wealth of the United States. The sporadic bursts of dazzling technical virtuosity by which the United States offset the grim perseverance of the Soviet Union have been marvellously impressive in their own right. But the fundamental point remains. After the expenditure of so much spirit and will, so much treasure and genius, and despite the acquisition of forces with range, speed, and destructiveness on a scale unimaginable to military planners four decades ago, the essential stand-off is little changed.

### The Strategic Balance

The United States and the Soviet Union each had the ability in 1987 to deliver some 10,000 to 12,000 nuclear warheads against the other's homeland. The Soviet Union had by far the greatest deliverable megatonnage, but their newest weapons demonstrate the same trend toward smaller warheads that has long characterized the American arsenal, presumably reflecting steady improvements in guidance technology. The forces are not symmetrical. About two thirds of the Soviet warheads were deployed on land-based missiles. In all, the Soviets had 1,398 land-based missiles with about 6,660 warheads. Of the total missiles, 668 were modern MIRVed SS-18s and SS-19s, with 5,240 warheads, all of which theoretically had the capability of attacking a hardened missile silo. As of 1987, the Soviets were testing a new MIRVed, possibly eight-warhead, solid-fuelled, possibly rail-mobile missile, the SS-24, and were replacing older SS-11s with a new solid-fuelled, apparently very accurate, mobile SS-25. (The introduction of two new missiles is in apparent violation of the SALT II restriction to only one new type; the Soviets insist, with straight faces, that the SS-25 is merely a modernization of the unsuccessful 1960s-vintage mobile SS-13.)

The United States' land-based missile component is much smaller, still basically consisting of the 1,000 Minutemen—450 one-warhead Minuteman IIs and 550 three-warhead Minuteman IIIs. Three hundred of the Minuteman IIIs carried the advanced Mark 12A warhead, which had the capability of attacking any hardened Soviet target; the remainder carried the Mark 12, a less powerful and less accurate warhead, although conservative Soviet planners probably regard it as a hard-target weapon. The old Titans were all scheduled to be phased out by late in 1987, and fifty Minutemen are being replaced with ten-warhead MXs. Even with the MX, the American land-based missile force deployed less than half the warheads of the Soviets, and 3-4,000 fewer hard-target warheads, depending on the counting conventions used.

The Soviet Union had considerably more nuclear missile submarines than the United States in 1987, 62* to 37, and more missiles, 940 to 640, but the United States deployed almost twice as many warheads, 5,728 to 3,084. The gradual replacement of the Poseidon ten-warhead MIRV with the Trident I-C4 eight-warhead MIRV will reduce the American sea-based warhead total, but the Tridents are far more powerful and accurate weapons. The new Trident II-D5, expected to be deployed near the end of the decade, will be the first submarine missile with a hard-target capability. The missiles on Soviet Delta-class submarines have longer ranges than American ones, reflecting the Soviet preference for basing their nuclear submarines in protected home waters. The basing preference probably stems from the comparative noisiness of Soviet submarines; conservative Soviet planners could not regard them as entirely secure from American acoustical tracking technology and new *Los Angeles*-class attack submarines. At the same time, submarines have long represented an area of intense Soviet interest and rapid progress. Most analysts anticipate that the new Soviet Typhoon-class submarines, huge boats similar to the American *Ohio* class, will have the ability to maintain long on-duty cruises under the Arctic ice and will be much quieter than the Deltas. The American Navy has considerable confidence that its own submarine missile fleet will remain invulnerable to Soviet countermeasures for the foreseeable future. Soviet submarine forces are also usually at a much lower state of readiness than American forces—only about 25 percent are out of port at any one time, compared to a 55–65 percent on-station rate for the United States.

The Soviet bomber force did not pose a plausible threat to the American mainland in 1987 although, in theory, the lumbering Bear bombers, which were being outfitted with new AS-15 cruise missiles, could mount an attack on the United States. The impending deployment of a Soviet B-1 lookalike, the "Blackjack" bomber, however, would represent a substantial change in Soviet capabilities, and one that would throw into sharp relief the long neglect of American continental

---

*There are an additional fifteen old diesel "Hotel" and "Golf" class submarines with 39 tactical nuclear missiles that are not counted as strategic weapons under the SALT rules.

air defenses. A substantial portion of American strategic nuclear power, by contrast, is deployed on bombers. Two hundred and forty-one B-52s dispose of a mix of cruise missiles, gravity bombs, and other air-launched missiles that add perhaps another 2,500 deliverable warheads to the American total. A further 150-odd nuclear bombs could be delivered by F-111s based in Europe. If all B-52s were credited with their maximum nuclear bomb loads, the Americans would have a deliverable warhead advantage in the 1,000–3,000 range; but the B-52s are not so armed, and, in any case, since bombers would almost certainly be subject to attrition by defensive systems, gravity bombs and missile warheads are not easily comparable on a strict one-for-one basis. The first squadrons of a planned 100 B-1B penetrating supersonic bombers were entering service in 1987, and work was proceeding apace on a new "Stealth" penetrating bomber for deployment in the mid-1990s.

The official counts of "strategic" forces overlook a number of additional weapon systems. The 270 SS-20s in western Russia in 1987 carried 810 warheads that could blanket targets anywhere in Western Europe. With the addition of a third stage—one that is readily available, some American conservatives argue—the SS-20s could reach the United States, although such an additional capability would seem to serve little purpose. By the same token, the United States had deployed over 400 Pershing II and ground-based cruise missiles in Europe by mid-1987, each with a single warhead capable of reaching western Russia. All of these weapons will be phased out under the new "INF" treaty.

Both countries were also moving rapidly to outfit their surface and submarine fleets with nuclear-capable cruise missiles that would be available as a strategic second-strike force or as tactical nuclear weapons in a theater war anywhere in the world. The Americans planned to deploy about 4,000 sea-launched cruises, of which about 750 would have a strategic nuclear capability; Soviet deployments are expected to be of comparable size.* Finally, although the British and French nuclear forces are, strictly speaking, independent, the Soviets quite reasonably regard them as part of the available Western arsenal in a nuclear war. The British deployed 4 submarines with 64 Polaris missiles in 1987, each with 3 separate, but not independently targetable, war-

*Strategists have not completely digested the implications of the cruise. In place of the traditional strategic "triad," it may now be more accurate to speak of a strategic "pentad"—land-based and submarine-based ballistic missiles, penetrating bombers, and air-launched and sea-launched cruises. There is no practical way, short of continuous inspection, to verify whether cruises carry nuclear warheads or not.

heads, while the French had another 180 warheads, on submarines, on Mirage jet bombers, and on short-range Pluton and Hades missiles.

Although the number of deliverable warheads is roughly the same, the asymmetry in the arsenals—the great preponderance of accurate Soviet land-based warheads—is a source of serious instability. As the Soviets continue to improve the reliability and the accuracy of their missiles, the theoretical possibility of a successful Soviet "coercive" first strike becomes more difficult for responsible American planners to ignore. By 1987, the Soviets could launch three highly accurate warheads against each American silo and still have an equal number of hard-target warheads available for a second countersilo salvo. An American President, the reasoning goes, would then have no choice but to capitulate: his bombers and sea-based missiles would be either too slow or too inaccurate to attack the remaining Soviet missiles, but initiating a city exchange after the quickest-reacting and most reliable leg of the American triad had already been disabled would be tantamount to suicide.

The concentration of nuclear power in the land-based fleet, however, creates a corresponding vulnerability for the Soviet Union. Even with the planned fifty MXs, the United States does not have enough hard-target warheads to mount a two-on-one attack against Soviet silos. But it has more than enough to take out the nearly 700 MIRVed missiles that carry more than *half* of the total Soviet warhead inventory. Almost certainly, somewhere in the bowels of the Kremlin, a Soviet version of Albert Wohlstetter is calculating that a first strike against the Soviet MIRVs would leave the United States with a two-to-one warhead advantage and a clear upper hand in the ensuing global staring contest.

Surprise attack scenarios are wildly implausible. With its limited first-strike capability, an American attack on Soviet MIRVs would be insane. And even with their huge advantage in hard-target warheads, the uncertainties of a Soviet mass attack are still so overwhelming that it can hardly be considered a serious policy alternative. The much more important effect of the powerful Soviet missile fleet is that it undercuts the plausibility of American escalatory threats in a crisis; NATO can no longer count on a cheap victory in Europe by threatening massive retaliation. Even more seriously, the mutual vulnerability of the two land-based fleets could be dangerously destablilizing. The Soviets have made it plain for many years that, in a time of great tension, they would not hesitate to "launch on warning" upon receiving evidence that their strategic arsenal was under attack, or about to come under attack.* Partly to counter the perceived Soviet first-strike advantage, the Reagan administration has issued similar warnings. The asymmetry in land-based missile forces, in short, combined with the increasing vulnerability of fixed silos, could lead to a perilously hair-trigger firing posture in a time of great tension. The point need not be overmade: for many years now, through a wide variety of conflicts and confrontations, with the possible exception of the Cuban missile crisis when the United States held all the advantages, the two adversaries have always managed to stay well away from a confrontation that would justify a full-scale nuclear alert, presumably because the political leadership in each country is acutely aware of the dangers. Still, the asymmetry is a source of festering doubts and justifiable suspicions of the kind that could, at a critical time, explode into paranoia and catastrophe.

There are two other areas of "strategic" weapons—antiballistic missile defenses, or ABM defenses, antisatellite weapons, and "exotic" technologies, like particle-beam weapons. The 1972 ABM Treaty did not rule out research, and there is every indication that the Soviets have maintained a vigorous program of ABM development, while the United States virtually discontinued research for the decade after the treaty was signed. The current Soviet program is more impressive for its breadth and perseverance than for its technical accomplishments. The Soviets have clearly improved their phased-array radar technology and their battle management systems. They have succeeded, with about a decade's lag, in mastering high-acceleration launchers, like the American Sprint missile. High-acceleration missiles greatly simplify the battle management task, because they permit the defender to wait until the atmosphere has stripped away the chaff and decoys from incoming warheads. Finally, and perhaps most important, the dogged Soviet investment in SAM defenses, which has continued without abatement for

*Although both sides casually invoke "launch-on-warning" tactics, a number of analysts have pointed out that a true launch under surprise attack is far more difficult than is sometimes portrayed. American negative control procedures (that protect against an improper launch) decentralize the launch process among hundreds of officers who must act in a coordinated fashion. It is generally assumed that, under normal conditions, the Soviets have similar control systems. It would be very difficult actually to override all the negative controls upon notice of a surprise attack. The danger of a full alert, of course, is that so many of the normal negative controls would have to be dismantled to ensure that any missiles could be launched at all that the risk of a panicked mis-launch would increase by some real amount, however small. In the same vein, it is at least possible (see Chapter 19) that the United States, and possibly the Soviet Union as well, would be unable to respond at all after a relatively small counterforce strike because of overlapping problems of negative controls and communication disruptions.

almost twenty-five years, may within the decade produce a genuine "SAM Upgrade" issue. The addition of portable phased-array radars to SAM sites and faster reacting missiles, perhaps like the SA-10, may some day give the Soviets a plausible defense against tactical ballistic missiles, like the Pershing, although not against ICBMs. Tactical missile defenses, it should be noted, are permitted under the ABM Treaty.

The Soviets have also pursued an extensive program of antisatellite research and testing, another area that was relatively neglected by the United States until the Reagan administration—annual funding during the Carter years, for instance, varied between $40 million and $110 million, or the price of a fighter plane or two. Like their ABM program, Soviet antisatellite development is more impressive for its determination than its accomplishments. By the early 1980s, they had successfully intercepted several low-earth-orbit satellites with ground-based interceptors. All militarily important American satellites, however, are in geosynchronous or higher orbits, or about twenty times higher than the satellites the Soviets have managed to intercept thus far. The United States announced a vigorous research and development program in 1982, and is expected to begin testing prototypes in 1987–88. The Soviets, apparently in some alarm, almost immediately proposed an antisatellite treaty, which was rejected by the Reagan administration. Talks did ultimately begin, but were suspended with the Soviet walkout from Geneva. In general, a good antisatellite agreement would appear to be in the American interest, since United States forces make much greater use of satellite communications than the Soviets do and are correspondingly more vulnerable to effective antisatellite weapons.

Finally, it also is generally assumed that the Soviets have pressed ahead with research in laser, particle-beam—proton or neutron beams—and perhaps even radio-frequency weapons. Soviet laser technology, in fact, is considered quite good, and they have made significant contributions to the field. There are allegations, in addition, that in the mid-1970s the Soviets successfully blinded several American early warning satellites with earth-based laser beams. The Soviets, however, are laggard in many of the technologies that will be essential to creating usable beam weapons—particularly ones in outer space—such as microelectronics and high-speed computers. American research in all beam weapon technologies was vastly accelerated with the announcement of President Reagan's "Star Wars" program in 1983, again to the great alarm of the Soviets.

The American research program has raised the legal question of the extent to which "exotic" technologies are permitted by the ABM Treaty. The treaty is unfortunately ambiguous. Article V bans sea-based, space-based, air-based, or mobile land-based ABM systems. Article II defines "ABM systems" as launchers, missiles, and radars. An "Agreed Statement" promises that "exotic" technologies will be referred for discussion. The Reagan administration proposed that since space-based laser weapons did not meet the definition of "ABM systems" in Article II, they were not banned, but were only subject to discussion under the "Agreed Statement." Senator Sam Nunn has presented an overwhelmingly documented brief showing that the Nixon administration and the treaty's negotiators unanimously interpreted the treaty to the Congress to mean that space-based ABM systems of any kind were absolutely banned; "exotic" components could be developed only for land-based fixed sites, but could not be deployed. Paul Nitze, who concurred with the "traditional" interpretation in 1972, has subsequently changed his view, although he is the only member of the SALT I team to do so. As this book was going to press, the administration's reply to Nunn was not yet available.

It is worth noting that "Star Wars" will be a serious obstacle to an agreement to reduce ICBM inventories, an objective announced by both the Soviet and American leadership. Proliferating warheads is the easiest way to overwhelm missile defenses. By strict RAND logic, the Soviets would be foolish to reduce their warhead inventory if the United States appeared on the verge of a successful defense of its land-based missiles. Indeed, a transition to a "defense-stable" standoff, the avowed goal of some "Star Wars" enthusiasts, may be difficult or even impossible. As missiles are reduced in number, the side with the best defenses gains a major advantage. On the other hand, if missiles are to be reduced by large numbers, there would appear to be less need for expensive defenses in the first place.

## The Conventional Balance

Assessing the conventional balance of forces is much more difficult than totting up strategic missiles, for the counting principles are not nearly so clear. For example, the Soviet Union in 1987 had about 5.3 million men under arms compared to 2.15 million men for the United States. But total NATO and Warsaw Pact troops are much closer in number— 6.44 million for the Warsaw Pact and 5.1 million for NATO. And much, if not all, of the Warsaw Pact's numerical edge is drained away by Soviet deployments in the Far Eastern theater—53 army divisions with per- haps 14,500 tanks, and a substantial portion of its navy and air force— against the threat, real or imagined, posed by China's 3.9 million soldiers. Depending on which forces are weighed in the balance, the Soviet position can be presented either as one of overwhelming superi- ority, or of relative equality, or perhaps even one of some strain.

Maintaining a conventional balance is critical for NATO's doctrine of "flexible response." Since the 1960s, deterring a Soviet attack on Europe without resorting to nuclear weapons has been a central objec- tive of American policy.* The current Soviet superiority in pre-emptive nuclear striking forces underlines the necessity for conventional deter- rence. If NATO's forces collapsed under the first wave of a Soviet assault, it is hard to imagine, given the enormous quick-reacting power of the SS-18s and 19s, that the United States could force a Soviet climb- down with the threat of a homeland missile strike. On the other hand, Soviet doctrine steadfastly maintains that a protracted war in Europe will almost inevitably escalate into an all-out nuclear war. Without the assurance of a quick, clean victory, they are extremely unlikely to initi- ate a conventional test of arms.

The critical confrontation would take place on Europe's central front, stretching from the Baltic Sea in the north through the long West German border with East Germany, Czechoslovakia, and Austria, and anchored in the south by the Swiss Alps.† In the mid-1980s, NATO's

---

*It is worth noting again that this is primarily an *American* objective. There is still a strong undercurrent of opinion in Europe that would prefer the threat of central nuclear war to come into play sooner rather than later. It is not an altogether unreason- able view. Given the great power of modern conventional weapons, Europeans are likely to find the effects of a protracted conventional war only marginally distinguishable from those of a nuclear exchange. Putting the American home territory at risk is also a lot cheaper for Europeans than buying standing armies. The United States, obviously, de- spite decades of fervently declaring its eagerness to commit suicide for its European friends, would much prefer to keep a war confined to the European continent. The difference in viewpoint, although it is rarely stated so baldly, lies at the root of most American-European policy disputes. Over the longer run, particularly as American eco- nomic interests become more involved with Asia, it will inevitably force the dreaded (to Europeans) "decoupling" of American and European military policy.

†There are two other possible areas of confrontation: the so-called "northern flank" across the Baltic on Norway's north coast facing northern Finland and the Soviet Kola Peninsula; and the "southern flank," where Hungary, Romania, and Bulgaria face Yugo- slavia and Italy on the west and Greece and Turkey to the south. The north cape of Norway is considerably north of the Arctic Circle, and is only lightly defended. It is generally assumed that Soviet troops would occupy northern Norway for the sake of improving the defenses of its northern fleet, and particularly its nuclear missile subma- rines, based in the Barents Sea. In the south, the bad blood between Greece and Turkey makes a land defense problematic, but at the same time the mountainous Balkan terrain, and the anomalous position of Yugoslavia, would greatly complicate a Soviet offensive. It is generally assumed that, perhaps after some nasty fighting, the American Sixth Fleet and the French Navy would control the southern flank by blocking the Turkish Straits and

defensive array on the central front presented a number of troubling problems, but the overall picture is hardly one to justify alarm. Once again, counting conventions are critical. Counting only troops on the ground in Germany on the Western side, and in East Germany, Poland, and Czechoslovakia on the Pact side, NATO forces actually have a slight manpower edge, just over a million men to just under a million for the Warsaw Pact, although the Pact forces have half again as many tanks and twice as much artillery. Counting the 37½ Soviet divisions and support units in western Russia, on the other hand, troops that are clearly intended for a war in Europe, and assuming that "Category Two" divisions, some two thirds of the total, are fully manned and equipped, raises the Pact total by another 450,000 men and some 13,000 tanks. Mobilizing East European reserve units would further increase the Pact's striking power.

But calling up reserves, manning the "Category Two" divisions, and moving Soviet troops to the NATO front would take from two weeks to a month, at least, and would be a highly visible operation. A NATO countermobilization could wipe out any Pact advantage. Equipment for five American divisions is pre-positioned in Europe, the French could move in at least another 200,000 men, while the West Germans could theoretically mobilize 1 million well-trained reserves in less than a week. Conservative estimates—which heavily discount NATO's mobilization abilities—indicate that the Pact would enjoy no more than a 1.2:1 manpower edge at the outset of the fighting. The Pact advantage could rise as high as 1.9:1 during the first weeks of the war, but would quickly settle back to roughly the 1.2:1 level by the end of the first month. It is important to stress that these are conservative assumptions. If Soviet mobilization schedules suffer the rate of snafus that are usually assumed for NATO, NATO could plausibly enjoy a manpower advantage at almost every stage of the fighting.*

bottling up the Soviet Black Sea Fleet. Because of the natural barriers of the Baltic and the Alps, events on the central front could be relatively isolated, at least in the first weeks of a war, from those on the northern and southern flanks.

*Not surprisingly, given their political ramifications, estimates of the shifting force balance under various mobilization schedules are highly controversial. The essential point here is that the range of possible estimates is quite wide. Conventional Western estimates for staffing out a Soviet "Category Two" division, which is maintained at 25–50 percent strength, are usually given as three days, which seems implausible, certainly for all twenty-three such divisions in western Russia. In addition, even the Soviet "Category One" divisions, the most combat-ready, are normally maintained at only about 75 percent strength. Under NATO rules, most "Category One" divisions would be listed as "not ready." If Soviet generals are anything like their Western counterparts, they would almost certainly adopt the most pessimistic assumptions regarding their own ability to move troops to the front and the most optimistic ones for NATO's. References to a range of opinion are given in the notes.

Imponderables and intangibles are more important than numerical comparisons. Their unified command and equipment structure must count as a major Pact advantage. The Soviet commanders can also adjust Pact deployments to fit their battle plan. NATO deployments still reflect the arbitrary termination points of the various national components of the Allied armies at the end of World War II. One of the prime Pact attack routes—through the North German Plain to the Ruhr—is defended by an admixture of British, Dutch, Belgian, and German troops, not nearly so strong an array as the crack German and American divisions defending the other two major attack routes to the south—the Fuld Gap toward Frankfurt (perhaps the most likely of all) and the Hof Corridor toward Stuttgart.

NATO is further disadvantaged by its Babel of equipment and organizations. Attempts to unify procurement are usually defeated by the competing interests of national arms manufacturers. It is taken for granted that the French will live up to their obligations under the NATO Treaty, but the separate French command will inevitably create coordination problems. Since most NATO troops are stationed somewhat behind the defensive lines, rapid mobilization after a surprise assault could create a wild criss-crossing snarl as different national units spread out to their positions. Severe as NATO's command problems may be, the Soviets' may be even worse; mutinies are not a major concern for NATO. The necessity for Soviet commanders to keep a wary eye on Polish and Czech troops would inevitably degrade offensive operations. The dangers of revolutions in the satellites also limit Soviet tactical choices: a war of attrition would create serious rear-area security problems.

By adopting a defensive posture, NATO has conceded the initiative to the Pact, and the political necessity for a "forward defense" further limits NATO's options. Since about 25–30 percent of West Germany's population and industry are within 60 miles of the border, a traditional "defense in depth"—conceding space for time, waiting for the attacker's logistics to falter before counterattacking—is simply out of the question. But a defensive posture has a number of advantages. A rule of thumb is that an attacker needs a local force advantage of three to one for a successful breakthrough. It is widely assumed, therefore, that the Soviets will probe for weak points all along the defensive lines, quickly mass for local breakthroughs, and exploit the breakthroughs with highly mobile "Operational Maneuver Groups"—probably armored or motorized rifle brigades—that will disrupt the NATO rear and turn small cracks in the defense into floodgates. But that is a highly demanding attack scenario, one requiring great speed, superb communications, and great initiative on the part of local commanders, attributes not normally associated with Soviet forces. Christopher Donnelly has commented that there is not even a native Russian word for "initiative." The Soviet Army has "considered one of its strengths its iron discipline and high-level centralized command system combined with a universal military doctrine." The *blitzkrieg* attack often envisioned by Western analysts may be the most difficult of all for the Pact to mount.

The darkest NATO scenarios usually assume that the Soviets will achieve breakthroughs at a large number of dispersed points along the front; it is not at all clear, however, that either geography or Pact force levels would permit such a strategy. As William Kaufmann has pointed out, the clash will not occur "somewhere on an infinite flat plain." The German terrain is much hillier, more heavily forested, with more river crossings than the smooth open expanses of western France that lay before the Nazi *Panzer* units crossing the Meuse. The natural attack routes into West Germany are fairly well defined and will be heavily reinforced by NATO defenses. And the more breakthrough points the Pact forces attempt, the more difficult it will be to achieve the required breakthrough mass, and the easier it will be for NATO to cover with adjoining units. NATO's "force to space" ratios, moreover, are generally quite good, even in the more thinly defended northern sector. Because there are limits to the amount of force an attacker can concentrate at any one point, it is usually assumed that a single defensive brigade can block most attacks across a front 7–15 kilometers wide. There are enough troops in the northern sector to cover every seven kilometers with roughly one brigade; even assuming that a third of the defensive brigades are kept in reserve, the brigade to space ratio is still only 1:11 kilometers, which should be enough to stop the first onslaught, even on the unlikely assumption that every point on the front is equally open to attack.

The necessity to mass an attacking force against specific pressure points in the defensive lines also limits the usefulness of the Pact's big quantitative advantages in tanks and artillery. Bringing superior numbers to bear on a small front—the traditional naval problem of "crossing the T"—places the burden of maneuver on the offense. Without outstanding Pact generalship, the numbers of tanks and artillery actually firing at each other in combat may be almost equal. The quality of the

Pact's armored equipment is also open to serious question. Although the Warsaw Pact as a whole has an enormous advantage in tanks—some 50,000 to 25,000—Soviet tank quality has slipped badly since the 1950s. Of the 14,000 tanks in the non-Soviet Pact countries, about 85 percent are T-54/55/62 versions or worse; Pact totals even include some 2,000 T-34s in storage in Eastern Europe, vehicles that are more than forty years old and almost certainly useless in a war. Soviet divisions have a larger number of more modern T-72/80 tanks, most of which are deployed in Europe, but the second-echelon forces still depend heavily on the older models.

The main NATO tanks—the M60A3, the new Abrams M-1, the British Challenger, and, probably best of all, the German Leopard Is and IIs—are far superior to anything the Soviets can put in the field. NATO tanks are more heavily armored and can withstand most Soviet antitank munitions, while all of the Soviet tanks are vulnerable to NATO tank cannon and antitank weapons—or at least were considered to be so until the revelation of Soviet acquisition of "reactive" armor. NATO tanks carry more ammunition, have firing rates roughly twice that of most Soviet tanks, and firing ranges 50–75 percent longer. A massed tank assault against Western armor and antitank weapons could be a disaster for the Pact forces, as it more or less has always been in the Middle East.

There is some evidence, in addition, of extensive tactical debates within the Soviet Union about proper deployments against NATO. On the one hand, nuclear "war-fighting" doctrine requires that tank forces be widely dispersed across a broad front to limit exposure to tactical nuclear weapons. *Blitzkrieg* tactics, on the other hand, require massed armor. In addition, since the Yom Kippur war, armored tactics have emphasized the use of combined infantry-armor sweeps to provide screening fire and infantry attacks against antitank missile emplacements. But combined infantry-armor tactics slow the *blitzkrieg* momentum. The "steamroller" tactics feared by some Western analysts are actually the opposite of the *blitzkrieg* tactics feared by others—the one signifies a ponderous assault across a broad front, the other highly focused, high-speed, breakthrough tactics. The apparent confusion among Western analysts is probably a good reflection of the controversy within the Soviet military.

Including tactical aircraft available for rapid deployment from the United States and France, NATO, and Pact fighter/ground attack air forces are roughly equal in number, although the Pact forces have a large advantage in shorter-range defensive interceptors. American analysts claim that the latest Soviet airplanes, the MiG-29 and 31, and the Su-27 are equivalent to the newest Western models, but such claims have been often made in the past and it is difficult to know whether to take them seriously. In any case, the new planes have been deployed only very slowly, possibly because of problems with their advanced electronic systems. In mid-decade the great bulk of the Pact air forces, including the Soviets', still consists of MiG-21s and 23s (with some Korean War–vintage MiG-15s and 17s thrown in) and much smaller numbers of Su-7s, 17s, and 24s. NATO planes are mostly F-15s and 16s, with some F-4s and A-10 close-support planes. The kill ratios achieved by F-4s, 15s, and 16s against MiG-21s and 23s in the Middle East have been nothing short of extraordinary.

Whether NATO will make best use of its tactical air arm, however, is a subject of some controversy. The standard assumption is that NATO will follow a deep interdiction mission, primarily against Pact airfields. But airfields, particularly ones hardened with reinforced concrete hangars, are difficult targets that are easily repaired, and Warsaw Pact airfields will be heavily defended. The Air Force has resisted attacking airfields with missiles, which might be far less expensive than risking airplanes, on the grounds, it is sometimes alleged, that Air Force tradition requires attacks with piloted aircraft. The Air Force is also accused of neglecting the close-support mission, because the A-10—an inexpensive, subsonic, low-altitude, armored antitank plane—is a boring weapon. Absent significant Air Force support, the Army has filled out its close-support needs with much more costly and vulnerable helicopters. Under pressure, the Air Force has apparently agreed to convert some F-15s and 16s to close-support duties, a mission for which they may be ill-suited. Mach-plus speeds are of little use in the close support mission, and high-performance aircraft have very thin skins which can be easily pierced by a machine-gun bullet.

If NATO withstands the first onslaught, its chances of winning a conventional war appear quite respectable. A critical requirement will be for the American Atlantic Fleet to secure the sealanes to Europe. The Soviet fleet, in fact, is poorly deployed to have much impact in a European war. The large deployments in the Far East and the Indian Ocean will be of little help, and the Black Sea Fleet should be denied passage of the Turkish Straits. In order to reach the North Atlantic, the Northern Fleet, based at Murmansk, must traverse a series of narrow passages around Greenland, Iceland, and the United Kingdom, where it could be engaged by the American Navy outside the range of most of its shore-based air support. Sealane protection, in short, should be well within NATO's capabilities—that is, if it does not exhaust its naval power with forays into the Russian home waters, as the "maritime strategy" seems to call for.

The staying power of the Pact divisions, on the other hand, may be highly questionable. Pact logistics and support structure are still very light, relying heavily on complete replacement by second-echelon units. (After forty-eight hours, according to one American general, the Soviets "drag [a division] into the weeds and bring on another.") Interdiction attacks against follow-on forces could be severely disruptive to the Pact battle plans. And NATO, for all its shortcomings, is probably better placed to meet the enormous materiel requirements of modern warfare. Critical supplies are likely to be short in all the Eastern European countries, and backup equipment is quite poor. If the Soviet first armored wave fails, for example, almost all their remaining tanks will be T-54/55s and T-62s, which will be sitting ducks for NATO defenses. At the same time, failure to achieve a quick victory should greatly increase the possibility of armed uprisings in Eastern Europe.

There is, of course, much that could go wrong for NATO. Successful Soviet deep attacks on airfields, communication centers, repair and supply depots, and storehouses for pre-positioned American equipment would be very damaging. It is easy to imagine how communication and coordination snarls might utterly befoul a defensive mobilization. Soviet airborne "Spetsnaz" troops might disrupt NATO's rear early in the hostilities. Worst of all, and the recurring nightmare of NATO commanders, is the worry whether the NATO political leadership has the will to begin a mobilization in response to aggressive Soviet moves—such as moving the western Russian divisions into Europe for the sake of "large-scale exercises." Refraining from mobilization out of fear of appearing "provocative"—one can almost hear the frightened cacophony in parliaments across Europe—could leave the NATO front desperately vulnerable to a sudden thrust and seriously compromise the possibility of organizing an effective response without resort to nuclear weapons.

Neither side has much to gain from using tactical nuclear weapons. The Warsaw Pact has the advantage in sheer numbers, about 8,000 to 5,250, but at those levels, numerical advantages are meaningless—on average, tactical nuclear weapons are comparable to the Hiroshima bomb. NATO, in fact, has been consciously reducing its nuclear stockpile, because the surplus of weapons adds little marginal capability, but complicates planning and diverts troops to stockpile guard duty. It is unlikely that the Soviets would initiate the use of tactical nuclear weapons: they have insisted for too long that, once the nuclear "firebreak" is crossed, escalation will be uncontrollable. At the same time, it is almost certain that Western commanders would demand authority to use nuclears if the Pact forces were on the verge of a major breakthrough. Weapon for weapon, the Soviet tactical nuclear array is a superior force to the primarily aircraft-delivered NATO weapons. The actual usefulness of the weapons in war, however, is open to considerable question; the most important function of NATO's tactical nuclears is merely to create additional doubts in Soviet minds about the wisdom of a conventional assault.

NATO's position is hardly a cause for complacency, and there is much more that could be done at relatively low cost. Building antitank barriers, for example, if it could ever be made politically acceptable, would help channel Pact attack routes and facilitate defense. Buying more A-10s, and transferring them to the Army, would improve antitank close-support capabilities and would be much cheaper than buying more helicopters. Improved sealift would greatly add to NATO's staying power.

The precariousness of the balance, in addition, creates very difficult problems for the arms control objective of reducing conventional forces in Europe, a far more important goal, by general consent, than reducing missile inventories. Current NATO forces arguably provide adequate coverage against a Soviet assault, but with little additional margin. Almost *any* NATO force reduction, therefore, will have a significant impact on defensive capabilities. Even highly asymmetric force reductions—say, a 600,000-man Pact reduction and a 300,000-man NATO reduction—would leave significant gaps in the NATO lines, and *increase* the advantages on the attacking side. To preserve the possibility of a conventional defense, the Pact reductions would need to be far more disproportionate than the politics of arms negotiations usually permit.

In the main, however, the legend of Warsaw Pact "overwhelming conventional superiority" does not stand up to close analysis. The Pact may indeed be superior, although that is at best an arguable point. As the London Institute of Strategic Studies cautiously concluded in late 1987: "... under a wide range of circumstances general military aggression is a high-risk option with unpredictable consequences, particularly where the possibility of nuclear escalation exists." The interaction between the two force structures, the Institute decided, would be so complex, and would depend on so many unknown, and unknowable, variables, that it would be impossible to predict the outcome of an all-out conventional war.

# CHAPTER 23

# Lessons and Reflections

The greatest accomplishment of the nuclear age, perhaps, is that we have survived it. Paradoxically, the very presence of nuclear weapons contributed to that survival. It is hard to imagine that the Western powers and the Soviet Union could have avoided a third great European war in this century absent the fear of nuclear holocaust. Four decades without a major power war is an undeniable accomplishment. But it has been achieved only at the price of amassing enormous, bristling, dreadfully dangerous stocks of weapons—conventional weapons that could raze all of Europe in just a few days, and nuclear weapons that could quite literally destroy civilized society in the entire world, hardly a matter for enthusiastic self-congratulation.

It is quite possible that we could manage to avoid catastrophe indefinitely, for another forty or for another hundred years, in a state of restlessly armed and competitively arming confrontation, always at the risk that some accident, some temporary epidemic of insanity, some unpredictable concatenation of crises will push the world off the cliff. The hope, quite naturally, is that we can do better than that. Offering advice on achieving such a hope is beyond the pretensions of this book. But understanding the dynamics of the arms competition itself may offer some clues, or at least some cautions, as statesmen address the larger problems.

Over the last forty years, although the the United States and the Soviet Union have achieved a remarkable degree of crisis stability, the arms balance itself has been quite *un*stable. On the one hand, no imbalance in armed power has ever been sufficient to cause one superpower or the other to push a confrontation to war; indeed, with the possible exception of the Cuban missile crisis, the two countries have warily skirted direct military confrontations. But still, thirty years of arms negotiations have failed to achieve the cherished goal of arms control theory: that the two sides could achieve a balance of nuclear and conventional weapons that is intrinsically stable on its own terms, a balance of weapons that is in the perceived best interests of *both* sides to preserve.

Achieving a stable balance of *weapons* is, of course, a secondary objective compared to maintaining actual crisis stability between the superpowers. Common sense and the postwar record argue, however, that severe arms imbalances will make the world more crisis-prone. The quest for this elusive arms balance—defined by Robert McNamara as the state of "stable, mutual assured destruction"—has been a central theme of American weapons planning, and has provided the terms of reference and fundamental logic for American, and to a lesser extent, Soviet, arms negotiators in successive rounds of SALT talks.

In the confident search for a mutually advantageous, semi-permanent balance of weaponry, classical arms control theory has a number of points of analogy with classical economics before the Great Depression—before the unhappy events of the 1930s, and the work of John Maynard Keynes, demonstrated that markets rarely, if ever, achieve the persisting state of grace anticipated by conventional marginal utility theory. "The animal spirits" of investors, among a host of other unpredictable factors, virtually assure continued cycles of economic instability, or worse, a perduring pathological stasis, represented in the 1930s by high and continued unemployment. In the world of classic arms control theory, the endless spiral of dangerous weapons accumulation is the analogy to embedded unemployment in Keynes's critique of classical economics; and, like entrepreneurs' "animal spirits," there are a host of irrational and semi-rational impulses that drive the arms race in ways that cannot be accommodated by conventional analytic models.

In the first place, there are powerful internal political impulses in both countries toward maintaining an apparent margin of military superiority. Dwight Eisenhower occasionally spoke of the requirement for a "sufficiency" of weapons, but when forced to defend his military policies, he stressed America's fundamental superiority. Robert McNamara in his 1967 San Francisco speech defended his proposed "assured destruction" policy on the grounds of the great American *superiority* in strategic warheads—it was the American superiority that ensured that the Soviets could not upset the balance. There are very few cases where statesmen were willing to embrace an *inferior* military position in the name of stability. The Senate doves who fought against MIRVs in the early 1970s may have been willing to do so. Khrushchev may have done so in the early 1960s, and perhaps President Carter in the early part of his administration, each, of course, with a singular lack of success.

Theory aside, in a hostile world, superiority *feels* much better than inferiority—or even "parity," on the unlikely assumption that "parity" could ever be precisely defined. American "assured destruction" advocates, like McNamara, have never denied that a position of military superiority was a much happier place to be during the Cuban missile crisis. Similarly, the forceful self-confidence of the Soviet Union in the 1970s, and its greater willingness to confront the United States, could not have been unrelated to the large enhancements in its military capabilities over the previous decade. More recently in the United States, Paul Nitze's definition of "high-quality deterrence"—sufficient to deny the Soviets victory from any conceivable first strike—necessarily implies a substantial American weapons superiority, a position wholeheartedly adopted by Ronald Reagan and Caspar Weinberger. Theoreticians can dispute the usefulness of "overkill" military capabilities; politicians, whether in the United States or the Soviet Union, who attempt to sell something less can expect heavy political weather. And given the stakes involved, perhaps they should.

But even if there were political willingness to embrace a self-denying state of stable balance, the inherent ambiguity of the military balance makes it virtually impossible to identify such a position with confidence. For one thing, assessments of the military balance are, to a substantial degree, psychological. Occasionally, the imprecision of assessments may help reduce weapons outlays. The upsurge in national self-confidence that attended Ronald Reagan's first term allowed him to wave away the "window of vulnerability" problem—a problem largely of his own making, of course—and deploy the new MX missiles in silos that only shortly before had been declared dangerously vulnerable. Defense analysts rightly protested that nothing essential had changed, and that the silos were still theoretically vulnerable; but with a strong President, who appeared both willing and able to resort to force in a showdown, the immense American strategic establishment appeared formidable enough.

Much more frequently, uncertainty of assessment leads to greater investment. Military leaders *must* give the benefit of the doubt to the opponent's forces; to do otherwise is feckless. But the process by which the military leaders of both sides routinely underrate their own abilities and overrate those of the other will of necessity produce a highly unstable competitive arming process. Only a supremely confident politician like Dwight Eisenhower, who had served as a superior to almost all of his key military officers, could consistently overrule military worst-case judgments, as Eisenhower did during the late 1950s missile scare. And even Eisenhower ultimately lost the argument about how large a strategic establishment the United States needed for its own safety.

The ambiguity operates on many different levels. Lawrence Freedman has pointed out in a recent illuminating discussion that *defensive* objectives almost always require *offensive* capabilities. Troops in a castle under siege would regularly sally forth to disrupt the opponent's attack. What the Soviet Union calls "forward defense"—and, who knows, perhaps they really mean it—looks very much like deployment for aggressive *blitzkrieg* war on NATO. The American quest for a guaranteed "assured destruction" capability in the 1960s appeared to the Soviets as a drive for first-strike superiority; similarly, in the 1970s, the Soviets protested their innocent, and purely defensive, intentions when Americans became so alarmed at the rapid buildup of powerful Soviet MIRVs.

Weapons systems themselves are inherently ambiguous. Almost always, it is the weapon system's use, rather than its inherent capabilities, that determines whether it is offensive or defensive. From the American point of view, nuclear attack submarines are primarily defensive weapons, to be used either to seek out and destroy Soviet missile-carrying submarines or to defend American shipping. But when attack submarines are charged with engaging Soviet missile submarines in their home ports, as the American "Maritime Strategy" suggests, it requires only a faintly suspicious mind to see them as part of a coordinated, counterforce, first-strike strategy. Arming attack submarines with cruise missiles that can attack military installations from short-range offshore launch positions further clouds the issue.

By the same token, the Soviets claim their new mobile missiles will contribute to a stable balance because they are easier to defend; but they are harder to count, and Americans worry, as well they should, about a rapid and surreptitious Soviet force buildup. ABM systems, as Alexei Kosygin protested in the late 1960s, are obviously defensive weapons; who could object to defenses? But good defenses reduce the risk of offensive action and may thereby increase the confidence of an aggressor. President Reagan's "Star Wars" program is the ultimate exercise in ambiguity. Any weapon that can knock out an opposing missile during its boost phase would be an ideal adjunct to an all-out countersilo missile strike.

The ambiguity of weapons, deployments, and strategies is so pervasive that it is a persistent source of confusion even among the NATO allies, let alone the United States and the Soviet Union. When the United States presses for conventional force buildups in Europe, does that mean it is more willing or less willing to fight a war with the Soviets? Will strong conventional forces deter the Soviets from attacking? Or merely underline an American nuclear disengagement, and therefore *entice* a Soviet attack? The fact that some of the most intelligent people in the world have argued all sides of these questions for forty years, and argued them with a religious fervor and ferocity, is a clue that there are no answers. The inherent ambiguity of weapons and deployments, coupled with the powerful political impulse toward military superiority, virtually ensures a continued arms racing instability. Even if the natural political impulse toward superiority were held in check, the other side's deployments would as often not *look* sufficiently threatening to elicit an offsetting response.

But there are further difficulties. Forty years' history makes it clear that technology itself is an independent determinant of the pace and direction of the arms race, quite apart from the intentions or hopes of politicians and strategists. Time and again, technological breakthroughs have radically altered, or threatened to radically alter, the military balance. As the Soviet armies swept toward the Elbe in 1945, Stalin had reason to believe that his vast and still-building conventional power had made the Soviet Union impregnably secure, and possibly strong enough to overmaster the entire continent. The American long-range atomic bomber trumped the Soviet conventional power; and a decade later, the promise of Soviet thermonuclear-tipped intercontinental missiles trumped the American bomber. MIRV technology permitted the inexpensive proliferation of accurate warheads that swept away any hope of stabilizing the missile balance at McNamara's calculated balance of sufficiency. Accurate submarine-launched missiles, like the Trident II D-5, could lead to an immense, and apparently invulnerable, American counterforce threat. Guided antitank missiles threaten the obsolescence of the vast Soviet armored establishment in central Europe; Soviet breakthroughs in armor technology threaten the integrity of NATO defenses; the advent of the homing anti-SAM missile, as Israel demonstrated in the Bekaa Valley, increases the nervousness of *both* NATO and Soviet commanders.

The uncanny accuracy of the newest generations of weapons still on the drawing board, coupled with potential breakthroughs in chemical explosives, may someday offer the possibility of *non-nuclear* counterforce silo attacks, perhaps increasing the attractiveness, because reducing the risk, of a first strike. Reasonably sized shaped-charge chemical weapons can bore through 30 feet of concrete, and could probably disable a hardened silo if the warhead were sure of impacting directly on the silo lid. Once rockets achieve essentially zero CEP, in short, both the conventional and the strategic balance will almost certainly be reshuffled in dramatic and unpredictable ways. Similarly, although the American "Star Wars" program almost certainly will not work as planned, just as certainly, it will produce new generations of weapons—lasers, particle beams, jamming devices, no one can be sure—that will either sharply alter the military balance, or at the very least provide grounds for suspicious Soviet Marshals to *argue* that the balance has been sharply altered.

Self-denying technological abstinence is not the answer. As often as not, as the history of the American MIRV suggests, the great significance of a new weapon system is not perceived until it is virtually ready for deployment. Leaving aside the few obvious cases, like the hydrogen bomb and the long-range missile, most individual weapons appear to be developed with only a limited appreciation of their strategic significance. The entire American strategic triad, for example, which occupies so honored a position in military theory, was more an accident of technology and interservice politics than a conscious development. More important, so long as a major technological breakthrough by the other side is *possible,* the military establishment is obligated to press its own technological development, just to forestall the possibility of a sudden major military disadvantage.

It is a gloomy picture. Technology, the internal political impulse toward a safe margin of superiority, and the inherent ambiguity of most military force deployments, all conspire to produce a continuing arms race. Several hundred hydrogen bombs looked like a grotesquely excessive overkill force in the 1950s. A decade later, excess was measured in the thousands. Two decades later still, with more than 10,000 strategic warheads on each side, forces are so massive as to be strategically meaningless, and still there is no end in sight. The conclusion is inescapable: *within its own terms of reference,* the arms race can neither be ended nor reach a point of enduring stability.

That does not mean that the process of competitive, aggressive arming by the United States and the Soviet Union can never be ended. It means that the problem is of exquisitely greater difficulty than merely calculating the "right" balance of retaliatory nuclear and conventional force, whatever that may be. The arms race is fundamentally a *political* problem, a symbol of the political confrontation between two super-powers with thoroughly inimical beliefs and value systems. It may be expected to continue until the political tensions, the clash of interests, between the United States and the Soviet Union are reduced to the point that both countries, presumably over a very long period of time, jointly conclude that the prospect of war is very remote—so remote that military preparations are steadily reduced until they cease to be-come the important element in the superpower relation.

Stranger things have happened. Who would have predicted forty years ago that France and Germany would be among the closest of European allies? Almost all of the major industrialized countries have in recent history engaged in savage military conflict against one or more of their fellows. Only fifteen years ago, relations between the United States and the People's Republic of China were steeped in mutual hatred. As the Soviet Union takes its place among the major industrial powers of the world, there are wide areas where its interests converge with those of the United States: safely harnessing the newest technolo-gies for energy production, avoiding a worldwide recession or environ-mental disaster, building industrial structures that can compete with the energetic new "tiger" economies of the Pacific rim, curbing the runaway spread of AIDS or narcotics, dealing with the problems of a rapidly aging population, integrating ethnic minorities without vio-lence or social disruption, working at the simple but mind-focusing task of getting richer.

The great promise of Mikhail Gorbachev is that he is the first Soviet leader, with the inconsistent exception of Khrushchev, to make the primary object of his energies—or at least of his rhetoric—just such problems as these, where the convergence of interests between the United States and the Soviet Union is striking and obvious. It is entirely conceivable, in short, that mutual American-Soviet interests could in-crease to the point where normal intercourse would not include im-plicit threats of nuclear missile attacks. Gradually, indeed, such threats might begin to sound silly. The most plausible scenario for ending the arms race, perhaps, is not with some grand agreement. More probably, with gradual resolution of political issues, the arms race, like Lenin's state, would simply wither away. (It might take many more years for governments to concede that their missile installations had become so old that they might as well be dismantled.)

There is no reason to expect that the political confrontation between the superpowers will end at any time soon. The conflicting interests between the two countries are as obvious as the convergences. Soviet geography implies clashing interests in Central Europe, the Middle East, and Asia; Soviet ideology attracts the most violent and terroristic military regimes in Africa; Soviet repressiveness in Eastern Europe, and its human rights record at home, will continue to make normal relations difficult, if not impossible; the vast military establishments on both sides immensely complicate the resolution of political problems; the fact that the Soviet Union has so few levers of world power beyond its armed might, particularly when compared to the United States, skews confrontations toward the military. (Japan and the United States, by contrast, threaten each other with trade or investment cutoffs.)

It is easy to be pessimistic. Since the war, neither superpower has shown itself capable of sustaining a creative, constructive, relation-building statecraft with the other. American policy has veered from extremes of confrontation to extremes of complacency. Henry Kissinger's and Richard Nixon's attempt to weld an arms negotiation process into a larger effort toward improving overall political relations is one of the few instances where the United States even came close to forging a consistent long-range policy, and the effort was a notably short-lived one. Previous Soviet efforts to open the country to outside influences and ideas, as Gorbachev seems to be trying to do, have been firmly squelched by a military-political elite who cling grimly to the Stalinist legacy of a rigid, centralized society, relentlessly arming against a sea of real or imagined invaders. There can be no great confidence that Gorbachev can succeed where all others have failed, if indeed his intentions are in accord with the most optimistic interpretations of them in the West.

In the final analysis, perhaps, only a few simple lessons emerge. The first is that efforts to control the arms race without reference to the sources of broader political tensions will almost necessarily fail. In an atmosphere of political enmity, arms control agreements may often just make things worse—as both sides push treaty interpretations to their pettifogging limits and bend all their technological powers to exploit each loophole in the treaty language. The Soviet proliferation of MIRVs during the first SALT regime and the American military's defense spending "SALT II windfall" are recent cases in point.

Arms control agreements, on the other hand, can powerfully reinforce an atmosphere of easing political tensions. Gorbachev's new willingness to make significant arms bargaining concessions is less important for the concessions themselves—although giving up the SS-20 is an important, if minor, step toward safer force configurations—than as a step toward a broader political dialogue. Major reductions in the number of strategic warheads would similarly be of little military importance—5 billion megatons could destroy civilized society about as effectively as 10 billion megatons—but, again, could provide additional support for a less confrontational politics. Missiles, however, are cheap currency in the age of mega-overkill. Arms reductions will not become significant in their own right until there is a substantial reduction of conventional forces in Central Europe. The true test of Gorbachev's intentions, perhaps, will be his willingness to ratchet down the conventional threat; reductions in Soviet armored divisions, for instance, would genuinely reduce the possibility of nuclear confrontation. For reasons indicated in the previous chapter, however, the technical obstacles to reaching such agreements are daunting.

Finally, both superpowers have amply demonstrated that, regardless of cost, they will not allow themselves to be bested in a weapons-building contest. At least four times in the course of the last four decades, one or the other side has embarked on a major military buildup while the other side was relaxing, if not actually reducing, its own pace of armament. Stalin began a force buildup in Europe while the Western Allies were actively disarming at the end of the war, but his margin of security was swept away by Truman's belated response in the 1950s. The American missile buildup in the early 1960s when Soviet force postures were in a static or declining mode was overborne by the vast Soviet force accretion of the 1970s. Whatever advantage the Soviets may have gained by the end of the 1970s was negated as the Carter, and much more forcefully, the Reagan administration remilitarized American spending priorities in turn. Any hopes that Americans may harbor of gaining a permanent margin of security with a burst of technological weapons development, of the "Star Wars" variety, are similarly doomed to disappointment. Or as Seweryn Bialer has put it, the history of the American-Soviet competition leads to a "blunt conclusion: it is unwise and counterproductive for either superpower to 'kick' the other" when it is down. If only that lesson has been learned from the bitter, and expensive, experience of four decades of arms racing, it would be grounds for considerable long-term optimism.

# Notes

All works are cited by the full title in the initial reference and by short title thereafter. A complete listing of works cited appears after the Notes.

## Introduction

The sources for the material in this section are given in the notes to the relevant chapters below; most quantities in this Introduction are rounded. The "thirty-five" submarines is based on normal on-station rates.

## Chapter 1: The Uncertain Alliance

### The Big Three

For general accounts of the beginnings of the Cold War, see Herbert Feis, *Churchill, Roosevelt, Stalin: The War They Waged and the Peace They Sought* (Princeton: Princeton University Press, 1957); Louis J. Halle, *The Cold War as History* (New York: Harper & Row, 1967); Daniel Yergin, *Shattered Peace: The Origins of the Cold War and the National Security State* (Boston: Houghton Mifflin, 1977); John Lewis Gaddis, *The United States and the Origins of the Cold War: 1941–1947* (New York: Columbia University Press, 1972); Adam B. Ulam, *The Rivals: America and Russia Since World War II* (New York: Viking Press, 1971); and Hugh Thomas, *Armed Truce: The Beginnings of the Cold War: 1945–1946* (New York: Atheneum, 1987). Other important sources include Adam B. Ulam, *Expansion and Coexistence: The History of Soviet Foreign Policy: 1917–1967* (New York: Praeger, 1968); George F. Kennan, *Memoirs: 1925–1950* (New York: Atlantic, Little, Brown, 1967); and Winston Churchill, *Triumph and Tragedy* (Boston: Houghton Mifflin, 1953). See also Arthur M. Schlesinger, Jr., "Origins of the Cold War," *Foreign Affairs* (October 1967), pp. 22–52, and Joseph R. Starobin, "Origins of the Cold War: The Communist Dimension," *Foreign Affairs* (July 1969), pp. 681–696. Roosevelt's Yalta trip and associated comment is from the *New York Times;* the details of the setting are

445

in Diane Shavers Clemens, *Yalta* (New York: Oxford University Press, 1970), pp. 111–117.

For Roosevelt as war leader, see Eric Larabee, *Commander in Chief: Franklin Delano Roosevelt, His Lieutenants, and Their War* (New York: Harper & Row, 1987); the "sunbeam" quote and Churchill's "strategist" assessment are from p. 644; the "possibility" quote, p. 625. Roosevelt on "handling Stalin," "soul of Russia," "young powers," and Yalta agreement are in Hugh Thomas, *Armed Truce*, pp. 171–172; but for his more realistic view, and Stalin's wary appreciation, see Larabee, *op. cit.*, pp. 632–634.

The account of Churchill and Stalin's division of Europe is in Churchill, *op. cit.*, pp. 227–228.; for Harriman's assignment, Adam Ulam, *The Rivals*, p. 48. Larabee defends Eisenhower and Marshall on the Ljubljana Gap proposal in his *op. cit.*, pp. 495–498; on the final lines in Berlin and Austria, see *ibid.*, p. 506, and Thomas, *op. cit.*, pp. 326–330. Churchill's own wavering on the Russians, and the illustrative quotes, are from Thomas, *op. cit.*, pp. 501–505; his "reasonable" quote on Poland is from the *New York Times*, February 23, 1944.

The Soviet side of the Warsaw Rising is in Alexander Werth, *Russia at War: 1941–45* (New York: Avon edition, 1965), pp. 788 ff., and see Schlesinger, *op.cit.*, p. 33. Djilas's and the other quotes on Stalin's criminality are in Thomas, *op. cit.*, p. 39. The rural terror is from Robert Conquest, *The Harvest of Sorrow: Soviet Collectivization and the Terror Famine* (New York: Oxford University Press, 1986), particularly pp. 195–198, 299–307, and 320. For a history of the broader Terror, see Robert Conquest, *The Great Terror: Stalin's Purge of the Thirties*, rev. ed. (New York: Macmillan, 1973); pp. 699–713 contain Conquest's statistical estimates. A more personalized account is in Anton Antonov-Ovseyenko, *The Time of Stalin: Portrait of a Tyranny* (New York: Harper & Row, 1981). The "official" version of Stalin's tyranny, of course, is Khrushchev's "Secret Speech" to the Twentieth Party Congress, which is reprinted in Bertram Wolfe, *Khrushchev and Stalin's Ghost* (New York: Praeger, 1957).

For Bukharin's trial and Stalin's involvement in the procedure, see Stephen F. Cohen, *Bukharin and the Bolshevik Revolution: A Political Biography: 1888–1938* (New York: Oxford University Press, 1980), pp. 372–380. The quote from Aleksandr Solzhenitsyn is from *The Gulag Archipelago: An Experiment in Literary Investigation* (New York: Harper & Row, 1973), p. 101n. Comparative casualties and General Deane's quote are from Gaddis, *op. cit.*, pp. 80, 84. The quote from a Russian official on lend-lease is in Werth, *op. cit.*, p. 577. Roosevelt's "vile" quote is in Gaddis, *op. cit.*, p. 93. The quotes on American leanings toward the Russians are from Adam Ulam, *The Rivals*, p. 20, Hugh Thomas, *op. cit.*, p. 161, and Eric Larabee, *op. cit.*, pp. 632, 636. The "America and Britain: Rivals or Partners" article, by William S. Wasserman, is in the *New York Times Magazine* of February 4, 1945; the C. L. Sulzberger quote is from "The Three Who Shape the Future" in the same edition, p. 52. The two quotes on British decline are from Thomas, *op. cit.*, p. 193; and De Gaulle's quote on the same subject is in Larabee, *op. cit.*, p. 635. The Russian approaches to American and British diplomats are from Thomas, *op. cit.*, pp. 192, 193.

## Yalta

For the Yalta Conference, see Diane Shavers Clemens, *Yalta.* Clemens offers an illuminating analysis of the quid pro quo bargaining that was neglected by Feis and earlier writers. A collection of American documents from Yalta and various minutes and notes from the meetings are in United States Department of State, *Foreign Relations of the United States: The Conferences at Malta and Yalta, 1945* (Washington, D.C.: USGPO, 1955). Cadogan's "woolly and bibulous" and "drivelling" quotes are from Thomas, *op. cit.,* pp. 501, 504; his quote on the leaders is in Yergin, *op. cit.,* p. 62. Stalin's quote on his word is in Thomas, *op. cit.,* p. 544.

The "whirlwind offensive" is from the *New York Times,* February 2, 1945. Harriman's quote on "words" is in Schlesinger, *op. cit.* p. 34, and Roosevelt's "boner" on Germany is in Gaddis, *op. cit.,* p. 120. Stalin's "algebra" quote is in Schlesinger, *op. cit.* p. 30. The exchange between Churchill and Stalin on eagles and small birds is in Clemens, *op. cit.,* p. 130. For the "black legend," see Thomas, *op. cit.,* pp. 418–419. For background on Soviet-Polish relations, see Ulam, *Expansion and Coexistence,* pp. 106–110. For the treatment of Poland by the Soviet troops, the treatment of Polish prisoners, and Pilsudski's and Beria's quotes, see Thomas, *op. cit.,* pp. 239–246. The Katyn Forest story is in J. K. Zawodny, *Death in the Forest* (South Bend, Ind.: University of Notre Dame Press, 1962). The Churchill quote to Poles is in Clemens, *op. cit.,* p. 26. Roosevelt's "high morality" quote is in Gaddis, *op. cit.,* p. 136. Stalin's "less Russian" quote is in Clemens, *op. cit.,* p. 184. American and British quotes at conclusion of Yalta are in *ibid.,* p. 268.

## First Frosts

For Soviet occupation behavior, and the Stalin and Churchill quotes, see Thomas, *op. cit.,* pp. 320–321, 355. The Rumanian episode is in *ibid.,* pp. 283–285, and Ulam, *The Rivals,* p. 58. Churchill's "invincible colossus" quote is in Ulam, *The Rivals,* p. 7. The encounter between Molotov and Truman is in Yergin, *op. cit.,* p. 83. Molotov's assurances on the imprisoned Poles are in Ulam, *Expansion and Coexistence,* p. 383. The Lippmann quote on deterioration of relations is in Yergin, *op. cit.,* p. 99.

For Kennan's view on aid to the Soviets, see his September 1944 memo, "Russia—Seven Years Later," reprinted in his *Memoirs,* pp. 503–531, and particularly pp. 508–510. Harriman's quote on economic aid to the Soviets is in Gaddis, *op. cit.,* p. 189. Truman's quote on Hopkins's mission is in *ibid.,* pp. 235–236. For the Potsdam Conference generally, see Charles L. Mee, Jr., *Meeting at Potsdam* (New York: Evans, 1975), and United States Department of State, *Foreign Relations of the United States: The Conference of Berlin, 1945* (Washington, D.C.: USGPO, 1960). Mee argues in great detail that all the essential Cold War divisions were frozen at Potsdam and assigns blame equally between Truman and Stalin. The "gibbering" quote is from Thomas, *op. cit.,* p. 196. The exchange between Churchill and Stalin at Potsdam is in Ulam, *Expansion and Coexistence,* p. 390; between Molotov and Byrnes, in

Yergin, *op. cit.*, p. 118; and Churchill on Truman's behavior at Potsdam in *ibid.*, p. 115.

## Chapter 2: The Beginning of the Cold War

### Six Fateful Weeks

For the data on public opinion toward the Soviet Union and related quotations, see Gaddis, *op. cit.*, pp. 155–156, 230–233, and 320–321. Truman's "fine man" quote on Stalin is in Gregg Herkin, *The Winning Weapon: The Atomic Bomb and the Cold War* (New York: Knopf, 1980), p. 52. Byrnes's quote on the London Conference is in Gaddis, *op. cit.*, p. 266. The events of February and March 1946 are summarized in Hugh Thomas, *Armed Truce*, pp. 481–499; Stalin's speech is in *ibid.*, pp. 3–17. The Sevareid and Douglas reactions are in Gaddis, *op. cit.*, p. 300. Lippmann's reaction and the *Business Week* quote are in Thomas, *op. cit.*, p. 483. Thomas, *ibid.*, p. 465, has Fuchs passing information on the bomb to the Soviets in June. Some accounts place Fuchs's action after Potsdam, but Zhukov confirmed in his diary that Stalin had advance information of the bomb—see Thomas W. Wolfe, *Soviet Power And Europe: 1945–1970* (Baltimore, John Hopkins, 1970) p. 36. The Tom Clark quote and the JCS quotes are in Thomas, *op. cit.*, p. 485.

Kennan tells of the background to his "Long Telegram" in his *Memoirs*, pp. 271–297. The text as received in the State Department is in Thomas H. Etzold and John Lewis Gaddis, *Containment: Documents in American Policy and Strategy, 1945–1950* (New York: Columbia University Press, 1978), pp. 50–63. The "Mr. X" article is "The Sources of Soviet Conduct," *Foreign Affairs* (July 1947), pp. 566–582. The quote from Vandenberg's speech is in Gaddis, *op. cit.*, p. 295; from Churchill's Fulton speech, *ibid.*, p. 308. The story of the Iranian confrontation is in Ulam, *Expansion and Coexistence*, pp. 425–428, and Thomas, *op. cit.*, pp. 495–499; the Truman and Lippmann quotes on Churchill's speech are in *ibid.*, p. 509. The details of the Acheson-Lilienthal-Baruch initiative on atomic sharing are in *ibid.*, pp. 536–538 (Oppenheimer's quote is on p. 537) and Michael Mandelbaum, *The Nuclear Revolution: World Politics Before and After Hiroshima* (Cambridge: Cambridge University Press, 1981), pp. 190–191.

### The Truman Doctrine

A detailed, if unsympathetic, account of the origin of the Truman Doctrine is in Richard M. Freeland, *The Truman Doctrine and the Origins of McCarthyism* (New York: Knopf, 1972). Kennan's quote on Greece is in his *Memoirs*, p. 316. The meeting of Marshall, Truman, and the congressional leadership on Greece and related quotations are in Dean Acheson, *Present at the Creation: My Years at the State Department* (New York: Norton, 1969), pp. 218–220. Marshall's biographer suggests that Acheson retrospectively inflated his role: see Forrest C. Progue, *George C. Marshall, Statesman, 1945–1949* (New York: Viking, 1987), pp. 164–165. Truman's address is in Gaddis, *op. cit.*, p. 351.

Stalin's quote on Greece is in Milovan Djilas, *Conversations with Stalin* (New York: Harcourt, Brace, 1962), p. 182.

## The Marshall Plan

The account of the Marshall Plan generally follows that of Forrest Pogue, *op. cit.,* pp. 197–257. Adam Ulam on Soviet suspicions of the Marshall Plan is in *Expansion and Coexistence,* pp. 447 and 433–434. The "chilling" quote and the Bohlen quote are from Pogue, *op. cit.,* pp. 190, 196; the negative Soviet reactions, *ibid.,* p. 220; the Bidault quote, p. 224; and Marshall's "struggle" quote, p. 249. For American hopes for Soviet non-participation in Marshall aid, see Kennan, *Memoirs,* pp. 325–353. Lippmann's reply to Kennan's "X" article is collected in Walter Lippmann, *The Cold War,* Ronald Steel, ed. (New York: Harper & Row, 1972), and is extensively excerpted in Walter Lippmann, "The Cold War," *Foreign Affairs* (Spring 1987), pp. 869–884. For the attack on Browder, see Harvey Klehr, *The Heyday of American Communism: The Depression Decade* (New York: Basic Books, 1984), pp. 411–412.

Claire Sterling's *The Masaryk Case* (New York: Harper & Row, 1968) presents the detailed evidence for Masaryk's murder. His *"Finis Bohemiae"* quote is on p. 30. For the speculation on the source of Clay's alarm, see Jean Edward Smith, ed., *The Papers of General Lucius D. Clay,* Vols. I and II (Bloomington, Ind.: University of Indiana Press, 1974), Vol. II, p. 586. For Maclean and Hiss, see Hugh Thomas, *op. cit.,* pp. 515, 527, and 553–554. For Hiss's probable guilt, see Allan Weinstein, *Perjury: The Hiss-Chambers Case* (New York: Knopf, 1978). Kennan's quotation "paragons . . ." is in George F. Kennan, "The Russian Revolution—Fifty Years After: Its Nature and Consequences," *Foreign Affairs* (October 1967), p. 15.

The interpretation followed here, as is clear from the text, follows essentially the current "post-revisionist" trend of scholarship and assigns considerably less responsibility for the Cold War to the United States than the 1960s and early 1970s revisionist historians were wont to do. The seminal revisionist history of the Cold War is William Appleman Williams, *The Tragedy of American Diplomacy* (Cleveland: World Publishers, 1959), and a more extreme version is David Horowitz, *Free World Colossus: A Critique of American Foreign Policy in the Cold War* (New York: Hill and Wang, 1965). For a devastating critique of the methods of the revisionists, see Robert Maddox, *The New Left and the Origins of the Cold War* (Princeton: Princeton University Press, 1972); a short critique is also in Oscar Handlin, *Truth in History* (Cambridge, Mass.: Harvard University Press, 1979), pp. 145–160.

### Chapter 3: "An Action Short of War"

## The Snows of Russia and the Cliffs of Dover

For a sober contemporary assessment of Soviet gains since the war, and the source of the "quasi-official" count, see Hanson W. Baldwin, *The Price of Power* (New York: Harper, 1948), a study prepared for the Council on Foreign Relations. An excellent discussion of the state of mind of the American leadership in the face of Soviet aggressiveness is in Richard H. Rovere, "Reflections: A New Situation in the World," *The New Yorker,* February 24, 1968, pp. 45–78. Rovere makes the point that Marshall and others were equally concerned with containing irresponsible calls for nuclear attacks on Russia from such unlikely sources as Bertrand Russell, Harold Urey, and Leo Szilard as they were worried about Stalin's behavior. The Kennan quote on "violent means" is in William Taubman, *Stalin's American Policy: From Entente to Detente to Cold War* (New York: Norton, 1982), pp. 201–202.

The best contemporary source for the view from inside the Washington policymaking establishment is Walter Millis, ed., *The Forrestal Diaries* (New York: Viking Press, 1951); see p. 392 for the reaction to Bevin's request for military aid. For a careful summary of Soviet military policy in Stalin's last years, see Thomas W. Wolfe, *Soviet Power and Europe,* pp. 32–49. For a more recent assessment that stresses the defensive character of Stalin's arming, see Michael MccGwire, *Military Objectives in Soviet Foreign Policy* (Washington, D.C.: Brookings, 1987), pp. 13–20, 67–71. The "greatest crash" quote is from Walter A. McDougall, . . . *the Heavens and the Earth: A Political History of the Space Age* (New York: Basic Books, 1985), p. 51. Stalin's comment on Lenin's "collision" quote is in Raymond Garthoff, "Ideological Conceptions in Soviet Foreign Policy," *Problems of Communism* (May 1953), pp. 1–9, at p. 7. The Djilas quote on Stalin is in his *Conversations with Stalin,* pp. 114–115. The "joke" quote on American intelligence is in Thomas Powers, *The Man Who Kept the Secrets: Richard Helms and the CIA* (New York: Knopf, 1979), p. 27. Roosevelt's and Churchill's intelligence efforts are in Hugh Thomas, *Armed Truce,* pp. 162, 211–212.

For contemporary estimates of Soviet forces, see, for example, Colin Clark, "Soviet Military Potential," *Soundings* (September 1947), pp. 38–45, and Hanson W. Baldwin, *The Great Arms Race* (New York: Praeger, 1958). The high estimate of 5.6 million Soviet troops in 1948 is in Malcolm Mackintosh, *Juggernaut: The Russian Forces, 1918–1966* (New York: Macmillan, 1967), pp. 270–272. In 1960, Khrushchev gave the following figures for the Soviet military establishment: 1948, 2.8 million men; 1955, 5.5 million men; 1960, 4.6 million men. This is the only time the Soviet Union has ever published official figures on its armed forces. The best American estimates showed relatively flat Soviet force levels between 1948 and 1955, and there was no evidence of the massive buildup required to double force levels in that period as Khrushchev had claimed—which tends to support the suspicion that he was fitting his numbers to his polemics. Critics of American policy who cite Khrushchev's figures for 1948 as evidence of the American penchant for overestimating Soviet strength usually ignore the fact that his figures for 1955, if true, would mean that U.S. intelligence was seriously *under*estimating Soviet force levels at that time. For a discussion, see Thomas W. Wolfe, *Soviet Power and Europe,* p. 10. A detailed review of the 1948 estimation process is in Matthew Evangelista, "Stalin's Postwar Army Reappraised," *International Security* (Winter 1982–83), pp. 110–129. Paul Nitze concludes that, even with hindsight, and accepting Khrushchev's numbers,

Stalin still had by far the more powerful forces because of his superior reinforcement position (interview with author).

For the recovery of the Soviet Air Force during World War II, see John Greenwood, "The Great Patriotic War," in Robin Hingham and Jacob Kipp, eds., *Soviet Aviation and Air Power: A Historical View* (Boulder, Colo.: Westview Press, 1977), pp. 69–137. For American weaknesses at the end of the war, see Thomas, *op. cit.*, pp. 189–190, and Arthur T. Hadley, *The Straw Giant, Triumph and Failure: America's Armed Forces* (New York: Random House, 1986), pp. 29–73. Churchill's "snows" quote is in Herkin, *op. cit.*, p. 18. Bradley's "Shoes" quote is in Hadley, *op. cit.*, p. 123.

For examples of American war-fighting plans, see JCS 1844/13 "Brief of Short-range Emergency War Plan" (July 21, 1948) and JSPC 877/59 "Brief of Joint Outline Emergency War Plan" (May 26, 1949), both reprinted in Thomas H. Etzold and John Lewis Gaddis, eds., *Containment.* For the Air Force's vision of the coming war, see Gen. Carl Spaatz, "Evolution of Air Power," *Journal of the American Military Institute* (Fall, 1947), pp. 3–16. For the limited number of American nuclear weapons, see Gregg Herken, *The Winning Weapon*, pp. 288–289; Daniel Yergin, *Shattered Peace*, p. 465n; and Arthur T. Hadley, *The Straw Giant*, p. 62. A recent chronology is in Donald B. Cotter, "Peacetime Operations Safety and Security," in Ashton B. Carter, John Steinbruner, and Charles A. Zraket, eds., *Managing Nuclear Operations* (Washington, D.C.: Brookings, 1987), pp. 17–74, at pp. 25–27, 63–64. Dulles on the possibility of a general war is quoted in Robert Osgood, *NATO: The Entangling Alliance*, (Chicago: Univ. of Chicago Press, 1962) p. 50. The Truman cabinet discussion on possible Soviet initiatives in Europe is in Walter Millis, *The Forrestal Diaries*, pp. 320–321. Truman's quote on "trigger-happy Russian" and Lovett's on "bubbles" are in Ari Shlaim, *The United States And The Berlin Blockade, 1948–1949: A Study In Crisis Decision-Making* (Berkeley, Univ. of Calif. Press, 1983), pp. 12, 182. Stalin's quote on Finland is in Milovan Djilas, *Rise and Fall* (New York: Harcourt Brace, 1985), p. 155.

## The Berlin Blockade

Shlaim *op. cit.* contains an extremely detailed account of crisis decision making. The background to the crisis is in W. Phillipps Davison, *The Berlin Blockade* (Princeton: Princeton University Press, 1958). Forrestal's diaries are the basic source for the decision making in Washington, and detailed documentation of American decision making on the scene is in Jean Edward Smith, ed., *The Clay Papers*. For a summary of events from Marshall's perspective, see Forrest C. Pogue, *George C. Marshall*, pp. 297–315, 404–412. For discussions of Stalin's Berlin policy in the context of his overall policies toward Europe, see Marshall D. Shulman, *Stalin's Foreign Policy Reappraised* (Cambridge, Mass.: Harvard University Press, 1963), and William Taubman, *Stalin's American Policy*.

Clay's quote on doing business with the Russians is in John Lewis Gaddis, *The Origins of the Cold War*, p. 242. Dratvin's note is quoted in Jean Edward Smith, ed., *The Clay Papers*, Vol. II, pp. 600–601. Washington's reaction to

Molotov's publication of the Smith overture is in Walter Millis, *The Forrestal Diaries*, pp. 441–444. A recent analysis supporting the conclusion of Soviet bad faith is in William Taubman, *op. cit.*, pp. 185–186. Daniel Yergin, consistent with the post-Vietnam revisionist view, treats the episode as a Soviet peace initiative, relying, it appears, on contemporary American press interpretations; see *Shattered Peace*, pp. 371–372.

For the exchanges between Clay, Royall, and Bradley on the appropriate response to the blockade, see Jean Edward Smith, ed., *The Clay Papers*, Vol. II, pp. 607–746. The quotes from Howley and Clay on staying in Berlin are in Shlaim, *op. cit.*, pp. 199–200. The meeting between Clay, Reuter, and Brandt and related quotes is in *ibid.* p. 203. For the process of reaching a decision in Washington and the contrast between Truman's decisiveness and the uncertainties of his advisers, see *The Forrestal Diaries*, pp. 451–491; the quote in the text is on p. 454. The quotes on the Smith-Stalin meeting are in Shlaim, *op. cit.*, p. 314, and Forrestal's machine politician view of Stalin is in *The Forrestal Diaries*, p. 402. The Reuter and Neumann quotes are in W. Phillipps Davison, *op. cit.*, pp. 188–189; the quote from the plaque and on Clay's departure from Berlin are in *ibid.*, pp. 169, 203.

## Chapter 4: From Berlin to the Yalu

### The Shambles of Stalin's Foreign Policy

Churchill's quote on the perversity of Stalin's policies is in Marshall D. Shulman, *Stalin's Foreign Policy Reappraised*, p. 13. Vojtech Mastry, "Stalin And The Militarization of The Cold War" *International Security* (Winter, 1984–1985) pp. 109–129, is a recent review of Stalin's misjudgements. For the Varga/Vosnesensky episodes, see *ibid.*, pp. 33–36 and 44–46; for the Cachin/Thorez episode, *ibid.*, pp. 58–62; for the East European purges, *ibid.*, pp. 36–40, and Zbigniew Brzezinski, "The Pattern of Political Purges," *Annals of the American Academy of Political and Social Sciences* (May 1958), pp. 79–87. For an analysis of the Vosnesensky episode in terms of the Soviet dynastic struggle, see Robert Conquest, *Power and Politics in the USSR: A Study in Soviet Dynastics* (London: Macmillan, 1961), pp. 88 ff.

### The Battle Over American Defense Spending

Daniel Yergin's *Shattered Peace* is the best and most thorough of the revisionist statements for this period. For a detailed study of the battle over defense spending, see Werner Schilling, "The 1950 Defense Budget," in Werner Schilling, Paul Y. Hammond, and Glenn H. Snyder, *Strategy, Politics and Defense Budgets* (New York: Columbia University Press, 1962), pp. 1–266. (The budget being worked on for submission to Congress in the fall of 1948 was for the fiscal year that began in July 1949 and ran through June 1950; in Washington shorthand, and most histories of the controversy, it is known as the "1950 budget.") See also Paul Y. Hammond, "Super-carriers and B-36 Bombers," in Harold

Stein, ed., *American Civil-Military Decisions* (Birmingham, Ala.: University of Alabama Press, 1963), pp. 465–568, and Robert J. Donovan, *The Presidency of Harry S. Truman, 1949–1953.* Vol. II, *The Tumultuous Years* (New York: Norton, 1982), pp. 53–65 and 105–113. Forrestal's view of the struggle is in Walter Millis, *The Forrestal Diaries,* pp. 375–550. Arthur T. Hadley gives a damning account of the behavior of almost all the involved parties in his *Straw Giant,* pp. 90–99. Marshall's reluctance to rearm is in *The Forrestal Diaries,* pp. 432. Forrest C. Pogue in his *George Marshall,* citing Gen. Alfred Gruenther, has Marshall less strongly opposed than Forrestal saw him, but confirms that he declined to support the chiefs' budget (p. 408).

The "Finletter Report" is Air Policy Commission, *Survival in the Air Age: A Report to the President* (Washington, D.C.: USGPO 1948). Forrestal's quote in defeat is in *The Forrestal Diaries,* p. 199. The "China White Paper" was published as U.S. Department of State, *U.S. Relations with China, with Special Reference to the Period 1944–1949* (Washington, D.C.: USGPO, 1949). For the reaction to the fall of China, see Dean Acheson, *Present at the Creation.* Acheson's quote on Alger Hiss is in *ibid.,* p. 360, and for background to the Hiss controversy, see Allan Weinstein, *Perjury,* and Robert J. Donovan, *The Tumultuous Years,* pp. 131–138 and 162–170. The quotes from the Navy hearings are in *ibid.,* pp. 110–113.

A detailed chronology of the drafting of NSC-68 is in Paul Y. Hammond, "NSC-68: Prologue to Rearmament," in Werner Schilling, *et al., Strategy, Politics and Defense Budgets,* pp. 267–358. A more recent review is Samuel Wells, "Sounding the Tocsin: NSC-68 and the Soviet Threat," *International Security* (Fall 1979), pp. 116–158, and see the comments by John Lewis Gaddis and Paul H. Nitze, "NSC-68 and the Soviet Threat Reconsidered," in *ibid.* (Spring, 1980), pp. 164–176. See also Paul H. Nitze, "U.S. Foreign Policy, 1945–1955," *Foreign Policy Association Headline Series* (April 1956), p. 54. The document itself is reprinted in Thomas H. Etzold and John Lewis Gaddis, *Containment,* pp. 385–442. Nitze's quotes in the text are from an interview with the author. The quote from Bradley on defense spending is in Hammond, "NSC-68," p. 304, and the quote on its "historical interest" is in *ibid.,* p. 370.

### The Korean War

A detailed account of the military course of the Korean War and casualty estimates are in Vol. 3 of the official U.S. Army history of the war: James F. Schnabel, Office of the Chief of Military History, U.S. Army, *The United States Army in the Korean War: The First Year* (Washington, D.C., 1972). The Army history takes quite a harsh view of MacArthur after Inchon. For general histories, see John W. Spanier, *The Truman-MacArthur Controversy and the Korean War* (New York: Norton, 1965); Allen Whiting, *China Crosses the Yalu: The Decision to Enter the War* (New York: Macmillan, 1960); and Martin Lichterman, "To the Yalu and Back," in Harold Stein, ed., *American Civil-Military Decisions.* pp. 569–642. For the political background, see Dean Acheson, *Present at the Creation,* pp. 355–360. Robert J. Donovan, *The Tumultuous Years,* pp. 187–268; and Forrest C. Pogue, *George C. Marshall,* pp. 441–490.

The disenchantment of the Chinese with the Soviet Union after Korea and Stalin's insistence that Mao pay for his arms is in Ross Terrell, *Mao* (New York: Harper & Row, 1980), pp. 210–211. The necessity to canvass Chinese schoolchildren is in Raymond Garthoff, *Soviet Military Policy* (New York: Praeger, 1966), p. 176. I. F. Stone's *The Hidden History of the Korean War* (New York: Monthly Review Press, 1952) is an ingenious reconstruction of events from a left-wing perspective. For the die-hard American left view that the South initiated the war, see *ibid.*, p. 13, and David Horowitz, *The Free World Colossus*, p. 121. Khrushchev's account of the Kim-Stalin conversation prior to the attack is in Strobe Talbott, ed. and trans., *Khrushchev Remembers* (Boston: Little, Brown, 1970), pp. 367–368.

MacArthur's description of the first days of the American intervention is quoted in John W. Spanier, *The Truman-MacArthur Controversy*, pp. 34–35. The Inchon quotes are in *ibid.*, pp. 79, 80. A negative view of American performance during the first days of the war—I think an unnecessarily waspish one, considering the odds—is given in Arthur Hadley, *Straw Giant*, pp. 100–108. The Soviet hints of a possible settlement in October are in William Taubman, *Stalin's American Policy*, pp. 218–219. MacArthur's "oriental psychology" quote is in John W. Spanier, *op. cit.*, p. 74. Allan Whiting, *op. cit.*, takes the position that the Chinese withdrawal in November was not a signal, but merely a tactical retreat prior to launching the all-out assault.

For MacArthur's turnabout after the second Chinese attack, see James F. Schnabel, *op. cit.*, p. 298; the description of the retreat and the handover of the command to Ridgeway, pp. 298–339, gives the impression that MacArthur abdicated in the face of the sudden reverse. The Baldwin quote is from his *Power and Politics* (Claremont, Calif.: Claremont College Press, 1950), pp. xii–xiii. Nitze's "terrible risk" quote is from an interview.

## Chapter 5: In Stalin's Wake

### Two Successions

An account of Eisenhower's inaugural and election campaign is in Emmett Hughes, *The Ordeal of Power: A Political Memoir of the Eisenhower Years* (New York: Atheneum, 1975). The liveliest, if not always reliable, source for Khrushchev's career is his memoir, *Khrushchev Remembers.* Also see Edward Crankshaw, *Khrushchev: A Career* (New York: Viking Press, 1966); Myron Rush, *The Rise of Khrushchev* (Washington, D.C.: Public Affairs Press, 1958); and Roy and Zhores Medvedev, *Khrushchev: The Years in Power* (New York: Columbia University Press, 1976). The most complete analysis of the struggle for succession is in Robert Conquest, *Power and Policy in the USSR.* A detailed contemporary analysis of Beria's overthrow is in Boris Nicolaevsky, *Power and the Soviet Elite* (Ann Arbor, Mich.: University of Michigan Press, 1975); see particularly the essays, "Russia Purges the Purgers," pp. 120–129; "The Meaning of the Beria Affair," pp. 130–147; and "The Liquidation of Beria's 'Agents' in Georgia," pp. 175–186. The "moral vacuum" quote from Kennan is in his introduction to Nicolaevsky's book, p. xvi. The quote from Nicolaevsky is in *ibid.*, p. 18.

## A Note on Soviet Government Organization

The government of the Soviet Union operates through an overlapping structure of official government and Party organs. The real power generally rests with the Party. The Central Committee of the Party has grown since Lenin's time to the size of a small parliament. Day-to-day Party administration is carried out by a permanent Secretariat, and overall policymaking is the province of the Politburo. Officially, power rests in the bicameral elected parliament, the Supreme Soviet. Ministers of the government departments are nominally chosen from the Supreme Soviet, and the Council of Ministers is the nominal equivalent of the British cabinet, so Malenkov's position as president of the Council of Ministers was equivalent to that of a British prime minister, or head of the government and chief administrator of the government departments. There is also a president of the Supreme Soviet, but the position is largely an honorary one.

The key governing body, virtually for the entire period since the revolution, has been the Politburo. Politburo members have always held a variety of government and Party, or less frequently, military posts, and are men who have achieved significant stature in their own right, with a claim to the leadership independent of their particular positions at the time. After Stalin's death, the first Politburo consisted of Beria, Bulganin, Kaganovich, Khrushchev, Malenkov, Mikoyan, Molotov, and Voroshilov, as well as two industrial technocrat/ managers, M. G. Pervuhkin and M. Z. Saburov. The new men whom Stalin had brought into the leading party and government organizations at the Nineteenth Congress were mostly dropped. The Politburo's name was also changed to the more democratic-sounding "Praesidium of the Central Committee." The name was changed back again to "Politburo" after Khrushchev's fall. Unless otherwise indicated, references to the "Praesidium" during Khrushchev's rule are to this body. See Helene Carrère d'Encausse, *Confiscated Power: How Soviet Russia Really Works* (New York: Harper & Row, 1982).

Khrushchev's version of Beria's overthrow is in *Khrushchev Remembers,* pp. 319–341; the revelations of his crimes are on p. 338. The complete text of his indictment and sentence is in Robert Conquest, *Power and Politics,* pp. 440–447. Khrushchev's unofficial account of Beria's execution is in Bertram Wolfe, *Khrushchev and Stalin's Ghost,* pp. 316–317. Khrushchev's quote on Yagoda is in *Khrushchev Remembers,* p. 94. The story of his career in the Ukraine is in Edward Crankshaw, *Khrushchev,* pp. 113–125.

## The American Defense Buildup

Tables of United States defense expenditures are in United States Senate, Subcommittee on Appropriations, *Department of Defense Appropriations* (Washington, D.C.: USGPO, various years). The statistics and quotations on the U.S. Korean War and post-Korea buildup are from the Department of Defense,

*Semiannual Report of the Secretary of Defense* (later *Annual Report*) (Washington, D.C.: USGPO, various years).

## A Note on Military Terminology

The division is the basic army unit of organization, essentially comprising a self-sufficient fighting unit, with its own headquarters, staff, and support organization. A NATO division, fully manned, has about 16,000 men—with German divisions ranging up to 20,000. Soviet divisions are smaller—between 10,000 and 12,000 men in 1953, making division comparisons somewhat misleading. Roughly two divisions make up a corps and two or more corps an army, or in Soviet terminology, a "front." Divisions subdivide progressively into brigades, then to regiments, then to battalions. An armored division, for the sake of illustration, will normally comprise two or three tank brigades, each containing two or three tank battalions of fifty-four tanks each and one or two mechanized infantry battalions. Actual divisional strength and composition, however, will vary widely over time and at any given time. The twenty American Army divisions in 1953, for example, comprised only 1.6 million men, or substantially less than what full-strength manning would have called for. The divisions in Korea were at reasonably full complements, those in Europe rather less so, and those at home at essentially skeletal levels.

In U.S. Air Force terminology in 1953, a bomber "wing" comprised about forty-five planes—bombers, escorts, and tankers—and a fighter wing seventy-five planes. Although the terminology was not identical, the total buildup to 143 wings envisioned by the outgoing Truman administration would have roughly doubled the Finletter 70-squadron target. But again organizational terminology is misleading; many wings were under strength, and the Eisenhower administration eliminated ten wings that had no planes at all assigned to them.

Finally, the Navy was divided into four fleets, each with about 100 major surface vessels. In the U.S. Navy, consistent with its force projection mission, the fleets were organized into carrier groups of some sixteen vessels each, that is, an aircraft carrier and supporting cruisers, destroyers, minesweepers, and other vessels. See John Keegan, *World Armies* (London: Macmillan, 1979).

The early problem of NATO communications is in United States Senate, Committee on Foreign Relations, *Statement of General Alfred M. Gruenther, March 26, 1955* (Washington, D.C.: USGPO, 1955). For the European buildup, see Robert Osgood, *NATO, the Entangling Alliance,* pp. 52–101.

For a thorough contemporary discussion of Soviet strategic conceptions, see Raymond Garthoff, *Soviet Strategy in the Nuclear Age* (New York: Praeger, 1956). Garthoff was a leading exponent of the "Stalinist stagnation" hypothesis; for the contrary view, see Asher Lee, *The Soviet Air Force* (New York: Day, 1962), p. 196. See Garthoff, *op. cit.,* pp. 82–84, for the "permanently operating factors," and pp. 86–87 for Soviet attitudes toward nuclear attacks. The "improved WWII" quote is from Michael MccGwire, *Military Objectives,* p. 71.

B. H. Liddell-Hart's *The Soviet Army* (London: Weidenfeld and Nicolson,

1956) is a complete analysis of contemporary Soviet Ground Forces. For infantry tactics and equipment, see Col. Louis Ely, "A General Assessment," pp. 197–212; for Soviet armored forces, see R. M. Ogarkiewicz, "Soviet Tanks," pp. 295–306, and Capt. N. Galay, "Recent Trends," pp. 306–322. The lineage of the Soviet tank force is also in Ray Bonds, ed., *The Soviet War Machine: An Encyclopaedia of Russian Military Equipment and Strategy* (London: Hamlyn, 1976). For the Soviet Air Force, see Asher Lee, ed., *Soviet Air and Rocket Forces* (New York: Praeger, 1959), including the essay by Sir Phillip Joubert, "Long-range Air Attack," pp. 101–116, for the early attempts to build a long-range air fleet. The development of Soviet air doctrine is in Robin Hingham and Jacob Kipp, eds., *Soviet Aviation and Air Power.* See particularly the essays by John Greenwood, "The Great Patriotic War," pp. 69–136, and Alfred L. Monks, "The Soviet Strategic Air Force and Civil Defense," pp. 213–239.

For the performance characteristics of individual aircraft, see *Jane's All the World's Aircraft* (London: Marston & Co., various years). The story of Tupolev's prison design team is in Walter McDougall, . . . *the Heavens and the Earth,* pp. 38–39. For the development of the Soviet Navy, see Michael MccGwire, Ken Booth, and John McDonnell, eds., *Soviet Naval Policy: Objectives and Constraints* (New York: Praeger, 1975), Robert Waring Herrick, *Soviet Naval Strategy: Fifty Years of Theory and Practice* (Annapolis, Md.: U.S. Naval Institute, 1968), and David Woodward, *The Russians at Sea* (London: Kimber, 1965). The quote on contesting for command of the seas is from Raymond Garthoff, *Soviet Military Doctrine* (Glencoe, N.Y.: The Free Press, 1953), p. 363. The Gorshkov quotation is in Robert Waring Herrick, *op. cit.,* p. 62; and the Khrushchev quote on the *Sverdlov* cruisers is in David Woodward, *op. cit.,* p. 229.

For Clausewitz's doctrines, see Karl von Clausewitz, *On War* (Harmondsworth, Middlx.: Penguin, 1968), particularly pp. 254–296. For the Soviet regard for Clausewitz, see Byron Dexter, "Clausewitz and Soviet Strategy," *Foreign Affairs,* (October, 1950), pp. 41–55. The German view of Soviet bullheadedness is in B. H. Liddell-Hart, *The Soviet Army,* p. 6. A discussion of the Soviet "defensive" positioning of their Ground Forces is in Lt. Col. F. O. Mischke's "Geography and Strategy" in Liddell-Hart, *ibid.,* pp. 249–250. See Walter McDougall, *op. cit.,* p. 47, for the prewar Soviet nuclear program. For background on the development of thermonuclear weapons, see Robert Divine, *Blowing on the Wind: The Nuclear Test Ban Debate, 1954–1960* (New York: Oxford University Press, 1978), and Norman Moss, *Men Who Play God: The Story of the H-Bomb and How Men Came to Live with It* (New York: Harper & Row, 1968). The "containment" quotes are from Kennan's "X" article, "The Sources of Soviet Conduct," pp. 576, 581.

## Chapter 6: Eisenhower

A detailed study of the Eisenhower "New Look" is in Glenn H. Snyder, "The 'New Look' of 1953," in W. Schilling, *et al.,* eds., *Strategy, Politics, and Defense Budgets,* pp. 383–524. There is also a thorough treatment in Stephen Ambrose's biography, *Eisenhower,* Vol. II, *The President* (New York: Simon and Schuster, 1984). See also Robert Divine, *Eisenhower and the Cold War* (New York: Oxford University Press, 1981), and for the effect of the presidential campaign, his *Foreign Policy and U.S. Presidential Elections* (New York: New Viewpoints, 1974), pp. 3–85. Eisenhower's own account of his policy is in his memoir, *Mandate for Change: 1953–1956* (Garden City, N.Y.: Doubleday, 1963), pp. 445–458. My understanding of the period also benefited greatly from interviews with Robert Bowie, who was chief of Policy Planning at the State Department during Eisenhower's first term, and Andrew Goodpaster, Eisenhower's assistant and confidant.

The quotations from George Kennan on Eisenhower's intellect are in his *Memoirs: 1950–1963,* Vol. II (New York: Pantheon Books, 1972), pp. 184–187. Eisenhower's quote on Dulles's ability is in Emmett Hughes, *Ordeal of Power,* p. 251. His letter on a non-military successor is reprinted in his *Mandate for Change,* p. 455. The assessment of Wilson is in Stephen Ambrose, *Eisenhower,* p. 36; Dulles's quote on licking the Chinese is in Emmett Hughes, *Ordeal of Power,* p. 105; the Humphrey quotes are in *ibid.,* pp. 72–73. For the Eisenhower peace speech, see Stephen Ambrose, *Eisenhower,* pp. 92–95; for the Korean settlement, see *ibid.,* pp. 97–106, and *Mandate for Change,* pp. 171–191.

Sir John Slessor's view of strategic airpower is in his "Air Power and World Strategy," *Foreign Affairs* (October 1954), pp. 43–53. The quotes from Dulles's January 1954 speech are in Robert Divine, *Eisenhower and the Cold War,* p. 38; his *Foreign Affairs* article is "Policy for Security and Peace" (April 1954), pp. 353–364. Harriman's response to Dulles's speech is his "Leadership in World Affairs" *Foreign Affairs* (July 1954), pp. 525–540. Henry Kissinger's quote is in his "Military Policy and the Defense of 'Grey Areas,'" *Foreign Affairs* (April 1955), pp. 416–428, at p. 425. Eisenhower's "year of maximum danger" quote is in Stephen Ambrose, *Eisenhower,* p. 89. The mid-1954 date stemmed from NSC-68's assumption that the Soviet Union would have 200 atomic bombs by mid-1954, enough, theoretically, to disable the United States. The quote from NSC 162/2 is in Glenn H. Snyder, "The 'New Look,' " p. 436. Eisenhower's quotes on the limitations of the bomb and the possibility of a nuclear war are in Stephen Ambrose, *Eisenhower,* pp. 34–35, 51–52, 70, 88–89, 144, and 184, and in his *Mandate for Change,* p. 453.

The discussion of "containment" relies on a number of sources. John Lewis Gaddis, *Strategies of Containment: A Critical Appraisal of Postwar National Security Policy* (New York: Oxford University Press, 1982), is a book-length study. A shorter version is in Gaddis's "Containment: Its Past and Future," *International Security* (Spring 1981), pp. 74–102. Barton Gellman's *Contending With Kennan: Toward a Philosophy of American Power* (New York: Praeger, 1984) is a provocative discussion. The argument in the note on the rapid obsolescence of Kennan's original formulation of containment relies on John Van Oudenaren, "Containment: Obsolete and Enduring Features," in Arnold C. Horelick, ed., *U.S.-Soviet Relations: The Next Phase* (Ithaca, N.Y.: Cornell University Press, 1986), pp. 27–54. For the Radford-Ridgeway controversy, see Glenn H. Snyder, "The 'New Look.' " The LeMay bombing strategy and reprints of the briefing summaries are in David Alan Rosenberg, "A Smoking Radiating Ruin at the End of Two Hours: Documents on the American Plan for

Nuclear War with the Soviet Union, 1954–55," *International Security* (Winter 1981–82), pp. 3–38.

## The "New Look" and the Arms Race

Oppenheimer's "technically sweet" quote is in Norman Moss, *Men Who Played God,* pp. 53–54. The story of the Japanese fishermen is in Robert Divine, *Blowing on the Wind,* pp. 3–31. For an early statement of the effects of fallout, see Ralph Lapp, " 'Fall-out'—Another Dimension in Atomic Killing Power," *The New Republic,* February 14, 1955, pp. 8–12. The Wilson quote on the Soviet aerial threat is in the June 1953 *Semiannual Report* of the Defense Department, p. 249, and the Quarles quotation is in the December 1953 *Report,* p. 215. The *Military Review* report on the alleged I1-38s is in the May 1954 issue, p. 68; it is a summary of the report in *Aviation Week.* Robert Oppenheimer's article is "Atomic Weapons and American Policy," *Foreign Affairs* (July 1953), pp. 525–535; the "20–30%" quote is on p. 534—he is citing Air Force Chief of Staff Hoyt Vandenberg, who was a tireless publicist for the alleged Soviet threat.

For Stewart Alsop on the "bomber gap," see his columns in the *New York Herald Tribune,* May 16 and 27, 1955. A useful summary of the controversy is in Myron Rush and Arnold C. Horelick, *Strategic Power and Soviet Foreign Policy* (Chicago: University of Chicago Press, 1966), pp. 17–31; the quotation on the effect of the Bison demonstration is on p. 28. The alarmist *New Republic* editorial is in the issue of June 27, 1955, pp. 3–4; it also quotes the *New York Times* editorial. (The editorials are based on pre-Aviation Day practice flights.) For an example of the persistence of the "bomber gap," see *The Communist Bloc and the Free World: The Military Balance 1959* (London: Institute for Strategic Studies, 1959, cited hereafter as *The Military Balance*). In its 1962–63 report, the Institute reduced its estimate of Bears and Bisons to a fourth of its 1959 estimate, more in line with the current view.

## Brinkmanship, Geneva, Budapest

Eisenhower's quote on Vietnam is in Stephen Ambrose, *Eisenhower,* pp. 176–177. Eisenhower wrote these lines in a draft of his memoirs, but excised them so as not embarrass the Kennedy administration. There was also a strong thread of anticolonialism in Eisenhower's views; in the memoir draft, he cited his moral objections to intervening in Vietnam—"the moral position of the United States is more to be guarded than the Tonkin Delta, indeed than all of Indochina"—but, again, and perhaps indicative of the drift of American policy, felt he had to excise them to avoid embarrassing Kennedy. His lecture to Radford on war in Asia is in Robert Divine, *Eisenhower and the Cold War,* p. 57.

The summary of the Formosan crisis is drawn from both Ambrose, pp. 213–214, 229–245, and Divine, pp. 55–70. The homily on war is in Ambrose, pp. 229–230. Churchill's quote on the new Russian regime is in Bertram Wolfe, "A New Look at the Soviet 'New Look,' " *Foreign Affairs* (January 1955), pp.

184–198. Eisenhower's response to the Soviet inspection proposal is in Ambrose, p. 247. Khrushchev's anxieties about the summit are in *Khrushchev Remembers*, pp. 392–400. His quote on "open skies" and Eisenhower's closing address are in Ambrose, pp. 265–266. *The New Republic*'s appraisal of the summit is in Michael Straight, "How Ike Reached the Russians at Geneva," August 1, 1955, pp. 7–11. The other media quotations are in Divine, *op. cit.*, p. 123. For the details of Khrushchev's secret speech and the text, from which the quotations are drawn, see Bertram Wolfe, *Khrushchev and Stalin's Ghost.*

For Khrushchev's problems in Eastern Europe, see Adam B. Ulam, *Expansion and Coexistence*, pp. 580–603. The actual events of the uprisings are drawn for the most part from contemporary reports in the *New York Times*. The quote "unquestionably existing grievances" is from "Proclamation of the Chairman of the Council of Ministers, Cyrankiewicz, to the People of Poznan, June 29, 1956," in Paul E. Zinner, ed., *National Communism and Popular Revolt in Eastern Europe* (New York: Columbia University Press, 1956), pp. 131–136, and the quotes from Gomulka's speech are from "Address by Wladislaw Gomulka Before the Central Committee of the Polish United Workers' Party," in *ibid.*, pp. 197–239. Zinner's *Revolution in Hungary* (New York: Columbia University Press, 1962) is a detailed, scholarly account; the quotation on Rakosi as self-confessed murderer is on p. 213. Endre Marton's *The Forbidden Sky* (Boston: Little, Brown, 1971) is an eyewitness account by a Hungarian who was imprisoned by Rakosi, and Janos Radvanyi's *Hungary and the Superpowers* (Stanford, Calif.: Hoover Institution, 1972) tells the story from the standpoint of a former Party official. Melvin Lasky's *The Hungarian Revolt: A White Book* (New York: Praeger, 1957) is a collection of eyewitness accounts.

Eisenhower's response to both the Hungarian uprising and the Suez crisis is in Stephen Ambrose, *op. cit.*, pp. 347–375. A defensive account of England's role in Suez is in Anthony Eden, *Memoirs: Full Circle* (Boston: Houghton Mifflin, 1960), pp. 210–270. See Leslie Bain, *The Reluctant Satellites* (New York: Macmillan, 1960), pp. 186–208, for a scathing critique of American policy toward Hungary and the role of Radio Free Europe in the rising.

## Chapter 7: The Technological Imperative

*Sputnik*

The account of the Sputnik launching and of the Soviet and American space and missile programs in the 1950s relies heavily on Walter McDougall's splendid . . . *the Heavens and the Earth;* see particularly pp. 41–227; quotes and details not specifically cited to other sources will be found in McDougall. See also Paul Stares, *The Militarization of Space: U.S. Policy, 1945–84* (Ithaca, N.Y.: Cornell University Press, 1985), pp. 22–57. For the reactions to the Sputnik launching cited in the text, see *Newsweek*, October 14 and November 11, 1957; *The New Republic*, October 14 and 21 and November 4 and 11; the *Denver Post*, October 9; and the *New York Times*, October 5–10. All other quotations of Sputnik reactions are drawn from McDougall.

The CIA's role in the development of the U-2 and surveillance satellites is told in Thomas Powers, *The Man Who Kept the Secrets*, pp. 95–97. For missile gap estimates and further citations to contemporary sources, see Brig. Gen. (Ret.) Thomas R. Phillips, "The Growing Missile Gap," *The Reporter*, (January 8, 1959), pp. 12–16, and Asher Lee, *Soviet Air and Rocket Forces*, pp. 146–159; see also John Kennedy, "When the Executive Fails to Lead," *The Reporter*, (September 18, 1958), pp. 14–19. John Prados, *The Soviet Estimate: U.S. Intelligence and Russian Military Strength* (New York: Dial, 1982), pp. 96–114, and Lawrence Freedman, *U.S. Intelligence and the Soviet Strategic Threat* (London: Macmillan, 1977), pp. 62–80, are good discussions.

The production rate estimate implied by Joseph Alsop was from two to five times the best the Americans could do; see Freedman, *op. cit.*, p. 78. Alsop, who coined the term "missile gap," never relented from his accusations: since at least *some* people in the intelligence community believed there might be a missile gap, he argued almost two decades later, Eisenhower "was fecklessly, even wickedly wrong in his dealings with the 'missile gap'—although the gap finally turned out not to exist—thank God!" *Foreign Policy*, "Comment by Joseph Alsop" (Fall 1974), pp. 83–88, at p. 88. For a detailed review of the information readily available on the true state of the Soviet missile program— and a conclusion that the Democrats knew the "missile gap" was a fabrication— see Desmond Ball, *Politics and Force Levels: The Strategic Missile Program of the Kennedy Administration* (Berkeley: University of California Press, 1980), especially pp. 42–62. The "thorough, suspicious" U-2 hearing is in McDougall, *op. cit.*, p. 220. The operational details on both Soviet and American weapons systems are drawn for the most part from *Jane's All the World's Aircraft* for 1958–59 and 1959–60. Schlesinger's quote on "stark choice" is in his pamphlet *The Big Decision: Private Indulgence or National Power* (New York: privately printed, 1960), p. 3. McDougall has an excellent discussion of the growing pressures toward centralized technocratic state management—it is the major theme of his book, and one of the best statements of the thesis I have found. I made a similar argument in my *A Time of Passion: America, 1960–1980* (New York: Harper & Row, 1984).

## The Years of High Theory

The foreign correspondent's description of the defense intellectuals as "Jesuits" is quoted in Fred Kaplan, *The Wizards of Armageddon* (New York: Simon and Schuster, 1983), p. 11, possibly the most complete analysis of the defense intellectuals' influence. For a sampling of Bernard Brodie's work, see *The Absolute Weapon: Atomic Power and World Order* (New York: Harcourt, Brace, 1946), and *Strategy in the Missile Age* (Princeton: Princeton University Press, 1959). See also his "Nuclear Weapons: Strategy or Tactical," *Foreign Affairs* (January 1954), pp. 217–229; "Unlimited Weapons and Limited War," *The Reporter*, (November 18, 1954), pp. 16–21; "More About Limited War," *World Politics* (October 1957), pp. 112–122; and "Defense Policy and the Possibility of Total War," *Daedalus* (Fall 1962), pp. 733–748. And see William W. Kaufmann, "The Requirements of Deterrence" and "Limited War" in William Kaufmann, ed., *Military Policy and National Security* (Princeton: Princeton University Press, 1956) pp. 12–38 and 102–136. For Thomas Schelling, see "Bargaining, Communication, and Limited War," *Journal of Conflict Resolution* (March 1957), pp. 19–36; "Strategy of Conflict," *ibid.* (September 1958), pp. 203–264; *Strategy of Conflict* (Cambridge, Mass.: Harvard University Press, 1960), and *Arms and Influence* (New Haven: Yale University Press, 1966). The bargaining quotations in the text are from *Arms and Influence*, pp. 112–116.

For Herman Kahn, see *On Thermonuclear War*, 2nd ed. (Princeton: Princeton University Press, 1961); the table reproduced in the text is on p. 184. See also *Thinking About the Unthinkable* (New York: Horizon, 1962), and *On Escalation* (New York: Praeger, 1965). In addition to Kaplan's *Wizards*, for general histories, see Michael Mandelbaum, *The Nuclear Question: The United States and Nuclear Weapons: 1946–1976* (Cambridge: Cambridge University Press, 1979), and Lawrence Freedman, *The Evolution of Nuclear Strategy* (New York: St. Martin's Press, 1981). Robert Bowie (interview with author) was a member of the late-term Eisenhower review of force structures. For the early RAND studies, see E. S. Quade, *Analysis for Military Decision-making* (Chicago: Rand-McNally, 1964), particularly his "Selection and Use of Strategic Air Bases: A Case History," pp. 24–63; and Donald B. Cotter, "Peacetime Operations," and Albert Wohlstetter and Richard Brody, "Continuing Control as a Requirement for Deterring," both in Ashton B. Carter, *et al.*, eds., *Managing Nuclear Operations*, at pp. 42–54 and 142–196.

For a useful analysis of some of the dimensions of the signalling problem, see Philip A. G. Sabin, "Shadow or Substance? Perceptions and Symbolism in Nuclear Force Planning," Adelphi Paper No. 222 (London: IISS, Summer 1987). MacArthur's interpretation of the Chinese signals is in Forrest C. Pogue, *George Marshall*, p. 457. The quote in Lawrence Freedman is in his "Strategic Defense in the Nuclear Age," Adelphi Paper No. 224 (London: IISS, Autumn 1987), p. 18. His observation on the "psychological" aspect of deterrence is, in turn, a quote from Robert Jervis.

Kissinger's recommendation for tactical nuclear weapons is in his *Nuclear Weapons and Foreign Policy* (New York: Harper & Row, 1957). For his successive recantations, see Stephen Graubard, *Kissinger, Portrait of a Mind* (New York: Norton, 1973), pp. 182–185. For critical contemporary views of the tactical nuclear weapon argument, see the two-part review of Kissinger's book by James King in *The New Republic*, July 1 and 15, 1957, pp. 18–21 and 16–18, and William Kauffmann, "The Crisis in Military Affairs," *World Politics* (July 1958), pp. 579–603. Kissinger was, in general, not trusted by the RAND intellectuals, who suspected him of trimming his views to support his own political ambitions. Raymond Aron's *The Great Debate* (New York: Anchor, 1963) offers a penetrating analysis of the contradictions inherent in the new theories of nuclear deterrence and war. For Michael Mandelbaum's "free trade" comparison, see *The Nuclear Revolution*, pp. 117–146. Bundy's quote is in Philip A. G. Sabin, *op. cit.*, p. 30. Further contemporary analysis is in Malcolm Hoag, "On Stability in Deterrence Races," *World Politics* (April 1961), pp. 505–527; Seyom Brown, "Invulnerable Retaliatory Capacity and Arms Control," *ibid.* (April 1961), pp. 528–543; and Thomas Schelling, "War Without Pain and Other

Models," *ibid.* (March 1962), at p. 477, which is an early admission that the intellectuals might have been more cautious about proclaiming "missile gaps."

Dinerstein's article, "The Revolution in Soviet Strategic Thinking," appeared in the January 1958 issue of *Foreign Affairs,* pp. 241–252. It was published in book form as *War and the Soviet Union: Nuclear Weapons and the Revolution in Soviet Military and Political Thinking* (New York: Praeger, 1959). The quotes in the text are drawn from the book; see pp. 184–187, 200–211, 223–229, 238–241, and 243–246, except for the "glittering" quote which is the last sentence of his article. Wohlstetter's article appeared as "The Delicate Balance of Terror," *Foreign Affairs* (January 1959), pp. 211–234; all of the quotes in the text are from the article. The quote on the "sensation" caused by Wohlstetter's article is from Fred Kaplan, *The Wizards of Armageddon,* p. 172. The "milestone" quote is in Schelling's "What Went Wrong with Arms Control," *Foreign Affairs* (Winter 1985–86), pp. 219–233.

## The Intellectual as Hero

The Kissinger quotes are drawn in the main from his *Necessity for Choice* (New York: Harper & Row, 1961); see pp. 3, 8–9, 94–97, and 340–358. In addition, see his *Foreign Affairs* articles, "Reflections on American Diplomacy" (October 1956), pp. 37–56; "Strategy and Organization" (April 1957), pp. 379–394; and "Missiles and the Western Alliance" (April 1958), pp. 383–400. For the Fallaci interview, see Bernard and Marvin Kalb, *Kissinger* (Boston: Little, Brown, 1974), pp. 399–400. The Dean Rusk quotation is from "The President," *Foreign Affairs* (April 1960), p. 369. The Tobin quotations are from a March 1958 article in the *Yale Review,* "The Eisenhower Economy and National Security: Defense, Dollars, and Doctrines," reprinted in Dean Albertson, *Eisenhower as President* (New York: Hill and Wang, 1963), pp. 133–145.

The quote from Klaus Knorr on defense requirements is from his "Is the American Defense Effort Enough?" Center for International Studies: Memorandum Number Fourteen (Princeton: Princeton University Press, 1957), p. 35. The quotations from Wassily Leontief are from his "The Decline and Rise of Soviet Economic Science," *Foreign Affairs* (January 1960), pp. 261–272. For contemporary assessments of Soviet economic potential, see Marshal I. Goldman, "The Soviet Standard of Living and Ours," *Foreign Affairs* (July 1960), pp. 625–637; while Philip Mosely's "Khrushchev's New Economic Gambit," *Foreign Affairs* (July 1958), pp. 557–568, is a relatively realistic assessment of Soviet economic problems. A puzzled traveller's account of Soviet backwardness despite the claims for technological superiority is in Peter Paul Stender, "The Paradox of Soviet Power," *Daedalus* (Fall 1962), pp. 766–782. The Herman Kahn "contemptuous" quote is in Lester B. Pearson, "After the Paris Debacle," *Foreign Affairs* (July 1960), pp. 537–546. The remaining Kahn quotes are from his *On Thermonuclear War,* pp. 477, 564, and 568. For Klaus Knorr on "war potential," see his *The War Potential of Nations* (Princeton: Princeton University Press, 1956); the quotes are from pp. 6 and 142–160.

## Chapter 8: The Failure of Dwight Eisenhower

Kissinger's conversation with Dobrynin is in *The White House Years* (Boston: Little, Brown, 1979), p. 113. For an analysis of Khrushchev's political problems, see Carl Linder, *Khrushchev and the Soviet Leadership, 1957–64* (Baltimore: Johns Hopkins Press, 1966), pp. 43–48, 53–57, and 72–89. For his Chinese problems, and the quotes from Mao and Zhou, see Adam Ulam, *Expansion and Coexistence*, pp. 623–624 and 628–630; for one of the earliest thorough analyses of the Sino-Soviet split, see Edward Crankshaw, *The New Cold War: Moscow vs. Pekin* (Baltimore: Penguin, 1963). For his agricultural programs, see Roy and Zhores Medvedev, *Khrushchev*, pp. 58–65, 94–101, and 117–128.

### A Note on Khrushchev's Force Reductions

Khrushchev's cutbacks were announced in four stages: one in 1955 estimated at 640,000 men; a second in 1957 estimated at 1,200,000 men; the third in 1958 estimated at 300,000 men; and the last in 1960 of another 1,200,000 men. The last cut was never fully implemented because of the 1961 confrontation with the Kennedy administration over Berlin. In 1963, Khrushchev announced another series of cuts, apparently designed to complete the 1960 cuts and go even further, but was deposed before the program could be carried out. The estimates of the forces involved in the cuts are of the grossest variety. The main source of information is Khrushchev himself, who provided detailed figures for the Soviet military establishment for various years in 1960. There is reason to believe that Khrushchev may have significantly overstated the size of the Soviet forces in 1955 to inflate the scale of his cutbacks—his figure was much bigger than the one generally accepted by Western analysts. To a substantial degree, the cutbacks were militarily justified, producing a leaner, more mobile, much better equipped force structure. But Khrushchev was clearly pressing the cuts to a point that made the professional soldiers uneasy. Resistance to the cuts was probably an important element in the surprise dismissal of Marshal Zhukov in favor of Malinovsky in 1957; Zhukov's position had been presumed to be well entrenched since he had played a key role in supporting Khrushchev against the attempted Praesidium coup led by Malenkov and Molotov in the same year. Although the cutback program was closely followed by Western specialists, it received little public or official recognition and did not lead to a general reassessment of Soviet fighting capabilities until about 1963. See Lincoln Bloomfield, *Khrushchev and the Arms Race*, pp. 90–104; Thomas W. Wolfe, *Soviet Power and Europe*, pp. 160–194 and 217–236; Thomas W. Wolfe, *Soviet Strategy at the Crossroads* (Cambridge, Mass.: Harvard University Press, 1964), pp. 139–160; and Malcolm Mackintosh, *Juggernaut*, pp. 290–305.

For the economic cost of Soviet military expenditures, see the detailed, although controversial, tables in W. T. Lee, *The Estimation of Soviet Defense Expenditures, 1955–75: An Unconventional Approach*, (New York: Praeger, 1977), pp. 105–106. The "testicles" quote on Berlin is in Michael R. Beschloss,

*MayDay: Eisenhower, Khrushchev and the the U-2 Affair* (New York: Harper & Row, 1986), p. 172. The account of the Berlin crisis generally follows Jack Schick, *The Berlin Crisis, 1958–62* (Philadelphia: University of Pennsylvania Press, 1971); see p. 15 for Khrushchev's November 1958 note. Adam Ulam's theory on a Chinese-German nuclear deal is in *Expansion and Coexistence*, pp. 623 and 629. The numerous quotations from Eisenhower's press conferences and his comments to aides in the latter months of his administration are taken from Volume II of Stephen Ambrose's *Eisenhower: The President*, pp. 502–614. Khrushchev's threat to Harriman is quoted in Thomas Schelling, *Arms and Influence*, p. 39.

The historical verdict on Eisenhower's handling of the Berlin crisis is a good example of the re-evaluation of his presidency. Adam Ulam, writing in the 1960s, is scathing, interpreting Eisenhower's blandness in the face of Khrushchev's threats as simple ignorance and sloth. Jack Schick, some five years later, was more muted in his criticism, but concludes that Eisenhower's failure to send more American troops to Europe, as the "flexible response" theorists were urging, left him with no credible backup to his diplomacy. More recently, Stephen Ambrose insists that Eisenhower's Berlin diplomacy was a "bravo performance." He kept the alliance together, he avoided a confrontation, he continued to reduce the military budget, and Khrushchev still came up empty-handed. Even making generous allowance for the biases of a biographer, if policy is to be judged by its results, Ambrose's judgment seems more nearly the correct one.

For the U-2 episode, Beschloss's account is the definitive one; see, in addition, Stephen Ambrose, pp. 569–579, and David Wise and Thomas B. Ross, *The U-2 Affair* (New York: Random House, 1962). Eisenhower's quote on the U-2 dangers is in Michael Beschloss, *op. cit.*, p. 233; Khrushchev's on the problems they caused him on pp. 238–239. Eisenhower on "free government" and the "elite" is in Walter McDougall, . . . *the Heavens and the Earth*, pp. 138, 229. The "sagging with future memories" and "rearguard and vanguard" phrases are McDougall's. The full text of Eisenhower's "Farewell Address" is in the *New York Times*, January 18, 1960.

### Chapter 9: The Summons of the Trumpet

The chapter title is a paraphrase of Kennedy's inaugural address: "Now the trumpet summons us again [to] . . . a long twilight struggle," *New York Times*, January 21, 1961. The setting for the Vienna meeting is described in the *New York Times* and in Hugh Sidey, *John F. Kennedy, President* (New York: Atheneum, 1964), pp. 192–200. The "blunt survey" and the "hour after hour" quotes are in *ibid*. "Visibly shaken" and the quote from George Kennan are in Lewis Paper, *Kennedy: The Promise and the Performance* (New York: Crown, 1974), pp. 85, 338. For Kennan's admiration of Kennedy, see Vol. II of his *Memoirs*, p. 317. The official memoranda of the summit meeting are still inexplicably classified; requests to reclassify them were refused. The quotations from Kreisky and Khrushchev are in Strobe Talbott, ed. and trans., *Khrushchev Remembers: The Last Testament* (Boston: Little, Brown, 1974), pp. 496–500.

For Kennedy's foreign policy, see Arthur M. Schlesinger, Jr., *A Thousand Days: John F. Kennedy in the White House* (Boston: Houghton Mifflin, 1965), and Theodore C. Sorenson, *Kennedy* (New York: Harper & Row, 1965), the official histories. Roger Hilsman, *To Move a Nation: The Politics of Foreign Policy in the Administration of John F. Kennedy* (Garden City, N.Y.: Doubleday, 1967), is also an insider's view. Lewis Paper's *Promise and Performance* is an even-handed and generally favorable treatment, while Bruce Miroff's closely argued *Pragmatic Illusions* (New York: MacKay, 1974) is more critical. Henry Fairlie, *The Kennedy Promise* (Garden City, N.Y.: Doubleday, 1973), is quite critical of Kennedy's foreign policy brinkmanship, while Richard J. Walton, *Cold War and Counterrevolution* (New York: Viking Press, 1972), is representative of the New Left view. For Kennedy's pragmatist heritage, see my *A Time of Passion,* pp. 5–11, and the sources cited therein particularly Morton White, *Pragmatism and the American Mind* (New York: Oxford University Press, 1972).

The adviser remarking on Eisenhower's view of the national "crisis" was Walt W. Rostow, quoted in Bruce Miroff, *Pragmatic Illusions,* p. 38. For an excellent discussion of the appeal of the space program to Kennedy's technocratic instincts, see Walter A. McDougall, . . . *the Heavens and the Earth,* pp. 301–324. Schlesinger's quote on "oblivion" is in his *The Big Decision,* p. 3. Theodore White on "lack of crisis" is in *The Making of the President, 1960* (New York: Atheneum, 1961), p. 378; the Rovere quote is in Lewis Paper, *Promise and Performance,* p. 232. Sorenson's catalogue of crises is in his *Kennedy,* pp. 292–293. The quote on Kennedy's sharpness during the Berlin crisis is in Hugh Sidey, *John F. Kennedy,* p. 63. Kennedy's "nose in dirt" quote to James Wechsler is quoted in Richard Walton, *Cold War,* p. 116. Sorenson's "no appetite" quote is in *Kennedy,* p. 624.

On "wars of national liberation" and Khrushchev's Third World problems, see Thomas W. Wolfe, *Soviet Strategy at the Crossroads,* pp. 1–11. Thomas Powers, *The Man Who Kept the Secrets,* pp. 112–118, chronicles the Bay of Pigs invasion; the "sitting ducks" quote is on p. 114. The Dean Acheson "Price Waterhouse" quote is in Bruce Miroff, *Pragmatic Illusions,* p. 44. Herbert Dinerstein carefully analyzes the Soviet view of the Bay of Pigs in *The Making of a Missile Crisis: October, 1962* (Baltimore: Johns Hopkins Press, 1976), pp. 127–135; Khrushchev's note is quoted on p. 130. The Eisenhower involvement, which Eisenhower later attempted to deny, is in Stephen Ambrose, *op. cit.,* pp. 608–610 and 637–640.

For the confrontation in Laos, see William J. Rust, *Kennedy in Vietnam: American Vietnam Policy, 1960–1963* (New York: Scribner's, 1985), pp. 28–32. Kennedy's "Thank God" quote is in Herbert Dinerstein, *Making of a Missile Crisis,* p. 136. Robert M. Slusser, *The Berlin Crisis of 1961* (Baltimore: Johns Hopkins Press, 1973), is a superbly detailed account. See also Jack Schick, *The Berlin Crisis, 1958–62.* Khrushchev's invasion anniversary speech is quoted in Thomas W. Wolfe, *Soviet Power and Europe,* p. 93. His complaint about the Western arms buildup is in Robert Slusser, *The Berlin Crisis,* p. 55. The "holy terror" quote is in Jack Schick, *The Berlin Crisis,* p. 155.

The fallout shelter mania is recounted in Theodore Sorenson, *Kennedy,* p.

615, and in Fred Kaplan, *The Wizards of Armageddon,* pp. 307–314. The symmetric quotes from Acheson and Khrushchev are in Robert Slusser, *The Berlin Crisis,* pp. 32, 118, and 126. The Rusk quote is in *ibid.,* p. 135, and the Mikoyan quote is in Jack Schick, *The Berlin Crisis,* p. 178. The account of the Cuban missile crisis draws primarily from Herbert Dinerstein, *The Making of a Missile Crisis.* Graham Allison provides an interesting decisional analysis in *The Essence of Decision: Explaining the Cuban Missile Crisis* (Boston: Little, Brown, 1971); and see Robert F. Kennedy, *Thirteen Days: A Memoir of the Cuban Missile Crisis* (New York: Norton, 1969). For Kennedy's advertised "cool precision," see, for example, "The Cool Precision of JFK," editorial, *The Reporter,* (February 16, 1961), p. 22. The intelligence failure is analyzed in John Prados, *The Soviet Estimate,* pp. 130–134. See also Stuart Novins, "The Invasion That Could Not Succeed," *The Reporter,* (May 11, 1961), pp. 19–22.

Rusk's revelations on a possible missile trade are in J. Anthony Lukas, "Class Reunion: Kennedy's Men Relive the Cuban Missile Crisis," *The New York Times Magazine,* August 30, 1987, p. 58. See Glenn T. Seaborg, *Kennedy, Khrushchev and the Test Ban* (Berkeley: University of California Press, 1981) for the Limited Test Ban Treaty; the American University speech and Khrushchev's reaction are on pp. 213–219. Kennedy's micromanagement in Berlin is in Arthur Hadley, *Straw Giant,* pp. 141–142. The submarine incidents, and the quote from Steinbruner are in John D. Steinbruner, "Choices and Tradeoffs," in Ashton B. Carter, *et al.,* eds., *Managing Nuclear Operations,* pp. 542–543; the details are in Scott D. Sagan, "Nuclear Alerts and Crisis Management," *International Security* (Spring 1985), pp. 99–139, at pp. 112–118.

McNamara's claim for the role of the conventional force buildup in the Berlin crisis was made explicitly in U.S. Department of Defense (Office of Freedom of Information, cited hereafter as DOD/FOI), "Remarks of Secretary McNamara, NATO Ministerial Meeting, 5 May 1962, Restricted Session." For Brodie's change of heart on "flexible response," see his "The McNamara Phenomenon," *World Politics* (April 1965), pp. 672–686, and "What Price Conventional Capabilities in Europe?" *The Reporter,* (May 23, 1963), pp. 25–33, where McNamara's quote on Cuba appears. George Quester is quoted in Desmond Ball, *Politics and Force Levels,* p. 199. Henry Kissinger's worries about Khrushchev's irrationality are in his "Reflections on Cuba," *The Reporter,* (November 22, 1962), pp. 21–24.

## Chapter 10: Winning the Arms Race

### The Search for Rationality

A general account of Robert McNamara in the Pentagon is in Henry Trewhitt, *McNamara and the Ordeal of the Pentagon* (New York: Harper & Row, 1971). For the RAND influence, see Fred Kaplan, *The Wizards of Armageddon,* pp. 249–257; the Enthoven quote is on p. 254. The quote from Colin Gray is in his "What Hath RAND Wrought" *Foreign Policy* (Fall 1971), pp. 111–129, p. 119. The background for PPBS was set out in Charles Hitch and Roland

McKeon, *The Economics of Defense in the Nuclear Age* (Cambridge, Mass.: Harvard University Press, 1960). For illustrative readings on the systems analytic method applied to defense issues, see Stephen Enke, *Defense Management* (Englewood Cliffs, N.J.: Prentice-Hall, 1967), and E. S. Quade, *Analysis for Military Decision-Making.*

More general surveys, all written by insiders and lavish in their praise of McNamara are Charles Hitch, *Decision Making for Defense* (Berkeley: University of California Press, 1965); William W. Kaufmann, *The McNamara Strategy* (Cambridge, Mass.: MIT Press, 1964) (Kaufmann never reveals in this book that he was a key adviser to McNamara or that he wrote many of the McNamara statements he so admires); and Alain Enthoven and K. Wayne Smith, *How Much Is Enough: Shaping the Defense Program, 1961–1969* (New York: Harper & Row, 1971). McNamara's own version of his tenure is in *The Essence of Security: Reflections in Office* (New York: Harper & Row, 1968). For a critical inside view, see Nathan B. Twining, *A Hard Look at U.S. Military Policy* (New York: Holt, Rinehart, Winston, 1966), and Clark Murdock's *Defense Policy Formation* (Albany, N.Y.: State University of New York, 1974). The anecdotes on defense briefings are in Murdock, pp. 77–81. McNamara's "argument is wrong" quote is in his November 21, 1962, "Draft Memorandum for the President," (DOD/FOI). The two quotations from Charles Hitch on centralization are from his *Decision-making for Defense,* p. 39, and his *Economics of Defense in the Nuclear Age,* pp. 237–238.

## Creating a "Missile Gap"

Eisenhower's strategic legacy is in Desmond Ball, *Politics and Force Levels,* pp. 42–46. The key strategic memorandums from McNamara—and the source of the quotations in the text—are the Draft Memorandums for the President of September 23, 1961, November 21, 1962, and December 6, 1963 (DOD/FOI). McNamara's Athens speech is "Remarks by Secretary McNamara, NATO Ministerial Meeting, 5 May 1962, Restricted Session"; his Ann Arbor speech is reprinted in the *New York Times,* June 17, 1962. For a further discussion, see Desmond Ball, "The Development of the SIOP, 1960–1983," in Desmond Ball and Jeffrey Richelson, eds., *Strategic Nuclear Targeting* (Ithaca, N.Y.: Cornell University Press, 1986), pp. 57–83. The "diminishing returns" quote is drawn from the December 6, 1963, Draft Memorandum for the President. The numbers of American and Soviet strategic weapons and their characteristics are drawn from the Draft Memorandums for the President cited; the *Annual Report of the Secretary of Defense* (Washington, D.C.: USGPO, various years); Institute for Strategic Studies, *The Military Balance,* various years; and *Jane's All the World's Aircraft* and *World Weapon Systems,* various years. The count of Soviet missiles, however, is from William T. Lee and Richard F. Staar, *Soviet Military Policy Since World War II* (Stanford, Calif.: Hoover Institution, 1986). Paul Nitze confirms that the SS-4s and 5s were not generally viewed as a force superior to the NATO bomber fleet (interview). Where there are discrepancies in the sources, I have followed McNamara's internal estimates.

The criticism of the McNamara missile procurement program follows that in Desmond Ball, *Politics and Force Levels.* See also William Niskanen, "The Defense Resource Allocation Process," in Stephen Enke, ed., *Defense Management,* pp. 3–22; James Schlesinger, "The Changing Environment for Systems Analysis," in *ibid.,* pp. 89–111 (for the "royal road" quote); and E. S. Quade, "Pitfalls in Systems Analysis," in his *Analysis for Military Decision-making,* pp. 300–316. For the White House reaction to McNamara's dismissal of the "missile gap," see Lewis Paper, *Promise and Performance,* pp. 136–137. For Air Force reaction and McNamara centralization of defense intelligence agencies, see John Prados, *The Soviet Estimate,* pp. 116–119. Thomas Schelling on the "missile gap" is from his "Managing the Arms Race," pp. 601–616, at p. 608, in David Abshire and Richard Allen, eds., *National Security: Political, Military, and Economic Strategies in the Decade Ahead* (New York: Praeger, 1963). The quotations in the remainder of this section are from Desmond Ball, *op. cit.,* pp. 178, 233, 275, 183, 197, and 126.

## The Other Gap

Alistair Buchan's 1962 quote is in his "The Reform of NATO," *Foreign Affairs* (January 1962), pp. 165–182, at p. 167. Henry Kissinger's quotes are in his "The Unsolved Problems of European Defense," *Foreign Affairs* (July 1962), pp. 515–541, at pp. 517 and 532. Edgar O'Ballance, *The Red Army* (London: Faber & Faber, 1964), pp. 204–226, is a typical contemporary overstatement of Soviet capabilities. McNamara's reassessment of the conventional military balance is in his Draft Memorandum for the President, December 19, 1963. The memorandum's analysis is extremely detailed; unless otherwise noted, the discussion in the text and the quotations from McNamara are drawn from this memorandum. The fifty-five division analysis is in William W. Kaufmann, "Planning Conventional Forces: 1950–1980" (Washington, D.C.: Brookings 1982). R. T. Rockingham-Gill's controversial article, "The New East-West Military Balance," *East Europe* (April 1964), pp. 3–9, was one of the earliest non-classified reassessments, and see his exchange with Philip Windsor of the Institute for Strategic Studies in the July 1964 issue, pp. 31–33. See also Sir Anthony Buzzard, "The Possibilities of Conventional Defense," Adelphi Paper, (London: IISS, December 1963). The contemporary appraisals of NATO and Soviet tanks are from *Jane's World Weapon Systems.* The analysis of comparative NATO-Soviet tactical air capabilities is in a Draft Memorandum for the President, October 1, 1966. The resistance by the Army and Joint Chiefs to the conventional reassessment is quoted in footnotes to McNamara's December 19, 1963, memorandum. McNamara's congressional testimony is quoted in R.T. Rockingham-Gill, *op. cit.,* p. 3.

For NATO politics and background, F. W. Mulley, *The Politics of Western Defence* (London: Thames and Hudson, 1962), is a solid discussion by a British parliamentarian and official NATO *rapporteur;* see also Timothy Stanley, *NATO in Transition* (New York: Praeger, 1963). The background to the multilateral force is in John D. Steinbruner, *The Cybernetic Theory of Decision: New Dimensions of Political Analysis* (Princeton: Princeton University Press, 1974), and see Henry Kissinger, "The Skybolt Affair," *The Reporter,* (January 17, 1963), pp. 22–26. The quotation from Thomas Schelling is from his "Managing the Arms Race," pp. 601–616, at pp. 614–615, in David Abshire and Richard Allen, eds., *op. cit.*

Alistair Buchan's reassessment of Soviet power is quoted in R. T. Rockingham-Gill in his July 1964 exchange with Philip Windsor, p. 32. Walter Lippmann's quote is from *The Washington Post,* December 3, 1963. Thomas Wolfe's assessment of Soviet intentions is in his *Soviet Strategy at the Crossroads,* pp. 18–25; and that of Malcolm Mackintosh is in his "Development of Soviet Military Doctrine Since 1918," in Michael Howard, ed., *The Theory and Practice of War* (London: Cassell, 1973), p. 267. The Hudson Institute Report is quoted in C. G. Jacobsen, *Soviet Strategy and Soviet Foreign Policy* (Glasgow: Mackelose, 1972), pp. 52–53.

### Chapter 11: Vietnam Prelude: The Road from Bandung

For a collection of resolutions adopted at Bandung and the attending countries, see *Bandung: The Revolutionary Flame of Bandung* (Djakarta: The Executive Command: Tenth Anniversary of the First Asian-African Conference, 1965). Most of the details of the conference, the quotes from the Western reporter, and from Zhou Enlai's speeches are drawn from Christopher Rand, "Four Hours by Rail from Djakarta," *The New Yorker,* (June 11, 1955), pp. 39–78. See also Peggy Durdin, "Behind the Facade of Asian Unity," *New York Times Magazine,* (April 17, 1955), pp. 24–28. The quote from Sukarno is from Leo Mates, *Nonalignment* (Belgrade: Institute of Politics and Economics, 1972), p. 239.

Bruce D. Porter's *The USSR in Third World Conflicts: Soviet Arms and Diplomacy in Local Wars, 1945–1980* (New York: Cambridge University Press, 1984) is an excellent survey, and see also Andrzej Korbonski and Francis Fukuyama, *The Soviet Union and the Third World: The Last Three Decades* (Ithaca, N.Y.: Cornell University Press, 1987). Khrushchev's policy shift after Bandung is in Francis Fukuyama, "Soviet Strategy in the Third World," *ibid.,* pp. 24–44, at p. 41. For background specific to the Soviet involvement in the Middle East, see Walter Z. Lacquer, *The Struggle for the Middle East: The Soviet Union and the Middle East, 1958–1968* (New York: Penguin, 1972); J. B. Kelly, *Arabia, the Gulf, and the West* (New York: Basic Books, 1980); pp. 458–475, Ammon Sella, *Soviet Policy and Military Conduct in the Middle East* (New York: St. Martin's Press, 1981); Aryell Y. Yodfat, *The Soviet Union and the Arabian Peninsula* (New York: St. Martin's Press, 1983); and Galia Golan, "The Soviet Union and the Middle East After Thirty Years," in Korbonski and Fukuyama, eds., *op. cit.,* pp. 178–207. (Golan gives a good summary of the tangled skein of Soviet motivations in the area. Many different policy threads are apparent at all times, although certain ones tended to dominate at particular times.)

For other specific Soviet Third World involvements during this period, see Edgar O'Ballance, *The Secret War in the Sudan, 1955–1972* (London: Faber & Faber, 1977), and his *The War in the Yemen* (Hamden, Conn.: Archon, 1971). The Palmerston quote is in J. B. Kelly, *Arabia,* p. 459. The Dulles quote on "serious development" is in Alexander L. George and Richard Smoke, *Deter-*

*rence in American Foreign Policy: Theory and Practice* (New York: Columbia University Press, 1974), p. 317.

The background to the Nasser arms deal is from Muhammed Heikel, *The Sphinx and the Commissar: The Rise and Fall of Soviet Influence in the Arab World*, (London: Collins, 1978) pp. 55–65. For the French and Soviet arms deliveries and their use in the Suez fighting, see Jon D. Glassman, *Arms for the Arabs: The Soviet Union and War in the Middle East* (Baltimore: Johns Hopkins Press, 1975), pp. 6–21; the quote from Zhukov is on p. 15. For the stepped-up Soviet efforts in the Third World after 1955, see Bruce D. Porter, *The USSR in Third World Conflicts*, pp. 18–21. Franklin A. Lindsay, "Unconventional Warfare," *Foreign Affairs* (January 1962), pp. 264–276, is an example of the tendency to assume that the Soviets were skilled manipulators of the Third World countries. For Nasser's exploitation of Soviets, see Muhammed Heikel, *Sphinx and Commissar*, pp. 25–35. For Khrushchev's run-ins with Sukarno, see Paul Johnson, *Modern Times* (New York: Harper & Row, 1983), p. 479, and Adam Ulam, *Expansion and Coexistence*, p. 562. The quotes from Nasser on "road to Moscow" and "Red Crescent" are from Walter Z. Lacquer, *The Struggle for the Middle East*, pp. 58, 84. The *Pravda* quotes on Yemen are from Bruce D. Porter, *op. cit.*, p. 72; the one on Turkey is from Walter Z. Lacquer, *op. cit.*, p. 37. The Kosygin quote is from Muhammed Heikel, *op. cit.* p. 174.

For the "Eisenhower Doctrine," see Alexander L. George and Richard Smoke, *Deterrence*, pp. 309–360. See, in addition, for the Lebanese intervention, William B. Quandt, "U.S. Intervention in Lebanon," in Barry M. Blechman and Stephen S. Kaplan, eds., *Force Without War: U.S. Armed Forces as a Political Instrument* (Washington, D.C.: Brookings, 1978), pp. 225–256. The details on the decision process are in Stephen Ambrose, *Eisenhower the President*, pp. 469–475; the "most relaxed" quote is on p. 470. For Khrushchev's reaction, see William B. Quandt, *op. cit.*, pp. 250–251. For the Chinese anger at Khrushchev's summit proposal, see Adam Ulam, *Expansion and Coexistence*, p. 616. For the intervention in Laos, see Roger Hilsman, *To Move a Nation*, pp. 130–146; David K. Hall, "The Laos Crisis, 1960–1961," in Alexander L. George, David K. Hall, and William E. Simons, eds., *The Limits of Coercive Diplomacy: Laos, Cuba, Vietnam* (Boston: Little, Brown, 1971), pp. 36–85; and David K. Hall, "The Laotian War of 1962," in Barry M. Blechman and Stephen S. Kaplan, eds., *op. cit.*, pp. 135–174. Khrushchev's quotes to the Chinese and Vietnamese are in *ibid.*, p. 152. For the data on Soviet involvement in India, see Robert C. Horn, "The Soviet Union and South Asia: Moscow and New Delhi Standing Together," in Korbonski and Fukuyama, eds., *op. cit.*, pp. 208–227, at p. 212; Colin Legum, "USSR Policy in Sub-Saharan Africa," in *ibid.*, pp. 228–246, summarizes the ups and downs of Soviet involvement in that area.

## Chapter 12: Hubris

### *"Pleikus Are Streetcars"*

For the history of the commitment of American forces to Vietnam, I follow for the most part George McT. Kahin, *Intervention: How America Became*

*Involved in Vietnam* (New York: Knopf, 1986), based on an enormous mass of recently declassified documents. Robert Shaplen, *The Lost Revolution,* rev. ed. (New York: Harper & Row, 1966), and Leslie H. Gelb, *The Irony of Vietnam: The System Worked* (Washington, D.C.: Brookings, 1979), are also excellent. Dave R. Palmer, *The Summons of the Trumpet* (San Rafael, Calif: Presidio Press, 1978), is a lucid military history. And see also Roger Hilsman, *To Move a Nation;* Townsend Hoopes, *The Limits of Intervention* (New York: David MacKay, 1973); David Halberstam, *The Best and the Brightest* (New York: Random House, 1972); and Herbert Schandler, *The Unmaking of a President: Lyndon Johnson and Vietnam* (Princeton: Princeton University Press, 1977).

The State Department report on the 1956 election outlook is quoted in George Kahin, *op. cit.,* p. 89. For Ho Chi Minh's famine, see *ibid.,* p. 465. American opponents of the war in Vietnam, to strengthen their case, tended to overlook, or actually to romanticize, the brutalities of Southeast Asian communism until the late 1970s, when it was no longer possible to ignore the horrors of Khmer Rouge rule in Cambodia or the imperial militarism of North Vietnam. Confusingly for abstract categorizers, Ho was both a genuine national liberation leader and a committed hard-line Stalinist. The near-famine in the North appears to have stemmed from heavy-handed agricultural collectivization on Stalinist lines. The degree of the "bloodbath" in the North was grossly exaggerated by anti-Communists, but there do appear to have been a large number of executions of "kulaks" and other bourgeoisie. The best known romantic version of Ho and the Viet Cong is probably Frances FitzGerald's *Fire in the Lake: The Vietnamese and the Americans in Vietnam* (Boston: Atlantic, Little, Brown, 1972).

For the early 1960s interest in guerrilla warfare, see, e.g., Franklin A. Lindsay, "Unconventional Warfare," and Raymond Garthoff, "Unconventional Warfare a Communist Strategy," *Foreign Affairs* (July 1962), pp. 566–576. Morton Halperin presents a summary of academic thinking and an annotated bibliography on limited war in his *Limited War,* (Cambridge, Mass.: Harvard University Press, 1962). For Kennedy's enthusiasm, see Theodore Sorensen, *Kennedy,* pp. 632–633. Bernard Brodie's quote on civilian strategists is in his "Why We Were So Wrong," *Foreign Policy* (Winter 1971), pp. 151–161, at pp. 151–152. The quote from McNamara on guerrilla war is in William W. Kaufmann, *The McNamara Strategy,* p. 77. Maxwell Taylor's book was *The Uncertain Trumpet* (New York: Harper, 1959); his quote on Vietnam as a "laboratory" is in Bruce Miroff, *Pragmatic Illusions,* p. 146. Rostow's book is *The Stages of Economic Growth: A Non-Communist Manifesto* (Cambridge: Cambridge University Press, 1961), and see his "The Third Round," *Foreign Affairs* (October 1963), pp. 1–10, an extraordinary article. His speech to the Green Berets is in Henry Fairlie, *The Kennedy Promise* (Garden City, N.Y.: Doubleday, 1973), p. 132.

De Gaulle's warning is quoted in Lewis Paper, *The Promise and the Performance,* p. 186. William Kaufmann on "multiple options" is in his *The McNamara Strategy,* p. 261. Rostow's "Junior Prom" quote is in George Kahin, *Intervention,* p. 131. John Kenneth Galbraith on the Sioux is quoted in Andrew F. Krepinevich, *The Army and Vietnam* (Baltimore: Johns Hopkins Press, 1986). Roger Hilsman on strategic hamlets is quoted in Bruce Miroff, *Pragmatic*

*Illusions,* p. 159. Kennedy's decision memorandum is quoted in George Kahin, *op. cit.,* p. 137. The quote from Colonel Vann on body counts is in Andrew Krepinevich, *op. cit.,* pp. 83–84. Tho's quote on "peaceful coexistence" is in George Kahin, *op. cit.,* p. 185; McNamara's "very disturbing," *ibid.,* p. 193; General Harkins's "eligible officers," *ibid.,* p. 202; McNamara to Johnson on negotiation, *ibid.,* p. 208; Rusk to the American Embassy, *ibid.,* p. 211; Bundy on commitment, *ibid.,* p. 218. For the possibility of American deception on the second Tonkin Gulf attack, see *ibid.,* pp. 219–225. Bundy on the "underlying difficulties" is in *ibid.,* p. 273; Kahin and Galucci on the adviser's self-interest, *ibid.,* p. 245; Clifford and Ball on same topic, *ibid.,* p. 387; Bundy on "street-cars," *ibid.,* p. 277; McNaughton on "measured, controlled, sequence," *ibid.,* p. 281, and for "progressive squeeze" see Fred Kaplan, *The Wizards of Armageddon,* pp. 332–335.

For Colin Gray on the Cuban parallel, see his "What Hath RAND Wrought." Lodge's quote on Rolling Thunder is in Leslie Gelb, *The Irony of Vietnam,* pp. 135–136. The McNaughton statistical analyses on war outcomes are in George Kahin, *op. cit.,* pp. 313, 357. For McNamara's bleak assessment, see *ibid.,* p. 362. Kahin has pieced together the decision record on sending combat troops from three recently declassified transcripts, *ibid.,* pp. 397–399; all of the quotations are from the Kahin compilation. For the growth of the American troop commitment, see *ibid.,* p. 399, and *The Military Balance, 1968–1969.* A question of considerable interest to historians of the period is whether Johnson's elaborate consultative process was a charade, intended to present the image of a broad consensus, or a genuine searching for the right alternative. George McT. Kahin's researches in recently declassified records of the meetings indicate that Johnson was by far the most reluctant of the warriors. If he was acting for the record, it was an extraordinarily skillful job.

## Imbalance of Power

The quote on military maneuvers with atomic weapons is from Col. Louis B. Ely, in B. H. Liddell-Hart's *The Soviet Army,* p. 209. The Malinovsky quote is in William and Harriet Scott, *The Soviet Art of War: Doctrine, Strategy, Tactics,* (Boulder, Colo.: Westview Press, 1968), p. 170. For the development of air mobility doctrine in the United States, see Andrew Krepinevich, *The Army and Vietnam,* pp. 112–127. The role of the air-mobile division in Vietnam is one more element fuelling the still-fierce debate within professional military circles on the military's tactics in that engagement. Col. Harry G. Summers is a persuasive advocate of the view that a misguided civilian belief that the war in Vietnam was a "guerrilla" war led to violations of basic rules of combat, long after the North Vietnamese had converted the war to an essentially conventional test of arms. Maj. Andrew Krepinevich makes the converse case that the fixation on concepts, like the air-mobile division, that were originally designed for the European theater prevented the military from ever developing an effective counterinsurgency capability.

Both men make telling points, but neither view is entirely convincing. Summers is arguably right that the Army could have won a Carthaginian victory by full-scale application of conventional war-fighting methods—by paving the jungle, if necessary, to engage the enemy—but he makes no allowance for a possible Chinese entry into the war, which would seem to have been inevitable under his scenario. Krepinevich scores with his criticisms of the military's constant search for a "technological fix," but his suggestion that the Army could have gone into the villages and the jungle and won a guerrilla war on the Viet Cong's terms must also be received with considerable skepticism. See Andrew Krepinevich, *op. cit.*, and Harry G. Summers, Jr., *On Strategy: A Critical Analysis of the Vietnam War* (Novato, Calif.: Presidio Press, 1982). The *Jane's* quote on the armed helicopter is from the 1969 edition of *All the World's Aircraft*, p. ii. The quote from a helicopter commander is cited in Lt. Gen. John H. Hay, Jr., *Tactical and Materiel Innovations* (Washington, D.C.: Dept. of the Army, 1974), p. 6. The operating and ordnance characteristics of the helicopters and other weapons systems cited are from *Jane's All the World's Aircraft* and *World Weapon Systems* for the appropriate years.

For descriptions of tactical and materiel innovations in the Vietnam War, see Lt. Gen. John H. Hay, *op. cit.;* Gen. Donn A. Starry, *Mounted Combat in Viet Nam* (Washington, D.C.: Dept. of the Army, 1978); and the U.S. Air Force *Southeast Asia Monograph Series* (Washington, D.C.: Dept. of the Air Force, 1976), particularly Maj. A. C. Lavelle, "Tale of Two Bridges," "The Battle for the Skies over North Viet Nam," and "The Vietnamese Air Force, 1951–1975: An Analysis of Its Role in Combat." For the decision to bomb the North during Kosygin's visit, see George Kahin, *Intervention*, pp. 277–280.

For a history of the Six-Day War, see Edgar O'Ballance, *The Third Arab-Israeli War* (London: Faber & Faber, 1972), and Jon D. Glassman, *Arms for the Arabs*, pp. 22–64. The comparisons for Israeli and Arab weapons are drawn from Glassman. The Heikel quote is from his *Sphinx and Commissar*, p. 201. The quotations from Nasser and the Soviet Central Committee meeting are from Glassman, *op. cit.*, pp. 52 and 59.

## Chapter 13: Decisions in the Kremlin

The story of the *Vokshod* launching and Korolev's quote are from Walter McDougall, . . . *the Heavens and the Earth*, pp. 292–293. For details on Khrushchev's fall, see Adam Ulam, *Expansion and Coexistence*, pp. 693–694. The best contemporary analysis of the Kremlin's "Great Debate" is in Thomas W. Wolfe, *Soviet Strategy at the Crossroads*, and see his "Shifts in Soviet Strategic Thought," *Foreign Affairs* (April 1964), pp. 475–486. More recent analyses are William T. Lee and Richard F. Staar, *Soviet Military Policy*, especially pp. 23–40; Michael MccGwire, *Military Objectives in Soviet Foreign Policy*, pp. 36–58; and Harriet and William F. Scott, *The Armed Forces of the USSR*, 3rd ed. (Boulder, Colo.: Westview Press, 1984), pp. 42–56. MccGwire's reconstruction of Khrushchev's missile plans is in *op. cit.*, pp. 477–492; a detailed history is in Robert P. Berman and John C. Baker, *Soviet Strategic Forces: Requirements and Responses* (Washington, D.C.: Brookings, 1982).

For background on Khrushchev's 1960 statement to the Supreme Soviet, see Thomas Wolfe, *Soviet Strategy at the Crossroads*, p. 31, and David Holloway,

*The Soviet Union and the Arms Race,* 2nd ed. (New Haven: Yale University Press, 1984), p. 38. The quotations from Marshal Zhukov are in Walter McDougall, . . . *the Heavens and the Earth,* p. 265. Khrushchev's address to the October 1961 Party Congress amd Malinovsky's rejoinder are in William and Harriet Fast Scott, *The Soviet Art of War,* pp. 165–170. The Rotmistrov quote is in Thomas Wolfe, *Soviet Strategy at the Crossroads,* p. 142. McNamara's testimony on "virtually any Soviet target" and Malinovsky's reply are quoted in C. G. Jacobsen, *Soviet Strategy and Soviet Foreign Policy,* pp. 58–59.

Sokolovsky's *Military Strategy* was published in the West in two translations: V. D. Sokolovsky, *Soviet Military Strategy,* translated and with an introduction by Thomas Wolfe, Herbert Dinerstein, and Leon Gouré (Englewood Cliffs, N.J.: Prentice-Hall, 1963), the "RAND translation," and, with the same title, translated and with an introduction by Raymond Garthoff (New York: Praeger, 1963). The 1962 and 1963 editions, together with a 1967 edition, are collected in an annotated version edited by Harriet Fast Scott, *Soviet Military Strategy* (New York: Stanford Research Institute, 1968). The quotations in the text are from the RAND translation. The quote on "veil" is from p. 274; on "world coalitions," p. 287; on "terrible disasters," p. 279; on "no quiet areas," p. 444; on "entire territory," p. 445; and on "losses six to eight times as great," p. 449.

The review of Western military and economic power is in a chapter entitled "The Military Strategy of the Imperialist States and Their Preparation of New Wars," pp. 141–208. The military figures cited in the book appear to be drawn primarily from the Institute for Strategic Studies' *Military Balance* series. The "Strategic Missile Forces" quote is from p. 299. The analysis of "flexible response" is on pp. 190–194. Bernard Brodie's quote is in Fred Kaplan, *Wizards of Armageddon* p. 340. The contradictory Sokolovsky quotes on the inevitability of escalation are in *op. cit.,* pp. 121 and 299. For the later Soviet view of conventional warfare, see Michael MccGwire, *op. cit.,* pp. 31–35. The Malinovsky quote on "general rocket war" is in William and Harriet Scott, *The Soviet Art of War,* p. 169; his quote on "highly maneuverable combat actions" is in *ibid.,* p. 170. The Sokolovsky quote on doctrinal "trends" is in *op. cit.,* p. 349; on "technical and material basis," p. 432; on "mobilization," p. 433; on "military bases" and "strategically important regions," p. 341; on nuclear war "rules," p. 192; for quotes and discussion on surprise attack, see pp. 159, 339, and 388–394.

Interview data collected by Fred Kaplan indicate that the Pentagon analysts, at McNamara's and Kennedy's request, did in fact prepare an American surprise attack scenario in the early 1960s. Game theory, of course, suggested that it was a reasonable option. Reassuringly, the overwhelming, but not unanimous, reaction in the White House and in the Pentagon to the study's conclusion that a surprise attack was feasible was one of outrage and horror. The outrage stemmed from moral considerations, of course. But, interestingly enough, even with the overwhelming American strike advantage, nobody had much confidence in the calculations of first-strike damage; see Kaplan's *Wizards of Armageddon,* pp. 298–301.

For analyses of Khrushchev's motives in Cuba, see Adam Ulam, *Expansion and Coexistence,* pp. 669–671, and Arnold C. Horelick, "The Cuban Missile

Crisis: An Analysis of Soviet Calculations and Behavior," *World Politics* (April 1964), pp. 363–389. The quote from Marshal Chuikov is in David Holloway, *The Soviet Union and the Arms Race*, p. 41. And see Thomas Wolfe, *Soviet Strategy at the Crossroads*, pp. 145–150, for the view that Khrushchev was reasserting control.

### Chapter 14: "Mad Momentum"—ABMs, MIRVs and SS-9s

The quotes from McNamara's San Francisco speech are from the version reported in the *New York Times*, September 19, 1967; the speech also appears in Robert McNamara, *The Essence of Security*, pp. 51–67. Interestingly, McNamara edited out the conclusion of his speech recommending a "thin" ABM system and presented it as an Appendix, *ibid.*, pp. 163–166. For McNamara's "rewriting of history," see Lawrence Freedman, *U.S. Intelligence and the Soviet Strategic Threat*, p. 119. The public announcement of the MIRV was in January 1967; see the *New York Times*, January 20, 1967. The "space-craft" quotation is from John Foster, director of Defense Research and Engineering, *New York Times*, December 14, 1967.

*ABM Deployment*

The quote from Henry Jackson on the ABM proposal is from the *New York Times*, September 19, 1967. The quote from Richard Russell is from John Newhouse, *Cold Dawn: The Story of SALT* (New York: Holt, Rinehart, Winston, 1973), p. 97; and see *ibid.* for McNamara quote: "Russians are sophisticated." His "further defense" quote is from the San Francisco speech. The history of McNamara's struggle against the ABM follows, in general, Morton Halperin, "The Decision to Deploy the ABM: Bureaucratic and Domestic Politics in the Johnson Administration," *World Politics* (October 1972), pp. 62–95, supplemented by Lawrence Freedman, *U.S. Intelligence*, pp. 85–101; and John Prados, *The Soviet Estimate*, pp. 151–171. The Malinovsky and Khrushchev quotes are in Freedman, p. 87.

For Soviet ABM systems, see Sayre Stevens, "The Soviet BMD Program," in Ashton B. Carter and David N. Schwarz, eds., *Ballistic Missile Defense* (Washington, D.C.: Brookings, 1984), pp. 182–220. McNamara's 1962 estimate of Soviet ABM capability is from his November 21, 1962, Draft Presidential Memorandum. The Soviet "impregnable defense" quotation is from the *New York Times*, February 21, 1967. Talensky's article is Nicolai Talensky, "Antimissile Systems and Disarmament," *The Bulletin of the Atomic Scientists*, (February, 1965), pp. 26–29. For the operations of phased-array radars, see Eli Brookner, "Phased-Array Radars," *Scientific American* (February 1985), pp. 94–102. The ABM as a "symbol of the arms race" quote is from Morton Halperin, "The Decision to Deploy the ABM," p. 72. Johnson's letter to Kosygin is quoted in Lyndon B. Johnson, *The Vantage Point: Perspectives of the Presidency, 1963–1969* (New York: Popular Library, 1971), pp. 479–480. Kosygin's implied criticism of McNamara is quoted in William T. Lee and Richard F.

Staar, *Soviet Military Policy,* p. 200. The story of Kosygin's mistranslated remarks is in Raymond Garthoff, "BMD and East-West Relations," in Ashton B. Carter and David N. Schwarz, eds., *op. cit.,* pp. 275–329, at pp. 295–296. Johnson's account of the Glassboro meeting is in *op. cit.,* pp. 481–485, and see John Newhouse, *Cold Dawn,* pp. 92–95, for McNamara's "passionate" speech and Soviet lack of interest.

The account of the development of the MIRV, including the argument for its apparent inevitability, follows generally Ted Greenwood, *Making the MIRV* (Cambridge, Mass.: Ballinger, 1975). For the opposition in the Senate, see "Statement by the Hon. Edward Brooke," *Hearings Before the U.S. Senate Committee on Foreign Relations,* May–June 1970, pp. 2–19. See Greenwood, *op. cit.,* pp. 25–35, for early RAND and contractor interest.

The Navy's view of nuclear strategy underwent a series of interesting mutations. When the budget battle between the Navy supercarrier and Air Force B-36 raged in the 1950s (see Chapter 4), the Navy condemned the Air Force city-bombing strategy as immoral, arguing that its carriers could concentrate on military targets. The Navy enthusiastically adopted an "assured destruction" countercity strategy, however, when it became clear that this was the only role suitable for its new Polaris missile. It shifted back again as soon as it appeared that Poseidon might fulfill a counterforce role (Poseidon was, in fact, never accurate enough to target a hardened Soviet missile silo, although it clearly could attack military bases with considerable precision). See Greenwood, *ibid.,* p. 54.

Hanson Baldwin's criticisms of weapons development pace is summarized in his "Slowdown in the Pentagon," *Foreign Affairs* (January 1965), pp. 262–280. For the growth of the American target list and McNamara's resistance to more missiles, see Desmond Ball, "The Development of the SIOP, 1960–1983," in Desmond Ball and Jeffrey Richelson, eds., *Strategic Nuclear Targeting,* pp. 57–83, at pp. 66–68. For concern about the Soviet ABM tests and the effectiveness of the Polaris A3, see Lawrence Freedman, *U.S. Intelligence,* pp. 86–89. For an analysis of the multiplicity of factors that drive weapons procurement decisions, see James Kurth, "Why We Buy the Weapons We Do," *Foreign Policy* (Summer 1973), pp. 33–56.

For compilations of intelligence estimates of Soviet strategic missile intentions, see Lawrence Freedman, *U.S. Intelligence,* pp. 101–117, and John Prados, *The Soviet Estimate,* pp. 183–199. The detailed analysis of McNamara's early estimates in the text, however, as well as the characteristics of early Soviet submarine missiles, are drawn primarily from his Draft Presidential Memorandums of November 21, 1962, December 6, 1963, and December 3, 1964. I have followed McNamara's memoranda wherever they disagree with the secondary sources. McNamara's quote on the Soviets dropping out of the quantitative arms race is in Colin Gray, "The Arms Race Phenomenon," *World Politics* (October 1971), pp. 39–79, at p. 69. The quote from his interview is in John Prados, *op. cit.,* p. 190. The Pentagon's quote is in Lawrence Freedman, *op. cit.,* p. 111.

Wohlstetter's critique was printed as a pamphlet entitled *Legends of the Strategic Arms Race,* and reprinted in the form of two articles in *Foreign Policy,*

"Is There a Strategic Arms Race?" (Summer 1974), pp. 3–20, and "Rivals But No Race" (Fall 1974), pp. 48–81. For countercritiques of Wohlstetter, see John Prados, *op. cit.*, pp. 197–199, and Morton Halperin and Jeremy Stone, "Reply to Albert Wohlstetter," *Foreign Policy* (Fall 1974), pp. 88–92. Counts of Soviet missiles in the mid-1960s are drawn from William T. Lee and Richard F. Staar, *Soviet Military Policy*, p. 64. The vulnerability of the clustered Soviet SS-7 sites is in John Prados, *op. cit.*, p. 187.

For the sudden shift in pressures against the American ABM, see John Newhouse, *Cold Dawn*, pp. 145–160, and Henry Kissinger, *The White House Years* (Boston: Little, Brown, 1979), pp. 204–210. For the liberal critique of the ABM, see Abram Chayes and Jerome Weisner, eds., *ABM: An Evaluation of the Decision to Deploy an Antiballistic Missile System* (New York: Harper & Row, 1969). For the defection of long-time hawk Stuart Symington to the ranks of the more dovish senators, see his article "Department of Defense Exaggerates," *New York Times*, March 18, 1971. For Laird's ABM fight, see Lawrence Freedman, *U.S. Intelligence*, pp. 129–160, and John Prados, *The Soviet Estimate*, pp. 200–224. For the pressures on the CIA analysts, see Thomas Powers, *The Man Who Kept the Secrets*, pp. 211–212. The "Sam Upgrading" anecdote is in Prados, p. 168.

Laird's quote, "The Soviets are going for . . ." and his quote on submarine warfare are from Lawrence Freedman, *op. cit.*, pp. 132, 134; the quote on Minuteman survivability is in Benjamin Lambeth, "Deterrence in the MIRV Era," *World Politics* (January 1972), pp. 221–242, at p. 225. For critical analyses of the Safeguard ABM, see *Hearings Before the U.S. Senate Foreign Relations Committee*, May–June 1970, particularly the testimony of Dr. Herbert York, pp. 58–66; Dr. Wolfgang Panofsky, pp. 176–200; and Dr. Sidney Drell, pp. 534–549.

## Chapter 15: The Technology of Long-Range Destruction

### Ballistic Missiles

For the engineering of ballistic missiles, see Matthew Bunn and Kosta Tsipis, *Ballistic Missile Guidance and Technical Uncertainties of Countersilo Attacks.* MIT Program in Science and Technology for International Security (August 1983), Report No. 9; the quotation on technical breakthroughs is on p. 30. A less technical discussion is in Kosta Tsipis, "The Accuracy of Ballistic Missiles," *Scientific American* (July 1975), pp. 14–23, and Kosta Tsipis, *Arsenal: Understanding Weapons in the Nuclear Age* (New York: Simon and Schuster, 1983), pp. 102–129. The conservative complaint against sale of ball-bearing technology is in William T. Lee and Richard F. Staar, *Soviet Military Policy*, p. 81. For the problem of locating Soviet target sites, and the usefulness of nuclear weapons against industrial targets, see Frederic S. Nyland, "Exemplary Industrial Targets for Controlled Conflicts," in Desmond Ball and Jeffrey Richelson, eds., *Strategic Nuclear Targeting* (Ithaca, N.Y.: Cornell University Press, 1986), pp. 209–233.

For the guidance system advances incorporated into the MX and Trident II

D–5 missiles, see Thomas B. Cochran, William M. Arkin, and Milton M. Hoenig, *Nuclear Weapons Databook. Vol. I* (Cambridge, Mass.: Ballinger, 1984), pp. 121, 145; and Matthew Bunn and Kosta Tsipis, *Ballistic Missile Guidance,* pp. 99–100 (for NAVSTAR). Details are highly classified. For nose cone technology and maneuverable warheads, see Matthew Bunn, *Technology of Ballistic Missile Reentry Vehicles.* MIT Program in Science and Technology for International Security (March 1984), Report No. 11. For the accuracies of specific missiles cited throughout this section, see, e.g., Kosta Tsipis, "Ballistic Missile Accuracy"; John M. Collins, *American and Soviet Military Trends Since the Cuban Missile Crisis* (Georgetown: Center for Strategic and International Studies, 1978), pp. 91–93; John M. Collins, *U.S.-Soviet Military Balance. Book II. Strategic Nuclear Trends* (Washington, D.C.: Congressional Research Service, 1980), pp. 119–143; William T. Lee and Richard F. Staar, *Soviet Military Policy Since World War II* pp. 145–146; and for the more recent weapons, Thomas Cochran, *et al., Nuclear Weapons Databook* (entries under specific weapons).

Lee and Collins tend to credit missiles with greater accuracies than Tsipis does. Tsipis claims (interview with author) that his estimates reflect the CIA's, while Collins's and Lee's tend to be the Air Force's. Cochran and his co-authors give a wide range of citations for each of their entries. For a fascinating compilation of the wide range of accuracy estimates for both American and Soviet missiles (often by the same source), see Tom Gervasi, *The Myth of Soviet Military Superiority* (New York: Harper & Row, 1986), "Appendix C. Missile Accuracy: A Chronology of Estimates," pp. 360–371.

## The Effects of Nuclear Explosions

The basic textbook on nuclear blasts is Samuel Glasstone and Philip J. Dolan, *The Effects of Nuclear Weapons* (Washington, D.C.: USGPO, 1977), a joint publication by the Departments of Energy and Defense, and see also Matthew Bunn and Kosta Tsipis, *Ballistic Missile Guidance,* pp. 54–60, and Kosta Tsipis, *Arsenal,* pp. 29–74. For the blackout effects of a high-altitude blast, see Chapter X, "Radio and Radar Effects," and Chapter XI, "The Electromagnetic Pulse and Its Effects," in Glasstone and Dolan, *op. cit.,* particularly pp. 519–523. The city damage effects at various overpressures are from the charts and tables in *ibid.,* pp. 214–219. Minuteman silo characteristics are from Thomas Cochran, *et al., Nuclear Weapons Databook,* pp. 113, 117, and Kosta Tsipis, *Arsenal,* pp. 132–135. And see the overpressure curves against hardened silos in William T. Lee, "Soviet Nuclear Targeting," in Desmond Ball and Jeffrey Richelson, eds., *Strategic Nuclear Targeting,* p. 95.

There have been startling increases in estimates of theoretical silo hardness (to 100,000-plus psi) in recent years; see the compilation in Tom Gervasi, *The Myth of Soviet Military Supremacy,* pp. 377–379. For MX "superhardening," see Thomas Cochran, *et al., op. cit.,* p. 120. For estimates of high Soviet silo hardness, see in addition, e.g., "Soviets' Nuclear Arsenal Continues to Proliferate," *Aviation Week and Space Technology,* June 16, 1980, p. 28, and Clarence A. Robinson, Jr., "Soviets Testing New Generation of ICBM," *ibid.,* November 3, 1980, p. 28. Hardening to extremely high psi levels would actually offer little additional benefit. Once accuracies fall within the 150-meter range, weapon lethality quickly becomes arbitrarily high. For the lack of data on large nuclear blasts, see Bunn and Tsipis, *Ballistic Missile Guidance,* pp. 87–88. The consequences of different burst heights are in Glasstone and Dolan, *op. cit.,* pp. 26–63.

### A Note on the Effects of Yield and Accuracy on Lethality

The yield of an atomic weapon is adjusted by the two-thirds power, $Y^{2/3}$ to derive effective yield. (To get an intuitive appreciation of the two-thirds power rule: the two-thirds power of a number is computed by taking the square of the number's cube root. A nuclear blast dissipates over a sphere, which is a cubic quantity, but the target is a flat area of the earth's surface, expressed as square.) The key expression in the calculation of a missile's effectiveness adjusts the warhead's effective yield, $Y^{2/3}$ by dividing by the square of the CEP. Since CEP in the formula is squared, small reductions in CEP will generate large increases in weapon effectiveness. To illustrate, assume a weapon with a yield of 100 kilotons and a CEP of one mile. The formula $Y^{2/3}/CEP^2$ gives $100^{2/3}/1^2 = 21.5$, a number which can be taken as an index of the weapon's destructiveness. (In this formula, it is simply an index number, not a measure of overpressure.) Doubling the yield to 200 kilotons gives $200^{2/3}/1^2 = 34.2$, or a destructiveness index increase of only about 60 percent. Halving the CEP, however, while holding the yield of the weapon at 100 kilotons, gives $100^{2/3}/.5^2 = 86$. Comparing the relative effectiveness of the two missile improvement strategies, it can be seen that doubling the yield produces an increase in destructiveness of 12.7 (34.2 minus the original 21.5), while halving the CEP produces a destructiveness increase of 64.5 (86 minus 21.5). The improvement in accuracy, that is, produces five times as much destructiveness improvement as the improvement in yield.

As the CEP becomes very small, the killing power of the missile becomes meaninglessly large. As a practical matter, a missile has achieved its maximum lethality when the radius of its CEP is smaller than the radius of its crater. If the missile silo falls into the warhead crater, it is obviously out of the battle. The fact that CEP improvement is the most efficient way to increase the killing power of a weapon, however, doesn't always mean that it is the *easiest* way. Once CEPs have been reduced to the 300-meter range, further improvements may be very hard to come by. The continued Soviet emphasis on large-payload weapons probably reflects a realistic view of their guidance technology. Throughout the 1970s, at least, it was presumably much easier for them to build 10-megaton weapons with half-mile CEPs than 1-megaton missiles with 300-meter CEPs. The discussion here is based on the formulas in Bunn and Tsipis, *Ballistic Missile Guidance,* pp. 56–60, and Tsipis, *Arsenal,* "Appendix H: Derivation of Kill Probability Equation," pp. 305–308.

The overpressure/CEP relationships in the examples were calculated from the empirically derived formula given by Tsipis (*ibid.,* p. 305): Overpressure $= 14.7(Y/r^3) + 12.8(Y/r^3)^{1/2}$, where Y is the yield in megatons and r is the distance from the target in nautical miles. Note that this is not a kill probability formula for a missile launch, but merely an overpressure calculation assuming the warhead has *already impacted* within the stated distance. Different sources give slightly varying formulas.

For Jan Lodal's point on the narrow relevance of warhead size, see his "Assured Strategic Stability: An Alternative View," *Foreign Affairs* (April 1976), pp. 462–481. The discussion of uncertainty for the most part follows Bunn and Tsipis, *Ballistic Missile Guidance.* For American and Soviet testing procedures, see pp. 128–143; for the quote on launch sequence, p. 137; for the effects of bias, and the quotations in the text, pp. 61–67. The quotation from Seymour Zeiberg with James Fallows is in Fallows's *National Defense* (New York: Random House, 1980), pp. 153. For an exchange on the bias problem, see the discussion between J. E. Anderson and Gen. R. Marsh in *Strategic Review* (Spring 1982), pp. 35–43. The 100-meter error estimate is Bunn and Tsipis's, *op. cit.*, p. 68 (given in nautical miles); for the fratricide problem and various attacking maneuvers, including "pindown" tactics, pp. 70–81; for the calculation of the total effects of uncertainty, p. 93; for the Schlesinger quote, p. 65; and for caution about future developments, p. 97.

A compact argument that reaches the same conclusions as Tsipis and Bunn on slightly different assumptions is in John D. Steinbruner and Thomas M. Garwin, "Strategic Vulnerability: The Balance Between Prudence and Paranoia," *International Security* (Summer 1976), pp. 138–181. Steinbruner and Garwin suggest as well that a one-half power function, rather than two-thirds, is a more appropriate adjustment for larger yield weapons, which would reduce the effective killing power of the Soviet missile force considerably. They do not rely on this assumption in their calculations, however.

## Chapter 16: SALT and the Shifting Military Balance

### Agreement in Moscow

The basic history of the SALT I agreement from McNamara's San Francisco speech to the Moscow summit is John Newhouse, *Cold Dawn.* Except as noted, I follow Newhouse's chronology. The main source for the Moscow negotiations and the operations of the "backchannel" is Henry Kissinger, *The White House Years.* Ambassador Smith's version is in Gerard Smith, *Doubletalk: The Story of the First Strategic Arms Limitation Talks* (New York: Harper & Row, 1980). Raymond Garthoff, "Negotiating with the Russians: Lessons from SALT," *International Security* (Summer 1976), pp. 3–24, is an excellent brief history that, like Smith's book, is quite critical of the confusions introduced by the "backchannel." Paul Nitze, a senior member of the Smith team, is also quite critical (interview). Garthoff was a key member of Smith's team and the chief drafter of the actual treaties.

Additional chronologies and contemporary assessments are in Mason Willrich and John B. Rhinelander, eds., *SALT: The Moscow Agreements and Beyond* (Glencoe, N.Y.: The Free Press, 1974). See, particularly, Chalmers M. Roberts, "The Road to Moscow," pp. 3–33; Alton Frye, "U.S. Decision Making for SALT," pp. 66–100; and Marshall D. Shulman, "SALT and the Soviet Union," pp. 101–

123. For a view of Soviet diplomatic exigencies during the SALT period, see Adam Ulam, *Dangerous Relations: The Soviet Union in World Politics, 1970–1982* (New York: Oxford University Press, 1983), pp. 39–82. The events in Brezhnev's dacha and the associated quotations are from Henry Kissinger, *The White House Years*, pp. 1223–1235; the "out of the blue" quote regarding Smirnov, however, is from John Newhouse *Cold Dawn*, p. 252.

Adam Ulam, in his "Moscow Plays the Balance," *Foreign Policy* (Fall 1972), pp. 86–91, comments on the uniqueness of Brezhnez's signing the SALT treaties. Not even Stalin signed treaties when he was only General Secretary of the Party. A detailed, but highly readable account of the Czechoslovakia invasion is H. Gordon Skilling, *Czechoslovakia's Interrupted Revolution* (Princeton: Princeton University Press, 1976). The "Brezhnev Doctrine" quote is from U.S. Senate, Subcommittee on Internal Security, *Czechoslovakia and the Brezhnev Doctrine* (Washington, D.C.: USGPO, 1969). The anti-Chinese proposal at the Vienna opera is in Gerard Smith, *Doubletalk*, pp. 141–143. For a useful short summary of other arms negotiations, see Coit D. Blacker, *Reluctant Warriors: The United States, The Soviet Union, and Arms Control* (New York: Freeman, 1987). For a counterforce calculation of Soviet interest in banning the ABM, see the essay "SALT in Soviet Military Policy—Narrowing the Gap," in William T. Lee and Richard F. Staar, eds., *Soviet Military Policy Since World War II*, pp. 199–218.

Lawrence Freedman, *U.S. Intelligence and the Soviet Strategic Threat*, gives a good summary of the events leading to Kissinger's Verification Panel, pp. 161–168. Kissinger's "proudest hour" quote is in *The White House Years*, p. 551; and see pp. 810–823 for his account of the "ABM-only" treaty pressure in Congress. Herbert Scoville on Nixon is from "The Latest Red Scare," *The New Republic*, May 15, 1971, pp. 16–19, at p. 17. For the Kistiakowsky and Rathjens statement, see the *New York Times*, January 27, 1971; and also April 5, 1971, for the editorial on ABM and MIRVs. The Fulbright and Humphrey quotations are from Kissinger, *op. cit.*, pp. 811–812. And see "Congress Can Do It," *The New Republic*, February 27, 1971, p. 9. for the Soviet SS-9 "signal"; and Ronald Tammen, "Wolf at the Pentagon Door," *The New Republic*, March 20, 1971, pp. 13–14, at p. 14 for the "missile gap" quote on Senator Jackson. Kissinger's quote on a MIRVed world is in Lawrence Freedman *U.S. Intelligence and the Soviet Strategic Threat* p. 177. The texts of the SALT I treaties and associated agreements are in U.S. Arms Control and Disarmament Agency, *Arms Control and Disarmament Agreements* (Washington, D.C.: USGPO, 1980), pp. 132–163. For hard-line Soviet reactions to SALT, see Thomas W. Wolfe, *The SALT Experience* (Cambridge, Mass.: Ballinger, 1979), pp. 18–22. The quote from Gerald Ford is in *ibid.*, p. 16.

## The Rusting American Military Machine

For the changing economic impact of defense spending, and overall American defense levels, see: "The New Look in Defense" and "Assessing U.S. Military Requirements," in Barry M. Blechman, Edward M. Gramlich, and Robert W. Hartman, *Setting National Priorities: The 1975 Budget* (Washington, D.C.:

Brookings, 1974), pp. 62–98, 99–132; Philip Odeen, "In Defense of the Defense Budget," *Foreign Policy* (Fall 1974), pp. 93–108; and Barry M. Blechman, *et al.*, *The Soviet Military Buildup and U.S. Defense Spending* (Washington, D.C.: Brookings, 1977), and Stephen Cimbala, "New Myths and Old Realities: Defense and Its Critics," *World Politics* (October 1971), pp. 127–157. The GAO studies are cited in Blechman, *et. al.*, *The 1975 Budget*, p. 125, and see pp. 80–84 for the service requests for F-14s and 15s. The quote on the MBT-70 tank is from the 1973 edition of *Jane's World Weapon Systems*. For the downtime for the F-14, see James Fallows, *National Defense*, p. 41. The Defense Science Board report mentioned in the note is cited in Seymour J. Deitchman, *Military Power and the Advance of Technology: General Purpose Military Forces for the 1980s and Beyond* (Boulder, Colo.: Westview Press, 1983), p. 224; and the 1979 GAO report is cited in John M. Collins, *U.S.-Soviet Military Balance* (Washington, D.C.: Congressional Research Service, 1980), "Book III: General Purpose Forces," p. 104n.

## The Shifting Missile Balance

Details on the production, deployment rates, and operational characteristics of Soviet missiles are drawn from John M. Collins, *op. cit.*, "Book II: Strategic Nuclear Trends" (see particularly the tables on pp. 120–122); William T. Lee and Richard F. Staar, *Soviet Military Policy*, particularly pp. 135–155; Robert P. Berman and John C. Baker, *Soviet Strategic Forces* (Washington, D.C.: Brookings, 1982), particularly pp. 113–126 for counterforce capabilities; and the *Military Balance*, various years. The most precise information on American missiles is in Thomas Cochran, *et al.*, *Nuclear Weapons Databook*. Raymond Garthoff's version of the missile silo volume negotiations is in his *Detente and Confrontation*, pp. 171–172n. Nitze gave a similar, though much less splenetic version in an interview with the author. Smith on the SS-19 is in his "Wrestling with the Plowshare Problem," the *New York Times*, January 16, 1976. My thanks to Walter Slocombe for helping me understand this issue. Nixon's promise on counterforce is cited in, e.g., Alton Frye, "Decision-making for SALT," p. 97.

## A Note on Soviet Theoretical First-strike Capability

By the end of 1979, 218 of the 240 SS-18s were MIRVed, for 1,712 warheads (assuming 8, not 10 warheads per missile), and 210 SS-19s carried 1,260 warheads, or 6 each. In addition, another 480 warheads were deployed on 120 MIRVed SS-17s. In theory, then, 2,000 accurate warheads could be launched against the Minuteman silos while holding another 1,000 in reserve. The Soviet Union continued to make accuracy improvements on its MIRVed SS-18s and SS-19s in the early 1980s as it tested and deployed the "Mod 4" and "Mod 3" versions, respectively. Lee, who is a strong critic of the results of the detente era, assumes that only the latest versions of the SS-18 and 19 MIRVs are accurate and reliable enough to constitute a plausible hard-target threat. Brookings analysts similarly concluded that "the overall survivability of the Minuteman force will become open to question by the mid-1980s." All of these appraisals, of course, are subject to the uncertainties of a massive ballistic missile strike detailed earlier, and, of course, the political uncertainty that the United States would, in any case, launch on warning in a crisis. Their significance is more as an indicator of the shift of the weight of strategic power than as an alarm bell of immediate American vulnerability.

Raymond Garthoff argues correctly that, with the completion of the Minuteman III Mark 12A upgrade in 1983, the United States had the ability to mount a first strike against all of the Soviet SS-17s, 18s, and 19s, thus taking out all of the Soviet Union's most accurate missiles and a larger *percentage* of their warheads than a Soviet first strike against the Minutemen (because of the large number of small warheads on the American Poseidon submarines). It was not an argument that could be counted upon to impress even the more reasonable defense conservatives. For one thing, between roughly 1978 and 1983, before the Mark 12A upgrade was finished, the Soviets did have a clear, although not necessarily usable, counterforce advantage; secondly, as the SS-19s continued to replace the SS-11s—and the Soviets pressed ahead on developing even newer missiles in the 1980s—the potential for squeezing more capability out of the Minutemen inevitably lagged the Russian progress; and, finally, the Minutemen themselves were becoming rather long in the tooth (in 1980 it was twenty years since the first Minuteman flight). See John Collins, *op. cit.*; Robert P. Berman and John C. Baker, *op. cit.*, p. 125; Raymond Garthoff, *Detente and Confrontation,* p. 798. For a similar picture of the Soviet view of American weapon capabilities, see Marshal D. Shulman, "SALT Through the Looking Glass," in William H. Kincade and Jeffrey D. Porro, *Negotiating Security* (New York: Carnegie Endowment for International Peace, 1979), pp. 20–23.

The public perception of the growing imbalance in nuclear striking forces was greatly heightened by Paul H. Nitze's immensely influential article, "Assured Strategic Stability in an Era of Detente," *Foreign Affairs* (January 1976), pp. 207–232; but see the response by Jan M. Lodal, "Assured Strategic Stability: An Alternative View." For a slightly different analysis that reaches Nitze's conclusions, see Jacqueline K. Davis, "End of the Strategic Triad," *Strategic Review* (Winter 1978), pp. 36–43, a clearly written summary.

### The Shifting Conventional Balance

The data on Soviet Ground Force development is drawn from the following sources: John M. Collins, *op. cit.*, "Book III: General Purpose Forces," and "Book V: NATO and the Warsaw Pact"; the *Military Balance,* various years; Jeffrey M. Record, *Sizing Up the Soviet Army* (Washington, D.C.: Brookings, 1975); a series of articles by John Erikson in *Strategic Review*—"European Security: Soviet Preferences and Priorities," (Winter 1976), pp. 37–44; "The Northern Theater: Soviet Capacities and Concepts" (Summer 1976), pp. 67–82; "Trends in Soviet Combined Arms Doctrine" (Winter 1977), pp. 32–52; "The Ground Forces in Soviet Military Doctrine" (Winter 1978), pp. 64–79—Walter F. Hahn, "NATO's Qualitative Crisis," *Strategic Review* (Summer 1977), pp. 26–39; and Barry Blechman, *et al., The Soviet Military Buildup.*

For the confrontations with China, see Thomas W. Robinson, "The Sino-Soviet Border Conflict," in Stephen S. Kaplan, *Diplomacy of Power*, pp. 265–313. The quote on the Su-24 is from the entry in the 1974 *Jane's World Aircraft* (the Su-24 was designated as the Su-19 at that time). The section on the Soviet naval buildup is drawn from Barry M. Blechman, *The Changing Soviet Navy* (Washington, D.C.: Brookings, 1973), and *Control of Naval Armaments* (Washington, D.C.: Brookings, 1975); John M. Collins, *op. cit.*, "Book III: General Purpose Forces," pp. 143–159. Data on displacement and armaments of individual ships are in *Jane's Fighting Ships* and *The Military Balance*, various years. Admiral Gorshkov is quoted in Barry Blechman, *The Changing Soviet Navy*, p. 22. The quote from the American Sixth Fleet admiral (Worth Bagley) is in Bruce G. Blair, "Alerting in Crisis and Conventional War," in Ashton B. Carter, *et al.*, eds., *Managing Nuclear Operations*, pp. 75–120, at p. 95.

For a non-alarmist review of the mid-seventies conventional balance in Europe, see, e.g., Blechman, *et al.*, *The Soviet Military Buildup*, pp. 26–27. Lee's cautious assessment is in his *op. cit.* p. 161; for Soviet readiness, see John M. Collins, *op. cit.*, "Book V: NATO and the Warsaw Pact," pp. 34–35. The numerical American-Soviet tank comparison is from Jeffrey Record, *Sizing Up the Soviet Army*, p. 27. For the T-62's deficiencies, see the summary of the Yom Kippur hostilities in the next chapter, and, in addition, Alexander Cockburn, *The Threat: Inside the Soviet Military Machine* (New York: Random House, 1983)—a frequently hilarious account; for the T-62, pp. 118–123; for Soviet airplanes, pp. 139–156; and for missile reliability, pp. 195–212. (Cockburn cites claims that Soviet missile reliability may be as low as 30 percent, which would reduce the effectiveness of a first strike to the vanishing point. Defense planners, of course, cannot rely on such low-ball assumptions, however plausible they might be.)

The Air Force quote on the Foxbat and the Viktor Belenko incident are both in the 1979 MiG-25 entry in *Jane's World Aircraft*. The Air Force also credited the MiG-25 with the first genuine "look-down/shoot-down" capability on any Soviet plane. "Look-down" radar is a daunting technical feat, because of the necessity of separating a target from the background clutter of radiation reflection. Belenko's plane had no such capability. (The Air Force mused darkly about a possible Soviet "disinformation" ploy.) A decade later, the Pentagon dubbed the new MiG-31 as the "first true look-down/shoot-down-capable aircraft in the Soviet inventory." The "look-down" speculation for the MiG-25 appeared in the 1976 entry in *Jane's;* the MiG-31 assessment is in the Defense Department's 1984 edition of *Soviet Military Power* (Washington, D.C.: USGPO, 1984), p. 37. The "naval analyst" quote is from Barry Blechman, *The Changing Soviet Navy*, p. 36. The Soviet quantitative force holdings at the outbreak of World War II are in Barry Blechman, *The Changing Soviet Navy*, p. 58; for the historical Soviet predilection for excessive forces, see George Kennan, "The United States and the Soviet Union, 1917–1976," *Foreign Affairs* (July 1976), p. 680.

The CIA revisions were publicly reported in the *New York Times* on December 26, 1976. For a discussion of dollar-ruble costing problems, see John M. Collins, *op. cit.*, "Book I: Organizations, Budgets, Manpower, Technology," pp. 58–70. And see also U.S. Central Intelligence Agency, *A Dollar Cost Comparison of Soviet and U.S. Defense Activities, 1968–1978* (Washington, D.C.:

USGPO, 1979). For Lee's method, see his *The Estimation of Soviet Defense Expenditures, 1955-1975: An Unconventional Approach* (New York: Praeger, 1977), particularly pp. 131-151 for a summary of his method and findings and "Appendix E," pp. 335-339, for Lee's speculations on the political background to Soviet defense budget reporting. Franklyn D. Holzman, "Are the Soviets Really Outspending the U.S. on Defense?", *International Security* (Spring, 1980) pp. 85-104, is an excellent overview of the comparability problem. The 1977 Brookings quote is from Blechman, *et al.*, *The Soviet Military Buildup*, p. 20. Robert Tucker's comments are from his "Beyond Detente," *Commentary* (March 1977), pp. 42-50.

## Chapter 17: The Bear Stretches

### Global Reach

The chronology of the Yom Kippur War is drawn from the *New York Times* and from Jon D. Glassman, *Arms for the Arabs*, pp. 125-176; Bruce D. Porter, *The USSR in Third World Conflicts*, pp. 113-146; and Henry Kissinger, *Years of Upheaval* (Boston: Little, Brown, 1982), pp. 450-544. Walter Laqueur, *Confrontation: The Middle East and World Politics* (New York: Bantam, 1974), is a good survey of the background issues. For the scale of the Soviet shipments to the Arabs, see Glassman, *op. cit.*, pp. 105-106, 115-116; the quotes from the Israeli flier and tank commander are from *ibid.*, pp. 127, 129. For Israeli armaments, see *The Military Balance, 1973-1974*, and 1974-*1975*—which, based on a comparison of the figures for Arab countries with the detailed estimates of Glassman and Porter, are of questionable reliability.

### A Note on Soviet/American Aircraft Performance

The F-4 Phantom was the key plane in the Israeli inventory. It was a powerful Mach 2 fighter bomber, and probably the best plane in the American inventory. It could carry a bomb load almost as big and almost as far as Egypt's subsonic Tu-16 Badgers, and was vastly superior to the other attack bombers in the Arab inventory, the Il-28s, Su-7s, and MiG-17s. At the same time, it could engage and defeat the best interceptor the Arabs had, the MiG-21, and—most embarrassingly for the Soviets—scored impressive kill ratios even when the MiG-21s were flown by Soviet and North Korean pilots. (In the air-to-air battles over the Suez, after the SA-6 sites were disabled, the Israeli score against MiG-21s and Su-7s was a dispiriting—for the Soviets—200 to 3.) Soviet interceptors were much too short-ranged to escort the Badgers—which would be sitting ducks if they attempted an attack on their own—so as a result the Arabs had no deep-strike capabilities, while the Israeli Phantoms could reach most major Arab cities.

The United States had developed electronic countermeasures for the Phantom against the SA-6, but had not provided them to the Israelis. The Soviets had recently deployed a new interceptor, the MiG-23, which could fly higher and faster than the Phantom; it was almost purely a defensive aircraft, but had the range to provide escort for the Badgers. Sadat pleaded for MiG-23s, but was consistently, and disdainfully, refused on the ground that it would take his pilots "more than five years" to learn how to fly them. The Soviets also had a detachment of supersonic Tu-22 medium bombers (the "Blinder") in Iraq, which would have had greater penetration ability—although they were not the equal of the Phantoms—but the planes were never released to the Arabs; the Israelis reciprocated by not attacking the Tu-22 airfield. For detailed performance data, see the respective entries in *Jane's World Aircraft.*

The agreement on preventing nuclear war is quoted from *Arms Control and Disarmament Agreements,* p. 159. The "trend for peace" quote is from the *New York Times,* June 24, 1973. The chronology of the Watergate events is also from the *New York Times.* Brezhnev's behavior at the summit is from Henry Kissinger, *Years of Upheaval,* pp. 297–299. The quote on the Soviet resupply effort is from Bruce Porter, *op. cit.*, p. 132. The quote from Theodore White is from his *Breach of Faith* (New York: Harper & Row, 1975), p. 269. The quotes from the Soviet note of the 12th and Kissinger's reply are in Henry Kissinger, *op. cit.*, p. 510. His quotes on Soviet behavior are from the *New York Times,* October 13. The "furious arguments" between Kissinger and Schlesinger are from Theodore White, *op. cit.*, pp. 258–259.

For Soviet worries about their tanks, see John Erikson, "Trends in Soviet Combined Arms Doctrine," *Strategic Review* (Winter 1977), pp. 32–52. The newspaper quotes on Nixon's resignation are in Theodore White, *op. cit.*, p. 269. The note from Brezhnev to Nixon is quoted in Jon Glassman *op. cit.*, p. 160; the language of the note quoted by Glassman appears in all of the sources I reviewed, except for Henry Kissinger, who gives a slightly different version in his *op. cit.*, p. 583. The full text has still not been released. The "credible threat" quote is from Bruce Porter, *op. cit.*, p. 141. For details of the American alert, see the *New York Times,* October 25, and Bruce D. Blair, "Alerting in Crisis and Conventional War," in Ashton B. Carter, *et al., eds., Managing Nuclear Operations,* pp. 87–92. For the dangers of an alert, see Scott D. Sagan, "Nuclear Alerts and Crisis Management," *International Security* (Spring 1985), pp. 99–139. The quote from Dayan is in Glassman, *op. cit.*, p. 165.

Kissinger's press conference quotes on the alert are from the *New York Times,* October 25. His account of the incident is in his *op. cit.*, pp. 585–591. The Reston quote is from the *New York Times,* October 26. Harry Gelman's *The Brezhnev Politburo and the Decline of Detente* (Ithaca, N.Y.: Cornell University Press, 1984) is an in-depth assessment of Soviet internal politics during the period covered here. The Soviet official quoted on detente is Boris Ponomarev, Deputy Foreign Minister, cited in John Erickson, "European Security: Soviet Preferences and Priorities," *Strategic Review* (Winter 1976), p. 37. For the impact of the Chilean intervention, see Glassman, *op. cit.*, pp. 118, 123. Bruce Porter and Jon Glassman, for example, draw different conclusions from the evidence for Soviet connivance in Sadat's attack planning.

For Kissinger's view of "existential" diplomacy, see Peter Dickson, *Kissinger and the Meaning of History* (New York: Cambridge University Press, 1975). For the 1974 Moscow summit, see Henry Kissinger, *Years of Upheaval,* pp. 1151–

1173. The Khrushchev quote in Vienna is an indirect quote by Adam B. Ulam in "Forty Years of Troubled Coexistence," *Foreign Affairs* (Fall 1985), pp. 12–32, at p. 29. General Dung's quotation is from Harry Summers, *On Strategy*, pp. 136–137. The chronology of the North Vietnamese attack is drawn from the *New York Times*. For Kissinger's "cannot abandon" quote, see the *Times*, March 27, 1975; for Ford's "will not be honored," April 4; for "finished," April 23; for the details of the embassy withdrawal, April 29–May 2; and for Kissinger's "some help," April 30. The 1973 newspaper quotations on the possibility of renewed bombing are quoted in Henry Kissinger, *Years of Upheaval*, pp. 305–306, and see pp. 1236–1243 for a listing of additional contemporary statements on the possibility of renewed bombing.

## The End of Detente

The account of the Afghan invasion is drawn primarily from the *New York Times*. There is also a detailed account in Raymond Garthoff, *Detente and Confrontation*, pp. 887–965. The quotations from the Soviets on the invasion are from *ibid.*, pp. 928, 929; additional Soviet quotes on the invasion and the hostage-taking in Iran are from Adam Ulam, *Dangerous Relations*, pp. 253, 256–257. Zbigniew Brzezinski's account is in *Power and Principle: Memoirs of the National Security Adviser, 1977–1981* (New York: Farrar, Straus & Giroux, 1983), pp. 486–500; and see Cyrus Vance, *Hard Choices: Critical Years in America's Foreign Policy* (New York: Simon and Schuster, 1983), pp. 408–413.

For the shift in Soviet Third World policy, see Francis Fukuyama, "Soviet Strategy in the Third World," in Francis Fukuyama and Andrzej Korbonski, eds., *The Soviet Union and the Third World: The Last Three Decades* (Ithaca, N.Y.: Cornell University Press, 1987), pp. 24–45. Colin Legum's analysis of Soviet purposes is in his "USSR Policy in Sub-Saharan Africa," in *ibid.*, pp. 228–246. The quote on Soviet policy in the Horn of Africa is from Paul Henze, "Getting a Grip on the Horn: The Emergence of the Soviet Presence and Future Prospects," in Walter Z. Laqueur, *Patterns of Soviet Conduct in the Third World* (New York: Praeger, 1983), pp. 150–186, at p. 152. The background material is drawn from a number of sources: see Laqueur's "Introduction," pp. 1–39; Bruce Porter, *The USSR in Third World Conflicts*, pp. 1–59; and "Kissinger's Critique," *The Economist*, February 3, 1979, p. 17.

For Soviet policy in Africa, see Colin Legum, "Angola and the Horn of Africa," in Stephen S. Kaplan, *Diplomacy of Power: Soviet Armed Forces as a Political Instrument* (Washington, D.C.: Brookings, 1980), pp. 570–637. For the war in Angola, see Bruce Porter, *op. cit.*, pp. 147–181; Arieh Eilar, "Soviet Diplomacy in the Third World," in Walter Laqueur, *op. cit.*, pp. 42–80, at pp. 63–66; Neil C. Livingston and Manfred von Nordheim, "The U.S. Congress and the Angolan Crisis," *Strategic Review* (Spring 1977), pp. 34–43, and p. 40 for the Cranston quote. For the Ogaden war, see Bruce Porter, *op. cit.*, pp. 182–215; Arieh Eiler, *op. cit.*; and Peter Vanneman and Martin James, "Soviet Thrust into the Horn of Africa: The Next Targets," *Strategic Review* (Fall 1978), pp. 33–38 (for, in particular, the role of the Cubans and strains over the Cuban role in Eritrea—the Cubans did not like fighting Eritrean rebels). For the scale of Soviet arms shipments to Africa, see Raymond W. Copson, "The Soviet Union in Africa: An Assessment," in Walter Laqueur, *op. cit.* pp. 187–207, at pp. 198–199.

The mildest view of Soviet intentions in Africa, and a capably argued one, is in Raymond Garthoff, *Detente and Confrontation,* pp. 630–652 (dealing with the Horn of Africa); Robert Legvold, "The Super Rivals: Conflict in the Third World," *Foreign Affairs* (Spring 1979), pp. 755–778, makes a similar argument. Donald Zagoria's quote is from his "Into the Breach: New Soviet Alliances in the Third World," *Foreign Affairs* (Spring 1979), pp. 733–754, at p. 741. Kissinger reflects on the implication of the Western failure to respond to Soviet Third World probes in "East Asia, the Pacific, and the West: Strategic Trends and Implications: Part I," Adelphi Paper No. 216, Conference Report of the International Institute for Strategic Studies (London: IISS, Spring 1987), pp. 3–10.

### Chapter 18: Arms Control Revisited

#### *The Demise of SALT*

The most complete history of the SALT II Treaty is Strobe Talbott, *Endgame: The Inside Story of SALT II* (New York: Harper & Row, 1979); the text of the treaty is reprinted on pp. 279–310. Except as noted, the account in my text, although not the analysis of the treaty, follows Talbott's. Vance's account is *op. cit.,* pp. 99–109 and 349–367, and Garthoff's is *op. cit.,* pp. 801–827. The detailed technical provisions produced more than the usual fencing over verification and data requirements. The United States argued, and won, a point on the indistinguishability of SS-19 and SS-11 silos, once those missiles were intermixed. The Soviets made the same argument with respect to Minuteman IIs and IIIs, but conceded the point. The fact was, as everyone knew, the contents of American missile silos could be verified simply by reading congressional hearings or the reports in *Aviation Week and Space Technology*—the Soviets hardly needed satellites. The argument over the Minuteman identification was one of the first times that the Soviets implicitly accepted the fact of "information asymmetry."

There was similar byplay over encryption. At one point during the encryption discussions, the Soviets conducted a missile test in which almost everything important was encrypted. When the United States protested, the Soviets asked for specifics, apparently to test American monitoring capabilities. On at least two occasions, the Americans delayed protests so as not to reveal how rapidly they could analyze and interpret data on Soviet test flights.

#### *A Note on Cruise Missile Guidance*

Currently deployed cruise missiles use the TERCOM (for "terrain contour matching") guidance system. It is known as a "line correlator" approach. A radar on the bottom of the cruise looks directly down on the ground and measures the height of the terrain features it is passing over. The on-board computer then compares the height undulations of the measured terrain line with maps stored in its memory and steers the cruise to a predetermined course. Currently deployed cruises reportedly carry up to ten pre-selected target maps in their memory; conceivably targets could be changed during flight. Computer memory capacity limits the resolution of the map features to about 30–70 meters, although as memory storage technology improves, resolutions could be much finer. To conserve memory and fuel, the cruise will fly on inertial guidance at a high altitude for the early part of its flight; when it comes within range of air defenses, it will shift to radar guidance and descend to its ground-hugging flight path for the last leg of its journey. The resolution of the guidance map is finer as the cruise approaches the target; a cruise approaching land from sea, for example, is likely to be a good distance off course—TERCOM is obviously useless over water—so it will need a broadly gauged map-scan to get reoriented.

Some experts suggest that the actual CEP of a cruise is likely to be closer to 100 meters than 30, which is still outstandingly good. The missile reportedly will switch back to inertial guidance for the last 30 kilometers or so of its flight to avoid being confused by missile craters from previous attacks, which may reduce its final accuracy slightly; it could also be thrown off course by heavy snow conditions or small mapping errors. More sophisticated guidance systems are under development that will, e.g., make an area radar scan rather than a line scan as TERCOM does, or use infrared sensors to read the infrared characteristics of the overflown terrain.

In the mid-1980s, the Defense Department ended cruise procurement and shifted emphasis to an "Advanced Technology Cruise" that should begin deployment in the late 1980s. It will have roughly double or even triple the range and even greater homing capacity, will be somewhat faster, will have more advanced path-finding and route-selection abilities, and will incorporate the latest "Stealth" or electronic defense technology, to increase its invisibility to Soviet aircraft defenses. The advanced cruise will cost from two to six times more than the first-generation weapons. See Matthew Bunn, *Technology of Ballistic Missile Reentry Vehicles,* MIT Program in Science and Technology for International Security, Report No. 11 (March 1984), pp. 53–56, and Kosta Tsipis, "Cruise Missiles," *Scientific American* (February 1977), pp. 20–29. Information on the "Advanced Technology Cruise" is from Thomas Cochran, *et al., Nuclear Weapons Databook.*

The JCS "modest but useful" quote is in *Aviation Week and Space Technology,* July 16, 1979, p. 25. The "cosmetic" congressional quote is from Alton K. Marsh, "House Panel Urges Rejection of SALT," *Aviation Week and Space Technology,* January 1, 1979, pp. 16–17. For the events leading to the Vladivostok summit and Kissinger's problems with Jackson and Perle, see Henry Kissinger, *Years of Upheaval,* pp. 979–1031. Richard Neustadt and Ernest R. May, *Thinking in Time: The Uses of History for Decision-makers* (Glencoe, N.Y.: The Free Press, 1986), give a scathing account of Carter's early SALT initiative, pp. 111–133. For the effect of SALT on the eight-point Committee on the Present Danger program, see Jan M. Lodal's "SALT II and American Security," *Foreign*

*Affairs* (Winter 1978–79), pp. 245–268, generally considered the most authoritative statement of the case for ratification.

The JCS "nothing differently" quote is in Strobe Talbott, *Deadly Gambits* (New York: Vintage, 1985), p. 226. Fred C. Iklé's "SALT and the Nuclear Balance in Europe," *Strategic Review* (Spring 1978), pp. 18–22, is a lukewarm defense. For the spending impact of SALT and "windfall" quote, see David R. Griffiths, "Defense Spending Demands Spur Needs List," *Aviation Week and Space Technology*, (August 13, 1979), p. 14–15. The Schlesinger quote on SALT violations is in *Aviation Week and Space Technology*, December 1, 1975, p. 21. For sophisticated conservative opposition, see William Van Cleave, "SALT on the Eagle's Tail," *Strategic Review* (Spring 1976), pp. 44–51—for both the Zumwalt view and the Gray "Western invention" quote—and Colin Gray, "SALT: Time to Quit," *Strategic Review* (Fall 1976), pp. 14–22. Additional critical quotations are from Robert Hotz, "Pitfalls of SALT," *Aviation Week and Space Technology*, (November 24, 1975), p. 7. A recent assessment of the Krasnoyarsk radar is in Bruce Parrot, "The Soviet Union and Ballistic Missile Defense," SAIS Papers in International Affairs No. 14 (Boulder, Colo.: Westview Press, 1987), pp. 41–43; and see Miroslav Nincic, "Can The U.S. Trust the U.S.S.R.?", *Scientific American* (April 1986), pp. 33–41, for a thorough assessment of compliance issues on both sides. Americans who were allowed to see the half-finished site in 1987 confirmed that it was probably not an ABM battle management radar, and were struck by its crudity (*New York Times,* September 6–10, 1987).

Kissinger's "conscience-bound" and "fatigue" quotes are in William H. Gregory, "The Voice of Experience," *Aviation Week and Space Technology*, August 13, 1979, p. 9. The Soviet quote on cruises as a first-strike weapon is in Strobe Talbott, *Deadly Gambits,* p. 132n. Clarence A. Robinson, Jr., "MX Racetrack Questioned in Congress," *Aviation Week and Space Technology*, November 12, 1979, pp. 17–18, describes the various MX basing schemes and left-right alliances; transporter-erector details are in Thomas Cochran, *et al., Nuclear Weapons Databook.* The "Scowcroft Report" is the Report of the President's Commission on Strategic Forces (Washington, D.C.: USGPO, 1983).

## A Note on Theoretical American First-strike Capability with 200 MXs

Assuming 2:1 warhead coverage on Soviet hardened targets, replacing 200 Minuteman IIIs with MXs would make more than 3,000 accurate warheads available against some 1,500 Soviet silos (200 MX × 10 = 2,000; 350 Minuteman III × 3 = 1,050). The 450 Minuteman IIs would remain as a second-wave strike force, or perhaps as an additional first-strike force against command and control targets. The addition of the accurate Trident II D-5 will add further margin. The accuracy of the MX, if it works (there have been reports of early problems) will be truly phenomenal—at about 100 meters, much better than anything the Soviets have achieved. The warhead finally chosen, the W87/ Mark 21, is actually slightly smaller, at 300 kilotons, than the Minuteman III's W78/Mark 12A configuration. Larger warheads were considered, but were rejected in favor of accuracy and other technical considerations. The high accuracy makes warhead size unimportant; the MX will have a 99+ percent kill capability against any Soviet hardened target. The *theoretical* American first-strike capability with the MX, of course, makes it no more practical or less risky than the theoretical Soviet capability against the United States. (MX performance and warhead characteristics are from Thomas Cochran, *et al.*, *Nuclear Weapons Databook.*)

### The Dual Track and START: Breaking Off Arms Control

For the neutron bomb incident, see Raymond Garthoff, *Detente and Confrontation*, pp. 851–853, and Zbigniew Brzezinski, *Power and Principle*, pp. 301–306. Technical characteristics are in Steven T. Cohen, "Enhanced Radiation Warheads: Setting the Record Straight," *Strategic Review* (Winter 1978), pp. 11–18. Military spending patterns for the NATO allies are drawn from the *Military Balance*, various years. George Kennan's criticisms of the Europeans are in his "Europe's Problems, Europe's Choices," *Foreign Policy* (Spring 1974), pp. 3–16, at pp. 15–16.

The most complete history of the "Theater Nuclear Forces" debate is Strobe Talbott's *Deadly Gambits;* and see Raymond Garthoff, *op. cit.,* pp. 849–886; Zbigniew Brzezinski, *op. cit.,* pp. 307–311; and Helmut Schmidt, "A Policy of Reliable Partnership," *Foreign Affairs* (Spring 1981), pp. 743–755. SS-20 characteristics and deployments and those of the opposing NATO forces are from *The Military Balance*, various years. Brzezinski's quote on military value of TNF is in Garthoff, *op. cit.,* p. 859n.; the origin of the 572 number is in *ibid.,* p. 862; and for the Soviet reaction, *ibid.,* pp. 881–883. For the Pershing II, see Thomas Cochran, *et al., Nuclear Weapons Databook.* The Pershing II warhead failed almost all of its tests before deployment; whether it would have been deployed at all absent the enormous political momentum behind the Euromissiles is open to question. The Soviet insistence that the actual range of the Pershing II is about 1,500 miles—the American military says it is 1,000 miles—is in marked contrast to their almost uniform practice of accepting Western characterizations of their weapons. A 1,500-mile range would be required for the Pershing II to reach Moscow and the key command and control centers east of Moscow. Soviet fears about the Pershing illustrate the value of the cruise, however. The Soviets cannot plausibly protest the cruises as a first-strike threat. For the maneuverable warhead, see Matthew Bunn, *Technology of Ballistic Missile Reentry Vehicles*, pp. 60–61. For the official Soviet characterization of the Pershing II as a "first-strike" weapon, see *Whence the Threat to Peace* (Moscow: Military Publishing House, 1984), p. 20.

Perle's quotes on Euromissiles are in Strobe Talbott, *Deadly Gambits*, p. 44. Garthoff's "killed the prospect" quotes are from his *op. cit.,* pp. 1023, 1024. Nitze "singlehandedly" is from Talbott, *op. cit.,* p. 210; and the "walk in the woods" deal is in *ibid.,* pp. 122–130.

### Chapter 19: Images of War

### War-fighting Doctrine and "Assured Destruction"

Articles developing the Soviet war-fighting thesis include Richard E. Pipes, "Why the Soviet Union Thinks It Could Fight and Win a Nuclear War," *Com-*

mentary (July 1977), pp. 21–34; Walter Z. Laqueur, "Confronting the Problems," *Commentary* (March 1977), pp. 33–41; Edward N. Luttwack, "Defense Reconsidered," *Commentary* (March 1977), pp. 51–59, and "Churchill and Us," *Commentary* (June 1977), pp. 44–50; Fritz Ermath, "Contrasts in American and Soviet Strategic Thought," *International Security* (Fall 1978), pp. 138–155; Colin Gray, "Foreign Policy—There Is No Choice," *Foreign Policy* (Fall 1976), pp. 114–127; Colin Gray and Keith S. Payne, "Victory Is Possible," *Foreign Policy* (Summer 1980), pp. 14–27; and the exchange between Colin Gray and Michael Howard, "Perspectives on a Future Nuclear War," *International Security* (Summer 1981), pp. 185–187. See also Paul Nitze, "Assured Strategic Stability," Robert Tucker, "Beyond Detente," and Robert Conquest, "A New Russia? A New World?" *Foreign Affairs* (January 1975), pp. 482–497.

The "Team B" quotes are from John Prados, *The Soviet Threat*, p. 252. For a description of the exercise, see *The National Intelligence Estimates A-B Team Episode Concerning Soviet Strategic Capabilities and Objectives*, Senate Select Committee on Intelligence (Subcommittee Report) (Washington, D.C.: USGPO, 1978). The Sokolovsky quotes are from Harriet Fast Scott, ed., *Soviet Military Strategy*, pp. 190, 192, 202–203, 284–285, and 210; the Lomov quotes are from N. A. Lomov, *Scientific Technical Progress and the Revolution in Military Affairs* (U.S. Air Force translation) (Washington, D.C.: USGPO, 1973), pp. 143, 147. The third Soviet text is quoted in Albert Wohlstetter and Richard Brody, "Continuing Control as a Requirement for Deterring," in Ashton B. Carter, *et al.*, eds., *Managing Nuclear Operations*, pp. 142–196, at p. 155. The Grechko quote is in Thomas W. Wolfe, *The SALT Experience*, p. 21. The Ustinov quote is in John Van Oudenaren, "Deterrence, War-Fighting, and Soviet Military Doctrine," Adelphi Paper No. 210 (London: IISS, 1986), p. 11.

A recent much-publicized statement of the "no-first-use" argument by ten defense experts (McGeorge Bundy, Morton Halperin, William W. Kaufmann, George F. Kennan, Robert S. McNamara, Madalene O'Donnell, Leon V. Sigal, Gerard C. Smith, Richard H. Ullman, and Paul C. Warnke) is "Back from the Brink," *The Atlantic* (August 1986), pp. 35–41. The military implications of a "no-first-use" posture—again, like "assured destruction" it is more of a "posture" than a "strategy"—are in John D. Steinbruner and Leon V. Sigal, eds., *Alliance Security: NATO and the No-First-Use Question* (Washington, D.C.: Brookings, 1983). Colin Gray's "bitter article" is his "National Styles in Strategy: The American Example," *International Security* (Fall 1981), pp. 21–48.

Paul Nitze on the Soviet view of military strength is in *op. cit.,* p. 216. Colin Gray, in "What Hath RAND Wrought," *Foreign Policy* (Fall 1971), pp. 111–129, is one of the first to make this argument. For Kissinger's "strategic superiority" press conference, see his *Years of Upheaval*, p. 1175. The McNamara "war-fighting" quotes are from his Athens speech. The "management tool" quote is in Ted Greenwood, *Making the MIRV*, p. 70. For Herbert Scoville on "assured destruction," see, for example, his "Flexible MADness," *Foreign Policy* (Summer 1974), pp. 164–177. The "rigidified . . . quantified" quote is in Colin Gray, "What Hath RAND Wrought," pp. 120–121. The quote from Lambeth is in Lawrence Freedman, *The Evolution of Nuclear Strategy*, p. 260. Fred Iklé's quotes are from his "Can Nuclear Deterrence Last Out the Century?", *Foreign*

*Affairs* (January 1973), pp. 267–285, at pp. 279–280, an extremely influential article.

For a detailed treatment of arms race theories, casting doubt on simplistic action–reaction cycles, see Colin Gray, *The Soviet-American Arms Race* (Lexington, Mass.: Lexington, 1976), and his excellent shorter summary, "The Arms Race Phenomenon," *World Politics* (October 1971), pp. 39–79. The "muffled, lagged, and complex" phrase is quoted without attribution by Albert Wohlstetter in his "Is There a Strategic Arms Race?," p. 8. (It is a frequently cited phrase; I found the original source, but cannot locate it in my notes.) Nitze on MIRV/ ABM interaction is in his "Comment" on Wohlstetter's article, *Foreign Policy* (Fall 1974), pp. 82–83. An alternative and much-cited view—if perhaps an excessively schematic one—is in Roman Kolkowicz, "Strategic Parity and Beyond: A Soviet Perspective," *World Politics* (April 1971), pp. 431–451. Kolkowicz suggests that the Soviets imitate American arms policies with a five-year lag. For Lee on the onset of the Soviet buildup, see *The Estimation of Soviet Defense Expenditures*, pp. 146–149. For a concise history of the development of strategic targeting, see David Alan Rosenberg, "U.S. Nuclear War Planning, 1945–1960," and Desmond Ball, "Development of the SIOP, 1960–1983," in Desmond Ball and Jeffrey Richelson, *Strategic Nuclear Targeting*, pp. 35–56 and 57–83. The quote from George Ball is on p. 70.

The clearest outline of the evolution of McNamara's strategic thinking is in his Draft Presidential Memoranda. Warner Schilling's "United States Strategic Nuclear Concepts in the 70s: The Search for Sufficiently Equivalent Countervalue Parity," *International Security* (Fall 1981), pp. 49–79, is an unusually sensible discussion from a long-time student of practical policymaking. For a series of official statements on the counterforce role for the new MIRVs, see John Newhouse, *Cold Dawn*, pp. 31–32, 68–69. The Nixon quote on policy continuity is in Desmond Ball, *op. cit.*, p. 73. The *New York Times* quote is in Thomas W. Wolfe, *The SALT Experience*, p. 145. Schlesinger's "porous deterrent" quote is in his "The Evolution of American Policy Toward the Soviet Union," *International Security* (Summer 1976), pp. 37–48, at p. 43. His "reassurance" quote is in Thomas W. Wolfe, *ibid*, p. 137. For additional contemporary discussions, see Ted Greenwood and Michael F. Nacht, "The New Nuclear Debate: Sense or Nonsense" *Foreign Affairs* (July 1974), pp. 761–780, and Wolfgang Panofsky, "The Mutual Hostage Relationship Between America and Russia," *Foreign Affairs* (October 1973), pp. 109–118.

Brown's quotes are from his commencement address at the Naval War College, August 20, 1980 (United States Department of Defense, Office of Public Affairs). The quotes from Harold Brown and Colin Gray on "damage limitation" are from Gray's "Targeting Problems in Central War," in Desmond Ball and Jeffrey Richelson, *Strategic Nuclear Targeting*, pp. 171–193, at pp. 171, 175. Wohlstetter's quote is from his "Continuing Control," p. 180; Colin Gray on being "outbid" is in *op. cit.*, p. 172.

## Nuclear War Fighting and Reality

Paul Bracken on "missile farms" is from his "War Termination," in Ashton B. Carter, *et al.*, eds., *Managing Nuclear Operations*, pp. 197–214, at p. 200.

Schlesinger on "existential circumstances" is quoted in Bruce G. Blair, *Strategic Command and Control: Redefining the Nuclear Threat* (Washington, D.C.: Brookings, 1985), p. 214. The discussion of the problems of maintaining control over nuclear forces follows, in the main, Blair, *ibid.;* the technical details, in particular, unless otherwise indicated, are drawn from Blair. The additional citations below supplement Blair. Daniel Ford, *The Button* (New York: Simon and Schuster, 1985), is a more popularly written account on the same theme— although Ford's conclusion that American forces are in a "hair-trigger" status is probably overdrawn. Paul Bracken, *The Command and Control of Nuclear Forces* (New Haven: Yale University Press, 1983), pays particular attention to the problems of limited nuclear war in the NATO context. And see John D. Steinbruner, "Choices and Tradeoffs," and Ashton B. Carter, "Assessing Command System Vulnerability" and "Sources of Error and Uncertainty," in Ashton B. Carter, *et al.*, eds., *Managing Nuclear Operations,* pp. 535–554, 555–610, and 611–640; John D. Steinbruner, "Launch Under Attack," *Scientific American* (January 1984), pp. 37–47; and Ashton B. Carter, "The Command and Control of Nuclear War," in *ibid.* (January 1985), pp. 35–46.

For direct political contact with local commanders, see Bruce G. Blair, *ibid.*, p. 74, and Albert Wohlstetter and Richard Brody, "Continuing Control," p. 185. The general's "not enough time" quote is in Blair, *ibid.*, p. 235. For a description of a recent confused mobilization exercise, see William J. Broad, "Philosophers at the Pentagon," *Science,* October 24, 1980, pp. 409–410. For the multiplicity of options, see Walter Slocombe, "Preplanned Operations," in Ashton B. Carter, *et al.*, eds., *Managing Nuclear Operations,* pp. 121–141. For delegation of authority, see Paul Bracken, "Delegation of Nuclear Command Authority," in *ibid.*, pp. 352–372, and Daniel Shuchman, "Nuclear Strategy and the Problem of Command and Control," *Survival* (July–August 1987), pp. 336–360—an article which argues that delegation has been quite extensive in the past. For radio blackout and electromagnetic pulse effects, see Samuel Glasstone and Philip J. Dolan, *The Effects of Nuclear Weapons,* particularly Chapters X and XI. The quote from the Defense Science Board on EMP is in Bruce G. Blair, *op. cit.*, p. 134. The characteristics of the available radio-spectrum media are summarized in Ashton B. Carter, "Communications Technologies and Vulnerabilities," in Ashton B. Carter, *et al.*, eds., *op. cit.*, pp. 217–281. Carter's discussion of vulnerabilities is in his "Assessing Command System Vulnerability"—his case for the complexity of Soviet targeting, even given the serious weaknesses in the C$^3$I system, is more convincing than Blair's somewhat apocalyptic assessment.

For a commonsense review of the recent vulnerability debate, see Daniel Shuchman, "Nuclear Strategy and the Problem of Command and Control." For the dangers of an alert, see Bruce G. Blair, "Alerting in Crisis and Conventional War," and Scott D. Sagan, "Nuclear Alerts and Crisis Management." The "readiness will gravitate" quote is from Blair, "Alerting in Crisis," p. 106. For the practical problems of authorizing battlefield weapons, see in addition to Paul Bracken's *Command and Control,* Catherine McArdle Kelleher, "NATO Nuclear Operations," in Ashton B. Carter, *et al.*, eds., *op. cit.*, pp. 445–469, and Leon V. Sigal, "No First Use and NATO's Nuclear Posture" and "Political Prospects for No First Use," in John D. Steinbruner and Leon V.

Sigal, eds., *Alliance Security: NATO and the No-First-Use Question,* pp. 106–133, 134–146. For Soviet policies, see Stephen E. Meyer, "Soviet Nuclear Operations," in Ashton B. Carter, *et al.,* eds., *op. cit.,* pp. 470–533; Wohlstetter and Brody take a different view on essentially a priori grounds in their "Continuing Control."

For the problem of retinal damage, see Theodore Postol, "Targeting," in Ashton B. Carter, *et al.,* eds., pp. 373–406, at p. 403. Wohlstetter's Iran scenario is in his *op. cit.,* pp. 159–160. And see Michael Howard, "On Firing a Nuclear Weapon," *International Security* (Spring 1981), pp. 3–17. The "leading scholar" quote on command and control is from Bruce G. Blair, *Strategic Command and Control,* p. 287. For alternative "quote-mongering" exercises, see Raymond Garthoff's Brookings Staff Paper, "Perspectives on the Strategic Balance" (Washington, D.C.: Brookings, 1983), and pp. 768–785 of his *Detente and Confrontation;* see also Christopher D. Jones, "Soviet Military Doctrine: The Political Dimension," and Robert Arnett, "Soviet Views on Nuclear War," pp. 11–115 and 116–122 in William H. Kincade and Jeffrey D. Porro, *Negotiating Security.*

For sampling of NATO "war-fighting" writings, chosen almost at random from the pages of *Strategic Review,* see, for example, Col. Marc Geneste, "The Nuclear Land Battle" (Winter 1976), pp. 79–85; Capt. Eugene D. Bétit, "Soviet Tactical Doctrine and Capabilities and NATO's Strategic Defenses" (Summer 1976), pp. 95–107; and Steven T. Cohen, "Enhanced Radiation Warheads: Setting the Record Straight" (Winter 1978). LeMay on a pre-emptive attack is frequently cited in slightly varying versions. The quote here is in Daniel Schuchman, *op. cit.,* p. 348. The Lomov and Sokolovsky citations of Western sources for war-fighting doctrine are in *op. cit.,* respectively, p. 144 and pp. 279–282. And see Lawrence Freedman, *The Evolution of Nuclear Strategy,* p. 269, for an authoritative quote on the "morale-building" aspect of Soviet military doctrine. A recent Wohlstetter article on war-fighting theory, "Between an Unfree World and None," *Foreign Affairs* (Summer 1985), pp. 962–994, highlights another problem with the quote-mongering approach. Wohlstetter quotes liberally from official Soviet military writings to buttress his war-fighting argument; but, of nine citations, six date from 1970 or earlier, one from the mid-seventies, and two from the 1980s, one of which is apparently complaining about the *American* ability to wage limited war with precision-guided weapons. Even granting that the Soviets have generally shown much greater consistency of military theory and purpose than the United States, it is difficult to assess the value of twenty-year-old writings in buttressing an argument about current intentions and capabilities.

For Wohlstetter on Soviet command and control, see his "Continuing Control," pp. 156–157. His "substantial flexibility" quote is on p. 190. For a less sanguine view on Soviet command and control intelligence, see Stephen E. Meyer, *op. cit.,* pp. 478–482. John Van Oudenaren's analysis is in his "Deterrence, War-Fighting, and Soviet Military Doctrine." For the Sokolovsky quote on military theory, see *op. cit.,* p. 258. The Hanson quote is from Donald W. Hanson, "Is Soviet Strategic Doctrine Superior?", *International Security* (Winter 1982–83), p. 77. Arthur Schlesinger and Soviet "ignorance" is in his *Thousand Days,* p. 301; for Herbert Scoville and "self-denial," see, for example, his

"Beyond SALT One," *Foreign Affairs* (April 1972), pp. 488–501, where he recommends, for instance, the development of a long-range submarine-launched missile, but one that is not too accurate.

## Chapter 20: Rearming America

### The Spending Window

Stockman's account of defense budget development is in *The Triumph of Politics: Why the Reagan Revolution Failed* (New York: Harper & Row, 1986), pp. 105–109, 276–299. Richard Stubbings gives a somewhat different version of the same events in *The Defense Game* (New York: Harper & Row, 1986), pp. 374–375. The various figures on defense spending and defense spending shares are from *The Budget of the United States Government,* various years; *The Economic Report of the President,* various years; and United States House of Representatives, Committee on Appropriations, *Department of Defense Appropriations* (Washington, D.C.: USGPO, various years). The "shuddering halt" quote is from *Strategic Survey: 1985–1986* (London: IISS, 1986), p. 67. The "peacetime war" quote is in Richard Stubbings, *op. cit.,* p. 30; for the allocation of new funds in the Reagan administration, see the table in *ibid.,* p. 44.; and for the Pentagon quote, *ibid.,* p. 375.

Weinberger's "exorbitant price" quote is from House Committee on Appropriations, *op. cit.* (1985), p. 94. Edward Luttwack's quote is from his *The Pentagon and the Art of War* (New York: Simon and Schuster, 1985), p. 17; the Stubbings quote is from *op. cit.,* p. 43; the *Wall Street Journal* quote is from Stanley A. Weiss, "True Worth of a Defense Dollar," May 14, 1987. The readiness improvement data are from "The Report of the Secretary of Defense Caspar Weinberger to the Congress," February 1984 (Washington, D.C.: USGPO, 1984), pp. 64–79, 210–231. For recent exercise performance, see, for example, Arthur T. Hadley, "Back to the Front," *The New Republic,* November 16, 1987, pp. 16–18. In competitive NATO exercises, American troops have consistently been placing first or second since about 1982, compared to consistent last-place finishes in the late 1970s. Actual force structure and equipment changes are drawn from *The Military Balance,* various years. The Soviet production numbers for tanks and armored vehicles are in *Soviet Military Power, 1985* (Washington, D.C.: USGPO, 1985), p. 75. And see the table on tactical aircraft production in Richard Stubbings, *op. cit.,* p. 49. The congressional quote on readiness is from Surveys and Investigations Staff, Report to the Committee on Appropriations, U.S. House of Representatives on the Readiness of the U.S. Military—U.S. Army, Vol I. March 1983 (Washington, D.C.: USGPO, 1983), p. 1.

Deployment histories of the F-4 and F-111 airplanes are from Thomas Cochran, *et al., Nuclear Weapons Databook.* For the F-14, see Stubbings, *op. cit.,* pp. 150–151 and Luttwack, *op. cit.,* pp. 216–218; for Phoenix missile problems, Franklin C. Spinney, *Defense Facts of Life: The Plans/Reality Mismatch* (Boulder, Colo.: Westview Press, 1985), p. 165. Weapons costs are drawn, generally, from the schedules in the *Defense Department Appropriations,* various years, or Thomas Cochran, *et al., Nuclear Weapons Databook* (which includes deployment histories of all nuclear-capable planes and ships). See Edward Luttwack, *op. cit.,* pp. 58–60, for the performance of the A-6 in Lebanon. For airlift and sealift, see John M. Collins, *U.S.-Soviet Military Balance,* Vol. IV, "Airlift and Sealift," pp. 40–49, for the data on transport inventories and carrying capacity. For additional lift procurement in the Reagan administration, see Stubbings, *op. cit.,* pp. 31–42; and Luttwack, *op. cit.,* pp. 218–219. For the history of the Bradley, the Patriot, and the Sergeant York, see Stubbings, *op. cit.,* pp. 46, 136–139, and 184–186; for the Patriot's unit costs, Franklin C. Spinney, *op. cit.,* p. 238, and see *The Economist,* May 4, 1985, p. 49, for the weapon's capabilities.

## The Wide Blue Oceans

For the Reagan naval program, see Richard Stubbings, *op. cit.,* pp. 117–123; Edward Luttwack, *op. cit.,* pp. 220–222, 262–263; Jack Beatty, "In Harm's Way: America's Scary, and Expensive, New Naval Strategy," *The Atlantic* (May 1987), pp. 37–53; John Mearsheimer, "A Strategic Misstep: The Maritime Strategy and Deterrence in Europe," *International Security* (Fall 1986), pp. 3–57; and Barry R. Posen, "Inadvertent Nuclear War: Escalation and NATO's Northern Flank," *ibid.* (Fall 1982), pp. 28–54. And see Seymour Deitchmann, *Military Power,* pp. 91–121, for an excellent, detached discussion of naval issues. The counterargument is in Linton F. Brooks, "Naval Power and National Security: The Case for the Maritime Strategy," *International Security* (Fall 1986), pp. 58–88. The Weinberger quote is in Jack Beatty, *op. cit.,* p. 52. The *Stark* episode, Lehman's comment on the Exocet, and Kaufmann's "idle talk" quote are drawn from the accounts of the incident in the *New York Times,* May 26–31. For the capabilities of antiship missiles and defenses, and the effects of nuclear weapons, see Paul F. Walker, "Smart Weapons in Naval Warfare," *Scientific American* (May 1983), pp. 53–61. For a discussion of the pros and cons of Soviet use of nuclear weapons against a surface fleet, see Donald C.F. Daniel, "The Soviet Navy and Tactical Nuclear War at Sea," *Survival* (July/August, 1987), pp. 318–335 and Desmond Ball, "Nuclear War at Sea," *International Security,* (Winter, 1985/86), pp. 3–31.

## Technology and the Shape of War

The discussion in this section is drawn for the most part from Seymour J. Deitchmann's *Military Power,* the most consistently intelligent and levelheaded discussion I have found. Except as noted, the specific examples are taken from Deitchmann's book. There is also a useful collection of articles in *New Technology and Western Security Policy,* Part I, Part II, and Part III, Adelphi Papers Nos. 197, 198, and 199 (London: IISS, 1985). Current deployments of the United States and Soviet forces are taken from *The Military Balance* or *Soviet Military Power.* The quote on the F-111 is from Alexander Cockburn, *The Threat,* p. 224.

The argument on airplane reusability does not apply to the B-52/cruise combination versus the B-1; in *strategic* warfare each weapon will presumably be used only once, so the theoretical reusability of the B-1 does not create any savings, a point discussed further below. The economics of tactical warfare might shift in favor of the cruise missile over the airplane if the cruises were produced in sufficient quantities to lower unit costs significantly. Since cruises carrying nuclear weapons are indistinguishable from conventionally armed ones, however, production in such numbers would be extremely alarming to the Soviets. Finally, although bombs are still cheaper than missiles, high-speed, low-level attack patterns have greatly increased the complexity of bomb design. Sighting and fuzing become difficult problems, and if the bomb is nuclear, its descent must be slowed by parachute or other means to allow the plane time to escape. The troubled development of the B83, one of "the most complicated and expensive" bombs in the American inventory, is a case in point. Designed for the B-1B, it is a 1-megaton weapon that can be released from as low as 150 feet or as high as 50,000 feet at Mach 2 speeds with a CEP of 200 meters or less, about twice the CEP of the MX—see Thomas Cochran, *et al., Nuclear Weapons Databook.*

The details of the Israeli Bekaa Valley campaign are from Clarence A. Robinson, Jr., "Surveillance Integration Pivotal in Israeli Successes," *Aviation Week and Space Technology,* July 5, 1982, pp. 22–24. For a criticism of American drone policy, see Richard Stubbings, *op. cit.,* pp. 146–149. Grechko's quote is in Paul F. Walker, "Precision-guided Munitions," *Scientific American* (August 1981), pp. 36–45, at p. 37. For the arguments in favor of a high-tech, "Deep Strike"-type of NATO strategy, see, for instance, Donald B. Cotter, "New Conventional Force Technology and the NATO-Warsaw Pact Balance: Part II," in *New Technology and Western Security Policy, Part II, op. cit.,* pp. 25–39; for the counterargument, see Steven L. Canby, "New Conventional Force Technology and the NATO-Warsaw Pact Balance: Part I," *ibid.,* pp. 7–24; and John Mearsheimer, "Maneuver, Mobile Defense and the NATO Central Front," *International Security* (Winter 1981–82), pp. 104–122. See also Carl H. Builder, "The Prospects and Implications of Non-Nuclear Means for Strategic Conflict," Adelphi Paper No. 200 (London: IISS, Summer 1985), pp. 9–13.

It is worth noting that although critics of the defense industry frequently blame the military and defense contractors for excessive weapons claims, much of the impetus, or at least publicity, behind precision-guided weapons comes from the arms control community. The availability of precision-guided weapons, they hope, will raise the threshold for nuclear war: if the submunition concept actually worked as advertised, it would seem to eliminate the necessity to respond to an overwhelming Soviet conventional attack with tactical nuclear weapons. It is that promise, perhaps, rather than their actual test performance that colors the assessment of some of their more enthusiastic proponents. Successful tests of "Assault Breaker"-type weapons tend to be carried out in the desert, where tanks are easy to spot. How they would operate in crowded, afforested Central Europe is not at all clear. At the same time, the necessity to move tanks along lines of natural cover would inevitably complicate Soviet planning and slow an advance. A typical article is Alek Gliksman, "Deterrence Without Nukes," *New York Times*, May 18, 1987.

For a review of antisubmarine warfare technology, and the relative effectiveness of Soviet and American boats, see Randolph J. Steer, *Understanding Anti-Submarine Warfare Technology*. MIT Program in Science and Technology for International Security (June 1984), Report No. 12. For the "black box repair problem," see Franklin Spinney, *Defense Facts of Life*, pp. 32–35. The Libyan assault is described in Seymour Hersh, "Target Qaddafi," *New York Times Magazine*, February 22, 1987, p. 6. Speculation on the causes of Ogarkov's firing is in Bruce Parrot, *The Soviet Union and Ballistic Missile Defense*, pp. 13–14, 40–44. The B-1B's development problems are detailed in United States House of Representatives, Committee on Armed Services, "The B-1B: A Program Review" (Washington, D.C.: USGPO, March 30, 1987).

The President's "Star Wars" speech quotes are from the *New York Times*, March 24, 1983. General Keegan's quote is in Dietrich Schroeer, "Directed-Energy Weapons and Strategic Defense: A Primer," Adelphi Papers No. 221 (London: IISS, Summer 1987), p. 52. Schroeer's paper is a useful technical review. Freeman Dyson's quotes are from his *Weapons and Hope* (New York: Harper & Row, 1984), pp. 280, 296. In addition, see: Daniel O. Graham, *The Non-Nuclear Defense of Cities: The High Frontier Space-based Defense Against ICBM Attack* (Cambridge, Mass.: Abt, 1983); Ashton B. Carter, *Directed Energy Missile Defense in Space (A Background Paper)* (Washington, D.C.: Office of Technology Assessment, 1984). See also the following reports from the MIT Program in Science and Technology for National Security: M. Callaham and K. Tsipis, "High Energy Laser Weapons: A Technical Assessment" (Report No. 6, November 1980); G. Bekefi, B. T. Feld, J. Parmentola, and K. Tsipis, "Particle Beam Weapons" (Report No. 4, December 1978); and Peter Stein, "The SDI Battle Management Program" (Report No. 14, December 1985). And for the recent report of the American Physical Society, see C. Kumar, N. Patel, and Nicolaas Bloembergen, "Strategic Defense and Directed Energy Weapons," *Scientific American* (September 1987), pp. 39–45. See also Colin Gray, "A Case for Strategic Defense"; Harold Brown, "The Strategic Defense Initiative: Defensive Systems and the Strategic Debate" (two opposing views); and SDI Director Lt. Gen. James Abrahamson's statement to Congress of May 9, 1984, all collected in the March–April 1985 issue of *Survival*, pp. 50–54, 55–64, and 75–78, respectively. The Abrahamson statement is a good summary of the research program.

For the achievability of "conventional" antimissile defense, see Stephen Weiner, "Systems and Technology," and Ashton B. Carter, "BMD Applications: Performance and Limitations," in Ashton B. Carter and David N. Schwartz, eds., *Ballistic Missile Defense* (Washington, D.C.: Brookings, 1983), pp. 49–88 and 98–181; also Deborah Nutter Miner and Alan H. Rutan, "What Role for Limited BMD?", *Survival* (March–April 1987), pp. 118–136, and Dean Wilkening, Kenneth Watman, Michael Kennedy, and Richard Darilek, "Strategic Defences and First-Strike Stability," *ibid.*, pp. 137–165. Both articles, and particularly the latter, make a compelling case for the difficulty of transitioning to a "defense-stable" environment. If long-range forces are reduced, the side with the best defense could enjoy a significant, temporary, first-strike advantage. The redirection of the SDI program is reviewed in Douglas C. Waller and James T. Bruce, "SDI's Covert Reorientation: Short-term Gains Over Long-term Prospects," *Arms Control Today* (June 1987), pp. 2–8. A useful and objective policy review is The Aspen Strategy Group, *The Strategic Defense Initiative and American Security* (Lanham, Md.: University Press, 1987).

## Chapter 21: New Opportunities?

The brief capsule of recent events is drawn except as indicated from news accounts in the *New York Times* and *The Economist.* Bruce Parrott's *The Soviet Union and Ballistic Missile Defense* also summarizes recent arms negotiations. The case against the INF Treaty was made most persuasively by Richard Nixon and Henry Kissinger in their "To Withdraw Missiles We Must Add Conditions," *Los Angeles Times,* April 26, 1987. One of the conditions that Nixon and Kissinger propose, that the Soviet missiles in Asia be covered by the treaty, was in fact met. The more important condition, of linking the treaty to conventional force reductions, was not. Gorbachev's United Nations speech was printed in *Pravda* on September 17, 1987; the quotations are from an English translation furnished to me in typescript by staff to Governor Mario Cuomo.

For a recent history of Soviet politics, see Seweryn Bialer, *The Soviet Paradox: External Expansion, Internal Decline* (New York: Knopf, 1986). Gorbachev's rise to power is in Zhores A. Medvedev, *Gorbachev* (New York: Norton, 1986). Details of Soviet economic problems are in Bialer, *op. cit.,* pp. 57–80, supplemented by the many reports in *The Economist.* The 17 percent outside estimate of the military burden on the Soviet economy is in *The Military Balance, 1986–1987,* p. 32; see pp. 32–33 for trends in recent Soviet military budgets. Marshal Goldman, *Gorbachev's Challenge: Reform in the Age of High Technology* (New York: Norton, 1987), makes a powerful case for the hopelessness of the Soviet Union's competitive position in high technology absent drastic reform.

The CIA revisions are in Richard F. Kaufman, "Causes of the Slowdown in Soviet Defense," *Survival* (July–August 1985), pp. 179–192. For shifting policy in the Third World, see Francis Fukuyama, *Moscow's Post-Brezhnev Reassessment of the Third World* (RAND Report R-3337-USDP, Santa Monica, February 1986); the Mozambique quote is from p. 62, and Gorbachev's "sympathies" quote is on p. 45. Shmelev's quote is from *The Economist "Glasnost II,"* July 25–31, 1987, p. 27. Seweryn Bialer's "Gorbachev's Move," *Foreign Policy* (Fall 1987), pp. 59–87, is a catalogue of the impressive odds stacked against Mr. Gorbachev. For a more bullish view, see Roy Medvedev writing from Moscow, *"Perestroika:* Toward a Soviet 'Miracle,' " *Los Angeles Times,* July 5, 1987.

## Chapter 22: The Military Balance, 1987

The $15 trillion arms-spending estimate is derived by taking the constant-dollar American arms spending since 1945 and simply doubling it. John Lewis Gaddis reviews the crisis-stability of the arms standoff in his "The Long Peace:

Elements of Stability in the Postwar International System," *International Security* (Spring, 1986), pp. 99–147.

## The Strategic Balance

Except as specifically indicated, the counts of American-Soviet weapons follow those in *The Military Balance* for 1986–87. American naval cruise missile deployments are estimated in Thomas Cochran, *et al.*, *Nuclear Weapons Databook*. It is worth noting here that, as the Scowcroft Commission pointed out, the Soviet surplus of accurate warheads is of little marginal usefulness because of the deployment characteristics of American forces. ICBMs are not of great utility against bomber bases. In contrast to missiles, which must wait in their silos until the last minute upon an indication of a possible Soviet strike, bombers are quick-alert weapons. Since they could take off upon ambiguous notice of a Soviet strike, they would clear their bases before ICBMs could reach them. The Soviets could successfully attack alerted bomber bases with shorter trajectory submarine-launched missiles, but unless the timing was improbably perfect, the Americans would launch their land-based missiles upon confirmation of the bomber base attacks. The Scowcroft Commission concluded that a surprise attack scenario that would leave intact two of the three legs of the strategic triad is too implausible to warrant substantial counterinvestment. For the difficulties of a true "launch on warning," however, see John D. Steinbruner, "Launch Under Attack."

The Soviet ABM summary is drawn from Sayre Stevens, "The Soviet BMD Program," in Ashton B. Carter and David N. Schwarz, eds., *Ballistic Missile Defense*, pp. 182–220; and Bruce Parrott, *The Soviet Union and Ballistic Missile Defense*. Stevens is generally more pessimistic about the Soviet capabilities than Parrott. Paul B. Stares, *The Militarization of Space*, is an excellent detailed discussion of the antisatellite and beam weapon programs of both countries. Carter's spending figures are on p. 209; the satellite "blinding" incident is on p. 146. Senator Nunn's brief on "exotic" ABM technologies is in the *Congressional Record*, March 11–13, 1987. For a detailed review of the treaty controversy, see William J. Durch, "The Future of the ABM Treaty," Adelphi Paper No. 223 (London: IISS, Summer, 1987).

## The Conventional Balance

The counts of Warsaw Pact and NATO military establishments are from the 1986–87 *Military Balance*. For a detailed discussion of the NATO–Pact front, see John M. Collins, *U.S.-Soviet Military Balance*, "Book V. NATO and the Warsaw Pact," and his *U.S.-Soviet Military Balance, 1980–1985* (McLean, Va.: Pergamon-Brassey, 1985), especially pp. 99–132. There is also an excellent, detailed survey in *The Economist*, "The Sentry at the Gate: A survey of NATO's Central Front," September 5, 1986. *The Economist*'s survey most usefully separates forces immediately available on the central front from NATO and Pact totals. And see William P. Mako, *United States Ground Forces and the Defense of Europe*, (Washington, D.C.: Brookings, 1983). Complete orders of battle for the two sides and extensively detailed mobilization schedules are in Tom Gervasi, *The Myth of Soviet Military Superiority,* "Appendix H: Ground Forces and Conventional Weapons in Europe," pp. 440–486. Gervasi's discussion, pp. 184–207, is the most optimistic portrayal of the European balance I have found, but a well-documented one.

Detailed mobilization and endurance estimates are in William Kaufmann, "Nonnuclear Deterrence," in John D. Steinbruner and Leon V. Sigal, eds., *Alliance Security,* pp. 43–90; his "flat plain" quote is on p. 51. The detailed mobilization estimates in the text and the discussion of "force-to-space" ratios are drawn from John Mearsheimer, "Why the Soviets Can't Win Quickly in Central Europe," *International Security* (Summer 1982), pp. 3–39. The discussion of Soviet tactical problems relies on John Mearsheimer, *Conventional Deterrence* (Ithaca, N.Y.: Cornell University Press, 1986), an indispensable volume. A less optimistic view is in Steven L. Canby, "The Alliance and Europe, Part IV. Military Doctrine and Technology," Adelphi Paper No. 109 (London: IISS, 1974–75). The comment in the note on "Category One" readiness is from John M. Collins, "NATO and the Warsaw Pact," p. 35. The quote on Soviet initiative is in Mearsheimer, *op. cit.,* p. 36. For a critical view of NATO's tactical air strategy, see Gregg Easterbrook, "Voices for the Defense," *Los Angeles Times,* May 3, 1987, and William Kaufmann, "Nonnuclear Deterrence," pp. 77–79, which also contains a good discussion of sealane protection, pp. 45–51. The "drag in the weeds" quote is from *The Economist*'s survey, p. 17. The concluding quote is from *The Military Balance, 1987–1988,* p. 230.

## Chapter 23: Lessons and Reflections

Paul Nitze's quote on the required margin for safe second-strike deterrent is in Donald W. Hanson, "Is Soviet Strategic Doctrine Superior?", p. 69. John Lewis Gaddis makes an optimistic argument for the primacy of political issues in his "How the Cold War Might End," *The Atlantic* (November 1987), pp. 88–100, as does Lawrence Freedman in his "Strategic Defense in the Nuclear Age," particularly pp. 63–65. The quotation from Seweryn Bialer is from his "Lessons of History: Soviet-American Relations in the Postwar Era," in Arnold C. Horelick, ed., *U.S.-Soviet Relations: The Next Phase,* pp. 86–110, at p. 92.

# Works Cited

*Works with multiple authors are listed only once under the name of the first author. All sources cited are listed, with the exception of unsigned articles in newspapers of general circulation.*

Lt. Gen. James Abrahamson, "Statement to Congress of May 9, 1984," *Survival* (March–April 1985), pp. 75–78.

David Abshire and Richard Allen, eds., *National Security: Political, Military, and Economic Strategies in the Decade Ahead* (New York: Praeger, 1963).

Dean Acheson, *Present at the Creation: My Years at the State Department* (New York: Norton, 1969).

Air Policy Commission, *Survival in the Air Age: A Report to the President* (Washington, D.C., 1948).

Graham Allison, *The Essence of Decision: Explaining the Cuban Missile Crisis* (Boston: Little, Brown, 1971).

Joseph Alsop, "Comment by Joseph Alsop," *Foreign Policy* (Fall 1974), pp. 83–88.

Stephen Ambrose, *Eisenhower*. Vol. II, *The President* (New York: Simon and Schuster, 1984).

J. E. Anderson and General R. Marsh, "Discussion on Missile Accuracy," *Strategic Review* (Spring 1982), pp. 35–43.

Anton Antonov-Ovseyenko, *The Time of Stalin: Portrait of a Tyranny* (New York: Harper & Row, 1981).

Robert Arnett, "Soviet Views on Nuclear War," in William H. Kincade and Jeffrey D. Porro, *Negotiating Security: An Arms Control Reader* (Washington, D.C.: Carnegie Endowment for International Peace, 1979), pp. 116–122.

Raymond Aron, *The Great Debate* (New York: Anchor Books, 1963).

The Aspen Strategy Group, *The Strategic Defense Initiative and American Security* (Lanham, Md.: University Press, 1987).

Leslie Bain, *The Reluctant Satellites* (New York: Macmillan, 1960).

Hanson W. Baldwin, *The Great Arms Race* (New York: Praeger, 1958).

———, *Power and Politics* (Claremont, Calif.: Claremont College Press, 1950).

———, *The Price of Power* (New York: Harper, 1948).

———, "Slowdown in the Pentagon," *Foreign Affairs* (January 1965), pp. 262–280.

Desmond Ball, *Politics and Force Levels: The Strategic Missile Program of the Kennedy Administration* (Berkeley: University of California Press, 1980).

———. "Nuclear War At Sea" *International Security* (Winter, 1985/1986), pp. 3–31.

———. "The Development of the SIOP, 1960–1983," in Desmond Ball and Jeffrey Richelson, eds., *Strategic Nuclear Targeting* (Ithaca, N.Y.: Cornell University Press, 1986), pp. 57–83.

*Bandung: The Revolutionary Flame of Bandung* (Djakarta: The Executive Command: Tenth Anniversary of the First Asian-African Conference, 1965).

Jack Beatty, "In Harm's Way: America's Scary, and Expensive, New Naval Strategy," *The Atlantic* (May 1987), pp. 37–53.

G. Bekefi, B. T. Feld, J. Parmentola, and K. Tsipis, *Particle Beam Weapons.* MIT Program in Science and Technology for National Security, Report No. 4 (December 1978).

Robert P. Berman and John C. Baker, *Soviet Strategic Forces: Requirements and Responses* (Washington, D.C.: Brookings, 1982).

Michael R. Beschloss, *MayDay: Eisenhower, Khrushchev and the the U-2 Affair* (New York: Harper & Row, 1986).

Capt. Eugene D. Bétit, "Soviet Tactical Doctrine and Capabilities and NATO's Strategic Defenses," *Strategic Review* (Summer 1976), pp. 95–107.

Seweryn Bialer, *The Soviet Paradox: External Expansion, Internal Decline* (New York: Knopf, 1986).

———, "Lessons of History: Soviet-American Relations in the Postwar Era," in Arnold C. Horelick, ed., *U.S.-Soviet Relations: The Next Phase* (Ithaca, N.Y.: Cornell University Press, 1986), pp. 86–110.

———, "Gorbachev's Move," *Foreign Policy* (Fall 1987), pp. 59–87.

Coit D. Blacker, *Reluctant Warriors: The United States, the Soviet Union, and Arms Control* (New York: Freeman, 1987).

Bruce G. Blair, *Strategic Command and Control: Redefining the Nuclear Threat* (Washington, D.C.: Brookings, 1985).

———, "Alerting in Crisis and Conventional War," in Ashton B. Carter, John D. Steinbruner, and Charles A. Zraket, eds., *Managing Nuclear Operations* (Washington, D.C.: Brookings, 1987), pp. 75–120.

Barry M. Blechman, *The Changing Soviet Navy* (Washington, D.C.: Brookings, 1973).

———, Edward M. Gramlich, and Robert W. Hartman, *Setting National Priorities: The 1975 Budget* (Washington, D.C.: Brookings, 1974).

———, *Control of Naval Armaments* (Washington, D.C.: Brookings, 1975).

———, *The Soviet Military Buildup and U.S. Defense Spending* (Washington, D.C.: Brookings, 1977).

——— and Stephen S. Kaplan, *Force Without War: U.S. Armed Forces as a Political Instrument* (Washington, D.C.: Brookings, 1978).

Ray Bonds, ed., *The Soviet War Machine: An Encyclopaedia of Russian Military Equipment and Strategy* (London: Hamlyn, 1976).

Paul Bracken, *The Command and Control of Nuclear Forces* (New Haven: Yale University Press, 1983).

———, "War Termination" and "Delegation of Nuclear Command Authority," in Ashton B. Carter, John D. Steinbruner, and Charles A. Zraket, eds., *Managing Nuclear Operations* (Washington, D.C.: Brookings, 1987), pp. 197–214 and 352–372.

William J. Broad, "Philosophers at the Pentagon," *Science,* October 24, 1980, pp. 409–410.

Bernard Brodie, ed., *The Absolute Weapon: Atomic Power and World Order* (New York: Harcourt, Brace, 1946).

———, "Nuclear Weapons: Strategic or Tactical?", *Foreign Affairs* (January 1954), pp. 217–229.

———, "Unlimited Weapons and Limited War," *The Reporter,* (November 18, 1954), pp. 16–21.

———, "More About Limited War," *World Politics* (October 1957), pp. 112–122.

———, *Strategy in the Missile Age* (Princeton: Princeton University Press, 1959).

———, "Defense Policy and the Possibility of Total War," *Daedalus* (Fall 1962), pp. 733–748.

———, "What Price Conventional Capabilities in Europe?", *The Reporter,* (May 23, 1963), pp. 25–33.

———, "The McNamara Phenomenon," *World Politics* (April 1965), pp. 672–683.

———, "Why We Were So Wrong," *Foreign Policy* (Winter 1971), pp. 151–161.

Eli Brookner, "Phased-Array Radars," *Scientific American* (February 1985), pp. 94–102.

Linton F. Brooks, "Naval Power and National Security: The Case for the Maritime Strategy," *International Security* (Fall 1986), pp. 58–88.

Harold Brown, "The Strategic Defense Initiative: Defensive Systems and the Strategic Debate," *Survival* (March–April 1985), pp. 55–64.

Seyom Brown, "Invulnerable Retaliatory Capacity and Arms Control," *World Politics* (April 1961).

Zbigniew Brzezinski, "The Pattern of Political Purges," *Annals of the American Academy of Political and Social Sciences* (May 1958), pp. 79–87.

———, *Power and Principle: Memoirs of the National Security Adviser, 1977–1981* (New York: Farrar, Straus & Giroux, 1983).

Alistair Buchan, "The Reform of NATO," *Foreign Affairs* (January 1962), pp. 165–182.

Carl H. Builder, "The Prospects and Implications of Non-Nuclear Means for Strategic Conflict," Adelphi Paper No. 200 (London: IISS, Summer 1985), pp. 9–13.

McGeorge Bundy, Morton Halperin, William W. Kaufmann, George F. Kennan, Robert S. McNamara, Madalene O'Donnell, Leon V. Sigal, Gerard C. Smith, Richard H. Ullman, and Paul C. Warnke, "Back from the Brink" *The Atlantic* (August 1986), pp. 35–41.

Matthew Bunn and Kosta Tsipis, *Ballistic Missile Guidance and Technical Uncertainties of Countersilo Attacks.* MIT Program in Science and Technology for International Security, Report No. 9 (August 1983).

———, *Technology of Ballistic Missile Reentry Vehicles.* MIT Program in Science and Technology for International Security, Report No. 11 (March 1984).

Sir Anthony Buzzard, "The Possibilities of Conventional Defense," Adelphi Paper (London: IISS, December 1963).

M. Callaham and K. Tsipis, *High Energy Laser Weapons: A Technical Assessment.* MIT Program in Science and Technology for National Security, Report No. 6 (November 1980).

Steven L. Canby, "The Alliance and Europe, Part IV. Military Doctrine and Technology," Adelphi Paper No. 109 (London: IISS, 1974–75).

———, "New Conventional Force Technology and the NATO-Warsaw Pact Balance: Part I," in *New Technology and Western Security Policy, Part II.* Adelphi Paper No. 198 (London: IISS, 1985), pp. 7–24.

Ashton B. Carter and David N. Schwarz, eds., *Ballistic Missile Defense* (Washington, D.C.: Brookings, 1984).

———, *Directed Energy Missile Defense in Space (A Background Paper)* (Washington, D.C.: Office of Technology Assessment, 1984).

———, "The Command and Control of Nuclear War," *Scientific American* (January 1985), pp. 35–46.

———, John D. Steinbruner, and Charles A. Zraket, eds., *Managing Nuclear Operations* (Washington, D.C.: Brookings, 1987), including Ashton B. Carter, "Assessing Command System Vulnerability" and "Sources of Error and Uncertainty", pp. 535–554, 555–610.

Abram Chayes and Jerome Weisner, eds., *ABM: An Evaluation of the Decision to Deploy an Antiballistic Missile System* (New York: Harper & Row, 1969).

Winston Churchill, *Triumph and Tragedy* (Boston: Houghton Mifflin, 1953).

Stephen Cimbala, "New Myths and Old Realities: Defense and Its Critics," *World Politics* (October 1971), pp. 127–157.

Colin Clark, "Soviet Military Potential," *Soundings* (September 1947).

Karl von Clausewitz, *On War* (Harrandsworth, Middlesex: Penguin, 1968).

Diane Shavers Clemens, *Yalta* (New York: Oxford University Press, 1970).

Thomas B. Cochran, William M. Arkin, and Milton M. Hoenig, *Nuclear Weapons Databook.* Vol. I (Cambridge, Mass.: Ballinger, 1984).

Stephen F. Cohen, *Bukharin and the Bolshevik Revolution: A Political Biography: 1888–1938* (New York: Oxford University Press, 1980).

Steven T. Cohen, "Enhanced Radiation Warheads: Setting the Record Straight," *Strategic Review* (Winter 1978), pp. 11–18.

Alexander Cockburn, *The Threat: Inside the Soviet Military Machine* (New York: Random House, 1983).

John M. Collins, *American and Soviet Military Trends Since the Cuban Missile Crisis* (Georgetown: Center for Strategic and International Studies, 1978).

———, *U.S.-Soviet Military Balance.* Books I–VII (Washington, D.C.: Congressional Research Service, 1980).

———, *U.S.-Soviet Military Balance, 1980–1985* (McLean, Va.: Pergamon-Brassey, 1985).

Robert Conquest, *Power and Politics in the USSR: A Study in Soviet Dynastics* (London: Macmillan, 1961).

———, *The Great Terror: Stalin's Purge of the Thirties,* rev. ed. (New York: Macmillan, 1973).

———, "A New Russia? A New World?", *Foreign Affairs* (January 1975), pp. 482–497.

———, *The Harvest of Sorrow: Soviet Collectivization and the Terror Famine* (New York: Oxford University Press, 1986).

Raymond W. Copson, "The Soviet Union in Africa: An Assessment," in Walter Z. Laqueur, ed., *Patterns of Soviet Conduct in the Third World* (New York: Praeger, 1983), pp. 187–207.

Donald B. Cotter, "New Conventional Force Technology and the NATO-Warsaw Pact Balance: Part II," in *New Technology and Western Security Policy, Part II.* Adelphi Paper No. 198 (London: IISS, 1985), pp. 25–39.

———, "Peacetime Operations Safety and Security," in Ashton B. Carter, John Steinbruner, and Charles A. Zraket, eds., *Managing Nuclear Operations* (Washington, D.C.: Brookings, 1987), pp. 17–74.

Edward Crankshaw, *The New Cold War: Moscow vs. Pekin* (Baltimore: Penguin, 1963).

———. *Khrushchev: A Career* (New York: Viking Press, 1966).

Donald C.F. Daniel, "The Soviet Navy and Tatical Nuclear War at Sea" *Survival,* (July/August, 1987) pp. 318–335.

Jacqueline K. Davis, "End of the Strategic Triad," *Strategic Review* (Winter 1978), pp. 36–43.

W. Phillipps Davison, *The Berlin Blockade* (Princeton: Princeton University Press, 1958).

Seymour J. Deitchman, *Military Power and the Advance of Technology: General Purpose Military Forces for the 1980s and Beyond* (Boulder, Colo.: Westview Press, 1983).

Helene Carrère d'Encausse, *Confiscated Power: How Soviet Russia Really Works* (New York: Harper & Row, 1982).

Byron Dexter, "Clausewitz and Soviet Strategy" *Foreign Affairs* (October, 1950), pp. 41–55.

Peter Dickson, *Kissinger and the Meaning of History* (New York: Cambridge University Press, 1975).

Herbert Dinerstein, "The Revolution in Soviet Strategic Thinking," *Foreign Affairs* (January 1958), pp. 241–252.

———, *War and the Soviet Union: Nuclear Weapons and the Revolution in Soviet Military and Political Thinking* (New York: Praeger, 1959).

———, *The Making of a Missile Crisis: October, 1962* (Baltimore: Johns Hopkins Press, 1976).

Robert Divine, *Foreign Policy and U.S. Presidential Elections* (New York: New Viewpoints, 1974).

———, *Blowing on the Wind: The Nuclear Test Ban Debate, 1954–1960* (New York: Oxford University Press, 1978).

———, *Eisenhower and the Cold War* (New York: Oxford University Press, 1981).

Milovan Djilas, *Conversations with Stalin* (New York: Harcourt, Brace, 1962).

———, *Rise and Fall* (New York: Harcourt, Brace, 1985).

Robert J. Donovan, *The Presidency of Harry S. Truman, 1949–1953.* Vol. II. *The Tumultuous Years* (New York: Norton, 1982).

John Foster Dulles, "Policy for Security and Peace," *Foreign Affairs* (April 1954), pp. 353–364.

William J. Durch, "The Future of the ABM Treaty" Adelphi Paper No. 223 (London: IISS, Summer, 1987).

Peggy Durdin, "Behind the Facade of Asian Unity," *New York Times Magazine,* April 17, 1955, pp. 24–28.

Freeman Dyson, *Weapons and Hope* (New York: Harper & Row, 1984).

Gregg Easterbrook, "Voices for the Defense," *Los Angeles Times,* May 3, 1987.

Anthony Eden, *Memoirs: Full Circle* (Boston: Houghton Mifflin, 1960).

Arieh Eilar, "Soviet Diplomacy in the Third World," in Walter Z. Laqueur, ed., *Patterns of Soviet Conduct in the Third World* (New York: Praeger, 1983), pp. 150–186.

Dwight D. Eisenhower, *Mandate for Change: 1953–1956* (Garden City, N.Y.: Doubleday, 1963).

Col. Louis Ely, "A General Assessment," in B. H. Liddell-Hart, *The Soviet Army* (London: Weidenfeld and Nicolson, 1956), pp. 197–212.

Stephen Enke, *Defense Management* (Englewood Cliffs, N.J.: Prentice-Hall, 1967).

Alain Enthoven and K. Wayne Smith, *How Much Is Enough: Shaping the Defense Program, 1961–1969* (New York: Harper & Row, 1971).

John Erikson, "European Security: Soviet Preferences and Priorities," *Strategic Review* (Winter 1976), pp. 37–44.

———, "The Northern Theater: Soviet Capacities and Concepts," *Strategic Review* (Summer 1976), pp. 67–82.

———, "Trends in Soviet Combined Arms Doctrine," *Strategic Review* (Winter 1977), pp. 32–52.

———, "The Ground Forces in Soviet Military Doctrine," *Strategic Review* (Winter 1978), pp. 64–79.

Fritz Ermath, "Contrasts in American and Soviet Strategic Thought," *International Security* (Fall 1978), pp. 138–155.

Thomas H. Etzold and John Lewis Gaddis, *Containment: Documents in American Policy and Strategy, 1945–1950* (New York: Columbia University Press, 1978).

Matthew Evangelista, "Stalin's Postwar Army Reappraised," *International Security* (Winter 1982–83), pp. 110–129.

Henry Fairlie, *The Kennedy Promise* (Garden City, N.Y.: Doubleday, 1973).

James Fallows, *National Defense* (New York: Random House, 1980).

Herbert Feis, *Churchill, Roosevelt, Stalin: The War They Waged and the Peace They Sought* (Princeton: Princeton University Press, 1957).

Frances FitzGerald, *Fire in the Lake: The Vietnamese and the Americans in Vietnam* (Boston: Atlantic, Little, Brown, 1972).

Daniel Ford, *The Button* (New York: Simon and Schuster, 1985).

Lawrence Freedman, *U.S. Intelligence and the Soviet Strategic Threat* (London: Macmillan, 1977).

———, *The Evolution of Nuclear Strategy* (New York: St. Martin's Press, 1981).

———, "Strategic Defense in the Nuclear Age," Adelphi Paper No. 224 (London: IISS, Autumn 1987).

Richard M. Freeland, *The Truman Doctrine and the Origins of McCarthyism* (New York: Knopf, 1972).

Francis Fukuyama, *Moscow's Post-Brezhnev Reassessment of the Third World,* RAND Report R-3337-USDP (Santa Monica, Calif., February 1986).

———, "Soviet Strategy in the Third World," in Andrzej Korbonski and Francis Fukuyama, eds., *The Soviet Union and the Third World: The Last Three Decades* (Ithaca, N.Y.: Cornell University Press, 1987), pp. 24–44.

Alton Frye, "U.S. Decision Making for SALT," in Mason Willrich and John B.

Rhinelander, eds., *SALT: The Moscow Agreements and Beyond* (Glencoe, N.Y.: The Free Press, 1974), pp. 66–100.

John Lewis Gaddis, *The United States and the Origins of the Cold War: 1941–1947* (New York: Columbia University Press, 1972).

—— and Paul H. Nitze, "NSC-68 and the Soviet Threat Reconsidered," *International Security* (Spring, 1980), pp. 164–176.

——, "Containment: Its Past and Future," *International Security* (Spring 1981), pp. 74–102.

——, *Strategies of Containment: A Critical Appraisal of Postwar National Security Policy* (New York: Oxford University Press, 1982).

——. "The Long Peace: Elements of Stability in the Postwar International System," *International Security* (Spring, 1986), pp. 99–142.

——, "How the Cold War Might End," *The Atlantic* (November 1987), pp. 88–100.

N. Galay, "Recent Trends," in B. H. Liddell-Hart, *The Soviet Army* (London: Weidenfeld and Nicolson, 1956), pp. 306–322.

Raymond Garthoff, "Ideological Conceptions in Soviet Foreign Policy," *Problems of Communism* (May 1953), pp. 1–9.

——, *Soviet Military Doctrine* (Glencoe, N.Y.: The Free Press, 1953).

——, *Soviet Strategy in the Nuclear Age* (New York: Praeger, 1956).

——, "Unconventional Warfare a Communist Strategy," *Foreign Affairs* (July 1962), pp. 566–576.

——, ed. and trans. of V.D. Sokolovsky, ed., *Soviet Military Strategy* (New York: Praeger, 1963).

——, *Soviet Military Policy* (New York: Praeger, 1966).

——, "Negotiating with the Russians: Lessons from SALT," *International Security* (Summer 1976), pp. 3–24.

——, "Perspectives on the Strategic Balance" (Washington, D.C.: Brookings, 1983).

——, "BMD and East-West Relations," in Ashton B. Carter and David N. Schwarz, eds., *Ballistic Missile Defense* (Washington, D.C.: Brookings, 1984), pp. 275–329.

——, *Detente and Confrontation: American-Soviet Relations from Nixon to Reagan* (Washington, D.C.: Brookings, 1985).

Leslie H. Gelb, *The Irony of Vietnam: The System Worked* (Washington, D.C.: Brookings, 1979).

Barton Gellman, *Contending with Kennan: Toward a Philosophy of American Power* (New York: Praeger, 1984).

Harry Gelman, *The Brezhnev Politburo and the Decline of Detente* (Ithaca, N.Y.: Cornell University Press, 1984).

Col. Marc Geneste, "The Nuclear Land Battle," *Strategic Review* (Winter 1976), pp. 79–85.

Alexander L. George, David K. Hall, and William E. Simons, eds., *The Limits of Coercive Diplomacy: Laos, Cuba, Vietnam* (Boston: Little, Brown, 1971).

Alexander L. George and Richard Smoke, *Deterrence in American Foreign Policy: Theory and Practice* (New York: Columbia University Press, 1974).

Tom Gervasi, *The Myth of Soviet Military Superiority* (New York: Harper & Row, 1986).

Jon D. Glassman, *Arms for the Arabs: The Soviet Union and War in the Middle East* (Baltimore: Johns Hopkins Press, 1975).

Samuel Glasstone and Philip J. Dolan, *The Effects of Nuclear Weapons* (Washington, D.C.: USGPO, 1977).

Alek Gliksman, "Deterrence Without Nukes," *New York Times*, May 18, 1987.

Galia Golan, "The Soviet Union and the Middle East After Thirty Years" in Andrzej Korbonski and Francis Fukuyama, eds., *The Soviet Union and the Third World: The Last Three Decades* (Ithaca, N.Y.: Cornell University Press, 1987), pp. 178–207.

Marshal I. Goldman, "The Soviet Standard of Living and Ours," *Foreign Affairs* (July 1960), pp. 625–637.

———, *Gorbachev's Challenge: Reform in the Age of High Technology* (New York: Norton, 1987).

Daniel O. Graham, *The Non-Nuclear Defense of Cities: The High Frontier Space-based Defense Against ICBM Attack* (Cambridge, Mass.: Abt. 1983).

Stephen Graubard, *Kissinger, Portrait of a Mind* (New York: Norton, 1973).

Colin Gray, "What Hath RAND Wrought" *Foreign Policy* (Fall 1971), pp. 111–129.

———, "The Arms Race Phenomenon," *World Politics* (October 1971), pp. 39–79.

———, "SALT: Time to Quit," *Strategic Review* (Fall 1976), pp. 14–22.

———, *The Soviet-American Arms Race* (Lexington, Mass.: Lexington, 1976).

———, "Foreign Policy—There Is No Choice," *Foreign Policy* (Fall 1976), pp. 114–127.

——— and Keith S. Payne, "Victory Is Possible," *Foreign Policy* (Summer 1980), pp. 14–27.

——— and Michael Howard, "Perspectives on a Future Nuclear War," *International Security* (Summer 1981), pp. 185–187.

———, "National Styles in Strategy: The American Example," *International Security* (Fall 1981), pp. 21–48.

———, "A Case for Strategic Defense," *Survival* (March–April 1985), pp. 50–54.

———, "Targeting Problems in Central War," in Desmond Ball and Jeffrey Richelson, eds., *Strategic Nuclear Targeting* (Ithaca, N.Y.: Cornell University Press, 1986), pp. 171–193.

John Greenwood, "The Great Patriotic War," in Robin Hingham and Jacob Kipp, eds., *Soviet Aviation and Air Power: A Historical View* (Boulder, Colo.: Westview Press, 1977), pp. 69–137.

Ted Greenwood, *Making the MIRV* (Cambridge, Mass.: Ballinger, 1975).

——— and Michael F. Nacht "The New Nuclear Debate: Sense or Nonsense?", *Foreign Affairs* (July 1974), pp. 761–780.

William H. Gregory, "The Voice of Experience," *Aviation Week and Space Technology*, August 13, 1979, p. 9.

David R. Griffiths, "Defense Spending Demands Spur Needs List," *Aviation Week and Space Technology*, August 13, 1979, pp. 14–15.

Arthur T. Hadley, *The Straw Giant, Triumph and Failure: America's Armed Forces* (New York: Random House, 1986).

———, "Back to the Front," *The New Republic*, (November 16, 1987), pp. 16–18.

Walter F. Hahn, "NATO's Qualitative Crisis," *Strategic Review* (Summer 1977), pp. 26–39.

David Halberstam, *The Best and the Brightest* (New York: Random House, 1972).

David K. Hall, "The Laos Crisis, 1960–1961," in Alexander L. George, David K. Hall, and William E. Simons, eds., *The Limits of Coercive Diplomacy: Laos, Cuba, Vietnam* (Boston: Little, Brown, 1971), pp. 36–85.

———, "The Laotian War of 1962," in Barry M. Blechman and Stephen S. Kaplan, *Force Without War: U.S. Armed Forces as a Political Instrument* (Washington, D.C.: Brookings, 1978), pp. 135–174.

Louis J. Halle, *The Cold War as History* (New York: Harper & Row, 1967).

Morton Halperin, *Limited War,* (Cambridge, Mass.: Harvard University Press, 1962).

———, "The Decision to Deploy the ABM: Bureaucratic and Domestic Politics in the Johnson Administration," *World Politics* (October 1972), pp. 62–95.

——— and Jeremy Stone, "Reply to Albert Wohlstetter," *Foreign Policy* (Fall 1974), pp. 88–92.

Paul Y. Hammond, "NSC-68: Prologue to Rearmament," in Werner Schilling, Paul Y. Hammond, and Glenn H. Snyder, eds., *Strategy, Politics and Defense Budgets* (New York: Columbia University Press, 1962), pp. 267–358.

———, "Super-carriers and B-36 Bombers," in Harold Stein, ed., *American Civil-Military Decisions* (Birmingham, Ala.: University of Alabama Press, 1963), pp. 465–568.

Oscar Handlin, *Truth in History* (Cambridge, Mass.: Harvard University Press, 1979).

Donald W. Hanson, "Is Soviet Strategic Doctrine Superior?" *International Security* (Winter 1982–83), pp. 65–88.

Averill L. Harriman, "Leadership in World Affairs," *Foreign Affairs* (July 1954), pp. 525–540.

Lt. Gen. John H. Hay, Jr., *Tactical and Materiel Innovations* (Washington, D.C.: Dept. of the Army, 1974).

Muhammed Heikel, *The Sphinx and the Commissar: The Rise and Fall of Soviet Influence in the Arab World,* (London: Collins, 1978).

Paul B. Henze, "Getting a Grip on the Horn: The Emergence of the Soviet Presence and Future Prospects," in Walter Z. Laqueur, ed., *Patterns of Soviet Conduct in the Third World* (New York: Praeger, 1983), pp. 150–186.

Gregg Herkin, *The Winning Weapon: The Atomic Bomb and the Cold War* (New York: Knopf, 1980).

Robert Waring Herrick, *Soviet Naval Strategy: Fifty Years of Theory and Practice* (Annapolis, Md.: U.S. Naval Institute, 1968).

Seymour Hersh, "Target Qaddafi," *New York Times Magazine,* February 22, 1987, p. 6.

Roger Hilsman, *To Move a Nation: The Politics of Foreign Policy in the Administration of John F. Kennedy* (Garden City, N.Y.: Doubleday, 1967).

Robin Hingham and Jacob Kipp, *Soviet Aviation and Air Power: A Historical View* (Boulder, Colo.: Westview Press, 1977).

Charles Hitch and Roland McKeon, *The Economics of Defense in the Nuclear Age* (Cambridge, Mass.: Harvard University Press, 1960).

————, *Decision Making for Defense* (Berkeley: University of California Press, 1965).

Malcolm Hoag, "On Stability in Deterrence Races," *World Politics* (April 1961), pp. 505–527.

David R. Holloway, *The Soviet Union and the Arms Race.* 2nd ed. (New Haven: Yale University Press, 1984).

Franklyn D. Holzman, "Are the Soviets Really Outspending the U.S. on Defense?" *International Security* (Spring, 1980), pp. 86–104.

Townsend Hoopes, *The Limits of Intervention* (New York: David Mackay, 1973).

Arnold C. Horelick, "The Cuban Missile Crisis: An Analysis of Soviet Calculations and Behavior," *World Politics* (April 1964), pp. 363–389.

————, ed., *U.S.-Soviet Relations: The Next Phase* (Ithaca, N.Y.: Cornell University Press, 1986).

Robert C. Horn, "The Soviet Union and South Asia: Moscow and New Delhi Standing Together," in Andrzej Korbonski and Francis Fukuyama, *The Soviet Union and the Third World: The Last Three Decades* (Ithaca, N.Y.: Cornell University Press, 1987), pp. 208–227.

David Horowitz, *Free World Colossus: A Critique of American Foreign Policy in the Cold War* (New York: Hill and Wang, 1965).

Robert Hotz, "Pitfalls of SALT," *Aviation Week and Space Technology,* (November 24, 1975), p. 7.

Michael Howard, ed., *The Theory and Practice of War* (London: Cassell, 1973).

————, "On Firing a Nuclear Weapon," *International Security* (Spring 1981), pp. 3–17.

Emmett J. Hughes, *The Ordeal of Power: A Political Memoir of the Eisenhower Years* (New York: Atheneum, 1975).

Fred C. Iklé, "Can Nuclear Deterrence Last Out the Century?", *Foreign Affairs* (January 1973), pp. 267–285.

————, "SALT and the Nuclear Balance in Europe," *Strategic Review* (Spring 1978), pp. 18–22.

C. G. Jacobsen, *Soviet Strategy and Soviet Foreign Policy* (Glasgow: Mackelose, 1972).

*Jane's All the World's Aircraft* (London: Marston & Co., various years).

*Jane's Fighting Ships* (London: Marston & Co., various years).

*Jane's World Weapon Systems* (London: Marston & Co., various years).

Lyndon B. Johnson, *The Vantage Point: Perspectives of the Presidency, 1963–1969* (New York: Popular Library, 1971).

Paul Johnson, *Modern Times* (New York: Harper & Row, 1983).

Christopher D. Jones, "Soviet Military Doctrine: The Political Dimension," in William H. Kincade and Jeffrey D. Porro, eds. *Negotiating Security: An Arms Control Reader,* (Washington, D.C.: Carnegie Endowment for International Peace, 1979) pp. 111–115.

Sir Phillip Joubert, "Long-range Air Attack," in Asher Lee, ed., *Soviet Air and Rocket Forces* (New York: Praeger, 1959), pp. 101–116.

George McT. Kahin, *Intervention: How America Became Involved in Vietnam* (New York: Knopf, 1986).

Herman Kahn, *On Thermonuclear War.* 2nd ed. (Princeton: Princeton University Press, 1961).

————, *Thinking About the Unthinkable* (New York: Horizon, 1962).

————, *On Escalation* (New York: Praeger, 1965).

Bernard and Marvin Kalb, *Kissinger* (Boston: Little, Brown, 1974).

Fred Kaplan, *The Wizards of Armageddon* (New York: Simon and Schuster, 1983).

Stephen S. Kaplan, *Diplomacy of Power: Soviet Armed Forces as a Political Instrument* (Washington, D.C.: Brookings, 1980).

Richard F. Kaufman, "Causes of the Slowdown in Soviet Defense," *Survival* (July–August 1985), pp. 179–192.

William W. Kaufmann, "The Crisis in Military Affairs," *World Politics* (July 1958), pp. 579–603.

————, *The McNamara Strategy* (Cambridge, Mass.: MIT Press, 1964).

————, ed., *Military Policy and National Security* (Princeton: Princeton University Press, 1956, including William W. Kaufmann, "The Requirements of Deterrence" and "Limited War"), pp. 12–38, 102–136.

————, "Planning Conventional Forces: 1950–1980" (Washington, D.C.: Brookings, 1982).

————, "Nonnuclear Deterrence," in John D. Steinbruner and Leon V. Sigal, eds., *Alliance Security: NATO and the No-First-Use Question* (Washington, D.C.: Brookings, 1983).

John Keegan, *World Armies* (London: Macmillan, 1979).

Catherine McArdle Kelleher, "NATO Nuclear Operations," in Ashton B. Carter, John D. Steinbruner, and Charles A. Zraket, eds., *Managing Nuclear Operations* (Washington, D.C.: Brookings, 1987).

J. B. Kelly, *Arabia, the Gulf, and the West* (New York: Basic Books, 1980).

George F. Kennan, ("X"), "The Sources of Soviet Conduct," *Foreign Affairs* (July 1947), pp. 566–582.

————, "The Russian Revolution—Fifty Years After: Its Nature and Consequences," *Foreign Affairs* (October 1967).

————, *Memoirs: 1925–1950* (Boston: Atlantic, Little, Brown, 1967).

————, *Memoirs: 1950–1963* (Boston: Atlantic, Little, Brown, 1970).

————, "Europe's Problems, Europe's Choices," *Foreign Policy* (Spring 1974), pp. 3–16.

————, "The United States and the Soviet Union, 1917–1976," *Foreign Affairs* (July 1976), pp. 670–690.

John F. Kennedy, "When the Executive Fails to Lead," *The Reporter,* (September 18, 1958), pp. 14–19.

Robert F. Kennedy, *Thirteen Days: A Memoir of the Cuban Missile Crisis* (New York: Norton, 1969).

William H. Kincade and Jeffrey D. Porro, eds., *Negotiating Security: An Arms Control Reader* (Washington, D.C.: Carnegie Endowment for International Peace, 1979).

James King, review of Henry A. Kissinger, *Nuclear Weapons and Foreign Policy* in *The New Republic,* (July 1 and 15, 1957), pp. 18–21 and 16–18.

Henry A. Kissinger, "Military Policy and the Defense of 'Grey Areas,' " *Foreign Affairs* (April 1955), pp. 416–428.

————, "Reflections on American Diplomacy," *Foreign Affairs* (October 1956), pp. 37–56.

————, "Strategy and Organization," *Foreign Affairs* (April 1957), pp. 379–394.

————, *Nuclear Weapons and Foreign Policy* (New York: Harper & Row, 1957).

————, "Missiles and the Western Alliance," *Foreign Affairs* (April 1958), pp. 383–400.

————, *Necessity for Choice* (New York: Harper & Row, 1961).

————, "The Unsolved Problem of European Defense," *Foreign Affairs* (July 1962), pp. 515–541.

————, "Reflections on Cuba," *The Reporter,* (November 22, 1962), pp. 21–24.

————, "The Skybolt Affair," *The Reporter,* (January 17, 1963), pp. 22–26.

————, *The White House Years* (Boston: Little, Brown, 1979).

————, *Years of Upheaval* (Boston: Little, Brown, 1982).

————, "East Asia, the Pacific, and the West: Strategic Trends and Implications: Part I," Adelphi Paper No. 216, *Conference Report of the International Institute for Strategic Studies* (London: IISS, Spring 1987), pp. 3–10.

Harvey Klehr, *The Heyday of American Communism: The Depression Decade* (New York: Basic Books, 1984).

Klaus Knorr, *The War Potential of Nations* (Princeton: Princeton University Press, 1956).

————, "Is the American Defense Effort Enough?", Center for International Studies: Memorandum Number Fourteen (Princeton: Princeton University Press, 1957).

Roman Kolkowicz, "Strategic Parity and Beyond: A Soviet Perspective," *World Politics* (April 1971), pp. 431–451.

Andrzej Korbonski and Francis Fukuyama, *The Soviet Union and the Third World: The Last Three Decades* (Ithaca, N.Y.: Cornell University Press, 1987).

Andrew F. Krepinevich, *The Army and Vietnam* (Baltimore: Johns Hopkins Press, 1986).

C. Kumar, N. Patel, and Nicolaas Bloembergen, "Strategic Defense and Directed Energy Weapons," *Scientific American* (September 1987), pp. 39–45.

James Kurth, "Why We Buy the Weapons We Do," *Foreign Policy* (Summer 1973), pp. 33–56.

Walter Z. Lacquer, *The Struggle for the Middle East: The Soviet Union and the Middle East, 1958–1968* (New York: Penguin, 1972).

————, *Confrontation: The Middle East and World Politics* (New York: Bantam, 1974).

————, "Confronting the Problems," *Commentary* (March 1977), pp. 33–41.

————, *Patterns of Soviet Conduct in the Third World* (New York: Praeger, 1983).

Benjamin Lambeth, "Deterrence in the MIRV Era," *World Politics* (January 1972), pp. 221–242.

Ralph Lapp, " 'Fall-out'—Another Dimension in Atomic Killing Power," *The New Republic,* (February 14, 1955), pp. 8–12.

Eric Larabee, *Commander in Chief: Franklin Delano Roosevelt, His Lieutenants, and Their War* (New York: Harper & Row, 1987).

Melvin Lasky, *The Hungarian Revolt: A White Book* (New York: Praeger, 1957).

Maj. A. C. Lavelle, "Tale of Two Bridges," *Southeast Asia Monograph Series* (Washington, D.C.: Dept. of the Air Force, 1976).

————, "The Battle for the Skies over North Viet Nam," *Southeast Asia Monograph Series* (Washington, D.C.: Dept. of the Air Force, 1976).

————, "The Vietnamese Air Force, 1951–1975: An Analysis of Its Role in Combat," *Southeast Asia Monograph Series* (Washington, D.C.: Dept. of the Air Force, 1976).

Asher Lee, ed., *Soviet Air and Rocket Forces* (New York: Praeger, 1959).

————, *The Soviet Air Force* (New York: Day, 1962).

William T. Lee, *The Estimation of Soviet Defense Expenditures, 1955–1975: An Unconventional Approach* (New York: Praeger, 1977).

———— and Richard F. Staar, *Soviet Military Policy Since World War II* (Stanford, Calif.: Hoover Institution, 1986).

————, "Soviet Nuclear Targeting," in Desmond Ball and Jeffrey Richelson, eds., *Strategic Nuclear Targeting* (Ithaca, N.Y.: Cornell University Press, 1986), pp. 84–108.

Colin Legum, "Angola and the Horn of Africa," in Stephen S. Kaplan, ed., *Diplomacy of Power: Soviet Armed Forces as a Political Instrument* (Washington, D.C.: Brookings, 1980), pp. 570–637.

————, "USSR Policy in Sub-Saharan Africa," in Andrzej Korbonski and Francis Fukuyama, eds., *The Soviet Union and the Third World: The Last Three Decades* (Ithaca, N.Y.: Cornell University Press, 1987), pp. 228–246.

Robert Legvold, "The Super Rivals: Conflict in the Third World," *Foreign Affairs* (Spring, 1979), pp. 755–778.

Wassilly Leontief, "The Decline and Rise of Soviet Economic Science," *Foreign Affairs* (January 1960), pp. 261–272.

Martin Lichterman, "To the Yalu and Back," in Harold Stein, ed., *American Civil-Military Decisions* (Birmingham, Ala.: University of Alabama Press, 1963), pp. 569–642.

B. H. Liddell-Hart, *The Soviet Army* (London: Weidenfeld and Nicolson, 1956).

Carl Linder, *Khrushchev and the Soviet Leadership, 1957–64* (Baltimore: Johns Hopkins Press, 1966).

Franklin A. Lindsay, "Unconventional Warfare," *Foreign Affairs* (January 1962), pp. 264–276.

Walter Lippmann, *The Cold War,* ed. Ronald Steel (New York: Harper & Row, 1972).

Neil C. Livingston and Manfred von Nordheim, "The U.S. Congress and the Angolan Crisis," *Strategic Review* (Spring 1977), pp. 34–43.

Jan M. Lodal, "Assured Strategic Stability: An Alternative View," *Foreign Affairs* (April 1976), pp. 462–481.

————, "SALT II and American Security," *Foreign Affairs* (Winter 1978–79), pp. 245–268.

N. A. Lomov, *Scientific Technical Progress and the Revolution in Military Affairs* (U.S. Air Force translation) (Washington, D.C.: USGPO, 1973).

J. Anthony Lukas, "Class Reunion: Kennedy's Men Relive the Cuban Missile Crisis," *The New York Times Magazine,* August 30, 1987, p. 22.

Edward N. Luttwack, "Defense Reconsidered," *Commentary* (March 1977), pp. 51–59.

————, "Churchill and Us," *Commentary* (June 1977), pp. 44–50.

————, *The Pentagon and the Art of War* (New York: Simon and Schuster, 1985).

Malcolm Mackintosh, *Juggernaut: The Russian Forces, 1918–1966* (New York: Macmillan, 1967).

————, "Development of Soviet Military Doctrine," in Michael Howard, ed., *The Theory and Practice of War* (London: Cassell, 1973).

Robert Maddox, *The New Left and the Origins of the Cold War* (Princeton: Princeton University Press, 1972).

Walter A. McDougall, . . . *the Heavens and the Earth: A Political History of the Space Age* (New York: Basic Books, 1985).

Michael MccGwire, Ken Booth, and John McDonnell, eds., *Soviet Naval Policy: Objectives and Constraints* (New York: Praeger, 1975).

————, *Military Objectives in Soviet Foreign Policy* (Washington, D.C.: Brookings, 1987).

Robert S. McNamara, *The Essence of Security: Reflections in Office* (New York: Harper & Row, 1968).

William P. Mako, *United States Ground Forces and the Defense of Europe* (Washington, D.C.: Brookings, 1983).

Michael Mandelbaum, *The Nuclear Question: The United States and Nuclear Weapons: 1946–1976* (Cambridge: Cambridge University Press, 1979).

————, *The Nuclear Revolution: World Politics Before and After Hiroshima* (Cambridge: Cambridge University Press, 1981).

Alton K. Marsh, "House Panel Urges Rejection of SALT," *Aviation Week and Space Technology*, January 1, 1979, pp. 16–17.

Endre Marton, *The Forbidden Sky* (Boston: Little, Brown, 1971).

Vojtech Mastry, "Stalin and the Militarization of the Cold War" *International Security* (Winter, 1984/1985) pp. 109–129.

Leo Mates, *Nonalignment* (Belgrade: Institute of Politics and Economics, 1972).

John J. Mearsheimer, "Maneuver, Mobile Defense and the NATO Central Front," *International Security* (Winter 1981–82), pp. 104–122.

————, "Why the Soviets Can't Win Quickly in Central Europe," *International Security* (Summer 1982), pp. 3–39.

————, *Conventional Deterrence* (Ithaca, N.Y.: Cornell University Press, 1986).

————, "A Strategic Misstep: The Maritime Strategy and Deterrence in Europe," *International Security* (Fall 1986), pp. 3–57.

Roy and Zhores Medvedev, *Khrushchev: The Years in Power* (New York: Columbia University Press, 1976).

Roy Medvedev, *"Perestroika:* Toward a Soviet 'Miracle,' " *Los Angeles Times*, July 5, 1987.

Zhores A. Medvedev, *Gorbachev* (New York: Norton, 1986).

Charles L. Mee, Jr., *Meeting at Potsdam* (New York: Evans, 1975).

Stephen E. Meyer, "Soviet Nuclear Operations," in Ashton B. Carter, John D. Steinbruner, and Charles A. Zraket, eds., *Managing Nuclear Operations* (Washington, D.C.: Brookings, 1987).

*The Military Balance* (London: Institute for Strategic Studies, annually beginning in 1959).

Walter Millis, ed., *The Forrestal Diaries* (New York: Viking Press, 1951).

Deborah Nutter Miner and Alan H. Rutan, "What Role for Limited BMD?", *Survival* (March–April 1987), pp. 118–136.

Bruce Miroff, *Pragmatic Illusions* (New York: David MacKay, 1974).

Lt. Col. F. O. Mischke "Geography and Strategy," in B. H. Liddell-Hart, *The Soviet Army* (London: Weidenfeld and Nicolson, 1956), pp. 245–260.

Alfred L. Monks, "The Soviet Strategic Air Force and Civil Defense," in Robin Hingham and Jacob Kipp, eds., *Soviet Aviation and Air Power: A Historical View* (Boulder, Colo.: Westview Press, 1977), pp. 213–239.

Charles R. Morris, *A Time of Passion: America, 1960–1980* (New York: Harper & Row, 1984).

Philip Mosely, "Khrushchev's New Economic Gambit," *Foreign Affairs* (July 1958), pp. 557–568.

Norman Moss, *Men Who Play God: The Story of the H-Bomb and How Men Came to Live with It* (New York: Harper & Row, 1968).

F. W. Mulley, *The Politics of Western Defence* (London: Thames and Hudson, 1962).

Clark Murdock, *Defense Policy Formation* (Albany, N.Y.: State University of New York, 1974).

Richard Neustadt and Ernest R. May, *Thinking in Time: The Uses of History for Decision-makers* (Glencoe, N.Y.: The Free Press, 1986).

John Newhouse, *Cold Dawn: The Story of SALT* (New York: Holt, Rinehart, Winston, 1973).

Boris Nicolaevsky, *Power and the Soviet Elite* (Ann Arbor, Mich.: University of Michigan Press, 1975).

Miroslav Nincic, "Can the U.S. Trust the U.S.S.R.?", *Scientific American* (April 1986), pp. 33–41.

William Niskanen, "The Defense Resource Allocation Process," in Stephen Enke, ed., *Defense Management* (Englewood Cliffs, N.J.: Prentice-Hall, 1967), pp. 3–22.

Paul H. Nitze, "U.S. Foreign Policy, 1945–1955," *Foreign Policy Association Headline Series* (April 1956).

———, "Comment," *Foreign Policy* (Fall 1974), pp. 82–83.

———, "Assured Strategic Stability in an Era of Detente," *Foreign Affairs* (January 1976), pp. 207–232.

Richard Nixon and Henry Kissinger, "To Withdraw Missiles We Must Add Conditions," *Los Angeles Times,* April 26, 1987.

Stuart Novins, "The Invasion That Could Not Succeed," *The Reporter,* (May 11, 1961), pp. 19–22.

Senator Sam Nunn, "Interpretation of the ABM Treaty," Parts I–III, *Congressional Record,* March 11–13, 1987.

Frederic S. Nyland, "Exemplary Industrial Targets for Controlled Conflicts," in Desmond Ball and Jeffrey Richelson, eds., *Strategic Nuclear Targeting* (Ithaca, N.Y.: Cornell University Press, 1986), pp. 209–233.

Edgar O'Ballance, *The Red Army* (London: Faber & Faber, 1964).

———, *The War in the Yemen* (Hamden, Conn.: Archon, 1971).

———, *The Third Arab-Israeli War* (London: Faber & Faber, 1972).

———, *The Secret War in the Sudan, 1955–1972* (London: Faber & Faber, 1977).

Philip Odeen, "In Defense of the Defense Budget," *Foreign Policy* (Fall 1974), pp. 93–108.

R.M. Ogarkiewicz, "Soviet Tanks," in B. H. Liddell-Hart, *The Soviet Army* (London: Weidenfeld and Nicolson, 1956), pp. 295–306.

Robert Oppenheimer, "Atomic Weapons and American Policy," *Foreign Affairs* (July 1953), pp. 525–535.

Robert Osgood, *NATO: The Entangling Alliance* (Chicago: University of Chicago Press, 1962).

Dave R. Palmer, *The Summons of the Trumpet* (San Rafael, Calif: Presidio Press, 1978).

Wolfgang Panofsky, "The Mutual Hostage Relationship Between America and Russia," *Foreign Affairs* (October 1973), pp. 109–118.

Lewis Paper, *Kennedy: The Promise and the Performance* (New York: Crown, 1974).

Bruce Parrot, "The Soviet Union and Ballistic Missile Defense," *SAIS Papers in International Affairs No. 14* (Boulder, Colo.: Westview Press, 1987).

Lester B. Pearson, "After the Paris Debacle," *Foreign Affairs* (July 1960), pp. 537–546.

Brig. Gen. (Ret.) Thomas R. Phillips "The Growing Missile Gap," *The Reporter,* (January 8, 1959), pp. 12–16.

Richard E. Pipes, "Why The Soviet Union Thinks It Could Fight and Win a Nuclear War," *Commentary* (July 1977), pp. 21–34.

Forrest C. Pogue, *George C. Marshall, Statesman, 1945–1959* (New York: Viking Press, 1987).

Bruce D. Porter, *The USSR in Third World Conflicts: Soviet Arms and Diplomacy in Local Wars, 1945–1980* (New York: Cambridge University Press, 1984).

Barry R. Posen, "Inadvertent Nuclear War: Escalation and NATO's Northern Flank," *International Security* (Fall 1982), pp. 28–54.

Theodore Postol, "Targeting," in Ashton B. Carter, John D. Steinbruner, and Charles A. Zraket, eds., *Managing Nuclear Operations* (Washington, D.C.: Brookings, 1987), pp. 373–406.

Thomas Powers, *The Man Who Kept the Secrets: Richard Helms and the CIA* (New York: Knopf, 1979).

John Prados, *The Soviet Estimate: U.S. Intelligence and Russian Military Strength* (New York: Dial, 1982).

E. S. Quade, "Selection and Use of Strategic Air Bases: A Case History" and "Pitfalls in Systems Analysis," in E. S. Quade, ed., *Analysis for Military Decision-making* (Chicago: Rand-McNally, 1964), pp. 24–63 and pp. 300–316.

William B. Quandt, "U.S. Intervention in Lebanon," in Barry M. Blechman and Stephen S. Kaplan, eds., *Force Without War: U.S. Armed Forces as a Political Instrument* (Washington, D.C.: Brookings, 1978), pp. 225–256.

Janos Radvanyi, *Hungary and the Superpowers* (Stanford, Calif.: Hoover Institution, 1972).

Christopher Rand, "Four Hours by Rail from Djakarta," *The New Yorker,* (June 11, 1955), pp. 39–78.

Jeffrey M. Record, *Sizing Up the Soviet Army* (Washington, D.C.: Brookings, 1975).

Report of the President's Commission on Strategic Forces (Washington, D.C.: USGPO, 1983).

Chalmers M. Roberts, "The Road to Moscow," in Mason Willrich and John B. Rhinelander, eds., *SALT: The Moscow Agreements and Beyond* (Glencoe, N.Y.: The Free Press, 1974), pp. 3–33.

Clarence A. Robinson, Jr., "MX Racetrack Questioned in Congress," *Aviation Week and Space Technology,* November 12, 1979, pp. 17–18.

———, "Soviets Testing New Generation of ICBM," *Aviation Week and Space Technology*, November 3, 1980, p. 28.

———, "Surveillance Integration Pivotal in Israeli Successes," *Aviation Week and Space Technology*, July 5, 1982, pp. 22–24.

Thomas W. Robinson, "The Sino-Soviet Border Conflict," in Stephen S. Kaplan, ed., *Diplomacy of Power: Soviet Armed Forces as a Political Instrument* (Washington, D.C.: Brookings, 1980), pp. 265–313.

R. T. Rockingham-Gill, "The New East-West Military Balance," *East Europe* (April 1964), pp. 3–9.

———, "Exchange with Philip Windsor," *East Europe* (July 1964), pp. 31–33.

David Alan Rosenberg, "A Smoking Radiating Ruin at the End of Two Hours: Documents on the American Plan for Nuclear War with the Soviet Union, 1954–55," *International Security* (Winter 1981–82), pp. 3–38.

———, "U.S. Nuclear War Planning, 1945–1960," in Desmond Ball and Jeffrey Richelson, eds., *Strategic Nuclear Targeting* (Ithaca, N.Y.: Cornell University Press, 1986), pp. 35–56.

Walt W. Rostow, *The Stages of Economic Growth: A Non-Communist Manifesto* (Cambridge: Cambridge University Press, 1961).

———, "The Third Round," *Foreign Affairs* (October 1963), pp. 1–10.

Richard H. Rovere, "Reflections: A New Situation in the World," *The New Yorker*, (February 24, 1968) pp. 45–78.

Myron Rush, *The Rise of Khrushchev* (Washington, D.C.: Public Affairs Press, 1958).

——— and Arnold C. Horelick, *Strategic Power and Soviet Foreign Policy* (Chicago: University of Chicago Press, 1966).

Dean Rusk, "The President," *Foreign Affairs* (April 1960), p. 369.

William J. Rust, *Kennedy in Vietnam: American Vietnam Policy, 1960–1963* (New York: Scribner's, 1985).

Philip A. G. Sabin, "Shadow or Substance? Perceptions and Symbolism in Nuclear Force Planning," Adelphi Paper No. 222 (London: IISS, Summer 1987).

Scott D. Sagan, "Nuclear Alerts and Crisis Management," *International Security* (Spring 1985), pp. 99–139.

Herbert Schandler, *The Unmaking of a President: Lyndon Johnson and Vietnam* (Princeton: Princeton University Press, 1977).

Thomas C. Schelling, "Bargaining, Communication, and Limited War," *Journal of Conflict Resolution* (March 1957), pp. 19–36.

———, "Strategy of Conflict," *Journal of Conflict Resolution* (September 1958), pp. 203–264.

———, *Strategy of Conflict* (Cambridge, Mass.: Harvard University Press, 1960).

———, "War Without Pain and Other Models," *World Politics* (March 1962), pp. 477–00.

———, "Managing the Arms Race," in David Abshire and Richard Allen, eds., *National Security: Political, Military, and Economic Strategies in the Decade Ahead* (New York: Praeger, 1963), pp. 601–616.

———, *Arms and Influence* (New Haven: Yale University Press, 1966).

———, "What Went Wrong with Arms Control," *Foreign Affairs* (Winter 1985–86), pp. 219–233.

Jack Schick, *The Berlin Crisis, 1958–62* (Philadelphia: University of Pennsylvania Press, 1971).

Werner Schilling, Paul Y. Hammond, and Glenn H. Snyder, *Strategy, Politics and Defense Budgets* (New York: Columbia University Press, 1962).

———, "United States Strategic Nuclear Concepts in the 70s: The Search for Sufficiently Equivalent Countervalue Parity," *International Security* (Fall 1981), pp. 44–79.

Arthur M. Schlesinger, Jr., *The Big Decision: Private Indulgence or National Power* (New York: privately printed, 1960).

———, *A Thousand Days: John F. Kennedy in the White House* (Boston: Houghton Mifflin, 1965).

———, "Origins of the Cold War," *Foreign Affairs* (October 1967), pp. 22–52.

James R. Schlesinger, "The Changing Environment for Systems Analysis," in Stephen Enke, ed., *Defense Management* (Englewood Cliffs, N.J.: Prentice-Hall, 1967), pp. 89–111.

———, "The Evolution of American Policy Toward the Soviet Union," *International Security* (Summer 1976), pp. 37–48.

Helmut Schmidt, "A Policy of Reliable Partnership," *Foreign Affairs* (Spring 1981), pp. 743–755.

James F. Schnabel, U.S. Army, *The United States Army in the Korean War: The First Year* (Washington, D.C.: Office of the Chief of Military History, 1972).

Dietrich Schroeer, "Directed-energy Weapons and Strategic Defense: A Primer," Adelphi Paper No. 221 (London: IISS, Summer 1987).

Harriet Fast Scott, ed. and trans. of V. D. Sokolovsky, ed., *Soviet Military Strategy* (New York: Stanford Research Institute, 1968).

——— and William F. Scott, *The Soviet Art of War: Doctrine, Strategy, Tactics* (Boulder, Colo.: Westview Press, 1968).

——— and William F. Scott, *The Armed Forces of the USSR.* 3rd ed. (Boulder, Colo.: Westview Press, 1984).

Herbert Scoville, "The Latest Red Scare," *The New Republic,* May 15, 1971, pp. 16–19.

———, "Beyond SALT One," *Foreign Affairs* (April 1972), pp. 488–501.

———, "Flexible MADness," *Foreign Policy* (Summer 1974), pp. 164–177.

Glenn T. Seaborg, *Kennedy, Khrushchev and the Test Ban* (Berkeley: University of California Press, 1981).

Ammon Sella, *Soviet Policy and Military Conduct in the Middle East* (New York: St. Martin's Press, 1981).

Robert Shaplen, *The Lost Revolution,* rev. ed. (New York: Harper & Row, 1966).

Ari Shlaim, *The United States and The Berlin Blockade, 1948–1949: A Study In Crisis Decision-making* (Berkeley: Univ. of Calif. Press, 1983).

Daniel Shuchman, "Nuclear Strategy and the Problem of Command and Control," *Survival* (July–August 1987), pp. 336–360.

Marshall D. Shulman, *Stalin's Foreign Policy Reappraised* (Cambridge, Mass.: Harvard University Press, 1963).

———, "SALT and the Soviet Union," in Mason Willrich and John B. Rhinelander, eds., *SALT: The Moscow Agreements and Beyond* (Glencoe, N.Y.: The Free Press, 1974), pp. 101–123.

———, "SALT Through the Looking Glass," in William H. Kincaid and Jeffrey D. Porro, eds., *Negotiating Security: An Arms Control Reader* (Washington, D.C.: Carnegie Endowment for International Peace, 1979), pp. 20–23.

Hugh Sidey, *John F. Kennedy, President* (New York: Atheneum, 1964).

Leon V. Sigal, "No First Use and NATO's Nuclear Posture" and "Political Prospects for No First Use," in John D. Steinbruner and Leon V. Sigal, eds., *Alliance Security: NATO and the No-First-Use Question* (Washington, D.C.: Brookings, 1983), pp. 106–133, 134–146.

H. Gordon Skilling, *Czechoslovakia's Interrupted Revolution* (Princeton: Princeton University Press, 1976).

Sir John Slessor, "Air Power and World Strategy," *Foreign Affairs* (October 1954), pp. 43–53.

Walter Slocombe, "Preplanned Operations," in Ashton B. Carter, John D. Steinbruner, and Charles A. Zraket, eds., *Managing Nuclear Operations* (Washington, D.C.: Brookings, 1987), pp. 121–141.

Robert M. Slusser, *The Berlin Crisis of 1961* (Baltimore: Johns Hopkins Press, 1973).

Gerard C. Smith, "Wrestling with the Plowshare Problem," *New York Times* January 16, 1976.

———, *Doubletalk: The Story of the First Strategic Arms Limitation Talks* (New York: Harper & Row, 1980).

Jean Edward Smith, ed., *The Papers of General Lucius D. Clay.* Vols I and II (Bloomington, Ind.: University of Indiana Press, 1974).

Glenn H. Snyder, "The 'New Look' of 1953," in Werner Schilling, Paul Y. Hammond, and Glenn H. Snyder, eds., *Strategy, Politics and Defense Budgets* (New York: Columbia University Press, 1962), pp. 383–524.

Aleksandr Solzhenitsyn, *The Gulag Archipelago: An Experiment in Literary Investigation* (New York: Harper & Row, 1973).

Theodore C. Sorenson, *Kennedy* (New York: Harper & Row, 1965).

General Carl Spaatz, "Evolution of Air Power," *Journal of the American Military Institute,* (Fall, 1947) pp. 3–16.

John W. Spanier, *The Truman-MacArthur Controversy and the Korean War* (New York: Norton, 1965).

Franklin C. Spinney, *Defense Facts of Life: The Plans/Reality Mismatch* (Boulder, Colo.: Westview Press, 1985).

Timothy Stanley, *NATO in Transition* (New York: Praeger, 1963).

Paul Stares *The Militarization of Space: U.S. Policy, 1945–84* (Ithaca, N.Y.: Cornell University Press, 1985).

Joseph R. Starobin, "Origins of the Cold War: The Communist Dimension," *Foreign Affairs* (July 1969), pp. 681–696.

Gen. Donn A. Starry, *Mounted Combat in Viet Nam* (Washington, D.C.: Dept. of the Army, 1978).

Randolph J. Steer, *Understanding Anti-Submarine Warfare Technology.* MIT Program in Science and Technology for International Security, Report No. 12 (June 1984).

Harold Stein, ed., *American Civil-Military Decisions* (Birmingham, Ala.: University of Alabama Press, 1963).

Peter Stein, *The SDI Battle Management Program*. MIT Program in Science and Technology for National Security, Report No. 14 (December 1985).

John D. Steinbruner, *The Cybernetic Theory of Decision: New Dimensions of Political Analysis* (Princeton: Princeton University Press, 1974).

—— and Thomas M. Garwin, "Strategic Vulnerability: The Balance Between Prudence and Paranoia," *International Security* (Summer 1976), pp. 138–181.

—— and Leon V. Sigal, eds., *Alliance Security: NATO and the No-First-Use Question* (Washington, D.C.: Brookings, 1983).

——, "Launch Under Attack" *Scientific American* (January 1984), pp. 37–47.

——, "Choices and Tradeoffs," in Ashton B. Carter, John D. Steinbruner, and Charles A. Zraket, eds., *Managing Nuclear Operations* (Washington, D.C.: Brookings, 1987), pp. 542–543.

Peter Paul Stender, "The Paradox of Soviet Power," *Daedalus* (Fall 1962), pp. 766–782.

Claire Sterling, *The Masaryk Case* (New York: Harper & Row, 1968).

Sayre Stevens, "The Soviet BMD Program," in Ashton B. Carter and David N. Schwarz, eds., *Ballistic Missile Defense* (Washington, D.C.: Brookings, 1984), pp. 182–220.

David R. Stockman, *The Triumph of Politics: Why the Reagan Revolution Failed* (New York: Harper & Row, 1986).

I. F. Stone, *The Hidden History of the Korean War* (New York: Monthly Review Press, 1952).

Michael Straight, "How Ike Reached the Russians at Geneva," *The New Republic*, (August 1, 1955), pp. 7–11.

Richard Stubbings, *The Defense Game* (New York: Harper & Row, 1986).

C. L. Sulzberger, "The Three Who Shape the Future," *New York Times Magazine*, (February 4, 1945), p. 9.

Harry G. Summers, Jr., *On Strategy: A Critical Analysis of the Vietnam War* (Novato, Calif.: Presidio Press, 1982).

Stuart Symington, "Department of Defense Exaggerates," *New York Times*, March 18, 1971.

Strobe Talbott, ed. and trans., *Khrushchev Remembers* (Boston: Little, Brown, 1970).

——, ed. and trans., *Khrushchev Remembers: The Last Testament* (Boston: Little, Brown, 1974).

——, *Endgame: The Inside Story of SALT II* (New York: Harper & Row, 1979).

——, *Deadly Gambits* (New York: Vintage, 1985).

Nicolai Talensky, "Antimissile Systems and Disarmament," *The Bulletin of the Atomic Scientists*, (February, 1965) pp. 26–29.

Ronald Tammen, "Wolf at the Pentagon Door," *The New Republic*, (March 20, 1971), pp. 13–14.

William Taubman, *Stalin's American Policy: From Entente to Detente to Cold War* (New York: Norton, 1982).

Maxwell Taylor, *The Uncertain Trumpet* (New York: Harper, 1959).

Ross Terrell, *Mao* (New York: Harper & Row, 1980).

Hugh Thomas, *Armed Truce: The Beginnings of the Cold War: 1945–1946* (New York: Atheneum, 1987).

James Tobin, "The Eisenhower Economy and National Security: Defense, Dollars, and Doctrines," in Dean Albertson, ed., *Eisenhower as President* (New York: Hill and Wang, 1963).

Henry Trewhitt, *McNamara and the Ordeal of the Pentagon* (New York: Harper & Row, 1971).

Kosta Tsipis, "The Accuracy of Ballistic Missiles," *Scientific American* (July 1975), pp. 14–23.

———, "Cruise Missiles," *Scientific American* (February 1977) pp. 20–29.

———, *Arsenal: Understanding Weapons in the Nuclear Age* (New York: Simon and Schuster, 1983).

Robert Tucker, "Beyond Detente," *Commentary* (March 1977), pp. 42–50.

Nathan B. Twining, *A Hard Look at U.S. Military Policy* (New York: Holt, Rinehart, Winston, 1966).

Adam B. Ulam, *Expansion and Coexistence: The History of Soviet Foreign Policy: 1917–1967* (New York: Praeger, 1968).

———, *The Rivals: America and Russia Since World War II* (New York: Viking Press, 1971).

———, "Moscow Plays the Balance," *Foreign Policy* (Fall 1972), pp. 86–91.

———, *Dangerous Relations: The Soviet Union in World Politics, 1970–1982* (New York: Oxford University Press, 1983).

———, "Forty Years of Troubled Coexistence," *Foreign Affairs* (Fall 1985), pp. 12–32.

U.S. Arms Control and Disarmament Agency, *Arms Control and Disarmament Agreements* (Washington, D.C.: USGPO, 1980).

U.S. Central Intelligence Agency, *A Dollar Cost Comparison of Soviet and U.S. Defense Activities, 1968–1978* (Washington, D.C.: USGPO, 1979).

U.S. Department of Defense, Draft Memorandums for the President (Robert S. McNamara to John F. Kennedy and Lyndon B. Johnson, 1961–67).

———, "Remarks of Secretary McNamara, NATO Ministerial Meeting, 5 May 1962, Restricted Session."

———, "Remarks Prepared for Delivery by the Honorable Harold Brown, Secretary of Defense, at the Convocation Ceremonies for the 97th Naval War College Class, Naval War College, Newport, Rhode Island, Wednesday, August 20, 1980."

———, *Semiannual Report of the Secretary of Defense* (also *Annual Report*) (Washington, D.C.: USGPO, various years).

———, *Soviet Military Power* (Washington, D.C.: USGPO, various years).

U.S. Department of State, *U.S. Relations with China, with Special Reference to the Period 1944–1949* (Washington, D.C.: USGPO, 1949).

———, *Foreign Relations of the United States: The Conferences at Malta and Yalta, 1945* (Washington, D.C.: USGPO, 1955).

———, *Foreign Relations of the United States: The Conference of Berlin, 1945* (Washington, D.C.: USGPO, 1960).

U.S. House of Representatives, Committee on Appropriations, *Department of Defense Appropriations* (Washington, D.C.: USGPO, various years).

———, Surveys and Investigations Staff, Report to the Committee on Appropriations, U.S. House of Representatives on the Readiness of the U.S. Military—U.S. Army, Vol. I, March 1983 (Washington, D.C.: USGPO, 1983).

————, Committee on Armed Services, "The B-1B: A Program Review" (Washington, D.C.: USGPO, March 30, 1987).

U.S. Senate, Committee on Foreign Relations, "Statement of General Alfred M. Gruenther, March 26, 1955" (Washington, D.C.: USGPO, 1955).

————, Subcommittee on Internal Security, *Czechoslovakia and the Brezhnev Doctrine* (Washington, D.C.: USGPO, 1969).

————, Committee on Foreign Relations, "Statement by the Hon. Edward Brooke," May–June 1970 (Washington, D.C.: USGPO, 1970).

————, Select Committee on Intelligence, *The National Intelligence Estimates A-B Team Episode Concerning Soviet Strategic Capabilities and Objectives* (Washington, D.C.: USGPO, 1978).

————, Subcommittee on Appropriations, *Department of Defense Appropriations* (Washington, D.C.: USGPO, various years).

Cyrus Vance, *Hard Choices: Critical Years in America's Foreign Policy* (New York: Simon and Schuster, 1983).

William Van Cleave, "SALT on the Eagle's Tail," *Strategic Review* (Spring 1976), pp. 44–51.

Peter Vanneman and Martin James, "Soviet Thrust into the Horn of Africa: The Next Targets," *Strategic Review* (Fall 1978), pp. 33–38.

John Van Oudenaren, "Containment: Obsolete and Enduring Features," in Arnold C. Horelick, ed., *U.S.-Soviet Relations: The Next Phase* (Ithaca, N.Y.: Cornell University Press, 1986), pp. 27–54.

————, "Deterrence, War-Fighting, and Soviet Military Doctrine," Adelphi Paper No. 210 (London: IISS, 1986).

Paul F. Walker, "Precision-guided Munitions," *Scientific American* (August 1981), pp. 36–45.

————, "Smart Weapons in Naval Warfare," *Scientific American* (May 1983), pp. 53–61.

Douglas C. Waller and James T. Bruce, "SDI's Covert Reorientation: Short-term Gains Over Long-term Prospects," *Arms Control Today* (June 1987), pp. 2–8.

Richard J. Walton, *Cold War and Counterrevolution* (New York: Viking Press, 1972).

William S. Wasserman, "America and Britain: Rivals or Partners?", *New York Times Magazine*, February 4, 1945 p. 10.

Stephen Weiner, "Systems and Technology," in Ashton B. Carter and David N. Schwartz, eds., *Ballistic Missile Defense* (Washington, D.C.: Brookings, 1983), pp. 49–88.

Allan Weinstein, *Perjury: The Hiss-Chambers Case* (New York: Knopf, 1978).

Stanley A. Weiss, "True Worth of a Defense Dollar," *Wall Street Journal*, May 14, 1987.

Samuel Wells, "Sounding the Tocsin: NSC-68 and the Soviet Threat," *International Security* (Fall 1979), pp. 116–158.

Alexander Werth, *Russia at War: 1941–45* (New York: Avon edition, 1965).

*Whence the Threat to Peace* (Moscow: Military Publishing House, 1984).

Morton White, *Pragmatism and the American Mind* (New York: Oxford University Press, 1972).

Theodore H. White, *The Making of the President, 1960* (New York: Atheneum, 1961).

————, *Breach of Faith* (New York: Harper & Row, 1975).

Allen Whiting, *China Crosses the Yalu: The Decision to Enter the War* (New York: Macmillan, 1960).

Dean Wilkening, Kenneth Watman, Michael Kennedy, and Richard Darilek, "Strategic Defences and First-strike Stability," *Survival* (March–April 1987), pp. 137–165.

William Appleman Williams, *The Tragedy of American Diplomacy* (Cleveland: World Publishers, 1959).

Mason Willrich and John B. Rhinelander, eds., *SALT: The Moscow Agreements and Beyond* (Glencoe, N.Y.: The Free Press, 1974).

David Wise and Thomas B. Ross, *The U-2 Affair* (New York: Random House, 1962).

Albert Wohlstetter, "The Delicate Balance of Terror," *Foreign Affairs* (January 1959), pp. 211–234.

———, "Is There a Strategic Arms Race?", *Foreign Policy* (Summer 1974), pp. 3–20.

———, "Rivals But No Race," *Foreign Policy* (Fall 1974), pp. 48–81.

———, "Between an Unfree World and None," *Foreign Affairs* (Summer 1985), pp. 962–994.

——— and Richard P. Brody, "Continuing Control as a Requirement for Deterring," in Ashton B. Carter, John D. Steinbruner, and Charles A. Zraket, eds., *Managing Nuclear Operations* (Washington, D.C.: Brookings, 1987), pp. 142–196.

Bertram Wolfe, "A New Look at the Soviet 'New Look,' " *Foreign Affairs* (January 1955), pp. 184–198.

———, *Khrushchev and Stalin's Ghost* (New York: Praeger, 1957).

Thomas W. Wolfe, Herbert Dinerstein, and Leon Gouré, eds. and trans. of V. D. Sokolovsky, ed., *Soviet Military Strategy* (Englewood Cliffs, N.J.: Prentice-Hall, 1963).

———, *Soviet Strategy at the Crossroads* (Cambridge, Mass.: Harvard University Press, 1964).

———, "Shifts in Soviet Strategic Thought," *Foreign Affairs* (April 1964), pp. 475–486.

———, *Soviet Power and Europe: 1945–1970* (Baltimore: Johns Hopkins Press, 1970).

———, *The SALT Experience* (Cambridge, Mass.: Ballinger, 1979).

David Woodward, *The Russians at Sea* (London: Kimber, 1965).

Daniel Yergin, *Shattered Peace: The Origins of the Cold War and the National Security State* (Boston: Houghton Mifflin, 1977).

Aryell Y. Yodfat, *The Soviet Union and the Arabian Peninsula* (New York: St. Martin's Press, 1983).

Donald Zagoria, "Into the Breach: New Soviet Alliances in the Third World," *Foreign Affairs* (Spring 1979), pp. 733–754.

J. K. Zawodny, *Death in the Forest* (South Bend, Ind.: University of Notre Dame Press, 1962).

Paul E. Zinner, ed., *National Communism and Popular Revolt in Eastern Europe* (New York: Columbia University Press, 1956).

———, *Revolution in Hungary* (New York: Columbia University Press, 1962).

# Index

A-10 planes, 431
A-6E Intruder bomber, 379
ABM (Anti-Ballistic Missile) system, 354, 361, 362, 423–24
  anti-Chinese justification for, 247, 249
  McNamara and, 247–54, 264
  Nixon administration and, 264–68
  SALT I and, 290–95
  Soviet development of, 249–51, 265–66
  "Star Wars" program and, 399, 400
ABM Treaty, 290–95, 351, 406, 423, 424
Acheson, Dean, 33, 34, 96, 101*n*, 110, 152, 168, 174
  Berlin crisis and (1961), 170–71
  China policy and, 63–64
  Hiss case and, 64–65
  Korean War and, 70, 76
  NSC-68 and, 67
Adenauer, Konrad, 151–54, 172–73
Afghanistan, 203
  Soviet invasion of, 327–29
Africa, 21
Agnew, Spiro, 268, 317
Aircraft carriers
  American, 381–86
  Soviet, 307
Air Force, Soviet, 44. *See also specific aircraft*
  in 1960s, 188, 195
  "bomber gap" and, 107–9
  current strength of, 420–21
  in early 1950s, 88–91
  in World War II, 89
Air Force, U.S., 85, 97, 378, 431. *See also specific aircraft*
  airlift capability of, 379–80
  "bomber gap" and, 107–9
  Eisenhower and, 102–4
  Finletter Report and, 62

Air Force *(cont.)*
  McNamara and, 181, 182, 187, 189–90
  military spending debate and (1948), 62
  MIRVs and, 257
  Reagan administration and, 376
  SALT I and, 291
  spending cuts of 1960s and 1970s and, 299–300
Air forces (air warfare)
  current balance of power, 430–31
  in Six-Day War in Middle East (1967), 230
  technology and, 387–90
Air interdiction campaigns, 386–87
Airlift capability, 379–80
Air mobility doctrine, 227
Albania, 31, 59
Allende, Salvador, 323
Almond, Maj. Gen. Edward, 72
Alsop, Joseph, 127
Alsop, Stewart, 107, 320
Ambrose, Stephen, 114
American Physical Society, 401
Amin, Hafizullah, 328
Andropov, Yuri, 118–19, 408, 414
Angola, 330–31, 333
Antiaircraft defenses, 388–89
Antimissile missiles. *See also* ABM (Anti-Ballistic Missile) system, Soviet, 188
Anti-Semitism, Soviet, 59–60
Antiship missiles, 383–84
Antitank weapons, 391–94, 430
Apache (AH-64) helicopters, 392
Ap Bac, battle of (1962), 217
Argentina, 12, 19
Arif, Abdel, 205
Armed forces, Soviet, 300–1. *See also* Air Force, Soviet; Army, Soviet; Navy, Soviet

Armed forces (cont.)
  in late 1940s, 43–44
  in early 1950s, 86–93
  in 1970s, 304–11
Armored personnel carriers, 392–93
Armored units, Soviet, 88
Armored warfare, 391–94. See also Tanks
Arms and Influence (Schelling), 138n
Arms limitations treaties, 289–90
Arms race. See also specific types of
    weapons, weapon systems, and
    other topics
  in 1960s, 244–45
  "action-reaction" cycle of, 354–55
  current status of, 418–34
    conventional balance, 425–26
    strategic balance, 419–25
  lessons of, 435–43
Arms sales
  by Czechoslovakia to Egypt, 201–2
  by France to Israel, 202
Army, Soviet. See also Military strategy,
    Soviet
  in early 1950s, 87–88
  in 1960s, 193–96
  in 1970s, 304–5
Army, U.S., 85, 103. See also Military
    strategy, American
  Patriot air defense system of, 380–81
Asia, Yalta Conference (1945) and, 13–14
Assad, Haifez al-, 318
Assault Breaker weapons, 393–94
"Assured destruction" strategy, 352–56,
    358, 399, 436
  McNamara and, 185–86, 191, 246–47,
    250, 259, 262, 263
Aswan Dam, 203, 205
Atlas missiles, 128–29, 187, 273
Atomic bomb. See also Nuclear weapons
  first successful explosion of (1945), 22
Atomic energy, United Nations and
    development of, 30
Austria, 5, 6, 16, 113–14
Aviation Week and Space Technology,
    107, 127, 338

B-1 bombers, 389
B-1B bombers, 376, 397–98, 421
B-36 bombers, 85, 90
B-47 bombers, 103, 104, 109, 187
B-52 bombers, 103, 104, 129, 136, 187,
    421
B-58 bombers, 187
B-70 bombers, 181, 191, 251
Backfire bombers, 304, 335, 383
Baghdad Pact, 202
Balance of power. See also specific topics
  in early 1960s, 210–11
  current, 418–34
    conventional balance, 425–26
    strategic balance, 419–25

Baldwin, Hanson, 77, 257
Balkans, 32, 33
  post-World War II influence over, 5–6
Ball, Desmond, 189, 191
Ball, George, 219, 224–25, 355
Ball-bearing technology, 271–72, 274
Bandung Conference (1955), 199–200
Barre, Siad, 325
Baruch, Bernard, 30–31
Bekaa Valley campaign (1982), 389–91
Belenko, Viktor, 308
Benelux countries, 57
Beneš, Edvard, 38–39
Beria, Lavrenti, 15, 59n, 82–84
Berlin, 6
  1961 crisis over, 169–73, 177
  Khrushchev's foreign policy and,
    150–52, 154, 169–73
  Soviet blockade of (1948), 40
Berlin, University of, 48–49
Berlin airlift, 52–56
  "baby," 50
Berlin Blockade, 47–56
  American diplomatic initiative of April
    20 and, 50–51
  background of, 47–51
  "creeping blockade," 49–50
  start of, 51–52
Berlin Wall, 172
Beschloss, Michael, 155, 156
Bevin, Ernest, 39, 42, 70
Bialer, Seweryn, 415, 443
Bidault, Georges, 36–37
Bikini atoll, 105
Bissell, 168
Bizonia, 48
Blackjack bomber, 420
Blitzkrieg tactics, 429, 430, 438
BMP-76 armored personnel carriers, 305
Bogan, Adm. Gerald, 66
Bohlen, Charles "Chip," 5, 32, 35, 50, 56,
    67
Bomarc missiles, 129
"Bomber gap," 107–9
Booster rockets, 270
Bracken, Paul, 359
Bradley, Gen. Omar, 45, 52, 66, 68, 224
Bradley armored vehicle, 380, 392
Brandt, Willy, 52, 172
BRAVO, 105–6
Brewster, Owen, 64
Brezhnev, Leonid, 302, 316–17, 326, 328,
    413
  SALT II and, 335, 336
  Yom Kippur War (1973) and, 320, 321
Bridges, Styles, 64
Brodie, Bernard, 131–33, 177, 185, 191,
    196, 214, 220, 241–42, 244
Brooke, Edward, 255, 264
Browder, Earl, 38
Brown, Harold, 357–58

Brzezinski, Zbigniew, 344
Buchan, Alistair, 192–93
Bukharin, Nikolai, 8n
Bulganin, Nikolai, 115, 118, 200, 203
Bulgaria, 5, 21, 24, 59
Bullpup missiles, 229
Bundy, McGeorge, 139, 183, 191,
    218–21, 223
Bush, George, 348
Bush, Vannevar, 30, 123
*Business Week*, 25
Byrnes, James, 13, 22, 28, 29
    atomic-sharing proposals and, 24–25
    at Foreign Minister's conferences
        (1945), 24–25

C-5 transport planes, 379–80
Cachin, Marcel, 58
Cadogan, Sir Alexander, 10, 11
Camp David peace treaty (1977), 325
Canada, 26, 57
Capehart, Homer, 64
Cargo planes, 379–80
Carpatho-Ukraine, 21
Carrier task groups, U.S., 381–86
Carter, Jimmy, 397
    Afghanistan and, 328
    NATO countries and, 341–45
    neutron bomb proposal and, 342
    SALT II and, 333–41, 335, 336
Castro, Fidel, 167–68, 173
Catholic Church, American, 64
Central Intelligence Agency (CIA), 39,
    108
    ABM system and, 250–52
    Soviet defense estimates of (1976),
        309–10
    Team B group and, 348–49
    U-2 affair and, 154, 155
CEP (circular error probable), 277–79,
    281
Chambers, Whittaker, 64–65
Chamoun, Camille, 206
Chernenko, Konstantin, 396, 408
Chiang Kai-shek, 73, 111, 112
Chile, 323
China, 22, 68, 113, 194, 195, 288, 289.
    *See also* Sino-Soviet split
    ABM system and, 247, 249
    communist takeover in, 39, 63–64
    Formosan crisis and (1954–1955), 111,
        112
    Korean War and, 73–77, 96, 134, 137
    Laotian crisis of 1961–62 and, 208–9
    Truman and, 63–64
    Vietnam War and, 109, 110
    White Paper on, 64
    Yalta Conference (1945) and, 13–14
China Lobby, 64, 73, 98, 110
*Christian Science Monitor,* 264
Chuikov, Marshal, 245

Church, Frank, 264, 293
Churchill, Sir Winston, 31, 43, 45, 97,
    113, 138n
    "iron curtain" speech (1946), 29
    postwar settlement with Stalin, 5
    Potsdam Conference and (1945), 21
    on Roosevelt, 4
    Soviet Union as viewed by, 17, 18
    on Stalin, 5–6, 57
    at Yalta Conference (1945), 11–17
Circular error probable (CER), 277–79, 281
Civil defense, 107, 170
Clark, Mark, 95
Clark, Tom, 26
Clay, Gen. Lucius, 39, 42, 46–47, 172
    Berlin Blockade and, 49–56
Clementis, Vladimir, 59
Clifford, Clark, 224
"Coercive" strategy, McNamara's,
    184–86, 268
Cold War, 66, 98, 143, 164
    beginning of, 23–41
        Kennan's "Long Telegram" (1946),
            26–27
        Marshall Plan, 34–40
        Truman Doctrine, 31–34
"Combined arms" doctrine, Soviet, 305,
    368, 370
Cominform (Communist Information
    Bureau), 38, 58, 60
Command and control systems, limited
    nuclear war and, 363–72
Committee on the Present Danger, 337,
    348
Communication systems, limited nuclear
    war and, 363–72
Communism, Truman on democracy vs.,
    33
Communist parties (or movements)
    European, Marshall Plan and, 38–39
    in Middle East, 205
    in Western Europe, 46–47
Communist party, French, 58–59
Communist party, Soviet
    Khrushchev and, 148
    Stalin and, 7
Congo, 167
Conquest, Robert, 7
Containment, doctrine of, 60, 93, 98,
    100, 101, 101–2n, 210
Conventional warfare (limited wars). *See
    also specific wars*
    1970s shift in balance of forces, 304–11
    air interdiction campaigns in, 386–87
    balance of forces in 1987, 425–34
        aircraft, 430–31
        manpower, 425–27
        naval forces, 431–32
        scenarios, 426–29
        tactical nuclear weapons, 432–33
        tanks and artillery, 429–30

Conventional warfare *(cont.)*
 defense intellectuals and, 138
 McNamara and, 193–94
 rapid maneuver, 226–27
 Sokolovsky book on, 242–43
Council on Foreign Relations, 132
Counterforce strategy, 133, 137, 185,
 186, 191, 198, 355
Counterinsurgency capability, 214,
 226–27
Cranston, Alan, 333
Crommelin, Capt. John, 65–66
Cruise missiles, 377, 388, 405, 421
 SALT II and, 335, 339–40
Cuba, 210
 Angola and, 331
 Bay of Pigs invasion of, 167–69
 Ethiopia and, 332
Cuban missile crisis (1962), 173–78, 245
Curzon Line, 16
Cyprus, 205
Czechoslovakia, 21, 37, 59, 201
 Communist putsch in (1948), 38–39
 Soviet invasion of (1968), 290

"Damage-limiting" nuclear policy, 355,
 357–59
Dardanelles, 30
Davies, Joseph, 23
Dayan, Moshe, 321
Dean, Arthur, 224
Dean, Gen. John, 9, 71
"Deep Strike" strategy, 393
Defense, U.S. Department of, under
 McNamara, 179–83, 188–89
Defense intellectuals, 131–46, 176–77
 in 1970s, 348–59
 in McNamara's Pentagon, 180
 Vietnam War and, 219–20
Defense spending. *See* Military spending
Defense strategy. *See* Military strategy
 (or doctrine)
De Gaulle, Charles, 3, 10, 58–59, 152–54,
 156–58, 172, 196, 197, 215
Deitchmann, Seymour, 395
"Delicate Balance of Terror, The"
 (Wohlstetter), 140–41, 359
Denfield, Adm. Louis, 66
*Denver Post,* 120
De-Stalinization, 113, 116
Detente, 327
 Yom Kippur War (1973) and, 322–23
Deterrence, 137, 357
 Brodie on, 132, 133
 minimum, McNamara on, 185
Developing countries. *See also* Third
 World
 Bandung Conference of (1955),
 199–200
 Soviet policy toward, 200–1, 203–4
DEW system, 129

Diem, Ngo Dinh, 110, 212–13, 216
Dillon, Douglas, 156
Dinerstein, Herbert, 131, 140, 142, 143,
 168
Djilas, Milovan, 5, 7, 34, 43, 47
Dobrynin, Anatoly, 147, 173, 287, 288,
 293, 324
Dodge, Joseph, 102
Domino theory, 32, 109–10
Donnelly, Christopher, 429
Donovan, Robert, 115
Douglas, Donald, 124
Douglas, William O., 25
Douhet, Giulio, 88
Dratvin, Gen. Mikhail, 49–50
Drones, 390
"Dual track," 345
Duclos, Jacques, 38
Dulles, Allen, 130, 155, 168
Dulles, John Foster, 18, 46, 97, 111, 114,
 122, 136, 151, 152, 201–2, 207
 Eisenhower's relationship with, 94–95
 Korean War and, 96, 97
 massive retaliation policy and, 98
Dung, Gen. Van Tien, 326
Dyson, Freeman, 399

E-2C radar planes, 389, 390
Early warning radar system, 103, 108
Early warning systems, limited nuclear
 war and, 361–62
East Berlin, 54, 55, 116
Eastern Europe, 21, 23, 24
 Gorbachev's reforms and, 416
 Marshall Plan and, 37–38
 purges in (1948–1952), 59–60
 Soviet divisions in, in 1970s, 304–5
East Germany, 42, 47, 58, 416
 Berlin crisis of 1961 and, 169–73
 currency reform in (1948), 51
 Khrushchev's foreign policy and,
 150–52, 169–70
 refugees from, 171
 Sovietization of, 48
EC-135 aircraft, 365
*Economics of Defense in the Nuclear
 Age, The* (Hitch), 180
Economy, the, 144
 Soviet, 145, 149, 409–16
Eden, Anthony, 6, 12
Egypt, 118
 in 1967 Six-Day War with Israel, 229,
 230
 Korean War and, 315–21
 Soviet Union and, 201–5
Eisenhower, Dwight D. (Eisenhower
 administration), 81, 93–119, 183,
 436
 Dulles's relationship with, 94–95
 as elder statesman, 169*n*
 Farewell Address of, 160

Eisenhower *(cont.)*
  foreign policy of, 94, 95
  Formosan crisis and (1954–1955),
    111–12
  Hungarian uprising and, (1956), 118
  Kennedy's view of, 165
  Khrushchev and, 151–60
    Berlin crisis (1959), 151–52, 154, 171
    Camp David talks (1959), 154
    Paris summit (planned but not held),
      154–58
  Korean War and, 95–97
  Lebanon intervention and (1958),
    206–7
  massive retaliation policy and, 98–99,
    101, 104
  Middle East policy of, 206
  military spending and, 95–96, 99,
    102–3, 158–60
  missile and rocket development under,
    123, 128–31
  nuclear policy of, 98–99, 101, 103–4,
    136, 138n, 141
    rejection of recommendations to use
      nuclear weapons, 109–12
  overall appraisal of, 94–95
  space program and, 123–26
  Suez Canal crisis and (1956), 118
  summit conference of 1955 and,
    114–15
  Truman administration and, 95–96
  U-2 affair and, 154–58
  as unmilitaristic president, 95
  Vietnam War and, 109–10, 212
  in World War II, 5, 6, 11
Eisenhower Doctrine, 206
Electromagnetic pulse, 274–75, 364
Ellsberg, Daniel, 180
Emergency Rocket Command System,
  367
"Emerging Technologies" program, 393
Enthoven, Alain, 179, 180, 182, 191, 252
Ermath, Fritz, 348
Ethiopia, 330–33
Euromissiles, 345–47
European Recovery Program, 37–38
Exocet missiles, 383–84
Explorer I, 126
Extremely Low Frequency (ELF)
  systems, 364n

F-4 Phantom fighters, 299, 316, 377, 431
F-14 fighters, 300, 378, 384, 385
F-15 fighters, 299–300, 431
F-16 fighters, 378, 431
F-86 Saberjet, 85, 89
F-111 (TFX) fighter bombers, 378, 382,
  388
F/A-18 fighter/attack plane, 378–79
Fail-safe procedure, 136
Falklands War, 384, 385

Fallaci, Oriana, 144
Fallout shelter program, 158
Finland, 47, 113
Finletter, Thomas, 62
First use of nuclear weapons (first-strike
    strategy), 101, 244
  "assured destruction" balance and,
    246–47
  attainability of, 284–85
  counterforce strategy and, 133
  defense intellectuals and, 133, 134
  Khrushchev's military strategy and,
    237, 238
  McNamara and, 184–85, 191
  Soviet military writings on, 351–52
  surprise attack scenarios, 139–43
"Flexible response" strategy, 170,
    177–78, 185, 186, 196, 197, 214,
    226, 426
  Sokolovsky book and, 241–43
FNLA (Angola), 330, 331
"Follow-on Forces" strategy, 393
Ford, Gerald, 297, 327, 336
*Foreign Affairs* (journal), 37, 98, 99, 140
Foreign Minister's conferences (1945),
    24–25
Formosa. *See* Taiwan
Forrestal, James V., 28, 52–54, 61
*Forrestal* (aircraft carrier), 85
Foster, John, 265, 266
France, 40, 42, 48, 51, 56, 57, 289, 332,
    405, 422, 428. *See also* De Gaulle,
    Charles
  arms contract with Israel, 202
  German rearmament and, 110, 112–13
  Suez crisis and (1956), 118, 203
  Vietnam war and, 109, 110
  Yalta Conference (1945) and, 12, 13
Freedman, Lawrence, 137, 246, 438
Free trade, 139
Fuchs, Klaus, 26
Fulbright, William, 264, 293

Galbraith, John Kenneth, 216
Galosh missile, 252
Game theory, 133, 133–34n, 139–41
Garthoff, Raymond, 302, 346
Garwin, Richard, 282
Gates, Thomas, 155
Gavin, Gen. James, 132, 227
Gelb, Leslie, 220
Geneva summit conference (1955),
    113–15
Geneva Conference (1954), 212
George, Walter, 67
*George Washington* (submarine), 129
Germany. *See also* East Germany; West
    Germany
  Cold War and, 40
  currency reform proposals for (late
    1940s), 49, 51–55

Germany *(cont.)*
    Marshall Plan and, 35, 36
    reparations after World War II, 13, 18,
        21, 40
    reunification of, 151, 152, 172
    World War II and, 6, 10, 11, 16
    Yalta Conference (1945) and, 12–13
Gilpatric, Roswell, 238
*Glasnost* policy, 407, 414–16
Glassboro summit meeting (1967), 254
Goldwater, Barry, 257
Golem missile, 128
Gomulka, Wladislaw, 59, 116
Goodpaster, Gen. Andrew, 154, 299
Gorbachev, Mikhail, 405–8, 441–43
    economic policies of, 410–16
Gorshkov, Adm. Sergei, 91, 307
Gouzenko, Igor, 26
Graham, Gen. Daniel O., 348, 399
Gray, Colin, 180, 220, 338, 348, 352, 358
Great Britain, 56, 57, 60, 75, 76, 421–22.
    *See also* Churchill, Sir Winston
    Greek communist insurgency and
        (1947–1948), 31–32
    Iran and, 29
    post-World War II credits to, 19–20
    Suez crisis and (1956), 118, 203
    U.S. relations with, during World War
        II, 10
    World War II and, 5–6
*Great Soviet Encyclopedia,* 84
Grechko, Marshal, 351, 370, 391–92
Greece, 5, 12, 16, 57
    communist insurgency in (1947–1948),
        31–34
Gromyko, Andrei, 29, 153, 238, 287
Groves, Gen. Leslie, 30, 43
Gruenther, Alfred, 108
Gryphon missiles, 250–51
Guerrilla warfare, 214
GULAG, 48
Gyroscopes, 271–2

Hagerty, James, 111
Haig, Alexander, 322
Hansen, Donald, 372
Harkins, Paul, 218
Harriman, Averell, 5, 12, 18, 19, 21, 35,
    96, 110, 153, 216
    on massive retaliation policy, 99
Heikel, Muhammed, 203, 204, 231
Helicopters
    Soviet, 306
    in Vietnam War, 227–28
Herter, Christian, 156
"High Frontier" lobby, 399
Hill, Lister, 127
Hilsman, Roger, 216
Hiroshima, 22
Hiss, Alger, 26, 41, 64–65
Hiss, Donald, 64

Hitch, Charles, 180, 182–83
Ho Chi Minh, 222–23
Hoffman, Frederick, 180
Honest John missiles, 130
Hoover, Herbert, 35
Hoover, J. Edgar, 26
Hopkins, Harry, 10, 12, 13, 16
    meetings with Stalin (1945), 20–21
Hot line, 289
Hounddog missiles, 130, 187, 197
Howard, Michael, 369
Howley, Col. Frank, 52
HueyCobra helicopters, 227–28
Hughes, Harold, 293
Humphrey, George, 96
Humphrey, Hubert, 293
Hungary, 5, 21, 37, 59, 416
    1956 uprising in, 117–19
Hussein, King of Jordan, 206, 207

ICBMs (Intercontinental-range Ballistic
    Missiles), 124, 127, 143, 183. *See
    also specific missiles*
    SALT I and, 295–96
    Soviet buildup of (1960s), 258–63
Iklé, Fred, 136, 354, 358
Il-28 bombers, 89, 195, 202–3
Il-38 bombers, 107–8
India, 210, 289
Indochina, 100
    Eisenhower's refusal to intervene in,
        109–10
Indonesia, 203, 204
INF (Intermediate-range Nuclear Force)
    treaty, 405, 421
Infantry, Soviet, 87, 88
Institute for Strategic Studies, 108
Intellectuals, defense. *See* Defense
    intellectuals
Intelligence agencies, Western, 43, 44
International Geophysical Year
    (1957–1958), 125
Iran, 33, 59, 205–6
    abdication of the Shah of, 329
    Soviet policy toward (1946), 29
Iranian hostage crisis (1979–80), 329
Iraq, 150, 203, 205, 206, 230
Isolationism, 32, 38
Israel, 205
    in 1967 Six-Day War with Arab
        countries, 229–31
    Bekaa Valley campaign (1982), 389–91
    French arms sale to, 202
    Korean War and, 315–25
    Suez Canal crisis and (1956), 118, 202
Italy, 21, 32, 38, 42, 45, 46, 59
*Izvestia,* 82

Jackson, Henry, 107, 121, 249, 336
Japan, 21, 24, 60, 68
    Korean War and, 69–71

Japan *(cont.)*
World War II and, 9, 13, 20, 22, 387
Yalta Conference (1945) and, 13
Jaruzelski, Gen. Wojciech, 409
Javits, Jacob, 264
Jessup, Philip, 56
Johnson, Kelly, 125
Johnson, Louis, 65, 66, 77
Johnson, Lyndon B., 121, 130, 172
ABM system and, 253, 254
arms limitation treaties and, 289, 290
MIRV and, 257
Six-Day War in Middle East (1967)
and, 230–31
Vietnam War and, 136, 219–25, 229
Johnston, Eric, 19
Joint Chiefs of Staff
1946 assessment of world military
situation, 26
budget request of (1948), 62–63
Jordan, 207, 208
in 1967 Six-Day War with Israel, 229,
230
Judd, Walter, 64
Jupiter-C booster, 126

Kadar, Janos, 117, 119
Kahn, Herman, 131–32, 134–37, 145–46,
185, 198
Karmal, Babrak, 328
Katyn Forest massacre (1940), 15
Kaufmann, William, 131, 180, 185, 215,
383, 429
Kazhakstan, 7
Keating, Kenneth, 174
Keegan, Gen. George, 399
Kennan, George, 19, 32, 34, 41, 42, 47,
50, 59, 67, 76, 82, 144, 343n
on containment doctrine, 93
on Eisenhower, 94
on Kennedy-Khrushchev meetings,
163–64
"Long Telegram," 26–28, 49
"X" article, 26, 101, 101–2n
Kennedy, John F. (Kennedy
administration), 99, 110, 121, 122,
159. *See also* McNamara, Robert
Berlin crisis and (1961), 169–73, 177
as command-post President, 176–77
crisis orientation of, 165–67
Cuban missile crisis (1962) and, 173–78
on Eisenhower, 165
invasion of Cuba and, 167–69
Laos and, 169, 208–10
McNamara and, 179, 183
as pragmatist ideologue, 164–65
Vienna summit and (1961), 163–64,
169–70
Vietnam War and, 169, 214–18
Kennedy, Robert, 172, 173n, 175, 214
Keynes, John Maynard, 20

Keyserling, Leon, 67
Khanh, Maj. Gen. Nguyen, 219, 220
Khomeini, Ayatollah, 329
Khrushchev, Nikita, 44, 59n, 69, 91, 113,
145, 250, 320
Cuban invasion by the United States
and, 168–69
Cuban missile crisis (1962) and,
173–78, 245
economic policies of, 149
fall from power, 235–36
foreign policy of, 150–58
Berlin and Germany, 150–54, 169–73
Berlin crisis (1959), 151–52, 154, 171
Paris summit (planned but not held),
154–58
Hungarian uprising and, (1956), 118,
119
internal problems of, 147–49
Laotian crisis and (1962), 209
Lebanon crisis and (1958) and, 207–8
military cutbacks and, 149–50, 153,
170, 236, 238, 245
military strategy of, 236–45
Sokolovsky book on and, 239–44
missile and rocket development under,
121–24, 127
Sino-Soviet split and, 148
at summit conference of 1955, 114–15
Third World policy of, 200–1, 204
transfer of power after Stalin's death
and, 82–85
U-2 affair and, 154–58
Vienna summit and (1961), 163–64,
169–70
visit to America (1959), 153–54
Killian, James, 124
Killian Report, 124–25
Kim Il-Sung, 69
King, Adm. Ernest, 4
Kirov, Sergei, 7
Kissinger, Henry, 132, 147, 178, 263,
333, 353, 356, 442
ABM system and, 264, 268
diplomatic style of, 325
on massive retaliation policy, 99
*Necessity for Choice,* 143–44
on nuclear warfare, 137–38
SALT I and, 287–94, 302, 338–39
SALT II and, 336
Vietnam War and, 327
Yom Kippur War (1973) and, 316,
318–25
Kistiakowsky, George, 293
Knorr, Klaus, 132, 145, 146
Knowland, William, 64, 73
Kobayama, Aikichi, 105, 106
Koestler, Arthur, 8n
Kommandatura, 48
Korean War, 44, 68–77, 89, 100, 109
China and, 96, 134, 137

Korean War *(cont.)*
  decision to cross 38th parallel in, 73–74
  start of, 68–69
  United Nations and, 70, 73–75
Kornilev, Sergei, 122, 123
Korolev, Sergei, 235
Kostov, Traicho, 59
Kosygin, Alexei, 205, 229, 230, 289–90,
    319, 438
  ABM system and, 253–54
Kozlov, Frol, 148
Kreisky, Bruno, 164
Krock, Arthur, 68
Kvitsinksy, Yuli, 346
Kwajalein test range, 281
Ky, Nguyen Cao, 222

Laika, 120
Laird, Melvin, 263–68, 292, 370
  ABM system and, 264–68
Lambeth, Benjamin, 348, 353
Land, Edwin, 124
Lansdale, Edwin, 214, 216
Laos, Kennedy administration and, 169,
    208–10
Lapp, Ralph, 105
Laser technology, 424
Lebanon, 150
  American intervention in (1958), 206–7
  Bekaa Valley campaign (1982) in,
    389–91
Lee, Asher, 127
Lee, Robert E., 112
Lee, William T., 309–10, 354–55
Legum, Colin, 330
Lehman, John, 381, 384
LeMay, Gen. Curtis, 104, 181, 237,
    370
  Berlin airlift and, 52–54
*Le Monde*, 115
Lend-lease aid to Soviet Union, 9, 20
Lenin, V. I., 14, 43, 91, 200
Leontieff, Wassilly, 145
Lie, Trygve, 73
*Life* (magazine), 23, 120–21, 170
Ligachev, Yegor, 416
Lilienthal, David, 30
Limited Nuclear Test Ban Treaty (1962),
    176, 250, 289
Limited wars. *See also* Conventional war;
    Nuclear warfare, limited; Nuclear
    warfare, tactical
  Brodie on, 133
Lippmann, Walter, 19, 25, 29, 37, 98,
    198
Loans to Soviet Union, after World War
    II, 19–20
Lockheed, 125, 380
Lodal, Jan, 279
Lodge, Henry Cabot, 222, 225
Lomov, Col. Gen. N. A., 350

London Institute of Strategic Studies,
    433–34
"Long Telegram" (Kennan), 26–28, 49
Lovett, Robert, 47, 52, 54, 96
Luce, Henry, 158
*Lucky Dragon* (fishing boat), 105
Luftwaffe, 89
Lumumba, Patrice, 167
Lunik II, 128
Luttwack, Edward, 348, 375

M-60 tank, 299
MacArthur, Gen. Douglas, 23, 95, 137
  Korean War and, 69–77
McCarthy, Joseph, 65
MccGwire, Michael, 237
McCloy, John, 224
McCormack, John, 121
McDougall, Walter, 159
McGovern, George, 293
Mach 2 Blinder bombers, 188
Mackintosh, J. M., 198
Maclean, Donald, 41, 43
Macmillan, Harold, 152–54, 196–97, 207
McNamara, Robert, 174, 241, 246–65, 365
  ABM system and, 247–54, 264
  arms limitation treaties and, 289–90
  "assured destruction" balance and,
    246–47, 250, 259, 262, 263,
    352–56, 436
  conservative defense intellectuals's
    criticisms of, 352–56
  MIRV and, 248, 252, 254–57
  on nuclear warfare, 184–86, 192, 239
  San Francisco speech of (1967),
    246–48, 352–54, 436
  Soviet missile buildup and, 258–63
McNaughton, John, 180, 221–23
Malenkov, Georgi, 59n, 60, 113, 119, 149
  transfer of power after Stalin's death
    and, 82–85
Malik, Jacob, 56
Malinovsky, Rodion, 149, 157, 226, 238,
    239, 245, 250
Manchuria, 22
  Korean War and, 73, 74
Mandelbaum, Michael, 139
Mansfield, Mike, 224
Mao Zedong, 14, 69, 76, 148, 208
Maritime strategy, 383–86
Mark 12 warhead, 419–20
Mark 12A warhead, 419–20
Marshall, George C., 4, 5, 32–33, 41, 49,
    53–54, 61, 95
  China and, 64
  Korean War and, 73–74, 76
  military spending debate and (1948),
    63
Marshall Plan, 34–40, 49, 50
  American motivations for, 35
  Congressional approval of, 37–38

Masaryk, Jan, 38, 39
Massive retaliation, policy of, 98–99, 101,
    104
  credibility issue and, 133
  Kissinger on, 99
  Khrushchev's, 236
Matthews, Francis, 66
McNamara, Robert, 177–97
  "assured destruction" policy and,
    185–86, 191, 246–47, 250, 259,
    262, 263
  Defense Department under, 179–83,
    188–89
  on guerrilla warfare, 214
  "missile gap" and, 189–90
  non-nuclear forces and, 192–97
  strategic defense postures and, 184–86
  strategic missile buildup under, 187,
    189–92
  "2½ war" strategy of, 193–94
  Vietnam War and, 218–19, 223, 224
  weapons procurement schedule
    proposed by, 183–84, 186–87, 189,
    190
Mechanized (motor rifle) divisions,
    Soviet, 88
Medvedev, Zhores, 415
*Memoirs* (Kissinger), 147
Mengistu, Col., 331–32
Menon, V. K. Krishna, 199
MGB (formerly NKGB), 83*n*
Michael, King of Rumania, 18
Middle East, 31
  1956 Suez crisis in, 118
  1967 Six-Day War in, 229–31
  Eisenhower administration and,
    206
  Soviet policy toward, 201–6
  Yom Kippur War (1973) in, 315–25
MiG-15s, 85, 89, 202
MiG-21s, 389, 390, 431
MiG-23s, 389, 390, 431
MiG-25s, 308–9
MiG-29s, 431
MiG-31s, 431
Mikoyan, Anastas, 117, 151, 172
Military aid, Soviet, 203, 204
Military-industrial complex, Eisenhower
    on, 160
*Military Review*, 107
Military Sealift Command, 379–80
Military spending
  Soviet, 67
    Khrushchev and, 126, 128, 149–50,
      153, 170, 245
    methods for calculating, 309
  United States
    1948–1950, 60–68
    1950–1953, 85–86
    1951, 77
    1960s–1970s decline in, 298–300

Military spending *(cont.)*
  Carter and, 341–42
  Eisenhower and, 95–96, 99, 102–3,
    158–60
  McNamara and, 183–84, 186–87, 189
  NSC-68 (1950) and, 66–68
  Reagan administration and, 373–82
  under Truman, 95–96
  Western European, 1950–1953, 86
Military strategy (or doctrine). *See also*
    Nuclear warfare; *and specific
    strategies and policies*
  American. *See also* Defense
    intellectuals
    Eisenhower's "New Look," 97–109
    late 1940s, 45–46
    McNamara on, 184–86
  Soviet
    early 1950s, 86–87, 92
    in 1970s, 348–52
    under Khrushchev, 236–45
    Sokolovsky book on, 239–44,
      349–50
    in World War II, 91–92
*Military Strategy* (Sokolovsky), 239–44,
    349–50
Minh, Gen. Duong Van, 327
Minh, Ho Chi, 222–23
Minimax principle, 134*n*
"Minimum deterrence" strategy, 185
Minuteman missiles, 129, 187, 189–92,
    271, 291
  as first-strike weapon, 244
  Launch Control Centers for, 266–67,
    363, 364
Minuteman I missiles, 273
Minuteman II missiles, 303, 334, 419
Minuteman III missiles, 254, 278, 283,
    303, 334, 419
Minuteman silos, 279
  ABM development and, 265–68
MIRV (Multiple Independently targeted
    Re-entry Vehicles), 271, 354–55,
    362
  development of, 254–57
  McNamara and, 248, 252, 254–57
  SALT I and, 290–93
  SALT II and, 334–37
  Soviet, 301–3
"Missile gap," 121–22, 127–31, 159,
    189–90
Missiles. *See also* ABM (Anti-Ballistic
    Missile) system; ICBMs; MIRV
    (Multiple Independently targeted
    Re-entry Vehicles); "Missile gap";
    *and specific missiles*
  accuracy of, 273–74, 277–79, 281–83,
    287
  antiship, 383–84
  antitank, 392
  cruise, 335, 339–40, 377, 388, 405

Missiles *(cont.)*
  Eisenhower administration and, 123,
    128–31
  Kennedy administration's strategic
    buildup, 187, 189–90
  with maneuverable warheads, 273
  MIRVed, 254–57
  Soviet, 305
    in 1960s, 187–88, 244, 249, 258–63
    accuracy of, 287
    Khrushchev's military strategy and,
      236–37, 244
    shifting balance in 1970s, 301–4;
      301–4
    submarine missiles, 303
  tactical aircraft compared to, 389
  technology and performance of,
    269–74
  testing procedures for, 280–81
  uncertainties of successful counterforce
    launching of, 279–85
    reliability, 280–81
    systematic biases in guidance
      calibrations, 281–83
    timing of launches, 283–84
Missile silos, 249, 250, 269
  effects of a nuclear explosion against,
    275–79
Mitchell, Billy, 88
Mitscher, Adm. Marc, 387
Molotov, Vyacheslav M., 4, 16, 18–20, 24,
    60, 82, 85, 119
  Berlin Blockade and, 50–51, 53, 55
  Marshall Plan and, 36–37
Morozov, Pavel, 8
Motorized rifle divisions, Soviet, 305, 306
Mozambique, 414
MPLA (Angola), 330–31
Muller, Herbert, 105
Multilateral Force, 197
Murphy, Robert D., 49, 51, 52, 207, 208
Muskie, Edmund, 293, 337
MVD (formerly NKVD), 83n
MX missiles, 272, 376, 420
  basing plans for, 340–41
  SALT II and, 334, 337, 339–41
Mya-4 (Bison) bombers, 90–91, 108, 188
Mystère jets, 202

Nagasaki, 22
Nagy, Imre, 37, 117–19
Nam Tha, battle of (1962), 208
Nasser, Gamal Abdel, 199, 203–5, 231
  Lebanon crisis and (1958) and, 207–8
National Emergency Airborne Command
  Posts, 365, 366
National Intelligence Estimates, 258,
  260–61
National Liberation Front (Viet Cong),
  213, 219, 221, 222
  "body counts" of Viet Cong killed, 217

National Security Council (NSC), 100
NATO (North Atlantic Treaty
    Organization), 118, 130, 240, 241,
    308, 388
  armored warfare and, 393, 394
  Carter administration and, 341–45
  conventional balance of forces in 1987
    and, 425–33
  Eisenhower's mst and, 101
  first use of nuclear weapons and,
    351n
  Khrushchev and, 150–52
  in mid-1960s, 193–97
  tactical (battlefield) nuclear weapons
    and, 368, 369
Naval Research Laboratory, 126
Navy, Soviet, 311, 385
  in 1950s, 91
  in 1970s, 306–7
  conventional balance of power and,
    431–32
Navy, U.S., 85, 129, 300, 387, 397
  carrier task groups of, 381–86
  Eisenhower administration and, 103,
    104
  maritime strategy of, 383–86
  McNamara and, 181, 191
  military spending debate and (1948),
    62, 65–66
  MIRVs and, 257
  Reagan administration and, 381–86
  sealift capability of, 379–80
  Soviet Navy compared to, 306–7
  vulnerability of, 382–86
*Necessity for Choice* (Kissinger), 143–44
Nehru, Jawaharlal, 199
Neto, Augustinho, 330
Neumann, Franz, 54–55
Neutron bomb, 342
"New Look," 97–109, 114
*New Republic*, 108–9, 115, 121, 293
*Newsweek*, 121
*New Yorker, The*, 121
*New York Times*, 10, 23, 98, 108, 264,
    287, 293, 316, 356
Nhu, Ngo Dinh, 218
Nicaragua, 407
Nicolaevsky, Boris, 82
Niebuhr, Reinhold, 23
Nitze, Paul, 179–80, 302, 346, 352–54,
    425
  NSC-68 and, 67–68
Nixon, Richard M., 64, 156, 159, 263,
    303, 326, 442
  1960 campaign and, 158
  ABM system and, 264–68
  military spending under, 398–300
  SALT I and, 290–95
  Watergate and, 319, 320, 322
  Yom Kippur War (1973) and, 318–25
NKVD, 15, 23

North Atlantic Treaty (1949), 57–58
North Atlantic Treaty Organization. *See*
　NATO
North Korea, 25, 69. *See also* Korean
　War
North Vietnam
　bombing of, 136, 220–23, 229, 288, 326
　Laotian crisis of 1961–62 and, 208–9
　Tonkin Gulf incidents and, 220
Norway, 42
Nose cones, 272–73
NSC-68 (1950), 66–68, 99–101
NSC-141, 96
NSC-162/2, 101
Nuclear deterrence. *See* Deterrence
Nuclear energy, 10
Nuclear Non-Proliferation Treaty, 289
Nuclear test ban treaty, 114
　Eisenhower and, 154
　Limited Nuclear Test Ban Treaty
　　(1962), 176, 250, 289
Nuclear tests, 276
　in 1950s, 105–7
　in 1961, 173, 237
Nuclear warfare. *See also* Military
　strategy
　Brodie on, 132–33
　conservative defense intellectuals' view
　　of, 348–59
　game theory and, 133, 133–34*n*,
　　139–41
　Kahn on, 134–36
　Kissinger on, 137–38
　Khrushchev's military strategy and,
　　236–37
　limited, 359–72
　　airborne command post system,
　　　365–67
　　alert conditions, 367–68
　　command and control systems,
　　　363–72
　　delegation of launch authority, 363
　　early warning systems, 361–62
　　tactical (battlefield) nuclear weapons,
　　　368–69
　　tight central control over nuclear
　　　forces, 360–61, 363
　　time available to a President for
　　　responding in, 362
　McNamara on, 184–86, 192, 239
　Schelling on, 134
　Sokolovsky book on, 240–44
　strategy, 353–59
　survivability of nuclear forces and,
　　136
　tactical, 137–38, 241–42
　"war fighting" strategy, 353–59, 371,
　　372
Nuclear weapons. *See also* Nuclear
　warfare
　1987 strategic balance and, 419–25

Nuclear weapons *(cont.)*
　American. *See also* Massive retaliation,
　　policy of
　Eisenhower's military strategy,
　　98–101, 103–4
　Eisenhower's rejection of
　　recommendations to use nuclear
　　weapons, 109–12
　first use of. *See* First use of nuclear
　　weapons
　military spending debate and (1948),
　　62, 65–66
　military strategy of late 1940s and,
　　45–46
　thermonuclear weapons in 1950s,
　　92–93
　effects of explosion of, 274–79
　Korean War and, 75, 76
　Soviet
　　development of atomic bomb, 43
　　first test of an atomic weapon, 63, 92
　　thermonuclear weapons in 1950s, 92,
　　　93
　tactical, 130, 137, 368–69, 432–33
　　Kissinger on, 193
　　McNamara on, 193
　　in naval warfare, 385
　United Nations and, 30–31
　West Germany and, 151
*Nuclear Weapons and Foreign Policy*
　(Kissinger), 137–38
Numeiry, Col. Jaafar al-, 325
Nunn, Sam, 425

October War. *See* Yom Kippur War
Office of Systems Analysis, 181–82
Ogarkov, Marshal Nikolai, 396
*On Escalation* (Kahn), 135–36
*On Thermonuclear War* (Kahn), 135
"Open Skies" aerial inspection proposal,
　114, 115
Operation Strangle, 386
Oppenheimer, Robert, 30, 105, 108
"Option 1 and ½," 98

Packard, David, 369
Palmerston, Lord, 201
Paris summit conference (planned for
　1959), 154–58
Pathet Lao, 208
Patriot air defense system, 380–81
Pauling, Linus, 105
Peace movement, communist emphasis
　on (1949), 60
Pearson, Drew, 26
Perle, Richard, 336, 346
Pershing II missiles, 273, 344–45, 405
Personnel carriers, armored, 392–93
Phalanx anti-missile gun, 384, 385
Phased-array radar, 252, 361–62
Philby, H.A.R. ("Kim"), 43

Phoumi Nosavan, 208, 209
Pilsudski, Joseph, 14
Pipes, Richard, 348, 349
Poland, 18, 40, 59, 116, 408–9, 416
  anti-Communist underground of, 19
  under Gomulka, 116
  Lublin government of, 15–17, 19–21
  World War II and, 6
  Yalta Conference (1945) and, 14–17
Polaris missiles, 129, 187, 191, 257, 344
Portugal, 57
Poseidon missiles, 254, 257, 344
Potsdam Conference (1945), 21–22
Powers, Francis Gary, 130, 155, 157, 158
PPBS (Program Planning and Budgeting
  System), 180–82
*Pravda*, 36, 84, 121, 170, 205, 235
"Prisoner's Dilemma," 133–34n
Proxmire, William, 293

Qaddafi, Col. Muammar, 396
Quarles, Donald, 107
Quemoy and Matsu, crisis over
  (1954–1955), 111–12
Quester, George, 178
Quwatli, Shukrih al-, 203

Radar
  early warning system, 103, 108
  limited nuclear war and, 361–62
  phased-array, 252, 361–62
  SALT I and, 295
Radford, Adm. Arthur, 66, 97, 98, 102–3
Radiation poisoning, 105, 106
Radiation sickness, 274n
Radio Free Europe, 119
Rajk, Lazslo, 59, 117
Rakosi, Matyos, 117
RAND Corporation, 131, 136, 139–41,
  179, 185, 256. *See also* Defense
  intellectuals
RAND reports (1946 and 1950), 124,
  125
Rapid Deployment Force, 376
Rapid-maneuver warfare, 226–27
Rathjens, George, 293
*Reader's Digest*, 37
Reagan, Ronald (Reagan administration)
  Euromissiles and, 346–47
  INF treaty and, 405
  military spending under, 373–82
  Navy and, 381–86
  "Star Wars" program of, 347, 396–402,
    400–1, 405, 406, 424–25, 438–40
Reedy, George, 130
*Reporter* (magazine), 127
Republican party (Republicans), 25, 114
Resor, Stanley, 224
Reston, James, 98, 322
Reuter, Ernst, 52, 54, 56
"Revolt of the Admirals" (1949), 65–66

"Revolution in Soviet Strategic Thinking,
  The" (Dinerstein), 140
Rhee, Synghman, 69, 97
Ridgeway, Matthew, 76, 103, 111
Roberto, Holden, 330
Roberts, Frank, 28
Robertson, Gen. Sir Brian, 52
Rockefeller, Nelson, 114, 126, 158, 159
Rockets. *See also* Missiles
  booster, 270
  Soviet, in 1950s, 121–24
Rogers, Gen. Bernard P., 393
Rogers, William, 288
Rokossovsky, Konstantin, 6n
Rolling Thunder bombing program,
  222–23
Roosevelt, Franklin D., 20, 43
  on Stalin, 4–5
  World War II and, 4, 10
  at Yalta Conference (1945), 3–4, 11–17
Rostow, Walt, 183, 215–16, 218, 223
Rotmistrov, Marshal, 238
Rovere, Richard, 115, 165
Rowen, Henry, 179
Royall, Kenneth, 51–52
Rumania, 5, 18, 21, 24, 37, 416
Rumsfield, Donald, 360–61
Rusk, Dean, 73, 144, 172, 174, 175n,
  216, 218, 219
Russell, Bertrand, 372
Russell, Richard, 249

SA-6 missiles, 315–17, 319
SA-10 missiles, 388
SA-12 missiles, 388
Sadat, Anwar al-, 315, 319, 324
Safeguard system, 264, 267–68. *See also*
  ABM (Anti-Ballistic Missile) system
Sagan, Scott, 322
SAGE system, 129
"Sagger" antitank missiles, 316, 317
Sakharov, Andrei, 93
Salinger, Pierre, 189
SALT I (first Strategic Arms Limitation
  Treaty), 287–98, 336–40
  ABM system and, 290–95
  backchannel negotiations on, 287–88
  groundwork for, 289–90
  offensive weapons and, 293–97
  SALT II compared to, 334, 336
  shifting missile balance and, 300–3
  Soviet "cheating," 337–38
  "Unilateral Statements" appended to,
    296–97
SALT II (second Strategic Arms
  Limitation Treaty), 333–41, 419
SAM missiles, 388
"Sandstone" tests, 46
San Francisco Conference (1945), 18–19
"Sanger plane," 127–28
Sarit Thanarat, 208

Satellites, 120–21, 125, 126
Savimbi, Jonas, 330, 331
Schelling, Thomas, 131, 133–34, 137,
    140, 180, 185, 198, 219
Schlesinger, Arthur, Jr., 131, 165, 171,
    183, 191, 372
Schlesinger, James, 190, 284, 285, 318,
    321, 322, 338, 356, 357, 359
Schmidt, Helmut, 341–43
Scoville, Herbert, 292–93, 353, 355,
    372
Scowcroft Commission, 341
Scud missiles, 319, 323
Sealift capability, 379–80
SEATO (Southeast Asia Treaty
    Organization), 110
Selassie, Haile, 331
Semenov, Vladimir, 287
Sentinel system, 264. *See also* ABM
    (Anti-Ballistic Missile) system
Sergeant York antiaircraft gun, 381
Sevareid, Eric, 25
Sharon, Ariel, 319
Sherman, Adm. Forrest, 66, 71–72
Shmelev, Nikolai, 414
Sidewinder missiles, 130
Silos. *See* Missile silos
Sino-Soviet split, 14, 148
SIOP (Single Integrated Operational
    Plan), 184
Skybolt missiles, 182, 196–97
SKYWATCH program, 107
Slansky, Rudolf, 59, 82
Slessor, Sir John, 97
Smirnov, Leonid, 287, 288
Smith, Gerard, 287–88, 289, 302
Smith, Walter Bedell, 50–51, 53, 55
Sokolovsky, Gen. Vasily, 51, 54, 239–44,
    349–50, 370, 371
Solidarity labor movement, 408, 409
Somalia, 325, 331, 332
Sorenson, Theodore, 166, 183
"Sources of Soviet Conduct, The"
    (Kennan), 37
Southeast Asia Treaty Organization
    (SEATO), 110
South Korea, 103. *See also* Korean War
South Vietnam, 211. *See also* Vietnam
    War
    Diem regime in, 212–14, 217, 218
    military coups in (1963), 218
Soviet Union. *See also* Brezhnev, Leonid;
    Gorbachev, Mikhail; Khrushchev,
    Nikita; Stalin, Joseph; *and specific
    topics*
    Anglo-American frictions after World
        War II and, 10–11
    anti-Semitism in, 59–60
    de-Stalinization in, 113, 116
    Eastern Europe and. *See* Eastern
        Europe

Soviet Union *(cont.)*
    economy of, 145, 149, 409–16
    Korean War and, 68–70, 73
    lend-lease aid to, 9, 20
    loans to, after World War II, 19–20
    Middle East and, 201–6
        1967 Six-Day War, 229–231
    Third World policy of, 329–33, 413–14
    trade with, 19
    underdeveloped countries and, 200–1,
        203–4
    World War II and, 8–12
Space program. *See also* Satellites
    Eisenhower administration and,
        123–26
    Kennedy administration and, 165
Spain, 57
Spartan missiles, 267
Spies, Soviet, 26, 41
Sprint missiles, 267
Sputnik, 120–21
SS-4 missiles, 188
SS-5 missiles, 188
SS-6 missiles, 187, 274
SS-7 missiles, 187, 244, 261–62, 274, 296
SS-8 missiles, 187, 261–62, 274, 296
SS-9 missiles, 259, 260, 265–67, 274, 278,
    296, 302
SS-11 missiles, 259, 260, 266, 278, 296
SS-12/22 missiles, 405
SS-17 missiles, 302
SS-18 missiles, 301, 303
SS-19 missiles, 301–2
SS-20 missiles, 343–46, 405, 421
SS-23 missiles, 405
SS-24 missiles, 419
SS-25 missiles, 419
SS-N-18 missiles, 303
*Stages of Economic Growth* (Rostow),
    215
Stalin, Joseph, 23, 26, 89$n$, 99, 200
    Anglo-American frictions and, 10–11
    Berlin Blockade and, 47–48, 52, 54, 56
    Churchill on, 5–6, 57
    Churchill's postwar settlement with, 5
    Cold War and, 25, 29–35, 37, 40–41,
        46
    death of, 81–82
        transfer of power after, 82–85
    "doctors' plot" and, 82
    expansionist foreign policy of, 31, 42
    foreign policy of (1949), 57–60
    Hopkins's meetings with (1945), 20–21
    Khrushchev's denunciation of (1956),
        116
    Korean War and, 69, 76
    military buildup of late 1940s and,
        42–43
    military strategy of, 91, 92
    Poland and, 6
    Potsdam Conference and (1945), 21

Stalin *(cont.)*
  rocket development under, 122, 123
  Roosevelt on, 4–5
  terror policy of, 7–8, 82
  World War II and, 9, 10, 11–12
  at Yalta Conference (1945), 3–4, 11–17
*Stark* (frigate), 384
START (Strategic Arms Reduction Talks), 347
"Star Wars" program, 347, 396–402, 405, 406, 424–25, 438–40
  "layered" defense concept and, 400–1
State Department, U.S., 18, 20, 23, 28, 32
Steinbruner, John, 177
Stettinius, Edward, 10, 16
Stevenson, Adlai, 124, 167
Stevenson, Adlai, Jr., 336
Stimson, Henry, 18
Stockman, David, 373
Strategic Air Command (SAC), 103, 187, 321
Strategic Defense Initiative, 347
"Strategic hamlet" program, 216–17
Strategic Rocket Forces (Soviet Union), 236
*Strategy in the Missile Age* (Brodie), 132
Strontium-90, 106
Stubbings, Richard, 375
Su-17 fighters, 306
Su-24 fighters, 306, 388
Su-27 fighters, 431
Submarine missiles, 303–4
Submarines
  American, 177, 303
    current forces (1987), 420
    maritime strategy and, 383
    *Ohio*-class (Trident missile), 377
    Polaris-class, 129, 187, 197
  communication with, 364–65
  Soviet, 91, 188, 177, 303
    current forces (1987), 420
  technology and, 394–95
Sudan, 325
Suez Canal, 1956 crisis over, 118, 202–3
Sukarno, 199, 203
Sulzberger, C. L., 10
Summit conference(s)
  1955 (Geneva), 113–15
  1960 (Paris; planned but not held), 154–58
  1961 (Vienna), 163–64, 169–70
  1967 (Glassboro), 254
  1968 (Moscow; planned but not held), 290
  1974 (Moscow), 326
Suslov, Mikhail, 148, 149
Suzuki, Shinzo, 105
Symington, Stuart, 63, 65, 107, 109, 121, 124, 190, 264, 293

Syria, 203, 206
  in 1967 Six-Day War with Israel, 229, 230
  Korean War and, 315
  Yom Kippur War (1973) and, 317–19

T-1 rocket, 123, 128
T-2 rocket, 123, 128
T-34 tanks, 88
T-54 tanks, 88, 230
T-55 tanks, 230
T-62 tanks, 308
T-64 tanks, 308
TACAMO aircraft, 365, 366
Tachen Islands, 111
Tactical nuclear weapons, 130, 137
  Kissinger on, 193
  McNamara on, 193
Taft, Robert, 95
Taiwan (Formosa), Eisenhower and, 109–12
Talensky, Gen. Nikolai, 251
Tank divisions, Soviet, 88, 304–6
Tanks, 429–30
  American, 376
  antitank weapons and, 391–94
  NATO, 430
  in Six-Day War in Middle East (1967), 230
  Soviet, 87–88, 194–95, 230, 308, 391–92, 430
  in Yom Kippur War (1973), 319
Taraki, Nur Mohammed, 327–28
Taylor, Gen. Maxwell, 132, 152, 191, 214–16, 221
Team B exercise, 309, 348, 349
Technology, military, 387–402, 424–25, 439–40. *See also specific topics;* "Star Wars" program
  air warfare and, 387–90
  armored warfare and, 391–94
  defensive systems and, 388–90
  overview of, 377–81
  submarine and antisubmarine warfare and, 394–95
Teheran Conference (1943), 14, 15
Teller, Edward, 105, 121, 400
Thailand, 208
Theater Nuclear Forces (TNF), 343
Thermonuclear weapons (hydrogen bombs), 92–93. *See also* Nuclear weapons
Third World, 385
  Soviet policy toward, 329–33, 413–14
Tho, Nguyen Ngoc, 218
Thompson, Llewelyn, 156
Thorez, Maurice, 58–59
Thor missile, 128
*Time* (magazine), 29
Titan missiles, 128, 129, 187, 273
Tobin, James, 144–45

Togliatti, Palmiro, 38, 46, 58
Tonkin Gulf Resolution, 220
Trade, 19, 139
Transport planes, 379–80
Trident missiles, 272, 273, 304, 420
Trinkl, Frank, 180
"Trollope ploy," 175
Trotsky, Leon, 89n
Truman, Harry S., 13, 18, 28, 46, 81, 123
  atomic-sharing proposals and, 24–25
  Berlin airlift and, 52–53
  Berlin Blockade and, 55
  Cold War and, 30
  on communism vs. democray, 33
  Eisenhower and, 95–96
  Hopkins-Stalin talks and (1945), 20–21
  Korean War and, 72–74, 76
  Marshall Plan and, 37
  military spending and, 60–61, 63, 65, 77
  Potsdam Conference and (1945), 21, 22
  Stalin as viewed by, 23
Truman Doctrine, 31–34, 61, 64
Tu-4 bombers, 90
Tu-16 (Badger) bombers, 90, 108, 188, 230
Tu-26 (Backfire) bomber, 304, 335
Tu-95 (Bear) bombers, 90, 108, 188
Tucker, Robert, 311
Tudeh Party, 29
Tukachevsky, Mikhail N., 89n
Tupolev, 90, 122
*Tupolevskaya Sharaga*, 90
Turkey, 21, 29–30, 32, 33, 57, 174–75n, 175, 205
"2½ war" strategy, 193–94

Ukraine, 7
Ulam, Adam, 35, 151
Ulanova, Galina, 204
Ulbricht, Walter, 152, 171, 172
UNITA (Angola), 330, 331
United Arab Republic, 206
United Nations, 26
  atomic energy and, 30
  Berlin Blockade and, 55
  Korean War and, 70, 73–75
  nuclear weapons and, 30–31
  San Francisco Conference (1945) and, 18–19
  Yalta Conference (1945) and, 16
United States. *See names of presidents and other high officials*
*United States* (aircraft carrier), 65
Uranium-238, 106
Ustinov, D. F., 351
U-2 affair, 154–58
U-2 planes, 125–27, 130, 175, 250

Vandenberg, Arthur, 18, 24, 28, 33, 37
Vanguard, 121, 126
Vann, Lt. Col. John Paul, 217

Van Oudenaren, John, 371
Varga, Eugene, 58
Verification Panel, 292
Very Low Frequency (VLF) transmitters, 364–65
Viet Cong. *See* National Liberation Front
Vietminh, 109, 110
Vietnam War, 214–27. *See also* National Liberation Front (Viet Cong); North Vietnam
  American takeover of the ground war in the South, 223–25
  decision for military intervention in, 219–20
  defense intellectuals and, 219–20
  Eisenhower's refusal to intervene in, 109–10
  end of, 326–27
  helicopters in, 227–28
  Johnson administration and, 136, 219–25, 229
  Kennedy administration and, 138, 169, 214–18
  military advisers in, 216
  Soviet Union and, 225–26
  "strategic hamlet" program in, 216–17
Viking rocket, 126
Vladivostok "mini-summit" (1974), 336–37
Vokshod I, 235
Von Braun, Wernher, 122, 123, 126
Von Neumann, John, 133
Voznesensky, Nikolai, 58, 59n
Vyshinsky, Andrei, 8, 16, 57, 60

Walesa, Lech, 409
Wallace, Henry, 4–5
*Wall Street Journal, The*, 375
Walsh, J. B., 282
*War and the Soviet Union* (Dinerstein), 140
Warfare. *See* Conventional warfare; Limited wars; Nuclear warfare
War Powers Act, 318, 327
Warsaw Pact, 113, 193, 195
  conventional balance of forces in 1987 and, 425–33
Warsaw Rising (1944), 6
*Washington Post, The*, 98, 264, 320
Watergate, 317, 319, 320, 322
Weinberger, Caspar, 373–76, 381
West Berlin. *See also* Berlin; Berlin Blockade
  Khrushchev's foreign policy and, 150–52, 154, 169–73
Western Europe. *See also* NATO (North Atlantic Treaty Organization)
  economic recovery in, 58
  Marshall Plan and, 35–40
  military strategy of late 1940s and, 45–46

West Germany, 45, 289, 428, 429. *See also* Germany
  currency reform in, 51, 58
  formation of government of, 56, 57
  Khrushchev's foreign policy and, 150–53
  rearmament of, 110, 112–13
Westmoreland, Gen. William, 227
Wheeler, Gen. Earle, 225, 231
White, Harry Dexter, 26
White, Theodore H., 165, 318
"Why the Soviet Union Thinks It Can Fight and Win a Nuclear War" (Pipes), 348, 349
Williams College, 124
Wilson, Charles, 96, 102–4, 107, 108
"Window of vulnerability," 284–85
Wohlstetter, Albert, 131, 136, 140–41, 145, 180, 244, 279
  "The Delicate Balance of Terror," 260–63, 359
  on limited nuclear war, 369, 371
Wolfe, Thomas W., 198, 348
World War II, 4–6, 386–88, 391
  in the Pacific, 22, 387
  Soviet Union and, 8–12

Xoxe, Gen. Koci, 59

Yalta Conference (1945), 3–4, 11–18
  Asia and, 13–14
  Polish question at, 14–17
  reparations issue at, 13, 18
Yemen, 203, 205
Yevtushenko, Yevgeny, 204
Yezhov, Nikolai, 82, 83n
Yom Kippur War (1973), 315–25
  alert status of American and Soviet forces, 321–22
  cease-fire in, 320
  Egyptian armored assault in, 318–19
  Soviet resupply airlift in, 317, 318
Yugoslavia, 5, 31, 34, 58, 59

Zagoria, Donald, 333
Zeiberg, Seymour, 282
Zero option policy, 346
Zhdanov, Andrei, 38, 59n, 60
*Zhdanovshchina*, 47
Zhou Enlai, 64, 73, 97, 112, 199, 200
Zhukov, Marshal Georgi K., 6, 50, 203, 237–38
Zorin, Valerian, 38
Zumwalt, Adm. Elmo, 338

## About the Author

Charles R. Morris is a partner in an investment banking firm. This is his third book. *A Time of Passion: America, 1960–1980* explored two decades of social, political, economic, and intellectual upheaval in the United States. *The Cost of Good Intentions,* selected as one of the "Best Books of 1980" by the *New York Times,* was a microscope on the social policies of the "Great Society." Mr. Morris has published many articles on national affairs and is a regular contributor to the editorial pages of the *Los Angeles Times.*